Communication Yearbook 40

302·205 COM

ONE WEEK LOAN

Communication Yearbook 40

**Edited by
Elisia L. Cohen**

international
communication
association

Published Annually for the
International Communication Association

Routledge
Taylor & Francis Group

NEW YORK AND LONDON

First published 2016
by Routledge
711 Third Avenue, New York, NY 10017

and by Routledge
2 Park Square, Milton Park, Abingdon, Oxon, OX14 4RN

Routledge is an imprint of the Taylor & Francis Group, an informa business

ISSN: 0147-4642
ISSN: 1556-7429

ISBN: 978-1-138-64729-9 (hbk)
ISBN: 978-1-315-62708-3 (ebk)

Typeset in Times
by Keystroke, Station Road, Codsall, Wolverhampton
Printed at CPI on sustainably sourced paper

Contents

The International Communication Association

The International Communication Association (ICA) was formed in 1950, bringing together academics and other professionals whose interests focus on human communication. The Association maintains an active membership of more than 4,000 individuals, of whom some two-thirds teach and conduct research in colleges, universities, and schools around the world. Other members are in government, law, medicine, and other professions. The wide professional and geographic distribution of the membership provides the basic strength of the ICA. The Association serves as a meeting ground for sharing research and useful dialogue about communication interests.

Through its divisions and interest groups, publications, annual conferences, and relations with other associations around the world, the ICA promotes the systemic study of communication theories, processes, and skills. In addition to *Communication Yearbook*, the Association publishes the *Journal of Communication*, *Human Communication Research*, *Communication Theory*, *Journal of Computer-Mediated Communication*, *Communication, Culture & Critique*, *A Guide to Publishing in Scholarly Communication Journals*, and the *ICA Newsletter*.

For additional information about the ICA and its activities, visit online at www.icahdq.org or contact Laura Sawyer, Executive Director, International Communication Association, 1500 21st Ave. NW, Washington, DC 20036 USA; phone 202-955-1444; fax 202-955-1448; email ica@icahdq.org.

Editors of the *Communication Yearbook* series:

Volumes 1 and 2, Brent D. Ruben
Volumes 3 and 4, Dan Nimmo
Volumes 5 and 6, Michael Burgoon
Volumes 7 and 8, Robert N. Bostrom
Volumes 9 and 10, Margaret L. McLaughlin
Volumes 11, 12, 13, and 14, James A. Anderson
Volumes 15, 16, and 17, Stanley A. Deetz
Volumes 18, 19, and 20, Brant R. Burleson
Volumes 21, 22, and 23, Michael E. Roloff
Volumes 24, 25, and 26, William B. Gudykunst
Volumes 27, 28, and 29, Pamela J. Kalbfleisch
Volumes 30, 31, 32, and 33, Christina S. Beck
Volumes 34, 35, and 36, Charles T. Salmon
Volumes 37, 38, 39 and 40, Elisia L. Cohen

Patricia Frances Phalen
Media Industry Studies IG Chair
George Washington University

Veronika Karnowski
Mobile Communication IG Chair
Ludwig Maximilians University,
Munich

Alison Hearn
Philosophy, Theory and Critique Div.
Chair
University of Western Ontario

Craig R. Scott
Organizational Communication Div.
Chair
Rutgers University

Jesper Stromback
Political Communication Div. Chair
Mid Sweden University

Melissa A. Click
Popular Communication Div. Chair
University of Missouri-Columbia

Chiara Valentini
Public Relations Div. Chair
Aarhus University

Andrew C. Billings
Sports Communication IG Chair
University of Alabama

Giorgia Aiello
Visual Communication Studies Div.
Chair
University of Leeds

Michael L. Haley
Executive Director (ex-officio)
International Communication
Association

Laura Sawyer
Executive Director (ex-officio)
International Communication
Association

DIVISION CHAIRS

Sahara Byrne
Children, Adolescents & the Media
Div. Chair
Cornell University

James A. Danowski
Communication & Technology Div.
Chair
University of Illinois at Chicago

Richard K. Popp
Communication History Div. Chair
University of Wisconsin-Milwaukee

Seamus Simpson
Communication Law & Policy Div.
Chair
University of Salford

Richard J. Doherty
Environmental Communication Div.
Chair
New England College

Federico Subervi
Ethnicity & Race in Communication
Div. Chair
Kent State University

Natalia Rybas
Feminist Scholarship Div. Chair
Indiana University East

Nicholas David Bowman
Game Studies Div. Chair
West Virginia University

Terry Flew
Global Comm/Social Change Div.
Chair
Queensland University of
Technology

Kevin B. Wright
Health Communication Div. Chair
George Mason University

Kevin Wise
Information Systems Div. Chair
University of Illinois Urbana-
Champaign

Aaron R. Boyson
Instructional/Developmental Div.
Chair
University of Minnesota-Duluth

Stephen Michael Croucher
Intercultural Communication Div.
Chair
University of Jyvaskyla

Ascan F. Koerner
Interpersonal Communication Div.
Chair
University of Minnesota

Matt Carlson
Journalism Studies Div. Chair
Saint Louis University

Alena L. Vasilyeva
Language & Social Interaction Div.
Chair
University of Massachusetts-
Amherst

Lance Holbert
Mass Communication Div. Chair
Temple University

Alison Hearn
Philosophy, Theory and Critique Div.
Chair
University of Western Ontario

Craig R. Scott
Organizational Communication Div.
Chair
Rutgers University

Jesper Stromback
Political Communication Div. Chair
Mid Sweden University

Melissa A. Click
Popular Communication Div. Chair
University of Missouri-Columbia

Chiara Valentini
Public Relations Div. Chair
Aarhus University

Giorgia Aiello
Visual Communication Studies Div.
Chair
University of Leeds

INTEREST GROUP CHAIRS

Eve C. Ng
Lesbian, Gay, Bisexual, Transgender
& Queer IG Chair
Ohio University

Travers Scott
Lesbian, Gay, Bisexual, Transgender
& Queer IG Chair
Clemson University

Janice Krieger
Intergroup Communication IG Chair
University of Florida

Patricia Frances Phalen
Media Industry Studies IG Chair
George Washington University

Veronika Karnowski
Mobile Communication IG Chair
Ludwig Maximilians University,
Munich

Andrew C. Billings
Sports Communication IG Chair
University of Alabama

Thomas Feeley	*SUNY, University of Buffalo, USA*
Edward L. Fink	*University of Maryland, USA*
Brooke Fisher Liu	*University of Maryland, USA*
Richard Fitzgerald	*University of Queensland, Australia*
Lewis A. Friedland	*University of Wisconsin–Madison, USA*
Brandi N. Frisby	*University of Kentucky, USA*
Shiv Ganesh	*Massey University, New Zealand*
Howard Giles	*University of California-Santa Barbara, USA*
G. Thomas Goodnight	*University of Southern California, USA*
Allison Scott Gordon	*University of Kentucky, USA*
James E. Grunig	*University of Maryland, USA*
Lutz M. Hagen	*Dresden University of Technology, Germany*
Naila Hamdy	*The American University in Cairo, Egypt*
Dale Hample	*University of Maryland*
Nancy G. Harrington	*University of Kentucky, USA*
Tyler Harrison	*University of Miami*
Jake Harwood	*University of Arizona, USA*
Magne Martin Haug	*Norwegian Business School, Norway*
Evelyn Y. Ho	*University of San Francisco, USA*
Thomas A. Hollihan	*University of Southern California, USA*
Andrea B. Hollingshead	*University of Southern California, USA*
Robert Huesca	*Trinity University, USA*
David Huffaker	*Northwestern University, USA*
Dal-Yong Jin	*Simon Fraser University, Canada*
Liz Jones	*Griffith University, Australia*
Amy B. Jordan	*University of Pennsylvania, USA*
Joo-Young Jung	*International Christian University, Japan*
Jennifer A. Kam	*University of California-Santa Barbara, USA*
Vikki S. Katz	*Rutgers University, USA*
Jody Koenig Kellas	*University of Nebraska, Lincoln, USA*
Marj Kibby	*University of Newcastle, Australia*
Youna Kim	*The American University of Paris, France*
Yong Chan Kim	*Yonsei University, South Korea*
Michael W. Kramer	*University of Oklahoma, USA*
Kenneth A. Lachlan	*University of Connecticut, USA*
Chih-Hui Lai	*University of Akron, USA*
Annie Lang	*Indiana University, USA*
Robert LaRose	*Michigan State University, USA*
Chin-Chuan Lee	*City University of Hong Kong, China*
Maria Len-Rios	*University of Georgia, USA*
Xigen Li	*City University of Hong Kong, China*
Anthony Limperos	*University of Kentucky, USA*
Maria Löblich	*Ludwig-Maximilians-Universität, Germany*
Monique M. Turner	*George Washington University, USA*
Robin Mansell	*London School of Economics and Political Science, UK*

Valerie Manusov   *University of Washington, USA*
Matthew M. Martin   *West Virginia University, USA*
Caryn Medved   *Baruch College, USA*
Rebecca Meisenbach   *University of Missouri, USA*
Vernon Miller   *Michigan State University, USA*
Michelle Miller-Day   *Chapman University*
Sheila Murphy   *University of Southern California, USA*
Kang Namkoong   *University of Kentucky, USA*
Robin Nabi   *University of California-Santa Barbara, USA*
Jeff Niederdeppe   *Cornell University, USA*
Seth M. Noar   *University of North Carolina at Chapel Hill, USA*

Mohammed Zin Nordin   *Universiti Pendidikan Sultan Idris, Malaysia*
Jon F. Nussbaum   *Pennsylvania State University, USA*
Amy O'Connor   *North Dakota State University, USA*
Thomas O'Gorman   *Northern Illinois University, USA*
Daniel J. O'Keefe   *Northwestern University, USA*
Mary Beth Oliver   *Pennsylvania State University, USA*
Sanne Opree   *Center of Research on Children, Adolescents and the Media, The Netherlands*
Mahuya Pal   *University of South Florida, USA*
John J. Pauly   *Marquette University, USA*
Wei Peng   *Michigan State University, USA*
Katie Place   *Saint Louis University, USA*
Marshall Scott Poole   *University of Illinois at Urbana-Champaign, USA*
Linda L. Putnam   *University of California-Santa Barbara, USA*
Jack Linchuan Qiu   *Chinese University of Hong Kong, China*
Brian L. Quick   *University of Illinois at Urbana-Champaign, USA*
Artemio Ramirez, Jr.   *University of South Florida, USA*
Rajiv N. Rimal   *George Washington University, USA*
Gertrude Robinson   *McGill University, Canada*
Clemencia Rodriguez   *University of Oklahoma, USA*
Randall Rogan   *Wake Forest University, USA*
Michael Roloff   *Northwestern University, USA*
Craig R. Scott   *Rutgers University, USA*
Dave Seibold   *University of California-Santa Barbara, USA*
Timothy Sellnow   *University of Kentucky, USA*
Michelle Shumate   *Northwestern University, USA*
Kami Silk   *Michigan State University, USA*
Aram Sinnreich   *Rutgers University, USA*
Michael Slater   *Ohio State University, USA*
Sandi W. Smith   *Michigan State University, USA*
Jordan Soliz   *University of Nebraska-Lincoln, USA*

Lisa Sparks	*Chapman University, USA*
Krishnamurthy Sriramesh	*Purdue University, USA*
Laura Stafford	*Bowling Green State University, USA*
Michael Stohl	*University of California-Santa Barbara, USA*
Ed S. Tan	*University of Amsterdam, Netherlands*
David Tewksbury	*University of Illinois at Urbana-Champaign, USA*
C. Erik Timmerman	*University of Wisconsin-Milwaukee, USA*
April R. Trees	*Saint Louis University, USA*
Monique Mitchell Turner	*George Washington University, USA*
Shari Veil	*University of Kentucky, USA*
Mina Tsay-Vogel	*Boston University, USA*
Sebastián Valenzuela	*Pontificia Universidad Católica, Chile*
Jens Vogelgesang	*University of Muenster, Germany*
Peter Vorderer	*University of Mannheim, Germany*
Joseph B. Walther	*Nanyang Technological University, Singapore*
Steve R. Wilson	*Purdue University, USA*
Werner Wirth	*University of Zurich, Switzerland*
Greg Wise	*Arizona State University, USA*
Saskia Witteborn	*Chinese University of Hong Kong, China*
Yariv Tsfati	*University of Haifa, Israel*
Y. Connie Yuan	*Cornell University, USA*
Marc Ziegele	*Johannes Gutenberg University Mainz, Germany*

Ad Hoc Reviewers

Alicia Alexander	*Southern Illinois University, Edwardsville, USA*
Jaime Banks	*West Virginia University, USA*
Jeff Bennett	*University of Iowa, USA*
Brenda Berkelaar	*University of Texas, Austin, USA*
Helena Bilandzic	*Augsburg University, Germany*
Graham D. Bodie	*Louisiana State University, USA*
Namjoo Choi	*University of Kentucky, USA*
Peter Chow-White	*Simon Fraser University, Canada*
Christopher Clarke	*George Mason University, USA*
Christine Davis	*University of North Carolina, Charlotte, USA*
Megan Dillow	*West Virginia University, USA*
Richard J. Doherty	*University of Leeds, UK*
Debbie Dougherty	*University of Missouri, USA*
John Downing	*Southern Illinois University, USA*
Kate Eddens	*University of Kentucky, USA*
Joshua Ewalt	*James Madison University, USA*
Patricia Geist-Martin	*San Diego State University, USA*
Carmen Gonzalez	*Rutgers University, USA*
Melanie Green	*SUNY, University of Buffalo, USA*
Craig Hayden	*American University, USA*
Katharine J. Head	*Indiana University Purdue, University Indianapolis, USA*
James K. Hertog	*University of Kentucky, USA*
Amanda Hinnant	*University of Missouri, USA*
Nick Iannarino	*University of Central Michigan, USA*
Bobi Ivanov	*University of Kentucky, USA*
James D. Ivory	*Virginia Tech University, USA*
Amy Johnson	*Ohio University, USA*
Susanne M. Jones	*University of Minnesota, USA*
Seok Kang	*University of Texas, San Antonio, USA*
Randall A. Lake	*University of Southern California, USA*
Mei-Chen Lin	*Kent State University, USA*
Erina MacGeorge	*Pennsylvania State University, USA*
Kelly McAninch	*University of Kentucky, USA*
Sharon Meraz	*University of Illinois, Chicago, USA*
Seungahn Nah	*University of Kentucky, USA*
Kimberly Parker	*University of Kentucky, USA*
Joshua Pederson	*Boston University, USA*
Elizabeth Petrun	*University of Maryland, USA*
Jeff Pooley	*Muhlenberg College, USA*
Shawn Powers	*Georgia State University, USA*
Kevin Real	*University of Kentucky, USA*
Matthew Savage	*University of Kentucky, USA*

Jennifer Scarduzio	*University of Kentucky, USA*
Travers Scott	*Clemson University, USA*
Robert Shapiro	*University of Kentucky, USA*
Fuyuan Shen	*Pennsylvania State University, USA*
Alan Sillars	*University of Montana, USA*
Keri Stephens	*University of Texas, Austin, USA*
Jennifer Stevens Aubrey	*University of Arizona, USA*
Jeannette Sutton	*University of Kentucky, USA*
Nurit Tal-Or	*University of Haifa, Israel*
Martin Tanis	*University of Amsterdam, Netherlands*
Jeffrey Treem	*University of Texas, Austin, USA*
Ben Triana	*University of South Carolina, Aiken, USA*
Riva Tukachinsky	*Chapman University, USA*
Maria Venetis	*Purdue University, USA*
Laura Young	*Butler University, USA*

Editor's Introduction

Elisia L. Cohen

Welcome to Volume 40 of the *Communication Yearbook*. This collection continues the format, which began with Volume 37, of publishing interdisciplinary and internationally diverse scholarship relating to communication in its many forms. The volume includes state-of-the-discipline literature reviews and meta-analyses that advance knowledge and understanding of communication systems, processes, and effects. Included essays provide a rigorous assessment of the status of a communication theory or body of communication inquiry, and offer new guidance for examining hypotheses, extending communication theory, or studying insights into communication systems, processes, policies and effects.

In the tradition of volumes that I edited previously, this volume of *Communication Yearbook* brings together essays from a group of international scholars to advance the field of communication research. This is also the last volume in the *Yearbook* series, which has been a 40-year publication effort by the International Communication Association. The latest volume completes the series supported and published by Linda Bathgate. While the Epilogue of this book describes *Communication Yearbook*'s journey over the years to its present form, I want to make special introductory note of Linda Bathgate who has been an exceptional steward of the *Yearbook* while at Lawrence Erlbaum, and later as Erlbaum became part of the Routledge, an imprint of Taylor and Francis. Without her unwavering support of this project over the past decade (and longer) reaching Volume 40 would not have been possible.

The *Yearbook* begins with a focus on media framing, media industry structure, and a reception study considering characteristics of contemporary quality television. In Chapter 1, Sophie Lecheler and Claes de Vreese conduct a systematic review of longitudinal news framing studies. Although much international communication research has demonstrated the effects of framing, how long such framing effects last—and the theoretical mechanisms that may be influential for their duration and influence on decision-making over time—is an empirical question worthy of additional exploration. In a broad review investigating the duration of news framing effects, Lecheler and de Vreese describe how most studies report effects on opinions beyond initial exposure, although little is known about the duration of behavioral and emotional responses.

The chapter that follows, from Nurit Tal-Or and Jonathan Cohen, advances narrative persuasion theory by reviewing comparative studies explicating transportation and identification as distinct forms of narrative engagement. After analyzing 56 studies exploring the antecedents and consequences of these two constructs, the authors identify the similarities and differences between these processes to highlight the contextual, structural, and personality factors contributing to their effects on attitudinal and behavioral outcomes. In so doing, the authors suggest different paths for transportation into the story from identification with its characters. Tal-Or and Cohen also identify several particularly vexing questions for theorists and persuasive message design by grappling with whether transportation and identification necessarily co-occur, or what type of narrative design would evoke one effect without the other.

Chapter 4 continues *Communication Yearbook*'s consideration of television, but considers its place in the connected world of evolving information and communication technologies (ICTs). Paul Murschetz offers a consideration of how the television industry is transforming, using the case of Germany, to demonstrate the economic and structural change in television broadcasting. With a focus on media convergence, industry analysis, and corporate-level strategic position, the author reviews the state of the literature to examine the nature of media convergence with respect to factors that drive or inhibit convergence toward Connected TV. Second, the chapter considers the drivers of industry transformation and the factors influencing broadcaster competition (and structure). Finally, the chapter identifies "winning" business models or economic strategies in Connected TV.

In an applied narrative context, what makes for high-quality entertainment TV is a question that Hollywood writers, producers, and scholars have been considering for the past several decades. In Chapter 3, Daniela Schlütz gives a systematic history of successful serial characteristics by detailing the features of the entertainment experience. In so doing, the author articulates quality TV as "a culturally bound, discursive construct" which "functions as a meta-genre with concrete implications for selection, experience and possible effects of entertaining quality TV" (p. 95).

The second section of *Communication Yearbook 40* reviews problems of strategic communication in interactions. First, Marya Doerfel and Patricia Moore's essay identifies how online discourse analysis can be used by communication scholars to identify how the Strength of Weak Ties theory (SoWT) can be applied to the affordances of social network ties via social networking sites, blogs, and message boards. Toward this end, the essay extends SoWT theory to propose that (a) homophilous online environments will generate communities of strong ties; (b) through texts reflective of tolerance for various opinions on a topic, an open network structure that welcomes new membership via spontaneous and latent ties (re)emerges; and (c) SNS-driven weak ties are deeply rooted in shared cultures resulting in outcomes akin to conventional ties.

Second, Carrie Anne Platt, Amber Raile, and Ann Burnett examine the current sex-specific conceptualization of relational aggression as a pathological trait in young girls, arguing that connections between research in psychology, education, media, and communication studies suggest relational aggression or "meanness" as a strategic, situation-specific communication strategy for different goals. Platt and her colleagues offer four recommendations for future research: the need to examine strategic aspects of relationally aggressive communication; to take a multimethod approach and effort to triangulate how and why participants communicate the way that they do; for research that includes diverse study populations; and for research that traces connections between offline and online relational aggression.

Chapter 7 provides a synthetic review of computer-mediated support research examining support acquisition and the outcomes of support acquired online. Since the advent of computer-mediated communication, cultural futurists have considered dystopian scenarios for human disconnection or alternatively, the utopian advantages of connection across time and distance. In reviewing the research evidence, the chapter addresses the following questions: (a) who seeks computer-mediated support? (b) why do people seek computer-mediated support? (c) are computer-mediated context viable resources for support? (d) what factors influence perceptions of computer-mediated support quality? (e) is participating in an online support community beneficial? and (f) is computer-mediated support associated with positive outcomes? In so doing, Stephen Rains and Kevin Wright's chapter also comments on three areas where the field has established understanding social support outcomes in specific contexts: older adults, educational audiences, and in the context of cultural adaptation. Across these three contexts, Rains and Wright argue that CMC has been established as a useful resource for social support and the chapter concludes by suggesting several avenues for researchers seeking to understand the role of computer-mediation in the broader ecological context of the social support provision process.

Erina MacGeorge, Bo Feng, and Lisa Guntzviller contribute the eighth chapter of this volume and focus their study on one communicative form of social support and influence: advice-giving. After reviewing communication scholarship identifying how recipients evaluate and respond to advice messages, the chapter turns to consider advice in interactions and social exchange relationships. In so doing, the chapter considers alternative paradigms for advice research, reviewing discursive, psychological, and network approaches to provide insight into the characteristics, functions, and outcomes of advice. In sum, the authors provide researchers with advice to advance research (a) observing advice-giving exchanges (rather than rely on researcher-constructed or recollected advice); (b) expanding the range of recipient outcomes under scholarly consideration; (c) with a broader range of advice content under consideration, specifically with attention to advice in professional settings and on non-intimate topics, with attention to the role and position of the advice-giver and recipient; (d) that considers sustained, relational outcomes for groups and organizations over time; and (e) considering ways that media and cultural context may matter.

The third section of the *Yearbook* presents contributions from scholars proposing several areas for growth in organizational communication research in examining workplace boundaries, place, and exchanges. Chapter 9 begins with an identification of the ways that extant literature on organizational space focuses on material conditions of organizing or socially constructed organizational places. Elizabeth Wilhoit's essay considers how place and space are both constitutive of, and constituted by, organizational communication, and briefly considers several areas for organizational communication research on space.

As modern workplace wellness programs become sites where workers' health issues are addressed, the boundaries between workers' personal space and the places in which they work has become less stable. In Chapter 10, Jessica Ford and Emily Scheinfeld extend Petronio's communication privacy management theory to the context of employee-employer framing of health-related boundary negotiations to examine the ways that cultural, privacy, confidentiality, and ethical boundaries are discursively permeated or weakened by workplace health promotions. The chapter concludes by broadly identifying the need for interpretive, critical, feminist, and postcolonial scholarship of workplace health promotion practices.

Chapter 11 follows with Brian Manata, Vernon Miller, Briana DeAngelis, and Jihyun Paik's examination of the importance of multi-level and cross-level theorizing for organizational socialization research. In so doing, they overview three broad methods of studying newcomer socialization as (a) contextual, (b) content-specific, and (c) what they identify as the (v) memorable message approach. They critique these three approaches to illustrate the multilevel nature of socialization, and then offer general principles to guide future research in this area.

The two chapters that follow examine openings for organizational communication scholars to strengthen their disciplinary inquiry. Leah Omilion-Hodges, Jennifer Ptacek, and Deidre Zerilli consider the evolution of leader-member exchange (LMX), coworker exchange (CWX), and team-member exchange (TMX) in the contextualized workgroup to present the case for more multilevel examinations of workgroup relationships in communication research that would examine these relationships in concert. Following this consideration of contextualized workgroup relationships as a multilevel problem, Chapter 13 considers the role of mixed-method research in organizational communication. In Chapter 13, Elizabeth Carlson, Katherine Cooper and Andrew Pilny examine the use of mixed-method research in recent organizational communication research. Specifically, a study of 201 mixed-method organizational communication articles published between 1994 and 2014 revealed four trends in the research: "(a) the dominance of single-paradigm, interpretive studies; (b) the preponderance of triangulation, complementarity, and development as purposes for mixing methods; (c) varied combinations of methods; and (d) a lack of mixed methods citations" (p. 395). In describing these trends, the authors discuss topical directions for robust mixed method organizational communication scholarship.

The final section of *Communication Yearbook 40* considers emerging or innovative areas of communication research. The first essay in this section,

"Communicating Energy in a Climate (of) Crisis," details the "awareness of and controversies about the connections between energy security, economic growth, and energy systems" in the twenty-first century. Danielle Endres, Brian Cozen, Joshua Barnett, Megan O'Byrne and Tarla Rai Peterson take a critical approach to communication about energy as an emerging subfield in the communication discipline that reflects a new context for theorizing and positions communication activities as a resource for social deliberations about energy policy and the role of energy in society. After identifying energy communication as a distinct subfield, the authors highlight three current themes in the development of crisis-framed energy communication research (media strategy, corporate strategy, and decision-making in energy crises), and suggest three areas for research that offer a broader understanding for energy communication as part of a broader, "context-responsive frame" for energy communication scholarship. Such scholarship would focus on the rhetoric of energy science, offer comparative studies across energy resources, and include a lifespan approach to energy in society.

The final chapter of the *Yearbook* includes a review of contemporary scholarship driven by the reconsideration and application of existing communication infrastructure theory. In Chapter 14, Seok Kang examines the literature on communication infrastructure and civic engagement in the era of information and communication technology. The chapter reflects on the ecological aspects of ICT to examine the contingencies of civic engagement by communication agents at multiple levels of analysis. By examining human and media storytelling networks in communication infrastructure against a backdrop of ICT in terms of its communication ecology, it synthesizes the contextual factors that may generate more or less civic engagement in the ICT era.

Editor's Postscript: The Future of *Communication Yearbook* and the Field

One of the pleasures in editing a series like *Communication Yearbook* is the opportunity to develop a more intimate relationship with the field of communication. Indeed, this is the greatest benefit to editing that I have heard and read several prior editors comment on. Reading widely across literature outside of my area of specialization has allowed me to see more clearly the communication field's dreams and concerns, growth and decay in scholarship, and areas for discovery and supposition in commonplaces considered well-trodden ground. I believe that the field of communication has much to contribute in addressing the emerging problems of the twenty-first century. By tracing the history of *Communication Yearbook* over time (as I do for readers in the Epilogue), it is clear to me that the field has moved from studying communication processes to identifying phenomena, to focusing deeply on explaining the constitution and effects of communication and their applications for addressing complex, multilevel social problems.

I am grateful to have had the opportunity to review the work of an outstanding group of international communication scholars and to gain new friendships in the process. I began to realize early-on in my editorship that there are no real strangers to me in this field, only friends who I have not yet met and relationships I have not yet established. I hope that my students who have worked with me on this project have also realized these benefits. *Communication Yearbook 40* would not have been possible without the steadfast editorial assistance of Rachael Record and Jenna Reno. In addition to making a tremendous editorial team by keeping up broadly with correspondence and editing minutiae, Rachael and Jenna have simultaneously balanced their obligations as editorial assistants, instructors, and researchers while completing their doctorate degrees. They have become trusted colleagues.

I am particularly grateful to the members of the ICA Publications Committee, and to current and former ICA Executive Committee members Wolfgang Donsbach, Amy Jordan, Cynthia Stohl, Peter Vorderer, and the inimitable Michael Haley for entrusting this publication to me over the past four years. Without their encouragement, and the support of J. Alison Bryant, Michael Cody, Nancy Harrington, Tom Hollihan, Dan O'Hair, and Michelle Shumate I would not have taken on this role. The role of editor has taught me as much about the diverse theoretical and applied research traditions in our field as it has about the community of scholars practicing within it. Over the course of four years I realized how truly fortunate I have been to have such excellent, international communication research to review as an editor. I appreciate my colleagues' willingness to entrust their work to the editorial process that I managed.

When I became editor of *Communication Yearbook*, I did so with a goal of advancing its scope of scholarly reach and editorial reach, in the hope that it would transition to an electronically available journal under a future editor's helm. Indeed, past editors of *Communication Yearbook*, particularly Chuck Salmon, had made a compelling case to the ICA Board in prior *Yearbook* reports. With this goal in mind, for the past four years *Communication Yearbook's* editorial process has been guided by the norms of blind, peer-review and the inclusion of the best "state-of-the-art" manuscripts advancing disciplinary communication research. In my solicitation of Editorial Board members and reviewers, I sought out referees who would provide an international perspective to communication research. I want to express appreciation to those who provided reviews for manuscripts in this volume. I am also grateful for the contributors of selected studies and for their cooperation in preparing their manuscripts for final production. We will all take joy in the knowledge that the new editor will have an online manuscript management system, and that David Ewoldsen rather than I will manage the manuscripts, revisions, and correspondence to authors and editors in this environment. As I detail in the Epilogue of this volume, I believe it is due to the success and strength of *Communication Yearbook* over its four-decade lifespan that it has piqued the interest of publishers as a viable, widely distributed electronic journal that will advance the International Communication Association's goals for many years to come.

Last, I want to thank my husband, Jeff, and my daughter, who supported the energy and commitment that I have made to *Communication Yearbook* over the past four years.

Part I

Media Framing, Structure, and Reception

CHAPTER CONTENTS

1 How Long Do News Framing Effects Last? A Systematic Review of Longitudinal Studies

Sophie Lecheler and Claes H. de Vreese

University of Amsterdam, The Netherlands

A growing number of experimental studies investigate the duration of news framing effects. This article presents a systematic review of the theoretical premises, experimental designs, and individual-level moderators in these studies. Our results suggest that most studies report effects that persist beyond initial exposure and that may be influential for subsequent decision-making over time, but that durability of effects heavily depends on whether individuals are exposed to competitive frames also. We also find that little is known about duration of news framing effects on behavior and emotional responses. We propose a research agenda for future longitudinal framing studies.

*T*ime is a key concept in news framing theory, but also a tricky one. When studying the effects of news frames on political attitudes and behavior, most researchers are—more or less explicitly—interested in describing substantial and thus lasting effects of news framing on citizens (Tewksbury & Scheufele, 2009). At the end of the day, if all framing effects were only short-term, immediate reactions to media messages with no further implications, the concept would probably not be so popular in communication science, political science, sociology, psychology, and public opinion research. To study over-time effects, a number of studies make use of panel survey designs and media content analysis data (cf. Iyengar & Simon, 1993). However, doing so makes researchers face the near impossibility of establishing an individual-level connection between frame exposure and effects on citizens.

Because framing effects research strongly relies on experimental survey designs, there are efforts within the field to combine the advantages of experiments (i.e., the assumption of causality, the controlled exposure) with the multiple measure perspective of panel designs. This is not surprising, given that framing experiments are usually designed to "*identify how citizens make decisions and respond to real-world political objects, in order to enhance understanding of politics*" (Gaines, Kuklinski, & Quirk, 2007, p. 2; emphasis in original). Experiments, just like all research designs (Campbell & Stanley, 1966), have limitations and can realistically only examine some aspects of (media) reality. For instance, experiments cannot at this point show how and why certain frames emerge in political discourse, nor can they fully explain why some frames gain and hold this prominence over long periods of time

(Carragee & Roefs, 2004; Entman, 2003). Yet, with the addition of longitudinal measurement of effects, framing experiments can provide us with an increased understanding of conditions under which frames really influence us over time. In this sense, time can be understood as a moderator variable in framing effects research.

So far, the literature on over-time experimental designs in framing research is in its infancy and therefore scattered. The field has not yet benefitted from the accumulation of theoretical evidence towards an answer to the question regarding the real-life relevance of framing effects over time. Existing framing experiments test the longevity of effects across varying and seemingly arbitrary time spans, or may not put full analytical and theoretical focus on their over-time designs (Baden & Lecheler, 2012). Therefore, we note that the available research on the duration of news framing effects has not yet attempted to establish a conceptual or empirical standard on how duration of framing effects should be measured, and when exactly a news framing effect could be described as long-, mid-, or short-term in nature. Also, there are many variables and aspects of effect duration yet to be explored in future studies.

In response, this article presents a systematic, albeit modest, review of experimental studies that test the persistence of framing effects over time and thus introduces time as a moderator of framing effects. We begin our argument by providing a short introduction into framing theory and the study of duration in framing research. Following, we systematically search and select relevant framing experiments that have included repeated or over-time measurements of effects. We, first, compare their theoretical premises, focusing on both independent (i.e., the frames) and dependent variables (i.e., the framing effects). Second, we evaluate their designs. Third, we assess the determinants of the duration of framing effects in the form of a review of individual-level moderators in the selected studies. Lastly, we evaluate whether authors themselves label framing effects as short-, mid- or long-lasting. The results of this review can function as an important guidepost for answering the central question of how long news framing effects last. Given the novelty of longitudinal framing experiments, we conceptualize this review not as a final but as a preliminary answer to the question of duration of framing effects. We hope that this review will aid future theoretical and methodological advances in media framing research.

Theoretical Foundations

Understanding Framing Theory

Framing as used in mediated communication research is a concept originating in both psychology and sociology (Carragee & Roefs, 2004; Entman, 1993; D'Angelo, 2002).[1] In psychology, framing research has roots in Kahneman and Tversky's (1979; 1984) prospect theory where decisions taken by individuals can be altered by presenting information in logically equivalent but semantically different ways. In sociology, Goffman (1974) also constructed the idea of framing on a micro-level. He suggested that individuals organize their daily experiences by means of "frameworks or schemata of interpretation" (p. 21). Most important among these are the so-called primary frameworks, which render "what would otherwise be a meaningless aspect of the scene into something that is meaningful" (p. 21).

Although the term "frame" has been used in mediated communication research for decades now, the question of what exactly constitutes a frame is contested (Matthes, 2009). Frames can be found in various parts of the communication process: within the originating political system through the sponsorship of frames by political actors, institutions, and social movements; through journalists or media institutions; and with recipients (de Vreese, 2002; Entman, 1993; Kinder & Sanders, 1996; Scheufele, 1999). Kinder and Sanders (1996) argue that frames "lead a double life," because they are present in political discourse, as well as in the mind as "cognitive structures that help individual citizens make sense of the issues that animate political life" (p. 164). Scheufele (1999) distinguishes between "media frames" in content and "individual frames" that are present in a person's mind as a result of either deep-rooted beliefs or short-term reference changes (pp. 106–107). The notion of the presence of frames in multiple locations has led to the understanding of framing as a process that stretches across all parts of the communication process (D'Angelo, 2002; Scheufele, 1999). De Vreese (2002) thus distinguishes between frame-building, the "process and factors that influence the structural qualities of news frames" and frame-setting, the "interaction between media frames and individuals' prior knowledge and predispositions" (p. 24).

On a macro-level, a frame "organizes everyday reality" within the media and is thereby "part and parcel of everyday reality" (Tuchman, 1978, p. 193). Frames are "persistent patterns of cognition, interpretation, and presentation, of selection, emphasis and exclusion by which symbol-handlers routinely organize discourse" (Gitlin, 1980, p. 7). In the news, a frame is often described as "a central organizing idea or story line that provides meaning to an unfolding strip of events, weaving a connection among them. The frame suggests what the controversy is about, the essence of the issue" (Gamson & Modigliani, 1987, p. 143; see also Reese, 2001). Entman (1993) highlights the selection aspect of frames in arguing that to

> frame is *to select some aspects of a perceived reality and make them more salient in a communicating context, in such a way as to promote a particular problem definition, causal interpretation, moral evaluation, and/or treatment recommendation* for the item described.
>
> (p. 52; emphasis in original)

Yet, this conceptual frame definition does not give much indication of the distinct elements that constitute a news frame or how to actually identify a frame in the news (cf. Matthes & Kohring, 2008). There are, to date, two very common classifications of news frames—both of which are used in studying the duration of framing effects. The first divides news framing into equivalency and emphasis frames (Druckman 2001). *Equivalency* frames refer to content that is similar or even identical in its logical message, but that is phrased differently (Kahneman & Tversky, 1984). *Emphasis* frames are closer to "real" journalistic news coverage and present "qualitatively different yet potentially relevant considerations" of an issue (Chong & Druckman, 2007, p. 114). Equivalency frames are not often used in mediated communication research, because this rather narrow conceptualization of framing limits its applicability in a social or political context. For that reason, many studies—including the majority of studies reported in this review—have made use of emphasis frames as more realistic translations of political news coverage (de Vreese, 2002; Sniderman & Theriault, 2004; but see Iyengar, 2010; Scheufele & Iyengar, in press). Among emphasis frames, there is a division between issue-specific frames and generic frames. Issue-specific frames are built explicitly for an issue, whereas generic frames are a recurring set of frames that can be applied to a variety of issues (de Vreese, Peter, & Semetko, 2001).

Based on these definitions, framing experiments most often define frames as patterns of interpretation that are used to classify information and that aid audiences in processing information efficiently. Media frames stress certain aspects of reality and push others into the background: they have a selective function. A framing effect is the influence a news frame has on an individual's framing of issues.

Studying News Framing Effects over Time

Framing effects are often studies using experimentation. Framing experiments are usually conducted online or in a laboratory and are based on survey designs. Participants are exposed to one or more media messages, featuring a particular news frame, and effects of this exposure are then tapped by means of a questionnaire. Such experimental designs are often considered methodologically superior, because they establish causal relationships between frame exposure and changes within the individual (Spencer, Zanna, & Fong, 2005). But, framing experiments are mere snapshots of reality, characterized by forced one-shot exposure to (often researcher-crafted) news messages in a highly artificial media use scenario. This limits their external validity considerably (Barabas & Jerit, 2010) and raises the simple but fundamental question whether framing experiments allow for assumptions about the real-life impact of news reporting on the individual (Baden & Lecheler, 2012; Kinder, 2007).

Still, the greater part of available news framing effects experiments emphasizes the relevance of their results for actual politics and individual decision-making (Lecheler & de Vreese, 2011; Tewksbury & Scheufele, 2009). However, a number of scholars have suggested alterations to the experimental designs used in testing framing effects (Barabas & Jerit, 2010; Kinder, 2007).

Gaines et al. (2007) argue that the potential of the survey experiment in political research can only be fulfilled once researchers start admitting 'real-life' factors into their experimental designs. These factors include controlling for pre-treatment exposure, including a control group, exposure to more than one treatment during an experiment, and the measurement of the longevity of effects. This suggests that assumptions about the genuine impact of news framing on the individual cannot be sustained without further investigation of the duration of results (Tewksbury & Scheufele, 2009). Consequently, a growing number of studies do just that: they test for the duration of news framing effects by employing over-time designs.

However, we argue that while there are a number of studies on the duration of news framing effects published, this empirical body of work does not yet allow for clear theoretical expectations for future studies (Baden & Lecheler, 2012). This is surprising, given that there are studies and reviews in other fields such as persuasion research that have accumulated knowledge regarding the duration of mediated communication effects (Hill, Lo, Vavreck, & Zaller, 2013; Hovland & Weiss, 1951; Iyengar & Kinder, 1987; Kleinnijenhuis, van Hoof, & Oegema, 2006; Mitchell, 2012; Wanta & Hu, 1994). Nevertheless, news framing is held to operate on different psychological processes than these theories of media effects (Scheufele, 2000), which warrants a review of the study of duration of framing effects specifically.

What Determines the Duration of News Framing Effects?

In the most general sense, duration is tested in framing effects studies by including additional delayed post-test measures of the dependent variable to a 'traditional' one-shot framing experiment (de Vreese, 2012). Valid conclusions about how long news framing effects actually last depend on a number of theoretical as well as empirical aspects of the respective experiment. Figure 1.1 summarizes these aspects and thus functions as the structural model of this review. The model shows that we consider three important groups of variables likely to empirically determine how long a framing effect lasts: (a) the theoretical foundation of the study; (b) its study and design characteristics; and (c) individual-level moderators tested within a study. In the following discussion, we introduce each of these factors.

When planning a news framing effects experiment, researchers must clearly define its *theoretical premise* or the independent (i.e., news frame) and dependent variables (i.e., what represents the "framing effect") within the design. Both aspects will influence how long reported effects last, because frames vary in strength (Aarøe, 2011) and framing effects on some attitudes, opinions and behaviors should be more or less durable than on others (Hill et al., 2013).

As discussed above, the question as to what exactly constitutes a 'news frame' as an *independent variable* remains contested (Matthes, 2009). So far, most framing experiments make use of emphasis frames (see Scheufele & Iyengar, in press) and both generic and issue-specific frames can be found in

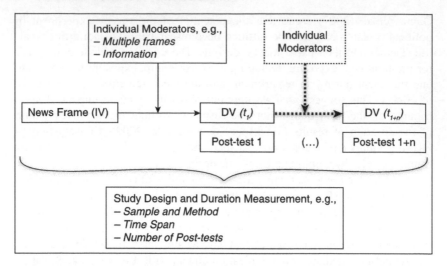

Figure 1.1 News Framing Effects over Time

these experiments. There is, however, evidence that some news frames can have stronger and therefore likely more durable effects on opinion. For example, Aarøe (2011) shows that generic episodic frames (i.e., frames that feature concrete cases and individuals) have stronger effects on opinions than thematic frames (i.e., frames that place an issue in a general of abstract context, see Iyengar, 1991), because they cause greater emotional responses (see also Gross, 2008).

In terms of *dependent variables*, framing researchers often focus on how news frames can affect our thinking about a certain political topic or event (Scheufele, 1999). Along these lines, some studies examine effects on information processing and how citizens interpret and "understand" a political issue or event (Nabi, 2003; Price, Tewksbury, & Powers, 1997; Shen, 2004; Valkenburg, Semetko, & de Vreese, 1999). However, most news framing scholars conceive this process as only a "mediating step on the way to some other effect" (Tewksbury & Scheufele, 2009, p. 26) and concentrate on effects of news frames on opinions (Haider-Markel & Joslyn, 2001; Slothuus, 2008), behavior (Schuck & de Vreese, 2006) and emotions (Gross, 2008). These studies usually report that opinions are susceptible to relatively strong news framing effects (Jacoby, 2000).

The duration of framing effects will also depend on characteristics connected to the overall *experimental design*. This, first, includes general study characteristics such as the decision to use a student sample (Mintz, Redd, & Vedlitz, 2006). Evidence suggests that this should matter for duration also, because there is evidence that survey experiments using student versus nonstudent samples in research related to politics produce results of varying magnitude (cf. Basil, 1996; Falk, Meier & Zehnder, 2013). Also, methodological decisions, such as conducting a study online or in the laboratory (cf. Wurm, Cano, & Barenboym, 2011), or with a within-subject (i.e., variability within an individual or sample) or between-subject (i.e., the difference between individuals or samples) comparison design (cf. Charness, Gneezy, & Kuhn, 2012), can play a role in how persistent a framing effect is.

When it comes to the elements of a study design that pertain to the actual measurement of duration, scholars are confronted with the question of how many measurement points should be employed and how maturation effects are handled. Naturally, the inclusion of two measurement points will only allow for linear result patterns, while more than two measurement points enables the analysis of more complex over-time changes in framing effects (cf. Zaller, 1992). Another important aspect is the overall time span of the longitudinal experiment. Obviously, a re-measurement after 15 minutes will produce different results than after two weeks. Baden and Lecheler (2012) argue that studies focusing on the duration of news framing effects have so far operated without theoretical guidelines as to 'when' a news framing effect should be re-measured. This renders the comparison of the overall time spans of longitudinal experiments paramount for future research.

Third, effect duration depends on a more conceptual aspect, namely which individual-level *moderator* variables are tapped in a study. Previous studies have identified a number of moderators of immediate news framing effects, such as individual-level knowledge (Nelson, Clawson, & Oxley, 1997; Schuck & de Vreese, 2006), values (Shen & Edwards, 2005) or emotions (Druckman & McDermott, 2008). Since these variables regulate how strongly an individual is influenced by a news frame, most or even all of them are also likely to play a role in how quickly a news framing effect dissipates.

A fourth determinant of framing effect duration not specified in Figure 1.1 is the question of how scholars themselves evaluate the relevance of news framing effects over time. Some authors might argue that a framing effect that lasts beyond initial exposure is sufficiently relevant, whereas others might only pass this judgment once an effect has been shown to translate into (voting) behavior. Inferences such as these determine as how pertinent news frames are perceived in future research.

Thus, in sum, we will review framing studies along four dimensions: First, we will evaluate the theoretical premises of longitudinal framing experiments (RQ1). Then we will examine how these experiments are designed and actually measure 'duration' (RQ2). Third, we will analyze which individual-level moderators influence the duration of news framing effects (RQ3). Lastly, we want to know if the authors of these studies themselves evaluate news framing effects as short-, middle- or long-term in nature (RQ4).

Method

Literature Search and Selection Criteria

For our review, we searched a number of databases for literature and examined the leading journals in the field (see Dundar & Fleeman, 2014) using the relevant keywords (e.g., *longitudinal experiments, delayed measurement, duration of framing effects*). Next, we checked the references section of all selected papers for further relevant studies. Also, we asked a number of experts in the field of news framing effects for help in finding further related works.[2]

We restrict our review to (a) experimental studies that operate (b) within the wider field of mediated communication research and news framing (including neighboring disciplines such as media studies, psychology, sociology, and political science) and that thus (c) empirically test the persistence of a news framing effect. This means that we only include studies where the researcher operationalized a framing effect in form of a (d) repeated-measure experiment. Because we are interested in classifying empirical results relating to the duration of news framing effects, this means we excluded purely theoretical papers, as well as studies that test other mass media effects, such as persuasion effects. Because longitudinal framing experiments have only recently gained popularity, we also include conference papers in this analysis. We initially selected 28 studies based on our search as detailed above. We then excluded studies that did not fulfil all of the above criteria (e.g., because they were actually panel surveys), and arrived at a final sample of 16 longitudinal experimental framing studies. These were published between 2000 and 2014, as no earlier studies could be found. Ten studies were conducted in the United States and six studies were conducted in Europe. The studies stem from research in communication science, political science, and psychology. We were not able to find eligible studies from other related fields, such as sociology.

Coding of Studies

Our codebook and coding procedure were based on previous reviews in the field of media effects (Roskos-Ewoldsen, Klinger, & Roskos-Ewoldsen, 2007; Mares & Woodard, 2007).

Based on our conceptual model (Figure 1.1), a graduate student coder was trained and coded the following variables within the selected experimental studies. For every selected article, the coder entered the appropriate items into a coding sheet according to the following coding schedule: First, we coded studies for (a) *general characteristics* such as author(s), if they were published, date of publication, and if the publication was in a journal or other academic outlet. Next, we focused on the (b) *theoretical approach* and the independent variables (either issue-specific or generic news frames). The coder then detailed the dependent variables in each study, categorizing them into attitudinal, affective or behavioral. The coder also recorded several variables pertaining to the (c) *measurement of duration* within each experiment, such as total number of post-tests, sample quality (non-student or student sample), sample size, method (online, laboratory experiment, quasi or full experiment, natural experiment), and overall time span of the experiment (in days).

We then coded which variables were used as (d) *moderators* within the selected studies with a list of moderators based on pre-existing framing experiments (e.g., values, emotions, information-processing variables, knowledge).

Lastly, the coder assessed (e) *duration according to authors* in three categories according to conclusions made by the authors as to how effects could be conceptualized: short (effects do not last), medium (effects have potential to be lasting), and long (effects are lasting). This variable was only coded, if duration was directly discussed in text (e.g., in the conclusion or discussion section). A random sample of three articles (> 10%) was used to test for intercoder reliability between two coders.[3] Overall percent agreement was .83; Cohen's kappa was .76.[4]

Results

The study of duration of news framing effects is a new and popular aspect of framing effects research. In recent years, there has been an increase in studies testing for duration and more studies are to be expected in the near future.

Theoretical Premises (RQ1)

Our review of the theoretical premises of duration experiments focused on the question which independent variables (i.e., which news frames?), and dependent variable were chosen (i.e., what will these news frames influence?). These choices will likely influence how long framing effects last within a study. Table 1.1 provides an overview of news frames and dependent variables used in the included studies. It shows that a majority of studies test how issue-specific news frames influence opinions ($n = 9$; 56.3%).

Independent Variables

Two groups of studies emerge: One in which issue-specific news frames are developed based on salient political issues or events (e.g., current policy debates; $n = 12$; 75%), and a second group where generic news frames are interpreted within a broader, sometimes non-salient, political or social context ($n = 4$; 25%). The first group argues that salient political contexts make their results more valid because reading about these issues feels realistic to participants. However, authors in the second group suggest that the use of broad and recurring news frames allows for greater generalizability of results beyond one issue contexts. Differences in use of generic versus issue-specific frames mirror the conceptual divide within framing research as discussed above (cf. Scheufele & Iyengar, in press).

Specifically, studies focusing on issue-specific frames develop frames from media content analysis or from public opinion data pertaining to the salience of a political issue. For example, Chong and Druckman (2010) report results from an experiment focusing on the U.S. Patriot Act "which was a piece of legislation enacted shortly after the terrorist attacks of September 11, 2001" (p. 666). Those examining the effects of generic frames base their designs on the conceptual importance of recurring journalistic angles, such as loss vs. gain frames (Boydstun & Ledgerwood, 2013; $n = 1$), the economic consequences

Table 1.1 Overview of Framing Experiments

Study	Total N	Sample[1]	Method[2]	Design[3]	Frames in Study	Dependent Var	Stimulus[3]	Control[4]
Boydstun & Ledgerwood (2013)	344	combination	laboratory	post-test	Loss/Gain frames	opinions	written	N
Chong & Druckman (2010)	1,302/749	combination	combination	post-test	Issue-Specific frames	opinions	written	Y
Chong & Druckman (2013)	794	non-student	online	post-test	Issue-Specific frames	opinions	written	Y
De Vreese (2004)	83	non-student	laboratory	post-test	Strategy frame	political cynicism/ opinions	audiovisual	N
Druckman & Leeper (2012)	985	combination	combination	post-test	Issue-Specific frames	opinions	written	Y
Druckman & Nelson (2003)	261	student	laboratory	post-test	Issue-Specific frames	opinions	written	Y
Druckman & Bolsen (2011)	621	non-student	combination	post-test	Issue-Specific frames	opinions	written	Y
Druckman et al. (2010)	416	non-student	laboratory	post-test	Issue-Sp. frames/Cues	vote choice	written	Y
Druckman et al. (2012)	547	combination	combination	post-test	Issue-Specific frames	opinions/ attitude certainty/	written	Y
Lecheler & de Vreese (2011)	1,324	non-student	online	post-test	Generic Frames	opinions	written	Y
Lecheler & de Vreese (2013)	625	non-student	online	post-test	Generic Frames	opinions	written	Y
Lecheler et al. (2015)	278	non-student	online	post-test	Issue-Specific frames	opinions	written	N
Matthes & Schemer (2012, study1)	236	student	online	post-test	Issue-Specific frames	opinions	written	N
Slothuus (2010)	1,636	non-student	natural/quasi	pre/post	Party/Issue-Sp. frames	opinions	combination	N
Tewksbury et al. (2000)	510	student	laboratory	post-test	Issue-Specific frames	issue evaluations	written	N
Vishwanath (2009)	129	student	combination	post-test	Issue-Specific frames	behav. intentions/ beliefs/importance	written	Y

Note: 1 Student/non-student sample or combination.
2 Type of experiment in study (laboratory/online/quasi/field/natural/other experiment, or combination).
3 Experimental design (DV measured pre/post-test, post-test only).
4 Type of stimulus (visual/audio-visual/written).
5 Was there a control condition (Y/N)?

frame (Lecheler & de Vreese, 2011; $n = 2$), and strategy news framing (i.e., frames that emphasize horse race, strategy, and tactics of politics; de Vreese, 2004; $n = 1$). For example, Lecheler & de Vreese (2011) test the effects of a positive or negative version of an economic consequences frame focusing on the role of new EU member states within the EU economy.

Overall, framing experiments have evaluated a range of political issues in connection to duration (e.g., international politics, terror, social policies), but only a limited number of generic news frames have been tested. There seems to be no systematic difference between the two groups in terms of how strong news framing effects are initially. However, studies using non-salient issues are able to detect longer-lasting framing effects, probably because there is less exposure to issue-relevant news in the interim period between initial and delayed post-tests (de Vreese, 2004). Also, other research on framing effects shows that framing effects are weaker, if the issue at stake has been important on the national news agenda before or during an experimental study (Lecheler, de Vreese, & Slothuus, 2009).

A large portion of both generic and issue-specific framing studies make use of "pro" and "con" versions of news frames (cf. Chong & Druckman, 2010; Druckman & Bolsen, 2011; Lecheler & de Vreese, 2013; Lecheler, Keer, Schuck, & Hänggli, 2015; Vishwanath, 2009), even if the used frames also differ along other content-related dimensions. One reason for the occurrence of valenced news frames in longitudinal framing experiments is the focus of a number of studies on competitive news framing over time (i.e., the exposure to news frames that are 'opposing'; $n = 7$). We discuss the impact of competitive news framing on duration testing below. Nevertheless, our review suggests that there are differences between pro and con frames in terms of duration: Vishwanath (2009) shows that negative news frames are likely to have stronger and therefore longer-lasting effects on opinions than positive news frames (see also Lecheler et al., 2015). This difference in longevity is likely related to a negativity bias in media effects. Negative information about politics has stronger effects, because it is easier understood and integrated into existing opinions and attitudes (Bizer, Larsen, & Petty, 2011; Soroka, 2006).

Dependent Variables

We find that a majority of studies were concerned with effects on *opinions* ($n = 14$; 87.5%), with a few studies reporting effects on issue interpretation ($n = 1$), voting choice ($n = 1$), and other behavioral intentions ($n = 1$). The concept of opinions includes a range of terms and issues used within these studies, such as opinions about emergent technologies (Druckman & Bolsen, 2011), support for increased investment in elderly care (Lecheler et al., 2015), and policy support (Slothuus, 2010). There is conclusive evidence that news frames will have initial (strong) effects on opinions, and that these effects dissipate over time.

As for other dependent variables, Druckman, Hennessy, St Charles, and Webber (2010) test framing effects on vote choice as a behavioral intent over time (*"Whom would you have voted for in this election?"* p. 139). Similarly, Vishwanath (2009) examines effects of frames on behavioral intentions connected to technology adaption, and finds strong initial and, to some extent, persistent effects. Yet, effects of news frames over time have only been tested on a relatively narrow sub-set of cognitive variables. Over-time designs provide the opportunity to tap real-life behavioral changes, which has so far been left widely unexplored.

All in all, we can argue that the theoretical premises (RQ1) of available over-time studies are homogenous. Most studies seem to compare the effects of pro or con frames on opinions. Results show that this initial cause-effect relationship is strong, and that negative (con) news frames have longer-lasting effects than positive (pro) news frames. The reason for this difference between valence frames is rarely an empirical focus within the reviewed studies, but it is likely connected to the negativity bias of media effects (Soroka, 2006). Our results suggest that, so far, there is no systematic difference in how fast issue-specific versus generic news framing effects dissipate. Also, framing effects pertaining to highly salient issues might dissipate more quickly as respondents are more likely to be exposed to dissonant media exposure later on, and because effects are weaker in the first place.

Experimental Designs (RQ2)

General Study Characteristics

Next, we evaluate the design of the included experiments. Table 1.1 shows that four of the reviewed studies made use of student samples, whereas the rest either employed a non-student sample ($n = 9$), or a combination of student and non-student participants ($n = 3$). Some studies reported samples of above 1,000 ($n = 3$), and typical sample size per condition was between 40 and 70 participants. Longitudinal experiments also showed a relatively even distribution between online survey questionnaires ($n = 5$), laboratory survey experiments ($n = 5$), or a combination of both ($n = 5$). Most studies were "full" survey experiments (i.e., randomized group allocation; $n= 15$), with one natural/quasi experiment (Slothuus, 2010). Table 1.1 also shows that all experiments except one were conducted using written newspaper article stimuli. Interestingly, all studies but one used news material that was made to look real, but which was constructed by the researchers. These articles often contained real facts, and the frames applied in them were obtained in preceding content analyses or pilot studies. Only Slothuus (2010), whose study is based on a natural experiment, taps duration of effects on published media reporting.

In terms of duration, there seems to be no difference between studies using student and non-student samples. However, unsurprisingly, studies using non-student or representative samples are more confident in asserting the generalizability of their results. Lab studies are able to implement more complex designs involving multiple frame exposure scenarios; this is more challenging when online designs are used.

Operationalization of duration

Table 1.2 provides a summary of aspects related to the measurement of duration. The variable *time* shows the total time elapsed between first or initial news frame exposure and the last re-measurement of the dependent variable in days. Time spans range from 0 to 77 days (Mdn_{time} = 14 days). With one exception (Slothuus, 2010; quasi/natural experiment), the duration of news framing effects is measured by post-test designs, where change between groups is compared over time. Most studies employed an overall design of two experimental sessions (n = 10; $Mdn_{session}$ = 2), with a frame exposure and post-test at T1, and one additional delayed post-test at T2. Yet, a number of studies employ more intricate designs: For instance, Matthes and Schemer (2012, study 1) report one immediate frame exposure and post-test at the start of the study, and one delayed exposure and again post-test ten days after the beginning of the study. Lecheler et al. (2015) employ four sessions and frame exposures, paired with three measures of the dependent variable per participant over the course of 42 days with an increasing time span in between delayed post-tests (*Inter1–4* = 1 day, 13 days, 14 days, 14 days). Druckman, Fein, and Leeper (2012) report results from four sessions across 21 days with seven days (*Inter1–3*) in between sessions.

A substantial portion of framing experiments includes multiple frame exposures over time in their design (n = 9; 56.3%). In doing so, these studies mimic a dynamic political discourse where participants are exposed to either competitive (n = 7) or repetitive (n = 4) news frames over time. Multiple frame exposures function as individual moderators of news framing effects, and are thus explored in the next section. Yet, even given these complex designs, most studies operate along relatively similar time spans of a couple of weeks. Only very few studies include either very short (e.g., Lecheler & de Vreese, 2011) or longer (e.g., Slothuus, 2010) designs. Authors generally do not explain their choice of time spans, but seem to base design decisions on previous studies. This suggests that the actual number of days or weeks between initial exposure and re-measurement might not be that relevant to scholars when planning longitudinal experiments.

In sum, the experimental design (RQ2) of available studies is based on full experimental survey designs using textual, news article-type, framing stimuli. Studies have tested effects across an average of two weeks, with few studies employing time delays below this average. However, there are studies that test framing effects across longer periods of time. Effects outlast initial exposure to some extent, but our review shows that authors do not often argue the question of how long in days or weeks an effect actually lasts.

Individual-level Moderators (RQ3)

Table 1.3 shows an overview of individual-level moderators tested in framing experiments included in this review. In this table, moderators are marked as either having been measured at baseline (i.e., in a pre-test by means

Table 1.2 How was duration measured?

Study	Total N	Time[1]	Session[2]	Measure[3]	Multiple[4]	Inter 1[5]	Inter 2	Inter 3	Inter 4	Duration[6]
Boydstun & Ledgerwood (2013)	344	0	2	2	competitive	0	—	—	—	—
Chong & Druckman (2010)	1,302/749	10/21	2	2	competitive	10	—	—	—	short
Chong & Druckman (2013)	794	24	2	2	competitive	10	14	—	—	short
De Vreese (2004)	83	14	2	2	—	14	—	—	—	short
Druckman & Leeper (2012, study1)	647	15	1	1	repetitive	5	5	5	—	short
Druckman & Nelson (2003)	261	10	2	2	—	10	—	—	—	short
Druckman & Bolsen (2011)	621	10	2	2	—	10	—	—	—	—
Druckman et al. (2010)	416	14	2	2	competitive	14	—	—	—	medium
Druckman et al. (2012)	547	21	4	2	combination	7	7	7	—	—
Lecheler & de Vreese (2011)	1,324	14	4	2	—	1	6	7	—	long
Lecheler & de Vreese (2013)	625	14	4	2	combination	1	6	7	—	medium
Lecheler et al. (2015)	278	42	4	3	repetitive	1	13	14	14	medium
Matthes & Schemer (2012, study1)	236	10	2	2	competitive	10	—	—	—	medium
Slothuus (2010)	1,636	77	11	1	—	7	7	7	7	—
Tewksbury et al. (2000)	510	21	2	2	—	21	—	—	—	—
Vishwanath (2009)	129	7	2	2	—	7	—	—	—	medium

Note: 1 Time elapsed between exposure and last delayed post-test measure; in days.
2 Number of sessions within experiment (e.g., either post-test only or post-test in combination with stimulus exposure, or only stimulus exposure).
3 Number of measurements DV per participant.
4 Multiple frame exposures; competitive (multiple exposure to competitive frames) or repetitive (multiple exposures to repetitive frames); combination (both competitive and repetitive exposures).
5 Time between t1 and t2; Inter2=t2→t3, Inter3=t3→t4; Inter4=t4-t5; in days.
6 Effect duration was divided in three categories according to the conclusion made by the authors as to how effects could be conceptualized: short (effects do not last), medium (effects have potential to be lasting), and long (effects are lasting); only coded if directly discussed in text (e.g., in conclusion section).

of trait/perception measures) or as manipulated within the experimental study design. Conceptually, scholars take two approaches towards testing what moderates the persistence of news framing effects. Some test if the duration of news framing effects depends on (a) multiple frame exposure scenarios (competitive/repetitive framing; frames with varying degrees of facts/information; self-selection of frames; $n = 9$), whereas others test how duration is influenced by an individual's state or trait (b) information-processing ($n = 5$).

Complex Frame Exposure Scenarios

Framing experiments including multiple news frame exposure scenarios mimic real-world media exposure. These studies can be classified into those testing the effects of (a) competitive or (b) repetitive exposure over time. Results from these studies provide convincing evidence as to how multiple frame exposure changes news framing effects: Studies focusing on competitive framing often conclude that news framing effects persist beyond initial exposure, but are relatively easily altered, sometimes only one day later, by competitive exposure (Chong & Druckman, 2010; Lecheler & de Vreese, 2013). Thus, most authors conclude that the relevance of news framing is limited by recency effects or the idea that opinions are often shaped by the latest frame an individual has been in contact with. The extent of recency depends on a frame's strength or power in changing opinions. This mechanism depends on individual-level information processing, which is discussed below.

Studies focusing on repetitive framing are less conclusive but suggest that repetitive news frame exposure strengthens the framing effect to some extent, perhaps because repetition causes an increase in attitude certainty (Druckman et al., 2012) or leads to actual longer-lasting effects (Lecheler et al., 2015). Some studies conceptualize multiple frame exposures in terms of 'pre-treatment effects'—news frame exposure prior to experimental treatment (Druckman & Leeper, 2012). In doing so, they offer insights as to how the magnitude of news framing effects produced in experimental studies may be interpreted. Also, Druckman et al. (2012) manipulate the extent to which media exposure is forced within their experiment, allowing participants to choose themselves which news frames they are exposed to over time. Results show that studying frame repetition over time matters, because participants tend to repeatedly choose attitude-consistent frames.

Information Processing

There is a group of studies focusing on the influence of online vs. memory-based message processing on framing effect duration ($n = 4$; Druckman et al., 2010). Generally, these studies demonstrate that online processors exhibit longer-lasting framing effects, because these individuals are able and willing to integrate a frame into their memory to be used at a later point in time. In a similar fashion, Matthes and Schemer (2012) find that framing effects on

Table 1.3 Individual Level Moderators of the Duration of Framing Effects

Study	Moderator
Boydstun & Ledgerwood (2013)	—
Chong & Druckman (2010)	competitive frame exposure[2]
	online/memory-based processing (need to evaluate)[1]
Chong & Druckman (2013)	competitive frame exposure[2]
	online/memory-based processing[2]
De Vreese (2004)	—
Druckman & Leeper (2012, study1)	online/memory-based processing[2]
Druckman & Nelson (2003)	—
Druckman & Bolsen (2011)	—
Druckman et al. (2010)	online/memory-based processing (need to evaluate)[1]
Druckman et al. (2012)	competitive frame exposure[2]
	repetitive frame exposure[2]
	information search behaviour[2]
Lecheler & de Vreese (2011)	political knowledge[1]
Lecheler & de Vreese (2013)	political knowledge[1]
	competitive frame exposure[2]
	repetitive frame exposure[2]
Lecheler et al. (2015)	political knowledge[1]
	repetitive frame exposure[2]
Matthes & Schemer (2012, study1)	opinion certainty[2]
	competitive frame exposure[2]
Slothuus (2010)	partisanship[1]
	issue beliefs[1]
Tewksbury et al. (2000)	—
Vishwanath (2009)	—

Note: 1   Measured at baseline (e.g., as trait/perception).
2   Manipulated in study design; only hypothesized, framing- and duration-related moderators; excludes "control variables" as moderators.

opinions paired with strong opinion certainty are less likely to be cancelled out by a competitive news frame than those paired with low opinion certainty. Another cluster of studies (Lecheler & de Vreese, 2011; $n = 3$) argues that the duration of framing effects depends on political knowledge. Results suggest that individuals with moderate knowledge will display the most persistent news framing effects, because they are most likely to integrate a news frame into their long-term memory. An exception to the focus on information processing is presented by Slothuus (2010), who shows that frame susceptibility is moderated by partisanship and issue beliefs—albeit within a natural quasi-experimental design.

In sum, the available research provides a comprehensive view of how duration of news framing effect is moderated by multiple frame exposures and information processing (RQ3). Competitive framing diminishes the influence of news frames—framing is susceptible to strong recency effects depending on how strong a news frame is. Repetitive framing leads to (somewhat) stronger news framing effects. Individuals who are online processors and those with high opinion certainty show greater opinion stability, which means longer-lasting effects. Also, those with moderate levels of political knowledge display the most durable news framing effects.

Lasting? Or Not? (RQ4)

We also examined if scholars themselves judge their framing effects as short-, mid- or long-term. Table 1.2 contains an overview of judgments found in the analyzed manuscripts. Almost all studies included in this analysis find news framing effects to last beyond initial exposure, but most authors are careful in producing clear statements as to the relevance of their results for political decision-making over time. Four studies characterized their effects as short-term or not lasting. For instance, de Vreese (2004) did not find a significant framing effect two weeks after initial exposure and concludes that framing effects are short-term. A second group of studies concluded that their effects were moderately durable, meaning that some effects may persist while others vanish ($n = 4$): Vishwanath (2009) studied the impact of news framing on technology adoption over time and posits that "framing effects attenuated over time" when it came to behavioral intent, but that effects did "persist" over time when it came to the influence of frames on beliefs (p. 197).

A third group of authors argues that their effects are long-lasting. For instance, Lecheler and de Vreese (2011) note that their effects were "surprisingly resistant to dilution," with substantial news framing effects two weeks after news frame exposure (p. 975). Notably, however, authors that did not test for moderators of duration are most willing to define effects as short- or long-term (or as relevant or not relevant for real-life politics and decision-making), whereas those testing for moderators produced more nuanced judgments. Importantly, Druckman et al. (2012) posit that news framing effect experiments should, in addition to over-time designs, also relax conditions of forced exposure within their experimental designs. Their first results illustrate that individuals will retreat to attitude-consistent news if given a choice. This has additional implications for how realistic framing effects from previous experiments actually are.

Overall, we find that most authors are cautious in their view of how long news framing effects last (RQ4). Yet, with increasing empirical data and growing insights into the dynamics of media use over time, effects seem to become smaller and less persistent. Empirical evidence also suggests that repetitive exposure to news frames causes stronger or lasting effects, and that frames still impact decision-making later on. This at least somewhat supports the idea of a powerful news framing effect.

Conclusion

The goal of this review was to provide a first and systematic answer to the question how long news framing effects last. Our results show that available longitudinal framing studies have already produced an important body of work. In sum, our review suggests the following:

- Theoretical premises (RQ1) of over-time studies are relatively homogenous. Most studies compare the effects of pro or con frames on opinions and find initial strong news framing effects. So far, results suggest that types of frames (e.g., generic vs. issue-specific) do not influence duration. There is data that shows, however, how negative news frames can have longer-lasting effects than positive news frames. Also, those studying salient political issues seem to report shorter-lasting framing effects compared to those focusing on non-salient issues. Similarly, we suggest that the duration of framing effects on dependent variables such as behavioral intentions or emotions should be similar to that on opinions. Yet, further study is required to show if this is actually the case.
- Experimental designs (RQ2) are typically full experimental survey designs using non-student samples and textual framing stimuli in the form of newspaper articles. Many studies test effects across two weeks, with only a few employing time delays below or above this average. Our review suggests that most studies do not emphasize how long in days or weeks exactly an over-time framing effect lasts. Also, studies provide little or no detail as to why a specific time span in a longitudinal experiment was chosen.
- The duration of news framing effect is moderated by multiple frame exposure and information processing (RQ3). Competitive frame exposure shows that recency effects dominate framing effects. Repetitive framing leads to stronger effects and greater attitude certainty. Online processors and those with high opinion certainty show greater opinion stability after a framing effect. Also, moderate levels of political knowledge lead to the most robust framing effects. There is so far no evidence on how other moderators of framing effects, such as values, beliefs, and emotional states and traits, influence duration.
- Most authors are careful when predicting how long their news frames last and if they are 'relevant' for real-life politics (RQ4). With increasing empirical data regarding the complexities of real-life media use, effects seem to become smaller and less durable. But, our review also shows that repetitive or pre-treatment exposure to news frames still to some extent impacts decision-making later on, which supports the idea that experiments can provide a useful picture of real-life mediated communication effects.

We appreciate that the focused nature of this study has provided us with both a US/European-biased sample and a small number of studies to review.

Our focus on experiments also renders it beyond the scope of this article to present an in-depth discussion of the benefits of experimentation in framing effects research versus other research designs, such as panel survey in combination with content analyses. We consciously tried to uncouple the studies discussed in this review from panel survey studies, simply because their claim for causality and their methods are different. We encourage future studies to not lose sight of existing and continuing threats to ecological validity in media effects research.

Future Research Agenda

Based on this review, we identify a number of future avenues for research on the duration of news framing effects. These are particularly important given the restricted number of studies available for our review at this point in time.

Compare News Frame Types

Framing experiments have tested longevity using a variety of issue-specific and generic news frames. What has been left untouched is the question if there are types of frames that differ across the board in how long they impact individual opinions, attitudes and behaviors. For instance, one could assume that episodic news frames, which have been shown to elicit stronger news framing effects due to their emotive qualities (Aarøe, 2011), might also lead to longer-lasting framing effects than thematic frames. Along the same lines, human interest or conflict frames might have substantially different effects over time (see Semetko & Valkenburg, 2000). For those interested in issue-specific news frames, we suggest that there could be differences at the issue-level. Our review suggests that issue saliency will impact duration, and there could be other important issue dimensions, such as issue contestation, framing within media hypes, and the connection between an issue and certain political values. Combinations of issue-specific and generic frames might also yield new insights as to the effects of competitive and repetitive frame exposure over time.

Test Visual Framing Effects

This review shows that almost all repeat-measure framing studies operated with textual, newspaper-style experimental stimuli. However, there is reason to believe that effects of textual information substantially differ from that of audio-visual stimuli (Geise & Baden, 2014; Messaris & Abraham, 2001; Powell, Boomgaarden, de Swert, & de Vreese, 2015). There is increasing interest in studying visual framing via qualitative and quantitative content analyses, and future studies can learn from other fields such as visual argumentation in their theoretical and methodological set-up (cf. Cloud, 2004; Greenwood & Jenkins, 2015; Smith & McDonald, 2011). These content analyses show different categories of visual representation in the news media that may be used in experimental studies. Along the same lines, studies using related theoretical approaches, such as persuasion and learning (Jackob, Roessing & Peterson, 2011), have plotted the effects of visuals. These studies should be followed up by evidence from framing research and in particular by studies using longitudinal research designs.

Also, there are suggestions that using visual rather than textual stimuli in framing experiments is more theoretically rigorous. Scheufele and Iyengar (in press) suggest that framing researchers move away from emphasis frames towards equivalency frames, and that they operationalize these frames by using visual cues. They point out that visual cues make up a majority of our daily media use and that visual stimuli offer researchers greater control as they allow for the clean variation of specific factors of a frame in an experimental setting.

Specify Results by Introducing Shorter Time Spans

The available studies test longevity across a time span of approximately two weeks. While an obvious extension might be to also examine framing effects across longer time spans, we also suggest the introduction of shorter delays. Shorter delays between frame exposure and re-measurement could be particularly insightful for those studying affective variables and arousal as a result of news framing. Also, shorter time spans allow for the inclusion of psychophysiological measures within laboratory designs. By studying bodily responses to news frame exposure, researchers may be able to disentangle the psychological processes that lead to (lasting) news framing effects. Studies might make use of both methodological as well as theoretical insights from neuroscience and psychology (cf. de Martino, Kumaran, Seymour, & Dolan, 2006).

Culture as a Variable

Many existing studies on duration are conducted within the United States or Western Europe. None of them takes an intercultural or comparative view on effect duration (see van Gorp, 2007). This is surprising, given the fact that the persistence and strength of media effects by no means only depends on individual level moderators, but is likely also related to media landscapes, the journalistic style of a country and the national salience of a political issue (Esser, Strömbäck, & de Vreese, 2012). Comparative research designs have the ability of showing if the information environment of news frames affect the duration of effects (Schuck et al., 2013).

Diversify Dependent Variables

Almost all framing studies in our review tested news framing effects on opinions. While testing effects on (public) opinion is at the center of understanding how news work within political discourse, this still leaves a big gap. The study of news framing effects over time offers the possibility to introduce measures of actual behavior and decision-making into experimental designs. This may happen both in a laboratory and online. For instance, in laboratory experiments, over-time designs allow for the observation of information searching and selection behaviors after frame exposure. When conducting research online, follow-up surveys could contain a variety of measures addressing real behavior between frame exposure and re-measurement. Beyond behavior, there is also the need to further study the role of emotions in the duration of news framing effects.

Go Beyond Information-Processing

We also suggest diversification regarding the individual-level moderators of the duration of news framing effects. There is plenty of evidence on moderators of immediate news framing effects (Borah, 2011). At the moment, information processing is the number one determinant of how well framing effects persist over time. However, duration might also depend on emotional states or mood when encountering a news frame (Druckman & McDermott, 2008). Also, how well a news frame corresponds to pre-existing values, beliefs and ideology is likely to influence duration, as will a range of personality traits from the psychological literature (Blais & St-Vincent, 2011; Blickle, 1996; Hastie & Kumar, 1979). Lastly, variables that are popular in public opinion research, such as partisanship, previous voting behavior, and cynicism should be tested when predicting framing effect duration (e.g., Schuck & de Vreese, 2012).

Use Real News Coverage as Stimulus Material

All but one study analyzed in this paper used constructed rather than actually published news material as a stimulus. The constructed news media stimuli often contained real facts, and the frames applied in them were obtained in preceding content analyses or pilot studies. Only Slothuus (2010), whose study is based on a natural experiment, taps duration of effects on real-life media reporting. Given that longitudinal framing studies are designed with the goal of increasing external validity, future studies should consider the possibility of using actually published news material as stimuli. This approach, naturally, is limited in that control for pre-treatment effects to published material is decreased (e.g., Druckman & Leeper, 2012). However, the use of actual news content may substantially increase awareness among framing scholars as to the actual complexity of news framing effects.

In sum, our results show that, even though the available studies stem from different academic fields, they are remarkably similar in their approach towards studying framing effects over time. This entails that many determinants of the duration of framing effects are still untested. We thus view this article not as a final account of the question posed in its title, but as an invitation for future research and the better integration of the variable 'time' into current theoretical models.

Notes

1 Parts of this introduction to framing theory have been derived from Lecheler (2010) and de Vreese and Lecheler (2012).
2 We searched databases such as Web of Science and web search engines such as Google Scholar; we consulted journals within mass communication research, e.g., *Communication Research, Communication Monographs* and *Journal of Communication* as well as journals in psychology and political science (e.g., *The Journal of Politics, American Journal of Political Science*); we contacted the authors of some of the articles (e.g., JD; DT), but also other experts in framing research (e.g., JM).
3 The second coder was one of the authors.
4 *Percentage*: General characteristics = 1.00; theoretical approach = .83; measurement of duration = 1.00; moderators = .66; duration according to authors = .66. *Cohen's kappa*: General characteristics = 1.00; theoretical approach = .77; measurement of duration = 1.00; moderators = .55; duration according to authors = .50.

References

Aarøe, L. (2011). Investigating frame strength: The case of episodic and thematic framing. *Political Communication, 28*(2), 207–226. doi: 10.1080/10584609.2011.568041

Baden, C., & Lecheler, S. (2012). Fleeting, fading, or far-reaching? A knowledge-based model of the persistence of framing effects. *Communication Theory, 22*, 359–382. doi: 10.1111/j.1468-2885.2012.01413.x

Barabas, J., & Jerit, J. (2010). Are survey experiments externally valid? *American Political Science Review, 104*(02), 226–242. doi: 0.1017/S0003055410000092

Basil, M. D. (1996). Standpoint: The use of student samples in communication research. *Journal of Broadcasting and Electronic Media, 40*(3), 431–440. doi: 10.1080/08838159609364364

Bizer, G. Y., Larsen, J. T., & Petty, R. E. (2011). Exploring the valence-framing effect: Negative framing enhances attitude strength. *Political Psychology, 32*(1), 59–80. doi: 10.1111/j.1467-9221.2010.00795.x

Blais, A., & St-Vincent, S. L. (2011). Personality traits, political attitudes and the propensity to vote. *European Journal of Political Research, 50*(3), 395–417. doi: 10.1111/j.1475-6765.2010.01935.x

Blickle, G. (1996). Personality traits, learning strategies, and performance. European *Journal of Personality, 10*(5), 337–352. doi: http://dx.doi.org/10.1006/ceps.1999.1042

Borah, P. (2011). Conceptual issues in framing theory: A systematic examination of a decade's literature. *Journal of Communication, 61*(2), 246–263. doi: 10.1111/j.1460-2466.2011.01539.x

Boydstun, A. E., & Ledgerwood, A. (2013, April). *On the limits of reframing effects: The asymmetric stickiness of loss and gain frames.* Paper presented at the Visions in Methodology Conference, Tallahassee, FL.

Campbell, D. T., & Stanley, J. C. (1966). *Experimental and quasi-experimental designs for research.* Chicago, IL: Rand McNally.

Carragee, K. M., & Roefs, W. (2004). The neglect of power in recent framing research. *Journal of Communication, 54*(2), 214–233. doi: 10.1111/j.1460-2466.2004.tb02625.x

Charness, G., Gneezy, U., & Kuhn, M. A. (2012). Experimental methods: Between-subject and within-subject design. *Journal of Economic Behavior & Organization, 81*(1), 1–8. doi: http://dx.doi.org/10.1016/j.jebo.2011.08.009

Chong, D., & Druckman, J. N. (2007). A theory of framing and opinion formation in competitive elite environments. *Journal of Communication, 57*(1), 99–118. doi: 10.1111/j.1460-2466.2006.00331.x

Chong, D., & Druckman, J. N. (2010). Dynamic public opinion: Communication effects over time. *American Political Science Review, 104*(4), 663–680. doi: http://dx.doi.org/10.1017/ S0003055410000493

Chong, D., & Druckman, J. N. (2013). Counterframing effects. *The Journal of Politics, 75*(01), 1–16. doi: http://dx.doi.org/10.1017/S0022381612000837

Cloud, D. L. (2004). "To veil the threat of terror": Afghan women and the clash of civilizations in the imagery of the US war on terrorism. *Quarterly Journal of Speech, 90*(3), 285–306. doi: 10.1080/0033563042000270726

D'Angelo, P. (2002). News framing as a multiparadigmatic research program: A response to Entman. *Journal of Communication, 52*(4), 870–88. doi: 10.1111/ j.1460-2466.2002.tb02578.x

de Martino, B., Kumaran, D., Seymour, B., & Dolan, R. J. (2006). Frames, biases, and rational decision-making in the human brain. *Science, 313*(5787), 684–687. doi: 10.1126/science.1128356

de Vreese, C. H. (2002). *Framing Europe: Television news and European integration.* Amsterdam, NL: Aksant Academic Publishers.

de Vreese, C. H. (2004). The effects of strategic news on political cynicism, issue evaluations, and policy support: A two-wave experiment. *Mass Communication & Society, 7*(2), 191–214. doi: 10.1207/s15327825mcs0702_4

de Vreese, C. H. (2012). New avenues for framing research. *American Behavioral Scientist, 56*(3), 365–375. doi: 10.1177/0002764211426331

de Vreese, C. H., & Lecheler, S. (2012). News framing research: An overview and account of new developments. In H. A. Semetko & M. Scammell (eds.). *The Sage Handbook of Political Communication* (pp. 292–306). London: Sage.

de Vreese, C. H., & Semetko, H. A. (2002). Cynical and engaged strategic campaign coverage, public opinion, and mobilization in a referendum. *Communication Research, 29*(6), 615–641. doi: 10.1177/009365002237829

de Vreese, C. H., Peter, J., & Semetko, H. A. (2001). Framing politics at the launch of the Euro: A cross-national comparative study of frames in the news. *Political Communication, 18*(2), 107–122. doi: 10.1080/105846001750322934

Druckman, J. N. (2001). On the limits of framing effects: Who can frame? *Journal of Politics, 63*(4), 1041–1066. doi: 10.1111/0022-3816.00100

Druckman, J. N., & Bolsen, T. (2011). Framing, motivated reasoning, and opinions about emergent technologies. *Journal of Communication, 61*(4), 659–688. doi: 10.1111/j.1460-2466.2011.01562.x

Druckman, J. N., & Leeper, T. J. (2012). Learning more from political communication experiments: Pretreatment and its effects. *American Journal of Political Science, 56*(4), 875–896. doi: 10.1111/j.1540-5907.2012.00582.x

Druckman, J. N., & McDermott, R. (2008). Emotions and the framing of risky choice. *Political Behavior, 30,* 297–321. doi: 10.1007/s11109-008-9056-y

Druckman, J. N., & Nelson, K. R. (2003). Framing and deliberation: How citizens' conversations limit elite influence. *American Journal of Political Science, 47*(4), 729–745. doi: 10.1111/1540-5907.00051

Druckman, J. N., Fein, J., & Leeper, T. J. (2012). A source of bias in public opinion stability. *American Political Science Review, 106*(2), 430–454. doi: 10.1017/S000305541 200012

Druckman, J. N., Hennessy, C. L., St Charles, K., & Webber, J. (2010). Competing rhetoric over time: Frames versus cues. *The Journal of Politics, 72*(01), 136–148. doi: http://dx.doi.org/10.1017/S0022381609990521

Dundar, Y., & Fleeman, N. (2014). Developing my search strategy and applying inclusion criteria. In A. Boland, M. G. Cherry, & R. Dickson (Eds.), *Doing a systematic review: A student's guide* (pp. 87–99). New York: Routledge.

Entman, R. M. (1993). Framing: Toward clarification of a fractured paradigm. *Journal of Communication, 43*(4), 51–58. doi: 10.1111/j.1460-2466.1993.tb01304.x

Entman, R. M. (2003). Cascading activation: Contesting the White House's frame after 9/11. *Political Communication, 20*(4), 415–432. doi: 10.1080/10584600390244176

Esser, F., Strömbäck, J., & de Vreese, C. H. (2012). Reviewing key concepts in research on political news journalism: Conceptualizations, operationalizations, and propositions for future research. *Journalism, 13*(2), 139–143. doi: 10.1177/1464884911427795

Falk, A., Meier, S., & Zehnder, C. (2013). Do lab experiments misrepresent social preferences? The case of self-selected student samples. *Journal of the European Economic Association, 11*(4), 839–852. doi: 10.1111/jeea.12019

Gaines, B. J., Kuklinski, J. H., & Quirk, P. J. (2007). The logic of the survey experiment reexamined. *Political Analysis, 15*, 1–20. doi: 10.1093/pan/mpl008

Gamson, W. A., & Modigliani, A. (1987). The changing culture of affirmative action. In R. G. Braungart & M. M. Braungart (Eds.), *Research in political sociology* (Vol. 3, pp. 137–177). Greenwich, CT: JAI Press.

Gamson, W. A., & Modigliani, A. (1989). Media discourse and public opinion on nuclear power: A constructionist approach. *American Journal of Sociology, 95*, 1–37.

Geise, S., & Baden, C. (2014). Putting the image back into the frame: Modeling the linkage between visual communication and frame-processing theory. *Communication Theory* (early view). doi: 10.1111/comt.12048

Gitlin, T. (1980). *The whole world is watching: Mass media in the making and unmaking of the new left*. Berkeley: University of California Press.

Goffman, E. (1974). *Frame analysis: An essay on the organization of experience*. New York: Harper and Row.

Greenwood, K., & Jenkins, J. (2015). Visual framing of the Syrian conflict in news and public affairs magazines. *Journalism Studies, 16*(2), 207–227. doi: 10.1080/1461670X.2013.865969

Gross, K. (2008). Framing persuasive appeals: Episodic and thematic framing, emotional response, and policy opinion. *Political Psychology, 29*, 169–192. doi: 10.1111/j.1467-9221.2008.00622.x

Haider-Markel, D. P, & Joslyn, M. R. (2001). Gun policy, opinion, tragedy, and blame attribution: The conditional influence of issue frames. *Journal of Politics, 63*(2), 520–543. doi: 10.1111/0022-3816.0007

Hastie, R., & Kumar, P. A. (1979). Person memory: Personality traits as organizing principles in memory for behaviors. *Journal of Personality and Social Psychology,37*(1), 25–38. doi: 10.1037/0022-3514.37.1.25

Hill, S. J., Lo, J., Vavreck, L., & Zaller, J. (2013). How quickly we forget: The duration of persuasion effects from mass communication. *Political Communication, 30*(4), 521–547. doi: 10.1080/10584609.2013.828143

Hovland, C. I., & Weiss, W. (1951). The influence of source credibility on communication effectiveness. *Public opinion quarterly, 15*(4), 635–650. doi: 10.1086/266350

Iyengar, S. (1991) *Is anyone responsible? How television frames political issues*. Chicago, IL: University of Chicago Press.

Iyengar, S. (2010). Framing research: The next steps. In B. F. Schaffner & P. J. Sellers (Eds.), *Winning with words: The origins and impact of framing* (pp. 185–191). New York: Routledge.

Iyengar, S., & Kinder, D. R. (1987*). News that matters: Agenda-Setting and priming in a television age.* Chicago, IL: University of Chicago Press.

Iyengar, S., & Simon, A. (1993). News coverage of the gulf crisis and public opinion: A study of agenda-setting, priming, and framing. *Communication Research, 20*(3), 365–383. doi: 10.1177/009365093020003002

Jackob, N., Roessing, T., & Petersen, T. (2011). The effects of verbal and nonverbal elements in persuasive communication: Findings from two multi-method experiments. *Communications, 36*(2), 245–271. doi: 10.1515/comm.2011.012

Jacoby, W. G. (2000). Issue framing and public opinion on government spending. *American Journal of Political Science, 44*(4), 750–767. doi: 10.2307/2669279

Kahneman, D., & Tversky, A. (1979). Prospect theory: An analysis of decisions under risk. *Econometrica, 47*(2), 263–291. doi: 10.2307/1914185

Kahneman, D., & Tversky, A. (1984). Choices, values, and frames. *American psychologist, 39*(4), 341. doi: 10.1037/0003-066X.39.4.341

Kinder, D. R. (2007). Curmudgeonly advice. *Journal of Communication, 57*(1), 155–162. doi: 10.1111/j.1460-2466.2006.00335.x

Kinder, D. R., & Sanders, L. M. (1996). *Divided by color: Racial politics and democratic ideals.* Chicago, IL: University of Chicago Press.

Kleinnijenhuis, J., van Hoof, A. M., & Oegema, D. (2006). Negative news and the sleeper effect of distrust. *The Harvard International Journal of Press/Politics, 11*(2), 86–104. doi: 10.1177/1081180X06286417

Lecheler, S. (2010). *Framing politics* (Doctoral dissertation). Retrieved from UvA-DAE Digital Academic Repository.

Lecheler, S., & de Vreese, C. H. (2011). Getting real: The duration of framing effects. *Journal of Communication, 61*(5), 959–983. doi: 10.1111/j.1460-2466.2011.01580.x

Lecheler, S., & de Vreese, C. H. (2013). What a difference a day makes? The effects of repetitive and competitive news framing over time. *Communication Research, 40*(2), 147–175. doi: 10.1177/0093650212470688

Lecheler, S., de Vreese, C., & Slothuus, R. (2009). Issue importance as a moderator of framing effects. *Communication Research, 36*(3), 400–425. doi: 10.1177/009365020933 3028

Lecheler, S., Keer, M., Schuck, A. R. T., & Hänggli, R. (2015). The effects of repetitive news framing on political opinions over time. *Communication Monographs* (ahead-of-print), 1–20. doi: 10.1080/03637751.2014.994646

Mares, M. L., & Woodard, E. H. (2007). Positive effects of television on children's social interaction: A meta-analysis. In R. W. Weiss, B. M. Gayle, N. Burrell, M. Allen, & J. Bryant (Eds.), *Mass media effects research: Advances through meta-analysis* (pp. 281–300), New York, NY: Routledge.

Matthes, J. (2009). What's in a frame? A content analysis of media framing studies in the world's leading communication journals, 1990–2005. *Journalism & Mass Communication Quarterly, 86*(2), 349–367. doi: 10.1177/107769900908600206

Matthes, J., & Kohring, M. (2008). The content analysis of media frames: Toward improving reliability and validity. *Journal of Communication, 58*(2), 258–279.

Matthes, J., & Schemer, C. (2012). Diachronic framing effects in competitive opinion environments. *Political Communication, 29*(3), 319–339. doi: 10.1080/10584609. 2012.694985

Messaris, P., & Abraham, L. (2001). The role of images in framing news stories. In S. Reese, O. Gandy, & A. Grant (Eds.), *Framing public life* (pp. 215–226), Mahwah, NJ: Lawrence Erlbaum.

Mintz, A., Redd, S. B., & Vedlitz, A. (2006). Can we generalize from student experiments to the real world in political science, military affairs, and international relations? *Journal of Conflict Resolution, 50*(5), 757–776. doi: 10.1177/0022002706291052

Mitchell, D. G. (2012). It's about time: The lifespan of information effects in a multiweek campaign. *American Journal of Political Science, 56*, 298–311. doi: 10.1111/j.1540-5907.2011.00549.x

Nabi, R. L. (2003). Exploring the framing effects of emotion. *Communication Research, 30*, 224–247. doi: 10.1177/0093650202250881

Nelson, T. E., Clawson, R. A., & Oxley, Z. M. (1997). Media framing of a civil liberties conflict and its effect on tolerance. *American Political Science Review, 91*(3), 567–583. Retrieved from www.jstor.org/stable/2952075

Nelson, T. E., Oxley, Z. M., & Clawson, R. A. (1997). Toward a psychology of framing effects. *Political Behavior, 19*(3), 221–246. doi: 10.1023/A:1024834831093

Powell, T. E., Boomgaarden, H. G., de Swert, K., & de Vreese, C. H. (2015, February). *A clearer picture: Unpacking the contribution of visuals and text to framing effects.* Paper presented at the Etmaal van de Communicatiewetenschap, Antwerp/Belgium.

Price, V., Tewksbury, D., & Powers, E. (1997). Switching trains of thought. *Communication Research, 24*(5), 481–506. doi: 10.1177/009365097024005002

Reese, S. D. (2001). Prologue—framing public life: A bridging model for media research. In S. D. Reese, O. H. Gandy, Jr., & A. E. Grant (Eds.), *Framing public life. Perspectives on media and our understanding of the social world* (pp. 7–32). Mahwah, NJ: Lawrence Erlbaum.

Roskos-Ewoldsen, D. R., Klinger, M. R., & Roskos-Ewoldsen, B. (2007). Media priming: A meta-analysis. In R. W. Weiss, B. M. Gayle, N. Burrell, M. Allen, & J. Bryant (Eds.), *Mass media effects research: Advances through meta-analysis* (pp. 53–80), New York, NY: Routledge.

Scheufele, D. A. (1999). Framing as a theory of media effects. *Journal of Communication, 49*(1), 103–122. doi: 10.1111/j.1460-2466.1999.tb02784.x

Scheufele, D. A. (2000). Agenda-setting, priming, and framing revisited: Another look at the cognitive effects of political communication. *Mass Communication and Society, 3*(2), 297–316. doi: 10.1207/S15327825MCS0323_07

Scheufele, D., & Iyengar, S. (in press). The state of framing research: a call for new directions. *The Oxford Handbook of Political Communication Theories.* New York, NY: Oxford University Press.

Scheufele, D. A., & Tewksbury, D. (2007). Framing, agenda setting, and priming: The evolution of three media effects models. *Journal of Communication, 57*(1), 9–20. doi: 10.1111/j.0021-9916.2007.00326.x

Schuck, A. R., & de Vreese, C. H. (2006). Between risk and opportunity: News framing and its effects on public support for EU enlargement. *European Journal of Communication, 21*(1), 5–23. doi: 10.1177/0267323106060987

Schuck, A. R., & de Vreese, C. H. (2012). When good news is bad news: Explicating the moderated mediation dynamic behind the reversed mobilization effect. *Journal of Communication, 62*(1), 57–77. doi: 10.1111/j.1460-2466.2011.01624.x

Schuck, A. R., Vliegenthart, R., Boomgaarden, H. G., Elenbaas, M., Azrout, R., van Spanje, J., & de Vreese, C. H. (2013). Explaining campaign news coverage: How medium, time, and context explain variation in the media framing of the 2009

European parliamentary elections. *Journal of Political Marketing, 12*(1), 8–28. doi: 10.1080/15377857.2013.752192

Semetko, H. A., & Valkenburg, P. M. (2000). Framing European politics: A content analysis of press and television news. *Journal of Communication, 50*(2), 93–109. doi: 10.1111/j.1460-2466.2000.tb02843.x

Shen, F. (2004). Chronic accessibility and individual cognitions: Examining the effects of message frames in political advertisements. *Journal of Communication, 54*(1), 123–137. doi: 10.1111/j.1460-2466.2004.tb02617.x

Shen, F., & Edwards, H. H. (2005). Economic individualism, humanitarianism, and welfare reform: A value-based account of framing effects. *Journal of Communication, 55*(4), 795–809. doi: 10.1111/j.1460-2466.2005.tb03023.x

Slothuus, R. (2008). More than weighting cognitive importance: A dual process model of issue framing effects. *Political Psychology, 29*(1), 1–28. doi: 10.1111/j.1467-9221.2007.00610.x

Slothuus, R. (2010). When can political parties lead public opinion? Evidence from a natural experiment. *Political Communication, 27*(2), 158–177. doi: 10.1080/10584 601003709381

Smith, C. M., & McDonald, K. M. (2011). The mundane to the memorial: circulating and deliberating the war in Iraq through vernacular soldier-produced videos. *Critical Studies in Media Communication, 28*(4), 292–313. doi: 10.1080/15295036.2011. 589031

Sniderman, P. M., & Theriault, S. M. (2004). The structure of political argument and the logic of issue framing. In W. E. Saris & P. M. Sniderman (Eds.), *Studies in Public Opinion* (pp. 133–165). Princeton, NJ: Princeton University Press.

Soroka, S. N. (2006). Good news and bad news: Asymmetric responses to economic information. *Journal of Politics, 68*(2), 372–385. doi: http://dx.doi.org/10.1111/ j.1468-2508.2006.00413.x

Spencer, S. J., Zanna, M. P., & Fong, G. T. (2005). Establishing a causal chain: Why experiments are often more effective than mediational analyses in examining psychological processes. *Journal of Personality and Social Psychology, 89*(6), 845. doi: 10.1037/0022-3514.89.6.845

Tewksbury, D., & Scheufele, D. (2009). News framing theory and research. In J. Bryant & M. B. Oliver (Eds.), *Media effects: Advances in theory and research* (pp. 17–33, 3rd edn). New York: Routledge.

Tewksbury, D., Jones, J. Peske, M. W., Raymond, A., & Vig, W. (2000). The interaction of news and advocate frames: Manipulating audience perceptions of a local public policy issue. *Journalism and Mass Communication Quarterly, 77*(4), 804–829. doi: 10.1177/107769900007700406

Tuchman, G. (1978). *Making news. A study in the construction of reality.* New York, NY: Free Press.

Valkenburg, P. M., Semetko, H. A., & de Vreese, C. H. (1999). The effects of news frames on readers' thoughts and recall. *Communication Research, 26*, 550–569. doi: 10.1177/009365099026005002

van Gorp, B. (2007). The constructionist approach to framing: Bringing culture back in. *Journal of Communication, 57*(1), 60–78. doi: 10.1111/j.0021-9916.2007. 00329.x

Vishwanath, A. (2009). From belief-importance to intention: The impact of framing on technology adoption. *Communication Monographs, 76*(2), 177–206. doi: 10.1080/03637750902828438

Wanta, W., & Hu, Y. W. (1994). The effects of credibility, reliance, and exposure on media agenda-setting: A path analysis model. *Journalism & Mass Communication Quarterly, 71*(1), 90–98. doi: 10.1177/107769909407100109

Wurm, L. H., Cano, A., & Barenboym, D. A. (2011). Ratings gathered online vs. in person: Different stimulus sets and different statistical conclusions. *Mental Lexicon, 6*(2), 325–350. doi: http://dx.doi.org/10.1075/ml.6.2.05wur

Zaller, J. (1992). *The nature and origins of mass opinion*. New York: Cambridge University Press.

CHAPTER CONTENTS

2 Unpacking Engagement

Convergence and Divergence in Transportation and Identification

Nurit Tal-Or and Jonathan Cohen

University of Haifa

This review proposes that transportation and identification are distinct forms of engaging with narratives, that they are enhanced by different factors and that they have distinct roles in narrative persuasion. By describing and analyzing 56 studies that explore the antecedents and consequences of transportation and identification, the ways in which these two processes are similar and different are highlighted. Following the review, new directions for research in this area are explicated. Finally, implications for both theory and message design are explored.

In recent years, communication research has demonstrated that an effective way to educate and persuade mass media audiences is through the use of narratives (Green & Brock, 2000; Slater, Buller, Waters, Archibeque, & LeBlanc, 2003). Several experiments comparing the effects of expository health and social messages to those embedded in entertaining narratives demonstrate that narrative messages seem to be remembered and adopted more than similar messages that are presented in an expository presentation (e.g., Braverman, 2008; Murphy, Frank, Chatterjee, & Baezconde-Garbanati, 2013). Thus, a major goal of media research has been to explain why people are often persuaded by narratives. Several theories have been suggested and tested to explain narrative persuasion. One theory is that stories are a better vehicle for social learning (Bandura, 2001). According to social cognitive theory, narratives evoke emotions that increase attentiveness, and they provide both characters that serve as social models and a more vivid context that makes modeled behavior seem more relevant. Another theory contends that the effectiveness of stories is due to the decreased tendency to resist messages when they come in narrative form (Moyer-Gusé, 2008; see also Slater & Rouner, 2002). Studies have shown that narratives reduce resistance to persuasive messages and the tendency to counter-argue with expository messages. Studies following both these theoretical approaches have focused on the psychological reactions people have to narratives and how such reactions lead to the persuasive effects of narratives. This essay attempts to compare and contrast two of the most important such reactions: Transportation and identification.

In the various studies that have explored the psychology of narrative persuasion, two psychological processes have emerged as central to persuasion. One is transportation (Gerrig, 1993), a concept that describes the way people tend to become immersed in the story world. Audience members feel as if they are removed from their immediate environment and present in the world of the narrative. The degree to which readers, viewers or listeners feel that they are transported into the narrative has been shown to predict their learning from the story, their counter-arguing and the likelihood that they will adopt its attitudes (Green & Brock, 2000). A second psychological process that has been demonstrated to be central to persuasion and behavior change is identification (Cohen, 2001). Identification is another form of engagement with a story that is focused on a specific character. When identifying with a character, an audience member imagines him or herself to be that character, and, thus, is more likely to model characters, adopt their point of view, goals and emotions.

Although these two processes are both avenues to narrative engagement and as such have many similar characteristics, the differences and the relationship between them are not well understood. Tal-Or and Cohen (2010) have demonstrated that these two processes are distinct and can be manipulated separately. Specifically, transportation was increased by increasing suspense whereas identification was more intense when the character was presented more positively. Like other studies, these findings reveal some important ways in which these two concepts are different, but the overall understanding of this distinction and the relationships between the two concepts remains incomplete.

Besides conceptual clarity, understanding how transportation and identification are different and how they interact is important for considerations of message design. If narratives are an effective tool for affecting attitude and behavior change, a closer understanding of the underlying mechanisms should allow for more effective stories to be created. First, knowing which narrative characteristics, contexts and audience features affect transportation and which affect identification will allow for creating more precisely designed narratives. Second, when designing a narrative intended to affect specific attitudes or behaviors and/or targeted to a specific audience or situation, it would be helpful to know the relative importance of transportation and identification to achieving these specific objectives.

Although many narratives may lead to high levels of both transportation and identification, when creating persuasive narratives there are situations where one must decide which may be of greater importance. For example, at an intuitive level it would seem that a multi-character narrative could potentially be more complex and suspenseful but that a story with a clear hero will create greater identification (although one can also suggest that multi-character narratives provide a wider range of opportunities to identify). A story with a clearly positive protagonist is likely to create greater identification, but a morally ambivalent character is likely to create more suspense and therefore transportation. In this review, the similarities and differences between transportation and identification are explored. Relevant studies in which both were measured are examined to determine under what circumstances transportation and identification seem to behave in a similar manner and when they differ. Because of the paucity of studies that measured both, we also reviewed many studies that measured either transportation or identification but that were relevant to the issues we raise. We examine which of the determinants and consequences of transportation and identification differ and which factors seem to affect and be affected by both in the same way. We do this to better understand the two concepts and the relationships between them and to understand how to create more persuasive narratives.

Defining Transportation and Identification

As stated above, transportation is a concept that describes the feeling of being in the story, part of the action and removed from the reading or viewing context. As explained by Green and Brock (2000), transportation is a "distinct mental process" whereby "all mental systems and capabilities become focused on events occurring in the narrative" (p. 701). Although there are different conceptions of transportation (e.g., absorption, presence) there is a common thread among all of these that is the degree to which audience members are engrossed in the story and are focused on the story world. Scholars have used different measures of transportation in their studies, each representing somewhat different understandings of transportation. The most commonly used scale was created and tested by Green and Brock (2000) and has 11 items measuring imagery, affect and attentional focus. Several studies, (e.g., de Graaf, Hoeken, Sanders, & Beentjes, 2011; Tal-Or & Cohen, 2010) have found that the attentional items seem to factor separately and so have used seven items. However, in most studies, these dimensions seem to be strongly connected and the scale is generally reliable (e.g., Moyer-Gusé & Nabi, 2010). More recently, Appel, Gnambs, Richter and Green (2015) developed and validated a short form of the transportation scale that includes six items and is based on a three facet conceptualization of transportation.

Busselle and Bilandzic (2009) have suggested and tested a scale of narrative engagement based on a mental models approach. This scale has 12 items that represent four factors: Understanding, attentional focus, presence, and emotional engagement. Engagement, as measured by this scale is a somewhat broader concept than transportation and includes understanding as well as attention and emotion. Also, replacing imagery with presence suggests that being engaged requires a feeling of being in the story rather than simply having a visual image of the story world.

Although related, transportation is distinct from various judgments or perceptions about the story such as perceived realism or relevance that compare the text to some external standard and from post-exposure judgments such as enjoyment. Transportation is the experience one feels, while viewing or reading, of being focused on the narrative and feeling part of it and removed from one's immediate environment.

As opposed to transportation, identification refers to a connection that audience members develop with characters rather than the story world as a whole. Although identification with a character brings audience members into the story world, identification is unique in that unlike transportation, identifying involves a merging of character and self, rather than engagement with the story as whole. Thus, identification necessarily involves a certain level of transportation, but one can be transported into a story as an observer rather than through a specific character. Identification is one of several concepts that refer to ways such connections form (Cohen, 2009). Identification involves merging and is, therefore, not an interactive relationship (like para-social relationships) and it is characterized by intimacy rather than a distanced adoration or fandom. It is also distinct from what may be predictors of identification such as perceptions of similarity, liking or attraction and concepts such as social comparison or imitation that may result from identification but are not part of it.

In regard to identification, there is some variety of conceptualization and measurement but for the most part dimensions of identification include sharing of a character's perspective, goals and feelings. Thus, measures such as similarity (e.g., Slater, Rouner, & Long, 2006) can be seen as capturing correlates of identification but not tapping the entire concept. Others (e.g., Eyal & Rubin, 2003; Murphy et al., 2013) have used more general measures that measure identification together with related constructs that may be causes of, or related to identification (e.g., liking, similarity, feeling like you know, and wanting to be like).

However, the most commonly used scale to measure identification with characters is based on Cohen's (2001) ten items scale and includes items tapping cognitive empathy (e.g., "I think I have a good understanding of character X"), affective empathy (e.g., "While viewing the show I could feel the emotions character X portrayed"), and adopting of goals (e.g., "When character X succeeded I felt joy but when he or she failed I was sad"). Although never formally tested, this scale has been used in many studies (e.g., Chung & Slater, 2013; de Graaf, 2014; Moyer-Gusé, Chung & Jain, 2011) and generally found reliable. As originally conceived, the scale included two items that measured absorption (i.e., "While viewing program X, I felt as if I was part of the action", "While viewing program X, I forgot myself and was fully absorbed") and overlapped transportation and thus the scale is often used with only eight items.

Theoretical Similarities and Empirical Convergence of Transportation and Identification

Because both transportation and identification are ways that audience members become involved in a narrative, it is not surprising that they are similar in many ways and that they often correlate quite strongly. Both are ways that viewers or readers experience psychological convergence with the text, a feeling of closeness to plot and characters. Both involve feelings as well as cognitions. When transported into the narrative, one is experiencing the story more vividly and thus has stronger feelings regarding what is taking place. One's attention and cognitive resources are also diverted away from one's self and immediate environment and focused on the story. Identification also entails both empathy (the sharing of feelings) and understanding of story events through the character's perspective.

Almost universally, the levels of transportation and identification are positively correlated, generally substantially. For example, So and Nabi (2013) found a correlation between transportation and identification of r = 0.49, and Green, Rozin, and Aldao, (2004*[1]) found that although the correlation differed across variations of text in three studies, these correlations were always significant and in the range 0.57 < r < 0.71. Typically, Bilandzic and Busselle (2011) found positive correlations across three films (crime: r = 0.54; science fiction: r = 0.63; romantic comedy: r = 0.58). In another interesting example, Himelowsky, Jain, Cohen, and Ewoldsen (2014*) measured the correlation between transportation and identification twice during exposure to the narrative. For half their sample they measured these variables both half-way through the film and again at the end and found that half-way through the film the correlation was practically the same r = 0.45 than at the end, r = .0.52. The correlation was stable even though the level of identification dropped significantly as the protagonist was revealed to be deranged and violent. Interestingly, transportation was also reduced from the half-way mark to the end of the film, but to a lesser degree than identification. Finally, Cohen, Tal-Or, and Mazor-Tregerman (2015) presented subjects with a story that had protagonists presenting opposing positions on a relevant and controversial topic. Although the identification with the two protagonists was negatively correlated, transportation was, regardless of prior position and virtue of either character, positively correlated with identification with both of the characters (r = 0.36. and 0.27). Thus, across various texts, genres and study conditions, transportation and identification are substantially and positively correlated although the strength of these correlations does vary quite a bit depending on the texts.

Theoretical and Empirical Convergence

Mutual Antecedents

Context

Several studies have provided evidence that transportation and identification share mutual antecedent factors. With regard to the context of viewing, two recent studies showed that the nature of co-viewers influence both identification and transportation. One of these studies demonstrated that when watching a war film, the gender of the co-viewer had similar effects on both transportation and identification (Tal-Or, in press, study 2), so that the participants were more transported to the movie and identified more with the male protagonist when watching with a male than when watching with a female. Similarly, Banjo et al. (2013) found that when Black viewers watched with Black co-viewers they were more transported and more strongly identified with characters on a Black-oriented comedy. Thus, both transportation and identification are sensitive to the context of reading or viewing, such that it seems that co-viewers that seem consonant with content increase involvement.

In another study (Tal-Or & Tsfati, in press) in which participants were exposed to a movie that ended in a rape scene, the reactions of the confederate co-viewers were manipulated. Some co-viewers showed enthusiasm and some showed signs of boredom and rejection of the movie. In this study, participants who viewed the movie with an enthusiastic confederate identified more with the male protagonist and were more transported into the narrative, both through the mediation of the perceived confederate co-viewer's enthusiasm.

Narrative Structure

The structure of the narrative also affects both transportation and identification. In a recent study Kuijpers (2014; study 2) found that narrative structure (either in a form of suspense—a classic narrative starting with an initiation event or curiosity—without an explicit initiating event) influenced both transportation and emotional engagement (which was measured using some of the identification items as well as others). Specifically, both transportation and identification were higher in the curiosity version than in both the control and the suspense versions.

Other studies demonstrated that removing various elements from the narrative affects both constructs. Green et al. (2004*; study 1) reported that removing physical details from a story reduced both transportation and identification. Similarly, Costabile and Terman (2013; study 1) found that removing the soundtrack from a film clip reduced both transportation and identification.

Personality Traits

Two studies found that similar personality traits predict both transportation and identification. Billandzic and Busselle (2011) examined the correlations between transportability and both transportation and identification and found that both were significantly correlated with transportability. Himelowsky et al. (2014*) showed participants the very violent film, *Falling Down*, in which the protagonist engages in many violent acts. They measured trait aggression and found that it was a predictor of both transportation and identification with the violent protagonist. Furthermore the regression coefficients were of similar size for transportation and identification. These findings suggest that similar types of people are likely to be transported into and to identify with protagonists for a given text.

Common Consequences

Knowledge, Attitudes and Behaviors

Many studies have found that transportation and identification have effects on persuasive outcomes or mediate the effects of exposure, or reactions to exposure, on perceptions, attitudes, behavioral intentions and behavior. For example, Murphy, Hether, Felt, and de Castro Buffington (2012) found both transportation and involvement with characters (measured somewhat differently but conceptually similar to identification) to predict changes in knowledge and behavioral intentions regarding immigration, sexual violence, and "conflict minerals" after watching a relevant episode of *Law & Order: SVU*. Similarly, Slater, Rouner, and Long (2006) found in one of two films they used that both identification and transportation predicted attitudes related to gay marriage.

Interestingly, in many of the regression models when either transportation or identification were entered alone they were significant predictors, but when both variables were entered together only one remained significant, suggesting a high degree of shared variance. For example, Murphy, Frank, Moran, and Pantoe-Woodley (2011) examined the effects of an entertainment education intervention regarding lymphoma using the popular TV show *Desperate Housewives*. When examined separately, both involvement with characters and transportation were predictors of knowledge, attitudes, information seeking, and talking with others. Using structural equation modeling, however, they suggested that identification may lead to transportation which, in turn, led to the aforementioned outcomes. In general, however, the effects of exposure on outcomes through identification were weaker than the mediated effects of transportation on knowledge, attitudes, information seeking, and talking with others.

Many other studies examined either the effects of identification or those of transportation on knowledge, attitudes and behavior and showed that both of them predict these variables. Accordingly, in their meta-analysis Tukachinsky and Tokunaga (2013) conclude that "transportation in the narrative and empathic identification with characters [have] the strongest influence over knowledge, attitudes and behaviors" (p. 311). For example, Moyer-Gusé, Chung, and Jain (2011) found that viewers of an episode of the HBO series *Sex and the City* that depicted talking about sexually transmitted diseases were more likely to report both intentions to talk to others as well as behavioral effects. They found that identification, through its impact on counter-arguing and self-efficacy had an effect on intentions and behavior but because they did not measure transportation, it is impossible to know whether transportation also had a similar effect. Igartua and Barrios (2012) report that identification with the protagonist of a film about the religious group Opus Dei was associated with beliefs that were consistent with those cultivated by the film, but this study also did not measure transportation. Similarly, de Graaf, Hoeken, Sanders, and Beentjes (2012) show that in two different studies about two separate social issues increasing identification had an effect on attitudes, but do not report effects of engagement (although these were measured). On the other hand, Green and Brock (2000) show that transportation had persuasive effects but they did not distinguish identification and transportation. Thus, although they do not necessarily operate in tandem, transportation and identification can play similar roles in the process of narrative persuasion.

Enjoyment

Many studies that examined identification and transportation separately also demonstrated their contribution to enjoyment (e.g., Hefner, Klimmt, & Vorderer, 2007; Krakowiak & Oliver, 2012; Nabi, Stitt, Halford, & Finnerty, 2006). In a recent study that examined these constructs together, Bilandzic and

Busselle (2011) found that both transportation and identification are correlated with enjoyment of crime dramas, romantic comedies and science fiction. Similar findings were obtained by Himelowsky et al. (2014*).

Given their conceptual similarity, one should not be surprised by the existence of mutual antecedents and consequences to identification and transportation. Both are psychological responses to a narrative and ways to become more involved with a story. Thus, it is to be expected that they are often substantially correlated and have somewhat similar roles in the process of narrative persuasion. However, what is perhaps more interesting and theoretically illuminating is to identify and consider their differences. Such differences can perhaps take us beyond considering involvement with narratives as important to persuasion to a consideration of the mechanisms through which audiences become involved and how these different mechanisms operate.

Theoretical and Empirical Divergence

Divergent Predictors

Textual Factors

Character's virtue. One of the major factors that seem to impact identification without influencing transportation into the narrative is the protagonist's virtue. People tend to identify more with a protagonist who is presented as good hearted, sincere, and likeable, than one who is presented as evil, a liar, and dislikeable. However, these differences in the depiction of the protagonist do not seem to influence the participants' involvement with the narrative as a whole. Tal-Or and Cohen (2010) demonstrated this point in a study in which the participants identified less with a protagonist when learning about his past or future marital infidelity compared with the same protagonist when learning about his past or future marital fidelity. The protagonist's faithfulness did not matter at all to the participants' level of transportation into the narrative. Similarly, in their recent study, Hoeken and Sinkeldam (2014) showed that participants identified more with a character described as suffering from brain damage after being hit by a cab when she was depicted as a likeable person than when she was portrayed as unlikeable. However, here again the character's likeability had no effect on the participants' transportation into the narrative.

While these studies manipulated the traits of the media character, in Tal-Or and Tsfati (2015*) the entire narrative was manipulated. In this study, Jewish Israeli participants watched a movie clip about a very sick Arab baby from Gaza who was hospitalized in an Israeli hospital. The movie presented the multifaceted and complicated situation in Israel and Gaza, and included scenes presenting Israelis more positively and the Arabs from Gaza more negatively and vice versa. The authors created two clips from the same movie that were either pro-Israeli or pro-Palestinian. These clips differed not only in the presentation of the protagonists, but also in the presentation of the suffering of the population—in one case, the Israelis and in the other case, the Palestinians.

Interestingly, in this case too, the type of clip affected the identification of the Jewish Israeli participants with the Arab and Jewish protagonists (more identification with the Arab protagonist in the pro-Palestinian clip and vice versa), but not their transportation into the narrative.

Because transportation and identification are related, the differential impact of character valence on identification and transportation needs to be explained. First, it might be hypothesized that manipulating the virtue of one character does not affect general transportation, as long as there are other characters in the narrative that can engender identification. Alternatively, because being transported may mean feeling that you yourself are inside the plot, and not necessarily through merging with one of the characters, the characters' traits do not matter much to this experience.

Suspense. While the virtue of the protagonist affects identification without affecting transportation, it is logical to assume that variations in the narrative that make it more or less suspenseful would have a stronger effect on transportation than on identification. Unfortunately, there has been almost no research on this possibility. One exception is Tal-Or and Cohen's (2010) study mentioned above that demonstrated that hints about future occurrences, regardless of whether they were positive or negative in nature, enhanced transportation without affecting the level of identification with the protagonist.

Modes of address. There are many ways in which a narrative can be told and this should have an effect on how people respond to narratives. Stories can be presented by one of the characters or by an omniscient narrator, in first person or third person voice, and the narrator can address the audience directly or ignore their presence. A number of recent studies have examined the effects of such modes of address on transportation and identification. For example, does it matter whether a narrative character narrates a voiceover or talks directly at the audience? These devices, called narrating (Semmler, Loof, & Berke, 2015), abound in prime time television and are believed to engage the viewers with the narrator (Keveney, 2005). A recent study tested this assumption by asking participants to watch one of several clips from the *House of Cards* series (Oliver et al., 2014*). These authors compared a condition in which the lead character directly talked to the audience to a condition in which he did not. They found that the participants were more transported into the narrative when the lead character spoke to the audience directly, but their level of identification with him did not vary whether he spoke to them directly or did not. Overall, levels of identification with the main character (Frank Underwood) were around the mid-point of the scale negating the possibility that the lack of difference in identification is due to the negative nature of the character.

Interestingly, in a seemingly similar study that compared two clips from the *Dexter* series (Semmler, Loof, & Berke, 2015), the participants identified more with the protagonist when hearing his voiceover describing his thoughts than when there was no voiceover. However, no effect on transportation emerged. In a third study, Tsay-Vogel and Oliver (2014) showed their participants a segment from MTV's *The Real World: Las Vegas* that focused on a target person. The target person disclosed personal information either directly to viewers or to another character. In a third, control, condition a narrator provided this information rather than the target person. The participants reported significantly greater identification in the character-to-viewer and character-to-character conditions than in the narrator-to-viewer condition. However, although modes of address affected transportation through the mediation of identification, there was no direct effect of modes of address on transportation.

To explain these seemingly conflicting results of a character's narration on identification we hypothesize an interaction of different modes of address and different genres in affecting identification. In general, it is possible to speculate that adding personal information should increase identification by increasing the sense of intimacy. In drama, a genre that creates the illusion that viewers are outside looking in, a character directly addressing the audience, even if adding personal information, may break that illusion by reminding audience members of themselves and therefore negate the positive effect of personal information on identification. However, in reality shows, or in cases of a voice over with no direct address, this effect should be found. This hypothesis, of course, is based on a small number of studies that are quite different from each other and therefore needs further testing in future research.

Narrative perspective. Even from within the story world, the perspective from which a story is told can have an effect. This was recently manipulated in two studies by de Graaf et al. (2012). These authors manipulated which of two protagonists told the story from his or her perspective. In two completely different narratives, this manipulation affected identification but not transportation. The participants tended to identify more with a character when the story was told from his or her perspective, but there was no difference in the level of transportation.

Based on de Graaf et al. (2012), we might expect that identification would be more sensitive to changes in perspective than transportation. However, it is possible to conjecture that when the narrative focuses on an issue about which the audience member has strong, clear attitudes the effect of telling the story from the perspective with which the audience member agrees may also affect transportation. We suggest, then, that hearing the story from the perspective of a character with which one agrees might lead to greater transportation than when hearing it from the perspective of an antagonistic character.

Vividness of the medium and sound effects. When we are exposed to a narrative, does our degree of involvement depend on the medium through which it is presented? Does it matter whether we read it, listen to it or both listen and watch it? Are we transported and identify with the characters more when we obtain all of the information directly through our senses, or are we more involved when there is room for our imagination to create our own image of the events and the figures? Unfortunately, there is little research on this topic. The only published study relating to this presented the participants with the same story in print and film form to assess their degree of transportation and found no difference between the media forms (Green et al., 2008).

Some unpublished studies also exist in this area. In a recent study comparing transportation and identification in response to either a video clip or a written version of the same narrative, the participants exhibited the same level of transportation but identified more with the protagonist in the audiovisual version (Cohen & Mazor Tregerman, 2012*). It should be noted that the actors in the clip were very attractive and quite well known, and seeing them may account for the greater identification in the film condition. Alternatively, the differences between the groups in their level of identification might be attributed to the vividness of the presentation, which is stronger in audiovisual depictions (Green et al., 2008). Another unpublished study examined the effects of vividness, and demonstrated that a narrative without physical details produces less transportation and identification than a narrative including such details (Green et al., 2004*).

Thus, the effect of the richness and vividness of modes of presentation on transportation is not yet clear. Some studies point to the advantages of more vivid text, while others have not discerned that this variable has any effect. Clearly the relationship between vividness and transportation involves other variables and is more complex. This complexity echoes vividness research investigating the persuasiveness of non-narrative messages that finds mixed results (e.g., Frey & Eagly, 1993; Taylor & Thompson, 1982).

Another aspect of vividness is music. According to Green et al. (2008), one of the advantages of film for engaging the audience is the musical soundtrack. As mentioned above, Costabile and Terman (2013) tested this hypothesis by comparing the levels of reactions to a movie clip with or without its original musical soundtrack and found more transportation and identification in the clip with the musical soundtrack. In their second study, they measured reactions to a movie clip that had no musical soundtrack, the same clip to which a soundtrack was added that was congruent with the affect displayed in the movie, and the same clip to which a soundtrack was added that was incongruent with the affect displayed in the movie. This time they found more transportation in the congruent condition than in the other two conditions but no direct effect on identification, although there was an indirect effect of condition on identification through transportation. Thus, congruence of message elements is one of the factors that seem to interact with vividness to impact engagement but more research is needed to explicate this relationship.

Environmental Factors

Distraction. Green and Brock (2000) were the first to show that distracting readers reduces their level of transportation. In their seminal study, they asked some of their participants to read a story carefully, whereas others were asked to read it while trying to find words that would not be understood by adults who knew English at a fourth grade level. This distraction allowed participants to understand the story, but it reduced their level of transportation. Two recent studies used similar distracting manipulations and found that they affected transportation but not identification (Cohen et al., 2015; de Graaf, Hoeken, Sanders, & Beentjes, 2009). Distraction that interferes with transportation might stem not only from activities that media consumers engage in while reading or watching, but also from their co-viewers.

Co-viewers. The experience of watching films or TV with others can be quite different than viewing alone. When viewing with others, the distraction caused by the presence of others as well as their reactions to narratives can influence people to be more or less engaged with the movie or with its characters. As mentioned above, research has demonstrated that the presence of co-viewers can affect both transportation and identification (e.g., Banjo et al., 2013*; Tal-Or, in press, study 2; Tal-Or & Tsfati, in press).While some studies document similar effects for the type and reactions of co-viewers on identification and transportation, others show the effect on only one of these. For example, in Tal-Or's (in press*) experiment, confederate co-viewers who displayed enthusiasm for a science fiction film influenced the participants to be more transported than co-viewers who showed boredom or a neutral response or in the solitary viewing control condition. However, participants watching with an enthusiastic co-viewer did not differ from those in the bored and neutral co-viewer conditions in their identification with the protagonist. In another study by Tal-Or and Tsfati (2015*), Jewish Israelis viewed pro-Palestinian or pro-Israeli clips taken from the same film in the company of a Jewish or Arab confederate co-viewer. They found that among those who watched the pro-Israeli movie, the co-viewers' ethnicity affected identification with the Arab protagonist, so that they identified more when they watched with an Arab confederate. However, the ethnicity of the co-viewer did not affect their transportation level.

We might suggest that the valence of the co-viewer's reactions generally influence transportation into the movie. However, this valence affects identification only when the protagonist is very dominant in the narrative, so that the reactions of the co-viewer are likely to be interpreted as a direct response to the protagonist. Viewers might imitate the reactions or the perceived reactions of their co-viewers so that when they believe that their co-viewer is transported and identifies with a protagonist, they too tend to be transported and identify with the protagonist. When they do not have a reason to assume that their co-viewer is more or less transported into a narrative or identifies with a protagonist, co-viewing does not influence their level of transportation and identification.

Regulatory fit. Recent studies (e.g., Vaughn, Hesse, Petkova, & Trudeau, 2009) have demonstrated that the psychological states people experience before being exposed to narratives affects transportation. Importantly, these psychological states have an impact even though they are completely unrelated to the narrative. For example, Vaughn and colleagues asked their participants to think about either their goals and aspirations or their duties and obligations. In a later task, participants in each of the groups were asked either to list strategies that would help them achieve their goals and aspirations or the strategies that would help them avoid situations that would make them neglect their duties and obligations. Thus, for some of the participants the two tasks fit with one another, and for some they did not. The researchers found that those who experienced regulatory fit were later more transported into an unrelated narrative. The authors explained that, as a result of experiencing regulatory fit or non-fit, people feel a general sense of "rightness" or "wrongness" that they attribute to the story. Additional research is needed to determine whether this general feeling of rightness or wrongness also affects identification.

Enhanced self-awareness. There are situations in life in which we are especially aware of ourselves. That would be the case, for example, when we enter a room and everybody looks at us. It is also the case when we see ourselves in the mirror. A recent study showed that this exact situation inhibits experience taking, which is an experience akin to identification (Kaufman & Libby, 2012). These authors showed that experience taking is reduced when a mirror was placed in front of the participants. The effect of self-focus on transportation, however, was not significant. Identification implies merging with the character, and focusing on the self, interferes with this action. However, given that people can be transported by imagining themselves inside the narrative, the focus on the self might be less detrimental to transportation. However, a focus on one's surrounding might disturb transportation. For example, we may speculate that a mirror reflecting not one's own face but the room in which they are located might inhibit transportation.

Moreover, it might be that enhanced self-awareness that is somehow related to the narrative enhances transportation. Indeed, in a series of experimental studies Escalas (2004; 2007) demonstrated that viewers of ads for athletic shoes that were instructed to imagine themselves using the product, as compared to viewers viewing the ad without these instructions, were more transported and evaluated the brand more positively.

Audience Factors

Personality traits. Most studies that have found personality correlates with narrative engagement have focused on parasocial interaction (e.g., Eyal & Rubin, 2003) or wishful identification (Hoffner, 1996; Hoffner & Buchanan, 2005). The studies that did examine personality correlates of identification and transportation mostly examined these constructs separately, or did not differentiate between them.

Dal Cin, Zanna, and Fong (2004) acknowledged that people differ in the degree to which they are transported into narratives and identify with media characters. To measure this tendency, they created a transportability scale. They demonstrated significant correlations between transportability and transportation into various specific narratives. Unfortunately, this scale measures both the tendency to be transported and the tendency to identify with media characters, making it impossible to differentiate between these constructs. Mazzocco, Green, Sasota, and Jones (2010) also found in two studies positive and significant correlations between transportability and transportation, but did not measure identification.

As mentioned above, Bilandzic and Busselle (2011) examined the correlations between transportability and transportation and identification separately, and found that both were significantly correlated with transportability. In another study, Greenwood and Long (2009) created a transportation scale that included items measuring identification with characters. They showed that solitude and the need to belong predicted transportation. However, given that they measured both identification and transportation in the same scale, we do not know whether the effect is true for both factors or for only one of them.

Other studies have investigated the individual differences that predict either identification or transportation but did not include both in the same study. For example, extroversion and affective empathy predicted identification (Tsao, 1996). Chory-Assad and Cicchirillo (2005) found the identification correlated with perspective taking, empathic concern and affective orientation. In one of two films regarding suicide Till, Vitouch, Herberth, Sonneck, and Niederkrotenthaler (2013) found a correlation between identification and empathy. The tendency to focus on oneself, called self-consciousness, correlated negatively with experience taking, which is a construct very similar to identification (Kaufman & Libby, 2012). Regarding transportation, Hall and Bracken (2011) found that transportation into a self-selected film was associated with trait fantasy empathy, although not with other dimensions of empathy and Appel and Richter (2010) found that need for affect was positively associated with transportation.

In sum, both transportation and identification seem to correlate with some personality traits but whether the same traits are related to both, or whether each is related to different personality traits, is yet undetermined. Exploring this seems like a worthwhile direction for research, especially in conjunction with various types of texts as it may help explain who is more likely to be transported and to identify with characters in a particular narrative, and perhaps provide a better understanding of why.

Similarity. It seems that both character traits and audience traits have a limited impact on transportation and identification, although these effects are far from consistent and are not well established. But does the similarity in traits between audiences and characters have an impact on identification and transportation? Do characters who share specific demographic traits with audience members elicit stronger responses? Importantly, whereas perceptions of similarity have been linked to identification, the effects of real similarity (shared traits) between narrative characters and audiences, has been tested less often.

As stated by social cognitive theory, role models who are similar to the individual are more influential (Bandura, 2001). Similarly, research on tailoring in health messages inform us that messages that are perceived as more relevant to the individual are more persuasive (Jensen, King, Carcioppolo, & Davis, 2012). Although there is evidence for the role of similarity and personal relevance on persuasion in advocacy messages, it is less clear whether this effect is true in narrative messages and is mediated by identification and transportation. There is limited evidence documenting the effect of the similarity between the media consumer and the media character on identification (Williams, 2010), but almost no research to date has examined the effect of similarity on transportation. In a recent study that tested the effect of similarity on both identification and transportation, the participants read a story about a university student diagnosed with intestinal cancer living either at home or in a dorm (de Graaf, 2014). De Graaf assessed the effects of the similarity in living conditions between the participants and the character in the story on perceived similarity, self-referencing, identification and engagement, determining that similarity did affect self-referencing but not identification or engagement. Similar findings were obtained by McKinley (2010). In this research, which used a TV episode regarding binge drinking, the author used a similarity manipulation describing the main character as either a college student (i.e., high similarity) or as a person whose parents had died (i.e., low similarity). This similarity manipulation influenced perceived similarity but not identification.

The findings were somewhat different in Eyal and Rubin (2003) who found a correlation between trait aggressiveness and identification with an aggressive TV character. Similar results were obtained by Himelowsky et al. (2014*) who found that trait aggressiveness predicted both identification with an aggressive character and transportation into a violent film.

Evidence for the similarity effects were also obtained in a recent study (Murphy et al., 2013) who found that a film about cervical cancer featuring a Hispanic family was more transporting and elicited stronger identification among Mexican-American viewers than among Caucasians or African-Americans. Because the film highlighted many cultural elements that were culturally specific it is impossible to conclude that it was similarity alone that accounted for these findings (rather than familiarity or cultural relevance). Similar results were obtained by another study about the effects of similarity in marital status on reactions to a safe-sex narrative (Ophir, 2013*). In this study, the participants read a story about a female protagonist who refused to have unprotected sex with her partner, and as a result they broke up. Several months later she found out that he suspected he had AIDS. Following exposure to this narrative, the participants completed measures assessing their narrative engagement and identification, among other variables. In this study, single women identified more than married women with the single female protagonist. However, marital status had no effect on engagement with the narrative. Importantly, neither of the two studies mentioned above was meant to test a similarity hypothesis, and therefore neither used a balanced design that would allow a strong conclusion. In sum, the findings regarding the importance of character similarity are mixed, although it seems that this is a much less important factor than previously assumed (e.g., Hoffner & Cantor, 1991).

The one type of similarity that does have a strong effect on identification is agreement or attitude similarity. To the extent that identification is related to attraction, this can be seen as a logical extension of the (attitude) homophily-attraction effect (Byrne, 1969). De Graaf et el. (2012) found that participants, who were generally pre-disposed to be favorable toward euthanasia, tended to identify more strongly with the character that was a proponent for euthanasia. Similarly, Cohen et al. (2015) found that participants tended to identify more strongly with the character who advocated the position they held prior to reading the story.

Familiarity. One explanation of why similarity should increase identification and transportation is that a story with similar characters should be more familiar to readers or viewers and thus induce greater emotional responses. Green (2004) tested the impact of familiarity with elements of the story world on transportation. She found that readers of a story about a homosexual man attending his fraternity reunion induced greater transportation among readers that were familiar with fraternities and those that had more homosexual acquaintances.

Divergent Consequences

Attitudes

The dominant models of narrative communication (e.g., Moyer-Gusé, 2008) regard both transportation and identification as important vehicles through which exposure to narratives changes attitudes. As outlined above, there is ample evidence of the contribution of these constructs to narrative persuasion. Still, in the studies that measured both transportation and identification, and examined their ability to predict attitudes, sometimes only one of them plays a significant role.

A good example is the study by Murphy et al. (2013) that examined the effect of a narrative vs. non-narrative text about cervical cancer on attitudes toward, and knowledge about, this type of cancer. In the narrative there were several female protagonists—two sisters and their mother's friend. The older sister is diagnosed with HPV. She informs the others about cervical cancer and pap tests, and tries to alleviate their fears. In this study, transportation was not a significant predictor of attitudes toward pap tests, nor was identification with two of the protagonists. However, identification with the older sister did predict positive attitudes about getting a pap test.

The effects of identification in this study are seemingly in contrast to those found in the lymphoma study mentioned above (Murphy et al., 2011) in which both transportation and identification with the sick character separately predicted attitudes. However, when tested together only transportation seemed to have independent predictive power. Similarly, in the Murphy et al. (2012) study mentioned above, in which participants viewed an episode of *Law & Order: SVU* about immigrants, both transportation and identification were correlated with knowledge, attitudes, and current and future behavior. However, identification was the stronger predictor of knowledge and behavior whereas transportation was the stronger predictor of attitudes. This is in line with a recent meta-analysis (van Laer, de Ruyter, Visconti, & Wetzels, 2014) that supported a positive link between transportation and both attitudes and beliefs.

It seems that transportation and identification as predictors of attitudes have a large shared variance. They usually predict attitudes when examined alone, but when examined together, only one of them remains significant. When the narrative is largely focused on the target protagonist, transportation seems to override identification. However, in narratives that include a number of protagonists which represent various perspectives (such as in Murphy et al., 2013), identification with a specific protagonist predict attitudes that accord with those presented by this character more than transportation into the narrative as a whole.

More evidence for this hypothesis comes from a recent research by Cohen et al. (2015) examining changes in attitudes following exposure to a narrative presenting two sides of a conflict equally. In their first studies, these authors manipulated the level of identification. They found that identification with a character whose attitudes were congruent with those of the participant polarized attitudes, while identification with the character whose attitudes were incongruent with those of the participant tempered attitudes. In their second study, they manipulated the level of transportation and found that it also tempered attitudes. As in Murphy et al.'s (2013) study, identification led to specific changes in attitudes in line with those of the particular character. Interestingly, transportation tempered attitudes, although the narrative contained equal number of arguments on both sides of the issue. The authors speculated that the existence of a character who presents the attitudes of the readers reduces their reactance to the narrative and the need to create their own counter-arguments. This, in turn, increases the willingness to accept the attitudes of the other side.

In two recent studies that examined the effects of co-viewers on attitudes through the mediation of transportation and identification, once again, identification, not transportation, predicted attitudes. In the first of these studies (Tal-Or & Tsfati, in press) that examined the effect of exposure to a film ending with a rape scene, identification with the rapist predicted rape myth acceptance but transportation had no direct predictive role. In Tal-Or and Tsfati (2015*), which examined the effect of exposure to a pro-Israeli or pro-Palestinian video clip on the Jewish participants' attitudes towards Arabs from Gaza, identification with the Arab protagonist again predicted more positive attitudes about Arabs and more peaceful attitudes concerning the Israeli-Palestinian conflict, but transportation did not.

Again, it seems that identification rather than transportation into the narrative is a better predictor of specific attitudes. Future research should investigate the ability of transportation and identification to predict general attitudes that are consistent with the narrative compared with more specific attitudes that are consistent with the perspective of a particular character.

Counter-Arguments

One of the leading explanations for the effect of engagement with narratives on story consistent attitudes is reduced counter-arguing (Moyer Gusé, 2008). Indeed, Green and Brock (2000) demonstrated that more transportation into a narrative was associated with less "false notes" detections. That is, those who were more transported found fewer parts in the story that seemed wrong to them. However, in their recent research about the effect of narrative concerning the problems associated with teen pregnancy, Moyer-Gusé and Nabi (2010) actually found a positive correlation between transportation and counter-arguing, such that those that were more transported produced more counter-arguments. They also report a positive correlation between identification and counter-arguing. The different findings of these two studies regarding the relationship between counter-arguing and transportation might be related to counter-arguing measurement. In the first study, actual negative responses to the narrative were counted while in the second study the participants answered a questionnaire in which they evaluated the degree to which they were engaged in counter-arguing. It is also likely that when asked in the Moyer-Gusé and Nabi study about their perceived counter-arguing, participants focused on counter-arguing with the reality reflected in the show rather than the show's presentation of that reality. In other words, viewers may have argued with the teens' decision to keep the baby or how they handled the situation, and thus being transported into the show increased this type of counter-arguing. In contrast, Green and Brock were clearer that they were looking for false notes in the plot. Thus, we would expect future research to show that transportation limits counter-arguments regarding narrative portrayals, but depending on the topic may increase counter-arguments regarding the realities being portrayed.

Perceived Knowledge, Actual Knowledge and Recall

Entertainment media attempt not only to change people's attitudes but also to educate them and make them more knowledgeable. Thus, it is very important to examine whether transportation and identification mediate the effect of narratives on knowledge acquisition. Some studies that have attempted to do so did not assess the effects on actual knowledge but on the perceived knowledge that the media consumer reported possessing. For example, Weinmann, Löb, Mattheiß, and Vorderer (2013) examined the ability of transportation and identification to predict the perceived knowledge gained about a science issue from educational entertainment. They found that each variable alone predicted perceived knowledge but when examined together, only transportation remained a significant predictor.

Interestingly, in a study that examined the effects on actual knowledge, Quintero, Harrison, and Quick (2013) documented that participants who reported being more transported into a health-related message recalled less health information. There was no significant correlation between identification and recall. In contrast, in a study in which participants randomly selected from the general population watched a movie about cervical cancer, Murphy et al. (2013) established a positive correlation between transportation and knowledge. Furthermore, identification with a character who was a middle-aged woman and knew little about cervical cancer was negatively correlated with knowledge (the identification with the younger characters was not correlated with knowledge).

It might be suggested that in Quintero et al.'s (2013) study, because the participants were students, they felt that they were being tested, so they concentrated on the film whether or not they were transported into it. Those who were not transported may have been able to process more information, because they were not emotionally involved in the film. In contrast, those who were transported were less attentive to the specific information because they were wrapped up in the story. However, in the Murphy et al. (2013) study, the participants were not students and viewed the film with no explicit expectation that they learn information. Thus, they were attentive only to the degree that they were engaged in the story and so learning was positively correlated with transportation.

Enjoyment

Very few studies have compared the effects of transportation and identification on enjoyment, but those that did produced conflicting results. As shown above, using three different genres, Bilandzic and Busselle (2011) demonstrated strong and significant correlations between both transportation and identification and enjoyment. However, in Tal-Or and Cohen (2010), the correlation between transportation and enjoyment was much larger ($r = 0.38$, $p < 0.001$) than that between identification and enjoyment ($r = 0.18$, $p > 0.10$), and only transportation significantly predicted enjoyment. We might suggest that since enjoyment is a general reaction to the film, it is more connected with transportation. However, in cases in which there is one leading protagonist which the plot is focusing on, identification is also likely to be related to enjoyment.

Self-Perception, Perceived Vulnerability and Personal Risk Perception

Sestir and Green (2010) tested the effects of transportation and identification on self-perception. Participants completed a "me/not me" test of self-perception and were then asked to watch a seven- to ten-minute clip of one of four movies. The authors manipulated both transportation and identification. In a postexposure me/not me test, they found that strong identification reduced reaction times for traits that were relevant to the clip suggesting that the character's traits were integrated into the self. However, transportation did not have a similar effect on self-perception.

In Ophir's (2013*) study of a safe-sex narrative mentioned above, identification predicted perceived vulnerability to AIDS but narrative engagement did not. Similarly, So and Nabi (2013) determined that both transportation and identification reduced the perceived social distance to a media character, which, in turn, influenced perceptions of personal risk. However, identification predicted perceived social distance to a greater extent than transportation. In a correlational study, Dunlop, Wakefield, and Kashima (2010) found that being transported into health messages increased self-referencing and in turn increased perceived risk. However, this study did not report findings regarding identification and so it is impossible to compare effects sizes or identify the effect of transportation controlling for identification.

A recent study by Appel (2011) suggests that media characters can also have negative effects on self-perception. Appel examined the effects of reading a story about a stupid character. He did not measure identification but rather focused on assimilation and contrast with characters. In this study, participants who were not instructed to find differences between them and the protagonist performed worse in a knowledge quiz than a group that received these instructions and a control group that read a different text. The most plausible explanation for this effect is that stupidity was primed but it is possible that part of the effect was a result of identifying with the stupid character.

Thus, it seems that with regard to the effects on self-perception and perceived vulnerability and personal risk, identification plays a more dominant role than transportation. This is in line with the entertainment overcoming resistance model (EORM; Moyer-Gusé, 2008), according to which identification with media characters overcomes the usual optimistic bias that leads us to believe that we are less at risk than others for experiencing various diseases and accidents. Identifying with a character that suffers from these diseases, is diagnosed as having them or experiences other life threatening occurrences, might make audience members feel as if it happened to them and, at least temporarily, make them feel vulnerable. Transportation by itself does not seem to have the same effect since while being transported, one can still maintain his or her selfhood and self-biases.

Conclusions and Implications

When discussing the differences between transportation and identification, Moyer-Gusé (2008) suggested that "The extent to which these differences matter for entertainment-education processing and persuasive effects remains an important empirical question for future research" (p. 410). This review takes up this challenge by examining the shared and distinctive consequences of each. The resounding answer to the question posed by Moyer-Gusé is "yes," these two concepts matter and they matter differently. Unfortunately, providing a clear answer as to how exactly they matter is still far off.

That said, the current review provides a good starting point to the understanding of the distinctiveness of these two processes. Looking at the findings summarized above, there seems to be a general pattern (see Figure 2.1). With regard to the predictors of transportation and identification, there appear to be factors that predict each exclusively and some that influence both. Identification is affected mainly by the traits of the character, such that more positive traits entail more identification. The perspective from which the narrative is told is also a predictor of identification as well as the sharing of a protagonist's thoughts through "voice over." As identification means merging with the media character, changes in self-awareness affects it so that enhanced self-awareness decreases identification.

Transportation, on the other hand, seems to be affected more by narrative characteristics that enhance suspense. It is also affected by environmental

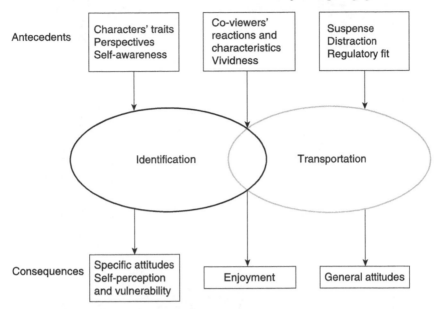

Figure 2.1 Conceptual Diagram of Antecedents and Consequences for Identification and Transportation

factors that distract the viewer or the reader and by environmental factors that cause the audience members to feel uneasy (i.e., low regulatory fit). While suspense motivates the audience to be involved with the narrative, feeling that something is right or wrong will most likely enable or disable the experience of flow in which one is fully absorbed into the narrative.

The factors that seem to affect both transportation and identification include the reactions and characteristics of co-viewers. The findings seem to show that viewers are more transported, and/or identify more with media characters, as long as there are hints that their co-viewers react these ways. Textual features that enhance the vividness of the narrative, as well as musical soundtracks, also seem to affect both transportation and identification, although there might be nuances in these textual features that might be more related to one process or the other. Lastly, personality factors affect these two constructs, but the only individual differences factor that had its relationship with both transportation and identification empirically tested is transportability, which was found to predict both (see Table 2.1 for a list of studies documenting the antecedents of transportation and identification).

With regard to consequences, it seems fair to conclude that both transportation and identification change attitudes, but the former is more influential on attitudes that are generally in-line with the narrative as a whole while the latter has a unique impact on attitudes that are representing the perspective of a specific character. When the narrative is largely focused on the protagonist, they

Table 2.1 Antecedents of Identification and Transportation

	Identification	Transportation
Textual factors		
Character's virtue	Tal-Or & Cohen (2010) Hoeken & Sinkeldam (2014) Tal-Or & Tsfati (2015)*	
Suspense		Tal-Or and Cohen (2010)
Modes of address	Kuijpers (2014; Study 2)	Kuijpers (2014; Study 2) Oliver et al. (2014)*
	Semmler, Loof, & Berke (2015) Tsay & Oliver (2014)	
Narrative perspective	de Graaf, Hoeken, Sanders & Beentjes (2012)	
Vividness of the medium and sound effects	Cohen & Mazor Tregerman (2012)*	
	Green, Rozin & Aldao (2004; Study 1)* Costabile & Terman (2013; Study 1) Costabile & Terman (2013; Study 2)	Green, Rozin & Aldao (2004; Study 1)* Costabile & Terman (2013; Study 1)
Environmental factors		
Distraction		Green & Brock (2000) Cohen, Tal-Or & Mazor Tregerman (2015) de Graaf, Hoeken, Sanders & Beentjes (2009)
Co-viewers	Banjo et al. (2013)* Tal-Or (in press) Tal-Or & Tsfati (in press) Tal-Or & Tsfati (2015)*	Banjo et al. (2013)* Tal-Or (in press) Tal-Or & Tsfati (in press)

Audience factors		
Regulatory fit		
Enhanced self-awareness	Kaufman & Libby (2012)	Vaughn, Hesse, Petkova & Trudeau (2009)
Personality traits	Himelowsky, Jain, Cohen & Ewoldsen (2014)	Himelowsky, Jain, Cohen & Ewoldsen (2014)
	Dal Cin, Zanna &Fong (2004)	Mazzacco, Green, Sasota & Jones (2010)
	Bilandzic & Busselle (2011)	Bilandzic & Busselle (2011)
	Greenwood & Long (2009)	Greenwood & Long (2009)
	Tsao (1996)	Hall &Bracken (2011)
	Chory-Assad & Cicchirillo (2005)	Appel & Richter (2010)
	Till, Herberth, Sonneck, Vitouch & Niederkrotenthaler (2013)	
	Kaufman & Libby (2012)	
Similarity	Williams (2010)	Himelowsky, Jain, Cohen & Ewoldsen (2014)
	Eyal & Rubin (2003)	
	Himelowsky, Jain, Cohen & Ewoldsen (2014)	
	Murphy, Frank, Chatterjee, & Baezconde-Garbanati (2013)	
	Ophir (2013)*	
	de Graaf, Hoeken, Sanders & Beentjes (2012)	
	Cohen, Tal-Or & Mazor Tregerman (2015)	
Familiarity	Green (2004)	

both appear to predict the same attitudes. While changes in attitudes seem to be affected by both processes, changes in the self tend to be more influenced by identification. Identifying with a protagonist seems to affect the way a person perceives him or herself, as well as their perception of their vulnerability to various threats. Lastly, enjoyment seems to be affected by both of these processes, though some evidence pinpoints to a precedence of transportation in this regard (see Table 2.2 for a list of studies documenting the consequences of transportation and identification).

Implications for Message Design

On the basis of our findings we can provide some cautious suggestions for designing persuasive narratives. When it comes to affecting attitudes there seem to be two ways to go about designing stories. One is to base the message on a specific protagonist, in which case identification will be crucial and the protagonist should be as attractive and desirable as possible. The second option is that the message is delivered through plot points or interaction among several characters, in which case it is likely to be determined by transportation. In such cases, suspense is a key factor; or perhaps, more specifically, curiosity.

Research shows that if the object of a narrative is to strengthen existing attitudes then identification is important and a strong character that advocates the existing positon is a good vehicle to achieve this aim. However, if the object is to allow people on both sides to seriously consider the opposite point of view, creating a transporting narrative with two virtuous characters that present both sides of the issue is an effective strategy.

Especially in the context of health communication, it is often desirable to increase feelings of vulnerability or to create some change in how people see themselves. In line with social cognitive theory (Bandura, 2001), the research reviewed above shows that message producers would do well to focus on creating characters with whom audiences will identify. Transportation, however, seems less important to such changes in self-perceptions.

Suggestions for Future Research

Most of the research reviewed above focuses on simple effects of various predictors on transportation and identification and simple effects of transportation and identification on various consequences. An important path for future research is the examination of the possible interactive effects leading to transportation and identification as well as the interactive effects of various factors with transportation and identification that may lead to different consequences. For example, one factor that may play into the vividness effect involves the mental effort that media consumers make or are motivated to make. People become transported when they create a mental image of the story by themselves (Green et al., 2008). However, since this process demands effort, not everyone is willing or able to do so. If they do not make the effort, they cannot be transported into

Table 2.2 Consequences of Identification and Transportation.

	Identification	Transportation
Attitudes and behavior	Moyer-Gusé, Chung & Jain (2011)	
	Igartua & Barrios (2012)	
	De Graaf, Hoeken, Sanders & Beentjes (2012)	
	Green & Brock (2000)	
	Slater, Rouner & Long (2006)	Slater, Rouner & Long (2006)
		Murphy, Frank, Moran & Pantoe-Woodley (2011)
	Murphy, Frank, Chatterjee, & Baezconde-Garbanati (2013)	Murphy, Frank, Moran & Patnoe-Woodley (2011)
	Murphy, Hether, Felt & de Castro Buffington (2012)	Murphy, Hether, Felt & de Castro Buffington (2012)
	Cohen, Tal-Or & Mazor Tregerman (2015)	Cohen, Tal-Or & Mazor Tregerman (2015)
	Tal-Or & Tsfati (in press)	
	Tal-Or & Tsfati (2015)*	
Counter-arguments	Moyer-Guse', Chung & Jain (2011)	Green and Brock (2000) (-)
	Moyer-Guse' & Nabi (2010)	Moyer-Guse' & Nabi (2010)

(Continued)

Table 2.2 (Continued)

	Identification	Transportation
Knowledge and recall	Murphy, Hether, Felt & de Castro Buffington (2012) Murphy, Frank, Moran & Pantoe-Woodley (2011) Murphy, Frank, Chatterjee, & Baezconde-Garbanati (2013)	Murphy, Hether, Felt & de Castro Buffington (2012) Murphy, Frank, Moran & Pantoe-Woodley (2011) Weinmann, Löb, Mattheiß & Vorderer (2013) Quintero, Harrison & Quick (2013) Murphy, Frank, Chatterjee, & Baezconde-Garbanati (2013)
Enjoyment	Hefner, Klimmt & Vorderer (2007) Busselle & Billandzic (2011) Himelowsky, Jain, Cohen & Ewoldsen (2014)	Krakowiak & Oliver (2012) Nabi, Stitt, Halford & Finnerty (2006) Bilandzic & Busselle (2011) Himelowsky, Jain, Cohen & Ewoldsen (2014) Tal-Or & Cohen (2010)
Self-perception and perceived risk and vulnerability	Sestir & Green (2010) Ophir's (2013)* So & Nabi (2013)	So & Nabi (2013) Dunlop, Wakefield & Kashima (2010)

the story. For unmotivated people it would be much easier to be transported into a very rich medium. Indeed, Green et al. (2008) provided evidence supporting this contention when they showed that people with a high need for cognition, who liked to exert mental effort, were more transported into print than into film, and vice versa for people with a low need for cognition.

In a recent study, attitude similarity between audience and media characters interacted with character's virtue in affecting identification (Cohen et al., 2015). Similarly, we suggest that there may be an interaction between attitude similarity and perspective on transportation such that transportation would be enhanced when the narrative is told from the perspective of a character as opposed of being told by an omniscient narrator, when the character's attitudes are concordant with those of the audience. However, when the character's attitudes are discordant, telling the narrative from his or her perspective would interfere with transportation.

Our review of the studies that examined the effect of transportation on knowledge gain suggests several speculations regarding possible interactive effects. The first interaction that should be considered is between the degree of motivation to process a narrative and transportation such that in high motivation situations, transportation interferes with knowledge gain while in low degrees of motivation, transportation enhances knowledge. There might also be different effects for transportation on recall, depending on the medium through which the narrative is presented. Transportation into audio-visual medium might lead to better recall of visual details while transportation into written narrative might lead to a better recall of terms and concepts. These and other interactive hypotheses still await testing and should further enhance our understanding of the unique roles of transportation and identification.

Future Theoretical Directions

A couple of new theoretical questions stem from this review. The first question is that of the causal order. Can we determine whether one of these psychological responses precedes the other or do they co-occur simultaneously? In other words, is identification with a character a precursor to transportation or does the more general transportation precede the development of identification with a specific character? This brings us to the question of whether they always co-occur. Is it possible to experience transportation but no identification? Is it possible to experience identification without being transported?

It is hard to imagine how one would empirically test the causal order of two related concepts that are both responses to narrative and neither has what we would currently consider physically noticeable manifestations. The only advance we can offer at this point is to point to the differences in focus between transportation and identification and suggest that narratives that begin with a major event around which the nature of characters is revealed would probably evoke transportation followed by identification. In contrast, narratives that highlight a specific person—perhaps even as a first-person narrator who slowly reveals the complication that drives the narratives—would evoke and depend on identification as a vehicle for transportation. That said, it should be noted that in none of the reviewed studies was a case reported in which a very low level of either transportation or identification was found where the other was at a meaningful level. This suggests that under ordinary circumstances transporting narratives also create identification and characters that elicit identification also create transportation.

As for the question of co-occurrence, no data exists to answer this question but a theoretical argument can be made suggesting that transportation alone may occur but not identification without transportation. It is possible to imagine a narrative that has no specific characters with which audiences can identify (i.e., perhaps a story about a group of people or an organization). It is also possible to think of narratives that have only unattractive characters that do not engender identification. If the plot is suspenseful enough such narratives could evoke substantial transportation with very little, or no, identification. This is possible if one is transported into the narrative as an observer rather than a character (Oatley, 1999). On the other hand, it is hard to see how audiences identify with a character without being transported into the narrative.

Limitations

One clear lesson that is forwarded by this review is that research on transportation and identification is a growing area of research that is fruitful and vibrant. However, findings are far from consistent, suggesting that there are multiple moderating variables that need to be considered. This review includes many explanations for conflicting findings, some of which are admittedly quite speculative. These explanations are not meant as a final word to explain away these conflicting results but rather as speculations that call for future tests of hypotheses. The review also includes several unpublished studies (e.g., conference papers, masters and doctoral theses). These findings, that have yet to go through the normal review process, should be critically evaluated but they have been included for the sake of gathering as many relevant data points and in an attempt to tell a coherent story from the data. We prioritize these goals as a way to raise questions that will encourage more research. We hope that as more studies are published, future reviews and formal meta-analyses will provide clearer answers to the important questions raised herein.

In the interest of future reviews and analyses, it should be noted that our task was made more difficult and speculative because of a few obstacles that we encountered with the existing literature. The first is the use of multiple scales that are conceptually similar but not always identical. The development of newer measures based on theoretical development (e.g., Busselle & Bilandzic, 2009) is certainly to be encouraged but all too often scholars create conceptual confusion by using scales that were meant to measure one construct and calling it by a different name. Although this may work for a scholar in a given situation, it prevents the field from moving forward by making it difficult to synthesize research from various scholars. Examples of this can be seen in Kaufman and Libby (2012) who use some items from the identification scale and label it perspective taking, or studies by Murphy and colleagues (2011; 2012) that use items measuring liking, perceived similarity, wishful identification, and parasocial interaction all together under the very general label of "involvement with characters." It cannot be determined to what extent the inconsistencies in some of the findings reported earlier can be attributed to the variations in measurement, but future research should test this possibility.

Another obstacle is created by studies that either did not measure or report both identification and transportation even when studying both, but which seem theoretically relevant. Finally, there were studies that included measures of both transportation and identification but they were reported as one construct (Dal Cin, Zanna, & Fong, 2004; Greenwood & Long, 2009). It is hoped that this review will advance the consolidation of the field of narrative persuasion at least in terms of the use of similar concepts and measures that will allow future scholars to compare findings across studies.

Our review has aimed not only to summarize and synthesize the many studies on transportation and identification but to lay out an ambitious agenda for the future direction of research. This agenda prioritizes process over impact and the synthesis of factors related to audience, message, medium and context. Teasing out the specifics of how narratives work to influence attitudes and behaviors promises to be a difficult task that will require great effort, but we have attempted to show that significant advances have already been made.

Researchers in this field are asking more complex and refined questions and developing more nuanced and insightful theories. There is every reason to hope that such advances will continue to take place in the years to come and that the many unanswered questions we have offered will be answered.

Note

1 Sources noted with an asterisk are unpublished sources including MA theses, conference papers and other unpublished data.

References

Appel, M. (2011). A story about a stupid person can make you act stupid (or smart): Behavioral assimilation (and contrast) as narrative impact. *Media Psychology, 14(2)*, 144–167. doi: 10.1080/15213269.2011.573461

Appel, M., & Richter, T. (2010). Transportation and need for affect in narrative persuasion: A mediated moderation model. *Media Psychology, 13*(2), 101–135. doi: 10.1080/15213261003799847

Appel, M., Gnambs, T., Richter, T., & Green, M. C. (2015). The Transportation Scale–Short Form (TS–SF). *Media Psychology, 18*(2), 243–266. doi: 10.1080/15213269.2014.987400

Bandura, A. (2001). Social cognitive theory of mass communication. *Media Psychology, 3*(3), 265–299. doi: http://dx.doi.org/10.1207/S1532785XMEP0303_03

Banjo, O., Appiah, O., Wang, Z. J., Brow, C., Walther, W., Tchernev, J., & Pierman, E. (2013, June). Coviewing effects of ethnic-oriented programming: An examination of in-group bias and racial comedy exposure. Paper presented at the meeting of ICA, London.

Bilandzic, H., & Busselle, R. W. (2011). Enjoyment of films as a function of narrative experience, perceived realism and transportability. *Communications, 36*(1), 29–50. doi: 10.1515/comm.2011.002

Braverman, J. (2008). Testimonials versus informational persuasive messages: The moderating effect of delivery mode and personal involvement. *Communication Research, 35*(5), 666–694. doi: http://dx.doi.org/10.1177/0093650208321785

Busselle, R., & Bilandzic, H. (2009). Measuring narrative engagement. *Media Psychology, 12*(4), 321–347. doi: 10.1080/15213260903287259

Byrne, D. (1961). Interpersonal attraction and attitude similarity. *The Journal of Abnormal and Social Psychology, 62*(3), 713. doi: 10.1037/h0044721

Byrne, D. (1969). Attitudes and attraction. *Advances in experimental social psychology, 4*, 35–89.

Chory-Assad, R. M., & Cicchirillo, V. (2005). Empathy and affective orientation as predictors of identification with television characters. *Communication Research Reports, 22*(2), 151–156. doi: 10.1080/00036810500130786

Chung, A. H., & Slater, M. D. (2013). Reducing stigma and out-group distinctions through perspective-taking in narratives. *Journal of Communication, 63*(5), 894–911. doi: 10.1111/jcom.12050

Cohen, J. (2001). Defining identification: A theoretical look at the identification of audiences with media characters. *Mass Communication and Society, 4*(3), 245–264. doi: 10.1207/S15327825MCS0403_01

Cohen, J. (2009). Mediated relationships and media effects: Parasocial interaction and identification. In R. L. Nabi, & M. B. Oliver (Eds.). *The Sage handbook of media processes and effects* (pp. 223–236). Thousand Oaks, CA: Sage.

Cohen, J., & Mazor Tregerman, M. (2012). *Medium effects: Love hurt.* Unpublished raw data.

Cohen, J., Tal-Or, N., & Mazor-Tregerman, M. (2015). The tempering effect of transportation: Exploring the effects of transportation and identification during exposure to controversial two-sided narratives. *Journal of Communication, 65*, 237–258. doi: 10.1111/jcom.12144

Costabile, K. A., & Terman, A. W. (2013). Effects of film music on psychological transportation and narrative persuasion. *Basic and Applied Social Psychology, 35*(3), 316–324. doi: http://dx.doi.org/10.1080/01973533.2013.785398

Dal Cin, S., Zanna, M. P., & Fong, G. T. (2004). Narrative persuasion and overcoming resistance. In E. S. Knowles, & J. A. Linn (Eds.). *Resistance and persuasion* (pp. 175–191). Mahwah, NJ: Lawrence Erlbaum Associates.

de Graaf, A. (2014). The effectiveness of adaptation of the protagonist in narrative impact: Similarity influences health beliefs through self-referencing. *Human Communication Research, 40*, 73–90. doi: 10.1111/hcre.12015

de Graaf, A., Hoeken, H., Sanders, J., & Beentjes, H. (2009). The role of dimensions of narrative engagement in narrative persuasion. *Communications, 34*(4), 385–405. doi: 10.1515/COMM.2009.024

de Graaf, A., Hoeken, H., Sanders, J., & Beentjes, J. W. J. (2012). Identification as a mechanism of narrative persuasion. *Communication Research, 39*(6), 802–823. doi: 10.1177/0093650211408594

Dunlop, S. M., Wakefield, M., & Kashima, Y. (2010). Pathways to persuasion: Cognitive and experiential responses to health-promoting mass media messages. *Communication Research 37(1)* 133–164. doi: 10.1177/0093650209351912

Escalas, J. E. (2004). Imagine yourself in the product: Mental simulation, narrative transportation, and persuasion. *Journal of advertising, 33(2)*, 37–48. doi: 10.1080/00913367.2004.10639163

Escalas, J. E. (2007). Self-referencing and persuasion: narrative transportation versus analytical elaboration. *Journal of Consumer Research, 33(4)*, 421–429. doi: http://www.jstor.org/stable/10.1086/510216

Eyal, K., & Rubin, A. M. (2003). Viewer aggression and homophily, identification, and parasocial relationships with television characters. *Journal of Broadcasting & Electronic Media, 47*(1), 77–98. doi: 10.1207/s15506878jobem4701_5

Frey, K. P., & Eagly, A. H. (1993). Vividness can undermine the persuasiveness of messages. *Journal of Personality and Social Psychology, 65*, 32–44. doi: http://dx.doi.org/10.1037/0022-3514.65.1.32

Gerrig, R. J. (1993). *Experiencing narrative worlds: On the psychological activities of reading*. New York, NY: Yale University Press.

Green, M. C. (2004). Transportation into narrative worlds: The role of prior knowledge and perceived realism. *Discourse Processes, 38*(2), 247–266. doi: 10.1207/s15326950dp3802_5

Green, M. C., & Brock, T. C. (2000). The role of transportation in the persuasiveness of public narratives. *Journal of Personality and Social Psychology, 79*(5), 701–721. doi: http://dx.doi.org/10.1037/0022-3514.79.5.701

Green, M. C., Rozin, P., & Aldao, A., (2004, August). Effect of story details on transportation into narrative worlds and identification with characters. Paper presented in IGEL, Edmonton.

Green, M. C., Kass, S., Carrey, J., Herzig, B., Feeney, R., & Sabini, J. (2008). Transportation across media: Repeated exposure to print and film. *Media Psychology, 11*(4), 512–539. doi: 10.1080/15213260802492000

Greenwood, D. N., & Long, C. R. (2009). Psychological predictors of media involvement: Solitude experiences and the need to belong. *Communication Research, 36*(5), 637–654. doi: http://dx.doi.org/10.1177/0093650209338906

Hall, A. E., & Bracken, C. C. (2011). "I really liked that movie": Testing the relationship between trait empathy, transportation, perceived realism, and movie enjoyment. *Journal of Media Psychology: Theories, Methods, and Applications, 23*(2), 90–99. doi: http://dx.doi.org/10.1027/1864-1105/a000036

Himelowsky, J., Jain, P., Cohen, J., & Ewoldsen, D. (2014, May). Looking deeper into the narrative interpretation process: Exploring the determinants and dynamics of reacting to and interpreting media stories. Paper presented to annual meeting of the Mass Communication Division of the International Communication Association Conference, Seattle, WA.

Hefner, D., Klimmt, C., & Vorderer, P. (2007). Identification with the player character as determinant of video game enjoyment. In L. Ma, M. Rauterberg, & R. Nakatsu (Eds.), *Entertainment computing – International Conference of Entertainment Computing* (pp. 39–48). Berlin: Springer.

Hoeken, H., & Sinkeldam, J. (2014). The role of identification and perception of just outcome in evoking emotions in narrative persuasion. *Journal of Communication, 64*, 935–955. doi: 10.1111/jcom.12114

Hoffner, C. (1996) Children's wishful identification and parasocial interaction with favorite television characters. *Journal of Broadcasting and Electronic Media, 40*(3), 389–402. doi: 10.1080/08838159609364360

Hoffner, C., & Buchanan, M. (2005). Young adults' wishful identification with television characters: The role of perceived similarity and character attributes. *Media Psychology, 7*(4), 325–351. doi: 10.1207/S1532785XMEP0704_2

Hoffner, C., & Cantor, J. (1991). Perceiving and responding to mass media characters. In J. Bryant & D. Zillmann (Eds.), *Responding to the screen: Reception and reaction processes* (pp. 63–103). Hillsdale, NJ: Lawrence Erlbaum Associates.

Igartua, J. J., & Barrios, I. (2012). Changing real-world beliefs with controversial movies: Processes and mechanisms of narrative persuasion. *Journal of Communication, 62*(3), 514–531. doi: 10.1111/j.1460-2466.2012.01640.x

Jensen, J. D., King, A. J., Carcioppolo, N., & Davis, L. (2012). Why are tailored messages more effective? A multiple mediation analysis of a breast cancer screening intervention. *Journal of Communication, 62*(5), 851–868. doi: 10.1111/j.1460-2466.2012.01668.x

Kaufman, G. F., & Libby, L. K. (2012). Changing beliefs and behavior through experience-taking. *Journal of Personality and Social Psychology, 103*(1), 1–19. doi: 10.1037/a0027525

Keveney, B. (2005, November 25). Shades of "Grey's Anatomy": Mix of comedy, drama, personality types—and a little sex—makes quirky hospital show a hit. *USA Today*, D1.

Krakowiak, K. M., & Oliver, M. B. (2012). When good characters do bad things: Examining the effect of moral ambiguity on enjoyment. *Journal of Communication, 62*(1), 117–135. doi: 10.1111/j.1460-2466.2011.01618.x

Kuijpers, M. M. (2014). Absorbing stories: The effects of textual devices on absorption and evaluative responses. (Unpublished doctoral dissertation). University of Utrecht, The Netherlands.

Mazzocco, P. J., Green, M. C., Sasota, J. A., & Jones, N. W. (2010). This story is not for everyone: Transportability and narrative persuasion. *Social Psychological and Personality Science*, 1(4), 361–368. doi: 10.1177/1948550610376600

McKinley, C. (2010). Examining dimensions of character involvement as contributing factors in television viewers' binge drinking perceptions. (Unpublished doctoral dissertation). University of Arizona, Tucson, AZ.

Moyer-Gusé, E. (2008). Toward a theory of entertainment persuasion: Explaining the persuasive effects of entertainment-education messages. *Communication Theory, 18*(3), 407–425. doi: 10.1111/j.1468-2885.2008.00328.x

Moyer-Gusé, E., & Nabi, R. L. (2010). Explaining the effects of narrative in an entertainment television program: Overcoming resistance to persuasion. *Human Communication Research, 36(1),* 26–52. doi: 10.1111/j.1468-2958.2009.01367.x

Moyer-Gusé, E., Chung, A. H., & Jain, P. (2011). Identification with characters and discussion of taboo topics after exposure to an entertainment narrative about sexual health. *Journal of Communication, 61(3),* 387–406. doi: 10.1111/j.1460-2466.2011.01551.x

Murphy, S. T., Frank, L. B., Chatterjee, J. S., & Baezconde-Garbanati, L. (2013). Narrative versus nonnarrative: The role of identification, transportation, and emotion in reducing health disparities. *Journal of Communication, 63*(1), 116–137. doi: http://dx.doi.org/10.1111/jcom.12007

Murphy, S. T., Frank, L. B., Moran, M. B., & Patnoe-Woodley, P. (2011). Involved, transported, or emotional? Exploring the determinants of change in knowledge, attitudes, and behavior in entertainment-education. *Journal of Communication*, *61*(3), 407–431. doi: 10.1111/j.1460-2466.2011.01554.x

Murphy, S. T., Hether, H. J., Felt, L. J., & de Castro Buffington, S. (2012). Public diplomacy in prime time: Exploring the potential of entertainment education in international public diplomacy. *American journal of media psychology*, *5*(1–4), 5–32.

Nabi, R. L., Stitt, C. R., Halford, J., & Finnerty, K. L. (2006). Emotional and cognitive predictors of the enjoyment of reality-based and fictional television programming: An elaboration of the uses and gratifications perspective. *Media Psychology*, *8*(4), 421–447. doi: 10.1207/s1532785xmep0804_5

Oatley, K. (1999). Meetings of minds: Dialogue, sympathy, and identification, in reading fiction. *Poetics, 26*(5), 439–454. doi: 10.1016/S0304-422X(99)00011-X

Oliver, M. B., Shade, D., Ferchaud, A., Bailey, E., Yang, C., Bilandzic, H., & Cohen, J. (2014). *The effects of direct address in House of Cards*. Unpublished raw data.

Ophir, Y. (2013). Pursuing the vividness effect— textual vividness, identification, transportation and the change of attitudes and behavioral intentions in the context of health communication. (Unpublished master's thesis). University of Haifa, Haifa, Israel.

Quintero, J. M., Harrison, K., & Quick, B. L. (2013). Understanding the effectiveness of the entertainment-education strategy: An investigation of how audience involvement, message processing, and message design influence health information recall. *Journal of Health Communication: International Perspectives*, *18*(2), 160–178. doi: 10.1080/10810730.2012.688244

Semmler, S. M., Loof, T., & Berke, C. (2015). The influence of audio-only character narration on character and narrative engagement. *Communication Research Reports*, *32*(1). doi: 10.1080/08824096.2014.989976

Sestir, M., & Green, M. C. (2010). You are who you watch: Identification and transportation effects on temporary self-concept. *Social Influence, 5*(4), 272–288. doi: 10.1080/15534510.2010.490672

Slater, M. D., & Rouner, D. (2002). Entertainment-education and elaboration likelihood: Understanding the processing of narrative persuasion. *Communication Theory, 12*(2), 173–191. doi: 10.1111/j.1468-2885.2002.tb00265.x

Slater, M. D., Rouner, D., & Long, M. (2006). Television dramas and support for controversial public policies: Effects and mechanisms. *Journal of Communication*, *56*(2), 235–252. doi: 10.1111/j.1460-2466.2006.00017.x

Slater, M. D., Buller, D. B., Waters, E., Archibeque, M., & LeBlanc, M. (2003). A test of conversational and testimonial messages versus didactic presentations of nutrition information. *Journal of Nutrition Education and Behavior, 35*(5), 255–259. doi: 10.1016/S1499-4046(06)60056-0

So, J., & Nabi, R. (2013). Reduction of perceived social distance as an explanation for media's influence on personal risk perceptions: A test of the risk convergence model. *Human Communication Research*, *39*(3), 317–338. doi: 10.1111/hcre.12005

Tal-Or, N. (in press). How co-viewing affects attitudes through transportation and identification. *Media Psychology*.

Tal-Or, N., & Cohen, J. (2010). Understanding audience involvement: Conceptualizing and manipulating identification and transportation. *Poetics, 38*, 402–418. doi: 10.1016/j.poetic.2010.05.004

Tal-Or, N., & Tsfati, Y. (2015). When Arabs and Jews watch TV together: Combining direct and mediated intergroup contact. Manuscript in preparation.

Tal-Or, N., & Tsfati, Y. (in press). Does the co-viewing of sexual material affect rape myth acceptance? The role of the co-viewer's reactions and gender. *Communication Research.*

Taylor, S. E., & Thompson, S. C. (1982). Stalking the elusive "vividness" effect. *Psychological Review, 89*(2), 155. doi: http://dx.doi.org/10.1037/0033-295X.89.2.155

Till, B., Vitouch, P., Herberth, A., Sonneck, G., & Niederkrotenthaler, T. (2013). Personal suicidality in reception and identification with suicidal film characters. *Death Studies, 37*(4), 383–392. doi: 10.1080/07481187.2012.673531

Tsao, J. (1996). Compensatory media use: An exploration of two paradigms. *Communication Studies, 47*(1–2), 89–109. doi: 10.1080/10510979609368466

Tsay-Vogel, M., & Oliver, M. B. (2014). Is watching others self-disclose enjoyable? An examination of the effects of information delivery in entertainment media. *Journal of Media Psychology: Theories, Methods, and Applications, 26*(3), 111–124. doi: http://dx.doi.org/10.1027/1864-1105/a000116

Tukachinsky, R., & Tokunaga, R. S. (2013). The effects of engagement with entertainment. In E. L. Cohen (Ed.). *Communication Yearbook 37* (pp. 287–321).

van Laer, T., de Ruyter, K., Visconti, L. M., & Wetzels, M. (2014). The extended transportation-imagery model: A meta-analysis of the antecedents and consequences of consumers' narrative transportation. *Journal of Consumer Research, 40*(5), 797–817. doi: 10.1086/673383

Vaughn, L. A., Hesse, S. J., Petkova, Z., & Trudeau, L. (2009). "This story is right on": The impact of regulatory fit on narrative engagement and persuasion. *European Journal of Social Psychology, 39*(3), 447–456. doi: 10.1002/ejsp.570

Weinmann, C., Löb, C., Mattheiß, T., & Vorderer, P. (2013). Approaching science by watching TV: What do entertainment programs contribute to viewers' competence in genetic engineering? *Educational Media International, 50*(3), 149–161. doi: 10.1080/09523987.2013.839152

Williams, K. D. (2010). The effects of homophily, identification, and violent video games on players. *Mass Communication and Society, 14*(1), 3–24. doi: 10.1080/15205430903359701

CHAPTER CONTENTS

3 Connected Television

Media Convergence, Industry Structure, and Corporate Strategies

Paul Murschetz

Alpen-Adria-University of Klagenfurt, Austria

This study offers an economic analysis of the television broadcasting industry at the convergence of broadcast and broadband connectivity. It finds that media convergence obscures rather than illuminates the complexity of the current changes in the industry. However, the structure-conduct-performance (SCP) model of industrial organization theory can fruitfully be applied to various questions of the fundamental transformation toward connected TV. Yet, the emerging ecosystem for connected TV in Germany is immature and each provider is struggling to realize an optimal corporate strategy and organizational form in the connected TV domain.

Television is reaching yet another tipping point in its industry evolution. Driven by the dynamic evolution of information and communication technologies (ICTs), transformations provoked by the convergence between television broadcast and Internet broadband allow for the boundary between television and the Internet to disappear. How is the television industry transforming, and who is in the driving seat to win the race for its future?

The issues surrounding structural change in television broadcasting are far from straightforward. The underlying economics are highly complex, but their importance to all stakeholders is evident. The seminal question of who will own the television audience and control the user interface is still an open one, and one important consideration therein will be the role that legacy broadcasters will play when being confronted with new competitors from outside the industry, mainly by companies such as Samsung, Apple, and Google.

In fact, investments in service improvements and content wealth allow these new players to displace TV industry incumbents and offer free online video libraries with entire seasons of current TV shows produced by the big networks and studios. As it stands, the television broadcasting networks and their most popular channels can still deliver to large audiences. But, as viewing habits have shifted and digitization has blurred the boundaries between previously distinct access networks and technologies (in media, telecom, and computing), industry architectures and business models used within this converged media ecosystem are greatly challenged. Media managers face the need to satisfy the changing expectations of the audiences and undertake convergence as competitive strategy to achieve both economies of scope and scale.

It is clear that these disruptive potentials, arising from convergence in its full dimensionality, evoke a nexus of research dimensions. These encompass issues of technological change and innovation; effects of the convergence on journalism and the newsroom; effects on the industry structure and the competitive behavior of broadcasters and their new rivals from outside the industry; the ever-more-important changes in audience behavior; and the creation of public policies to protect consumers. Frankly, it is notoriously difficult to deconstruct these many interrelated phenomena.

What Is Connected TV?

"Connected TV," sometimes referred to as smart TV or hybrid TV, is the new buzzword in home entertainment. It includes a wide range of technical solutions that bring linear TV and the internet world together, for example, TV sets with added Internet connectivity, set-top boxes delivering audiovisual content "over-the-top," connections to social media and networking services, and the ability to control and interact with gestures and voice commands, and so forth, connected TV may bring these services to large flat-screen TVs that have the processing power to display HDTV or 3DTV.

Connected TV is a good example of the merging of previously distinct media technologies and media forms resulting from digitization and computer networking, and an economic strategy in which the TV companies diversify and 'attack' the Internet domain (or, alternatively, defend their old territories). As for access to connected TV, a broadband connection is a necessary precondition. In Germany, 70.9% of all German TV households have a broadband connection to the Internet and, if equipped with connected TV hardware or other media streamers, can combine the strengths of broadcast and Internet worlds on their large screens in their living rooms. At least 75% of these households expect to be connected to broadband networks; cheap streaming media dongles and boxes also make physical connection an irrelevant issue (Gfk Retail and Technology GmbH, 2015).

For the purpose of this study, connected TV will be defined alongside the definition of the *Deutsche TV-Plattform* (English: "German TV platform"), an interdisciplinary forum for cross-sectoral exchange of information and opinions among developments in digital television in Germany. There, connected TV is rather widely defined as "television sets that can display broadcast programs and services from traditional broadcasting channels as well as content from the internet, so that both sources can be equally used as suppliers of information and/or entertainment" (Deutsche TV-Plattform, 2012, p. 6). Once connected, viewers can download connected TV software applications or apps from the propriety operating systems installed or update or install apps on demand via an "app store," in a similar manner to how the apps are integrated in modern smartphones. Popular apps are news apps (e.g., "Tagesschau" newscast app in Germany), apps offering the video libraries of the television networks, web TV apps (e.g., YouTube), social media apps (e.g., Facebook), or game apps.

Connected TV is different from HbbTV. HbbTV stands for "Hybrid Broadcast Broadband TV" and is both an industry standard (European Telecommunications Standards Institute, 2010) and promotional initiative for hybrid digital TV to harmonize broadcast, IPTV (i.e., television services delivered over the Internet), and broadband delivery of entertainment to the end consumer through connected TVs (smart TVs) and set-top boxes. Simply speaking, it connects linear broadcasts with interactive internet services on your TV screen, similar to the "Red Button" service on the remote control for certain digital television set-top boxes in the United Kingdom, Australia, Belgium, Hong Kong, Malaysia, Thailand, and by DirecTV and Comcast in the United States. Besides the traditional functions of TV sets and set-top boxes provided through traditional broadcasting media, most connected TVs have built-in apps for services like Netflix. Often, they have web browsers, games, and other "time sucks." Indeed, the Internet and the "online video revolution" also have substantially changed how we watch TV. This is due to the likes of Netflix, an American provider of on-demand Internet streaming media services, and other big-name providers such as Google's video-sharing platform YouTube; Hulu, an "over-the-top" (OTT) subscription service offering ad-supported on-demand streaming video of TV shows, movies, and webisodes; or Amazon's LoveFilm, a UK-based provider of streaming video on demand in the United Kingdom and Germany. Digital convergence is currently leading to a variety of new and innovative TV services.

But all is not rosy. The latest global privacy policy announcement of Samsung, the consumer electronics giant and leading provider of connected TV services, states that a user's personal conversations will be recorded by the device's microphone and transmitted to third parties (www.samsung.com/uk/info/privacy-SmartTV.html). But while this privacy policy has been called Orwellian and raises accusations of digital spying, it emphasizes that connected TV is to be associated not only with technology, but also with industrial and institutional structures, as well as with social and cultural norms that shape and are shaped by converging media.

Research Questions and Methodology

I will begin exploring the future of television and broadcasting by delineating the concept of media convergence as a key point of reference for the transition in the audiovisual media landscape toward connected TV. Essentially, I will offer an economic analysis of the structural transformations of television broadcasting toward the emerging connected TV industry and its dynamics. Theoretical focus is on media convergence, industry analysis, and corporate-level strategic positioning of media firms.

Research is based on a review of literature that explores media convergence and its impacts on industry evolution and strategic positioning. My own review of the comprehensive and necessarily interdisciplinary literature suggests that academia continues to wrestle with the substantial changes in the evolving connected TV landscape (Chan-Olmsted & Kang, 2003; Doyle, 2010;

Hacklin, 2008; Hacklin, Battistini, & Krogh, 2013; Hacklin, Klang & Baschera, 2013; Kind, Nilssen, & Sorgard, 2009; Wirth, 2006). In my view, a clear picture of the relationship between media convergence, industry transformation, and the strategic options of TV companies is only now emerging. A questionnaire was designed and used to test questions regarding the strategic choices available to broadcasters and other new players in connected TV. The issue of *strategic choice* is a major one within the structure-conduct-performance (SCP) framework's second model element *conduct* (i.e., the "C" of SCP). SCP is a main pillar of industrial organization (IO) theory, which was devised over half a century ago in an effort to contextualize and explain industry dynamics in an attempt to investigate how SCP can contribute to explaining emergent issues in the economics of connected TV. As shown in Figure 3.1, conduct is the behavioral variable of the model, specified by product and service strategies in connected TV offered by the players, among others. Germany was our case study for reasons of market size and data accessibility.

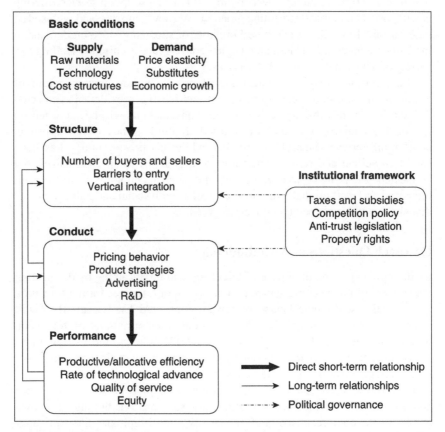

Figure 3.1 The SCP Framework of Industrial Organization Theory, Basic Elements, and their Relationships (adapted from Scherer & Ross, 1990).

The sample drew on all ordinary members of the German "Deutsche TV-Platform" (altogether 45; www.tv-plattform.de/de/ueber-uns/mitglieder. html), coming from all value-chain segments of the industry. The members were given a structured questionnaire containing a total of 10 questions. The participants were asked for their perception about macro environmental drivers of industry change, their connected TV strategies, and their current levels of revenue performance in their connected TV activities. I also conducted an in-depth interview with a key representative of "Deutsche TV-Platform."

Principally, I argue that in order to advance our thinking about media convergence and industry change in television, we are well advised to explore the industrial organization theory as a framework for coalescing and focusing on the ongoing and ever-more-intensified dynamic change that is blurring industry boundaries. And, further, we need to explore whether there are "game-winning" strategies and choices that broadcasters have to make in order to preserve and capture value in the ever-more-competitive environment of connected TV. Hence, I pose the following two research questions:

1   Regarding the nature of convergence: What defines media convergence and which factors drive or inhibit its development toward connected TV?
2   Regarding the drivers of industry transformation: What factors affect the industry's structure and, consequently, have an impact on the broadcasters' competitive behaviors and strategic positioning thereof?

Regarding the need to identify winning strategies in connected TV: How are strategies responding to the challenges of industry transformation? Are they driving the need for the development of new business models? Besides the literature review, I organized an in-depth interview with the head of research of a key proponent of the German private TV sector. This paper proceeds with revisiting the debate on media convergence. It will briefly describe the structure-conduct-performance model from industrial organization economics in an attempt to investigate how the model can contribute to explaining emergent issues in the economics of connected TV. The conclusion will sum up key findings and critically discuss the results.

Media Convergence Revisited

Convergence has gained an enormous amount of attention across disciplines within the last several years. In the media field, it is used to describe the merging of formerly distinct functions, markets, and fields of application, which has changed the way TV companies operate and consumers perceive and process media content. These transformations have not only led business practices to change and required companies to adapt to new conditions; they also continue to have a lasting impact on research in this area.

In their book *Media Convergence: Networked Digital Media in Everyday Life*, Meikle and Young (2012) define convergence alongside four dimensions:

- Technological—the combination of computing, communications, and content around networked digital media platforms,
- Industrial—the engagement of established media institutions in the digital media space, and the rise of digitally based companies such as Google, Apple, Microsoft, and others as significant media content providers,
- Social—the rise of social network media such as Facebook, Twitter and YouTube, and the growth of user-created content, and
- Textual—the reuse and remixing of media into what has been termed a 'transmedia' model, where stories and media content (for example, sounds, images, written text) are dispersed across multiple media platforms.

The empirical analysis below will mainly focus on the industrial side of convergence. However, it is evident that media convergence, in reality, is more than just a shift in technology which is changing industry. It alters relationships between industries, technologies, audiences, genres, and markets. Media convergence changes the rationality media industries operate in. It must be considered as a metaprocess. But while the impacts of convergence as detailed in "Preparing for a Fully Converged Audiovisual World" (the European Commission's 2013 green paper title for a direction of travel for identifying key aspects of policy and regulation) are far-reaching, they bring significant challenges too.

First, as already indicated above, ambivalence toward media convergence prevails (European Commission, 2013; Jin, 2012; Størsul & Stuedahl, 2007). The problems are manifold and the most pressing seems to be the nature of convergence itself, which remains multifaceted, difficult to operationalize, and dynamic in nature. When looking into the driving forces of media convergence, for example, it becomes evident that the convergence process is better viewed as being co-evolutionary in origin. This means "its direction and pace is determined by the reciprocal interplay of technological innovations, corporate strategies, political-legal reforms and changes in media reception patterns" (Latzer, 2013, p. 7). Latzer integrates media convergence with elements of innovation theory (Dogruel, 2013; Küng, 2013) and complexity theory (Schneider, 2012). Then, a larger-scale model of media change emerges, thus opening the convergence paradigm into new research domains. Other scholars argue that developments toward convergence follow a more restricted and monocausal "techno-economic paradigm" (Perez, 2010), a term to depict the notion that media development and change would stem from the constant interplay of technological innovations and entrepreneurial strategies for media to grow profitably. In sum, the proposition that only convergence would result from such a techno-economic paradigm—and not "de-convergence," a process whereby media disintegrate and differentiate their product portfolio—remains problematic or is, at best, speculative, and analyses based on it are not able to give valid inferences.

Second, on the supply side, media convergence affects all stages in the value chain of the traditional television and broadcasting sector. At the industry level, the TV value chain is reconfigured in various ways (Wirtz, 2001). The television sector is facing a profound restructuring, as players from formerly disparate sectors (such as TV, Internet, and equipment vendors) converge on the market. Since the economics of broadcast TV have been disrupted by the introduction of the networked digital video recorders (DVRs) (von Rimscha, 2006), the discussion of television broadcasting losing its dominance in video distribution is opened. The impacts of technology-driven changes puts enormous pressure on the existing broadcast TV value chain, from content production and editing, content aggregation, services programming and packaging, delivery and transmission, to platforms and end-user reception, and this has further intensified (Hess & Matt, 2013). Still, the question of who will win over the television audience and control the user interface is still open. One important aspect will be the role incumbent or "veteran" TV broadcasters (terrestrial, cable, and satellite) will play when confronted with new competitors from outside the industry (electronics companies, Internet aggregators, telecoms, and so on), each with their own distinctive source of competitive advantage to deliver video content to consumers.

A third challenge towards convergence concerns changes in the audiences' viewing behavior with regard to the offerings of these new convergent TV products and services. TV consumption is set to experience a variety of changes in usage and engagement modes from:

- Lean-back/passive to lean-forward/active viewing;
- Use of the remote control to use of voice and gesture control;
- Live broadcasts to time-shifted and on-demand TV modes;
- Single-screen to multiscreen usage ;
- Single-person viewing (in the child's room) to multi-person family viewing in the living room (where virtual co-viewers may be part of the viewing experience by means of online social networks; Xu & Yan, 2011).

However, while the majority of viewing is said to stay with the traditional broadcasting networks and their "big event TV," which includes programs such as the Super Bowl or the matches of the 2014 FIFA World Cup in Brazil, the seeds of change in TV viewing patterns have been planted by a series of technological innovations. There is now a plethora of TV apps, and viewers can increasingly customize their viewing to their own interests and on their own schedules.

While online video consumption via personal computers and portable devices has become increasingly mainstream, and the adaptation of content to these devices and to connected TV sets has become a prerequisite for ongoing market penetration, the fragmentation of the user experience is considered one of the biggest barriers to a more rapid adoption of connected TV services.

The question of convergence is also of long-standing interest to scientists in the field of media economics and management, who try to understand the promising, fascinating, and sometimes frightening opportunities of shifts in the contours of the new media world. The *Journal of Media Management*, then edited by the Institute for Media and Communications Management of the University of Sankt Gallen in Switzerland, commenced in 1999 with a series of articles devoted to various aspects of convergence. The *Journal* led the reader on a comprehensive *tour d'horizon* through the key issues involved in media convergence: types and dimensions (Stipp, 1999), processes of integration into the multimedia business (Wirtz, 2001), the need for alignment of convergence with innovation strategies (Thielmann & Dowling, 1999), and its application towards multimedia convergence in the newsroom (Palmer & Eriksen, 1999). If the general thrust of ideas about media convergence in this first issue seems rather naive, the *Journal* added another special issue on the topic in 2003, edited by Michael Wirth, revisiting the same theme more critically. There the *Journal* more lucidly traced the formation of convergence as a central ideology in business, politics, and the communications field (and beyond). It revealed that regulatory liberalization and convergence strategies within the information and communication technology (ICT) industries during the 1990s were largely political, leading to a large increase in mergers and acquisitions and to the formation of a myriad of convergence-based strategic alliances within the ICT industries (Dennis, 2003; Lawson-Borders, 2003; Noll, 2003). However, key authors of the volume concluded that industry convergence of this type (notably, the megamerger of Internet superstar AOL and media giant Time Warner after the turn of the millennium, and the French company Vivendi with Universal) had not been successful (Ozanich & Wirth, 2004).

Instead, during the past decade, many communication industry giants have adopted a corporate-wide strategy of focusing on a few core business areas while divesting from other fields, whether through sales, liquidation, or spin-off of a corporate division or subsidiary. Since then, scholars who are mainly informed by the critical political economy of communication studies perspective, have pontificated about various types of industry de-convergence or *divergence* accompanying and complementing convergence processes (Jin, 2012; Jin, 2013; Liestøl, 2007; Winseck, 2008). With these industry worries in mind, others opined pithily about convergence and suggested it to be a "dangerous word" (Silverstone, 1995, p. 11) because implicit in its use is a series of claims routinely made that are technologically deterministic in fashion. Hesmondhalgh (2007), who undertook various in-depth analyses into the "creative industries," criticized the concept and its promoters for the "promise of further wonders" (p. 261), as he assessed convergence. Jenkins, the author of a book on "convergence culture," recognized as a hallmark of research on trans-media storytelling, focuses very much on the notion that

> convergence is a word that manages to describe technological, industrial, cultural, and social changes, depending on who's speaking and what they think they are talking about. In the world of media convergence, every important story gets told, every brand gets sold, and every consumer gets courted across multiple media platforms. Right now, convergence culture is getting defined top-down by decisions being made in corporate boardrooms and bottom-up by decisions made in teenagers' bedrooms.
>
> (Jenkins, 2006, p. 3)

Seen this way, convergence would become a universal code for explaining monoculture, and for denouncing the lack of diversity in entertainment and news content fabricated by large media conglomerates.

> It is shaped by the desires of media conglomerates to expand their empires across multiple platforms and by the desires of consumers to have the media they want where they want it, when they want it, and in the format they want.
>
> (Jenkins, 2006, p. 2)

Industrial Organization Economics of Connected TV

The Structure-Conduct-Performance (SCP) Paradigm

Much of the literature in the field of media economics has traditionally taken neoclassical approaches, led by the industrial organization (IO) model (Caves, 1980; Scherer & Ross, 1990; Schmalensee, 1988; Tirole, 1988). The old IO model (or Bayesian framework of analysis) is based on the assumption that there is a causal and one-directional link from market structure to firm conduct to market and firm performance. The SCP paradigm, originally proposed by Mason (1949) and later adopted by Bain (1968), is the most representative of the old IO model and is a commonly used analytical framework in media economics. The basic tenet of the SCP paradigm to market analysis states that within the framework of certain *basic conditions* (which also includes the economic infrastructure and the *institutional framework* of government laws and policies; see Figure 3.1 on page 82), the structure of a market determines the conduct of its participants (buyers and sellers), which in turn influences its performance. External factors—or, following SCP jargon, basic conditions—refer to characteristics that are often exogenous to the market (e.g., infrastructure or legal and policy environment) but may also be endogenous (e.g., available technology, product durability or purchase methods). Basic conditions are macro-environmental factors and determine the structure of the market and the competitive process that results from it.

Usually, the institutional frameworks (Figure 3.1) represent the government policies which themselves will have an impact on either the market structure, or the conduct of the firms in the market. Government policies in TV broadcasting are principally related to (European Commission, 2013; European Parliament, 2013; Organization of Economic Cooperation and Development [OECD], 2013):

- Citizens' rights and consumer protection (e.g., protection of minors, privacy and personal data);
- Issues related to EU Single Market and cultural policies (e.g., technical standards, interoperability, access to broadband interactivity); and
- Antitrust and competition issues (e.g., monopolies and abuse of dominant position, competitive bottlenecks).

In the context of connected TV, government policies face the challenging task of securing a variety of choice for consumers and warranting identical conditions for the competition of platforms, while at the same time taking the specificities of each use into consideration with regard to its relevance to the formation of public opinion and the public interest. As it stands, however, there is no specific EU legislation for connected TV. Attempts to regulate this emergent field seem biased towards the interests of industry. But while it would be important to include all critical stakeholders in shaping this new digital future and to foster greater levels of citizen participation and empowerment, broadcasters are given free rein to develop their own business models regardless of societal impacts and responsibilities. Consequently, following this *de minimis* regulation approach, it is left to the market to determine how supply and demand will shape the connected TV future.

Market structure in the IO model is defined as "those characteristics of the organization of the market that seem to exercise strategic influence on the nature of competition and pricing within the market" (Bain, 1968, p. 7). Issues of market structure are complex and wide, and this chapter cannot possibly address them fully. Usually, the market structure refers to the number and size distribution of firms in relation to the size of the total market. In fact, the market structure is greatly determined by the presence or absence of barriers to entry faced by new firms (Baumol, Rogers, & Willig, 1982). These barriers mainly depend on:

- The number of sellers (producers) and buyers (which is a result of entry barriers);
- Vertical integration by one form that owns its upstream suppliers or its downstream buyers (which may obstruct or facilitate entry);
- The extent of product differentiation by distinguishing a product or service from others (which eases entry);
- Cost structures (which may obstruct entry); and
- Access to inputs (which may obstruct entry).

When clustering the key players of the emerging connected TV ecosystem in Germany, for example, the following types of key players and their strategies (which will be explicitly and more deeply examined in the next section) can be identified as follows:

- *Content owners and producers*: Hollywood studios (Disney, etc.) and other (independent) producers that partner with device-based or platform-based retailers (such as HBO with Sky, via the on-demand OTT pay TV service Snap). They face internal and external pressures of change on their core businesses (i.e., deep content libraries) and are in direct competition with giants from the manufacturing or advertising industry (Apple, Google) and established OTT players (Netflix).
- *Traditional free-to-air and pay television broadcasters*: Public service broadcasters (ARD, ZDF, etc.), private free-to-air (RTL, ProSiebenSat1),

and pay TV (Sky) competitors seek to position themselves in the connected TV world in order to leverage their trusted brand names and their large portfolio of (premium) content rights, all for extending reach with their properties.

- *Over-the-top (OTT) television and VOD services*: Services whose audiovisual content is delivered on the 'open' Internet rather than over a managed IPTV architecture (e.g., Netflix, Hulu, LoveFilm), which penetrate the market of pay TV providers by offering low-cost video services and thus spark fears of cord-cutting from premium cable and pay TV operators.

- *Internet Protocol Television (IPTV) service providers*: Services that combine premium video packages over managed facilities, or, alternatively, function as infrastructure access and service providers, such as "Entertain" from Deutsche Telekom in Germany, which control the delivery network (and hence the quality of digital bandwidth), thus operating as a powerful gatekeeper for securing access to mass audiences,

- *Video-sharing platforms*: Examples include the Google-owned YouTube, which diversified into "YouTube for TV" in January 2009, offering a version of the website tailored for set-top boxes and other TV-based media devices with web browsers, initially allowing videos to be viewed on the PlayStation 3 and Wii consoles. YouTube TV is most challenged by licensing premium catch-up TV from broadcasters and allowing for an easier access of its content on TV.

- *Consumer electronics manufacturers*: Examples include Apple TV, a digital media player, developed and sold by Apple Inc. and now in its third generation, allows consumers to use an HDTV set to watch video from the iTunes store, Netflix, Hulu Plus, and now many more content offerings. Notable competitors include Google TV, which itself offers a software platform for set-top-boxes and HDTV sets on the basis of its operating system, Android; and connected TVs from companies such as Sony, Samsung, LG Electronics and others.

- *TV set manufacturers*: Samsung, for instance, which manufactures end-user devices to display, store, and manage content, and also offers connected TV portals in order to monetize TV viewing by integrating more interactivity (gaming, social media) into the viewing experience (which IDATE consulting named the "TV app store model." In all, this cluster is challenged by a multiplicity of standards and inexperience in the content market.

- *Supporting services*: Advertising, electronic program guides, search analytics, and tools facilitate both revenue-generating business opportunities around digital content, but also serve as vehicles for communication among Social TV audiences (e.g., Couchfunk, Zapitano).

The number of producers is the primary characteristic that defines a market structure. Different forms of market structure range from a monopoly (one supplier), to an oligopoly (a few suppliers), to perfect competition (an infinite number of suppliers). The monopolist has the highest form of market power (i.e., the ability to price above marginal costs); suppliers in a perfect competitive market have no market power (i.e., price equals marginal costs). A monopolist is only able to retain his unique position if others face barriers to entering the market. The extent to which a supplier can exert market power is thus not only determined by the number of competitors, but also by the presence of entry barriers and, thus, by the number of possible competitors. Furthermore, as described above, the ability to raise price above marginal costs also depends on the availability of close substitutes. In other words, the extent of market power is determined by the contestability of a market and by the elasticity of demand. The market power of a monopolist can then better be defined as the extent to which he can set his price above marginal costs "without losing so many sales so rapidly that the price increase is unprofitable and must be rescinded" (Landes & Posner, 1981, p. 937)—for example, by encouraging new firms to enter the industry. To any firm with market power, the existence of entry barriers is of crucial importance whenever pricing and investment decisions are made. Bain (1956) was among the first to recognize the importance of entry barriers and defined them as

> the advantage of established sellers in an industry over potential entrant sellers. These advantages being reflected in the extent to which established sellers can persistently raise their prices above a competitive level without attracting new firms to enter the industry.
>
> (p. 3)

Bain implicitly states here that entry barriers cause market power. Bain (1956) defined conditions in the absence of which entry barriers may be found, these conditions being:

* Established firms having no absolute cost advantages over potential entrant firms;
* Economies of large-scale firms being absent;
* Established firms having no product differentiation advantages.

Conduct refers to the behavior of firms; for example, pricing and marketing policies and tactics, overt of tacit collusion or rivalry, and product or market-related R&D activities. The conduct of market participants is generally interpreted as being focused on maximizing profits. In the most general form, profit maximization entails pricing strategies, product strategies, location choices, advertising, and research and development.

There are a number of ways in which convergence can be expected to change the market structure of both broadcasting and Internet markets as well as the nature of competition in these markets. One of the most exciting issues refers to the question which new technologies and the dynamic effects of convergence are changing competition (OECD, 2013). Yet, companies are bound to a certain, often industry-specific conduct. To answer this, it is plausible to refer to Michael Porter's "five forces" framework for industry analysis and to look into one force more deeply; namely, the intensity of competitive rivalry as the major determinant of the competitiveness of the industry. Porter identified a series of determinants of industry rivalry and found that such rivalries will be more intense if "competitors are numerous and equal in size and power . . . industry growth is slow, precipitating fights for market share . . . the products or services lack differentiation . . . [and] fixed costs are high or the product is perishable" among others (Porter, 1979, p. 143). Naturally, creating and capturing value from interacting with audiences and advertisers in television broadcasting is a central tenet in strategic management research of broadcast media (Chan-Olmsted, 2006; Chan-Olmsted & Ha, 2003; Chan-Olmsted & Jung, 2001; Chan-Olmsted & Li, 2002; Chon, Choi, Barnett, Danowski, & Joo, 2003; Doyle, 2010; Liu & Chan-Olmsted, 2002; Rangone & Turconi, 2003).

Strategic alliances for content partnership and various concentration strategies in the market, notably vertical integration and horizontal growth, seem to be those IO-style strategies that reaffirm the approach of competitive conditions determining competitive behavior. On the one hand, some players forward-integrate their businesses and thus increase horizontal supplier market power, while others become vertically integrated and differentiate out into key specialists in niche markets. On the other hand, these challenges open ways for new supply chain partnerships (Waterman, Sherman, & Ji, 2012). Innovation and product differentiation strategies are called for today in media convergence thinking (Habann, 2010; Størsul & Krumsvik, 2013). Traditional broadcasters, for example, may still operate as value chain companies, but enduring innovation in digital technology may change their plans for delivery of information and entertainment content to the end consumer through connected TV. While holding rights and controlling access to a comprehensive range of desirable content, they may have to diversify their business model beyond linear broadcast TV and advance it into the new arena of on-demand TV, providing enhanced interactivity and enriched customer services through electronic program guides, video on demand, games, and information and transaction applications. Usually, performance is measured in terms of productive or allocative efficiency. In addition, innovation (i.e., the rate of technological advance) and quality are considered as further performance indicators. Neoclassical theory assumes that a competitive market maximizes the efficiency of resource allocation. Economic efficiency requires both allocative efficiency and productive (or technical) efficiency.

Finally, the SCP model coalesces with the performance of an industry. Performance is the outcome variable of the SCP model and basically refers to three concepts: economic efficiency, consumer welfare, and, when connected to TV broadcast competition, social benefits and costs associated with broadcast-broadband convergence (Wirth, 2006). Economic efficiency deals with the "size of the pie" (the pie being defined as the total amount of social welfare that is available), whereas equity deals with the "distribution of the pie." Because equity is a normative concept, its relevance to welfare strongly depends on political choices. However, when part of the consumers' surplus is transferred to producers because of market power, equity issues may play a role within competition policy. The extent to which one surplus is valued more than the other, however, remains a normative question. When looking into firm performance as an outcome variable of connected TV, my interview partner from a big commercial network TV station found that traditional broadcast strategies would fit the strategies in connected TV. Offering both linear programming over traditional network channels and nonlinear services over Connected TV (e.g., as apps) would be complementary strategies; the one would not cannibalize the other.

There are several causal relations running from structure to conduct and from conduct to performance. In addition, there are causal relations running from conduct to structure (e.g., pricing strategies may decrease the number of

Table 3.1 Key Players and Strategies in the Emerging Connected TV Ecosystem in Germany

Key Player	Strategy
Content owners and producers	Hollywood studios (Disney, etc.) and other (independent) producers that partner with device-based or platform-based retailers (such as HBO with Sky, via the on-demand OTT pay TV service Snap); they face internal and external pressures of change on their core businesses (i.e., deep content libraries) and are in direct competition with giants from the manufacturing or advertising industry (Apple, Google) and established OTT players (Netflix).
Traditional free-to-air and pay television broadcasters	Public service broadcasters (ARD, ZDF, etc.), private free-to-air (RTL, ProSiebenSat1), and pay TV (Sky) competitors seek to position themselves in the connected TV world in order to leverage their trusted brand names and their large portfolio of (premium) content rights, all for extending reach with their properties.
Over-the-top (OTT) television and VOD services	Services whose audiovisual content is delivered on the 'open' Internet rather than over a managed IPTV architecture (e.g., Netflix, Hulu, LoveFilm), which penetrate the market of pay TV providers by offering low-cost video services and thus spark fears of cord-cutting from premium cable and pay TV operators.
Internet Protocol Television (IPTV) service providers	Services that combine premium video packages over managed facilities, or, alternatively, function as infrastructure access and service providers, such as "Entertain" from Deutsche Telekom in Germany, which control the delivery network (and hence the quality of digital bandwidth), thus operating as a powerful gatekeeper for securing access to mass audiences.
Video-sharing platforms	Examples include the Google-owned YouTube, which diversified into "YouTube for TV" in January 2009, offering a version of the website tailored for set-top boxes and other TV-based media devices with web browsers, initially allowing videos to be viewed on the PlayStation 3 and Wii consoles. YouTube TV is most challenged by licensing premium catch-up TV from broadcasters and allowing for an easier access of its content on TV.

Key Player	Strategy
Consumer electronics manufacturers	Examples include Apple TV—a digital media player, developed and sold by Apple Inc. and now in its third generation—which allows consumers to use an HDTV set to watch video from the iTunes store, Netflix, Hulu Plus, and now many more content offerings. Notable competitors include Google TV, which itself offers a software platform for set-top-boxes and HDTV sets on the basis of its operating system, Android; and connected TVs from companies such as Sony, Samsung, LG Electronics, and others.
TV set manufacturers	Samsung, for instance, which manufactures end-user devices to display, store, and manage content, and also offers connected TV portals in order to monetize TV viewing by integrating more interactivity (gaming, social media) into the viewing experience (which IDATE consulting named the "TV app store model); in all, this cluster is challenged by a multiplicity of standards and inexperience in the content market.
Supporting services	Advertising, electronic program guides, search analytics, and tools facilitate both revenue-generating business opportunities around digital content, but also serve as vehicles for communication among Social TV audiences (e.g., Couchfunk, Zapitano).

competitors), from performance to conduct (e.g., lack of revenues may have an influence on product strategies), and from performance to structure (e.g., bad performance may lead to market exit).

Corporate Strategies

Eventually, for traditional broadcasters still seeking a viable business strategy (or model) for connected TV, the challenges of ubiquitous content and "TV everywhere" connectivity may compound their problems. Nonetheless, as technology-driven convergence processes urge for business model innovation, their challenge is how to reconfigure and reinvent value in this new domain (Küng, 2013; Picard, 2011). Industry proponents have been quick to grasp that commercial mass media would be struggling to find new revenue streams for the converged-media future. Their executives, supported by a fleet of experts, proposed that the broadcasting industry's future could only be safeguarded by large-scale experiments in product innovation, market development, monetization, business-model venturing, and strategic customer interaction (e.g., Accenture, 2011; Accenture, 2012; FutureScape, 2011; Networked & Electronic Media, 2012). For most traditional media companies this represents a major adaptive challenge. Media companies whose primary business models are based on advertising revenues, like television, find it increasingly difficult to reach a mass audience.

So far, the industry's responses have fallen into three categories: horizontal integration, vertical integration, and the search for new revenue sources. The strategic rationale behind horizontal and vertical integration is that in a fragmenting market, media companies can only reach a mass audience with a broad portfolio of media assets, each targeted at a different group that can be exploited along the distribution windows. In sum, media companies are trying to re-aggregate audiences by diversifying across types of media and by taking a portfolio approach to content. Moreover, the traditional rights windows, which gave broadcasters almost a monopoly over quality content, have multiplied, and business-to-business revenue models are now being supplanted by potentially superior business models that are based on a deeper and more direct relationship with the end consumer. In the sections that follow, I shall introduce some selected best-practice corporate strategies in connected TV in Germany.

The "TVplus" Strategy

In Germany, the age of connected TV started at the *International Broadcasting Exhibition* in Berlin (IFA) in 2010. Since then, all four major German "FreeTV" networks—ARD, ZDF, RTL, and ProSiebenSat1—have offered 'HbbTV' services. The public broadcasters focus on so-called "Mediathek" services: free, 7-day catch-up video library services, provided by ARD, ZDF, Arte, "Das Erste," RBB, Radio Bremen, and the "Tagesschau" (the television news service produced by Norddeutscher Rundfunk (NDR) on behalf of the German public-service television network ARD). While public broadcasters wish to secure their competitive prominence in the era of connected TV, the web portals of the private TV broadcasters have ventured into building up commercial video on-demand portals, from where TV programs can exclusively be downloaded in advance of the live broadcast on linear TV (e.g., RTL Now, Pro7 Connect). Both public service broadcasting (ARD, ZDF, regional PSBs), and private free-to-air (RTL, ProSiebenSat1) and pay-TV (Sky) networks are seeking to position themselves in the connected TV world in order to leverage their trusted brand names and their portfolio of (premium) content rights. The prime focus is on extending reach with their properties, a business model which industry consultant IDATE called the "TVplus" positioning model, whereby classic broadcast TV is enhanced with VOD and OTT services (IDATE, 2010).

Likewise, Germany's largest pay-TV operator, Sky Deutschland, expanded its platform in order to offer additional benefits to its customers in terms of interactivity and multi-platform experience. In 2007, Sky launched Sky Anytime, a (catch-up) video-on-demand service that provides instant access to the best premium programming and is free to Sky+ customers. Sky+ is a HD receiver and has recording functionalities through the hard disk recorder and the integrated Sky Guide. In September 2012, Sky announced that Sky Anytime and Sky+ would be merged and rebranded as On Demand. The service offers around 1,000 hours of content featuring 350 movies, 500 series episodes, 150 documentaries and 400 kids' programs. On Demand is offered free of charge to all Sky customers with Sky+ HD boxes, although access to premium content depends on the subscriber's package. Sky+ customers doubled to 929,000 in 2012, meaning that 27.6% of all Sky subscribers already use Sky+.

In July 2011, Sky Player and Sky Mobile TV were integrated and rebranded as Sky Go. The new platform allows customers to stream live channels depending on the Sky TV subscription at no additional cost, limited to two simultaneous devices (online, iPad, iPhone, Xbox 360). Sky Go is Sky's answer to the "over-the-top" (OTT) threat, whereby video is delivered over the Internet without a multiple-system operator being involved in the control or distribution of the content, thus ensuring greater flexibility and convenience for its customers. Integrating Sky Guide into Sky Go enables a whole host of new functions, such as remote programming for Sky+. With 33.3 million customer sessions in 2012, Sky Go seems to be part of a successful convergence strategy. In January 2013, download service Sky Go Extra was launched, allowing up to four users to download their programming to their laptop, smartphones, or tablet to view offline for an additional €5 per month.

In all, Sky Deutschland is facing hard times. Germany's pay TV market is very underdeveloped and, compared to France and the United Kingdom, has a market penetration rate of only 15% (as opposed to circa 50% in France and the UK). On top of this, Internet streaming services such as LoveFilm, Maxdome, and Watchever are directly competing for customers, while Netflix has entered the German market as well. Snap is Sky's response to these threats. Launched at the end of 2013, the online video library offers 4,000 films and TV series to Sky (€4.90 per month) and non-Sky customers (€9.90 per month).

The "Paid-Owned-Earned" Advertising Revenue Strategy

Until now, the TV business has been a fairly linear process: Journalists would gather facts and observations and turn them into stories, which were then committed to be broadcast over the air or via cable/satellite, and finally consumed by the audience. This "pipeline model" is the simplest metaphor for that process, wherein content distribution was organized around the broadcast tower. Now, at the confluence of industry convergence and the increasing penetration of consumers with connected TV devices and their properties, a new business model is emerging: the "paid-owned-earned advertising" revenue strategy model.

If we believe in the boundary-spanning nature of business models by emphasizing that organizations interact with their environments—which, fundamentally, create requirements for organizations that their managers address in part by adopting their business models (Amit & Zott, 2012)—then business models that used to support traditional media companies in the past appear not to work in the digital age. Addressing this business-model innovation gap raises the fundamental question of how commercial broadcast media will manage to survive as traditional sources of revenue (paid display ads, subscriptions, and transaction sales) shrink.

Solving this issue is vital, as the legacy revenue model through "paid" (i.e., all forms of advertising for which a media purchase is necessary) and "owned" (i.e., all content assets that a brand either owns or wholly controls) media is failing. Paid advertising has found many outlets, atomized into thousands of blogs, Facebook pages, and specialized television and radio stations, so that return on investment is becoming difficult to trace due to audience fragmentation. Social media enhancements are the best drivers of opportunity to complement paid and owned media revenue models. The latter are so-called "earned" media revenue-generation activities and are gained through user-generated content created and/or shared by users. Still, earned media are the most elusive of the three marketing channels (Altimeter, 2013).

The examples of RTLII's *Berlin – Tag & Nacht* and ProSiebenSat.1's *Dirty Dancing Double Date* suggest that social media enhances the television viewing experience and reconnects the medium with the typically hard-to-reach younger segment that can be monetized through advertising forms. In that context, earned and shared media support the traditional revenue models (advertising and viewer payments) which are still crucial in financing platform development. Broadcasters that are able to secure a key position in commercial models for connected TV, or even lead the development of such commercial models, could potentially become the dominant power in the next television revolution as connected TV gradually replaces traditional television. Broadcasters may still mainly operate as value chain companies following the pipeline model, but enduring innovation in digital technology will have an impact on the distribution and consumption of television content. Along with digital television technology, platform operators have started packaging channels in their platforms and providing enhanced interactivity and enriched customer services such as electronic program guides, video on demand, games, and information and transaction applications.

The "Platform" Strategy

German consumer electronics manufacturers such as Samsung, LG Electronics, Sony, Sharp, Panasonic, and Grundig are the strongest opponents to traditional broadcasting in the connected TV era. They position themselves as downstream players and pursue backward integration strategies by slipping into the role of portals and aggregators of content and services. Scholars in Internet and media economics call this model the "platform" model (Rochet & Tirole, 2003; Rysman, 2009). Likewise do IPTV and cable TV operators such as Deutsche Telekom, Kabel Deutschland, Unity Media, and Vodafone. Similarly, DVB-T (through Germany's largest distributor of audio-visual media, Media Broadcast) and the satellite network operator ASTRA Germany, a subsidiary of SES, a world-leading satellite operator with a fleet of 49 geostationary satellites, also create portal offerings, hoping to exploit the market of web content on the TV set. Sky Deutschland has secured the German rights to the second season of Netflix's original drama series *House of Cards* and will show it exclusively on its Sky Go mobile TV and Sky Anytime on-demand services. Sky has been broadcasting the complete second season of 13 episodes from February 14 on Sky Go and a day later on Sky Anytime, parallel to the US launch on Netflix. Sky Go subscribers have been able to view the show on the web, iPad, iPhone, iPod touch, and the Xbox 360, while Sky Anytime has been making the show available via the Sky+ HD DVR on-demand. Sky has also been making the first season of *House of Cards* available on Sky Go and Sky Anytime. Additionally, the consumer electronics giant Apple, very much a technology pioneer, leverages its competencies and market experience in order to establish a connected TV innovation platform aimed at complementary products and services.

In general, for players who have adopted a positioning devoted to seamless access to all content across devices, the television remains the central entertainment-delivery screen in the home, and is therefore the unified point of access for all digital content, regardless of provenance (broadcast stream, VoD, catch-up TV, Web, etc.). Google TV is a prime example of this strategy.

The "TV App Store" Strategy

Overall, there is a growing consensus that apps will replace TV channels as part of a natural evolution, as they will provide coherent branding and smooth user interfaces across the different associated services and companion devices. Adopted by Yahoo connected TV and Samsung Apps, the "TV app store" positioning model seeks to carry apps as substitutes to TV channels over to the TV set for the distribution of internet services. TV sets and STB manufacturers, such as Samsung that manufacture end-user devices to display, store, and manage content, also offer connected TV portals. They aim at monetizing TV viewing by integrating more interactivity (gaming, social media) into the viewing experience (which IDATE named the "TV app store model"); in all, this cluster is much challenged by a multiplication of standards and inexperience in the content market.

Parallel to its main competitor LG Electronics, Samsung launched its first connected TV system (named "Smart TV") in 2007, integrating the Internet and social media into television sets and set-top boxes. Initially, the service was rolled out under the name Power Infolink—an RSS feed service with content supplied by USA Today. Samsung's "Smart TV" service enabled the viewer to receive information from the Internet while at the same time watching linear television programming. Samsung later launched its Internet@TV and unveiled the upgraded version including 3D technology.

Samsung's "Smart TV" service offers free (or for-fee) download of applications from its Samsung Apps Store, in addition to existing services such as news, weather, stock market, YouTube videos, and movies. In addition to social media services like Facebook, Twitter, Skype, and Spotify, Samsung Deutschland has closed partnerships with local content providers including Die Welt, Bild, Audi, Maxdome, and the Berliner Philharmoniker. By the end of 2012, Samsung announced a multiyear partnership with Yahoo to add an interactive layer to the television experience. By means of widgets, Yahoo connected TV now provides interactive content like trivia, additional show insights, commerce or playable games to turn passive consumers into engaged viewers. This partnership also pens up opportunities for new forms of advertising by extending traditional 30-second commercials into immediate actions. With the Yahoo-enabled commercials, advertisers can embed calls to action for downloading apps or digital media, providing coupons, ordering samples, reading reviews or viewing product information via their connected TV. In return, Yahoo provides detailed insights and statistics to track and measure the performance of TV campaigns.

Conclusion

This chapter has shown that the television broadcasting industry is currently undergoing a fundamental transformation. Some believe that the television industry will change irrevocably. Given the findings of this research, I can reasonably conclude the following:

First, it is argued here that media convergence towards new forms of connected TV offerings is a complex process of transformation which can only be understood when its dynamisms of, and among, technological, industrial, organizational, political, and socio-cultural factors are taken into consideration. In any case, media convergence is hybrid in nature and plays an important role with regard to the future of TV broadcasting. Developments toward connected TV are driven by the interplay of the industry's creed in "technology push" and the viewers/users demand for "application pull." Academically, it seems that the convergence concept obscures rather than enlightens the complexities. It remains theoretically slippery and ambivalent and marginalizes other, perhaps more important, discourses—for example those of ownership concentration in the media, control over consumer experience, and content diversity.

Second, I explored the larger SCP framework of industrial organization economics, which, following a structural-functionalist paradigm, has occupied a strong position in media economics research (Albarran, 2010; Wirth & Bloch, 1995). I tried to show that the SCP paradigm provides a useful diagnostic tool to raise questions of the causal relationships between the structure of an industry, firm conduct, and market performance. Generally, I believe that SCP can fruitfully be applied to various questions of the fundamental transformation the television broadcasting sector is currently undergoing. I am also aware of the fact that the SCP paradigm has its weaknesses (Fu, 2003). Structure may not be exogenous, but may instead be the result of companies' behavior and product characteristics (Young, 2000). The traditional model does not capture the strategic dispositions of the media companies as such (Ramstad, 1997), and a more concentrated market structure could be the result of a better, more efficient industry performance, contrary to the predictions of the SCP model that market concentration leads to bad results. I can also conclude that both structural and behavioral factors will drive industry change. In the case of connected TV, I can in fact offer strong suggestive evidence that technological advances and media convergence are positively affecting the conditions of competition. Collectively, and in most general terms, technological innovation and the emergence of new products and services will render broadcasting markets more competitive as different market players are currently fighting for the central position in the living room on various levels and segments of the value chain.

Third, with regard to the need for identifying corporate strategies in connected TV, I stick to the notion that corporate strategies play an important role between technological convergence and value creation and capture. Obviously, empirical evidence of business models that are more than mere narratives and come to mediate between convergence and firm performance is hard to come by. Certainly, the growing technology adoption of connected TV in the home, the high level of broadband internet penetration, and the increasing consumption of content and services by connected TV devices and platforms is becoming a reality in many countries. In Germany, in fact, the number of TV households that own an internet-ready TV receiver has been continually on the rise in recent years. In 2014, 16% stated that they have at least one connected TV set (i.e., a TV set which can be directly connected to the internet) at home (die medienanstalten, 2014). This is an increase of around 45% within one year. Adding to that peripheral devices permanently connected to the TV which can feed content from the internet via their own internet connection (e.g., internet-ready set-top boxes, streaming boxes, Blu-Ray players, and games consoles), the share of TV households with connectable TV rises to 22.9%; this is some six percentage points higher than 2013 (die medienanstalten, 2014). This equals to some nine million connected TV households in Germany in 2014 (with 38.5 million TV households overall). However, despite the fact that the market continues to grow, old viewing habits are changing only slowly. Classical TV programs will remain popular, but nonlinear programs will, however, catch up.

Traditional broadcasters will continue to reach out for the mass market, but will also experiment with new platforms to broadcast their programs. Hence, their dominant connected TV strategy is "TVplus." Nontraditional players in connected TV, such as Apple, Microsoft (Xbox Live), and Samsung are in a strong position and may continue to focus on developing their service and differentiating it from the traditional TV user experience. These players dominate the "platform" and "TV app store" strategy model.

To conclude, the emerging ecosystem for connected TV services is immature and each provider is struggling to realize an optimal business model. Hence, the preliminary state of the industry evolution urges me to stress that corporate strategies and business models require permanent review in order to be fit for purpose in view of the current processes of media convergence, its effects on market structures and competitive dynamics. For now, the emerging connected TV industry ecosystem remains in a state of uncertainty.

References

Accenture (2011). *Bringing TV to life, issue II: The race to dominate the future of TV.* Retrieved from www.register.accenture.com/us-en/Pages/insight-bringing-tv-life-race-dominate-future-tv-summary.aspx

Accenture (2012). *Bringing TV to life, issue III: TV is all around you.* Retrieved from www.accenture.com/us-en/Pages/insight-bringing-tvto-life-tv-all-around-you summary.aspx

Albarran, A. B. (2010). *The media economy.* New York, NY: Routledge.

Altimeter (2013). *The converged media imperative: How brands must combine. Paid, owned, and earned media.* Retrieved from http://de.slideshare.net/Altimeter/the-converged-media-imperative

Amit, R., & Zott, C. (2012). Creating value through business model innovation. *Sloan Management Review, 53*(3), 41–49. Retrieved from http://sloanreview.mit.edu/article/creating-value-through-business-model-innovation/

Bain, J. S. (1956). *Barriers to new competition.* Cambridge, MA: Harvard University Press.

Bain, J. S. (1968). *Industrial organization.* New York, NY: John Wiley & Sons.

Baumol, W. J., Rogers, J. C., & Willig, R. D. (1982). *Contestable markets and the theory of industry structure.* New York, NY: Harcourt, Brace, Jovanovich.

Caves, R. E. (1980). Industrial organization, corporate strategy and structure. *Journal of Economic Literature, 18*(1), 64– 92. doi: 10.1007/978-1-4899-7138-8_16

Chan-Olmsted, S. M. (2006). Issues in strategic management. In A. B. Albarran, S. M. Chan-Olmsted, & M. O. Wirth (Eds.), *Handbook of media management and economics* (pp. 161– 181). Mahwah, NJ: Lawrence Erlbaum Associates.

Chan-Olmsted, S. M., & Ha, L. (2003). Internet business models for broadcasters: How television stations perceive and integrate the Internet. *Journal of Broadcasting & Electronic Media, 47*(4), 597–617. doi: 10.1207/s15506878jobem4704_7

Chan-Olmsted, S. M., & Jung, J. (2001). Strategizing the net business: How television networks compete in the age of the Internet. *International Journal on Media Management, 3.* Retrieved from www.mediamanagement.org/modules/pub/view.php/mediajournal-57

Chan-Olmsted, S. M., & Kang, J.-W. (2003). Theorizing the strategic architecture of a broadband television industry. *The Journal of Media Economics, 16*(1), 3–21. doi: 10.1207/S15327736ME1601_2

Chan-Olmsted, S. M., & Li, C. C. (2002). Strategic competition in the multichannel video programming market: An intra-industry strategic group analysis. *Journal of Media Economics, 15*(3), 153–174. doi: 10.1207/S15327736ME1503_2

Chon, B. S., Choi, J. H., Barnett, G. A., Danowski J. A., & Joo, S. H. (2003). A structural analysis of media convergence: Cross-industry mergers and acquisitions in the information industries. *Journal of Media Economics, 16*(3), 141–157. doi: 10.1207/S15327736ME1603_1

Dennis, E. E. (2003). Prospects for a big idea—Is there a future for convergence? *International Journal on Media Management, 5*, 7–11.

Deutsche TV-Plattform (2012). *White Book Hybrid-TV/Smart TV.* Arbeitsgruppe Smart-TV der Deutschen TV-Plattform, Version 2.0, August 2012. Retrieved from www.unternehmen.zdf.de/fileadmin/files/Download_Dokumente/DD_Technik/hybrid-tv_white-book_2012.pdf

die medienanstalten – ALM GbR (2014). *Digitisation 2014. Broadcasting and the internet – thesis, antithesis, synthesis?* (Digitalisierungsbericht 2014, English version). Retrieved from www.diemedienanstalten.de

Dogruel, L. (2013). Opening the black box: The conceptualizing of media innovation. In T. Størsul, & A. H. Krumsvik (Eds.), *Media innovations. A multidisciplinary study of change* (pp. 29–45). Göteborg, Sweden: Nordicom.

Doyle, G. (2010). From television to multi-platform: Less from more or more for less? *Convergence: The International Journal of Research into New Media Technologies*, *16*(4), 431–449. doi: 10.1177/1354856510375145

European Commission (2013). *Preparing for a fully converged audiovisual world: Growth, creation and values*. Brussels, 24.4.2013, COM(2013)231 final. Retrieved from http://eur-lex.europa.eu

European Parliament (2013). *The Challenges of Connected TV.* Retrieved from www.europarl.europa.eu/RegData/etudes/note/join/2013/513976/IPOL-CULT_NT%282013%29513976_EN.pdf

European Telecommunications Standards Institute (2010). *Hybrid Broadcast Broadband Television*, ETSI TS 102 796. Retrieved from www.etsi.org/deliver/etsi_ts/102700_102799/102796/01.01.01_60/ts_102796v010101p.pdf

Fu, W. (2003). Applying the structure Conduct-performance framework in the media industry analysis. *The International Journal of Media Management*, *5*(IV), 275–284.

FutureScape (2011). *How connected television transforms the business of TV*. A white paper based on the FutureScape strategy report Social TV. Retrieved from www.brandchannel.com/images/papers/530_futurescape_wp_connected_tv_0911.pdf

GfK Retail and Technology GmbH (April, 2015). *Wachstumsmarkt Smart TV und HbbTV in Deutschland*. Retrieved from www.tv-plattform.de/de/hbbtv-markt-2014.html

Habann, F. (2010). *Erfolgsfaktoren von Medieninnovationen*. Baden-Baden: Nomos.

Hacklin, F. (2008). *Management of convergence in innovation*, Heidelberg: Physica-Verlag.

Hacklin, F., Battistini, B., & Krogh, G. V. (2013). Strategic choices in converging industries, *MIT Sloan Management Review*. Retrieved from http://sloanreview.mit.edu/article/strategic-choices-in-converging-industries/

Hacklin, F., Klang, D., & Baschera, P. (2013). Managing the convergence of industries: archetypes for successful business models. In S. Diehl, & M. Karmasin (Eds.), *Media and Convergence Management* (pp. 25–36). Berlin Heidelberg: Springer-Verlag.

Hesmondhalgh, D. (2007). *The cultural industries* (2nd edn). London and Los Angeles: Sage.

Hess, T, & Matt, C. (2013). The Internet and the value chains of the media industry. In S. Diehl, & M. Karmasin (Eds.), *Media and convergence management* (pp. 37–57). Berlin Heidelberg: Springer-Verlag.

IDATE (2010). *Connected TV*. Retrieved from http://blog.idate.fr/connected-tv/

Jenkins, H. (2006). *Convergence culture: Where old and new media collide*. New York, NY: New York University Press.

Jin, D. Y. (2012). The new wave of de-convergence: A new business model of the communication industry in the 21st century. *Media, Culture and Society*, *34*(6), 761–772. doi: 10.1177/0163443712448952

Jin, D. Y. (2013). *De-convergence of global media industries*. New York: Routledge.

Kind, H. J., Nilssen, T., & Sorgard, L. (2009). Business models for media firms: Does competition matter for how they raise revenue? *Marketing Science*, *28*(6), 1112–1128.

Küng, L. (2013). Innovations, technology, and organizational change: Legacy media's big challenges: An introduction. In T. Størsul, & A. H. Krumsvik (Eds.), *Media innovations: A multidisciplinary study of change* (pp. 9–13). Göteborg: Nordicom.

Landes, W. M., & Posner, R. A. (1981). Market power in antitrust cases. *Harvard Law Review*, 94, 937–997.

Latzer, M. (2013). *Towards an innovation-co-evolution-complexity perspective on communications policy*. In M. Löblich, & S. Pfaff-Rüdiger (Eds.), *Communication and media policy in the era of digitization and the Internet: Theories and processes* (pp. 15–27). Baden-Baden: Nomos.

Lawson-Borders, G. (2003). Integrating new media and old media: Seven observations of convergence as a strategy for best practices in media organizations. *The International Journal on Media Management*, 5(2), 91–99.

Liestøl, G. (2007). The dynamics of convergence & divergence in digital domains. In T. Storsul, & D. Stuedahl (Eds.), *Ambivalence towards convergence: Digitalization and media change* (pp. 165–178). Stockholm: Nordicom.

Liu, F., & Chan-Olmsted, S. M. (2002). *Partnerships between the old and the new: Examining the strategic alliances between broadcast television networks and Internet firms in the context of convergence*. Paper submitted for presentation to the Media Management and Sales Division of the Broadcast Education Association, Las Vegas, Nevada.

Mason, E. S. (1949). The current state of the monopoly problem in the United States. *Harvard Law Review*, 62, 1265–1285.

Meikle, G., & Young, S. (2012). *Media convergence: Networked digital media in everyday life*. Basingstoke, Hampshire and New York: Palgrave Macmillan.

Networked & Electronic Media (2012). *Connected TV position paper*. Retrieved from www.nem-initiative.org/fileadmin/documents/PositionPapers/NEM-PP-015.pdf

Noll, M. (2003). The myth of convergence. *The International Journal on Media Management*, 1(5), 12–13.

Organization of Economic Cooperation and Development (2013). *Competition Issues in Television and Broadcasting*. Policy Roundtables, DAF/COMP/GF(2013)13. Retrieved from www.oecd.org/daf/competition/TV-and-broadcasting2013.pdf

Ozanich, G., & Wirth, M. (2004). Structure and change: An industry overview. In A. Alexander, J. Owers, R. Carveth, A. Hollifield, & A. Greco (Eds.), *Media economics: Theory and practice* (3rd edn; pp. 69–84). Mahwah, NJ: Lawrence Erlbaum Associates.

Palmer, J., & Eriksen, L. B. (1999). Digital news-paper: Broadcast and more convergence on the Internet. *International Journal on Media Management*, 1(1), 31–34.

Perez, C. (2010). Technological revolutions and techno-economic paradigms. *Cambridge Journal of Economics*, 34(1), 185–202.

Picard, R. G. (2011). *The economics and financing of media companies* (2nd edn). New York: Fordham University Press.

Porter, M. E. (1979). How competitive shape strategy. *Harvard Business Review*, 57, 137–156 (March–April).

Porter, M. E. (1981). The contributions of industrial organization to strategic management, *Academy of Management Review*, 6(4), 609–620. doi: 10.5465/AMR.1981.4285706

Ramstad, G. O. (1997). A model for structural analysis of the media market. *Journal of Media Economics*, 10(3), 45–50. doi: 10.1207/s15327736me1003_4

Rangone, A., & Turconi, A. (2003). The television (r)evolution within the multimedia convergence: a strategic reference framework. *Management Decision*, 41(1), 48–71. doi: 10.1108/00251740310452916

Rochet, J.-C., & Tirole, J. (2003). Platform competition in two-sided markets. *Journal of the European Economic Association*, 1(4), 990–1029.

Rysman, M. (2009). The economics of two-sided markets. *The Journal of Economic Perspectives*, 23(3), 125–143.

Scherer, F., & Ross, D. (1990). *Industrial market structure and economic performance* (3rd edn). Boston: Houghton Mifflin.

Schmalensee, R. (1988). Industrial economics: An overview. *The Economic Journal*, *98*(392), 643–681. doi: 10.2307/2233907

Schneider, V. (2012). Governance and complexity. In D. Levi-Faur (Ed.), *Oxford handbook of governance* (pp. 129–142). Oxford: Oxford University Press.

Silverstone, R. (1995). Convergence is a dangerous word: *Convergence. The International Journal of Research into New Media Technologies*, *1*(1), 11–14. doi: 10.1177/135485659500100102

Stipp, H. (1999). Convergence Now? *The International Journal on Media Management*, *1*(1), 10–14.

Størsul, T., & Krumsvik, A. H. (2013). What is media innovation? In T. Størsul, & A. H. Krumsvik (Eds.), *Media innovations: A multidisciplinary study of change* (pp. 13–16). Göteborg: Nordicom.

Størsul, T., & Stuedahl, D. (2007). *Ambivalence towards convergence: Digitization and media change*. Göteborg: Nordicom.

Thielmann, B., & Dowling, M. (1999). Convergence and innovation strategy for service provision in emerging web-TV markets. *The International Journal on Media Management*, *1*(1), 4–9.

Tirole, J. (1988). *The theory of industrial organization*. Cambridge, MA: MIT Press.

van Eimeren, B., & Frees, B. (2013). Rasanter Anstieg des Internetkonsums – Onliner fast drei Stunden täglich im Netz. *Media Perspektiven*, *7–8*, 358–372.

von Rimscha, B. (2006). How the DVR is changing the TV industry: A supply side perspective. *International Journal on Media Management*, *8*(3), 116–124.

Waterman, D., Sherman, R., & Ji, S. W. (2012). *The economics of online television: Revenue models, aggregation, and 'TV everywhere'*. Retrieved from http://ssrn.com/abstract=2032828

Winseck, D. (2008). The state of media ownership and media markets: Competition or concentration and why should we care? *Sociology Compass*, *2*(1), 34–47.

Wirth, M. O. (2006). Issues in media convergence. In A. B. Albarran, S. M. Chan-Olmsted, & M. O. Wirth (Eds.), *Handbook of media management and economics* (pp. 445–463). Mahwah, NJ: Lawrence Erlbaum Associates.

Wirth, M. O., & Bloch, H. (1995). Industrial organization theory and media industry analysis. *Journal of Media Economics*, *8*(2), 15–26. doi: 10.1207/s15327736me0802_3

Wirtz, B. W. (2001). Reconfiguration of value chains in converging media and communications markets. *Long Range Planning*, *34*(4), 489–506. doi: 10.1016/S0024-6301(01)00066-8.

Xu, H., & Yan, R.-N. (2011). Feeling connected via television viewing: Exploring the scale and its correlates. *Communication Studies*, *62*(2), 186–206.

Young, D. P. T. (2000). Modeling media markets: How important is market structure? *Journal of Media Economics*, *13*(1), 27–44. doi: 10.1207/S15327736Me1301_3

CHAPTER CONTENTS

4   Contemporary Quality TV

The Entertainment Experience
of Complex Serial Narratives

Daniela M. Schlütz

Hanover University for Music, Drama and Media

Lately, so-called quality TV series have been extremely successful—both in terms of audience shares and critical acclaim. Thus, the purpose of this chapter is to define the concept of quality serial television, giving a brief history of its development, systematizing its characteristics, and modeling the entertainment experience. I will argue that quality TV as a culturally bound, discursive construct functions as a meta-genre with concrete implications for selection, experience and possible effects of entertaining quality TV. This argument is summarized in a model of the quality TV entertainment experience.

A decade ago, Lucy Mazdon wrote in a book about (then) contemporary television series: "All of this—the quality of these programmes, their critical and commercial success and the questions they raise about the status of television, national industries and audiences—makes the contemporary prime-time television series/serial ripe for serious analysis" (Mazdon, 2005, pp. 4–5). Although being a decade old, this assessment has still not been put into practice—at least not by communication studies. Most of the scientific discourses dealing with complex quality television are rooted in the humanities (like film and television studies) and evolve around the texts themselves without linking them to comprehension and reception processes or possible effects (e.g., Jancovich & Lyons, 2003; Leverette, Ott, & Buckley, 2008; McCabe & Akass, 2007). Thus, the purpose of this chapter is to address this gap by defining the concept of quality serial television, giving a brief history of its development, systematizing its characteristics, and modeling the entertainment experience. I will argue that quality TV as a culturally bound, discursive construct functions as a meta-genre with concrete implications for selection, experience, and possible effects of entertaining quality TV. This argument is summarized in a model of the quality TV entertainment experience (for a more comprehensive discussion see Schlütz, in press).

Quality TV Series: Concept, History, and Characteristics

Lately, so-called quality TV series like *The Sopranos, The Wire,* or *Breaking Bad* have been extremely successful—both in terms of audience shares (Ernesto, 2013; Hibberd, 2013; Nielsen, 2014; Woollacott, 2014) and critical acclaim

(Nussbaum, 2009). These programs stand out due to their multi-level complexity, high production values, innovative cinematic techniques, and autonomous viewing habits. I will go into these characteristics in more detail below. Before doing so, however, I will clarify my understanding of serial television and its categories and describe the development of quality TV in the USA.

Serial Television: Definition and Taxonomy

Serial narratives are a "reigning principle of cultural production" (Dyer, 2002, p. 71). Since the early soap operas (Cantor & Pingree, 1983) both fictional and non-fictional formats have been the default of television content constituting its flow (Williams, 1974) and filling most of its program schedules (Creeber, 2004, p. 4). This chapter focuses on fictional (mostly dramatic) content although serial storytelling is not confined to it. However, as fictional narratives are processed somewhat differently from facts (Green, Garst, & Brock, 2004) this will help to clarify the argument. A *narrative* is an account of events bound by causality (Carroll, 2007). As opposed to single films, series are ongoing stories implying characteristics like lack of definite closure, use of cliffhangers, and sparse expositions (Allrath, Gymnich, & Surkamp, 2005, p. 3). Potential openness is an important aspect as it fosters audience engagement (Geraghty, 1981, p. 11) although some types of series strive for narrative closure (see below). In the following, a TV series/serial will be understood as a segmented sequence of confined but linked (fictional) films. By interlacing individual episodes in terms of form (time slot, opening credits, and theme), content (cast, plot, and setting), and structure (composition of story lines) a continuous narrative with an open structure is formed.

TV series can be distinguished according to their narrative structure in episodic series and continuous serials (Cantor & Pingree, 1983; Creeber, 2004; Ndalianis, 2005). (Note: I will use the term 'series' in the remainder of the chapter to denote serial narratives in general.) This differentiation is not a dichotomous one. Rather, one finds varying degrees of seriality as a function of character development and plot openness (Bock, 2013, p. 38). One can distinguish at least the following four types:

Anthology Series

Anthologies are a loose connection of episodes only bound by an overlaying theme (e.g., *ToonHeads, The Canterbury Tales*). They used to be a very popular serial form on the radio. Nowadays anthologies are rather rare.

Episodic Series

Series in the strict sense are shows like *Magnum, P.I., South Park,* or *The Simpsons* where every episode is more or less independent of each other. The narrative arcs are confined to one episode and there is hardly any character development.

The pure form of the series has become rather rare on contemporary television as well. More recent series like *Sherlock* or *Dexter* combine episodic plots (with a "murder of the week") and backstory arcs spreading across seasons or even the series as a whole (like Dexter's hunt for the Ice Truck Killer in Season 1). Newcomb (2004) termed this form cumulative narrative (p. 422). It has the advantage of appealing to both single-episode and regular viewers.

Continuous Serials

Serials tell an ongoing story with a (more or less) constant cast. They address the regular viewer. Examples are *Lost, The Wire,* or *The Killing.* Typical serial forms are sitcoms (*Modern Family*) or soap operas with an at least potentially indefinite run-time (*Dallas*). At any given time, old and new story lines are interwoven to keep the narrative running. Some serials like telenovelas (*Ugly Betty*) strive for narrative closure, though. Despite their name, miniseries (*Roots, True Detective*) can be subsumed into this category as well, because they tell an ongoing story, albeit in a predetermined and usually rather small number of episodes. Since the advent of the second season, though, *True Detective* is often termed an anthology.

Hybrid Forms

More complex shows like *ER* oscillate between long-term story arcs and stand-alone episodes (Mittell, 2006, p. 33). Nelson (2007) termed this form *flexi-narrative*. The line to cumulative narratives (see above) is somewhat blurred but many flexi-narratives strive for closure (like *Breaking Bad, Mad Men,* or *Boardwalk Empire*). These shows are not terminated for decreasing audience ratings but because the story has come to an end. This interplay between the demands of episodic and serial storytelling is "the hallmark of narrative complexity" (Mittell, 2006, p. 33). Quality TV series are usually flexi-narratives.

The Third Golden Age of Television: The Development of Quality TV

The label "quality television" was coined by US-American TV-critics in the mid-1970s with regard to shows like *Rich Man, Poor Man* and *Hill Street Blues.* Although it was not very well defined what quality television was, "people just seemed to know it when they saw it" (Thompson, 1996, pp. 12–13). Quality TV as a logo today marks a specific cultural status of television content (Newman & Levine, 2012, p. 21) as opposed to conventional television ("It's not TV, it's HBO"). Quality TV is complex television: It is intricate, complicated, and perplexing (Buckland, 2009, p. 3). It is demanding in terms of content, aesthetically ambitious and therefore attractive for certain target groups— it is both art and merchandise (Bignell, 2007). In this sense, the term quality TV functions as a unique selling proposition (USP; Nowell-Smith, 1994) in first-order market relations where goods are sold directly to the customer (Rogers, Epstein, & Reeves, 2002). From a distributor's point of view the label quality TV functions as a brand, from an audience's perspective it serves as a meta-genre (see below). Both aspects are a result (or a by-product) of the transformations that the US-American television market has undergone in the last 50 years (cf. Jenkins, 2008; Lotz, 2007). These changes fed back into financing, production, distribution, marketing, but also media use and content reception. Namely the rise of the pay TV channels (first and foremost HBO) was of paramount importance for the advent of quality TV productions like *The Sopranos* or *The Wire*. For analytical purposes, U.S. television history can be divided in distinct phases that are described below (Rogers et al., 2002, p. 48; see also Kompare, 2006; Reeves, Rodgers [*sic*], & Epstein, 1996; Reeves, Rogers, & Epstein, 2007; Santo, 2008).

TV I

The era of mass marketing (ca. 1950–1978) was dominated by the programming decisions of the three major networks—ABC, CBS, and NBC. They decided what was produced and broadcasted, aiming at the biggest audience possible (up to 90 percent combined market shares; Edgerton, 2008). In TV I, quality equaled popularity. A show like *Little House on the Prairie* is a good example for a then popular show. The market logic was an indirect one, audiences were "sold" to marketers; the more eyeballs, the better. Respect for advertisers and the need for syndication (as the two main sources of revenue; Kompare, 2009) favored shallow content and episodic formats. Innovative programs were not in demand: "The reluctance to innovate stemmed from the network executives' belief that the mass audience would immediately reject any show departing from the lowest-common denominator norm." (Pearson, 2005, p. 13)

TV II

The following phase (ca. 1978–1995) was distinguished by a multi-channel transition and corresponding niche marketing. Due to technological changes— like the introduction of the VCR and cable channels—the audience (or certain segments) gained autonomy in terms of time, space, and content. Furthermore, the audience grew more powerful because the market logic changed (at least partly) to a first-order relation: Viewers could purchase media content (more or less) directly by subscribing to a specific pay TV channel. As a whole, the market changes led to audience segmentation and the establishment of high-quality niche content with series like *Hill Street Blues* and *St. Elsewhere* (Thompson, 1996). Cable and satellite channels used their structural advantages (mainly independence from advertising) and legal pros (freedom from the NAB television code) for the production and distribution of quality shows (Creeber, 2004; Edgerton & Jones, 2008; Kelso, 2008). Additionally, the FCC Financial Interest and Syndication (fin-syn) Rules established in 1970 prevented the networks from owning any of the prime-time programming they aired. This breakup of vertical integration fostered the rise of independent production firms like MTM Enterprises that became "the modern cradle of quality television" (Martin, 2013, p. 171). These firms established new story telling modes like the flexi-narrative (Nelson, 1997, p. 32). It was also the beginning of the era of the writer-producer (Pearson, 2005) that was accompanied by greater artistic freedom in content and style. These *auteurs* or showrunners like Alan Ball (*Six Feet Under*), Aaron Sorkin (*The West Wing*), and Vince Gilligan (*Breaking Bad*), to name but a few, stand for aesthetic integrity. They are both "brand manager" and "lonely genius" (Newman & Levine, 2012, p. 54), merging art and business in their work.

TV III

The post-network era (ca. 1995–2010) was shaped by digitalization and media convergence. Its focus lay on brand marketing in order to build "value around specific narrative worlds, characters and personalities, seeking to encourage audience loyalty to these products" (Hills, 2007, p. 52). Due to the advent of new media, users became even more autonomous in terms of time, space, and devices. Thus, their relation to the producers and distributors changed. Comparable to other entertainment markets (like books or films) popularity now became "a function of satisfying the desires of the audience, rather than caring to the needs of advertisers" (Rogers et al., 2002, p. 46). Quality content—often distinguished by a "signature style" (C. Johnson, 2005, p. 64)—that matched the specific taste of discrete audience groups became a USP and a driver of demand (Lotz, 2007, p. 141). Programs like *Six Feet Under*, *Deadwood*, or *In Treatment* were distributed via cable, DVDs (Kompare, 2006), or streaming platforms. A supporting factor for the establishment of quality TV was its legitimization by critical discourse (Newman & Levine, 2012, p. 4). The resulting attributions were used for branding programs (Johnson, 2007, p. 20) and whole channels like HBO (cf. Feuer, 2007; Leverette et al., 2008; Rogers et al., 2002). As a consequence, these brands served as "class definers" and "primary currency of a system of distinction" (Rogers et al., 2002, p. 56).

TV IV

By now society has entered the next phase, the "third golden age of television" (Martin, 2013, p. 9). Premium cable channels like HBO, AMC, FX, and Showtime dominate the quality TV market with programs like *True Detective, Breaking Bad, The Americans,* and *Dexter*. Moreover, new players like the online platform Netflix have entered the competition with original serial programming (*House of Cards, Orange is the New Black, Sense8*) that is distributed via streaming only. Again, the balance of power is changing with media convergence allowing for even greater viewer agency: choice, control, convenience, customization, and community are, according to Lotz (2007, p. 245), the defining dimensions of current television. Thus, television use has changed "from flow to files" (Mittell, 2010, p. 422). This kind of media use is independent from constraints of space, time, and program schedules: "from appointment television to engagement television" (Jenkins, 2008, p. 121). Episodes can be viewed repeatedly and/or *en bloc* (so-called binge-watching; Brunsdon, 2010). This prolonged and highly concentrated reception mode suits complex, multi-layered narratives extremely well (McCabe, 2005, p. 208). It is the audio-visual equivalent to a page-turner: Like a book that one has to read from cover to cover in one session, quality TV is hard to turn off. Binge-watching might alter the viewing experience as it fosters comprehension and transportation.

Contemporary Serial Television: Characteristics of Quality TV

This chapter is about quality TV. But what does that mean exactly? Originally, the term quality denoted a feature that an object possessed (from Latin *qualitas* as opposed to *quantitas*; Nowell-Smith, 1994, p. 37). In everyday language, though, quality usually refers to high value or excellence. Thus, it has both a descriptive and an evaluative meaning (Rosengren, Carlsson, & Tagerud, 1996, p. 5). Sometimes quality implies a normative judgment as well when the term is used to define what good television should be like (cf. Ishikawa, 1996). My aim is less ambitious. I want to describe commonalities of television shows that are designated quality TV series. To carve out and systematize their similarities (provided there are any) and peculiarities is necessary groundwork for theorizing how viewers might make sense of the texts and experience them. To do so I draw on quality as a complex and multi-faceted concept (Garvin, 1984, p. 39): Quality is individually and historically bound (Mazdon, 2005, p. 4) and discursively constructed by relevant stakeholders. This social consensus is based on determinable (if not objective) features of the text, personal tastes, and social attributes like norms, standards, or conventions. Thus, quality is a notion deeply interwoven in the texture of culture and its hierarchies (Corner, 1997). This is why quality discourses often have a naturalizing effect where formerly subjective judgments became facts and assessments were framed as legitimate hierarchies (Newman & Levine, 2012, p. 6). As Rupert Murdoch put it: "Most of what passes for quality on British television . . . is no more than a reflection of the values of the narrow elite which controls it and has always thought that its tastes are synonymous with quality" (Creeber, 2004, p. 69). These assertions have factual consequences, however, on both social and individual level (Sewell, 2010). To label a text as quality TV rises its symbolic value and builds reputation (Garvin, 1987, p. 107), it increases its demand (albeit not necessarily so; cf. Costera Meijer, 2005), and frames the viewing experience by way of a meta-genre. I will come back to this after I have laid out the characteristics of quality TV.

The technological, economic, legal, and social developments described above prepared the ground for high quality television series like *Breaking Bad, Downton Abbey, Game of Thrones, House of Cards, Mad Men,* and *True*

Detective—the 2014 Emmy Award winners in the category outstanding drama series. Based on a literature research, I will now systemize what makes these series outstanding. In so doing I will show that quality TV series are comparable to literary fiction. This proximity suggests the necessity to adapt our theoretical understanding of audiovisual entertainment media to these characteristics.

Scholars agree that quality TV is demanding on several levels (Akass & McCabe, 2008; C. Johnson, 2005; McCabe, 2005): It is innovative and complex both in terms of content and form. It challenges viewing habits and genre expectations by breaking taboos, violating television customs, and expanding narrative rules. Additionally, it has high production values and a distinct visual style. I understand the concept of quality TV as follows: Serial quality TV is complex in terms of storytelling, cast, narrative ambiguity, and intertextuality. Due to realistic execution, controversial subjects, and ambiguous characters quality series appear authentic. Moreover, they stand out because of a signature style composed of high production values, distinctive visual style, and techniques fostering reflexivity. Quality TV addresses a special, highly autonomous audience segment. As a meta-genre it supports selection, frames comprehension, and channels interpretation. Quality serial television offers a cognitively and affectively challenging entertainment experience with added symbolic value. The central aspects of the definition are now explained in more detail, the resulting entertainment experience is modeled thereafter.

Complexity

Narrative complexity is at the core of quality television (Mittell, 2015). It can be understood as a distinct storytelling mode. This mode merges techniques of the serial and the series building a complex flexi-narrative. Manifold parallel and interlaced storylines (as in *Hill Street Blues*), a huge cast (the "social network complexity" of *The Wire*; S. Johnson, 2005, p. 109), and last but not least the prolongation that enables continuous storytelling and character development (like the 331 episodes of *ER*) make for a good series. Moreover, like any popular culture, quality TV series are embedded in a reference structure: "Contemporary television increasingly 'overflows' from the primary text across multiple platforms ... [constructing] an extended, immersive experience" (Brooker, 2001, p. 456; cf. Manovich, 2001). An example is the alternate reality game (ARG) *The Lost Experience*. This highly complex, interactive, transmedia hypertext was inspired by *Lost* and bridged the gap between the seasons of the show. With Fiske (1987) this phenomenon might be referred to as intertextuality (pp. 108–127) designating links both within the text and between the original text and surrounding works. Such ancillary content can be professional (like DVD extras, merchandise, comic books, ARGs, blogs, twitter accounts, websites, and the like) or user-generated (like fan art, wikis etc.; for examples see Barton, 2012; Gray, 2010; Lavery, 2007; Oernebring, 2007; Scott, 2013). Post-receptive social TV activities to connect with the community, producers, and characters and to evaluate the programs can be placed in this category as well (Buschow,

Schneider, & Ueberheide, 2014; Giglietto & Selva, 2014). These so-called *paratexts* add to the understanding of the characters (Kozloff, 1992, p. 92), the meaning of the original text, and its evaluation. Moreover, paratexts allow for user interaction, engagement, participation, and community building (Jenkins, 2008). They also grant credibility and aura (Gray, 2010, p. 82).

A by-product of narrative complexity is *ambiguity*: Quality series are ambiguous because the stories contain several blank spaces like cold opens (the chase at the very beginning of *Luther*), apparent contradictions, undisclosed motives, incomprehensible actions (like the medical dialogues in *ER*), and the like. In this they are comparable to literature. As a consequence, viewers need patience, the will, and the proficiency to fill in the blanks in order to construct meaning. The more blanks a text contains, the more elaboration (or reiteration) is necessary for decoding. This might be perceived as stimulating and entertaining or as arduous and boring. What is more, quality TV series often feature morally ambiguous characters (so-called "MACs"; Krakowiak & Oliver, 2012). Martin (2013) even calls the antihero trend "the signature for the decade's TV" (p. 267) because complex characters like John Luther (*Luther*), Jack Bauer (*24*), Walter White (*Breaking Bad*), or Carrie Mathison (*Homeland*) who superbly walk the thin line between good and evil are very common in contemporary serial television. Complexity and ambiguity lead to polysemy (Fiske, 1987) that renders the texts open to multiple, individually varying readings (Liebes & Katz, 1993, p. 140).

Authenticity

Despite their being fictional, contemporary TV series appear realistic in several ways: They are authentic in terms of subject matter (*Treme*, for instance, deals with the consequences of hurricane Katrina in New Orleans), content (the police procedural *Homicide: Life on the Street* is based on David Simon's observations as a police reporter in Baltimore), and style (like the resurrection of the 1960s in *Mad Men*). Authenticity is an important aspect as perceived realism is a moderator of media influence (Hall, 2003, p. 624) and is positively related to quality judgments (Greenberg & Busselle, 1996). Fictional authenticity contains several dimensions of realism that might enhance audience engagement (Busselle & Bilandzic, 2008). Hall (2003) identifies the following aspects of media reality: Factuality is comparable to the notion of the magic window (Busselle & Greenberg, 2000), like the display of Parkinson's disease symptoms in the *Michael J. Fox Show*. Narrative realism refers to the story's consistency. Plausibility, on the other hand, refers to credibility (how plausible is it, for instance, that the characters of *Friends* can afford the depicted lifestyle?). Typicality alludes to the question whether something is highly probable or not (like a chemistry teacher being able to cook top-notch methamphetamine). Even if all these dimensions are not met, the series can still be emotionally realistic (i.e., a teenager feeling different and excluded in *Buffy, the Vampire Slayer*). All aspects are supported by perceptual persuasiveness, that is a compelling visual illusion (like twentieth century

England in the period drama *Downton Abbey*). Additionally, quality TV often deals with controversial issues (like the war on drugs or torture) and contains multi-layered and therefore more credible characters (like the gay, scarred, duster wearing stick-up man Omar Little from *The Wire*).

Signature Style

Visual distinctiveness (like the light in *Six Feet Under*; Akass & McCabe, 2008, p. 79), stylistic features, and high production values are almost as important for quality TV series as complexity and depth of characters and scripts (C. Johnson, 2005, p. 59). Both semantic planes (content and style) reinforce each other because "themes and style are intertwined in an expressive and impressive way" (Cardwell, 2007, p. 6). Stylistic integrity is a key component for the appeal of quality series (Bignell, 2007). It contains, for instance, innovative techniques like cinematographic photography (i.e., widescreen and point-of-view shots in *Breaking Bad*), simultaneous and achronological narration (the split screen technique of *24* or and the flashbacks/flash-forwards in *A Young Doctor's Notebook*, respectively), multi-perspective storytelling (Rashomon effect; see for instance S05.E12 'Bad Blood' of *The X-Files*), and breaking the fourth wall (i.e., by directly addressing the audience like Frank Underwood in *House of Cards*). Genre conventions are often violated or toyed with; for instance, by staging a medical drama as a musical, a sci-fi program as a documentary (Lavery, 2004), or by mixing conventional genres (like soap opera and mafia movie in *The Sopranos*; Creeber, 2004, pp. 100–112). By this, contemporary narratives constantly undermine viewers' expectations, call attention to them and challenge them. Self-referencing forms can even take precedence over storytelling (Butler, 2013; Poulaki, 2014, pp. 38–46). When style and structure are foregrounded moments of reflexivity are offered to the viewer achieving "a double metafictional and metanarrational effect" (Poulaki, 2014, p. 39). Some of these effects will presumably enhance narrative engagement while others are prone to diminish it. On the other hand, by focusing "on both diegetic pleasures and formal awareness" (Mittell, 2006, p. 38–39) the dual-mode entertainment experience might be enriched.

Quality TV as Meta-Genre: Managing Expectations and Adding Value

Contemporary serial television is subtle, open, intellectually and emotionally challenging, and well done. Because of this, quality TV is hard to make sense of and sometimes hard to bear. One has to make an effort to successfully decode it. If this challenge is mastered, though, the experience is intellectually rewarding: "This kind of jigsaw puzzle or Lego set or computer game invites the metalinguistic viewer to anticipate the combinatorial possibilities and to stay with the program to prove himself [*sic*] right" (Liebes & Katz, 1993, p. 144). The feeling "that you made it" adds another layer to the entertainment experience:

For those who have acquired the cultural competence needed to adopt an aesthetic disposition, it is possible to look differently upon a television series: to perceive the artistic vision of an individual creator where once one may have seen stories with no discernable author; to reflect on the meaning of form even as one feels drawn into the pleasure of a gradually unfolding narrative; to recognize the threads of cultural and historical references woven into the fabric of a story; to appreciate the subtle subversion of genre conventions and audience expectations; and, most importantly, to celebrate the transcendence of the artwork over everyday experience and more mundane forms of popular culture. Television series have provoked many responses over the years, but only recently have they invited cultural consecration as works of art.

(Anderson, 2008, p. 25)

The complexity of quality TV content is mirrored by a multi-faceted entertainment experience. Its claim to artistic status, by an awareness of connoisseurship, adds value to this experience. Watching (even binge-watching) serial quality television is better than just watching "plain TV" because the quality designation carries cultural status (Newman & Levine, 2012, p. 32). This status is objectified (or even commodified; Kompare, 2006, p. 338) in the form of DVDs. They stand for "completeness" and "collectability" (Hills, 2007, p. 41), features that increase the value of the cultural object (Gray, 2010). Thus, quality TV comes with symbolic value. Its use and appreciation marks the self-proclaimed connoisseur—in his or her own view—as distinct from the "ordinary viewer." Quality TV consumption and follow-up communication (i.e., in blogs or forums) build symbolic capital if this action is acknowledged by relevant others (Bourdieu, 1985). If in former times TV was only suitable for distinction if one did *not* watch it, with the advent of quality TV this has changed: "In this manner, pay cable sells cultural capital to its subscribers, who are elevated above the riffraff that merely consume television" (Santo, 2008, p. 20; see also C. Johnson, 2007, p. 10).

Commonly, television genres are taxonomic categories with descriptive and organizing character. They are culturally constructed and historically bound (Feuer, 1992; Mittell, 2004). Genres reduce complexity and uncertainty by shaping expectations and viewing experiences. They classify and organize media experiences by linking them to concepts like cultural value and social function (Mittell, 2004, p. xii). Television genres are usually deduced from text traits and production standards. Quality TV series, however, "fit no discernible genre at all—except quality" (Martin, 2013, p. 271). Thus, quality TV can be seen as a meta-genre designating complex narratives, authenticity, signature style—and the surprising element that calls for a tolerant and flexible dual reception mode. The meta-genre quality TV is constructed discursively in a cultural context. Like a traditional genre it supports selection, frames comprehension, and channels interpretation. Moreover, it adds symbolic value to the viewing experience. It is important to note, however, that the classification as quality TV does not necessarily imply an individual judgment of taste: While the meta-genre quality TV might be acknowledged, the series in question may still be dismissed (Cardwell, 2007).

Making Sense of Complex Narratives: Modeling the Entertainment Experience of Quality TV Series

Quality TV series are complex in terms of story and characters. Thus, they lend themselves to narrative engagement including both presence in the narrative world and emotional engagement with characters (Busselle & Bilandzic, 2009). On the other hand they are stylistically distinct, calling for a mode of reception that is aware of the form. The complexity of quality TV in terms of content and style as well as intertextuality impedes decoding. The innovative visual and narrative style adds a further layer of meaning to the text, enhancing elaboration costs once more by calling for formal awareness. This might impact on narrative understanding and presence. The polysemy renders the text open to manifold readings. Authenticity might be beneficial for narrative engagement by fostering realism and credibility. On the other hand going against conventional stereotypes and story schema might have the opposite effect. Finally, as the meta-genre discussion indicates cultural aspects have to be taken into account when modeling the experience of quality TV.

I now want to propose a model of the quality TV entertainment experience (QTV-EE; see Figure 4.1). The model was developed to cater to quality TV series and their peculiarities as discussed above. It aims at advancing our theoretical understanding of the comprehension and reception of complex serial narratives by using an interdisciplinary approach. It integrates findings on comprehension processes from literary studies, insights on media reception from psychology and communication studies, a sociological perspective (regarding the person's social position) and findings from the humanities (with regard to the influence of culture on individual readings). The model is a first step towards an empirical study of quality TV. The comprehensive conceptual design enables a systematic operationalization of the elements based on a consistent frame of reference.

The QTV-EE model depicts a specific form of dual-mode entertainment reception that results (at best) in a meta-emotional, multi-dimensional entertainment experience. The experience comprises both hedonic (enjoyment) and non-hedonic (appreciation, elevation) dimensions of pleasure. These aspects are complemented by an aesthetic experience. This suggests the necessity for a complex dual reception strategy, a "'both-and' mode of engagement" (Nelson, 2007, p. 124). Experiencing high quality flexi-narratives is cognitively and affectively challenging and has symbolic value.

Empirically, the model focuses on the microscopic level. Influences of meso (i.e., production contexts) and macro level (i.e., socio-cultural context) are implicitly included as they determine the social position of the individual (Bourdieu, 1985) and establish the structures in which quality TV (as a work of

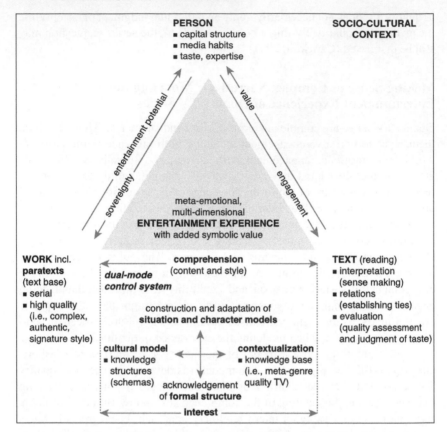

Figure 4.1 Model of the Quality TV Entertainment Experience (QTV-EE)

fiction, a meta-genre, and a reading) flourishes. The entertainment experience arises from an interaction of person and work realized as an individual reading (the text). The figure models the quality TV experience as an equilateral triangle denoting the equal importance of each of the three components: (a) the *person*, as a socially positioned and culturally shaped individual, (b) the structurally positioned and discursively constructed high quality *work* as defined above, and (c) the individual reading that is the valuable result of the interaction between, that is, the *text* (a) and (b). The cognitive and affective challenging entertainment experience with added value derives from a successful interplay between all three factors. The process of *comprehension* (as depicted below the hypotenuse of the triangle)—how the text earns personal relevance and value— is a crucial part of the model because this is where culture comes in. Cultural models contextualize the sense-making process by integrating knowledge about the world in general, and about narratives and stylistic techniques in particular. Depending on the complexity of the text, this construction might be strenuous and tedious. Thus focused, prolonged, and/or repeated viewing is required for the full experience. This is especially the case because one cannot always draw on preexisting schemas during the process of sense making (see below). Instead, models have to be reconfigured continuously while watching quality TV series. Comprehension of complex series is not confined to narrative information, though. The element of style inserts another plane of meaning that has to be decoded. This calls for a dual reception mode shaped by a specific control system. The control system develops by repeated contact with specific types of texts. In the moment of exposure it is triggered by certain text features like quality markers (i.e., elements of signature style). The enhanced engagement necessary for understanding complex texts is made sure by *interest* in the subjects, the personae, and the unfolding of the story (referenced at the left leg of the triangle). The return on investment is the *value* of the realized text (see right leg); that is, the cognitively and affectively challenging entertainment experience with symbolic value. This value is intrinsic and, thus, self-reinforcing.

The person in the model is thought of as active, autonomous, and engaged (see right leg). The extent to which this is the case might vary and, consequently, mediate the entertainment experience. Personality traits are not part of this model. It is plausible, though, that characteristics, like the need for cognition, moderate the interaction (Green et al., 2008; Henning & Vorderer, 2001). The reading of the text includes an assessment that has a textual and a social dimension. A quality assessment draws on criteria intrinsic to the text while the judgment of taste is reached by balancing these criteria with individual expectations resulting in a personal valuation. High personal value should result in repeated exposure and/or enhanced demand (as a volitional behavioral outcome; cf. Nabi & Krcmar, 2004). I will now describe the elements of the QTV-EE model and their interplay in more detail.

Experiencing Quality TV

Entertainment as Meta-Emotion

Quality TV texts might instigate enjoyment, pleasure, enlightenment (Dyer, 2002; Vorderer, 2001; Vorderer, Klimmt, & Ritterfeld, 2004; Zillmann & Bryant, 1994). Serial entertainment as described above (flexi-narratives dealing with controversial subjects) might also trigger suspense (Knobloch, 2003; Vorderer, Wulff, & Friedrichsen, 1996), melancholy or sadness (sad-film paradox; Hofer & Wirth, 2012; Oliver, 1993b), horror, disgust, and fear (Cantor, 2006; Oliver, 1993a; Tamborini, 2003), or they might confront the viewer with extreme violence (Miron, 2003). That these rather distressing feelings are— on the whole—enjoyed or appreciated by the viewer is usually explained by the concept of meta-emotions (Bartsch, Vorderer, Mangold, & Viehoff, 2008; Oliver, 1993b, 2008; Vorderer & Hartmann, 2009). A positive meta-emotion is the outcome of a monitoring process in which emotions that arise during exposure are appraised and responded to. In other words, it is some kind of retrograde emotional summation with an overall positive outcome. Nabi and Krcmar (2004) conceptualize this outcome as both affective and cognitive in nature. Considering its characteristics a combination of emotional experiences and cognitive challenges is probable for quality TV as well (Cardwell, 2007, p. 30; Cupchik, 2011; Latorre & Soto-Sanfiel, 2011; Tan, 1996, p. 229).

Multi-Dimensional Entertainment Experience

Watching quality TV series is not only a meta-emotional but also a multi-dimensional experience: Appreciation and elevation might supplement enjoyment as a result of a meaningful entertainment experience (Oliver & Bartsch, 2010, 2011; Oliver & Hartmann, 2010; Oliver & Raney, 2011; Wirth, Hofer, & Schramm, 2012) and even elicit physiological reactions like goose bumps, a lump in the throat, or chills (Oliver, Hartmann, & Woolley, 2012, pp. 362, 366). Meaningful experiences are more probable when the depiction is realistic (Hall & Bracken, 2011) and the characters are morally ambiguous (Krakowiak & Oliver, 2012)—both features of quality TV. Such experiences are indirectly rewarding (Bartsch, 2012). Traditional narratives privilege narrative engagement over the realization of the artifact (Tan, 1994, p. 13; 1996, p. 78) because the latter diminishes emotional reactions (Tan 1996; Visch & Tan, 2008). In quality TV series, however, style also bears meaning that needs to be decoded (Cupchik & Kemp, 2000). Thus, it is important to take both viewing modes—immersed and formally aware—into consideration for the model as both form and content are sources of pleasure (Klimmt, 2011). The decoding of both planes of meaning needs a lot of effort but—as with other aesthetic artifacts—it is self-rewarding. Preconditions for the enjoyment of this kind of entertainment are increased attention, certain cognitive capabilities, and the willingness to use them for the decoding of an entertainment show. This is motivated by interest and the appreciation of the artistic work (Tan, 1996; 2008). Interest is understood as an inclination to allocate attention. It can be experienced individually as fascination, enthrallment, suspense, transportation, and so forth (Tan, 1996, p. 86). It is tied to personal concerns and certain expectations and it "is determined by the relationship between investment and return" (Tan, 1996, p. 100). Interest is the motor that powers the dual-mode entertainment experience.

Engagement with Serial Narratives

As a rule, "seriality [is] an invitation to viewer involvement" (Liebes & Katz, 1993, p. 144). Involvement is a measure of intensity of information processing, of the cognitive and affective *engagement* with the text and its characters (Wirth, 2006). In the model, engagement is indicated at the right leg of the triangle. Narrative engagement consists of narrative presence (i.e., the feeling of being transported into a text; Oatley, 2002) and emotional engagement with characters (Busselle & Bilandzic, 2009). Perceived story authenticity is a prerequisite for both types. Both external and narrative realism are important for this perception (Busselle & Bilandzic, 2008, p. 267; Hall, 2003). Thus, quality TV series that are authentic in terms of content and characters should benefit from this. Narrative engagement is experienced as pleasurable (Busselle & Bilandzic, 2009, p. 326). Artistry or "craftsmanship" (Green & Brock, 2002, pp. 317, 328) supports transportation, whereas the foregrounding of stylistic features might be detrimental to it. Engagement with characters is also crucial for narrative experiences—be that empathy, sympathy, identification (Cohen, 2006; Klimmt, Hefner, & Vorderer, 2009; Tan, 1996), parasocial interaction (Giles, 2002), or interest (Tan, 1996). The reference point for any form of character relations is the persona. Serial narratives with their recurring ensemble and several chances for character development are especially prone to build relations (Pearson, 2007). Special textual cues (like voice-over or direct address) facilitate engagement with characters (Semmler, Loof, & Berke, 2015). Character relations foster suspense (Knobloch, 2003) and enjoyment in general (Hartmann & Goldhoorn, 2011; Tian & Hoffner, 2010). Quality TV series and their connected paratexts also hold challenges for this concept, though, as transmedia storytelling allows for character development in several different outlets. The viewer-persona relation might be enriched by manifold additional pieces of information and background stories on the Internet but it might also be disturbed when the sources are inconsistent or conflicting.

Complex Texts and the Construction of Meaning

Sense making is the basis for the entertainment experience of quality TV series. The comprehension of both content and style thus forms the hypotenuse of the triangle in the model. Media texts have to be understood in order to be enjoyed and/or appreciated. Decoding is an active process, even more so with quality TV: "Quality television . . . is about a complete cultural viewing experience that imagines proactive consumers owning the text—selecting when they will watch it and engaging in the meaning-making process" (McCabe, 2005, p. 221). Busselle and Bilandzic (2008) modeled the moment of sense making as the interplay of narrative comprehension and engagement resulting in specific outcomes, one of them enjoyment (Bilandzic & Busselle, 2011). Their model shows how recipients construct meaning from texts with the help of real-world knowledge and genre schemas. The smoother this sequence proceeds the more probable narrative engagement becomes and, as a consequence, enjoyment. Among other things, the success of the process is determined by the coherence and consistency of the text. Perceived realism renders engagement more likely (Ahn, Jin, & Ritterfeld, 2012; Hall & Bracken, 2011).

The interpretation process of quality TV commences by constructing culturally bound mental models guided by a text-specific control system. Modeling is based on both content and style information. The process is fueled by interest. It is rewarding in itself.

Dual-Mode Control System for Inconsiderate Texts

The process of sense making varies according to the kind of text that is processed (i.e., literary or informational). The control system guiding this process is a cognitive system that derives from repeated exposure to specific types of texts (Zwaan, 1996, pp. 241, 249) like complex narratives. It integrates knowledge with motivational and situational aspects and draws on relevant schemas (Zwaan, 1996). A control system for literary texts, for instance, might be activated by a specific surface structure (i.e., the meta-genre quality TV) or certain features of the text base (like flashbacks, flash-forwards, or unusual perspectives; Zwaan, 1996, p. 242). By this attention is drawn to the aesthetic characteristics of the text with possible detrimental effects for comprehension (Zwaan, 1996, pp. 246–247). Moreover, comprehension might be impeded by the text base itself because its sense is not immediately recognizable and the comprehension process has to be bottom-up (Zwaan, 1996, p. 247). Apparently, irrelevant details might become important during the course of the story. These details have to be kept in mind for further reference, thereby binding cognitive capacities. Open and complex narratives call for the construction of more than one situation model at a time or the postponement of its final design (see below). Only once enough information is gathered the final model can be constructed. Such "wrap-up moments" (Zwaan, 1996, p. 252) might be offered by repeated watching. Altogether, complex texts that are incoherent and ambiguous (so called "inconsiderate texts"; Zwaan, 1996, p. 247) make great demands on cognitive processing but they reward this demand directly by being interesting (Zwaan, 1996, p. 243) or indirectly by adding symbolic value to the experience.

Mental Models and Cultural Contextualization of Open Texts

Narrative comprehension—actively constructing meaning from a text—is based on a mental model (Busselle & Bilandzic, 2008, pp. 257–260). During the construction process the story is realized as an individually varying reading based on the text base (Cohen, 2002). Starting point is the construction of a situation model including the initial situation, the spatial setting, the characters and their relations based on the background information given at the beginning of most stories (exposition; Graesser, Olde, & Klettke, 2002, p. 258). Original construction and continuous adjustment of the mental model are guided by schemas and stereotypes (i.e., genres). The less conventional a narrative is, the harder or more tedious the model building should be. Imagine the following case:

> So there's a girl. She's walking down an alley. It's dark, the music is ominous, and everything we know about pop culture tells us she's going to be monster food in about 30 seconds.
>
> (Sepinwall, 2013, p. 191)

Thus, the viewer constructs a situation model according to the horror film genre in which young girls usually do not survive. But:

Only there's a guy [Joss Whedon, author of *Buffy, the Vampire Slayer*].
He's a third-generation screenwriter, an absolute sponge for pop culture,
and he likes nothing more than using our own expectations about how
these things work against us. What if, the guy wonders, the girl isn't the
victim, but the hero? What if the monster needs to be afraid of *her*?

(Sepinwall, 2013, p. 191; emphasis original)

That is what happens here: Buffy, the teenage girl, hunts monsters, not the other
way around. Thus, the schemas are in need of adaptation (unless the viewer
operated under the quality TV meta-genre in the first place and had been
prepared for the unexpected).

One feature of quality TV as discussed above is its ambiguity due to the blank
spaces in the text base. In order to understand viewers have to do a lot of filling
in (S. Johnson, 2005, p. 83). Comprehension models that deal with entertaining
works of literature or other aesthetic artifacts account for that. Zwaan (1996), for
instance, starts from the text base as the raw material of meaning. With reference
to real-world knowledge and other familiar text bases (like paratexts) a situation
model is constructed as an "amalgamation of information obtained from the
text and inferences constructed by the reader" (Zwaan, 1996, p. 244). Situation
models are multi-dimensional (in terms of time, space, and causality), even if
the story is not (Zwaan, Magliano, & Graesser, 1995). Blanks are filled in via
repeated exposure (Zwaan et al., 1995, p. 395). Discontinuity (like flashbacks)
can impede model construction leading to longer processing time (Zwaan et
al., 1995, p. 387). Media expertise, on the other hand, supports understanding.
Narrative knowledge and knowledge about cinematic presentation methods (like
cuts, sound, camera setting, editing, etc.) are consulted to create meaning (Ohler,
1994, p. 152). In the case of contemporary television series this knowledge is
available as the meta-genre quality TV.

Understanding and liking of popular culture is not possible without context.
Cultural discourses, media expertise, and individual tastes contribute to the
process of comprehension and enjoyment and/or appreciation. Schemas, scripts,
and stereotypes are rooted in culture (Tan, 1996, pp. 71, 73). Nevertheless,
most existing models do not account for this, at least not in so many words.
I want to explicitly incorporate culture into the QTV-EE model by drawing on
the concept of cultural models (Strasen, 2008, p. 265). The term denotes the
implementation of cultural influences and discourses into the sense making
process (Strasen, 2008, p. 274; see also Mittell, 2004). Cultural models connect
culturally shaped experiences with the individual cognitive system. By this,
culture as a symbolic system promotes contextualization and sense making
and converts a bunch of meaningless audiovisual information bits into a high
quality cultural artifact. For successful communication the cultural models of
the discourse communities (i.e., showrunner and viewers) have to be compatible
(Strasen, 2008, p. 273). This is interesting because although quality TV series
more often than not originate from the USA they are extremely successful in
other cultures as well (Schluetz & Schneider, 2014).

Among other things, quality TV series stand out due to their visual and narrative style. Mittel terms this "the narrative special effect" (2006, p. 35):

> These moments push the operational aesthetic to the foreground, calling attention to the constructed nature of the narration . . . this mode of formally aware viewing is highly encouraged by these programs, as their pleasures are embedded in a level of awareness that transcends the traditional focus on diegetic action typical of most viewers.
>
> (Mittel, 2006, pp. 35, 36)

To account for this effect it is necessary to include the decoding of stylistic aspects. To do so I draw on the model of aesthetic experience by Leder, Belke, Oeberst, and Augustin (2004). It shows the relevance of specific frames, control systems, and pre-existing knowledge (expertise) for understanding and appreciating art. The model distinguishes two ways of art reception leading to aesthetic pleasure and aesthetic judgment, respectively (Leder et al., 2004, p. 502).

Ambiguous Characters and Impression Formation

Morally ambiguous characters as described above complicate the construction of mental models because tried and tested schemas do not work on them. Sanders (2010) developed a model of character impression formation that accounts for this problem. The basic idea is that both category-based and attribute-based impression formation processes occur simultaneously and successively. They vary according to media content and individual factors moderated by inconsistency resolution. Sanders illustrates her model with reference to a quality TV series:

> An immediate impression of Tony Soprano can be that of a mobster. Viewers will thus check the fit of this label. Again, for many viewers this label will seem appropriate. . . . Yet viewers may also see him being a loving father, his frequent panic attacks, and his emotional reactions to murders he commits. These things seem discrepant with the idea or label of, mobster.' Based on this, a viewer may engage in inconsistency resolution. Viewers may use all of this information to come to an impression, . . . representing the first inconsistency resolution outcome. The second option is that viewers will integrate into the category of mobster, the idea that a mobster can be a doting father and be affected by the violence and death surrounding him. These characteristics become a part, either temporarily or permanently, of the label "mobster." Other viewers may disregard what he does for his family and the emotional toll his job has on him, simply viewing him as a mobster and using all of the associated affective information that goes with that label. Still others may disregard the label of "mobster," viewing this as just his occupation, while the other characteristics represent who he is as a character. Any of these options represents

the final inconsistency resolution outcome, a disregard of either the label or the attributes.

(Sanders, 2010, p. 160)

This process is much more extensive (both in terms of time and cognitive capacities) than usual schema-based impression formation (Raney, 2004), especially so because quality TV characters often develop during the course of the series.

Also relevant in the context of situation modeling and character impression formation are moral considerations (Zwaan, 1996, p. 245). Here cultural aspects are especially influential as values and norms are rooted deep in society and culture. Consequently, a large body of research has dealt with this (for an overview see Tamborini, 2013). Moral considerations have a direct bearing on enjoyment because they influence whether a viewer likes a character or not, roots for him or her or not and, consequently, enjoys the unfolding of the events (affective disposition theory; originally Zillmann & Cantor, 1976; for an overview see Raney, 2003, 2004). Thus, every story needs a likeable character to be enjoyable. Amazingly this recipe works for MACs as well (Schlütz, Schneider, & Zehrfeld, 2014) because the viewers find ways to like them (for instance by way of moral disengagement; Bandura, 2002). Quality TV series usually offer textual cues to facilitate this (Carroll, 2004; Pearson & Messenger-Davies, 2003). Morally complex characters might serve as points of moral orientation (Raney & Janicke, 2013): The viewer wishfully identifies with them, dissociates from, or looks down on them. Either way, engaging with these characters may have a reliving effect compensating for or satisfying needs that cannot be met in real life. Another possibility to explain enjoyment in the absence of likable characters is the notion of fascination (Smith, 2011, p. 82) denoting acute attention without moral engagement. Krakowiak and Oliver (2012) show empirically that MACs are less sympathized with but their stories are as engaging (and, as a consequence, enjoyable) as stories with good characters.

Conclusion: Reading Quality TV

The interaction of a person with a quality work brings into being an individual reading. The comprehension process as described above creates meaning and results in a specific interpretation of the text. At the same time it offers the chance to develop relationships with the personae and to assess the work in terms of quality and personal taste.

Interpretation

When dealing with ambiguous texts the viewer has to grapple with complex narrative structures and schemas. Over the course of time, he or she gets used to this. This is positive, as ambiguity tolerance is an important asset in dealing with the complexity of modern times (Krieger, 2010). Successful sense making calls for effort and expertise. Expertise, on the other hand, is built by repeated exposure. Moreover, literary texts that deviate from well-known schemas enhance processing expenses and call for more flexible and adjustable schemas. This is why such texts have the potential to renew schemas and mental models (Strasen, 2008, p. 252). For instance, repeated confrontation with MACs might enrich or reconfigure schemas (Raney, 2004; Shafer & Raney, 2012): "Over time, then, we learn to view antihero narratives through this lens, using a particular story schema that encourages moral disengagement" (Raney & Janicke, 2013, p. 160). This might not be altogether positive if this has implications for real-world behavior (like dimming the moral code; Raney, 2011, p. 22). Whether the effects from quality TV are beneficial or alarming (or both) is an empirical question worth addressing in the future.

Relations

Fictional media content is well suited for narrative persuasion (Green, Strange, & Brock, 2002; Shrum, 2004). Learning is often mediated or stimulated by social relations to media characters (Klimmt, Hartmann, & Schramm, 2006; Papa et al., 2000; Schiappa, Gregg, & Hewes, 2005; Slater, Johnson, Cohen, Comello, & Ewoldsen, 2014). The simulation of social experience is one function of complex, emotionally realistic fiction (Mar & Oatley, 2008). Complex narrative texts teach the viewer how the world and human relations work. Ambiguous stories provide the possibility to take alternative perspectives and to reflect on ourselves:

> By taking note of the pro-attitudes Tony [Soprano] elicits from us we may come to appreciate how subtly our moral compass can be demagnetized. Thus, by inciting us to care for Soprano, David Chase makes vivid our realization of the moral threat of rationalization.
>
> (Carroll, 2004, p. 136)

Evaluation

Quality TV is—at least according to the presented model—challenging and strenuous, both intellectually and emotionally, at times even aesthetically. It does not offer "instant gratification" (Martin, 2013, p. 15). It is worthwhile, however, because watching quality TV provides gratifications that light entertainment cannot offer. This is comparable to reading literary texts which is more costly than dealing with popular fiction as well (Zwaan, 1996). The more cognitive capacities a viewer is able or willing to invest, the more expertise she or he has acquired, the easier becomes the decoding of the text. By watching, understanding, and talking about quality TV one can show off this expertise, one's connoisseurship.

This chapter dealt with contemporary television, complex television series, so-called quality TV. The discussion showed that this kind of entertainment content is comparable to artistic artifacts in terms of structure and the surrounding quality discourse. I argued that the meta-genre, quality TV, serves as a heuristic for selection and reception and frames entertainment experiences and their assessment. In this manner quality entertainment offers a special, culturally bound experience that is intellectually challenging and at the same time rewarding—rewarding in the sense that it offers both direct effects and indirect outcomes (Bartsch, 2012). The direct impact is a positive meta-emotional and multi-dimensional entertainment experience. Indirectly, quality TV provides symbolic value and, thus, offers a profit of distinction (Bourdieu, 1985). As a consequence, the time spent with these series may not be perceived as wasted. Watching quality TV is not a "guilty pleasure" (Oliver & Raney, 2014; Reinecke, Hartmann, & Eden, 2014). Rather, it is comparable to curling up with a good book—a pastime that is rarely frowned upon. On the contrary, it is said that reading can make you a better person. And indeed reading literary fiction is supposed to add to your well-being and your cognitive capabilities (Cunningham & Stanovich, 2001; Rieger, Reinecke, Frischlich, & Bente, 2014). There is also evidence that being transported into a story fosters real life empathy (Bal & Veltkamp, 2013) and that reading literary fiction improves the understanding of other people's state of mind which in turn improves social interaction (Kidd & Castano, 2013). The same might hold true for complex contemporary television. Empirical studies show that serial television impacts on values in the long run (Eden et al., 2014; Weber, Tamborini, Lee, & Stipp, 2008) but many other research questions are still open for theoretical and empirical investigation. Communication studies should turn to them.

Acknowledgments

I would like to thank the anonymous reviewers for their thoughtful comments that substantially improved the quality of the manuscript.

References

Ahn, D., Jin, S.-A. A., & Ritterfeld, U. (2012). "Sad movies don't always make me cry". The cognitive and affective processes underpinning enjoyment of tragedy. *Journal of Media Psychology, 24*(1), 9–18. doi:10.1027/1864-1105/a000058

Akass, K., & McCabe, J. (2008). Six Feet Under. In G. R. Edgerton & J. P. Jones (Eds.), *The essential HBO reader* (pp. 71–81). Lexington, KY: Kentucky University Press.

Allrath, G., Gymnich, M., & Surkamp, C. (2005). Introduction: Towards a narratology of TV series. In G. Allrath & M. Gymnich (Eds.), *Narrative strategies in television series* (pp. 1–43). Houndsmille, NY: Palgrave Macmillan.

Anderson, C. (2008). Producing and aristocracy of culture in American television. In G. R. Edgerton & J. P. Jones (Eds.), *The essential HBO reader* (pp. 23–41). Lexington, KY: Kentucky University Press.

Bal, P. M., & Veltkamp, M. (2013). How does fiction reading influence empathy? An experimental investigation on the role of transportation. *PLoS ONE, 8*(1), e55341 doi: 10.1371/journal.pone.0055341

Bandura, A. (2002). Selective moral disengagement in the exercise of moral agency. *Journal of Moral Education, 31*(2), 101–119. doi: 10.1080/0305724022014322

Barton, K. M. (2012). Superpowers and super-insight: How back story and motivation emerge through the Heroes graphic novels. In D. Simmons (Ed.), *Investigating heroes. Essays on truth, justice, and quality TV* (pp. 66–77). Jefferson, NC: McFarland.

Bartsch, A. (2012). Emotional gratification in entertainment experience. Why viewers of movies and television series find it rewarding to experience emotions. *Media Psychology, 15*(3), 267–302. doi: 10.1080/15213269.2012.693811

Bartsch, A., Vorderer, P., Mangold, R., & Viehoff, R. (2008). Appraisal of emotions in media use: Toward a process model of meta-emotion and emotion regulation. *Media Psychology, 11*, 7–27. doi: 10.1080/15213260701813447

Bignell, J. (2007). Seeing and knowing: Reflexivity and quality. In J. McCabe & K. Akass (Eds.), *Quality TV: Contemporary American television and beyond* (pp. 158–170). London: Tauris.

Bilandzic, H., & Busselle, R. W. (2011). Enjoyment of films as a function of narrative experience, perceived realism and transportability. *Communications, 36*, 29–50. doi: 10.1515/comm.2011.002

Bock, A. (2013). *Fernsehserienrezeption: Produktion, Vermarktung und Rezeption US-amerikanischer Prime-Time-Serien* [Reception of television series: Production, marketing and reception of US-American prime-time series]. Wiesbaden, Germany: VS.

Bourdieu, P. (1985). The social space and the genesis of groups. *Theory and Society, 14*(6), 723–744. doi: 10.1007/BF00174048

Brooker, W. (2001). Living on Dawson's Creek: Teen viewers, cultural convergence, and television overflow. *International Journal of Cultural Studies, 4*(4), 456–472. doi: 10.1177/136787790100400406

Brunsdon, C. (2010). Bingeing on box-sets: The national and the digital in television crime drama. In J. Gripsrud (Ed.), *Relocating television: Television in the digital context* (pp. 63–75). London: Routledge.

Buckland, W. (2009). Introduction: Puzzle plots. In W. Buckland (Ed.), *Puzzle films: Complex storytelling in contemporary cinema* (pp. 1–12). Malden, MA: Wiley-Blackwell.

Buschow, C., Schneider, B., & Ueberheide, S. (2014). *Tweeting television: Exploring communication activities on Twitter while watching TV. Communications - The European Journal of Communication Research, 39*(2), 129–149. doi: 10.1515/commun-2014-0009

Busselle, R., & Bilandzic, H. (2008). Fictionality and perceived realism in experiencing stories: A model of narrative comprehension and engagement. *Communication Theory, 18*, 255–280. doi: 10.1111/j.1468-2885.2008.00322.x

Busselle, R., & Bilandzic, H. (2009). Measuring narrative engagement. *Media Psychology, 12*, 321–347. doi: 10.1080/15213260903287259

Busselle, R., & Greenberg, B. (2000). The nature of television realism judgments: A reevaluation of their conceptualization and measurement. *Mass Communication and Society, 3*(2-3), 249–268. doi: 10.1207/S15327825MCS0323_05

Butler, J. G. (2013). Mad Men: Visual style. In E. Thompson & J. Mittell (Eds.), *How to watch television* (pp. 38–46). New York, NY: New York University Press.

Cantor, J. (2006). Why horror doesn't die: The enduring and paradoxical effects of frightening entertainment. In J. Bryant & P. Vorderer (Eds.), *Psychology of entertainment* (pp. 315–327). Mahwah, NJ: Lawrence Erlbaum Associates.

Cantor, M. G., & Pingree, S. (1983). *The soap opera*. Beverly Hills, CA: Sage.

Cardwell, S. (2007). Is quality television any good? Generic distinctions, evaluations and the troubling matter of critical judgement. In J. McCabe & K. Akass (Eds.), *Quality TV: Contemporary American television and beyond* (pp. 19–34). London: Tauris.

Carroll, N. (2004). Sympathy for the devil. In R. Greene & P. Vernezze (Eds.), *The Sopranos and philosophy: I kill therefore I am* (pp. 121–136). Chicago, IL: Open Court.

Carroll, N. (2007). Narrative closure. *Philosophical Studies, 135*(1), 1–15. doi: 10.1007/s11098-007-9097-9

Cohen, J. (2002). Deconstruction Ally: Explaining viewers' interpretations of popular television. *Media Psychology, 4*, 253–277. doi: 10.1207/S1532785XMEP0403_03

Cohen, J. (2006). Audience identification with media characters. In B. Jennings & P. Vorderer (Eds.), *Psychology of entertainment* (pp. 183–197). Mahwah, NJ: Lawrence Erlbaum Associates.

Corner, J. (1997). 'Quality' and television: Histories and contexts. In M. Eide, B. Gentikow, & K. Helland (Eds.), *Quality television* (pp. 67–86). Bergen, Norway: University of Bergen, Department of Media Studies.

Costera Meijer, I. (2005). Impact or content? Ratings vs quality in public broadcasting. *European Journal of Communication, 20*, 27–53. doi: 10.1177/0267323105049632

Creeber, G. (2004). *Serial television: Big drama on the small screen*. London: BFI.

Cunningham, A. E., & Stanovich, K. E. (2001). What reading does for the mind. *Journal of Direct Instruction, 1*(2), S. 137–149. Retrieved from www.csun.edu/~krowlands/Content/Academic_Resources/Reading/Useful%20Articles/Cunningham-What%20Reading%20Does%20for%20the%20Mind.pdf

Cupchik, G. C. (2011). The role of feeling in the entertainment=emotion formula. *Journal of Media Psychology, 23*(1), 6–11. doi: 10.1027/1864-1105/a000025

Cupchik, G. C., & Kemp, S. (2000). The aesthetics of media fare. In D. Zillmann & P. Vorderer (Eds.), *Media entertainment: The psychology of its appeal* (pp. 249–264). Mahwah, NJ: Lawrence Erlbaum Associates.

Dyer, R. (2002). *Only entertainment* (2nd edn). London: Routledge.

Eden, A., Tamborini, R., Grizzard, M., Lewis, R., Weber, R., & Prabhu, S. (2014). Repeated exposure to narrative entertainment and the salience of moral intuitions. *Journal of Communication, 64*(3), 501–520. doi: 10.1111/jcom.12098

Edgerton, G. R. (2008). Introduction: A brief history of HBO. In G. R. Edgerton & J. P. Jones (Eds.), *The essential HBO reader* (pp. 1–20). Lexington, KY: Kentucky University Press.

Edgerton, G. R., & Jones, J. P. (2008). *The essential HBO reader*. Lexington, KY: Kentucky University Press.

Ernesto [*sic*]. (2013, December 25). 'Game of Thrones' most pirated TV-show of 2013. *TorrentFreak*. Retrieved from https://torrentfreak.com/game-of-thrones-most-pirated-tv-show-of-2013-131225/

Feuer, J. (1992). Genre study and television. In R. C. Allen (Ed.), *Channels of discourse, reassembled: Television and contemporary criticism* (pp. 138–160). London: Routledge.

Feuer, J. (2007). HBO and the concept of quality TV. In J. McCabe & K. Akass (Eds.), *Quality TV: Contemporary American television and beyond* (pp. 145–157). London: Tauris.

Fiske, J. (1987). *Television culture*. London: Routledge.

Garvin, D. A. (1984). What does 'product quality' really mean? *Sloan Management Review, 26*, 25–43. Retrieved from www.oqrm.org/English/What_does_product_quality_really_means.pdf

Garvin, D. A. (1987). Competing on the eight dimensions of quality. *Harvard Business Review, 65*(6), 101–109. Retrieved from http://cc.sjtu.edu.cn/G2S/eWebEditor/uploadfile/20130427091849944.pdf

Geraghty, C. (1981). The continuous serial—A definition. In R. Dyer, C. Geraghty, M. Jordan, T. Lovell, R. Paterson, & J. Stewart (Eds.), *Coronation Street* (pp. 9–26). London: BFI.

Giglietto, F., & Selva, D. (2014). Second screen and participation: A content analysis on a full season dataset of tweets. *Journal of Communication, 64*(2), 260–277. doi: 10.1111/jcom.12085

Giles, D. C. (2002). Parasocial interaction: A review of the literature and a model for future research. *Media Psychology, 4*, 279–305. doi: 10.1207/S1532785XMEP0403_04

Graesser, A. C., Olde, B., & Klettke, B. (2002). How does the mind construct and represent stories? In M. C. Green, J. J. Strange, & T. C. Brock (Eds.), *Narrative impact: Social and cognitive foundations* (pp. 229–262). Mahwah, NJ: Lawrence Erlbaum Associates.

Gray, J. (2010). *Show sold separately: Promos, spoilers and other media paratexts*. New York, NY: New York University Press.

Green, M. C., & Brock, T. C. (2002). In the mind's eye: Transportation-imagery model of narrative persuasion. In M. C. Green, J. J. Strange, & T. C. Brock (Eds.), *Narrative impact: Social and cognitive foundations* (pp. 315–341). Mahwah, NJ: Lawrence Erlbaum Associates.

Green, M. C., Garst, J., & Brock, T. C. (2004). The power of fiction: Determinants and boundaries. In L. J. Shrum (Ed.), *The psychology of entertainment media: Blurring the lines between entertainment and persuasion* (pp. 161–176). Mahwah, NJ: Lawrence Erlbaum Associates.

Green, M. C., Strange, J. J., & Brock, T. C. (Eds.) (2002). *Narrative impact: Social and cognitive foundations*. Mahwah, NJ: Lawrence Erlbaum Associates.

Green, M. C., Kass, S., Carrey, J., Herzig, B., Reeney, R., & Sabini, J. (2008). Transportation across media: Repeated exposure to print and film. *Media Psychology, 11*, 512–539. doi: 10.1080/15213260802492000

Greenberg, B. S., & Busselle, R. (1996). Audience dimensions of quality in situation comedies and action programmes. In S. Ishikawa (Ed.), *Quality assessment of television* (pp. 169–196). Luton, UK: John Libbey Media.

Hall, A. (2003). Reading realism: Audiences' evaluation of the reality of media texts. *Journal of Communication, 53*(4), 624–641. doi: 10.1093/joc/53.4.624

Hall, A. E., & Bracken, C. C. (2011). "I really liked that movie". Testing the relationship between trait empathy, transportation, perceived realism, and movie enjoyment. *Journal of Media Psychology, 23*(2), 90–99. doi: 10.1027/1864-1105/a000036

Hartmann, T., & Goldhoorn, C. (2011). Horton and Wohl revisited: Exploring viewers' experience of parasocial interaction. *Journal of Communication, 61*, 1104–1121. doi: 10.1111/j.1460-2466.2011.01595.x

Henning, B., & Vorderer, P. (2001). Psychological escapism: Predicting the amount of television viewing by need for cognition. *Journal of Communication, 51*, 100–120. doi: 10.1093/joc/51.1.100

Hibberd, J. (2013, September 30). 'Breaking Bad' series finale ratings smash all records. *Entertainment Weekly Online*. Retrieved from http://insidetv.ew.com/2013/09/30/breaking-bad-series-finale-ratings/

Hills, M. (2007). From the box in the corner to the box set on the shelf: TV III and the cultural/textual valorisations of DVD. *New Review of Film and Televison Studies, 5*(1), 41–60. doi: 10.1080/17400300601140167

Hofer, M., & Wirth, W. (2012). It's right to be sad: The role of meta-appraisals in the sad-film paradox—A multiple mediator model. *Journal of Media Psychology, 24*(2), 43–54. doi: 10.1027/1864-1105/a000061

Ishikawa, S. (Ed.) (1996). *Quality assessment of television*. Luton, UK: John Libbey Media.

Jancovich, M., & Lyons, J. (Eds.) (2003). *Quality popular television: Cult TV, the industry, and fans*. London: BFI.

Jenkins, H. (2008). *Convergence culture: Where old and new media collide*. New York, NY: New York University Press.

Johnson, C. (2005). Quality/cult television: The X-Files and television history. In M. Hammond & L. Mazdon (Eds.), *The contemporary television series* (pp. 57–74). Edinburgh: Edinburgh University Press.

Johnson, C. (2007). Tele-branding in TVIII: The network as brand and the programme as brand. *New Review of Film and Television Studies, 5*(1), 5–24. doi: 10.1080/17400300601140126

Johnson, S. (2005). *Everything bad is good for you: How popular culture is making us smarter*. London: Penguin.

Kelso, T. (2008). And now no word from our sponsor: How HBO puts the risk back into television. In M. Leverette, B. L. Ott, & C. L. Buckley (Eds.), *It's not TV: Watching HBO in the post-television era* (pp. 46–64). London: Routledge.

Kidd, D. C., & Castano, E. (2013). Reading literary fiction improves theory of mind. *Science, 342*(6156), 377–380. doi: 10.1126/science.1239918

Klimmt, C. (2011). Media psychology and complex modes of entertainment experiences. *Journal of Media Psychology, 11*(1), 34–38. doi: 10.1027/1864-1105/a000030

Klimmt, C., Hartmann, T., & Schramm, H. (2006). Parasocial interactions and relationships. In B. Jennings & P. Vorderer (Eds.), *Psychology of entertainment* (pp. 291–313). Mahwah, NJ: Lawrence Erlbaum Associates.

Klimmt, C., Hefner, D., & Vorderer, P. (2009). The video game experience as "true" identification: A theory of enjoyable alterations of players' self perception. *Communication Theory, 19*, 351–373. doi: 10.1111/j.1468-2885.2009.01347.x

Knobloch, S. (2003). Suspense and mystery. In J. Bryant & J. Cantor (Eds.), *Communication and emotion: Essays in honor of Dolf Zillmann* (pp. 379–395). Mahwah, NJ: Lawrence Erlbaum Associates.

Kompare, D. (2006). Publishing flow: DVD box sets and the reconception of television. *Television and New Media, 7*(4), 335–360. doi: 10.1177/1527476404270609

Kompare, D. (2009). The benefits of banality: Domestic syndication in the post-network era. In A. D. Lotz (Ed.), *Beyond prime time: Television programming in the post-network era* (pp. 55–74). London: Routledge.

Kozloff, S. (1992). Narrative theory and television. In R. C. Allen (Ed.), *Channels of discourse, reassembled: Television and contemporary criticism* (pp. 67–100). London: Routledge.

Krakowiak, K. M., & Oliver, M. B. (2012). When good characters do bad things: Examining the effect of moral ambiguity on enjoyment. *Journal of Communication, 62*(1), 117–135. doi: 10.1111/j.1460-2466.2011.01618.x

Krieger, V. (2010). "At war with the obvious": Kulturen der Ambiguität. Historische, psychologische und ästhetische Dimensionen des Mehrdeutigen ["At war with the obvious": Cultures of ambiguity. Historical, psychological, and aesthetical dimensions of the ambiguous]. In V. Krieger & R. Mader (Eds.), *Ambiguität in der Kunst: Typen und Funktionen eines ästhetischen Paradigmas* [Ambiguity in art: Types and functions of an aesthetic paradigm] (pp. 13–49). Cologne, Germany: Boehlau.

Latorre, J. I., & Soto-Sanfiel, M. T. (2011). Toward a theory of intellectual entertainment. *Journal of Media Psychology, 23*(1), 52–59. doi: 10.1027/1864-1105/a000033

Lavery, D. (2004). The X-Files. In G. Creeber (Ed.), *Fifty key television programmes* (pp. 242–246). London: Arnold.

Lavery, D. (2007). Read any good television lately? Television companion books and quality TV. In J. McCabe & K. Akass (Eds.), *Quality TV: Contemporary American television and beyond* (pp. 228–236). London: Tauris.

Leder, H., Belke, B., Oeberst, A., & Augustin, D. (2004). A model of aesthetic appreciation and aesthetic judgments. *British Journal of Psychology, 95*, 489–508. Retrieved from www.cognitivefluency.com/research/aesthetic.appreciation.judgements.pdf

Leverette, M., Ott, B. L., & Buckley, C. L. (Eds.), (2008). *It's not TV: Watching HBO in the post-television era*. London: Routledge.

Liebes, T., & Katz, E. (1993). *The export of meaning: Cross cultural readings of Dallas* (2nd edn). Cambridge, MA: Polity Press.

Lotz, A. (2007). *The television will be revolutionized*. New York, NY: New York University Press.

Manovich, L. (2001). *The language of new media*. London: The MIT Press.

Mar, R. A., & Oatley, K. (2008). The function of fiction is the abstraction and simulation of social experience. *Perspectives on Psychological Science, 3*, 173–192. doi: 10.1111/j.1745-6924.2008.00073.x

Martin, B. (2013). *Difficult men. From The Sopranos and The Wire to Mad Men and Breaking Bad: Behind the scenes of a creative revolution*. London: Faber and Faber.

Mazdon, L. (2005). Introduction: Histories. In M. Hammond & L. Mazdon (Eds.), *The contemporary television series* (pp. 3–10). Edinburgh, Scotland: Edinburgh University Press.

McCabe, J. (2005). Creating 'quality' audiences for ER on Channel Four. In M. Hammond & L. Mazdon (Eds.), *The contemporary television series* (pp. 207–223). Edinburgh, Scotland: Edinburgh University Press.

McCabe, J., & Akass, K. (Eds.) (2007). *Quality TV: Contemporary American television and beyond*. London: Tauris.

Miron, D. (2003). Enjoyment of violence. In J. Bryant & J. Cantor (Eds.), *Communication and emotion: Essays in honor of Dolf Zillmann* (pp. 445–472). Mahwah, NJ: Lawrence Erlbaum Associates.

Mittell, J. (2004). *Genre and television: From cop shows to cartoons in American culture*. New York, NY: Routledge.

Mittell, J. (2006). Narrative complexity in contemporary American television. *The Velvet Light Trap, 58*, 29–40. doi: 10.1353/vlt.2006.0032

Mittell, J. (2010). *Television and American culture*. New York, NY: Oxford University Press.

Mittell, J. (2015). *Complex TV: The poetics of contemporary television storytelling*. New York, NY: University Press.

Nabi, R. L., & Krcmar, M. (2004). Conceptualizing media enjoyment as attitude: Implications for mass media effects research. *Communication Theory, 14*(4), 288–310. doi: 10.1093/ct/14.4.288

Ndalianis, A. (2005). Television and the neo-baroque. In M. Hammond & L. Mazdon (Eds.), *The contemporary television series* (pp. 83–101). Edinburgh, Scotland: Edinburgh University Press.

Nelson, R. (1997). *TV drama in transition: Forms, values and cultural change*. Basingstoke, UK: Macmillan.

Nelson, R. (2007). *State of play: Contemporary 'high-end' TV drama*. Manchester, UK: Manchester University Press.

Newcomb, H. (2004). Narrative and genre. In J. D. H. Downing, D. McQuail, P. Schlesinger, & E. Wartella (Eds.), *The SAGE handbook of media studies* (pp. 413–428). London: Sage.

Newman, M. Z., & Levine, E. (2012). *Legitimating television: Media convergence and cultural status*. New York, NY: Routledge.

Nielsen. (Ed.) (2014, February). *This TV season's biggest moments on Twitter*. Retrieved from www.nielsen.com/us/en/newswire/2014/this-tv-seasons-biggest-moments-on-twitter.html

Nowell-Smith, G. (1994). 'Quality' television. In T. Elsaesser, J. Simons, & L. Bronk (Eds.), *Writing for the medium: Television in transition* (pp. 35–40). Amsterdam, The Netherlands: Amsterdam University Press.

Nussbaum, E. (2009, December 4). When TV became art: Good-bye boob tube, hello brain food. *New York Magazine*. Retrieved from http://nymag.com/arts/all/aughts/62513/

Oatley, K. (2002). Emotions and the story worlds of fiction. In M. C. Green, J. J. Strange, & T. C. Brock (Eds.), *Narrative impact: Social and cognitive foundations* (pp. 39–69). Mahwah, NJ: Lawrence Erlbaum Associates.

Oernebring, H. (2007). Alternate reality gaming and convergence culture: The case of Alias. *International Journal of Cultural Studies, 10*(4), 445–462. doi: 10.1177/1367877907083079

Ohler, P. (1994). *Kognitive Filmpsychologie: Verarbeitung und mentale Repräsentation narrativer Filme* [Cognitive film psychology: Information processing and mental representation of narrative films]. Muenster, Germany: MAkS-Publ.

Oliver, M. B. (1993a). Adolescents' enjoyment of graphic horror: Effects of viewers' attitudes and portrayals of victim. *Communication Research, 20*(1), 30–50. doi: 10.1177/009365093020001002

Oliver, M. B. (1993b). Exploring the paradox of the enjoyment of sad films. *Human Communication Research, 19*(3), 315–342. doi: 10.1111/j.1468-2958.1993.tb00304.x

Oliver, M. B. (2008). Tender affective states as predictors of entertainment preference. *Journal of Communication, 58*, 40–61. doi: 10.1111/j.1460-2466.2007.00373.x

Oliver, M. B., & Bartsch, A. (2010). Appreciation as audience response: Exploring entertainment gratifications beyond hedonism. *Human Communication Research, 36*, 53–81. doi: 10.1111/j.1468-2958.2009.01368.x

Oliver, M. B., & Bartsch, A. (2011). Appreciation of entertainment: The importance of meaningfulness via virtue and wisdom. *Journal of Media Psychology, 23*(1), 29–33. doi: 10.1027/1864-1105/a000029

Oliver, M. B., & Hartmann, T. (2010). Exploring the role of meaningful experiences in users' appreciations of "good movies". *Projections, 4*(2), 128–150. doi: 10.3167/proj.2010.040208

Oliver, M. B., & Raney, A. A. (2011). Entertainment as pleasurable and meaningful: Identifying hedonic and eudaimonic motivations for entertainment consumption. *Journal of Communication, 61*(5), 984–1004. doi: 10.1111/j.1460-2466.2011.01585.x

Oliver, M. B., & Raney, A. A. (2014). An introduction to the special issue: Expanding the boundaries of entertainment research. *Journal of Communication, 64*, 361–368. doi: 10.1111/jcom.12092

Oliver, M. B., Hartmann, T., & Woolley, J. K. (2012). Elevation in response to entertainment portrayals of moral virtue. *Human Communication Research, 38*, 360–378. doi: 10.1111/j.1468-2958.2012.01427.x

Papa, M. J., Singhal, A., Law, S., Pant, S., Sood, S., Rogers, E. M., & Shefner-Rogers, C. L. (2000). Entertainment-education and social change: An analysis of parasocial interaction, social learning, collective efficacy, and paradoxical communication. *Journal of Communication, 50*(4), 31–55. doi: 10.1093/joc/50.4.31

Pearson, R. (2005). The writer/producer in American television. In M. Hammond & L. Mazdon (Eds.), *The contemporary television series* (pp. 11–26). Edinburgh, Scotland: Edinburgh University Press.

Pearson, R. (2007). Anatomising Gilbert Grissom: The structure and function of the televisiual character. In M. Allan (Ed.), *Reading CSI: Crime TV under the microscope* (pp. 39–56). London: Tauris.

Pearson, R. E., & Messenger-Davies, M. (2003). 'You're not going to see that on TV': Star Trek: The Next Generation in film and television. In M. Jancovich & J. Lyons (Eds.), *Quality popular television: Cult TV, the industry, and fans* (pp. 102–117). London: BFI.

Poulaki, M. (2014). Puzzled Hollywood and the return of complex films. In W. Buckland (Ed.), *Hollywood puzzle films* (pp. 35–53). New York, NY: Routledge.

Raney, A. A. (2003). Disposition-based theories of enjoyment. In J. Bryant, D. Roskos-Ewoldson, & J. Cantor (Eds.), *Communication and emotion: Essays in honor of Dolf Zillmann* (pp. 61–84). Mahwah, NJ: Lawrence Erlbaum Associates.

Raney, A. A. (2004). Expanding disposition theory: Reconsidering character liking, moral evaluations, and enjoyment. *Communication Theory, 14*, 348–369. doi: 10.1093/ct/14.4.348

Raney, A. A. (2011). The role of morality in emotional reactions to and enjoyment of media entertainment. *Journal of Media Psychology, 23*(1), 18–23. doi: 10.1027/1864-1105/a000027

Raney, A. A., & Janicke, S. H. (2013). How we enjoy and why we seek out morally complex characters in media entertainment. In R. Tamborini (Ed.), *Media and the moral mind* (pp. 152–169). New York, NY: Routledge.

Reeves, J. L., Rodgers [*sic*], M. C., & Epstein, M. (1996). Rewriting popularity: The cult files. In D. Lavery, A. Hague, & M. Cartwright (Eds.), *Deny all knowledge: Reading the X-Files* (pp. 22–35). London: Faber.

Reeves, J. L., Rogers, M. C., & Epstein, M. M. (2007). Quality control: The Daily Show, the Peabody and brand discipline. In J. McCabe & K. Akass (Eds.), *Quality TV: Contemporary American television and beyond* (pp. 79–97). London: Tauris.

Reinecke, L., Hartmann, T., & Eden, A. (2014). The guilty couch potato: The role of ego depletion in reducing recovery through media use. *Journal of Communication, 64*(4), 569–589. doi: 10.1111/jcom.12107

Rieger, D., Reinecke, L., Frischlich, L., & Bente, G. (2014). Media entertainment and well-being—Linking hedonic and eudaimonic entertainment experience to media-induced recovery and vitality. *Journal of Communication, 64*(3), 456–478. doi: 10.1111/jcom.12097

Rogers, M. C., Epstein, M., & Reeves, J. L. (2002). The Sopranos as HBO brand equity: The art of commerce in the age of digital reproduction. In D. Lavery (Ed.), *This thing of ours: Investigating The Sopranos* (pp. 42–57). New York, NY: Columbia University Press.

Rosengren, K. E., Carlsson, M., & Tagerud, Y. (1996). Quality in programming: Views from the north. In S. Ishikawa (Ed.), *Quality assessment of television* (pp. 3–48). Luton, UK: John Libbey Media.

Sanders, M. S. (2010). Making a good (bad) impression: Examining the cognitive processes of disposition theory to form a synthesized model of media character impression formation. *Communication Theory, 20*(2), 147–168. doi: 10.1111/j.1468-2885.2010.01358.x

Santo, A. (2008). Para-television and discourses of distinction: The culture of production at HBO. In M. Leverette, B. L. Ott, & C. L. Buckley (Eds.), *It's not TV: Watching HBO in the post-television era* (pp. 19–45). London: Routledge.

Schiappa, E., Gregg, P. B., & Hewes, D. E. (2005). The parasocial contact hypothesis. *Communication Monographs, 72*(1), 92–115. doi: 10.1080/0363775052000342544

Schluetz, D., & Schneider, B. (2014). Does cultural capital compensate for cultural discount? Why German students prefer US-American TV series. In V. Marinescu, S. Branea, & B. Mitu (Eds.), *Critical reflections on audience and narrativity—New connections, new perspectives* (pp. 7–26). Stuttgart, Germany: ibidem.

Schlütz, D. (in press). *Quality TV als Unterhaltungsphaenomen: Entwicklung, Charakteristika, Nutzung und Rezeption komplexer Fernsehserien wie* The Sopranos, The Wire *oder* Breaking Bad. [Quality TV as an entertainment phenomenon: Development, characteristics, use, and reception of complex television series like *The Sopranos, The Wire*, or *Breaking Bad*]. Wiesbaden, Germany: VS.

Schlütz, D., Schneider, B., & Zehrfeld, M. (2014). America's favorite serial killer: Enjoyment of the TV serial 'Dexter'. In V. Marinescu, S. Branea, & B. Mitu (Eds.), *Contemporary television series: Narrative structures and audience perception* (pp. 115–132). Newcastle upon Tyne, UK: Cambridge Scholars Publishing.

Scott, S. (2013). Battlestar Galactica: Fans and ancillary content. In E. Thompson & J. Mittell (Eds.), *How to watch television* (pp. 320–329). New York, NY: New York University Press.

Semmler, S. M., Loof, T., & Berke, C. (2015). The influence of audio-only character narration on character and narrative engagement. *Communication Research Reports, 32*(1), 63–72. doi: 10.1080/08824096.2014.989976

Sepinwall, A. (2013). *The revolution was televised: The cops, crooks, slingers, and slayers who changed TV drama forever*. New York, NY: Touchstone.

Sewell, P. W. (2010). From discourse to discord: Quality and dramedy at the end of the classic network system. *Television & New Media, 11*, 235–259. doi: 10.1177/1527476409351289

Shafer, D. M., & Raney, A. A. (2012). Exploring how we enjoy antihero narratives. *Journal of Communication, 62*(6), 1028–1046. doi: 10.1111/j.1460-2466.2012.01682.x

Shrum, L. J. (2004). *The psychology of entertainment media: Blurring the lines between entertainment and persuasion*. Mahwah, NJ: Lawrence Erlbaum Associates.

Slater, M. D., Johnson, B. K., Cohen, J., Comello, M. L. G., & Ewoldsen, D. R. (2014). Temporarily expanding the boundaries of the self: Motivations for entering the story world and implications for narrative effects. *Journal of Communication, 64*(3), 439–455. doi: 10.1111/jcom.12100

Smith, M. (2011). Just what is it that makes Tony Soprano such an appealing, attractive murderer? In W. E. Jones & S. Vice (Eds.), *Ethics at the cinema* (pp. 66–90). Oxford, UK: Oxford University Press.

Strasen, S. (2008). *Rezeptionstheorien: Literatur-, sprach- und kulturwissenschaftliche Ansaetze und kulturelle Modelle* [Reception theory: Literary, linguistic and cultural studies approaches and cultural models]. Trier, Germany: WVT.

Tamborini, R. (2003). Enjoyment and social functions of horror. In J. Bryant & J. Cantor (Eds.), *Communication and emotion: Essays in honor of Dolf Zillmann* (pp. 417–443). Mahwah, NJ: Lawrence Erlbaum Associates.

Tamborini, R. (Ed.) (2013). *Media and the moral mind*. New York, NY: Routledge.

Tan, E. S.-H. (1994). Film-induced affect as a witness emotion. *Poetics, 23*, 7-32. doi: 10.1016/0304-422X(94)00024-Z

Tan, E. S.-H. (1996). *Emotion and the structure of narrative: Film as an emotion machine*. Mahwah, NJ: Lawrence Erlbaum Associates.

Tan, E. S.-H. (2008). Entertainment is emotion: The functional architecture of the entertainment experience. *Media Psychology, 11*, 28–51. doi: 10.1080/152132607018533161

Thompson, R. J. (1996). *Television's second golden age: From Hill Street Blues to ER*. New York, NY: Continuum.

Tian, Q., & Hoffner, C. A. (2010). Parasocial interaction with liked, neutral, and disliked characters on a popular TV series. *Mass Communication and Society, 13*(3), 250–269. doi: 10.1080/15205430903296051

Visch, V., & Tan, E. (2008). Narrative versus style: Effect of genre-typical events versus genre-typical filmic realizations on film viewers' genre recognition. *Poetics, 36*, 301–315. doi: 10.1016/j.poetic.2008.03.003

Vorderer, P. (2001). It's all entertainment, sure. But what exactly is entertainment? Communication research, media psychology, and the explanation of entertainment experiences. *Poetics, 29*, 247–261. doi: 10.1016/S0304-422X(01)00037-7

Vorderer, P., & Hartmann, T. (2009). Entertainment and enjoyment as media effects. In J. Bryant & M. B. Oliver (Eds.), *Media effects: Advances in theory and research* (3rd edn, pp. 532–550). Mahwah, NJ: Lawrence Erlbaum Associates.

Vorderer, P., Klimmt, C., & Ritterfeld, U. (2004). Enjoyment: At the heart of media entertainment.   *Communication Theory, 14*(4), 388–408. doi: 10.1093/ct/14.4.388

Vorderer, P., Wulff, H. J., & Friedrichsen, H. (Eds.) (1996). *Suspense: Conceptualizations, theoretical analyses, and empirical explorations*. Mahwah, NJ: Lawrence Erlbaum Associates.

Weber, R., Tamborini, R., Lee, H. E., & Stipp, J. (2008). Soap opera exposure and enjoyment: A longitudinal test of disposition theory. *Media Psychology, 11*(4), 462–487. doi: 10.1080/15213260802509993

Williams, R. (1974). *Television: Technology and cultural form*. London: Routledge.

Wirth, W. (2006). Involvement. In J. Bryant & P. Vorderer (Eds.), *Psychology of entertainment* (pp. 199–213). Mahwah, NJ: Lawrence Erlbaum Associates.

Wirth, W., Hofer, M., & Schramm, H. (2012). Beyond pleasure: Exploring the eudaimonic entertainment experience. *Human Communication Research, 38*, 406–428. doi: 10.1111/j.1468-2958.2012.01434.x

Woollacott, E. (2014, September 3). Breaking Bad piracy soars after Emmy wins. *Forbes*. Retrieved from http://www.forbes.com/sites/emmawoollacott/2014/09/03/breaking-bad-piracy-soars-after-emmy-wins/

Zillmann, D., & Bryant, J. (1994). Entertainment as media effect. In J. Bryant & D. Zillmann (Eds.), *Media effects: Advances in theory and research* (pp. 437–461). Mahwah, NJ: Lawrence Erlbaum Associates.

Zillmann, D., & Cantor, J. R. (1976). A disposition theory of humor and mirth. In A. J. Chapman & H. C. Foot (Eds.), *Humor and laughter: Theory, research and applications* (pp. 93–115). London: Wiley.

Zwaan, R. A. (1996). Toward a model of literary comprehension. In B. K. Britton & A. C. Graesser (Eds.), *Models of understanding texts* (pp. 241–255). Mahwah, NJ: Lawrence Erlbaum Associates.

Zwaan, R. A., Magliano, J. P., & Graesser, A. C. (1995). Dimensions of situation model construction in narrative comprehension. *Journal of Experimental Psychology: Learning, Memory, and Cognition, 21*(2), 386–397. doi: 10.1037/0278-7393.21.2.386

Part II

Personal and Strategic Communication in Social Interactions

CHAPTER CONTENTS

5 Digitizing Strength of Weak Ties

Understanding Social Network Relationships through Online Discourse Analysis

Marya L. Doerfel

Rutgers University

Patricia J. Moore

Purdue University

Strength of weak ties theory (SoWT) explains the social influences of weak ties as they facilitate access across social networks. An underlying assumption is that SoWT involves face-to-face interaction. Today, social media allow tie formation without necessarily being linked to time or place. We assert that building networks through online, text-based communication adds layers of complexity that are not fully part of the classic SoWT theory and application. We suggest discourse analysis constructs to extend SoWT to relationships formed and maintained with social media. We formulate propositions to extend SoWT to understand the consequences and opportunities afforded by online-only connections.

Communication scholarship has advanced a deeper understanding of the co-construction of relationships through communication processes while still accounting for broader social structures that are influenced by, and influence, relationship building, maintenance, and dissolution. Social network research, in particular, has been instrumental in advancing a deeper understanding of multi-level processes playing out (Monge & Contractor, 2003). At the relational level, the quality of communication links has been scrutinized for information flows through semantic network analyses (Carley & Kaufer, 1993; Danowski & Barnett, 1982; Doerfel & Barnett, 1999), through issue networks and convergence of dyadic attitudes (Contractor & Grant, 1996; Rice & Danowski, 1993), and through quantitatively derived indices that capture the ability for links to sustain themselves as their overall networks evolve (Monge, Heiss, & Margolin, 2008). Among system level dynamics, the quality of ties, especially regarding the strength of them, afford access to resources, information, and support. Since its inception, one of the most empirically tested and firmly established social network theories is the strength of weak ties (SoWT). But with the wide-spread adoption of social media—that is often text-based communication that happens over extended periods—the time is ripe for communication theory grounded in discourse to advance SoWT.

In 1973, Mark Granovetter wrote his seminal paper "The Strength of Weak Ties" (SoWT) in which he laid out the concept that weak social network ties play an important role in the dissemination of information and getting a job. Since its publication, his paper has been cited by over 15,000 published articles, resulting in one of the most generalizable assumptions about social networks. Granovetter began by laying out findings that demonstrated links between relational characteristics such as frequency of interaction and homophily and the strength of a connection between two people. Heider's (1958) theory of cognitive balance also resonates with SoWT because it not only confirms the idea of tie strength correlating with relative similarity between two people, but that two individuals who share a strong tie with a given individual are more likely to form a strong tie with each other.

Granovetter (1973) synthesized these ideas and posited that "small-scale interaction becomes translated into large-scale patterns, and that these, in turn, feed back into small groups" (p. 1360). Put another way, a circular pattern exists in which micro level interactions and macro level interactions feed and support each other. For example, a plant has three groups of workers: day shift, swing shift, and night shift. Because of the amount of time spent together and other perceived commonalities, each group's members form stronger social ties within their respective groups. However, the groups will also form weaker ties linking their shift to the other shifts. Over time, the iterative intragroup ties fuel group cohesion. The intergroup ties, while weaker, are the source of the movement of new information and ideas between the three groups of workers, for example if a particular machine will be replaced soon.

Granovetter began his defense by providing a framework of four correlated dimensions that determine the strength of a tie: (a) amount of time (the stronger the tie, the greater the investment of time in developing and maintaining the tie); (b) emotional intensity (the feeling of closeness between two people); (c) intimacy (mutual confiding); and (d) reciprocal services (the mutual provision of emotional support and aid within the relationship) (Granovetter, 1973; Marsden & Campbell, 1984). Granovetter did not specify a single formula or particular weak/strong threshold; however, the underlying assumption is that the higher the measure of each dimension, the stronger the tie. Close friends are considered strong ties, acquaintances and friends of friends are weak ties, and people who are known to a person but with whom there is no substantial tie are absent ties.

Granovetter's description of tie strength helped reveal the ways networks are both informational and instrumental. Weak ties provide access to information and resources beyond one's immediate social circle (Granovetter, 1983). Weak ties can speed up search times for knowledge across organizational units (Borgatti & Cross, 2003; Hansen, 1999), provide access to non-redundant information (Granovetter, 1983; Levin & Cross, 2004), and facilitate reliable technical support and advice (Constant, Sproull, & Kiesler, 1996). Meanwhile, strong ties set the stage for developing trust in others (Krackhardt, 1992) which then facilitates the motivation to share information with one another and have access to tacit knowledge (Gulati, 1995; Yuan, Fulk, Monge, & Contractor, 2010). In his seminal work, Granovetter cited cases that share a common feature, a tangible human element. An underlying implication is that the primary mode of tie formation and maintenance involve face-to-face communication. With the advent of Internet and communication technologies (ICTs) such as blogs, wikis, and other social media tools, however, relationships can be made and developed without the conventions of co-location.

Relationships and ICTs in the Twenty-First Century

When Granovetter wrote his paper, most dyadic partners usually communicated face-to-face, by phone, or through written correspondence.[1] Research on social networks in general, and weak ties theory in particular, predated social media and thus measuring tie strength has been mostly couched in terms of offline social networks. The three communication modes (face-to-face, phone, and writing) shared the common element of one person interacting directly with either the other person in the dyad or an artifact directly connected to that person (the words written on the page or the sound of their voice in real-time). In the 1980s and 90s, new modes of exchanging information were introduced to people. Personal computers allowed people to send email, connect to the Internet, and later, the World Wide Web (which provided more user-friendly access to the Internet-based information). According to the Pew Internet & American Life Project Surveys data (Rainie, Fox, & Maeve, 2014), in 1995 14% of Americans had Internet access at home, school, or work, by 2000, 50%; and by 2011, 78%. By 2009 Rainie et al.'s survey results showed that 81.9 million Americans had Internet access at home. Cell phones were also adopted at a ferocious pace. According to CTIA, The Wireless Association, in 1985 less than 1% (340,213) of Americans were cell phone subscribers and this continued to grow from 13% (33.8 million) of Americans having cell phone service to, in 1995, 96% (302.9 million) and, by the end of 2010, an 83% increase (CTIA, 2011).

Since 1973, computer-based communication modes, including email, online social networking, and mobile phone technologies, have become conventional parts of life. These new information and communication technologies (ICTs) expanded the number of choices people had for communicating and getting information. ICTs meant that a message to a relative could be written at 2:00 a.m. or 2:00 p.m. and sent as soon as it was written or at a later time; the recipient could read it right away or save it for later. A person placing a call was no longer tethered to a corded handset or base. A child could call a parent from the playing field if there was no payphone nearby. ICTs detached communication from time and place, changing the nature of social interaction, social influence, and creating new opportunities for relationships. An individual no longer had to be in a fixed location (Walther, 1996). As Baym (2010) stated, the Internet brought "the possibility of forming relationships that transcend space" (p. 100).

Because modern relationships transcend a conventionally face-to-face institution, SoWT has been complicated by the technological advances of the twenty-first century, yet traditional forms of connecting remain central to underlying assumptions about how ties are formed. For example, name generators, a common tool used to measure social network size, ask questions such as who the responder can depend on for assistance with household tasks such as painting (Marin & Hampton, 2007). While new media may not directly impact a users' centrality in their networks (Howard, 2002), social patterns change and emerge in line with tensions associated with the simultaneous existence of old and new media (Marvin, 1988; Hardey, 2008). To this point, the answer to "on whom do you depend for assistance" may still generate a Granovetter-esque weak tie name, but does not capture the patterns of social interaction that new media-sourced weak ties have changed.

New media have afforded additional and different ways to connect and engage in relationships, with the explosive growth of social networking sites (SNS). SNSs consist of personalized user profiles. Profiles are usually a combination of users' images (avatars), lists of interests and music, book, and movie preferences, and links to affiliated profiles ("friends"). Different sites impose different levels of privacy in terms of what information is revealed through profile pages to nonaffiliated visitors and how far "strangers" versus "friends" can traverse through the network of a profile's friends. Profile holders acquire new friends by browsing and searching through the site and sending friend requests. In this context of SNSs, new communication activities have emerged. As a result, other forms of relationship-formation and maintenance now exist (boyd & Ellison, 2008; Gruzd, Wellman & Takhteyev, 2011; Guo, 2008; Morrison, 2011; Stanley, 2004, p. 92; Wang & Wellman, 2010). SNSs have been around since the mid-1990s but SixDegrees.com was the first site that operated in the manner of the SNSs that became popular in the early decades of the twenty-first century. As noted by boyd and Ellison (2008), SixDegrees failed as a sustainable business. The story of their failure is told in the adoption rate of Internet usage in the United States. In 1997 less than 20% of Americans had Internet access at home so, even if a person had a SixDegrees profile, it was likely that not many others in their social network did.

Friendster.com rolled out in March 2003 and with its introduction there was a new Internet space that operated in the same manner as SNSs with which people are familiar today (Stanley, 2004). Friendster worked on an invite model and was based on existing users inviting others in their social network who were not on Friendster to set up a profile. Knowing someone on Friendster was necessary for setting up an account. By the time Friendster began gaining popularity, about 50% of Americans had Internet access thereby giving SNSs a critical mass of potential users. Friendster grew virally from 20 friends and acquaintances in the 2003 beta test to 300,000 by May 2003, then to almost six million a year later. That jump in users was triggered by mainstream media coverage of Friendster coupled with expanding requirements for membership. New members no longer needed an invite from an existing member to become part of the online community (boyd & Ellison, 2008). The sudden expansion in Friendster's membership caused issues, including, taxing site servers, an influx of people without previous ties to the original users that "upset the cultural balance" (boyd & Ellison, 2008), and new policies that angered users. As Friendster membership began to wane, another site, MySpace, was gaining in popularity, becoming America's SNS of choice in 2006 until Facebook assumed that position in 2008.

While small communities sprang up around message boards, Usenet, and other online outlets in the 1980s and 1990s, they were small and scattered because of their narrow appeal and a relative lack of potential participants. The introduction of SNSs introduced new dimensions to social influence and creating social networks. Profiles included information such as listings of interests, favorites, and demographics (gender, age, location); and the sites offered a feature where people on the site could search for and view other profiles based on that information. SNSs also changed ways to maintain relationships—they supported the ability to reconnect to others with whom people had lost touch. This is the point where some of the underlying assumptions of SoWT began to become strained.

As might be expected, individuals connected with people they knew through regular interaction, as observed in offline networks that formed prior to the proliferation of social media. In other words, people recreated their offline social networks online. Such relationships could readily be identified as strong or weak ties depending on the standard criteria. Using Granovetter's measures, it is easy to recognize a strong tie because it was assumed there was frequent interaction.[2] However, this is one of the areas where applying Granovetter to SNSs can become more complex. In addition to people connecting with others with whom they have regular face-to-face communication (Wellman & Hampton, 1999), people also connect with individuals from their past with whom they had lost touch, as well as people they did not know and with whom they shared no common acquaintances. In this last situation, two parties may have shared a particular interest but a social tie began to form when one stranger took the initiative to open up a line of communication with another stranger or their joint interaction in the same space led to mutual acquaintanceship (e.g., blog threads).

Example 1: Ann and Beth had a strong tie 12 years ago when they were in college but fell out of touch. They renewed their acquaintance through an SNS and now communicate several times a week through personal messages as well as messages which are broadcast to the communicator's social network on that site. How can Granovetter's dimension of "amount of time" or "intimacy" be assessed? This is an example of a dormant tie which is defined by Levin, Walter and Munighan (2011) as, "a relationship between two individuals who have not communicated with each other for a long time . . . as the option of a future reconnection continues to exist" (p. 923). While Levin et al. use this to illustrate the robustness of an alumni network, computer mediated communication (CMCs) have made it much easier and quicker for these types of dyadic pairs (ones without colocated histories) to reactivate a social network tie and/or maintain weakened connections that can be reactivated.

Example 2: Six months ago, Carl contacted Donna because Donna's name came up when Carl did a search for other people in the SNS who shared his interest in hiking. They added each other to their SNS networks and communicate occasionally within the site, but have never communicated outside of the site, effectively activating a latent tie. Haythornthwaite (2002) defined a latent tie as "a tie for which a connection is available technically [specifically through technology] but that has not yet been activated by social interaction" (p. 389). She continues, "[a]n important characteristic of this type of tie is that it is not established by individuals. Instead it depends on structures established organizationally by management of an organization, system administrators, or community organizers" (p. 389). Put another way, these ties are possible because individuals jointly use the same information systems, which make it possible for individuals to directly communicate with each other. Through such systems, the ties remain latent until the individuals directly communicate or collaborate with each other. In Example 2, it is unclear if the SNS is the managing entity that establishes that latent tie. Online activities like this have become commonplace, and we assert that social media is particularly suited to facilitate more spontaneous tie formation.

We argue that before ties have the potential to be latent, individuals come to find SNSs through their interest-based searches. They spontaneously enter into the information platform, and the spontaneous discovery of an information sharing site sets the stage for latent ties to form. A *spontaneous tie*, then, reflects the motivation to engage in a particular SNS when people without a common acquaintance or formal association (e.g., employment) motivate the presence on the social media site. With the promulgation of online social networking, a spate of literature has examined weak ties and online relationships (e.g., Ellison, Vitak, Gray, & Lampe, 2014; Kavanaugh, Reese, Carroll, & Rosson, 2005; Kavanaugh, Carroll, Rosson, Zin, & Reese, 2006; Wellman, Quan-Haase, Witte, & Hampton, 2001) and how communication technologies impact social networks (cf. Hampton, Sessions, Her, & Rainie, 2009). With few exceptions, these studies, like many of the offline studies predating SNSs, use surveys to poll users about the nature of their relationships, despite the unique qualities of online relationships and the methodological challenges that accompany them (Ellison & boyd, 2013). Indeed, in SNS contexts, relationships are built up through text-based interaction, where time spent and intimacy manifest differently than as reported in surveys and polls. This opens the door to a broader discussion of the role that CMCs plays in the four dimensions of tie strength.

How text-based relationships that occur within the context of SNSs relate to the SoWT is yet to be challenged and was not a part of Granovetter's original conception. While strangers met prior to the inception of social networking sites (Haring, 2007) and used multiple modes to stay in touch, the interaction between strangers on a social networking site consists primarily of written text, a different form of communication than face-to-face (Walther, 2011; Walther & Parks, 2002). A 1993 New Yorker magazine cartoon carried the now often-repeated line, "On the Internet nobody knows you're a dog" (Steiner, 1993). This humorous reminder underlined that online-only relationships lack or limit visual and aural cues, although increased usage of web camera sites may change this (Walther, 1996). For those who only communicate through text, both interactants take a leap of faith that others represent themselves honestly (Caspi & Gorsky, 2006; Ellison, Heino, & Gibbs, 2006). These relationships may remain online and yet this type of new connection, whether in mundane or profound ways, inevitably impacts relational patterns in both on- and off-line spaces (Baym, 1999). In short, online interactions underscore Marvin's (1988) thesis, that tensions associated with the simultaneity of new and old media can fundamentally change social patterns. Yet current theoretical and methodological treatment falls short of addressing this uniquely twenty-first century intermingling of social patterns. We thus assert the need to combine weak tie measurement and theory with communication centered theory that concerns itself with text-based discursive practices.

This chapter has thus far reviewed the evolution of online social networking and the challenges of categorizing tie formation with the vocabulary of face-to-face social networks. We proposed spontaneous ties as a new tie formation category and, through the use of examples and the ways ties are formed and maintained online, argued that SoWT needs to be reconsidered for these online contexts. Given that text-based interaction is a dominant communicative form online, this chapter turns to scholarship that focuses on texts, namely, discourse analysis.

Text-Based Communication and Discourse Analysis

To work toward a better understanding of how SoWT theory applies social ties within SNSs and other types of virtual communities it might be helpful to chronologically deconstruct the tie. This can be done by looking at how communication is constructed from the highest level and working downwards until reaching the dyad. Discourse analysis can be used to identify how the messages that build a relationship are constructed. At its most basic level, Fairhurst and Putnam (2006) explain that discourse analysis is a critical examination of talk and text in social practices and deals strictly with the textual aspects of communication. The textual emphasis is what makes it an appropriate vantage point for examining online social ties because communication through CMCs is still primarily text or image based. Approaching this issue from a Discursive Analysis approach is logical as, "the study of language in use and interaction process is the focus of discourse analysts. . . . [a] language emphasis distinguishes the discursive" (Fairhurst & Putnam, 2006, p. 7).

Discourses involve message and meaning construction. Language is a critical factor because it plays a role in the development of a shared context and message construction. In turn, shared contexts and message construction are critical in building and maintaining online relationships. Because there is little or no colocation, textual exchanges between dyads are the primary tool to form (or reform) a social tie.[3] The organizing mechanism here is joint interest in the same object, evoking Heider's (1958) balance theory that predicts mutual (dis)liking when both parties jointly (dis)like some third object or person. For example, Haas, Irr, Jennings, and Wagner's (2011) online negative enabling support group (ONESG) theory proposes six communication principles which, together, explain the co-construction of online groups that promote negative behaviors. One core ONESG theory principle is reconstructing mediated weak tie support into strong tie support, which proposes that individuals use the Internet to seek out, and easily find, "like-minded" others who share similar values and beliefs. We assert that such a group can be said to provide a homophilous environment. These individuals are therefore predisposed to share a "like-minded psychological connection" when they first interact online; which in the case of pro-anorexics leads to negative health outcomes.

But how do the users recognize as much? We depart from Haas et al.'s (2011) assertion and instead argue that the initial tie to that site is not merely about speedily moving from conventional Granovetter-esque weak-to-strong tie strength. Instead, the experience more closely reflects a latent tie (Haythornthwaite, 2002) that, through recognizing shared symbols and tacit meaning, jumps spontaneously to the strong tie state. The (perceived) similarities between the group's goals and the individual's goals nurtures and facilitate these ties. Yet strong spontaneous ties are not about a leap of faith; they are about the shared language, information, symbols, and tacit knowledge recognizable on such sites.

In her discussion of rhetorical tropes used in negotiations, Putnam (2004) focused on the literary tropes of metonymy (the use of the name of one thing for that of another of which it is an attribute or with which it is associated, such as "wheels" to describe a car) and synecdoche (the use of a part of something to stand in for the whole (as *fifty sails* for *fifty ships*), the whole for a part (as *society* for *high society*), the species for the genus (as *cutthroat* for *assassin*), the genus for the species (as *a creature* for *a man*), or the name of the material for the thing made (as *boards* for *stage*) to examine "the way that discourse shapes and is shaped" (2004, p. 39). Both metonymy and synecdoche reflect manifestations of a shared context that is constructed through language as they may not make sense to others outside of the group, but are used to convey meaning within the group. Putnam gives the example of a joke that is told in a group multiple times to the point that simply mentioning a few words triggers laughter among the insiders. Hence it is language which contributes to the creation of a shared context. Cultural awareness is revealed in and created by texts. Through iterative communicative processes, users observe and communicate through shared symbols, drawing in interlocutors and reifying shared contexts (Ligorio & Pugliese, 2004).

Both Gruzd et al. (2011) in their analysis of Twitter and Fine and van den Scott (2011) in their article on wispy communities make the point that jargon, slang, and other verbal constructs are an integral part of what forms a community. Mapping onto Granovetter, metonymy and synecdoche may be a text-based assessment of the weak/strong tie spectrum. Coding online texts then involves identifying the presence of these discursive acts, and their recurring presence indicates strong ties between communicators. This discursive property aligns with the network research regarding stronger relationships being facilitated by a culture that supports deeper trust and shared knowledge (Gulati, 1995; Krackhardt, 1992; Yuan et al., 2010). Context is the common history, preferences, idiosyncrasies, and other essential elements that the group members share and through that, builds unit cohesion. Barge (2003) also discusses the importance of language to create a shared context. He noted in his study, *Imagine Chicago*, how the first step of bringing a sense of hope back to residents was dropping negative vocabulary of community deficits and problems and embracing the positive notions of community assets and capacity. This change was transformative and residents started building a vocabulary of hope, co-creating a context fertile for positive change and social influence. The strong tie mechanism begins the group: It is the motivation to join; as opposed to previous networking where strong ties set the stage for trust. The built-up trust, then, leads to motivation to share information and access to tacit knowledge.

Putnam's (2004) and Barge's (2003) positions are complementary to Fairhurst and Putnam's (2006) *being orientation* of organization as constructed through discourse, in which the organization is portrayed as an almost living entity that is shaped by the interactions that occur within it. In this description an analogy could be made to Granovetter's four measures of tie strength. If the tie is considered a dyadic component of the broader organization (website; blog) the four measures of tie strength are all the result of actions that occur within the dyad with aggregated dyadic exchange, then co-constructing the organization (network). Those actions can create, maintain, or weaken the tie between the individuals; the actions shape the dyadic organization from within. If the relationship in question is being conducted online, those actions will by necessity be primarily textual because it is words (or their absence) that are the sole way of conveying the constant changing of those four measures.

The being orientation is not the only lens through which to view discursively constructed organizations. Two other orientations include the *object orientation* and the *grounded in action orientation*. Fairhurst and Putnam (2006) maintain that the being orientation does not exist in a vacuum but, that,

the object, becoming, and grounded in action orientations interrelate and presuppose inherent relationships with each other. Because all three possess a certain veridicality, collective inattention to these orientations prevents organizational discourse analysts from addressing questions that could further the field's theoretical development.

(p. 6)

Though different schools of philosophy may take a slightly different view of the object orientation (Berger & Luckman, 1966; Fairhurst & Putnam, 2006; Smith & Turner, 1995; Tsoukas, 2000), these viewpoints converge around the idea that the organization is already a structured, stable entity that shapes the way language is used. Because the thrust of the object orientation is about the structure imposing change on the malleable flow of discourse, this orientation is often invoked by scholars who address issues of the possession and imposition of power within the organizational structure.

In comparison, Fairhurst and Putnam (2006) explained that the grounded in action orientation views a mutually constitutive relationship between action and structure. Instead of a directional relationship between language, discourse, and the organization, this orientation can be viewed as being perpetually irregularly cyclical. The organization is constantly being created and recreated by the language that flows together to form the discourse. Organizational events become infused with a tangibility and transformed into myth, ritual, and other components that coalesce to form the organizational culture. This culture imparts a sense of concreteness to the organization. Within the outwardly concrete organization, language continues to flow between its members, continually repeating the process of formation and re-formation.

The being orientation complements SoWT by saying that discourse creates the organization in which the discourse occurs; however, the other two orientations view the organization as a creative and modifying force on the discourse. Tie formation has a temporal beginning and introduction (or in the case of a renewed tie, a reintroduction). Yet in treating social networks as organizations, when viewed through the being in action and object orientations, it seems as though the time-shaped language discourses that occur within the tie does not yet exist. Presumably language and other symbols and actions that create discourse would occur between the two people after they meet each other. Even in the case of a latent tie, Haythornthwaite (2002) explains that it is not established by individuals, per se, but instead by those individuals coexisting within the organization in which the potential tie resides (p. 389). The language of introduction leads to discourse and the creation of symbols, stories, rituals, and actions between the two individuals. However, in the case of online communities, if an orientation is adopted where the organization exerts influence on language, the question arises about how the organization can exert an influence if no organization yet exists. We assert that the answer is to reframe the elements of discourse, and thus, the spontaneous tie is the language of the have-yet-to become an actual tie. Moreover, the internet is a space where spontaneous ties can evolve and iteratively build up communities within which latent ties can then exist. An organizing mechanism, then, is that these spontaneous ties involve the interlocutors' preconceived mutual liking and strong tie formation because of their shared interests. On the other hand, in conventional SOWTs assessment, time spent and emotional intensity get built up.

Online actions like joining an SNS take place within a context. The context is what each person within the network brings and joins with others to form what both the group (macro) and individual (micro) tie is. Multilevel interactions that feed and support each other both before and after a network tie is formed facilitate a sense of closeness between some people and not others. Online groups are about common interests; shared interests get expressed both explicitly (joining the group, expressing a shared belief) and implicitly (a similar vocabulary or sense of humor) as texts that constitute the language that creates the discourse. For example, antique collectors may go online and find three different blogs on antiques. What may influence which one they engage with depends on visible elements such as the types of antiques the blog features or mechanical features, like the user interface. Intangibles also come into play, such as language complexity used by commenters or apparent user experience. As a coding guide, Table 5.1 summarizes the discursive elements and the ways they range to indicate processes that build up ties from strong to weak which also then contribute to the broader organization for spontaneity and latent tie transformation. These elements, which attract a person to a particular group, are what may create a homophilous environment online and would thus be additional features for assessing tie strength.

While the concept of homophily is applied to individuals, we suggest that a *homophilous environment* is a setting where there are enough perceived points of commonality between an individual and a given group that the individual is more favorably disposed to becoming a member and the group is more favorably disposed to accepting that individual. The homophilous environment sets the stage for strong spontaneous ties. The person is more likely to affiliate with that group to fill some need. This fulfillment is a part of McMillan and Chavis' (1986) definition of a sense of community. Their four criteria for defining a sense of community include: (a) membership (a feeling of belonging, being within the group boundaries); (b) influence (a sense of interdependence usually involving defining and maintaining group conformity); (c) integration and the fulfillment of needs (reinforcing the reasons a person joined); and (d) shared emotional connection (a sense of a shared history). These criteria define the elements that can transform a group of individuals into a community. If each group member goes through the process of assessing the potential group for a homophilous environment, joins, and becomes part of creating that sense of community, then we assert that there is a greater chance that the spontaneous ties will transform into latent ties and the latent ties will become active ones. This conclusion is based on the homophilous environment that attracts group members to that group (Haythornthwaite, 2002; Heider, 1958) and underscores homophily as a predictor of tie strength (McPherson, Smith-Lovin, & Cook, 2001).

Proposition 1: Homophilous online environments will generate communities of strong ties.

The strong tie side of SoWTs (e.g., Carpenter, Esterling, & Lazer, 2003; Krackhardt, 1992) applied to the online context, then, would involve the routine

Table 5.1 Discursive Elements as Indicators of Tie Strength

Grounded in Action	Discursive Signal	Explanation	Building Tie Strength
Iterative processes over time build up and constitute stronger ties and closure	Metonymy	Suggest Stronger Ties—frequent use sufficient but not necessary The use of the name of one thing for that of another of which it is an attribute or with which it is associated e.g.: "wheels" to describe a car	Strong
	Synecdoche	The use of a part of something to stand in for the whole e.g., *fifty sails for fifty ships*	
		Middle Range—frequent use necessary but not sufficient	
	Whole for a part	*Society* for *high society*	
	Species for the genus	*Cutthroat* for *assassin*	
	Genus for the species	*A creature* for *a man*	
	Name of the material for the thing made	*Boards* for *stage*	
	Veridicality	Low range—need to assert suggests lower levels of trust A signal of truthiness of the statement, ranging from asserting strongly of the truth—"She did write the book"—to questioning the truth—"She says she wrote the book" or "She may have written a book"	Weak

presence of particular participants, as well as the presence of threads indicative of metonymy and synecdoche.

A person's actions in joining the group or online social network, however, do not take place within a vacuum; they take place within a context. That context is formed by what individuals bring to the group while it forms, which in turn reinforces that context (Fairhurst, 2004; Fairhurst & Putnam, 2006; Giddens, 1984). This circular process of a homophilous set of people (re)forming their virtual community creates an organization through the act of lamination, a key feature of the grounded in action orientation. As described by Fairhurst and Putnam (2006), lamination occurs when a layering or lamination of past practices onto present practices occurs as conversations unfold (p. 17). Through lamination, the structure of the organization is created. So even spontaneous ties have the ability to engage, shape, and create interactions that evolve into recognizable structures.

In online social networks and communities, that lamination is comprised of the group's text-based communication which includes the repetition of group history, reinforcement of group norms, and other actions that create that sense of community (McMillan & Chavis, 1986). The lamination consists of the macro-level ties that connect the individuals to the group, be it a work team, message board, or a person's on-line network. The context created by the continual lamination process functions as the superstructure in which the organization sits. The individuals who are a part of that organization add to the lamination and continually create context through their collective actions. The organization sits within that context, which is the homophilous environment that attracts potential members to the group (Haas et al. 2011). We assert that for new media spaces, spontaneous links are more likely but the structures, by Haythornthwaite's definition, are contexts of latent ties, too. New members join and become part of the laminative process. Then, within the organization are the members and opportunities for building spontaneous and latent ties into observable network connections. Microlevel interactions which create and maintain social ties are the way in which dyads shape the group by creating context. Dyadic connections reinforce the super structure in which the organization sits and ultimately shape the organization, itself. Taking this analogy back into network terms, the layering of discussion reveals open or closed membership boundaries.

Proposition 2: Through texts reflective of tolerance for various opinions on a topic, an open network structure that welcomes new membership via spontaneous and latent ties (re)emerges.

Proposition 3: SNS-driven weak ties are deeply rooted in shared cultures resulting in outcomes akin to conventional strong ties.

Thus far this essay adapts SoWTs to consider community level contexts as organizing mechanisms of weak tie formation and emergence. The next section turns to the interaction-level, reflective of Granovetter's original conception.

As an independent variable, weak ties have been associated with unique access, innovation, and opportunities.

Strength of Weak Ties as Discursive Practice

From a social network point of view with a particular interest in understanding the implications of SoWTs, the ubiquity and pervasiveness of ICTs has changed the nature of social networks. SoWT considers strong ties and weak ties which serve different but necessary functions. The strong ties provide benefits such as emotional support and companionship (Wellman & Wortley, 1990) and the weak ties serve as conduits for innovations and new information between discrete social networks (Burt, 1992; Granovetter, 1973, 1982). Today, venues such as blogs and social networking sites allow people to build up networks through discursive practices and maintain contact through the mediated environments they co-construct. ICTs enable the expansion of a person's social network in two ways: they allow maintenance of otherwise dormant ties and they are a place for people to form spontaneous ties, transform latent ones, and are suited for those not physically co-located. But returning fully to the original weak ties thesis, so what? Do these online networks afford the same or similar opportunities as offline networks? Does the strength of weak ties thesis extend to the weak and strong tie relationships as measured through discourse analyses rather than the more frequently used self-report surveys?

Among a group of regular message board commenters, people may ask for help with a resume, announce good news or share information—activities that contribute to the shared context of that SNS. The text that people type on the screen is the primary source that creates shared context among the members, building a meaning-driven component into the network (Putnam & Cooren, 2004). Although text based, these interactions are different from semantic networks. Semantic networks have been used as a way to represent the structure of meaning (Carley & Kaufer, 1993; Doerfel & Barnett, 1999) or used to predict the convergence of meaning on social structures (Doerfel, 1998, 1999). In SNSs, the text based exchange is simultaneously meaningful relationally and the exchanges denote person-to-person linkage in the broader context. That broader context is more akin to a two-mode affiliation network (Borgatti & Everett, 1997; Davis, Gardner, & Gardner, 1941). Two members do not necessarily communicate directly with each other but they attend the same events and are thus socially engaged in similar ways. On the other hand, as members begin to actively engage in the thread, one-mode exchange networks form among those contributors. These threads, then, can offshoot to other networks. For example, in terms of blogs, while the range of topics discussed might be constrained by the blog topic, many message boards support off-topic discussion with designated secondary threads. Instead of two groups with occasional movement between the two camps (strong and weak ties), the traditional ties are joined by spontaneous, latent, and dormant ties, all of which are contingent upon technology.

SNSs hold structure that involve connection (Barabási, 2003) and discursive meaning. With discourse analysis, a critical assessment of the tone and content of threads can help reveal weak ties, marked by generally accepted norms and social scripts that guide relatively uncertain relationships (Berger & Calabrese, 1975), to relatively strong ties, marked by disclosure and references within conversation that point to richer histories and mutual knowledge, as in literary tropes of metonymy and synecdoche (Procter, 2004; Putnam, 2004; Weick, 1979, 1995; Yates & Orlikowski, 1992). Through iterative exchanges, the macro structures evolve and become recognizable as community or as organizing that amplifies online tie formation opportunities.

Granovetter's (1973) original thesis was that weak ties afforded opportunity. Since his seminal paper, the extant social network scholarship has grappled with strong-versus-weak tie advantages regarding social influence and concerns such as information flows, access, innovation, trust, and cohesion. With the formation of relationships through SNSs, we assert that weak and strong ties need to be evaluated differently and in doing so, outcomes associated with strength of weak ties theory need to be re-examined. Do online weak ties provide access to information and action, the way weak ties helped get MBA students a job (Granovetter, 1973); supported recovering organizations after disaster (Doerfel, Chewning, & Lai, 2013); or the way strong ties thwarted a union takeover (Krackhardt, 1992); or how CEOs friendships increased chances of joint ventures (Gulati & Westphal, 1999)? Indeed, online ties, even though pairs of people might not know each other, are not necessarily diverse. SNSs that bring together people with a common hobby or interest facilitate homogeneity around a shared interest; diversity is not easy to assess. Thus, in online groups, even though the ties are weak in the conventional, Granovetter-esque sense, do they afford the same benefits of access to broader networks of opportunities?

This evokes questions commonly asked in collective action theory, which consider how actors mobilize people through their (weak tie) networks to act on behalf of some public good or outcome (Castells, 1996; Gerlach, 2001; Oliver, 1993). Gladwell's (2000) *The Tipping Point*, for example, emphasizes the power of Paul Revere's weak tie network to inspire action. Likewise, communication scholars have also shown that collective action is fundamentally a communicative one (Bennett, 2003; Bimber, Flanagin, & Stohl, 2005, 2012; Flanagin, Stohl, & Bimber, 2006) where mobilizing people to coordinate and act is paramount to success. Common to Paul Revere and recent arguments about collective action is the advantage of the strength of weak ties to span networks of networks.

Yet the ability for one person to mobilize her network is limited by both her persuasive acumen and by her ability to maintain enough ties to make a differ-ence. Dunbar (1992, 1995) estimated that, based on the size of the human cortex, our social networks top off at around 150 others. There are times, however, like in attempting to mobilize for some collective action, when exceeding this 150 cap in one's network could be instrumental. Specifically, early work on public goods theory (Marwell & Ames, 1981; Olson, 1965) considered free riders, or the problem of larger group sizes undermining voluntary participation, along with thinking about how a critical mass of contributors could be built up to effect change or create a tragedy of the commons, whereby individual self-interest aggregates to disadvantages for the whole (Hardin, 1968). Online social media are a place where like-minded people find each other and through shared passions can be far more influential on collective actions.

Extending SoWT, we thus suggest an area to study would be to consider if latent, dormant, and spontaneous ties are Dunbar's number work-arounds. Dunbar used Christmas card lists to measure people's networks. McCarty, Killworth, Bernard, Johnsen, and Shelley (2001) used the scale up method to examine how many people someone knows within certain population subgroups (accountants, people named Joan, etc.). If Dunbar's thesis that 150 people is the upper limit of what humans can cognitively handle in social networks, do spontaneous ties serve as a reservoir for weak tie benefits?

> **Proposition 4**: SNSs become organizing spaces to support strong spontane-ous tie formation around single collective action issues.

This last proposition points to future research questions such as challenging whether SNSs facilitate storage of more strong spontaneous ties than capacities limited by conventional social networks; whether online weak tie networks facilitate easier access to non-redundant information, technical support, and advice; and in what ways do online strong tie networks co-construct an online cohesive network which then facilitate information sharing and access to tacit knowledge.

Conclusion

This chapter argues for updated theorizing about social networks in light of online social networking sites (SNSs) where text-based communication is at the center. SNSs provide a context for spontaneity and relationship building that no longer necessitates a conventional sense of mutual knowledge between people. In this way, relationships can be constructed and enacted solely through text-based interaction. And this text-based interaction and the emergent structuring of relationships, along with social outcomes associated with tie strength in a social network, do not align with the conventions of the original SoWT. This chapter thus introduces discourse analysis to grapple with the quality of online ties and offers propositions to advance SoWT to online contexts. We thus propose, too, that digitizing SoWTs necessitates the new dimension of tie strength, *strong spontaneous ties,* reflective of shared interest and familiarly with a topic, with intensity derived from discourse analysis. We treat getting to know others in these shared spaces, where *homophilous environments* are perpetuated, as organizing processes that shape, and are shaped by, the very contexts within which the interaction takes place. The idea that groups of people are tied together through interaction resonates with classic one-mode and two-mode social networks, yet brings meaning to the heart of understanding tie formation. Through discursive practices and through exchanges in the network, ties get created and, relatedly, tie strength can be seen in the texts shared by members of the network.

Notes

1 Note that the term "written correspondence" is being used instead of "writing a letter" because that term is more comprehensive and includes everything from business and personal letters to notes posted on a refrigerator.
2 Granovetter defined the frequency of contact categories in this manner as "often = at least twice a week; occasionally = more than once a year but less than twice a week; rarely equals once a year or less" (p. 1371).
3 Much of the literature on Discourse Analysis deals with communication within an organization but is more centered on processes of organizing as opposed to a container view of a place. For the purposes of this chapter a social tie is a relationship that engages in organizing and structuring through iterative communication. We thus view the process of organizing as salient and useful to understanding these online relationships as organizing processes, as well.

References

Barabási, A-L. (2003). *Linked: How everything is connected to everything else and what it means for business, science, and everyday life.* New York: Penguin.

Barge, J. K. (2003). Hope, communication, and community building. *Southern Communication Journal, 69*(1), 63–81. doi: 10.1080/10417940309373279

Baym, N. K. (1999). *Tune in, log on: Soaps, fandom, and online community* (Vol. 3). Thousand Oaks, CA: Sage.

Baym, N. K. (2010). *Personal connections in the digital age* (1st edn). Malden, MA: Polity Press.

Bennett, W. L. (2003). Communicating global activism: Strengths and vulnerabilities of networked politics. *Information, Communication, & Society, 6*(2), 143–168. doi: 10.1080/1369118032000093860

Berger, C. R., & Calabrese, R. J. (1975). Some explorations in initial interaction and beyond: Toward a developmental theory of interpersonal communication. *Human Communication Research, 1*(2), 99–112.

Berger, P., & Luckman, T. (1966). *The social construction of reality.* New York: Doubleday/ Anchor.

Bimber, B., Flanagin, A. J., & Stohl, C. (2005). Reconceptualizing collective action in the contemporary media environment. *Communication Theory, 15*, 365–388. doi: 10.1093/ct/15.4.365

Bimber, B., Flanagin, A., & Stohl, C. (2012). *Collective action in organizations: Interaction and engagement in an era of technological change.* Cambridge, UK: Cambridge University Press.

Borgatti, S. P., & Cross, R. (2003). A relational view of information seeking and learning in social networks. *Management Science, 49*(4), 432–445. doi: http://dx.doi.org/10.1287/mnsc.49.4.432.14428

Borgatti, S. P., & Everett, M. G. (1997). Network analysis of two-mode data. *Social Networks, 19*, 243–269. doi:10.1016/S0378-8733(96)00301-2 boyd, d. m., & Ellison, N. B. (2008). Social network sites: Definition, history, and scholarship. *Journal of Computer-Mediated Communication, 13*(1), 210–230. doi: 10.1111/j.1083-6101.2007.00393.x

Burt, R. S. (1992). *Structural holes: The social structure of competition.* Cambridge, MA: Harvard University Press.

Carley, K. M., & Kaufer, D. S. (1993). Semantic connectivity: An approach for analyzing symbols in semantic networks. *Communication Theory, 3,* 183–213. doi: 10.1111/j.1468-2885.1993.tb00070.x

Carpenter, D., Esterling, K., & Lazer, D. (2003). The strength of strong ties: A model of contact-making in policy networks with evidence from U.S. health politics. *Rationality and Society, 15*(4), 411–440. doi: 10.1177/1043463103154001

Caspi, A., & Gorsky, P. (2006). Online deception: Prevalence, motivation, and emotion. *CyberPsychology & Behavior, 9*(1), 54–59. doi:10.1089/cpb.2006.9.54

Castells, M. (1996). *The rise of the network society.* Oxford: Blackwell.

Constant, D., Sproull, L., & Kiesler, S. (1996). The kindness of strangers: The usefulness of electronic weak ties for technical advice. *Organization Science, 7*(2), 119–135. doi: 1047-7039/96/0702/0119

Contractor, N. S., & Grant, S. (1996). The emergence of shared interpretations in organizations: A self-organizing systems perspective. In J. Watt & A. VanLear (Eds.), *Cycles and dynamic processes in communication processes* (pp. 216–230). Newbury Park, CA: Sage.

CTIA, The Wireless Association (2011). Wireless and the environment: A review of opportunities and challenges. Retrieved from: www.bsr.org/reports/BSR_CTIA_Wireless_and_the_Environment.pdf

Danowski, J. A., & Barnett, G. A. (1982). A network analysis of the International communication Association. *Human Communication Research, 19*(2), 264–285. doi: 10.1111/j.1468-2958.1992.tb00302.x

Davis, A., Gardner, B. B., & Gardner, M. R. (1941). *Deep south.* Chicago: University of Chicago Press.

Doerfel, M. L. (1998). What constitutes semantic network analysis? A comparison of research and methodologies. *Connections, 21*(2), 16–26. Retrieved from: www.insna.org/PDF/Connections/v21/1998_I-2.pdf

Doerfel, M. L. (1999). Inter organizational networks: The convergence of cooperative competitors. *Communication Research Reports, 16,* 175–184. doi: 10.1080/08824099909388715

Doerfel, M. L., & Barnett, G. A. (1999). A semantic network analysis of the International Communication Association. *Human Communication Research, 25*(4), 589–603. doi: 10.1111/j.1468-2958.1999.tb00463.x

Doerfel, M. L., Chewning, L. V., & Lai, C-H. (2013, online first). The evolution of networks and the resilience of interorganizational relationships after disaster. *Communication Monographs, 80*(4), 533–559. doi: 10.1080/03637751.2013.828157.

Dunbar, R. I. M. (1992). Neocortex size as a constraint on group size in primates. *Journal of Human Evolution, 20,* 469–493. doi: 10.1016/0047-2484(92)90081-J

Dunbar, R. I. M. (1995). Neocortex size and group size in primates: A test of the hypothesis. *Journal of Human Evolution, 28,* 287–296. doi: 10.1006/jhev.1995.1021

Ellison, N. B. & boyd, d. (2013). Sociality through social network sites. In Dutton, W. H. (Ed.), *The Oxford Handbook of Internet Studies* (pp. 151–172). Oxford: Oxford University Press.

Ellison, N. B., Heino, R., & Gibbs, J. (2006). Managing impressions online: Self-presentation processes in the online dating environment. *Journal of Computer-Mediated Communication, 11*(2), 415–441. doi:10.1111/j.1083-6101.2006.00020.x

Ellison, N. B., Vitak, J., Gray, R., & Lampe, C. (2014). Cultivating social resources on social network sites: Facebook relationship maintenance behaviors and their role in social capital processes. *Journal of Computer-Mediated Communication, 19*(4), 855–870. doi: 10.1111/jcc4.12078

Fairhurst, G. T. (2004). Textuality and agency in interaction analysis. *Organization, 11*(3), 335–353. doi: 10.1177/1350508404041996

Fairhurst, G., & Putnam, L. (2006). Organizations as discursive constructions. *Communication Theory, 14,* (1), 5–26. doi: 10.1111/j.1468-2885.2004.tb00301.x

Fine, G. A., & van den Scott, L. J. (2011). Wispy communities, transient gatherings and imagined micro-communities. *American Behavioral Scientist, 55*(10), 1319–1335. doi: 10.1177/0002764211409379

Flanagin, A. J., Stohl, C., & Bimber, B. (2006). Modeling the structure of collective action. *Communication Monographs, 73,* 29–54. doi: 10.1080/03637750600 557099

Gerlach, L. P. (2001). The structure of social movements: Environmental activism and its opponents. In J. Arquilla, & D. Ronfeldt (Eds.), *Networks and netwars: The future of terror, crime, and militancy* (pp. 289–309). Santa Monica: Rand.

Giddens, A. (1984). *The constitution of society.* Berkeley, CA: University of California Press.

Gladwell, M. (2000). *The tipping point.* New York: Little, Brown and Company.

Granovetter, M. S. (1973). The strength of weak ties. *The American Journal of Sociology, 78* (6), 1360–1380. Retrieved from: www.jstor.org/stable/2776392

Granovetter, M. S. (1982). The strength of weak ties: A network theory revisited. *Sociological Theory,* 1, 201–233. DOI: 10.2307/202051

Gruzd, A., Wellman, B., & Takhteyev, Y. (2011). Imagining Twitter as an imagined community. *American Behavioral Scientist, 55*(10), 1294–1318. doi: 10.1177/0002764211409378

Gulati, R. (1995). Familiarity breeds trust? The implications of repeated ties on contractual choice alliances. *Academy of Management Journal, 38,* 85–112. doi: 10.2307/256729

Gulati, R., & Westphal, J. D. (1999). Cooperative or controlling? The effects of CEO-board relations and the content of interlocks on the formation of joint ventures. *Administrative Science Quarterly, 44*(3), 473–506. doi: 10.2307/2666959

Guo, R. M. (2008). Stranger danger and the online social network. *Berkeley Technology Law Journal, 23*(1), 617–644. Retrieved from: http://scholarship.law.berkeley.edu/btlj/vol23/iss1/26

Haas, S. M., Irr, M. E., Jennings, N., & Wagner, L. (2011). Communicating thin: A grounded model of Online Negative Enabling Support Groups (ONESGs) in the pro-anorexia movement. *New Media & Society, 13,* 40–57. doi: 10.1177/1461444810363910.

Hampton, K. N., Sessions, L. F., Her, E. J., & Rainie, L. (2009). How the internet and mobile phones impact Americans' social networks. Pew Research Internet Project, retrieved October 10, 2014, from: www.pewinternet.org/files/old-media/Files/Reports/2009/PIP_Tech_and_Social_Isolation.pdf

Hansen, M. T. (1999). The search-transfer problem: The role of weak ties in sharing knowledge across organization subunits. *Administrative Science Quarterly, 44,* 82–111. doi: 10.2307/2667032

Hardey, M. (2008). The formation of social rules for digital interactions. *Information, Communication & Society, 11*(8), 1111–1131. doi: 10.1080/13691180802109048

Hardin, G. (1968). The tragedy of the commons. *Science, 162*(3859), 1243–1248. doi: 10.1126/science.162.3859.1243

Haring, K. (2007). *Ham radio's technical culture.* Cambridge, MA: MIT Press.

Haythornthwaite, C. (2002). Strong, weak, and latent ties and the impact of new media. *Information Society, 18*(5), 385–401. doi: 10.1080/01972240290108195

Heider, F. (1958). *The psychology of interpersonal relations.* New York: Wiley.

Howard, P. N. (2002). Network ethnography and the hypermedia organization: New media, new organizations, new methods. *New Media & Society, 4,* 550–574. doi: 10.1177/146144402321466813

Kavanaugh, A. L., Reese, D. D., Carroll, J. M., & Rosson, M. B. (2005). Weak ties in networked communities. *The Information Society, 21,* 119–131. doi: 10.1080/01972240590925320

Kavanaugh, A. L., Carroll, J. M., Rosson, M. B., Zin, T. T., & Reese, D. D. (2006). Community networks: Where offline communities meet online. *Journal of Computer-Mediated Communication, 10*(4), article 3. doi: 10.1111/j.1083-6101.2005.tb00266.x

Krackhardt, D. (1992). The strength of strong ties: The importance of philos. In N. Nohria & R. Eccles (Eds.), *Networks and organizations: Structure, form, and action* (pp. 216–239). Boston, MA: Harvard Business School Press.

Levin, D. Z., & Cross, R. (2004). The strength of weak ties you can trust: The mediating role of trust in effective knowledge transfer. *Management Science, 50*(11), 1477–1490. doi: 10.1287/mnsc.1030.0136

Levin, D. Z., Walter, J., & Murnighan, J. K. (July/August 2011). Dormant ties: The value of reconnecting. *Organization Science, 22*(4), 923–939. doi: 10.1287/orsc.1100.0576

Ligorio, M. B., & Pugliese, A. C. (2004). Self-positioning in a text-based virtual environment. *Identity, 4*(4), 337–353. doi: 10.1207/s1532706xid0404_3

Marin, A., & Hampton, K. (2007). Simplifying the personal network name generator: Alternatives to traditional multiple and single name generators. *Field Methods, 19*(2), 163–193. doi: 10.1177/1525822X06298588

Marsden, P. V., & Campbell, K. E. (1984). Measuring tie strength. *Social Forces, 63*(2), 482–501. doi: 10.2307/2579058

Marvin, C. (1988). *When old technologies were new.* New York: Oxford University Press.

Marwell, G., & Ames, R. E. (1981). Economists free ride, does anyone else? Experiments on the provision of public goods, IV. *Journal of Public Economics, 15(3),* 295–310. doi: 10.1016/0047-2727(81)90013-X

McCarty, C., Killworth, P. D., Bernard, H. R., Johnsen, E. C., & Shelley, G. A. (2001). Comparing two methods for estimating network size. *Human Organization, 60 (1),* 28–39. doi: http://dx.doi.org/10.17730/humo.60.1.efx5t9gjtgmga73y

McMillan, D. W., & Chavis, D. M. (1986, January). Sense of community: A definition and theory. *Journal of Community Psychology, 14,* 6–23. doi: 10.1002/1520-6629(198601)14:1<6::AID-JCOP2290140103>3.0.CO;2-I

McPherson, M., Smith-Lovin, L., & Cook, J. M. (2001). Birds of a feather: Homophily in social networks. *Annual Review of Sociology, 27,* 415–444. doi: 0360-0572/01/0811-0415

Monge, P., Heiss, B. M., & Margolin, D. B. (2008). Communication network evolution in organizational communities. *Communication Theory, 18,* 449–477. doi: 10.1111/j.1468-2885.2008.00330.x

Monge, P. R., & Contractor, N. S. (2003). *Theories of communication networks*. New York: Oxford University Press.

Morrison, A. (2011). "Suffused by feeling and affect": The intimate public of personal mommy blogging. *Biography* 34(1), 37–55. University of Hawai'i Press. Retrieved April 29, 2013, from: https://muse.jhu.edu/login?auth=0&type=summary&url=/journals/biography/v034/34.1.morrison.html

Oliver, P. E. (1993). Formal models of collective action. *Annual Review of Sociology, 19*, 271–300. Retrieved from: www.jstor.org/stable/2083389

Olson, M. (1965). The logic of collective action. Cambridge, MA: Harvard University Press.

Procter, D. E. (2004). Building community through communication: The case for civil communion. *Journal of the Community Development Society, 35*(2), 53–72. doi: 10.1080/15575330409490132

Putnam, L. L. (2004). Dialectical tensions and rhetorical tropes in negotiations. *Organization Studies (01708406), 25*(1), 35–53. doi: 10.1177/01708413604038179

Putnam, L. L. (2005). Discourse analysis: Mucking around with negotiation data. *International Negotiation, 10*(1), 17–32. doi: 10.1163/1571806054741083

Putnam, L. L. (2010). Communication as changing the negotiation game. *Journal of Applied Communication Research, 38*(4), 325–335. doi: 10.1080/00909882.2010.513999

Putnam, L. L., & Cooren, F. (2004). Alternative perspectives on the role of text and agency in constituting organizations. *Organization, 11,* 323–333. doi: 10.1177/1350508404041995.

Rainie, L., Fox, S., & Maeve, D. (2014). *The Web at 25 in the U.S.* Pew Research Center, Washington, DC. Retrieved from: www.pewinternet.org/2014/02/27/the-web-at-25-in-the-u-s/

Rice, R. E., & Danowski, J. (1993). Is it really just like a fancy answering machine? Comparing semantic networks of different types of voice mail users. *Journal of Business Communication, 30*(4), 369–397. doi: 10.1177/002194369303000401

Smith, R. C., & Turner, P. K. 1995. A social constructionist reconfiguration of metaphor analysis: An application of "SCMA" to organizational socialization theorizing. *Communication Monographs*, 62: 152–181. doi: 10.1080/03637759509376354

Stanley, T. L. (2004, March). Jonathan Abrams. *Advertising Age, 75*, S-8. Retrieved from: http://adage.com/article/special-report-entertainment-marketers-of-the-year/jonathan-abrams/97833/

Steiner, P. (1993, July 5). Cartoon: On the internet, nobody knows you're dog. *The New Yorker, 69*, 61.

Tsoukas, H. (2000). False dilemmas in organization theory: Realism or social constructivism. *Organization, 7*(3), 531–535.

Walther, J. B. (1996). Computer-mediated communication: Impersonal, interpersonal, and hyperpersonal interaction. *Communication Research, 23*(1), 3–43. doi: 10.1177/009365096023001001

Walther, J. B. (2011). Theories of computer-mediated communication and interpersonal relations. In M. L. Knapp & J. A. Daly (Eds.), *The handbook of interpersonal communication* (4th edn, pp. 443–479). Thousand Oaks, CA: Sage. Retrieved from: www.sagepub.com/upm-data/42241_14.pdf

Walther, J. B., & Parks, M. R. (2002). Cues filtered out, cues filtered in: Computer-mediated communication and relationships. In M. L. Knapp & J. A. Daly (Eds.), *Handbook of interpersonal communication* (3rd edn, 529–563). Thousand Oaks, CA: Sage.

Wang, H., & Wellman, B. (2010). Social connectivity in America: Changes in adult friendship network size from 2002 to 2007. *American Behavioral Scientist, 53*(8), 1148–1169. doi: 10.1177/0002764209356247

Weick, K. E. (1979). *The social psychology of organizing.* New York: Random House.

Weick, K. E. (1995). *Sensemaking in organizations.* Thousand Oaks, CA: Sage.

Wellman, B., & Hampton, K. (1999). Living networked on and offline. *Contemporary Sociology, 28*(6), 648–654. Retrieved from: www.jstor.org/stable/2655535

Wellman, B., & Wortley, S. (1990). Different strokes from different folks: Community ties and social support. *American Journal of Sociology, 96*(3), 558–588. Retrieved from: www.jstor.org/stable/2781064

Wellman, B., Quan-Haase, A., Witte, J., & Hampton, K. (2001). Does the Internet increase, decrease, or supplement social capital? Social networks, participation, and community commitment. *American Behavioral Scientist, 45*(3), 436–455. doi: 10.1177/00027640121957286

Yates, J., & Orlikowski, W. J. (1992). Genres of organizational communication: A structurational approach to studying communication and media. *Academy of Management Review, 17,* 299–326. doi:10.5465/AMR.1992.4279545

Yuan, Y. C., Fulk, J., Monge, P. R., & Contractor, N. S. (2010). Expertise directory development, shared task-interdependence, and strength of communication network ties as multilevel predictors of expertise exchange in transactive memory groups. *Communication Research, 37*(1), 20–47. doi: 10.1177/0093650209351469

CHAPTER CONTENTS

6 Strategically Mean

Extending the Study of Relational Aggression in Communication

Carrie Anne Platt

North Dakota State University

Amber N. W. Raile

Montana State University

Ann Burnett

North Dakota State University

In this chapter we draw connections between current research on relational aggression in psychology, education, new media studies, and communication to make a case for extending the study of relational aggression by communication scholars. We also challenge the prevailing conceptualization of relational aggression as a pathological trait specific to young girls, arguing that it should be studied as a situation-specific communication strategy, employed by individuals of all ages for particular purposes and toward specific ends, using multiple modes of communication. We conclude with four recommendations for future research on relational aggression in the field of communication.

A preschooler tells another child that he is not allowed to play with their group in the sandbox. An elementary school child excludes someone from her birthday party. A teenager ignores the new student at school and then talks about her behind her back. A few college students create a Facebook group called, "Scott Sucks." Since the late 1990s, parents, teachers, and school administrators have become increasingly aware of the prevalence and severity of what scholars refer to as "relational aggression" in peer groups (Crick & Grotpeter, 1995; Simmons, 2002; Wiseman, 2002). This type of behavior can have fatal consequences; the past few years have seen multiple cases of teenagers committing suicide in response to relational aggression (see Bennett, 2010; Dahl, 2013; Dillon, 2010; Papadopoulos, 2014; Wolfe, 2014), and the subsequent proposal of state laws designed to address bullying (Hinduja & Patchin, 2014). The visibility of these cases in the media has increased public and scholarly interest in finding strategies to address and prevent relational aggression among young people.

This chapter is a call for communication researchers to expand the study of relational aggression in our field. In order to provide guidance for future inquiry, we start by defining and differentiating relational aggression from related concepts. After establishing this conceptual map, we synthesize and evaluate key studies of relational aggression in psychology and education. We then explore the state of research on this topic in the field of communication, considering how previous scholarship on verbal aggression, indirect aggression, and workplace bullying might inform future studies. We argue that, contrary to previous conceptualizations of relational aggression as an innate, pathological trait, it is more productive to view instances of such behavior as a situation-specific communication strategy, employed by individuals of all ages for particular purposes and toward specific ends, using multiple modes of communication. After establishing the current state of research across disciplines, we construct a blueprint for a theoretically grounded and communication specific approach to this phenomenon. We conclude by offering four recommendations for researchers based on our evaluation of previous research, to illustrate how communication scholars can most effectively extend the study of relational aggression in our field.

What Is Relational Aggression?

Scholars working in different fields have used a number of terms for this phenomenon, including "bullying" (Vaillancourt, Hymel, & McDougall, 2003), "indirect aggression" (Archer & Coyne, 2005; Coyne, Archer, & Eslea, 2006), "relational aggression" (Crick, 1997; Crick & Bigbee, 1998; Crick, Bigbee, & Howes, 1996; Crick & Grotpeter, 1995; Crick & Nelson, 2002; Crick, Ostrov, & Werner, 2006; Grotpeter & Crick, 1996; Werner & Crick, 1999), "social aggression" (Galen & Underwood, 1997), and "verbal aggression" (Willer & Cupach, 2011). "Cyberbullying" is also used when researchers focus on electronic means of communication. Some scholars have suggested that these various labels denote similar behavior (see Archer & Coyne, 2005), but they also seek to highlight distinctions (see Coyne et al., 2006). We argue that, in order to engage in more systematic investigations of relational aggression, it is important for communication scholars to work from a consistent definition of the term and to understand how relational aggression relates to other forms of aggression. In this section we articulate both connections and distinctions in order to create a conceptual map for future research.

Bullying involves various subtypes of aggression (Vaillancourt et al., 2003; Willer & Cupach, 2011) and can be physical, verbal, or relational (Johnson et al., 2013). Bullying has traditionally been defined by the use of verbal and physical aggression to intimidate others and is distinguished by the repetition of behavior and an imbalance of power between bully and target (Olweus, 1978). Relational aggression differs from physical and verbal bullying in both goal and methods. Although it can be viewed as a form of intimidation, the goal is more specific. Crick and Nelson (2002), pioneering scholars in the study of relational aggression, define the behavior as that in which "damage to relationships (or threat of damage) serves as the means of harm" (p. 599). Relational aggression may be focused on the relationship between the aggressor and the target (such as terminating a friendship) or directed toward the target's relationships with others in his or her peer group (Zimmer-Gembeck, Geiger, & Crick, 2005). In contrast to bullying, relational aggression does not typically involve physical aggression, may be singular in its occurrence, and can occur between those of relatively equal social status (boyd, 2014).

Social aggression has been defined as "actions directed at damaging another's selfesteem, social status or both" (Galen & Underwood, 1997, p. 589) and is the closest conceptual cousin to relational aggression, though the former term is used less frequently in the literature. A primary distinction between the two concepts is the inclusion of aggressive nonverbal behaviors in conceptualizations of social aggression (Archer & Coyne, 2005). We favor the term "relational aggression" for its definitional focus and greater possibilities for connecting research across fields, but encourage scholars to include aggressive nonverbal behaviors in their research.

Although distinct from the concepts discussed above, the remaining terms—indirect aggression, verbal aggression, and cyberbullying—can be understood as *methods* employed to achieve the *goals* of bullying and relational aggression. Indirect aggression has been defined as "attacking a target not directly, but circuitously, thereby remaining unidentified" (Björkqvist, Österman, & Lagerspetz, 1994, p. 28). It can take place anonymously, through intermediaries, or in a way that makes it difficult to ascribe malicious intent. Enlisting one or more confederates to threaten a target's social relationships is one example of how indirect aggression is used to enact relational aggression (Archer & Coyne, 2005; Crick, Casas, & Nelson, 2002; Miller-Ott & Kelly, 2013a). Verbal aggression, by contrast, consists of "insults, put-downs, ridicule, name-calling, malicious teasing, and explicit attacks on one's appearance, competence, or affiliations" (Willer & Cupach, 2011, p. 299). Explicit threats of damage to an important relationship illustrate how verbal aggression can also serve as a method of relational aggression.

The term "cyberbullying," defined as "willful and repeated harm inflicted through the medium of electronic text" (Patchin & Hinduja, 2006, p. 152), focuses on the medium rather than the message and can involve both indirect and verbal aggression. Young people's increasing access to mobile phones and social media has made it easier for them to engage in aggression through electronic channels (Agatston, Kowalski, & Limber, 2007; Beale & Hall, 2007; Kowalski, Limber, & Agatston, 2012; Raskaukas & Stoltz, 2007) and more likely to have such aggression go undetected by parents and other authority figures (Juvonen & Gross, 2008). Some research indicates that cyberbullying occurs less frequently than face-to-face aggression (Dehue, Bolman, & Völlink, 2008; Li, 2006; Wang, Iannotti, & Nansel, 2009), though more recent research indicates that cyberbullying reports have nearly doubled in the past ten years (Patchin & Hinduja, 2015).

The terms "indirect aggression" and "social aggression" are frequently used by communication researchers studying relationally aggressive behavior (see Miller-Ott & Kelly, 2013a; Willer & Cupach, 2008), but we recommend employing the broader term "relational aggression," as it encourages scholars to account for both the indirect and the direct verbal aggression that is used to damage relationships. The most common examples of relational aggression identified in previous literature—malicious gossip, sharing secrets told in confidence, intentionally spreading rumors, excluding a particular individual from a social outing, ostracizing someone from a peer group, or threatening to do any of the above unless the target complies with the aggressor (Crick & Bigbee, 1998; Crick & Gropeter, 1995; Ostrov & Crick, 2007)—support a theoretical conceptualization that includes direct and indirect, as well as verbal and nonverbal, forms of aggression. Communication scholars should account for as many of these forms as possible in order to study relational aggression in a systematic way.

Relational Aggression Research outside the Field of Communication

The majority of research on relational aggression has been undertaken in developmental psychology, social psychology, and education. This research has helped us to understand the frequency at which relational aggression occurs (see Coyne et al., 2006), sex differences in its use (see Card, Stucky, Sawalani, & Little, 2008; Zimmer-Gembeck et al., 2005), predictors of relationally aggressive behavior (see Crick et al., 1996; Crick & Grotpeter, 1995; Cullerton-Sen & Crick, 2005; Cullerton-Sen et al., 2008), effects of relational aggression on the target (see Crick & Bigbee, 1998), and perceptions of perpetrators (see Basow, Cahil, Phelan, Longshore, McGillicuddy-DeLisi, 2007). When relational aggression is discussed in the popular press, it is frequently in connection with youth suicides, or treated as a problem exclusive to young women. Thus, it is not surprising that much of the previous research has focused on the negative effects of relational aggression and sex differences in relationally aggressive behaviors.

Research on the psychological and social effects of relational aggression points to negative repercussions for both the aggressor and the target (Crick & Bigbee, 1998; Crick & Gropeter, 1995; Crick et al., 2006). Targets of relational aggression can suffer from diminished self-worth (Casey-Cannon, Hayward, & Gowen, 2001); emotional distress, loneliness, and vulnerability (Crick & Bigbee, 1998); and, in the case of ostracism, a heightened desire to correct faults so that reconnection can be made (Williams & Gerber, 2005). Cyberbullying has been linked to depression, withdrawal, aggression, rebellion, and other behavioral problems (Smith et al., 2008; Ybarra & Mitchell, 2007), suggesting that the broader reach of electronic channels amplifies negative effects. Although the rationale for research is frequently based on harms experienced by the target, aggressors are also at risk for social-psychological adjustment problems, including peer rejection and problems with friendships (Crick et al., 2006).

In terms of sex differences, much of the early research on relational aggression focused on female children and adolescents. Subsequent research took a comparative approach to relationally aggressive behavior among girls and boys. In line with conventional wisdom, relational aggression has been found to be more prevalent among girls than boys, and the consequences seem to be more serious for girls due to the smaller size of female peer groups, the increased importance placed on female friendships, and the fact that girls victimize their own friends more frequently than boys do (Casey-Cannon et al., 2001; Crick, 1997; Crick & Bigbee, 1998; Crick et al., 2002; Crick & Nelson, 2002; Galen & Underwood, 1997). By the sixth grade, girls are more likely to be relationally aggressive, whereas boys are more likely to be physically aggressive (Crick et al., 1996; Crick & Grotpeter, 1995; Cullerton-Sen & Crick, 2005). Sex differences have also been found in perceptions of relational aggression, with girls being more likely to perceive relationally aggressive behaviors as being wrong and harmful (Murray-Close, Crick, & Galotti, 2006), perhaps due to having more experience with these behaviors.

A defining feature of much of the previous research on relational aggression, particularly in studies conducted in developmental and social psychology, is the conceptualization of relational aggression as an innate and pathological personality trait. It is common methodological practice to use peer reports to first identify relationally aggressive individuals and then describe their behavior (see Abell & Brewer, 2014; Cairns, Cairns, Neckerman, Ferguson, & Gariépy, 1989; Crick, 1997; Crick & Bigbee, 1998; Crick & Nelson, 2002; Crick & Werner, 1998; Cullerton-Sen & Crick, 2005; Gropeter & Crick, 1996; Murray-Close & Crick, 2006; Werner & Crick, 2004). This approach suggests that some people are relationally aggressive by nature, while others—such as the targets of relational aggression—do not possess this trait. However, this assumption is not supported by empirical research.

Using the standard methodology of peer reports, Zimmer-Gembeck et al. (2005) found that only 10% of a class sample was *not* nominated by peers for being relationally aggressive. This ratio demonstrates that the majority of adolescents in their sample did engage in these behaviors and did so often enough to be identified by their peers as relationally aggressive. Additionally, because peer reports depend on behavioral salience, this result does not necessarily mean that the remaining 10% never engaged in such behaviors. While it is possible that certain people may be more prone to relationally aggressive behavior, conceptualizing relational aggression as a trait possessed by certain individuals limits our understanding of why those who would not typically be characterized as "relationally aggressive" might employ strategies associated with relational aggression.

The trait-based conceptualization of relational aggression also makes it difficult to account for the influence of context on behavior, such as the possibility of individuals being relationally aggressive in certain contexts but not others (e.g., an adolescent boy who engages in relationally aggressive behavior in his extracurricular activities but does not do so while in school, or a female college student who is relationally aggressive toward certain friends but not others). In order to account for both the prevalence of relational aggression identified in previous research and the influence of context, we argue that relational aggression should be viewed as a behavior rather than a trait, and as a behavior that most people engage in at some point or another. More specifically, we propose viewing relational aggression as a strategic communication strategy, used in particular circumstances and directed toward particular people, in pursuit of particular goals. This reconceptualization requires new theories and revised methodologies to better understand the strategic nature of this type of aggression. In the next section, we review the state of relational aggression research in our field in order to illustrate the value of taking a behavior-based, communication-focused approach.

Relational Aggression Research in the Field of Communication

Archer and Coyne (2005) have argued that the study of relational aggression must span disciplines in order to account for various facets of the phenomenon. Communication researchers are well positioned—both theoretically and methodologically—to contribute to the broader scholarly conversation on this topic. Although communication researchers do not generally use the term relational aggression, scholars in the field have been studying the communicative and sociological aspects of this type of aggression for nearly 30 years. Communication research on verbal aggression (see Infante & Rancer, 1996; Infante & Wigley, 1986; Nicotera, Steele, Catalani, & Simpson, 2012), indirect interpersonal aggression (see Chesbro & Martin, 2003), social ostracism (see Williams, 2001; Williams & Gerber, 2005), teasing (see Mills & Carwile, 2009; Mottet & Thweatt, 1997), workplace bullying (see Cowan, 2011; Lutgen-Sandvik, 2006, 2008; Lutgen-Sandvik & McDermott, 2011), cyberbullying (see Dehue et al., 2008), and the communicative aspects of psychological abuse (see Dailey, Lee, & Spitzberg, 2007) could and should be part of research on relational aggression.

In the field of communication, Willer and colleagues have conducted several studies on relational aggression (Willer & Cupach, 2008, 2011; Willer & Soliz, 2010). Initially focusing on face threats in adolescent social environments, Willer and Cupach (2008) found that aggressive acts carried out by more popular girls create greater levels of face threat and negative affect than similar acts carried out by girls who are equally as popular, or less popular, than the target. Willer and Soliz (2010) then applied the concept of face threats to relational aggression, finding that positive face needs and intragroup status tend to predict well-being; thus, potential face threat from relational aggression can negatively impact the target. Willer and Cupach (2011) have also used social identity theories from evolutionary psychology to explain girls' social aggression and argued for the creation of theory-based, flexible intervention strategies to combat relational aggression. Looking at the college context, Miller-Ott and Kelly (2013a, 2013b) found that relational aggression among female college students ranges from social exclusion or ostracism to direct confrontation, is typically a group-based phenomenon, and is frequently enacted through mediated communication technologies.

Communication scholars have also explored the discourse of relational aggression in contemporary media and culture. Ryalls (2012) has argued that phrases such as "mean girls" are problematic because they cast girls in a negative light and obscure the role boys might play in relational aggression. Martins and Wilson (2012a, 2012b) have explored the portrayal of relational aggression in popular children's television programs, finding that incidents of this type of aggression are frequent, tend to go unpunished, and can be used to justify aggressive behaviors on the part of viewers. Coyne, Robinson, and Nelson (2010) found that reality television programs contain especially high rates of relational aggression, suggesting that both children and adults are being exposed to representations of the phenomena on a regular basis.

The work of the aforementioned scholars demonstrates the value of studying relational aggression from a communication perspective and the need for further research. Early research on indirect aggression and teasing in our field has led to more recent research on what is now termed relational aggression. We call for communication scholars to continue this important work and to do so in a systematic way that facilitates our field's contribution to the broader scholarly conversation on the topic. Specifically, we recommend that researchers approach relationally aggressive behaviors as strategic in nature. The next section makes a case for the value of viewing relational aggression as strategic communication.

Reconceptualizing Relational Aggression as Strategic Communication

Given that relational aggression typically involves the use (or withholding) of communication, both verbal and nonverbal, to threaten or damage relationships and evoke distress in others, we argue that this phenomenon is *fundamentally communicative* and *goal-directed* in nature. Reconceptualizing relational aggression as strategic communication helps us see it as a behavior rather than a trait. In a strategic view of human interaction, we choose to engage in particular behaviors in order to achieve particular results (see Berger, 1997, 2008; Canary, Cody, & Manusov, 2000; Kellermann, 1992; Miller, Cody, & McLaughlin, 1994). Communication is not random or involuntary; we communicate with others to achieve our goals (Berger & Kellermann, 1994; Sanders, 1987), and the nature of our goals affects the strategies we select to achieve them (Cody, Canary, & Smith, 1994). Additionally, as goals typically differ by situation, a strategic communication perspective helps us to understand the context-specific nature of relationally aggressive communication.

Although generally grounded in a trait-based conceptualization of relational aggression, previous research on the topic also supports our contention that people make strategic choices about when to use relational aggression.

Proactive and reactive goals have been identified in previous relational aggression studies (see Little, Jones, Henrich, & Hawley, 2003; Ostrov & Crick, 2007), with Ostrov and Crick (2007) defining proactive aggression as "behaviors displayed to serve a goal-directed end" (p. 24). Although reactive aggression may not involve the same amount of strategic planning, some scholars argue that proactive and reactive aggression are not as dichotomous as originally thought. Even young children, who are typically viewed as reactive rather than purposeful actors, have been found to engage in goal-directed acts (Card & Little, 2006; Mathieson & Crick, 2010; Sanders, 2007).

The approach we are proposing adds more theoretical precision to the concept of relational aggression, particularly when it comes to questions of intention and rationality. First, though relationships can be threatened or damaged by interactions that unexpectedly escalate in emotional intensity, or by conversations in which someone says something unintentionally aggressive, we argue that relational aggression is defined by the intention to do harm to relationships (see Crick & Gropeter, 1995; Johnson et al., 2013). This distinction is important to practitioners because it calls for different strategies and solutions than keeping calm or being mindful of one's words. Second, viewing relational aggression as strategic communication helps scholars address questions of rationality, by explaining communicative behaviors that may not appear to be fully rational, particularly from the vantage point of adult observers.

As other researchers have noted, the selection of strategies is not necessarily dependent on the anticipated likelihood of success in the present situation (Wiemann & Daly, 1994). Berger (2008) asserts that people tend to rely on strategies that have been successful in the past, but the success of old tactics in a new situation will vary, due to "the dynamic nature of social interaction and social relationships" (p. 97). Recognizing this variance may shed new light on previous research on relational aggression, such as Crick and Werner's (1998) finding that girls who frequently engage in such behavior rate aggressive conflict responses as more positive than girls who do not rely on these strategies as often.

Finally, theories of strategic communication help to illuminate important variations in relationally aggressive behavior. If differences in behavior are related to differences in goals (Kellermann, 2004; Kellermann & Cole, 1994), it is likely that relational aggression varies according to the goal being pursued in a given situation. Goals can be self-presentational, relational, or instrumental (Canary et al., 2000), so a person might use different forms of relational aggression to make him or herself look better, to strengthen a relationship by targeting someone disliked by the other person, or as a means to gain something or someone they desire. Strategies may also vary when goals are co-constructed by people in a group (Wiemann & Daly, 1994), or when goals are proactive versus reactive (Cody et al., 1994). Co-constructed goals of two or more people might be more likely to result in social ostracism, while reactive goals may be more likely to perpetuate conflict (Cody et al., 1994).

In the remainder of this chapter, we outline a research agenda for communication scholars based on our reconceptualization of relational aggression as strategic communication, aspects of relational aggression and populations that are in need of further study, and best practices for research we have identified from previous studies.

Recommendations for Research

The primary goal of this chapter is to call for more research on the topic of relational aggression in the field of communication. To that end, we have brought together multiple lines of research—studies of relational aggression in fields outside of communication, studies of relational aggression and related concepts in our own field, and the literature on strategic communication—in order to show that relational aggression is a fundamentally communicative phenomenon that is strategic in nature, enacted by a majority of individuals at some point or another, and in need of more systematic study by communication scholars. The following recommendations for research provide guidance on *how* to study relational aggression as strategic communication. We begin by exploring theories of strategic communication that can be used to ground empirical research. We then discuss methodological issues associated with the study of relational aggression, focusing on the value of using multiple methods and diversifying our samples. We conclude by outlining a multimodal approach to relational aggression, designed to capture the increasing overlap between online and offline communication.

Recommendation 1: Look for Strategic Aspects of Relationally Aggressive Communication

When we view relational aggression as strategic communication, we recognize that this type of aggression is something that anyone might engage in at one time or another in pursuit of various social goals. This view of relational aggression contrasts directly with the individual pathology perspective taken in many of the previous studies reviewed but, as we have demonstrated, it is not inconsistent with their findings. Theories of strategic communication help us to understand relational aggression as a relatively common communication strategy rather than just a problematic personality trait. Though it is clear that some individuals engage in relational aggression more frequently than others, even studies taking a trait-based approach to relational aggression have provided support for our assertion that relational aggression is a goal-directed communication behavior in which most people occasionally engage.

If we use previous literature on strategic communication as a guide, scholars have several options for systematically investigating the strategic aspects of relational aggression. Before proceeding further, it should be noted that strategic communication is a conceptual approach to human interaction rather than a specific theory. But there are several well-established theories that can ground future research on relational aggression. One option is planning theory, which "seeks to explain how individuals arrive at an understanding of each other's goal-directed actions and discourse, and how individuals produce actions and discourse that enable them to attain their everyday goals" (Berger, 2008, p. 89). This theory is particularly useful for studying relational aggression because it helps us to understand both how aggressors use communication to threaten or damage relationships and how their targets (or bystanders to the aggression) understand the goals and motives behind this type of communication.

Planning theory proposes that goals motivate people to act in certain ways, that people use communication as a tool to achieve their goals, and that individuals have motives (broader abstract intentions) that may lead them to set goals (specific desired changes) that are pursued through sub-goals (specific actions; Berger, 1997, 2008; Dillard, 1989). Following planning theory, relational aggression can be conceptualized as a goal if the aggressor's ultimate aim is to threaten or damage relationships or as a sub-goal if the aggressor is attempting to damage relationships in order to achieve a broader goal, such as higher social status or the acquisition of a new romantic partner. Research grounded in planning theory—or similar theories—could therefore reveal new dimensions of relational aggression by asking respondents to reflect in greater detail on their goals and sub-goals when engaging in aggressive behaviors. This theoretical approach can also produce more applied research, as we need to understand when and why relational aggression is considered an appropriate strategy to achieve a goal if we wish to reduce people's reliance on it. Researchers should therefore include questions about goals, intended or perceived, when asking participants about their experiences with relational aggression. The next section addresses the methods we can use to identify and better understand the strategies used to pursue these goals.

Recommendation 2: Use both Quantitative and Qualitative Methods

To study relational aggression as strategic communication, scholars should employ research methods that avoid a trait-based approach and seek to illuminate *why* participants communicate the way they do and *how* they do it. Much of the previous research in psychology has been based on closed-ended surveys or self/peer/teacher/parent reports designed to identify relationally aggressive individuals and document their behavior (see Ostrov & Crick, 2007; Ostrov, Kamper, Hart, Godleski, & Blakely-McClure, 2014; Tackett & Ostrov, 2010), rather than treating relational aggression as a situation-specific communication strategy employed by a majority of individuals. There have also been fewer studies focusing on how participants understand their own experiences with relational aggression. If we wish to uncover the strategic dimensions of relational aggression, we need to ask participants why and how they communicated the way they did in particular situations, and what they hoped to achieve with that form of communication. Pairing closed-ended surveys with open-ended questions or interviews would provide a more detailed picture of the strategies, goals, and sub-goals of individuals engaging in relational aggression (see Merrell, Buchanan, & Tran, 2006 for sample assessments).

Communication researchers have provided us with several exemplars of using qualitative methods to study relational aggression. For example, semi-structured interviews have been used to understand target, aggressor, and bystander perceptions of relational aggression. Miller-Ott and Kelly (2013a, 2013b) have used interview protocols with questions designed to elicit personal explanations for, and understandings of, relational aggression. Rather than limiting participants to the recounting of specific instances of relational aggression, these studies provide insight into how women make sense of and account for such communicative behavior. Their findings provided rich information about various forms of relational aggression, communication channels used for relational aggression, and management of relational aggression. Lutgen-Sandvik (2006, 2008) has also used interviews to study reactions to the related issue of workplace bullying, with one investigation focusing specifically on understanding how victims pursue goals in reaction to instances of workplace bullying. Taken together, these studies illustrate the value of qualitative methods for understanding both how people enact relational aggression and how they make sense of it. The use of interviews in future research—to understand how communication strategies are selected and enacted in pursuit of particular goals—would provide valuable insights.

There are fewer exemplars of quantitative research consistent with our recommendation to treat everyone as capable of engaging in relational aggression. However, some multi-methodological studies on the topic can be used as models for studying relational aggression using quantitative methods. For example, Willer and Cupach (2008) asked participants to provide a written account of an experience as a relational aggression target and then had participants respond to questions about that experience. Though the questions focused primarily on the social status of the aggressor and bystanders, questions about target reactions were also included. Experimental survey designs using both written scenarios (Basow et al., 2007) and video prompts (Johnson et al., 2013) have also been used to understand how bystanders perceive aggressive behavior. The expansion of such protocols to include questions or methods designed to uncover the rationale and strategies behind the use of relational aggression would allow for predictions about when, why, and how individuals might use relationally aggressive tactics in pursuit of certain goals. In addition to expanding the methods used to study relational aggression, we must continue to diversify our study populations.

Recommendation 3: Diversify Study Populations

The reconceptualization of relational aggression as situation-specific communication strategies, employed by all types of individuals for particular purposes and toward specific ends, requires diversifying the populations we study. The majority of studies reviewed for this chapter focus on girls' and young women's enactment and experience of relational aggression (see Murray-Close & Crick, 2006; Ostrov & Crick, 2007; Werner & Crick, 2004 as representative examples), including the research that has been conducted in the field of communication (see Miller-Ott & Kelly, 2013a, 2013b; Willer & Cupach, 2008, 2011; Willer & Soliz, 2010). Studies documenting a higher frequency of relationally aggressive behavior among females as compared to males (see Crick et al., 2002; Cullerton-Sen et al., 2008; Ostrov & Crick, 2007) and the focus on identifying a "type" of person who is "relationally aggressive" in the trait-based approach have also contributed to the gendering of relational aggression in past research. The predominance of female study populations may reflect the view of relational aggression as a "girl problem" in the current cultural imagination (Ryalls, 2012; Simmons, 2002; Wiseman, 2002), where it is frequently presented in contrast to the physical aggression of boys.

However, previous research that includes boys and young men has shown that relational aggression is not exclusive to one biological sex (Bartlett & Coyne, 2014; Chesney-Lind, Morash, & Irwin, 2007; Faris & Felmlee, 2011; Henington, Hughes, Cavell, & Thompson, 1998), and demonstrated the value of diversifying our research populations. In a study of elementary school children, for example, Henington et al. (1998) found that boys engaged in both physical and relational aggression. Studies of college students have found that both males and females engage in and experience relational aggression, although females who use these strategies are perceived less favorably than males, suggesting a double standard of evaluation (Basow et al., 2007). Studies of adults suggest that sex differences in relational aggression largely disappear as men's use of relational aggression increases over time to match that of women (see Archer & Coyne, 2005 for summary). Based on their study of predictive factors of relational aggression, Faris and Felmlee (2011) argue that social status and cross-sex relationships may contribute to this type of aggression more than biological sex does.

Relational aggression is not just a middle school or high school phenomenon either. Relationally aggressive behavior has been documented in children as young as preschool age (Crick, Casas, & Mosher, 1997; Ostrov & Crick, 2007), in elementary aged children (Crick et al., 2002; Crick & Grotpeter, 1995; Werner & Crick, 2004), in college populations (Basow et al., 2007; Björkqvist et al., 1994; Miller-Ott & Kelly, 2013a, 2013b; Werner & Crick, 1999), and in adults (Andersson & Pearson, 1999; Pearson, Andersson, & Wegner, 2001; Salin, 2003; Sypher, 2004) through retirement age (Trompetter, Scholte, & Westerhof, 2011). Research suggests that adult incivility is on the rise, particularly in the workplace (Andersson & Pearson, 1999; Litwin & Hallstein, 2007; Williams, 2010). Of particular concern is an increase in workplace bullying, where relational aggression, manifesting itself in the form of gossip, sabotage, and/or emotional tirades, threatens workplace climates (Cowan, 2011; Lutgen-Sandvik, 2006; Lutgen-Sandvik & McDermott, 2011).

Research on adult populations has been particularly instructive when it comes to understanding variations in relationally aggressive communication, and how strategies shift over time. Björkqvist et al. (1994), for example, found that adult men tend to use what the researchers referred to as "rational-appearing aggression," such as interrupting or criticizing, judging someone's work harshly, or limiting opportunities for others to express an opinion; while women tend to use social manipulation strategies, including insulting personal choices, making insinuative glances, and spreading false rumors. This suggests that men transition from physical aggression to more nuanced relational aggression, while women continue to use the strategies they learned as girls. Given the professional and psychological implications of this behavior on both aggressors and targets, further study of adult aged populations is especially warranted.

The studies highlighted in this section have shown the value of studying populations outside the ages typically associated with relational aggression and of rejecting the idea that relational aggression is purely a female behavior. Using more diverse samples helps to increase both the representativeness and generalizability of our results, as well as uncover similarities and differences that are obscured when we limit our focus to young women. Previous research has also demonstrated that the communicative strategies associated with relational aggression differ by biological sex and age, a difference that may explain why the label is disproportionately applied to young women. By viewing relational aggression as strategic communication, as we advocate here, scholars are able to account for the use of different strategies in pursuit of the same social goal. Our final recommendation considers the strategic use of communication technologies in the enactment of relational aggression.

Recommendation 4: Trace Connections between Online and Offline Aggression

Relational aggression is no longer limited to the playground, the school halls, or the office. Communication technologies such as the web, email, text messaging, instant messaging, and social media provide individuals with the means to target others anywhere and any time.

A student can be targeted at home by those he or she knows at school, or have in-person acts of relational aggression relayed and amplified with technology. Coworkers can enact relational aggression through email or social media. In many incidents, offline and online communication serve to reinforce each other, creating a situation in which the target cannot escape his or her aggressors. Therefore, for our last recommendation, we highlight an important dimension of our definition of relational aggression: a situation-specific communication strategy, employed by individuals of all ages for particular purposes and toward specific ends, *using multiple modes of communication.* And we argue that research in relational aggression must, therefore, consider the multiplying points of contact between our online and offline lives.

Comparative studies on cyberbullying (i.e., those that contrast it with offline aggression) generally begin with the premise or end with the conclusion that cyberbullying is distinct from other forms of aggression. This conceptual approach has helped researchers identify what is unique about cyberbullying, but it has also obscured the many connections that exist between the online and offline communication of their participants. Previous research has found that adolescents use online communication media primarily to reinforce their offline relationships (Subrahmanyam & Greenfield, 2008), suggesting that young people use technology to develop and foster their social lives, while using the same technologies to sever relational ties and harass others. This multifaceted use of technology is not limited to children and adolescents. As researchers from the Pew Research Center have noted, the fastest growth in online media use over the past 10 years has occurred within adult populations, with significant jumps in social media usage indicating that adults are using technology to create, enhance, and possibly threaten offline relationships (Zickuhr, 2010).

As discussed previously, we believe it is more accurate to conceptualize cyberbullying as a method for enacting the broader goal of relational aggression. We therefore recommend that researchers trace connections between online and offline communication in order to capture the full scope of each incident. Previous studies that have considered multiple modes of communication have demonstrated the value of this approach, documenting how incidents of relational aggression are rarely restricted to just online or offline spaces. Juvonen and Gross (2008), for example, found that two-thirds of the cyberbullying targets they surveyed reported knowing the source of the electronic harassment, and half knew the bully from school. Mishna, Saini, and Solomon (2009) found that, although anonymity is generally seen as an integral part of cyberbullying, most incidents occur within the context of students' known social circles and peer groups. Other scholars have used network analysis to study the role that peer groups play in cyberbullying (see Dijkstra, Berger, & Lindenberg, 2011; Festl & Quandt, 2013; Low, Polanin, & Espelage, 2013; Neal & Cappella, 2012). Researchers have also found a correlation between offline aggression and cyberbullying (Hinduja & Patchin, 2008), suggesting that the dynamics of relational aggression operating in the offline context of school are spilling over, intensifying, or even beginning in online spaces.

Due to the fact that the majority of research on cyberbullying has focused on children and adolescents, less is known about adults' use of technology to enact relational aggression. Miller-Ott and Kelly (2013a, 2013b) found that college-aged women make frequent use of mediated channels when engaging in relational aggression, suggesting that there is definite value in studying connections between online and offline aggression in all age groups. Researchers working in the area of new media and emerging technologies have the experience, theories, and research tools necessary for tracing these connections (see Ellison, Steinfield, & Lampe, 2007; Haythornthwaite, 2005; Kavanaugh, Carroll, Rosson, Zin, & Reese, 2005; and Williams, 2006 for theories and methods), which is one more way the field of communication is well-positioned to contribute to the scholarly conversation on relational aggression. Given the increasing use of technology for social purposes, future research on relational aggression cannot afford to disregard these connections.

Conclusion

In this chapter we have argued for a reconceptualization of relational aggression as a situation-specific form of communication, enacted by most people at one time or another, in pursuit of particular social goals, using multiple modes of communication. We have called for communication scholars to further the study of relational aggression as strategic communication. To that end, we have synthesized relevant research both outside and inside of our field, in order to bring those who might wish to answer our call up to speed on the state of the literature. We have also made recommendations for future research based on: (1) our reconceptualization of relational aggression as strategic communication; (2) deficiencies in the trait-based approach used in much of the previous literature; and (3) best practices from researchers who have taken communication-focused approaches, documented variations in strategy through both qualitative and quantitative research methods, diversified their study populations, and/or considered the connections between online and offline communication. Using theories and methods that have been developed in our field, communication scholars can play an important role in understanding the strategic aspects of relational aggression, and creating effective programs to address this behavior in all walks of life. From an applied research perspective, we can think of no better way to have an impact than to contribute to combatting this serious social problem.

References

Abell, L., & Brewer, G. (2014). Machiavellianism, self-monitoring, self-promotion and relational aggression on Facebook. *Computers in Human Behavior, 36,* 258–262. doi: 10.1016/j.chb.2014.03.076

Agatston, P. W., Kowalski, R., & Limber, S. (2007). Students' perspectives on cyber bullying. *Journal of Adolescent Health, 41,* S59–S60. doi: 10.1016/j.jadohealth.2007.09.003

Andersson, L. M., & Pearson, C. M. (1999). Tit for tat? The spiraling effect of incivility in the workplace. *The Academy of Management Review, 24,* 452–471. doi: 10.2307/259136

Archer, J., & Coyne, S. M. (2005). An integrated review of indirect, relational, and social aggression. *Personality and Social Psychology Review, 9,* 212–230. doi: 10.1207/s15327957pspr0903_2

Bartlett, C., & Coyne, S. M. (2014). A meta-analysis of sex differences in cyberbullying behavior: The moderating role of age. *Aggressive Behavior, 40,* 474–488. doi: 10.1002/ab.21555

Basow, S. A., Cahill, K. R., Phelan, J. E., Longshore, K., & McGillicuddy-DeLisi, A. (2007). Perceptions of relational and physical aggression among college students: Effects of gender of perpetrator, target, and perceiver. *Psychology of Women Quarterly, 31,* 85–95. doi: 10.1111/j.1471-6402.2007.00333.x

Beale, A. V., & Hall, K. R. (2007). Cyberbullying: What school administrators (and parents) can do. *The Clearing House: A Journal of Educational Strategies, Issues, and Ideas, 81,* 8–12. doi: 10.3200/TCHS.81.1.8-12

Bennett, J. (2010, October 4). Phoebe Prince: Should school bullying be a crime? *Newsweek.* Retrieved from www.newsweek.com/phoebe-prince-should-school-bullying-be-crime-73815

Berger, C. R. (1997). *Planning strategic interaction: Attaining goals through communicative action.* Mahwah, NJ: Erlbaum.

Berger, C. R. (2008). Planning theory of communication: Goal attainment through communicative action. In L. A. Baxter & D. O. Braithwaite (Eds.), *Engaging theories in interpersonal communication* (pp. 89–103). Thousand Oaks, CA: Sage. doi: http://dx.doi.org/10.4135/9781483329529.n7

Berger, C. R., & Kellermann, K. (1994). Acquiring social information. In J. A. Daly and J. M. Wiemann (Eds.), *Strategic Interpersonal Communication* (pp. 1–32). Hillsdale, NJ: Erlbaum.

Björkqvist, K., Österman, K., & Lagerspetz, K. M. J. (1994). Sex differences in covert aggression among adults. *Aggressive Behavior, 20,* 27–33. doi: 10.1002/1098-2337

boyd, d. (2014). *It's complicated: The social lives of networked teens.* New Haven: Yale.

Cairns, R. B., Cairns, B. D., Neckerman, H. J., Ferguson, L. L., & Gariépy, J. L. (1989). Growth and aggression: 1. Childhood to early adolescence. *Developmental Psychology, 25,* 320–330. doi: 10.1037/0012-1649.25.2.320

Canary, D. J., Cody, M. J., & Manusov, V. L. (2000). *Interpersonal communication: A goals-based approach* (2nd edn). Boston: Bedford/St. Martin's.

Card, N. A., & Little, T. D. (2006). Proactive and reactive aggression in childhood and adolescence: A meta-analysis of differential relations with psychosocial adjustment. *International Journal of Behavioral Development, 30,* 466–480. doi: 10.1177/0165025406071904

Card, N. A., Stucky, B. D., Sawalani, G. M., & Little, T. D. (2008). Direct and indirect aggression during childhood and adolescence: A meta-analytic review of gender differences, intercorrelations, and relations to maladjustment. *Child Development, 79,* 1185–1229. doi: 10.1111/j.1467-8624.2008.01184.x

Casey-Cannon, S., Hayward, C., & Gowen, K. (2001). Middle-school girls' reports of peer victimization: Concerns, consequences, and implications. *Professional School Counseling, 5,* 138–147. Retrieved from http://eric.ed.gov/?id=EJ655177

Chesbro, J. L., & Martin, M. M. (2003). The relationship between conversational sensitivity, cognitive flexibility, verbal aggressiveness and indirect interpersonal aggressiveness. *Communication Research Reports, 20,* 143–150. doi: 10.1080/08824090309388810

Chesney-Lind, M., Morash, M., & Irwin, K. (2007). Policing girlhood? Relational aggression and violence prevention. *Youth Violence and Juvenile Justice, 5,* 328–345.doi: 10.1177/1541204007301307

Cody, M. J., Canary, D. J., & Smith, S. W. (1994). Compliance-gaining goals: An inductive analysis of actor's goal types, strategies, and successes. In J. A. Daly and J. M. Wiemann (Eds.), *Strategic interpersonal communication* (pp. 33–90). Hillsdale, NJ: Erlbaum.

Cowan. R. L. (2011). 'Yes, we have an anti-bullying policy, but. . .:' HR professionals' understandings and experiences with workplace bullying policy. *Communication Studies, 62,* 307–327. doi: 10.1080/10510974.2011.553763

Coyne, S. M., Archer, J., & Eslea, M. (2006). "We're not friends anymore! Unless. . .": The frequency and harmfulness of indirect, relational, and social aggression. *Aggressive Behavior, 32,* 294–307. doi: 10.1002/ab.20126

Coyne, S. M., Robinson, S. L., & Nelson, D. A. (2010). Does reality backbite? Physical, verbal, and relational aggression in reality television programs. *Journal of Broadcasting and Electronic Media, 54*, 282–298. doi: 10.1080/08838151003737931

Crick, N. R. (1997). Engagement in gender normative versus nonnormative forms of aggression: Links to social-psychological adjustment. *Developmental Psychology, 33*, 610–617. doi: 10.1037/0012-1649.33.4.610

Crick, N. R., & Bigbee, M. A. (1998). Relational and overt forms of peer victimization: A multiinformant approach. *Journal of Counseling and Clinical Psychology, 66*, 337–347. doi: 10.1037/0022-006X.66.2.337

Crick, N. R., & Grotpeter, J. K. (1995). Relational aggression, gender, and social-psychological adjustment. *Child Development, 66*, 710–722. doi: 10.2307/1131945

Crick, N. R., & Nelson, D. A. (2002). Relational and physical victimization within friendships: Nobody told me there'd be friends like these. *Journal of Abnormal Child Psychology, 30*, 599–607. doi: 10.1023/A:1020811714064

Crick, N. R., & Werner, N. E. (1998). Response decision processes in relational and overt aggression. *Child Development, 69*, 1630–1639. doi: 10.1111/j.1467-8624.1998.tb06181.x

Crick, N. R., Bigbee, M. A., & Howes, C. (1996). Gender differences in children's normative beliefs about aggression: How do I hurt thee? Let me count the ways. *Child Development, 67*, 1003–1014. doi: 10.2307/1131876

Crick, N. R., Casas, J. F., & Mosher, M. (1997). Relational and overt aggression in preschool. *Developmental Psychology, 33*, 579–588. doi: 10.1037/0012-1649.33.4.579

Crick, N. R., Casas, J. F., & Nelson, D. A. (2002). Toward a more comprehensive understanding of peer maltreatment: Studies of relational victimization. *Current Directions in Psychological Science, 11*, 98–101. doi: 10.1111/1467-8721.00177

Crick, N. R., Ostrov, J. M., & Werner, N. E. (2006). A longitudinal study of relational aggression, physical aggression, and children's social-psychological adjustment. *Journal of Abnormal Child Psychology, 34*, 131–142. doi: 10.1007/s10802-005-9009-4

Cullerton-Sen, C., Cassidy, A. R., Murray-Close, D., Chicchetti, D., Crick, N. R., & Rogosch, F. A. (2008). Childhood maltreatment and the development of relational and physical aggression: The importance of a gender-informed approach. *Child Development, 79*, 1736–1751. doi: 10.1111/j.1467-8624.2008.01222.x.

Cullerton-Sen, C., & Crick, N. R. (2005). Understanding the effects of physical and relational victimization: The utility of multiple perspectives in predicting social-emotional adjustment. *School Psychology Review, 34*, 147–160. Retrieved from www.nasponline.org/publications/spr/abstract.aspx?ID=1767

Dahl, J. (2013, October). Rebecca Sedwick case: Bullied girl and her tormentor both grew up in "disturbing" family situations, says sheriff. *CBS News*. Retrieved from www.cbsnews.com/news/rebecca-sedwick-case-bullied-girl-and-her-tormentor-both-grew-up-in-disturbing-family-situations-says-sheriff/

Dailey, R. M., Lee, C. M., & Spitzberg, B. H. (2007). Communicative aggression: Toward a more interactional view of psychological abuse. In B. H. Spitzberg & W. R. Cupach (Eds.), *The dark side of interpersonal communication* (pp. 297–326). Mahwah, NJ: Lawrence Erlbaum Associates.

Dehue, F., Bolman, C., & Völlink, T. (2008). Cyberbullying: Youngsters' experiences and parental perception. *Cyberpsychology and Behavior, 11*, 217–223. doi: 10.1089/cpb.2007.0008

Dijkstra, J. K., Berger, C., & Lindenberg, S. (2011). Do physical and relational aggression explain adolescents' friendship selection? The competing roles of network characteristics, gender, and social status. *Aggressive Behavior, 37,* 417–429. doi: 10.1002/ab.20402

Dillard, J. P. (1989). Types of influence goals in personal relationships. *Journal of Social and Personal Relationships, 6,* 293–308. doi: 10.1177/0265407589063004

Dillon, S. (2010, October 25). Help stop bullying, U.S. tells educators. *New York Times.* Retrieved from www.nytimes.com/2010/10/26/education/26bully.html

Ellison, N. B., Steinfield, C., & Lampe, C. (2007). The benefits of Facebook "friends:" Social capital and college students' use of online social network sites. *Journal of Computer-Mediated Communication, 12,* 1143–1168. doi: 10.1111/j.1083-6101.2007.00367.x

Faris, R., & Felmlee, D. (2011). Status struggles: Network centrality and gender segregation in same- and cross-gender aggression. *American Sociological Review, 76,* 48–73. doi: 10.1177/0003122410396196

Festl, R., & Quandt, T. (2013). Social relations and cyberbullying: The influence of individual and structural attributes on victimization and perpetration via the Internet. *Human Communication Research, 39,* 101–126. doi: 10.1111/j.1468-2958.2012.01442.x

Galen, B. R., & Underwood, M. K. (1997). A developmental investigation of social aggression among children. *Developmental Psychology, 33,* 589–600. doi: 10.1037/0012-1649.33.4.589

Grotpeter, J. K., & Crick, N. R. (1996). Relational aggression, overt aggression, and friendship. *Child Development, 67,* 2328–2338. doi: 10.2307/1131626

Haythornthwaite, C. (2005). Social networks and Internet connectivity effects. *Information, Communication & Society, 8,* 125–147. doi: 10.1080/13691180500146185

Henington, C., Hughes, J. N., Cavell, T. A., & Thompson, B. (1998). The role of relational aggression in identifying aggressive boys and girls. *Journal of School Psychology, 36,* 457–477. doi: 10.1016/S0022-4405(98)00015-6

Hinduja, S., & Patchin, J. W. (2008). Cyberbullying: An exploratory analysis of factors related to offending and victimization. *Deviant Behavior, 29,* 129–156. doi: 10.1080/01639620701457816

Hinduja, S., & Patchin, J. W. (2014, July). State cyberbullying laws: A brief review of state cyberbullying laws and policies. Retrieved from http://cyberbullying.us/state-cyberbullying-laws-a-brief-review-of-state-cyberbullying-laws-and-policies/

Infante, D. A., & Rancer, A. S. (1996). Argumentativeness and verbal aggressiveness: A review of recent theory and research. In B. R. Burleson (Ed.), *Communication Yearbook, 19,* (pp. 319–352). New York: Routledge.

Infante, D. A., & Wigley, C. J. (1986). Verbal aggressiveness: An interpersonal model and measure. *Communication Monographs, 53,* 61–69. doi: 10.1080/03637758609376126

Johnson, C., Heath, M. A., Bailey, B. M., Coyne, S. M., Yamawaki, N., & Eggett, D. L. (2013). Adolescents' perceptions of male involvement in relational aggression: Age and gender differences. *Journal of School Violence, 12,* 357–377. doi: 10.1080/15388220.2013.819557

Juvonen, J., & Gross, E. F. (2008). Extending the school grounds? Bullying experiences in cyberspace. *Journal of School Health, 78,* 496–505. doi: 10.1111/j.1746-1561.2008.00335.x

Kavanaugh, A., Carroll, J. M., Rosson, M. B., Zin, T. T., & Reese, D. D. (2005). Community networks: Where offline communities meet online. *Journal of Computer-Mediated Communication, 10,* doi: 10.1111/j.1083-6101.2005.tb00266.x

Kellermann, K. (1992). Communication: Inherently strategic and primarily automatic. *Communication Monographs, 59,* 288–300. doi: 10.1080/03637759209376270

Kellermann, K. (2004). A goal-directed approach to gaining compliance: Relating differences among goals to differences in behaviors. *Communication Research, 31,* 397–445. doi: 10.1177/0093650204266093

Kellermann, K., & Cole, T. (1994). Classifying compliance gaining messages: Taxonomic disorder and strategic confusion. *Communication Theory, 4,* 3–60. doi: 10.1111/j.1468-2885.1994.tb00081.x

Kowalski, R. M., Limber, S. P., & Agatston, P. W. (2012). *Cyberbullying: Bullying in the digital age,* 2nd edn. Hoboken, NJ: Wiley and Sons.

Li, Q. (2006). Cyberbullying in schools: A research of gender differences. *School Psychology International, 27,* 157–170. doi: 10.1177/0143034306064547

Little, T. D., Jones, S. M., Henrich, C. C., & Hawley, P. H. (2003). Disentangling the "whys" from the "whats" of aggressive behaviour. *International Journal of Behavioral Development, 27,* 122–133. doi: 10.1080/01650250244000128

Litwin, A. H., & Hallstein, L. O. (2007). Shadows and silences: How women's positioning and unspoken friendship rules in organizational settings cultivate difficulties among some women at work. *Women's Studies in Communication, 30,* 111–142. doi: 10.1080/07491409.2007.10162507

Low, S., Polanin, J. R., & Espelage, D. L. (2013). The role of social networks in physical and relational aggression among young adolescents. *Journal of Youth Adolescence, 42,* 1078–1089. doi: 10.1007/s10964-013-9933-5

Lutgen-Sandvik, P. (2006). Take this job and. . .: Quitting and other forms of resistance to workplace bullying. *Communication Monographs, 73,* 406–433. doi: 10.1080/03637750601024156

Lutgen-Sandvik, P. (2008). Intensive remedial identity work: Responses to workplace bullying trauma and stigmatization. *Organization, 15,* 97–119. doi: 10.1177/1350508407084487

Lutgen-Sandvik, P., & McDermott, V. (2011). Making sense of supervisory bullying: Perceived powerlessness, empowered possibilities. *Southern Communication Journal, 76,* 342–368. doi: 10.1080/10417941003725307

Martins, N., & Wilson, B. J. (2012a). Mean on the screen: Social aggression in programs popular with children. *Journal of Communication, 62,* 991–1009. doi: 10.1111/j.1460-2466.2011.01599.x

Martins, N., & Wilson, B. J. (2012b). Social aggression on television and its relationship to children's aggression in the classroom. *Human Communication Research, 38,* 48–71. doi: 10.1111/j.1468-2958.2011.01417.x

Mathieson, L. C., & Crick. N. R. (2010). Reactive and proactive subtypes of relational and physical aggression in middle childhood: Links to concurrent and longitudinal adjustment. *School Psychology Review, 39,* 601–611. Retrieved from www.nasponline.org/publications/spr/abstract.aspx?ID=1963

Merrell, K. W., Buchanan, R., & Tran, O. K. (2006). Relational aggression in children and adolescents: A review with implications for school settings. *Psychology in the Schools, 43,* 345–360. doi: 10.1002/pits.20145

Miller, L. C., Cody, M. J., & McLaughlin, M. L. (1994). Situations and goals as fundamental constructs in interpersonal communication. In M. L. Knapp & G. R. Miller (Eds.), *Handbook of interpersonal communication* (Vol. 2, pp. 162–198). Thousand Oaks, CA: Sage.

Miller-Ott, A. E., & Kelly, L. (2013a). Communication of female relational aggression in the college environment. *Qualitative Research Reports in Communication, 14,* 19–27. doi: 10.1080/17459435.2013.835338

Miller-Ott, A. E., & Kelly, L. (2013b). Mean girls in college: An analysis of how college women communicatively construct and account for relational aggression. *Women's Studies in Communication, 36,* 330–347. doi: 10.1080/17459435.2013.835338

Mills, C. B., & Carwile, A. M. (2009). The good, the bad, and the borderline: Separating teasing from bullying. *Communication Education, 58,* 276–301. doi: 10.1080/03634520902783666

Mishna, F., Saini, M., & Solomon, S. (2009). Ongoing and online: Children and youth's perceptions of cyber bullying. *Children and Youth Services Review, 31,* 1222–1228. doi: 10.1016/j.childyouth.2009.05.004

Mottet, T. P., & Thweatt, K. S. (1997). The relationships between peer teasing, self-esteem, and affect for school. *Communication Research Reports, 14,* 241–248. doi: 10.1080/08824099709388666

Murray-Close, D., & Crick, N. R. (2006). Mutual antipathy involvement: Gender and associations with aggression and victimization. *School Psychology Review, 35,* 472–492. Retrieved from www.nasponline.org/publications/spr/abstract.aspx?ID=1806

Murray-Close, D., Crick, N. R., & Galotti, K. M. (2006). Children's moral reasoning regarding physical and relational aggression. *Social Development, 15,* 345–372. doi: 10.1111/j.1467-9507.2006.00346.x

Neal, J. W., & Cappella, E. (2012). An examination of network position and childhood relational aggression: Integrating resource control and social exchange theories. *Aggressive Behavior, 38,* 126–140. doi: 10.1002/ab.21414

Nicotera, A. M., Steele, J., Catalani, A., & Simpson, N. (2012). Conceptualization and test of an aggression competence model. *Communication Research Reports, 29,* 12–25. doi: 10.1080/08824096.2011.639909

Olweus, D. (1978). *Aggression in the schools: Bullies and whipping boys.* Washington, DC: Hemisphere.

Ostrov, J. M., & Crick, N. R. (2007). Forms and functions of aggression during early childhood: A short-term longitudinal study. *School Psychology Review, 36,* 22–43. Retrieved from www. nasponline.org/publications/spr/abstract.aspx?ID=1862

Ostrov, J. M., Kamper, K. E., Hart, E. J., Godleski, S. A., & Blakely-McClure, S. J. (2014). A gender-based approach to the study of peer victimization and aggression subtypes in early childhood. *Development and Psychopathology, 26,* 575–587. doi: 10.1017/S0954579414000248

Papadopoulos, M. (2014). East Taunton family suspects cyberbullying is what led teen to commit suicide. *Taunton Daily Gazette.* Retrieved from www.tauntongazette.com/article/20140722/NEWS/140728915

Patchin, J. W., & Hinduja, S. (2006). Bullies move beyond the schoolyard: A preliminary look at cyberbullying. *Youth Violence and Juvenile Justice, 4,* 148–169. doi: 10.1177/1541204006286288

Patchin, J. W., & Hinduja, S. (2015, May 1). Summary of our research. Retrieved from http://cyberbullying.us/summary-of-our-research/

Pearson, C. M., Andersson, L. M., & Wegner, J. W. (2001). When workers flout convention: A study of workplace incivility. *Human Relations, 54(11),* 1387–1419. doi: 10.1177/00187267015411001

Raskaukas, J., & Stoltz, A. D. (2007). Involvement in traditional and electronic bullying among adolescents. *Developmental Psychology, 43,* 564–575. doi: 10.1037/0012-1649.43.3.564

Ryalls, E. (2012). Demonizing 'mean girls' in the news: Was Phoebe Prince 'bullied to death'? *Communication, Culture & Critique,* 5, 463–481. doi: 10.1111/j.1753-9137.2012.01127.x

Salin, D. (2003). Ways of explaining workplace bullying: A review of enabling, motivating and precipitating structures and processes in the work environment. *Human Relations, 56,* 1213–1232. doi: 10.1177/00187267035610003

Sanders, R. E. (1987). *Cognitive foundations of calculated speech: Controlling understandings in conversation and persuasion.* Albany, NY: State University of New York Press.

Sanders, R. E. (2007). The composition and sequencing of communicative acts to solve social problems: Functionality and inventiveness in children's interactions. *Communication Monographs, 74,* 464–491. doi: 10.1080/03637750701716628

Simmons, R. (2002). *Odd girl out: The hidden culture of aggression in girls.* New York: Harcourt.

Smith, P. K., Mahdavi, J., Carvalho, M., Fisher, S., Russell, S., & Tippett, N. (2008). Cyber bullying: Its nature and impact in secondary school pupils. *Journal of Child Psychology and Psychiatry, 49,* 376–385. doi: 10.1111/j.1469-7610.2007.01846.x

Subrahmanyam, K., & Greenfield, P. (2008). Online communication and adolescent relationships. *The Future of Children, 18,* 119–146. doi: 10.1353/foc.0.0006

Sypher, B. D. (2004). Reclaiming civil discourse in the workplace. *The Southern Communication Journal, 69,* 257–269. doi: 10.1080/10417940409373296

Tackett, J. L., & Ostrov, J. M. (2010). Measuring relational aggression in middle childhood in a multi-informant multi-method study. *Journal of Psychopathological Behavior Assessment, 32,* 490–500. doi: 10.1007/s10862-010-9184-7

Trompetter, H., Scholte, R., & Westerhof, G. (2011). Resident-to-resident relational aggression and subjective well-being in assisted living facilities. *Aging & Mental Health, 15,* 59–67. doi: 10.1080/13607863.2010.501059

Vaillancourt, T., Hymel, S., & McDougall, P. (2003). Bullying is power: Implications for school-based intervention strategies. *Journal of Applied School Psychology, 19,* 157–176. doi: 10.1300/J008v19n02_10

Wang, J., Iannotti, R. J., & Nansel, T. R. (2009). School bullying among adolescents in the United States: Physical, verbal, relational, and cyber. *Journal of Adolescent Health, 45,* 368–375. doi: 10.1016/j.jadohealth.2009.03.021

Werner, N. E., & Crick, N. R. (1999). Relational aggression and social-psychological adjustment in a college sample. *Journal of Abnormal Psychology, 108,* 615–623. doi: 10.1037/0021-843X.108.4.615

Werner, N. E., & Crick, N. R. (2004). Maladaptive peer relationships and the development of relational and physical aggression during middle childhood. *Social Development, 13,* 495–514. doi: 10.1111/j.1467-9507.2004.00280.x

Wiemann, J. M., & Daly, J. A. (1994). Introduction: Getting your own way. In J. A. Daly and J. M. Wiemann (Eds.), *Strategic interpersonal communication* (pp. vii–xiv). Hillsdale, NJ: Erlbaum.

Willer, E. K., & Cupach, W. R. (2008). When "sugar and spice" turn to "fire and ice": Factors affecting the adverse consequences of relational aggression among adolescent girls. *Communication Studies, 59,* 415–429. doi: 10.1080/10510970802473674

Willer, E. K., & Cupach, W. R., (2011). The meaning of girls' social aggression: Nasty or mastery? In W. R. Cupach & B. H. Spitzberg (Eds.), *The dark side of close relationships II* (pp. 297–326). New York, NY: Routledge.

Willer, E. K., & Soliz, J. (2010). Face needs, intragroup status, and women's reactions to socially aggressive face threats. *Personal Relationships, 17,* 557–571. doi: 10.1111/j.1475-6811.2010.01297.x

Williams, D. (2006). On and off the 'net: Scales for social capital in an online era. *Journal of Computer-Mediated Communication, 11,* 593–628. doi: 10.1111/j.1083-6101.2006.00029.x

Williams, K. D. (2001). *Ostracism: The power of silence.* New York: Guilford Press.

Williams, K. D., & Gerber, J. P. (2005). Ostracism: The making of the ignored and excluded mind. *Interaction Studies, 6,* 359–374. doi: 10.1075/is.6.3.04wil

Williams, R. (2010, August 21). Look out: Here comes "desk rage." In *Psychology Today online.* Retrieved from www.psychologytoday.com/blog/wired-success/201008/look-out-here-comes-desk-rage

Wiseman, R. (2002). *Queen bees & wannabes: Helping your daughter survive cliques, gossip, boyfriends, and other realities of adolescence.* New York: Three Rivers Press.

Wolfe, J. (2014). Young boy takes his life after being bullied about his size. *Opposing Views.* Retrieved from www.opposingviews.com/i/society/young-boy-takes-his-life-after-being-bullied-about-being-small

Ybarra, M. L., & Mitchell, K. J. (2007). Prevalence and frequency of Internet harassment instigation: Implications for adolescent health. *Journal of Adolescent Health, 41,* 189–195. doi: 10.1016/j.jadohealth.2007.03.005

Zickuhr, K. (2010, December 16). Generations online in 2010. Pew Research Internet Project. Retrieved from www.pewinternet.org/2010/12/16/generations-2010/

Zimmer-Gembeck, M. J., Geiger, T. C, & Crick, N. R. (2005). Relational and physical aggression, prosocial behavior, and peer relations: Gender moderation and bidirectional associations. *The Journal of Early Adolescence, 25,* 421–452. doi: 10.1177/0272431605279841

CHAPTER CONTENTS

7 Social Support and Computer-Mediated Communication

A State-of-the-Art Review and Agenda for Future Research

Stephen A. Rains

University of Arizona

Kevin B. Wright

George Mason University

Despite a great deal of speculation about the potential advantages and disadvantages of computer-mediated communication (CMC) for social support processes, few attempts have been made to summarize the findings from this body of scholarship. The present chapter reports a state-of-the-art review of research on computer-mediated support in an effort to determine whether the purported promise and peril of CMC has been realized. Empirical studies examining the use of CMC for acquiring social support and the outcomes of support acquired online are reviewed and synthesized. The review concludes with an agenda for future research identifying pressing questions for computer-mediated support scholarship.

Social support is central to well-being (Goldsmith, 2004; Uchino, 2004). Indeed, the benefits of social support have been demonstrated across a wide variety of contexts and populations (Burleson, Albrecht, & Sarason, 1994; Cohen, Underwood, & Gottlieb, 2000; Thoits, 2011). Although much of this research has been conducted in the context of face-to-face interaction, the use and implications of computer-mediated communication (CMC) for social support has been a longstanding topic of interest. Claims about the potential utility of computer-mediated support can be traced back to some of the earliest research examining the social implications of CMC. In reviewing a series of experiments they conducted during the early 1980s, Kiesler and colleagues suggested that, "It might be possible to turn computer networks into social support networks" (Kiesler, Siegel, & McGuire, 1984, p. 1131). Despite being made prior to the widespread adoption of the contemporary Internet, Kiesler and colleagues' prediction was quite prescient. Data from the Pew Internet and American Life Project (Fox, 2011) indicate that almost one in five adult Internet users in the United States have ventured online for health-related peer support.

Use of CMC among the lay public for exchanging social support has been matched by the growth in scholarship on this topic. Much has been written about the opportunities and pitfalls of CMC for acquiring and sharing support (e.g., Caplan & Turner, 2007; High & Solomon, 2011; Rains & Young, 2009; Tanis, 2008a; Walther & Boyd, 2002; Wright & Bell, 2003; Wright, Rosenberg, Egbert, Ploeger, & Bernard, 2013). Although there appears to be a fair amount of consensus about the *potential* implications of CMC for social support processes, few attempts have been made to synthesize existing quantitative and qualitative research and formally evaluate the uses and effects of CMC. The present chapter reports a state-of-the-art review of computer-mediated support research in an effort to bridge this gap and advance scholarship on this topic in two ways. First, empirical research will be summarized in an effort to evaluate claims about the potential support-related implications of CMC made in previous reviews (e.g., Caplan & Turner, 2007; Tanis, 2008a; Wright & Bell, 2003). We consider whether the results from existing empirical research are consistent with the purported benefits and limitations of CMC. Such a synthesis is critical to advance this body of research and better understand the degree to which the proposed promise and peril of CMC for social support has been realized. A second objective of this chapter is to outline an agenda for future research. We reflect on what is known about the implications of CMC for social support and offer an outline for additional scholarship on this topic. This effort will help provide a framework scholars can use to identify and pursue the most pressing questions regarding computer-mediated support.

The review will proceed as follows: We first define key terms, identify scope conditions, and discuss the procedures used to locate the research reports reviewed in this chapter. Next, we summarize existing empirical research on computer-mediated support. We focus specifically on scholarship examining support seeking in computer-mediated settings, outcomes of acquiring computer-mediated support, and the implications of computer-mediated support in three specific contexts. For each topic, we evaluate whether the proposed implications of CMC are consistent with the results of extant research. We conclude the review by sketching an agenda for future studies of computer-mediated support. Four specific avenues for scholarship will be considered.

Key Terms, Scope Conditions, and Research Report Identification

In discussing the body of research on computer-mediated support, it is important to define two key terms used throughout the review. First, social support is an umbrella term that generally involves providing assistance to others (Burleson & MacGeorge, 2002). In this review, social support is typically discussed in terms of the support individuals have received from others (i.e., received support) or the degree to which they perceive that others are available to serve as a support resource (i.e., perceived support). A few studies included in the review examine social support in terms of one's social connections (i.e., social integration). Second, we use the term CMC to refer to Internet-based technologies that make possible text-based interaction among dyads or groups. Various forms of CMC may serve as a means for exchanging social support. In addition to online discussion communities, social support has been studied among users of technologies such as e-mail, instant messaging, blogs, social network sites (SNSs), and massively multiplayer online games (MMOGs).[1]

In addition to defining key terms, it is important to consider some scope conditions for this project. This review largely focuses on support seeking and reception/outcomes. These two topics have been consistently studied in this body of research and have the potential to offer important insights about computer-mediated support processes. Space limitations prevent us from extensively reviewing other research detailing the development of support-focused interventions involving CMC or considering content analyses examining the explicit types of support messages shared in various computer-mediated contexts. Although we believe that such research is important, both topics have been addressed in other reviews (Rains, Peterson, & Wright, 2015; Rains & Young, 2009). A second scope condition stems from the tendency for research on computer-mediated support to focus on individuals coping with illness. Much of this review will rely on studies conducted in the context of health. However, we believe that the underlying support processes examined in these works are relevant beyond health contexts. In addition, we dedicate a section of the review to research conducted in other contexts, including among older adults, in facilitating cultural adaptation, and in educational settings.

In order to identify research reports for the review, we conducted a comprehensive literature search for articles published prior to 2014. We used the term "social support" along with the terms "computer-mediated communication," "online," or "Internet" to search a series of EBSCOhost databases (i.e., *Academic Search Complete*, *Communication and Mass Media Complete*, *ERIC*, *Medline*, *PsycArticles*, and *PsycInfo*) for published articles related to social support and CMC. The abstracts for all reports were reviewed to determine their relevance to the project. We also used the preceding terms and searched Google scholar, reviewing the first 100 results for additional reports. A follow-up search of EBSCOhost and Google scholar was conducted during January, 2015 to identify reports that were published during the prior year.

Seeking Computer-Mediated Support

The implications of CMC for support seeking have been a major focus of discussion and study in scholarship on computer-mediated support. CMC has been touted by several scholars as a particularly valuable context for acquiring social support (Caplan & Turner, 2007; Tanis, 2008a; Turner, Grube, & Meyers, 2001; Walther & Boyd, 2002; Wright & Bell, 2003). CMC is proposed to facilitate the support-seeking process by creating conditions under which individuals feel comfortable requesting help and have greater access to able and willing support providers. In examining the use and effects of CMC for support seeking, we consider research related to four questions involving: who seeks computer-mediated support, motivations for acquiring support online, the viability of computer-mediated support contexts, and factors influencing perceptions of computer-mediated support and providers. We synthesize existing research in an effort to evaluate claims about the utility of CMC in support acquisition.

Who Seeks Computer-Mediated Support?

As a foundation for evaluating the implications of CMC, it is worthwhile to first consider the prevalence and demographic characteristics of individuals who seek computer-mediated support. Use of CMC to acquire social support appears to be a fairly widespread phenomenon. Although the majority of research on this topic has tended to focus on support for physical and mental health issues, there is evidence that significant numbers of adult Americans have attempted to seek or share computer-mediated support. Research from the Pew Internet and American Life Project offers insights about the evolution of participation in computer-mediated support over the past 15 years. In 2001, 28 million adult Americans were estimated to have participated in an online support community dedicated to a medical condition or personal problem; as of 2004, the number increased to 36 million (Pew Internet and American Life Project, 2005). A survey conducted by the organization during 2010 offered evidence that 18% of adult Internet users have gone online specifically to find others with similar health concerns (Fox, 2011). Estimates of support-related Internet use were more modest when framed in terms of the last time respondents had a health concern. Among adult Internet users, only 13% used the Internet to seek information, care, or support from friends and family and 5% contacted others with the same condition. A more recent survey conducted by researchers at the National Cancer Institute (2012) indicated that an estimated 7.5 million adult Americans visited a health-related online support community during 2012.

Despite the volume of people seeking computer-mediated support, relatively few nationally representative surveys have been conducted to explore the demographics of this group. One exception is a recent survey of individuals who sought peer support online specifically for mental health problems (DeAndrea, 2014; DeAndrea & Anthony, 2013). Online support seekers were more likely to be female, white, and college-educated (DeAndrea & Anthony, 2013). Yet, participation in online support communities was substantially lower than face-to-face support groups/communities (DeAndrea, 2014). Relative to face-to-face support seekers, individuals who participated in online support communities were more likely to be female, white, and have greater levels of perceived distress. There were no consistent differences based on education. Among a convenience sample of Japanese women coping with breast cancer, women with greater education, who were more recently diagnosed and had higher levels of depression and anxiety, were more likely to participate in online support communities than face-to-face support groups (Setoyama, Yamazaki, & Nakayama, 2011). Researchers have also examined demographic differences in the ways online support communities are used. One study of women coping with breast cancer showed that, in the context of an online support-based intervention, Whites were more likely to actively contribute to group discussions than lurk, whereas the reverse trend was observed for African Americans (Han et al., 2012). Lurkers (i.e., people who read discussions but do not actively contribute) were also older and less likely to live alone. There were no differences in use of the community based on education or cancer stage.

Finally, researchers have considered the role of personality in seeking computer-mediated support. Attraction to computer-mediated support has been found to be positively associated with neuroticism and negatively associated with agreeableness and conscientiousness (Giota & Kleftaras, 2014). Other researchers showed that personality domains interacted with specific types of Internet use to predict general perceptions of support availability (Swickert, Hittner, Harris, & Herring, 2002). Individuals who scored high on neuroticism and engaged in higher levels of Internet use for technical reasons (e.g., visiting bulletin boards, creating webpages) and information exchange (e.g., e-mail, information seeking) reported perceiving less support available than individuals who scored high in neuroticism but engaged in lower levels of these types of Internet use as well as individuals who scored lower on neuroticism. Among individuals who engaged in greater levels of leisure Internet use (e.g., using instant messaging, playing games), those high in agreeableness reported greater support available than individuals who scored low on agreeableness as well as individuals who engaged in low levels of leisure Internet use.

Why Do People Seek Computer-Mediated Support?

Beyond demographic differences in support seekers, a number of interpersonal and situational factors have been argued to motivate individuals to seek computer-mediated support. The underlying rationale for many of these factors can be found in Turner and colleagues (Turner et al., 2001) adaptation of the optimal matching model (Cutrona, 1990). CMC is argued to create a context where individuals can acquire support that uniquely meets their needs and circumstances. We focus on those factors that have received the most attention in empirical research: limited access to support offline, stigma, accessibility, and interaction control. Across these factors, there is evidence to suggest the utility of CMC for meeting some of the unique needs of support seekers.

Limited Access to Support Offline

Online sources of social support have been argued to extend, and in some instances even replace, traditional offline support networks by overcoming some of the limitations of those networks (Tanis, 2008a; Wright & Bell, 2003). Online support is thought to be particularly attractive when one's traditional network lacks individuals who are willing and able to provide effective support. The results of research examining the status of one's offline support resources as a predictor of using CMC to acquire support are mixed. Several studies offer evidence demonstrating the importance of offline resource deficits. Among members of online support communities, satisfaction with offline support resources was inversely associated with respondents' preference for social interaction with online community members (Chung, 2013). In other research, the number of posts made to an online community (Kim et al., 2011) and time spent participating in a MMOG (Kaczmarek & Drazkowski, 2014) were inversely associated with offline support availability. Support community members have also been found to be significantly more satisfied with their online support networks than their offline networks (Wright, 2000a).

The preceding findings can be contrasted with research reporting no connection between access to offline resources and use of computer-mediated support. In a study of MMOGs, no significant relationships were found between time spent playing and players' perceptions of appraisal and belonging support available offline (Longman, O'Connor, & Obst, 2009). Among online support community members, satisfaction with their face-to-face support networks was not significantly correlated with time spent online (Wright, 1999). Researchers have also reported findings wholly inconsistent with the notion that limited access to offline resources drives support-related CMC use. Family cohesion was positively associated with use of an online support community in one study (Yoo et al., 2014). In the context of SNSs, respondents' satisfaction with their face-to-face support resources was positively associated with time spent using a SNS (Wright et al., 2013).

Perceived Stigma

Another variable that has been argued to be an important predictor of participating in computer-mediated support is the degree to which individuals feel stigmatized because of the issues they face. Stigma has been linked with a number of deleterious outcomes that can make it difficult to acquire social support (Rosman, 2004; Vanable, Carey, Blair, & Littlewood, 2006). Several scholars have argued that online support communities, in particular, may be valuable for individuals facing stigma as a means to gain access to weak ties (Tanis, 2008a; Wright & Bell, 2003; Wright & Rains, 2013). Although only a relatively small number of studies have examined this factor, researchers have reported tentative evidence that stigma may lead individuals to use CMC to acquire support.

Among a nationally representative sample of adults seeking assistance for mental health issues, respondents who were afraid others would find out about their condition and worried about being committed were significantly more likely to use online than face-to-face support communities (DeAndrea, 2014). However, there were no differences in seeking support online or offline based on respondents' concerns about being viewed negatively by members of the community in which they live. Other research offers indirect evidence of the role stigma may play as a motivating factor in seeking computer-mediated support. One group of scholars found greater member participation in online communities dedicated to marginalized concealable identities than in online communities dedicated to marginalized conspicuous identities or mainstream identities (McKenna & Bargh, 1998). Surveys of online community members showed that perceived stigma was positively associated with the degree to which members valued the text-based and anonymous aspects of their community (Tanis, 2008b) as well as members' preference for support from weak ties (Wright & Rains, 2013).

Accessibility

Computer-mediated support resources are unique from their face-to-face counterparts in that many forms are available all-day-every-day and do not require any travel. This increased accessibility offered by CMC has been highlighted as key factor encouraging its use (Tanis, 2008a; Walther & Boyd, 2002; Wright & Bell, 2003). There is some empirical evidence that accessibility is a reason individuals use CMC to acquire support. The accessibility of online communities has been found to be an important benefit in several qualitative studies (Colvin, Chenoeth, Bold, & Harding, 2004; Malik & Coulson, 2008; Yli-Uotila, Rantanen, & Suominen, 2014). In interviews with members of health-related *Second Life* support groups, for example, convenience was identified as a motivation for participation (Green-Haman, Eichorn, & Sherblom, 2011). Accessibility also emerged in surveys of online support community members (Walther & Boyd, 2002). One survey showed that mobility restriction among members was positively associated with the importance of text-based interaction and perceptions that community participation could help extend respondents' social network (Tanis, 2008b). Yet, a lack of time or physical accessibility did not differentiate users of online and face-to-face support communities dedicated to mental health (DeAndrea, 2014).

Interaction Control

Because interactions in computer-mediated environments are typically text-based, they are marked by the reduction in nonverbal cues that accompany face-to-face interaction and the potential for asynchronous exchanges. These two factors have been argued to be particularly beneficial in supportive interaction (Caplan & Turner, 2007; Tanis, 2008a; Walther & Boyd, 2002; Wright & Bell, 2003). More attention can be given to message construction as support seekers and providers have additional time to carefully craft their messages, and not having to see one's interaction partner may make individuals feel more comfortable sharing their experiences. Although the role of interaction control has received very little attention in empirical studies, there is evidence to tentatively suggest its promise as a predictor of seeking computer-mediated support. Among support community members, interaction management was one reason for their participation (Walther & Boyd, 2002). In another study, perceptions of the utility of text-based interaction were positively associated with the degree to which respondents used the community to help cope with their health condition (Tanis, 2008b). Researchers have also shown that perceptions of the interpersonal costs of seeking support from friends was inversely associated with support seeking face-to-face, but unrelated to the use of e-mail (Lim, Thompson, & Zhao, 2013).

Are Computer-Mediated Contexts Viable Resources for Support?

Given the volume of people venturing online and various motivations for seeking computer-mediated support, a relevant question involves whether it is possible to acquire meaningful levels of social support in these contexts. Claims about the potential of CMC for acquiring social support are typically grounded in broader ideas about the implications of CMC for interpersonal interaction. Whereas the cues-filtered-out perspective (Culnan & Markus, 1987) assumes that the reduced social cues (e.g., eye contact, facial expressions) create challenges for interpersonal interaction, the hyperpersonal communication model (Walther, 1996) suggests that CMC may lead to more personal interaction than occurs face-to-face. These two perspective are reflected in claims that CMC may be a particularly effective (Robinson & Turner, 2003; Turner et al., 2001; Wright & Bell, 2003) or ineffective (Lewandowski, Rosenberg, Parks, & Siegel, 2011) context for acquiring social support. Overall, the evidence from extant research tends to offer more support for the former claim and suggests that CMC can serve as meaningful resources for social support.

A few studies have shown that Internet use, in general, may have support-related benefits. A Pew Internet and American Life Project survey conducted during 2010 showed that Internet users perceived significantly greater levels of support available than did non-users—including greater availability of emotional, tangible, and companionship support (Hampton, Goulet, Rainie, & Purcell, 2011). A study of undergraduate students had commensurate findings (Liu & LaRose, 2008). The authors reported a positive association between perceived support available online and amount of time spent using the Internet. These findings can be contrasted with the results from a survey of women coping with infertility in which respondents reported desiring significantly more support than they received from online sources (High & Steuber, 2014). However, desiring more support than one received was not unique to online sources and extended to spouses and medical professionals as support resources.

Several groups of researchers have investigated the relationship between participation in online communities and social support. Time spent using online communities is associated with user size and satisfaction with their online support network (Wright, 2000b) as well as users' perceptions of informational and emotional support received in HIV/AIDS (Mo & Coulson, 2012) and weight-loss (Hwang et al., 2011) communities. Use of a Swedish online parenting community and regular contact with other members were positively associated with perceived support available from community members (Sarkadi & Bremberg, 2005). Yet, not all research has documented support-related benefits of online community participation. In one study of support community members, the relationship between respondents' amount of support-related Internet use and perceived support availability was not statistically significant (Eastin & LaRose, 2005). The size of respondents' online networks, however, was associated with their perceptions of support availability. Other research that provides evidence regarding the way in which these communities are used is important to consider. In the context of an online support intervention for women with breast cancer, lurkers—people who follow community discussions but do not actively make contributions—reported having significantly greater levels of social support available than participants who actively contributed to the discussions (Han et al., 2012).

Beyond online communities, researchers have documented the potential support-related benefits of using SNSs, blogs, MMOGs, and even instant messaging. A Pew Internet and American Life Project survey showed that individuals who used the SNS brand Facebook or authored a blog reported significantly greater levels of support availability compared with individuals who did not engage in those activities (Hampton et al., 2011). Other researchers have reported positive associations between SNS use by Taiwanese undergraduate students and perceived support available on the SNS (Liu & Yu, 2013) as well as the number of posts made by health bloggers over a six-week period and bloggers' perceptions of support available from their readers (Rains & Keating, 2011). Yet a study of new mothers resulted in more conflicting evidence (McDaniel, Coyne, & Holmes, 2012). Blogging frequency was associated with mothers' perceived support overall, and this relationship was mediated by perceived connections to extended friends and family. SNS use, however, was not associated with either variable. Research examining MMOGs has considered the implications of game participation for social support from gamers' in-game connections. In two studies, time spent playing MMOGs was positively associated with gamers' general perceptions of support available from other players (Kaczmarek & Drazkowski, 2014) as well as the availability of appraisal and belonging support (Longman et al., 2009). Finally, researchers examining instant messaging use among undergraduate students showed that time spent using instant messaging was associated with the amount of social support received by students during the previous month (Lin & Bhattacherjee, 2009).

What Factors Influence Perceptions of Computer-Mediated Support Quality?

Although the previously reviewed research offers evidence that various computer-mediated contexts can serve as valuable support resources, there is reason to believe that the quality of support received or available in these contexts is not uniform. Scholars have discussed several factors that may serve to influence perceptions of online support and support providers (Caplan & Turner, 2007; High & Solomon, 2011; Tanis, 2008a; Wright & Bell, 2003). We consider three factors that have received the most attention in research on computer-mediated support: the role of channel characteristics and contextual factors, perceived similarity, and perceived credibility. There is evidence that each factor can play a role in perceptions of social support in CMC.

Channel Characteristics and Contextual Factors

Despite significant discussion about the unique opportunities CMC offers for acquiring social support (Caplan & Turner, 2007; Tanis, 2008a; Wright & Bell, 2003), researchers have only recently begun to test its implications for perceptions of support messages and providers. Those studies that have been conducted, however, offer several important insights. Much of this work has focused on examining the implications of contextual features in computer-mediated supportive interactions occurring in online communities.

Research has been conducted to investigate the effects of a support seeker or provider's identity via their screen name and/or avatar picture. Relative to when support seekers had no picture and a non-name screen name (e.g., jmk76), participants wrote more person-centered and polite support responses when the support seeker included a picture and first name (e.g., Jamie) in their screen name (Feng, Li, & Li, 2013). Perceived social presence partially mediated the effect of identity information on person-centeredness but not politeness. In another study, participants were asked to judge a hypothetical supportive interaction in a support community in which the sex of the support provider (as indicated by a screen name) and person-centeredness of the support message were manipulated (Spottswood, Walther, Holmstrom, & Ellison, 2013). In the high person-centeredness support condition, male participants reported greater liking and perceived the support provider to be more effective when the provider had a male name than a female or ambiguous sex name. However, female participants liked and found more effective support providers who gave high person-centered support than low person-centered support, regardless of their apparent sex.

Research has also been conducted to examine how, in contexts like online support communities and SNSs, the nature of others' feedback to a support seeker impacts the quality of support messages produced by support providers. Researchers manipulated others' comments in an experimental study and found that, compared to when others' responses to the support seeker were unsupportive, participants who viewed supportive replies produced more effective action-focused and emotion-focused support messages (Li & Feng, 2014). A related study focusing specifically on SNSs examined the impact of the number of different features used to convey affect (High, Oeldorf-Hirsh, & Bellur, 2014). Participants who were exposed to a hypothetical SNS page in which emotional distress was communicated using a status message, the relationship feature, and profile picture were less willing to provide emotional and network support to the distressed person than when only one feature was used to convey distress.

Although CMC is argued to restrict some nonverbal information, scholars have investigated the support-related implications of those nonverbal cues that persist.

There is evidence that chronemic cues may be important (Ledbetter, 2009). In the context of supportive e-mail exchanges, the time delay between a support request and response influenced participants' perceptions of the provider and message. When the reply delay was shorter (i.e., one-hour delay vs. one-month delay), the support provider was rated as more immediate, similar, and receptive. In a second study, female participants rated the support provided as being of higher quality in the short delay condition (Ledbetter, 2009). Other cues, however, have been shown to be inconsequential. Cross-sectional and experimental studies showed that the presence of emotional cues in support messages received via e-mail did not impact the receivers' support satisfaction (Ledbetter & Larson, 2008). Beyond individual cues, language style matching—involving the degree to which speakers mimic one another's use of function words—has been shown to predict bloggers' perceptions of emotional support availability (Rains, 2015). Increased language style matching between health bloggers and their readers (via their comments) over a three-month period was positively associated bloggers' perceptions of emotional support available from readers.

Relatively little experimental research has been conducted to isolate the unique effects of CMC by comparing it with face-to-face supportive interactions. In one study, 24 undergraduate students completed a counselling session about anxiety conducted by a graduate student in counseling psychology either face-to-face or via instant messaging (Cohen & Kerr, 1999). Although there were no differences between the two conditions in perceptions of the counselor, nor the depth, smoothness, or positivity of the interaction, participants in the instant messaging condition reported lower arousal during the interaction. In a more recent study, dyads discussed a stressor either via instant messaging or face-to-face and one participant provided high, medium, or low levels of person-centered support (High & Solomon, 2014). Support providers in the face-to-face condition reported feeling significantly more self-presentational confidence than providers in the instant messaging condition. However, there were no differences in participants' perceptions of the ease of support message production. There were interaction effects involving participants' sex, message characteristics, and the communication medium for receivers' evaluations of the support messages. Whereas male and female receivers rated the high person-centered support they received from males as more sensitive in the instant messaging condition than face-to-face, low person-centered messages in female-female dyads were rated as being more sensitive face-to-face than in instant messaging. Women also rated the low person-centered support they received from other women in the instant messaging condition to be of lower quality than in the face-to-face condition.

Perceived Similarity

Another factor that has been argued to play a role in perceptions of support messages and providers in computer-mediated contexts is interactants' similarity with one another (Tanis, 2008a; Wright & Bell, 2003). Similarity in experiences with a stressor, as well as with the attributes of others, may encourage empathy and a sense of belonging. The results from several studies underscore the importance of similarity. Connecting with others who share similar experiences was a key motivation for participating in online support communities reported in several qualitative studies examining health-related communities (Haberstroh & Moyer, 2012; Holbrey & Coulson, 2013; Malik & Coulson, 2008; Yli-Uotila et al., 2014) as well as among caregivers (Colvin et al., 2004). In one experimental study, examining advice provided in the context of an online support community, perceived similarity of other community members influenced participants' perceptions of their credibility and, in turn, evaluations of the health information they provided (Wang, Walther, Pingree, & Hawkins, 2008). Two other cross-sectional studies offer evidence that perceived similarity of support community members was positively associated with perceived support available from the community (Campbell & Wright, 2002; Nambisan, 2011). Similarity of others has also been listed as a key advantage of participating in an online support community (Wright, 2002). Among SNS users, perceived attitudinal and background similarity with respondents' connections on the network were positively associated with evaluations of emotional support available from this group (Wright, 2012).

Perceived Credibility

A final factor that has been argued to influence perceptions of computer-mediated support providers and messages is credibility (Wright & Bell, 2003). The degree to which a support provider is knowledgeable and trustworthy could have substantial implications for perceptions of his or her advice and feedback. Although relatively little research has examined credibility, the studies that exist offer evidence of its importance. In experimental research, the credibility of support community members was found to be associated with participants' evaluations of the health information they received and, in turn, their intentions to act on that information (Wang et al., 2008). Survey research also offers evidence of the importance of credibility. Researchers conducting surveys of online support community members showed that two dimensions of source credibility—perceived competence and character—were associated with the size of and members' satisfaction with their online support network (Wright, 2000b) and their perceptions of emotional support available from other community members (Campbell & Wright, 2002). In the context of health blogs, the perceived credibility of blogs was a significant predictor of the degree to which they were used by cancer patients and their companions for problem solving as well as prevention and care (Chung & Kim, 2008). Other research offers indirect evidence of the importance of credibility. Researchers conducting a content-analysis of inaccurate information posted to an online support community showed that, although such information was relatively rare, it was typically identified by other members as inaccurate and updated or corrected (Esquivel, Meric-Bernstam, & Bernstam 2006). The results of interviews with SNS users suggest that the authenticity of support attempts in response to messages broadcast by users about their significant life events may be questioned (Vitak & Ellison, 2012).

Conclusions about Research Examining CMC for Seeking Support

Research investigating support seeking and CMC tends to be founded on the notion that CMC creates beneficial conditions for seeking and acquiring support. In addition to providing access to willing and able support providers, several structural characteristics of CMC serve to make individuals comfortable seeking support. The extant body of research examining support seeking provides some general support for these ideas. The conclusion that can be most confidently drawn from this body of research is that a variety of different forms of CMC can serve as viable resources for social support. In addition to online support communities, blogs, SNSs, and even MMOGs have all been documented to serve as support resources. Although the total number of studies examining many of the specific topics was small, there was also evidence to suggest stigma, accessibility, and interaction control were important factors in support seeking behavior. Additionally, contextual factors, credibility, and similarity appear to be factors that influence perceptions of the support available or provided in CMC. Yet, there are areas in which extant research was less consistent. Research examining the influence of one's offline support resources on support seeking behavior was largely mixed. Additionally, little is known about the demographics of support seekers. The only nationally representative research conducted to date that explored demographic factors was limited to mental health issues.

Scholarship examining the use of CMC for seeking support offers broader insights about social support processes. The noteworthy number of adults who seek support online—and the diversity of computer-mediated contexts in which it may be acquired—serves as compelling evidence of the important role that social support plays as a coping resource. The results from this body of research also demonstrate the notion that support seeking is a complex phenomenon. That stigma and interaction control were factors motivating the use of CMC highlights the challenges of seeking support. Attempting to acquire support is a more complex phenomenon than simply asking for assistance and several interpersonal and situational factors may encourage or discourage such efforts. The range of variables influencing support perceptions further highlights the nuanced nature of supportive communication. In addition to the content of the support messages shared, contextual factors and provider characteristics are important factors that may shape perceptions and outcomes of supportive interactions. Taken as a whole, research examining the role of CMC in seeking and acquiring social support underscores the importance and complexity of social support as a coping resource.

Outcomes of Computer-Mediated Support

The potential outcomes of acquiring social support online have received increased attention in recent years as scholars have worked to better understand if and how support acquired or available in computer-mediated contexts has salutatory effects. Much of this research is grounded in two general models about the effects of social support (for a review, see Cohen & Wills, 1985; Lakey & Cohen, 2000). One way in which support can have positive effects is by directly improving one's coping resources. Receiving advice or empathy, for example, can help a support seeker better manage a stressor. A second model focuses on perceived support availability. The knowledge that one has potential support providers available in computer-mediated contexts impacts support outcomes by influencing one's appraisal of a stressor. Perceiving that one could, if necessary, gain access to supportive others in online discussion communities, blogs, or SNSs may make stressors appear less severe and more manageable than if such resources were not available. There is evidence that both perceiving support to be available and receiving support in CMC is consequential for well-being.

Is Participating in an Online Support Community Beneficial?

Research examining the outcomes of support acquired in computer-mediated contexts has tended to focus on demonstrating positive outcomes among individuals participating in online support communities. Participation in support-focused CMC communities is considered a proxy for both perceiving available and receiving social support from community members. At the most general level, several studies offer evidence that simply participating in a support community can be beneficial. The results of panel studies have shown increased post-traumatic growth over six months among members of a breast cancer support community with Stage I and II cancer (Lieberman & Goldstein, 2006) as well as decreased rates of depression over the course of a year among depression community members (Houston, Cooper, & Ford, 2002). Use of health-related online support communities has also been linked with several "empowering processes" (Mo & Coulson, 2012, p. 446; Mo & Coulson, 2013). These processes, such as finding meaning and receiving information and support, are associated with positive outcomes such as self-efficacy and optimism (Mo & Coulson, 2012, 2013). Other research has considered outcomes related to members' perceived benefits or satisfaction with their community. In two studies, support community satisfaction was inversely associated with perceived stress (Wright, 2000a) and the perceived benefits of online support were positively associated with members' perceived coping ability (Seçkin, 2013). Yet, a few researchers have reported potentially negative outcomes of participation. For example, among individuals with visual impairment, negative associations were found between online support community participation and self-reports of physical well-being (Smedema & McKenzie, 2010).

Some inconsistencies in existing research might be accounted for by the way in which participation was evaluated. A survey of support community members in the Netherlands showed positive associations between the number of visits members made per week and social coping involving feelings of social connection, but a negative association between social coping and the total number of weeks members participated in the community (Tanis, 2008b).

The preceding findings are generally consistent with the results of qualitative research examining the experiences of support community members. Connecting with other members can be critical for mitigating isolation (Holbrey & Coulson, 2013), lessening the burden placed on offline support resources (Malik & Coulson, 2008), and acquiring novel information (Colvin et al., 2004; Yli-Uotila et al., 2014). Members of one online community reported that their experiences led them to feel greater efficacy when interacting with their health care provider (Holbrey & Coulson, 2013). Yet, there are also several significant limitations of support community participation. The most common involves stress resulting from hearing about difficulties experienced by other community members (Holbrey & Coulson, 2013; Malik & Coulson, 2008). Other drawbacks include social comparisons with others who are improving (Malik & Coulson, 2008), becoming overly focused on one's illness (Holbrey & Coulson, 2013), the inability to receive immediate feedback (Haberstroh & Moyer, 2012), the lack of physical and social cues (Colvin et al., 2004), and receiving limited or negative feedback (Yli-Uotila et al., 2014).

The way in which online communities are used—in the form of active participation versus lurking—also appears to be consequential. One survey of HIV/ AIDS community members showed a number of differences between lurkers and posters related to support outcomes (Mo & Coulson, 2010). Relative to lurkers, members who actively contributed were significantly more likely to report that they received social support and useful information from the community and were more likely to report being satisfied with other members. Other researchers have shown that active participants feel greater identification with their community and greater self-acceptance as a result of participating relative to lurkers (McKenna & Bargh, 1998). In a study of mental-health communities, active participants fared better in terms of stigma recovery than lurkers (Lawlor & Kirakowski, 2014). Yet, the authors also found that the frequency with which all respondents visited the community was inversely associated with stigma recovery. These findings can be contrasted with the results from an analysis of participation patterns in a computer-mediated support intervention (Han, Hou, Kim, & Gustafson, 2014). Although there were no differences after six weeks, lurkers were less depressed and reported marginally greater increases in functional well-being and social support at the three month follow-up than did individuals who actively participated in group discussions.

Finally, individual difference factors may impact the outcomes of participating in an online support community. Preference for weak-tie support is one such factor (Wright & Miller, 2010). This notion is drawn from Granovetter's (1973) ideas about weak ties but adapted to the context of social support.

Weak ties are argued to be valuable because they can offer access to novel information, less potential for role conflict, and represent less risky disclosure targets. Weak-tie support preference is an individual difference factor involving the degree to which individuals favor support from weak ties (Wright & Miller, 2010). Among members of health-related online support communities, weak-tie preference has been shown to be inversely related to perceived stress (Wright, Rains, & Banas, 2010) and anxiety (Wright & Miller, 2010) and positively associated with self-efficacy (Wright & Miller, 2010) and perceptions of the credibility of one's online support community (Wright & Rains, 2014). In another study examining online support community members, a significant interaction was found between weak-tie support preference and perceived stigma for depression and stress (Wright & Rains, 2013). The associations between stigma and both outcomes were weaker among respondents with a relatively greater preference for weak-tie support. The authors argue that, because participants who prefer weak-tie support are gaining access to this resource, the effects of stigma are less deleterious among this group.

Is Computer-Mediated Support Associated with Positive Outcomes?

Beyond the general benefits of participating in online communities, research has documented positive outcomes associated with support received or perceived from using specific forms of CMC. One experimental study showed that simply knowing that supportive others are available in computer-mediated contexts can be consequential (Feng & Hyun, 2012). Participants were assigned to read a hypothetical scenario in which they experienced a stressful event, logged into their instant messaging program, and then noticed that different groups of contacts were on or offline. Compared to participants who thought a target friend was offline, participants who perceived their target friend to be online reported higher levels of self-efficacy and lower stress.

Scholars conducting cross-sectional studies have also reported positive associations between well-being and support received or available from using online communities (Mo & Coulson, 2012; 2013; Oh & Lee, 2012), SNSs (Liu & Yu, 2013; Oh, Ozkaya, & LaRose, 2014; Wright et al., 2013), blogs (Ko & Kuo, 2009; Rains & Keating, 2011), microblogs (Liang, Ho, Li, & Turban, 2011), and MMOGs (Kaczmarek & Drazkowski, 2014; Longman et al., 2009). Most of these studies focused on perceived support availability. For example, in one study of online diabetes support communities, support perceived available from community members was positively associated with members' perceptions of health-related empowerment and, ultimately, their intention to actively communicate with their doctor (Oh & Lee, 2012). Among samples of student (Ko & Kuo, 2009) and health (Rains & Keating, 2011) bloggers, perceived support available from readers has been linked with various dimensions of well-being. The benefits of social support availability even extend to microbloggers' intentions to share and use consumer information from other microbloggers (Liang et al., 2011) and MMOG players' well-being (Kaczmarek & Drazkowski, 2014). The results from the few studies that have generally examined received support in CMC are more mixed. Although one group of researchers showed that supportive interactions on a SNS over the course of a five-day period predicted respondents' positive affect and, in turn, their life satisfaction (Oh et al., 2014), another scholar found that support received on a SNS was unrelated to life satisfaction (Kim, 2014).

Researchers have also examined the outcomes of receiving or perceiving available specific types of support. Receiving emotional support has been shown to have salutary effects in several studies (Kim et al., 2012; Oh, Lauckner, Boehmer, Fewins-Bliss, & Li, 2013; Turner et al., 2013; Yoo et al., 2014). Researchers, for example, examined the effects of emotional support messages communicated via e-mail during a health intervention for patients diagnosed with diabetes (Turner et al., 2013). They found that the proportion of providers' e-mails to patients that contained emotional support messages was associated with improved glycemic control among patients over the course of the intervention. Two studies examining a computer-mediated intervention for women with breast cancer showed that receiving emotional support message was associated with lower breast cancer concerns (Kim et al., 2012; Yoo et al., 2014). In one of the studies, however, this association was limited to women with moderate and high levels of emotional communication competence (Yoo et al., 2014). Perceived emotional support also appears to be beneficial. Among student SNS users, perceived emotional support available from one's SNS network was positively associated with health self-efficacy (Oh et al., 2013) and negatively associated with perceived stress (Wright, 2012). Researchers have considered a few other types of support with mixed results. Perceptions of appraisal support available from other MMOG members was inversely associated with psychological well-being, but the association between perceived belonging support and gamers' well-being was not statistically significant (Longman et al., 2009).

In addition to perceived and received support, there is evidence that the size of an individual's online social network is consequential. The number of connections one has in an SNS network (e.g., total "friends" on the popular SNS, Facebook) has been shown to be positively associated with well-being (Nabi, Prestin, & So, 2103). There is also evidence to suggest that expressing support has important potential outcomes. Three studies have been conducted to examine emotional support provision in the context of a computer-mediated support intervention among women coping with breast cancer. An examination of the messages constructed by participants showed that women who received emotional support messages were more likely to give emotional support to others (Kim et al., 2012). Emotional support expression was positively associated with positive reframing (Kim et al., 2011, 2012) and inversely associated with self-blame (Kim et al., 2011), but not associated with breast-cancer related concerns nor emotional well-being (Kim et al. 2012). The results from another intervention study indicated that, among individuals with higher levels of emotional competence, expressing emotional support was positively related to perceived quality of life (Yoo et al., 2014). However, emotional support expression and competence were not associated with participants' breast cancer concerns.

Relatively little research has been conducted to evaluate the consequences of computer mediation for support outcomes. In one experiment, participants engaged in a supportive interaction either face-to-face or via instant messaging (High & Solomon, 2014). Two weeks after the interaction, participants were asked to evaluate their perceptions of the stressor they had discussed. The results offered some evidence that support received in the instant messaging condition was less effective than in the face-to-face condition. Among female participants who received low person-centered support, those in the instant messaging condition reported less improvement in their situation than did women who received support face-to-face. These findings are commensurate with the results from a cross-sectional study (Lewandowski et al., 2011). Current and former military personnel were asked to estimate the level of disruption caused by a significant negative life event at the time of the event and at present along with the communication medium they primarily used to acquire support regarding the event. The reduction in disruption from the time of the event to the present was significantly greater among respondents who received support face-to-face than those who used a form of CMC. Put differently, participants who received support primarily via CMC did not report as much improvement as those who primarily received support face-to-face. Other researchers have found no differences between face-to-face and instant messaging in support outcomes. After completing a counseling session about anxiety, there was no difference in state anxiety change between participants in the instant messaging and face-to-face conditions (Cohen & Kerr, 1999).

Conclusions about Computer-Mediated Support Outcomes

Several conclusions can be drawn from research examining the outcomes of computer-mediated support. Perhaps most noteworthy, support available and received in computer-mediated contexts is generally associated with positive outcomes related to well-being. The results of research examining participation in online communities suggest a range of support-related benefits of participation as well as some potential limitations. Beyond online communities, there is a fair amount of evidence consistent with the notion that various forms of CMC can serve as valuable support resources. In cross-sectional research examining online support communities, blogs, microblogs, and MMOGs, positive associations have been found between perceived support available in these contexts and well-being. Received support—specifically, receiving emotional support—has also been connected with several outcomes linked with well-being. Yet, there is reason to question the role that CMC plays during supportive interactions. Although research explicitly comparing face-to-face and CMC are rare, those few studies that exist suggest that computer-mediated support may be no better—or even suboptimal—relative to commensurate face-to-face interaction.

Research examining the outcomes of computer-mediated support offers several insights about social support processes more broadly. The associations between well-being and both support availability and received support are a testament to the importance of social support as a coping resource. The variety of computer-mediated contexts in which support was shown to play an important role underscores the value and utility of this social resource. These various contexts also highlight the notion that supportive communication does not and need not occur solely in face-to-face interactions. Although non-verbal cues certainly can play an important role in communicating social support, the results from research on received emotional support in particular offers evidence that their presence is not a scope condition for effective comforting communication. Finally, research demonstrating the potential benefits of serving as a support provider suggests the importance of thinking more broadly about the settings in which support processes occur. Support seekers may also play the role of providers and interact with other seeker-providers—and such varying and multiplex roles may have important implications for supportive interactions.

Computer-Mediated Support in Special Contexts

Claims about the potential advantages and disadvantages of computer-mediated support extend to unique support contexts. Research has accumulated exploring the role of computer-mediated support among older adults, individuals adapting to a new culture, and in educational settings. Much of this work is grounded in the idea that computer-mediated support offers novel opportunities for coping with the variety of novel challenges that define each context. Scholarship examining computer-mediated support in each context is considered in the following paragraphs. Across all three contexts, there is evidence to suggest the utility of CMC as a resource for social support.

Older Adults

As the number of older adults in the United States continues to increase, CMC has been argued to create valuable opportunities for acquiring and sharing support among this group (Robinson & Turner, 2003; Wright, 2000c). Much of the extant research tends to focus on documenting the potential of CMC. There is some evidence to suggest that older adults' Internet use is generally associated with support perceptions. One group of scholars trained older adults to use the Internet over a four-month period and found that total time spent online was positively associated with participants' support perceptions (Cody, Dunn, Hoppin, & Wendt, 1999). However, this association did not extend to time spent using specific programs that foster interpersonal interaction such as chat and e-mail. Other researchers have reported more promising results regarding specific types of Internet use. Perceptions of support availability have been shown to be associated with older adults' frequency of Internet use for information, communication, and entertainment (Erikson & Johnson, 2011). In another study, social Internet use, defined as using instant messaging and discussion communities, was associated with positive health outcomes (Noel & Epstein, 2003). Respondents who engaged in greater amounts of social Internet use reported fewer health limits and better physical and mental health than those who engaged in smaller amounts of social Internet use. Among a sample of older adults residing in a retirement community, use of e-mail to communicate with adult children and friends was associated with perceptions that these two groups were available resources of advice and emotional support (Waldron, Gitelson, & Kelly, 2005). Notably, the results did not extend to perceptions of tangible or illness support availability. The findings from qualitative research further demonstrate the implications of different forms of CMC for social support. Interviews with a sample of older adults in China who used a particular website showed that the website's online community was used for acquiring informational support, whereas the instant messaging application was used for emotional support (Xie, 2008).

Several studies have been conducted to explore older adults' experiences in online support communities. A consistent finding is that such communities can be a valuable support resource for this group (Kanayama, 2003; Pfeil, Zaphiris, & Wilson, 2009; Wright, 2000d)—although one study showed that the benefits only extended to frequent Internet users (Wright, 2000c). Online support communities appear to serve several functions. An analysis of SeniorNet conversations revealed three discussion themes involving promoting community support, sharing life events, and offering advice disguised as self-disclosure (Wright, 2000d). Open-ended survey responses from SeniorNet members further suggested that the community served a wide range of support-related purposes from offering a little advice and emotional involvement to serving as a "surrogate family" (Wright, 2000d, p. 38). SeniorNet was particularly valuable for older adults to discuss their family with non-family members and as an avenue to work through difficulties by considering possible solutions. These results are consistent with more recent interview research in which older adults reported that online communities were seen as a useful resource for connection and comforting as well as for candid feedback (Pfeil et al., 2009). The potential to gain access to a large number of similar others was also identified as an important benefit. Yet, limitations of these communities and computer-mediated support more generally have also been reported. Interview respondents in one study indicated that the relative lack of nonverbal cues fostered misunderstandings and made them wary of information quality (Pfeil et al., 2009).

Cultural Adaptation

Research has been conducted with the aim of exploring the implications of computer-mediated support among individuals adapting to a new culture. CMC is argued to make it possible to maintain connections with one's established ties and, as a result, help buffer the stressors associated with adapting to new settings (Mikal, Rice, Abeyta, & DeVilbiss, 2013). A few studies have examined the use and relative importance of CMC for maintaining connections with one's home country. Interview and cross-sectional studies have shown that various forms of CMC are important, but less so than the telephone (Kim & McKay-Semmler, 2013; Kline & Liu, 2005). In one study, the number of minutes international students spent per week in contact with family members from their home country via phone was positively associated with self-reported stress (Kline & Liu, 2005). However, the association between e-mail contact and stress was not statistically significant. Among sojourners participating in a study abroad program, technologies such as e-mail, SNSs, and the telephone were important in maintaining existing supportive relationships and allowing them to feel that support resources were available (Mikal & Grace, 2012). Other research offers evidence of the difficulties associated with being unable to maintain existing offline connections. A qualitative study of Asian international students living in South Korea showed that some students experienced a reduction in their social networks due to underdeveloped technology infrastructure in their home country (Kim, Yun, & Yoo, 2009). The inaccessibility of CMC made it difficult for students to maintain the level of connection they desired with friends and family in their home country.

Researchers have also considered the implications of different types of support and support messages. In a study of Chinese international students, support-related relational messages were common in the e-mail and telephone exchanges between students and their families (Kline & Liu, 2005). Both e-mail and telephone were used for messages reflecting encouragement, caring, reassurance, and advice. Research examining Chinese nationals who had immigrated to Singapore showed that almost all of the migrants who had Internet access sought some form of support, with informational and tangible support being the most common (Chen & Choi, 2011). Immigrants who had been in their host country longer were less likely to seek emotional, tangible, and companionship support but not informational support. Seeking most types of support was inversely related to support available in immigrants' offline relationships. In other research, international students living in South Korea reported using SNSs like Cyworld for seeking informational support (Kim et al., 2009).

A fair amount of evidence exists to suggest that computer-mediated support can aid in cultural adaptation. A study of international students showed that CMC use for contacting members of their home country was positively associated with perceived support available from individuals in their home country and, in turn, psychological adaptation to living in the United States (Cemalciar, Falbo, & Stapleton, 2005). Other researchers have found positive associations between international students' use of the Internet for support-seeking purposes and their fear of victimization and perceived discrimination (Ye, 2005). Particular types of support also appear to have important implications for cultural adaptation. One cross-sectional study of immigrants found that respondents' overall levels of perceived support availability as well as specific support types (e.g., informational, emotional) were generally associated with socio-cultural, social, physical, and psychological adaptation (Chen & Choi, 2011). Among Chinese international students, another scholar found that informational and emotional support available from online ethic support groups was inversely associated with several dimensions of acculturative stress (Ye, 2006).

Education

The implications of computer-mediated support have also been considered in educational settings. Social support can be important in coping with the stressors that accompany formal education (Haythornthwaite, Kazmer, Robins, & Shoemaker, 2000). Much of this research involves distance learning in which students interact with one another and their instructors using various forms of CMC. Several studies have documented the benefits of computer-mediated support in such settings. Interviews with students participating in a distance-learning course showed that the support they received from other students was critical to their success (Haythornthwaite et al., 2000). The bonds students formed with one another and the exchange of informational support allowed them to feel greater efficacy about completing the class. Students who failed to make such connections reported a sense of isolation that furthered their existing anxieties about the course. A study of students in a teacher-education program had similar findings (Anderson, 2004). Support from others in the course was essential to overcome isolation and extended beyond class assignments to stressful life events experienced by class members. Students exchanged support on the shared message board for the course as well as by private e-mail.

Researchers have also examined the support-related content of messages exchanged in distance learning courses. In an analysis of two such courses, one-fifth of all messages included social support (Kucuk, Genc-Kumtepe, & Tasci, 2010). Support was conceptualized as messages intended to benefit social interaction such as expressing thanks or offering assistance. In other research examining students' technology use to communicate with one another outside of their online class, almost half of the respondents gave or received emotional support (Kearns & Frey, 2010). Social network analysis has been used to examine support message content. One such study found changes in advice networks over time as interaction tended to converge around designated teams within a distance-learning class (Haythornthwaite, 2001). Emotional support networks, by contrast, did not conform to team structures and were less stable than other networks. The individuals who contributed to emotional support over the semester changed. Face-to-face contact appeared to serve as a catalyst for computer-mediated emotional support at later time points. Other research has examined differences in support content based on the nature of the communication medium. Relative to information exchange, one study found that informational and emotional support messages were more common when students used synchronous forms of CMC than asynchronous forms (Hrastinski, 2008).

Special Contexts: Conclusions and Recommendations

Several trends are evident across research examining the implications of computer-mediated support among older adults, in cultural adaptation, and in distance education. Much of this work is rooted in the idea that CMC offers unique opportunities for exchanging social support. Across the three contexts, there is evidence to demonstrate the utility of CMC. The use of various forms of CMC was associated with support perceptions across all three contexts—although the findings related to individual technologies were more mixed. There is also evidence that support acquired in computer-mediated contexts is beneficial. Informational and emotional support, in particular, appears to play a significant role. More generally, the research on older adults and among individuals adapting to a new culture suggests the importance of CMC in overcoming distance and maintaining existing offline relationships with friends and family.

Research examining the support-related implications of CMC in specialized contexts offers several broader insights about social support processes. The results across these three contexts underscore the importance of strong-tie relationships with friends and family members as an indispensable resource for support. CMC proved critical for allowing access to one's existing strong-tie relationships and facilitating adaption to a new culture. Yet, this body of research also highlights the importance of CMC for connecting with weak ties. Online community members served as critical support resources among older adults as did classmates in online educational settings. Taken as a whole, the body of research examining computer-mediated support among older adults, in cultural adaptation, and in educational settings underscores that importance of considering the nature of the seeker and provider's relationship in understanding social support processes.

Agenda for Future Research

Research conducted to date on computer-mediated support offers valuable insights about factors that lead individuals to seek support online as well as the potential for achieving beneficial outcomes. In an effort to build from these findings, we propose an agenda for future scholarship. We highlight several issues that we believe will, if addressed, foster a more complete understanding of the uses and effects of computer-mediated support.

Better Understanding the Role of Computer-Mediation

One valuable avenue for future scholarship is to explore the implications of computer-mediation for computer-mediated support processes. Although a number of studies have demonstrated potential benefits of computer-mediated support, the implications of CMC have not been fully considered. Indeed, the various forms of CMC are typically studied as a constant in cross-sectional or longitudinal research. Such approaches make it difficult to isolate the implications stemming from the unique characteristics of computer-mediated interaction. Four aspects that transcend specific forms of CMC warrant consideration: synchronicity, availability of social cues, publicness, and network potential. Understanding the ways in which these characteristics are appropriated by users and with what effects would substantially help advance research on computer-mediated support.

Synchronicity

Computer-mediated support technologies vary in the degree to which they make possible synchronous interaction. Online discussion communities, for example, are typically asynchronous in that there can be a delay between constructing and sending a message. Instant messaging, in contrast, is more synchronous. The implications of (a)synchronicity for the construction and effects of support messages warrant additional empirical scrutiny. Although several scholars argue that the potential to take one's time in crafting support requests or attempts at providing support could foster more effective supportive interactions (Caplan & Turner, 2007; Wright & Bell, 2003), relatively little research has examined this issue. It would be valuable to more directly explore if and how the degree to which a technology is asynchronous influences the production and effects of support messages. Moreover, it would be useful to further examine how this particular characteristic is appropriated by support seekers and providers.

Availability of Social Cues

Another way that computer-mediated support is unique involves the availability of social cues such as facial expressions, eye contact, and vocalics. Social cues can extend to information about one's identity and include issues associated with anonymity. Different forms of CMC vary in the degree to which these cues are reduced or absent during interaction. This characteristic has been noted to have potentially significant implications for communicating support (Caplan & Turner, 2007; Tanis, 2008b; Wright & Bell, 2003), and studies conducted to date offers some evidence to support such claims (High & Solomon, 2014; Lewandowski et al., 2011). Additional research is essential to better understand the effects of reduced social cues on support processes and outcomes and as well as the mechanisms through which these cues bring about such effects. Formally manipulating the relative presence or absence of particular social cues in experimental research offers one potentially valuable approach. Qualitative studies considering the affordances stemming from the ways in which the reduction in social cues is appropriated by support seekers and providers would also be beneficial.

Publicness

Forms of CMC used to acquire and share support also vary in the degree to which they make possible public or private interaction. Whereas a technology such as e-mail can be used for dyadic communication, other technologies like blogs, SNSs, and online communities are public or semi-public in that the interactions that take place may be available to many people. The degree of publicness is important because it can dictate the type of audience to which a support seeker may have access. Although e-mail is valuable for connecting to known others such as family, friends, or health care providers, technologies that offer more public interactions can make it possible to connect with weak ties. Researchers have consistently highlighted the utility of technologies making possible more public interactions (High & Solomon, 2011; Tanis, 2008a; Wright & Bell, 2003) and scholars have demonstrated the benefits of support acquired via public technologies, such as blogs (Rains & Keating, 2011) and SNSs (Oh et al., 2014). Despite the value of such works, the unique contribution of publicness to the uses and effects of these technologies is not well understood. Research on computer-mediated support would benefit from sustained efforts at examining the implications of publicness for social support processes.

Network potential

A final dimension of CMC that is critical to consider involves the degree to which it is networked. Many popular forms of CMC relevant to social support such as online communities, SNSs, and blogs are distinct in that interactions take place among groups of interconnected individuals. Interaction occurs in the context of a broader network of actors also seeking and providing support. To date, however, little research has considered the implications of networks for computer-mediated support. Those studies that have been conducted offer important insights such as that structures of networks for different types of support vary over time (Haythornthwaite, 2001) and that networks in support communities can be highly centralized (Chang, 2009). Exploring computer-mediated support from a network perspective would generate insights about broader trends in supportive interactions and help to better understand how groups and communities function in fostering or mitigating particular support processes.

Summary

Examining the role of computer mediation in computer-mediated support is essential to help advance scholarship on this topic. As opposed to studying individual forms of CMC, scholars are encouraged to examine the implications of those characteristics that transcend particular technologies. Synchronicity, availability of social cues, publicness, and network potential are four characteristics that are particularly relevant to supportive interactions. Table 7.1 outlines a number of possible questions that might be investigated. Systematic and enduring efforts to study how these characteristics are used to seek and exchange support and with what effects will make it possible to more fully understand computer-mediated support.

Situating Online Support in the Context of Offline Resources

Another objective for scholarship on computer-mediated support involves adopting an ecological perspective of social support and CMC and considering

Table 7.1 Sample Questions for Examining the Implications of Computer Mediation for Computer-Mediated Support

Synchronicity	Availability of social cues	Publicness	Network potential
Under what conditions do support providers produce more effective support messages using more and less asynchronous technologies?	Under what conditions do support providers produce more effective support messages using reduced and increased-cue technologies?	How does the degree of publicness influence the nature and outcomes of support provision attempts?	Are there differences in the properties of networks for different types of social support (e.g., informational, emotional, esteem) in computer-mediated contexts?
Under what conditions do support seekers produce more effective support requests using more and less asynchronous technologies?	Under what conditions do support seekers produce more effective support requests using reduced and increased-cue technologies?	How does the degree of publicness influence the nature and outcomes of support seeking attempts?	What network properties in computer-mediated support contexts are associated with positive outcomes?
How are more and less asynchronous technologies appropriate by support seekers?	How are reduced and increased-cue technologies appropriated by support seekers?	How are more and less public technologies appropriated by support seekers?	What properties of offline support networks are associated with the use and outcomes of computer-mediated support?
Are asynchronous technologies used differently by support seekers and providers than synchronous technologies?	Are reduced-cue technologies used differently by support seekers and providers than increased-cue technologies?	What role do specific audiences play in support seeking behaviors and outcomes?	What factors explain how and why computer-mediated support networks change over time?
What individual difference factors are associated with a greater preference for using more and less asynchronous technologies for seeking social support?	What individual difference factors are associated with a greater preference for using reduced and increased-cue technologies for seeking social support?	What individual difference factors are associated with a greater preference for using more and less public technologies for seeking social support?	

those overlapping macro- and micro-level factors that could be significant. One specific avenue that might be pursued involves better understanding the implications of support seekers' online and offline support resources. In much of the research reviewed in this chapter that considers this issue, one's offline support resources are considered to be separate and unique from one's online resources. Membership in an online community, for example, may offer access to a network of weak ties that is wholly distinct from one's offline support resources consisting of friends and family members (i.e., strong ties). To date, several studies have documented the importance of such offline connections. Computer-mediated support may be particularly attractive (Chen & Choi, 2011) and valuable (Rains & Keating, 2011) when support in one's offline relationships is lacking. Beyond documenting this phenomenon, however, relatively little research has been conducted to explore how and why such effects occur. What is it about computer-mediated support that is uniquely beneficial when offline support is lacking? What role do the characteristics of the specific support medium (e.g., reduced social cues) play in bringing about such effects? Answering questions such as these would help to advance research on computer-mediated support by generating insights about its role and utility in the broader context of support seekers' offline relationships.

Beyond examining one's online and offline connections as two wholly distinct support resources, it would be valuable to examine the use and effects of CMC in the context of existing strong-tie relationships with friends and family members. For example, scholars have considered the importance of forms of CMC like e-mail as a means for international students to maintain their existing relationships in their home countries (Kline & Liu, 2005; Mikal & Grace, 2012). Although contexts such as this one are worthwhile to consider, it is also important to examine the use of CMC among friends and family members who frequently interact face-to-face. As mobile phones and Internet access become increasingly prevalent in our society, it is critical to consider the support-related implications of these technologies for existing strong-tie relationships. How and when is CMC used to acquire and share support with friends and family members with whom one routinely interacts face-to-face? Do the uses and effects of various forms of CMC for exchanging support among friends and family members vary? Through answering these and related questions it will be possible to better understand the implications of CMC in existing strong-tie relationships.

Considering what CMC Can Tell Us about Social Support Processes

In addition to the benefits of better understanding computer-mediated support for its own sake, examining CMC has the potential to advance our knowledge of basic social support processes. As was previously noted, much of the research on social support has been conducted in the context of face-to-face interaction. Because CMC is unique from face-to-face interaction in several important ways, it offers a novel vantage point from which to observe fundamental aspects of supportive communication. Research examining the implications of reduced social cues, for example, makes it possible to better understand the importance and role of nonverbal behavior during supportive interaction. Studies exploring individuals' motivations for seeking support from online communities help identify and offer insights about the potential limitations of acquiring support from strong ties such as family and friends. In research conducted to date, scholars have not consistently considered the implications of their findings for our understanding of social support more broadly. Future efforts to do so are essential to maximize the utility of studying computer-mediated support and better understanding basic social support processes.

Examining Contexts beyond Health

As evidenced by the studies reviewed in this chapter, research on computer-mediated support tends to be largely conducted in the context of health and among individuals coping with illness. Although it is absolutely critical to study health-related support, additional research would be valuable examining supportive exchanges in other settings. Social support is an important resource for coping with a range of life stressors, and additional research on computer-mediated support reflecting this diversity would be valuable. Indeed, research conducted among older adults, individuals adapting to new cultures, and educational settings offers evidence of the unique potential implications of computer-mediated support beyond health. Researchers would be well served to further explore these contexts as well as others where support is particularly critical. It may be that some dimensions of computer-mediated support are more or less influential in coping with particular types of stressors. More generally, such efforts would contribute to a more well-rounded understanding of the use and consequences of computer-mediated support.

Conclusion

It is reasonable to conclude that Kiesler and colleagues' (1984) forecast about the potential of CMC for social support has proven accurate. Multiple national surveys (Fox, 2011; National Cancer Institute, 2012) offer evidence that computer-mediated support is an important resource among American adults. Scholars have recognized this trend and an increasingly large body of research has accumulated on this topic. This chapter reviewed scholarship focusing on support seeking and the outcomes of computer-mediated support. Taken as a whole, the research reviewed in this chapter substantiates many of the purported benefits and limitations of CMC identified in previous reviews (e.g., Caplan & Turner, 2007; Tanis, 2008a; Wright & Bell, 2003). It should be noted, however, that several of the specific issues examined in this review have received relatively limited empirical attention. Moreover, important questions remain about the operating mechanisms and broader ecological factors contributing to the support-related implications of CMC. In this chapter an agenda for future research was presented in an effort to promote systematic and sustained efforts to address these issues. It is our hope that continued efforts studying this phenomenon will make it possible to better understand the use and effects of contemporary forms of CMC for exchanging support and be well-prepared for those new forms developed in the future.

Note

1   Research on MMOGs was included in the review because MMOGs tend to offer dyadic and group interaction and share important similarities with online communities.

References

Anderson, B. (2004). Dimensions of learning and support in an online community. *Open Learning: The Journal of Open, Distance, and e-Learning, 19,* 183–190. doi: 10.1080/0268051042000224770

Burleson, B. R., & MacGeorge, E. L. (2002). Supportive communication. In M. L. Knapp & J. A. Daly (Eds.), *Handbook of interpersonal communication* (3rd edn, pp. 374–424). Thousand Oaks, CA: Sage.

Burleson, B. R., Albrecht, T. L., & Sarason, I. G. (1994). *Communication of social support: Messages, interactions, relationships, and community.* Thousand Oaks, CA: Sage.

Campbell, K., & Wright, K. B. (2002). On-line support groups: An investigation of relationships among source credibility, dimensions of relational communication, and perceptions of emotional support. *Communication Research Reports, 19,* 183–193. doi: 10.1080/08824090209384846

Caplan, S. E., & Turner, J. S. (2007). Bringing theory to research on computer-mediated supportive and comforting communication. *Computers in Human Behavior, 23,* 985–998. doi: 10.1016/j.chb.2005.08.003

Cemalciar Z., Falbo, T., & Stapleton, L. M. (2005). Cyber communication: A new opportunity for international students' adaptation? *International Journal of Intercultural Relations, 29,* 91–110. doi: 10.1016/j.ijintrel.2005.04.002

Chang, H-I. (2009). Online supportive interactions: Using a network approach to examine communication patterns within a psychosis social support group in Taiwan. *Journal of the American Society for Information Science and Technology, 60,* 1504–1518. doi: 10.1002/asi.21070

Chen, W., & Choi, A. (2011). Leveraging computer-mediated communication for social support in immigrants' intercultural adaptation. *Cross-Cultural Communication, 7,* 167–176. doi: 10.1177/1461444810396311

Chung, D. S., & Kim, S. (2008). Blogging activity among cancer patients and their companions: Uses, gratifications, and predictors of outcomes. *Journal of the American Society for Information Science and Technology, 59,* 297–306. doi: 10.1002/asi.20751

Chung, J. E. (2013). Social interaction in online support groups: Preference for online social interaction over offline social interaction. *Computers in Human Behavior, 29,* 1408–1414. doi: 10.1016/j.chb.2013.01.019

Cody, M. J., Dunn, D., Hoppin, S., & Wendt, P. (1999). Silver surfers: Training and evaluating Internet use among older adult learners. *Communication Education, 48,* 269–286. doi: 10.1080/03634529909379178

Cohen, G. E., & Kerr, B. A. (1999). Computer-mediated counseling: An empirical study of a new mental health treatment. *Computers in Human Services, 15,* 13–26. doi: 10.1300/J407v15n04_02

Cohen, S., & Wills, T. A. (1985). Stress, social support and the buffering hypothesis. *Psychological Bulletin, 98,* 310–357. doi: 10.1037/0033-2909.98.2.310

Cohen, S., Underwood, L., & Gottlieb, B. (2000). *Social support measurement and interventions: A guide for health and social scientists.* New York: Oxford.

Colvin, J., Chenoeth, L., Bold, M., & Harding, C. (2004). Caregivers of older adults: Advantages and disadvantages of Internet-based social support. *Family Relations, 53,* 49–57. doi: 10.1111/j.1741-3729.2004.00008.x

Culnan, M. J., & Markus, M. L. (1987). Information technologies. In F. M. Jablin, L. L. Putnam, K. H. Roberts, & L. W. Porter (Eds.), *Handbook of organizational communication: An interdisciplinary perspective* (pp. 420–443). Newbury Park, CA: Sage Publications.

Cutrona, C. E. (1990). Stress and social support—In search of optimal matching. *Journal of Social and Clinical Psychology, 9,* 3–14. doi: 10.1521/jscp.1990.9.1.3

DeAndrea, D. C. (2014). Testing the proclaimed affordances of online support groups in a nationally representative sample of adults seeking mental assistance. *Journal of Health Communication.* Advanced online publication. doi: 10.1080/10810730.2014. 914606

DeAndrea, D. C., & Anthony, J. C. (2013). Online peer support for mental health problems in the United States: 2004–2010. *Psychological Medicine,* 43, 2277–2288. doi: 10.1017/S0033291713000172

Eastin, M. S., & LaRose, R. (2005). Alt.support: Modeling social support online. *Computers in Human Behavior, 21,* 977–992. doi: 10.1016/j.chb.2004.02.024

Erikson, J., & Johnson, G. M. (2011). Internet use and psychological wellness during adulthood. *Canadian Journal of Aging, 30,* 197–209. doi: 10.1017/S0714980811000109

Esquivel, A., Meric-Bernstam, F., & Bernstam, E. V. (2006). Accuracy and self-correction of information received from an Internet breast cancer list: Content analysis. *British Medical Journal, 332,* 939–943. doi: 10.1136/bmj.38753.524201.7C

Feng, B., & Hyun, M. J. (2012). The influence of friends' instant messenger status on individuals' coping and support-seeking. *Communication Studies, 63,* 536–553. doi: 10.1080/10510974.2011.649443

Feng, B., Li, S., & Li, N. (2013). Is a profile worth a thousand words? How online support-seekers profile features may influence the quality of received support messages. *Communication Research.* Advanced online publication. doi: 10.1177/ 0093650213510942

Fox, S. (2011). *Peer-to-peer healthcare.* Pew Internet and American Life Project. Retrieved from www.pewinternet.org

Giota, K. G., & Kleftaras, G. (2014). The discriminant value of personality, motivation, and online relationship quality in predicting attraction to online social support on Facebook. *International Journal of Human-Computer Interaction, 30,* 985–994. doi: 10.1080/10447318.2014.925770

Goldsmith, D. J. (2004). *Communicating social support.* New York: Cambridge University Press. doi: 10.1017/CBO9780511606984

Granovetter, M. S. (1973). The strength of weak ties. *American Journal of Sociology, 78,* 1360–1380. doi: 10.1086/225469

Green-Hamann, S. G., Eichhorn, K. C., & Sherblom, J. C. (2011). An exploration of why people participate in second life social support groups. *Journal of Computer Mediated Communication,* 16, 465–491. doi: 10.1111/j.1083-6101.2011.01543.x

Haberstroh, S., & Moyer, M. (2012). Exploring an online self-injury support group: Perspectives from group members. *The Journal for Specialists in Group Work, 37,* 113–132. doi: 10.1080/01933922.2011.646088

Hampton, K., Goulet, L. S., Rainie, L., & Purcell, K. (2011). *Social networking sites and our lives.* Pew Internet and American Life Project. Retrieved from www.pewinternet.org

Han, J. Y., Hou, J., Kim, E., & Gustafson, D. H. (2014). Lurking as an active participation process: A longitudinal investigation of engagement with an online cancer support group. *Health Communication, 29,* 911–923. doi: 10.1080/10410236.2013. 816911

Han, J. Y., Kim, J. H., Yoon, H. J., Shim, M., McTavish, F. M., & Gustafson, D. H. (2012). Social and psychological determinants of levels of engagement with an online breast cancer support group: Posters, lurkers, and nonusers. *Journal of Health Communication, 17,* 356–371. doi: 10.1080/10810730.2011.585696

Haythornthwaite, C. (2001). Exploring multiplexity: Social network structures in a computer-supported distance learning class. *The Information Society, 17,* 211–226. doi: 10.1080/01972240152493065

Haythornthwaite, C., Kazmer, M. M., Robins, J., & Shoemaker, S. (2000). Community development among distance learners: Temporal and technological dimensions. *Journal of Computer-Mediated Communication, 6.* doi: 10.1111/j.1083-6101.2000.tb00114.x

High, A. C., & Solomon, D. H. (2011). Locating computer-mediated social support within online communication environments. In K. B. Wright & L. M. Webb (Eds.), *Computer-mediated communication in personal relationships* (pp. 119–136). New York: Hampton Press.

High, A. C., & Solomon, D. H. (2014). Communication channel, sex, and the immediate and longitudinal outcomes of verbal person-centered support. *Communication Monographs, 81,* 439–468. doi: 10.1080/03637751.2014.933245

High, A. C., & Steuber, K. R. (2014). An examination of support (in) adequacy: Types, sources, and consequences of social support among infertile women. *Communication Monographs, 81,* 157–178. doi: 10.1080/03637751.2013.878868

High, A. C., Oeldorf-Hirsch, A., & Bellur, S. (2014). Misery rarely gets company: The influence of emotional bandwidth on supportive communication on Facebook. *Computers in Human Behavior, 34,* 79–88. doi: 10.1016/j.chb.2014.01.037

Holbrey, S., & Coulson, N. S. (2013). A qualitative investigation of the impact of peer to peer online support for women living with polycystic ovary syndrome. *BMC Women's Health, 13.* doi: 10.1186/1472-6874-13-51

Houston, T. K., Cooper, L. A., & Ford, D. E. (2002). Internet support groups for depression: A 1-year prospective cohort study. *American Journal of Psychiatry, 159,* 2062–2068. doi: 10.1176/appi.ajp.159.12.2062

Hrastinski, S. (2008). The potential of synchronous communication to enhance participation in online discussions: A case study of two e-learning courses. *Information & Management, 45,* 499–506. doi: 10.1016/j.im.2008.07.005

Hwang, K. O., Ottenbacher, A. J., Lucke, J. F., Etchegaray, J. M., Graham, A. L., & Thomas, E. J. (2011). Measuring social support for weight loss in an Internet weight loss community. *Journal of Health Communication, 16,* 198–211. doi: 10.1080/ 10810730.2010.535106

Kaczmarek, L. D., & Drazkowski, D. (2014). MMORPG escapism predicts decreased well-being: Examination of game time, game realism beliefs, and online social support for offline problems. *Cyberpsychology, Behavior, and Social Networking, 17,* 298–302. doi: 10.1089/cyber.2013.0595

Kanayama, T. (2003). Ethnographic research on the experience of Japanese elderly people online. *New Media & Society, 5,* 267–288. doi: 10.1177/146144480300500 2007

Kearns, L. R., & Frey, B. A. (2010). Web 2.0 technologies and back channel communication in an online learning community. *TechTrends, 54,* 41–51. doi: 10.1007/s11528-010-0419-y

Kiesler, S., Siegel, J., & McGuire, T. W. (1984). Social psychological aspects of computer-mediated communication. *American Psychologist, 39,* 1123–1134. doi: 10.1037/0003-066X.39.10.1123

Kim, E., Han, J. Y., Moon, T. J., Shaw, B., Shah, D. V., McTavish, F., & Gustafson, D. H. (2012). The process and effects of supportive message expression and reception in online breast cancer support groups. *Psycho-Oncology, 21,* 531–540. doi: 10.1002/pon.1942

Kim, E., Han, J. Y., Shah, D., Shaw, B., McTavish, F., Gustafson, D. H., & Fan, D. (2011). Predictors of supportive message expression and reception in an interactive cancer communication system. *Journal of Health Communication, 16,* 1106–1121. doi: 10.1080/10810730.2011.571337

Kim, H. (2014). Enacted support on social media and subjective well-being. *International Journal of Communication, 8,* 2201–2221.

Kim, K-H., Yun, H., & Yoo, Y. (2009). The Internet as a facilitator of cultural hybridization and interpersonal relationship management for Asian international students in South Korea. *Asian Journal of Communication, 19,* 152–169. doi: 10.1080/01292980902826880

Kim, Y. Y., & McKay-Semmler, K. (2013). Social engagement and cross-cultural adaptation: An examination of direct and mediated interpersonal communication activities of educated non-natives in the United States. *International Journal of Intercultural Relations, 37,* 99–112. doi: 10.1016/j.ijintrel.2012.04.15

Kline S. L., & Liu, F. (2005). The influence of comparative media use on acculturation, acculturative stress, and family relationships of Chinese international students. *International Journal of Intercultural Relations, 29,* 367–390. doi: 10.1016/j.ijintrel.2005.07.001

Ko, H. C., & Kuo, F. Y. (2009). Can blogging enhance subjective well-being through self-disclosure? *CyberPsychology & Behavior, 12,* 75–79. doi: 10.1089/cpb.2008.016

Kucuk, M., Genc-Kumtepe, E., & Tasci, D. (2010). Support services and learning styles influence interaction in asynchronous online discussions. *Educational Media International, 47,* 39–56. doi: 10.1080/09523981003654969

Lakey, B., & Cohen, S. (2000). Social support theory and measurement. In S. Cohen, L. Underwood, & B. Gottlieb (Eds.), *Measuring and intervening in social support* (pp. 29–52). New York: Oxford University Press.

Lawlor, A., & Kirakowski, J. (2014). Online support groups for mental health: A space for challenging self-stigma or a means of social avoidance? *Computers in Human Behavior, 32,* 152–161. doi: 10.1016/j.chb.2013.11.015

Ledbetter, A. M. (2009). Chronemic cues and sex differences in relational e-mail: Perceiving immediacy and supportive message quality. *Social Science Computer Review, 26,* 466–482. doi: 10.1177/0894439308314812

Ledbetter, A. M., & Larson, K. A. (2008). Nonverbal cues in e-mail supportive communication: Associations with sender sex, recipient sex, and support satisfaction. *Information, Communication, & Society, 11,* 1089–110. doi: 10.1080/13691180802109022

Lewandowski, J., Rosenberg, B. D., Parks, M. J., & Siegel, J. T. (2011). The effect of informal social support: Face-to-face versus computer-mediated communication. *Computers in Human Behavior, 27,* 1806–1814. doi: 10.1016/j.chb.2011.03.008

Li, S., & Feng, B. (2014). What to say to an online support-seeker? The influence of others' responses and support-seekers' replies. *Human Communication Research.* Advanced online publication. doi: 10.1111/hcre.12055

Liang, T. P., Ho, Y. T., Li, Y. W., & Turban, E. (2011). What drives social commerce: The role of social support and relationship quality. *International Journal of Electronic Commerce, 16,* 69–90. doi: 10.2753/JEC1086-4415160204

Lieberman, M. A., & Goldstein, B. A. (2006). Not all negative emotions are equal: The role of emotional expression in online support groups for women with breast cancer. *Psycho-Oncology, 15,* 160–168. doi: 10.1002/pon.932

Lim, V. K. G., Thompson, S. H. T., & Zhao, X. (2013). Psychological costs of support seeking and choice of communication channel. *Behavior & Information Technology, 32,* 132–146. doi: 10.1080/0144929X.2010.518248

Lin, C-P., & Bhattacherjee, A. (2009). Understanding online social support and its antecedents: A socio-cognitive model. *The Social Science Journal, 46,* 724–737. doi: 10.1016/j.soscij.2009.03.004

Liu, C., & Yu, C. (2013). Can Facebook induce well-being? *Cyberpsychology, Behavior, & Social Networking, 16,* 674–678. doi: 10.1089/cyber.2012.0301

Liu, X., & LaRose, R. (2008). Does using the Internet make people more satisfied with their lives? The effects of the Internet on college students' school life satisfaction. *CyberPsychology & Behavior, 11,* 310–319. doi: 10.1089/cpb.2007.0040

Longman, H., O'Connor, E., & Obst, P. (2009). The effect of social support derived from World of Warcraft on negative psychological symptoms. *CyberPsychology & Behavior, 12,* 563–566. doi: 10.1089/cpb.2009.001

Malik, S. H., & Coulson, N. S. (2008). Computer-mediated infertility support groups: An exploratory study of online experiences. *Patient Education and Counseling, 73,* 105–113. doi: 10.1016/j.pec.2008.05.024

McDaniel, B. T., Coyne, S. M., & Holmes, E. K. (2012). New mothers and media use: Associations between blogging, social networking, and maternal well-being. *Maternal Child Health Journal, 16,* 1509–1517. doi: 10.1007/s10995-011-0918-2

McKenna, K. Y. A., & Bargh, J. A. (1998). Coming out in the age of the Internet: Identity 'demarginalization' through virtual group participation. *Journal of Personality and Social Psychology, 75,* 681–694. doi: 10.1037/0022-3514.75.3.681

Mikal, J. P., & Grace, K. (2012). Against abstinence-only education abroad: Viewing Internet use during study abroad as a possible experience enhancement. *Journal of Studies in International Education, 16,* 287–306. doi: 10.1177/1028315311423108

Mikal, J. P., Rice, R. E., Abeyta, A., & DeVilbiss, J. (2013). Transition, stress and computer-mediated social support. *Computers in Human Behavior, 29,* 40–53. doi: 10.1016/j.chb.2012.12.012

Mo, P. K., & Coulson, N. S. (2010). Empowering processes in online support groups among people living with HIV/AIDS: A comparative analysis of 'lurkers' and 'posters'. *Computers in Human Behavior, 26,* 1183–1193. doi: 10.1016/j.chb.2010.03.028

Mo, P. K., & Coulson, N. S. (2012). Developing a model for online support group use, empowering processes and psychosocial outcomes for individuals living with HIV/AIDS. *Psychology & Health, 27,* 445–459. doi: 10.1080/08870446.2011.592981

Mo, P. K., & Coulson, N. S. (2013). Online support group use and psychological health for individuals living with HIV/AIDS. *Patient Education and Counseling, 93,* 426–432. doi: 10.1016/j.pec.2013.04.004

Nabi, R. L., Prestin, A., & So, J. (2013). Facebook friends with (health) benefits? Exploring social network site use and perceptions of social support, stress, and well-being. *Cyberpsychology, Behavior, and Social Networking, 16,* 721–727. doi: 10.1089/cyber.2012.0521

Nambisan, P. (2011). Information seeking and social support in online health communities: Impact on patients' perceived empathy. *Journal of American Medical Informatics Association, 18,* 298–304. doi: 10.1136/amiajnl-2010-000058

National Cancer Institute. (2012). Health Information National Trends Survey. Retrieved from http://hints.cancer.gov

Noel, J. G., & Epstein, J. (2003). Social support and health among senior Internet users: Results of an online survey. *Journal of Technology in Human Services, 21,* 35–54. doi: 10.1300/J017v21n03_03

Oh, H. J., & Lee, B. (2012). The effect of computer-mediated social support in online communities on patient empowerment and doctor-patient interaction. *Health Communication, 27,* 30–41. doi: 10.1080/10410236.2011.567449

Oh, H. J., Ozkaya, E., & LaRose, R. (2014). How does online social networking enhance life satisfaction? The relationships among online supportive interaction, affect, perceived social support, sense of community, and life satisfaction. *Computers in Human Behavior, 30,* 69–78. doi: 10.1016/j.chb.2013.07.053

Oh, H. J., Lauckner, C., Boehmer, J., Fewins-Bliss, R., & Li, K. (2013). Facebooking for health: An examination into the solicitation and effects of health-related social support on social networking sites. *Computers in Human Behavior, 29,* 2072–2080. doi: 10.1016/j.chb.2013.04.017

Pew Internet and American Life Project. (2005). *Internet: Mainstreaming of online life.* Retrieved from www.pewinternet.org

Pfeil, U., Zaphiris, P., & Wilson, S. (2009). Older adults' perceptions and experiences of online support. *Interacting with Computers, 21,* 159–172. doi: 10.1016/j.intcom.2008.12.001

Rains, S. A. (2015). Language style matching as a predictor of perceived social support in computer-mediated interaction among individuals coping with illness. *Communication Research.* Advanced online publication. doi: 10.1177/0093650214565920

Rains, S. A., & Keating, D. M. (2011). The social dimension of blogging about health: Health blogging, social support, and well-being. *Communication Monographs, 78,* 511–534. doi: 10.1080/03637751.2011.618142

Rains, S. A., & Young, V. (2009). A meta-analysis of research on formal computer-mediated support groups: Examining group characteristics and health outcomes. *Human Communication Research, 35,* 309–336. doi: 10.1111/j.1468-2958.2009.01353.x

Rains, S. A., Peterson, E., & Wright, K. B. (2015). Communicating social support in computer-mediated contexts: A meta-analytic review of content analyses examining support messages shared online among individuals coping with illness. *Communication Monographs.* Advanced online publication. doi: 10.1080/03637751.2015.1019530

Robinson, J. D., & Turner, J. W. (2003). Impersonal, interpersonal, and hyperpersonal social support: Cancer and older adults. *Health Communication, 15,* 231–239. doi: 10.1207/S15327027HC1502_10

Rosman, S. (2004). Cancer and stigma: Experience of patients with chemotherapy-induced alopecia. *Patient Education and Counseling, 52*, 333–339. doi: 10.1016/S0738-3991(03)00040-5

Sarkadi, A., & Bremberg, S. (2005). Socially unbiased parenting support on the Internet: A cross-sectional study of users of a large Swedish parenting website. *Child: Care, Health & Development, 31*, 43–52. doi: 10.1111/j.1365-2214.2005.00475.x

Seçkin, G. (2013). Satisfaction with health status among cyber patients: Testing a mediation model of electronic coping support. *Behaviour & Information Technology, 32*, 91–101. doi: 10.1080/0144929X.2011.603359

Setoyama, Y., Yamazaki, Y., & Nakayama, K. (2011). Comparing support to breast cancer patients from online communities and face-to-face support groups. *Patient Education and Counseling, 85*, 95–100. doi: 10.1016/j.pec.2010.11.008

Smedema, S. M., & McKenzie, A. R. (2010). The relationship among frequency and type of Internet use, perceived social support, and sense of well-being in individuals with visual impairments. *Disability and Rehabilitation, 32*, 317–325. doi: 10.3109/09638280903095908

Spottswood, E. L., Walther, J. B., Holmstrom, A. R., & Ellison, N. E. (2013). Person-centered emotional support and gender attributions in computer-mediated communication. *Human Communication Research, 39*, 295–316. doi: 10.1111/hcre.12006

Swickert, R. J., Hittner, J. B., Harris, J. L., & Herring, J. A. (2002). Relationships among Internet use, personality, and social support. *Computers in Human Behavior, 18*, 437–451. doi: 10.1016/S0747-5632(01)00054-1

Tanis, M. (2008a). What makes the Internet a place to seek social support. In E. A. Konijin, S. Utz, M. Tanis, & S. B. Barnes (Eds.), *Mediated interpersonal communication* (pp. 290–308). New York: Routledge.

Tanis, M. (2008b). Health-related online forums: What's the big attraction. *Journal of Health Communication, 13*, 698–714. doi: 10.1080/10810730802415316

Thoits, P. A. (2011). Mechanisms linking social ties and support to physical and mental health. *Journal of Health and Social Behavior, 52*, 145–161. doi: 10.1177/0022146510395592

Turner, J. W., Grube, J. A., & Meyers, J. (2001). Developing an optimal match within online communities: An exploration of CMC support communities and traditional support. *Journal of Communication, 51*, 231–251. doi: 10.1111/j.1460-2466.2001.tb02879.x

Turner, J. W., Robinson, J. D., Tian, Y., Neustadtl, A., Angelus, P., Russell, M., et al. (2013). Can messages make a difference? The association between e-mail messages and health outcomes in diabetes patients. *Human Communication Research, 39*, 252–268. doi: 10.1111/j.1468-2958.2012.01437.x

Uchino, B. N. (2004). *Social support and physical health: Understanding the health consequences of relationships*. New Haven, CT: Yale University Press. doi: 10.12987/yale/9780300102185.001.0001

Vanable, P. A., Carey, M. P., Blàir, D. C., & Littlewood, R. A. (2006). Impact of HIV-related stigma on health behaviors and psychological adjustment among HIV-positive men and women. *AIDS and Behavior, 10*, 473–482. doi: 10.1007/s10461-006-9099-1

Vitak, J., & Ellison, N. B. (2012). 'There's a network out there you might as well tap': Exploring the benefits of and barriers to exchanging informational and support-based resources on Facebook. *New Media & Society, 15*, 243–259. doi: 10.177/1461444812451566

Waldron, V. R., Gitelson, R., & Kelly, D. L. (2005). Gender differences in social adaptation to a retirement community: Longitudinal changes and the role of mediated communication. *Journal of Applied Gerontology, 24,* 283–298. doi: 10.177/0733464805277122

Walther, J. B. (1996). Computer-mediated communication: Impersonal, interpersonal, and hyperpersonal interaction. *Communication Research, 23,* 1–43. doi: 10.1177/009365096023001001

Walther, J. B., & Boyd, S. (2002). Attraction to computer-mediated social support. In C. A. Lin & D. Atkin (Eds.), *Communication technology and society: Audience adoption and uses* (pp. 153–188). Cresskill, NJ: Hampton Press.

Wang, Z., Walther, J. B., Pingree, S., & Hawkins, R. P. (2008). Health information, credibility, homophily, and influence via the Internet: Web sites versus discussion groups. *Health Communication, 23,* 358–368. doi: 10.1080/10410230802229738

Wright, K. B. (1999). Computer-mediated support groups: An examination of relationships among social support, perceived stress, and coping strategies. *Communication Quarterly, 47,* 402–414. doi: 10.1080/01463379909385570

Wright, K. B. (2000a). Social support satisfaction, on-line communication apprehension, and perceived life stress within computer-mediated support groups. *Communication Research Reports, 17,* 139–147. doi: 10.1080/08824090009388760

Wright, K. B. (2000b). Perceptions of on-line support providers: An examination of perceived homophily, source credibility, communication and support within on-line support groups. *Communication Quarterly, 48,* 44–59. doi: 10.1080/01463370009385579

Wright, K. B. (2000c). Computer-mediated social support, older adults, and coping. *Journal of Communication, 50,* 100–118. doi: 10.1111/j.1460-2466.2000.tb02855.x

Wright, K. B. (2000d). The communication of social support within an on-line community for older adults: A qualitative analysis of the SeniorNet community. *Qualitative Research Reports in Communication, 1,* 33–43.

Wright, K. B. (2002). Social support within an on-line cancer community: An assessment of emotional support, perceptions of advantages and disadvantages, and motives for using the community. *Journal of Applied Communication Research, 30,* 195–209. doi: 10.1080/00909880216586

Wright, K. B. (2012). Emotional support and perceived stress among college students using Facebook.com: An exploration of the relationship between source perceptions and emotional support. *Communication Research Reports, 29,* 175–184. doi: 10.1080/08824096.2012.695957

Wright, K. B., & Bell, S. B. (2003). Health-related support groups on the Internet: Linking empirical findings to social support and computer-mediated communication theory. *Journal of Health Psychology, 8,* 37–52. doi: 10.1177/1359105303008001429

Wright, K. B., & Miller, C. H. (2010). A measure of weak tie/strong tie support network preference. *Communication Monographs, 77,* 502–520. doi: 10.1080/03637751.2010.502538

Wright, K. B., & Rains, S. A. (2013). Weak-tie support network preference, stigma, and health outcomes in computer-mediated support groups. *Journal of Applied Communication Research, 41,* 309–324. doi: 10.1080/00909882.2013.792435

Wright, K. B., & Rains, S. A. (2014). Weak tie support preference and coping style as predictors of perceived credibility within health-related on-line support groups. *Health Communication, 29,* 281–287. doi: 10.1080/10410236.2012.751084

Wright, K. B., Rains, S., & Banas, J. (2010). Weak-tie support network preference and perceived life stress among participants in health-related, computer-mediated support groups. *Journal of Computer-Mediated Communication*, *15*, 606–624. doi: 10.1111/j.1083-6101.2009.01505.x

Wright, K. B., Johnson, A. J., Averbeck, J., & Bernard, D. (2011). Computer-mediated social support groups: Promises and pitfalls for individuals coping with health concerns. In T. L. Thompson, R. Parrott, & J. F. Nussbaum (Eds.), *Handbook of health communication* (pp. 349–362). Thousand Oaks, CA: Sage.

Wright, K. B., Rosenberg, J., Egbert, N., Ploeger, N., Bernard, D. R., & King, S. (2013). Communication competence, social support, and depression among college students. A model of Facebook and face-to-face support network influence. *Journal of Health Communication*, *18*, 41–57. doi: 10.1080/10810730.2012.688250

Xie, B. (2008). Multimodal computer-mediated communication and social support among older Chinese Internet users. *Journal of Computer-Mediated Communication*, *13*, 728–750. doi: 10.1111/j.1083-6101.2008.00417.x

Ye, J. (2005). Acculturative stress and use of the Internet among East Asian international students in the United States. *CyberPsychology & Behavior, 8*, 154–161. doi: 10.1089/cpb.2005.8.154

Ye, J. (2006). An examination of acculturative stress, interpersonal social support, and use of online ethnic social groups among Chinese international students. *Howard Journal of Communications*, *17*, 1–20. doi: 10.1080/10646170500487764

Yli-Uotila, T., Rantanen, A., & Suominen, T. (2014). Online social support received by patients with cancer. *CIN: Computers Informatics, Nursing, 32*, 118–126.

Yoo, W., Namkoong, K., Choi, M., Shah, D. V., Tsang, S., Hong, Y., . . . & Gustafson, D. H. (2014). Giving and receiving emotional support online: Communication competence as a moderator of psychosocial benefits for women with breast cancer. *Computers in Human Behavior*, *30*, 13–22. doi: 10.1016/j.chb.2013.07.024

CHAPTER CONTENTS

8 Advice

Expanding the Communication Paradigm

Erina L. MacGeorge

Pennsylvania State University

Bo Feng

University of California, Davis

Lisa M. Guntzviller

University of Illinois

Advice is a ubiquitous form of support and influence, exchanged in diverse contexts. Communication scholars have examined how advice recipients evaluate advice, but have done less to explore the breadth of effects it can have. We contrast the "message paradigm" for advice research with three alternative paradigms, each developed primarily by scholars from other disciplines. We then spotlight five directions for future research, integrating elements of the alternative paradigms with communication questions, perspectives, and methods of inquiry. By acquainting our discipline with existing theory and research on advice, we encourage bolder exploration of this consequential interpersonal phenomenon.

> it would be best by far
> for all people by nature to have complete knowledge,
> but if not, since that is not how things lean,
> then it is well that they learn from good advice
>
> Sophocles, *Antigone*[1]

People have problems. Many of those problems are more easily addressed with advice from others. Consequently, advice is a ubiquitous form of interpersonal communication,[2] exchanged in both personal and professional contexts (Lomi, Lusher, Pattison, & Robins, 2013; MacGeorge & Hall, 2014), in a wide range of relationship configurations (Feng & Magen, 2015; Koenig, 2011), in face-to-face and mediated interactions (Blank, Schmidt, Vangsness, Monteiro, & Santagata, 2010), and in diverse cultures (Chentsova-

Dutton & Vaughn, 2011; Feng, 2014b). Indeed, the impact of advice on recipients, advisors, relationships, groups, and organizations is evident in multiple life domains. To offer just a few examples: Grandmothers advise on infant feeding (Reid, Schmied, & Beale, 2010), young women advise one another on HPV vaccination (Miller-Ott & Durham, 2011), financial advisors recommend investment strategies (Marsden, Zick, & Mayer, 2011), and managers consult with other managers (Wong & Boh, 2014),

Communication scholars have emphasized that advice is both social support and social influence (MacGeorge, Feng, Butler, & Budarz, 2004; Wilson & Kunkel, 2000). In other words, advice has the capacity to reduce recipients' distress and improve their coping in tandem with persuading them to take particular problem-solving actions (MacGeorge, Guntzviller, Hanasono, & Feng, 2013). These positive consequences of advice are counter-balanced by its potential to threaten face or identity, increase distress, and generate resistance to the advised action (Goldsmith & Fitch, 1997). Indeed, most communication research on advice has focused on explaining how features of advice messages affect supportive and persuasive outcomes for recipients (for a review, see MacGeorge, Feng, & Burleson, 2011). This research agenda has produced valuable insight into the relationship between the design of advice messages and immediate effects on their intended targets. Yet it has also underestimated the complexity and the consequentiality of advice because of its relative inattention to other predictors and outcomes, reliance on a narrow range of methods and theoretical perspectives, and insufficient attention to the wide range of relationships and contexts in which advice is exchanged.

This chapter was written to encourage communication scholars to move beyond seeing advice as a social support or social influence "message," and explore the influence of person-to-person advising in interactions, relationships, organizations, cultures, and online. To open these directions for future research, we begin by reviewing and critiquing the central paradigm for communication research on advice—what we call the message paradigm of research on advice (see also MacGeorge et al., 2004). We then discuss three alternative paradigms of advice research conducted primarily (although not exclusively) by scholars from other disciplines, highlighting their strengths and limitations. In the final section, we recommend five future directions for research on advice. These directions reflect integrations of the existing paradigms, but also encourage a broader domain of topical focus and practical application, together with more diversity of theoretical perspective and research methods. Overall, we have two goals: acquainting communication scholars with the broad territory of existing theory and research on advice, and encouraging bolder exploration of this consequential interpersonal phenomenon.

The Message Paradigm

At present, the message paradigm for research on advice has two defining characteristics: (a) positioning advice as a type of message provided in supportive encounters, usually in personal relationships; and (b) focusing on the relationship between qualities of these advice messages and their effects on recipients (Goldsmith & MacGeorge, 2000). Indeed, most of this work fits within the broader tradition of studying social support from a "communication perspective" (MacGeorge et al., 2011), where advice is typically categorized as a form of informational or instrumental support and has been explicitly defined as messages that make recommendations about what to do, think, or feel in response to a problematic situation (MacGeorge, Feng, & Thompson, 2008). Researchers whose work contributes to the message paradigm principally come from departments of communication (but see Dalal & Bonaccio, 2010), but affiliation with a communication department is not a defining characteristic, as several 'COM' scholars have done work that makes important contributions to other paradigms and will be reviewed in later sections (e.g., Goldsmith, 2004).

In many respects, the message paradigm emerged from work by Goldsmith (1992; 1994), who encouraged focused interest in advice by arguing (based on politeness theory; Brown & Levinson, 1987), that variation in advice outcomes is a function of the threat it poses to recipients' face. Advice has the potential to threaten "negative face" when recipients perceive advice as "butting in" and constraining autonomy, and "positive face" when recipients perceive advice as implying a lack of knowledge or competence (Goldsmith, 1999; Goldsmith & Fitch, 1997). Multiple studies built on this theoretical foundation demonstrate that advice can threaten recipients' face (Wilson, Aleman, & Leatham, 1998; Wilson & Kunkel, 2000) and that perceptions of face threat or politeness influence message evaluations and interaction outcomes. Advice perceived by recipients as attending to their face needs (i.e., polite) is generally seen as more sensitive, appropriate, and effective than advice that is presented bluntly or explicitly threatens face (Feng & Feng, 2013; Goldsmith, 2000; MacGeorge et al., 2004; MacGeorge et al., 2013). Face concerns become particularly salient when advice is unsolicited (Goldsmith, 2000; Goldsmith & Fitch, 1997), which predicts poorer evaluations (Carlson, in press; Feng & MacGeorge, 2006). Advice recipients respond more positively to highly polite or "mitigated" advice than to either blunt or impolite ("aggravated") advice (Caplan & Samter, 1999; MacGeorge, Lichtman, & Pressey, 2002), though the effects of more subtle linguistic strategies are difficult to track (Goldsmith & MacGeorge, 2000).

Subsequent research extended beyond the framework of face and politeness to address the content features of advice. Recognizing that advice functions as both social support and social influence (Wilson & Kunkel, 2000), MacGeorge, Feng, and colleagues drew on theories of argumentation and persuasion (e.g., Social Judgment Theory; Sherif & Hovland, 1961) to identify several features of advice content that should influence recipients' responses to advice messages (MacGeorge et al., 2004; MacGeorge et al., 2008). Their series of studies has demonstrated that recipients' evaluations of an advised action's efficacy, feasibility, and lack of limitations, and the extent to which advice confirms previously-intended behavior, are positively associated with perceptions of advice quality, coping facilitation, and intention to implement the advised action (Feng, 2014b; Feng & Burleson, 2008; MacGeorge et al., 2013). In addition, advice messages containing explicit arguments about the advised action's efficacy, feasibility, and lack of limitations are evaluated more positively than advice messages without these arguments (Feng & Burleson, 2008).

Based on the expanding research, Feng and MacGeorge (2010) proposed a synthesis and extension of existing theory, which they termed advice response theory (ART). This theory drew together the pre-existing emphases on advice message content and politeness, but also began to integrate research examining the influence of advisor, recipient, and situational factors on advice outcomes (MacGeorge et al., 2013; see also later sections on psychological and network paradigms). In its current form, the theory proposes that message features (including both content and stylistic features such as politeness) are stronger influences on advice outcomes than are source characteristics such as expertise and trustworthiness, and predicts that the influence of source characteristics is mediated through their effects on perceptions of message features. In addition, drawing on dual-process models of persuasion and supportive communication (Bodie & Burleson, 2008), ART proposes that message features have a stronger influence on advice outcomes when recipients "process" or think about advice messages more carefully (e.g., when recipients perceive problems as very serious), and source characteristics become more influential when advice messages are thought about less carefully (e.g., when recipients perceive problems to be less serious). Initial testing of the theory largely supported these propositions (Feng & MacGeorge, 2010). Subsequent studies testing ART indicate that recipient characteristics such as culture and gender act as moderators on the effects of message features and advisor characteristics, and that the persuasive outcome of intention to implement is most strongly affected by message content, whereas the supportive outcome of facilitation of coping is more strongly affected by message politeness (Feng & Feng, 2013; MacGeorge et al., 2013).

Feng's integrated model of advice (IMA; Feng, 2009) steps beyond ART's current focus to theorize how advice functions in the broader context of supportive interactions. Drawing from the conversational appraisal theory of supportive communication (Burleson & Goldsmith, 1997), IMA emphasizes the role of emotional support and problem analysis in preparing a distressed person to consider advice. Feng's (2009, 2014b) experimental studies demonstrate that the impact of even high quality advice messages varies as a function of interaction sequence: advice offered following emotional support and problem analysis messages is perceived as higher in quality, more facilitative of the recipient's coping, and leads to stronger implementation intention than advice that does not follow this sequential pattern. Feng has also expanded ART's focus to consider the influence of national culture on advice, demonstrating similarities in Chinese and American patterns of advice evaluation and response, with relatively small effects explained by individualism and collectivism (Feng, 2014a; Feng & Feng, 2013).

Research in the message paradigm has principally employed one of two methodologies used by supportive communication scholars (Burleson & MacGeorge, 2002). The message perception method involves presenting participants with sets of messages designed to instantiate features of theoretical interest. The messages are typically embedded in researcher-constructed scenarios (e.g., MacGeorge et al., 2002). The foremost strength of this paradigm is its capacity to isolate effects from specific message features. Other research has employed a more naturalistic method that involves retrospective self-reports about supportive interactions that involved advice (e.g., MacGeorge et al., 2004). A major strength of this method is ecological validity; instances of naturally occurring advice giving and receiving are examined in the context of real and oftentimes substantial stressors.

In sum, research in the message paradigm has provided insight into features or characteristics of advice messages that affect how recipients evaluate and respond to advice, with some more recent attention to the interplay between features of advice messages, perceived characteristics of advisors and situations (MacGeorge et al., 2013), other types of messages that accompany advice in supportive interactions (Feng, 2009), and culture (Feng, 2014a). This work permits detailed "advice to the advisor" about constructing advice messages that support and persuade. However, we contend that this paradigm, as developed to date, is also remarkably and unnecessarily limited in ways that have obscured the importance and interest value of advice for communication scholars, perhaps especially for those whose research interests lie outside of interpersonal communication, social support, or close relationships. Researchers in the message paradigm have tended to concentrate on advice in close, peer relationships (often involving young, college adults), and given much less attention to advice in workplace or professional contexts, to relationships where partners differ in power or status, or to non-intimate relationships. Correspondingly, they have usually examined advice with regard to personal problems, as opposed to those that are professional or task-related, and to problems that evoke relatively high degrees of emotional distress (Feng & MacGeorge, 2010). The message paradigm has also concentrated on immediate outcomes for advice recipients, and done relatively little to address broader impacts, such as making health-related decisions, developing a relationship with an advisor, being productive in a working group, or sustaining an organizational culture—yet interpersonal advice can exert these influences and more.

Alternative Paradigms for the Study of Advice

Prior to or concurrent with the development of the message paradigm by communication scholars, other scholarly disciplines have also regarded advice as an important phenomenon, and contributed to three other research paradigms. The strengths and limitations of the message paradigm are thrown into sharper relief by comparison with these paradigms, helping to identify how communication scholars can expand "our" traditional questions and theories about advice to connect with a broader range of interactional, relational, organizational, cultural, and technological issues. Thus, in the following section, we review what we have termed the discourse, psychological, and network paradigms, introducing the distinctive theories and methods that characterize these paradigms and highlighting key findings.[3] A summary of all four paradigms is provided in Table 8.1.

The Discourse Paradigm

The discourse paradigm for research on advice is characterized by a focus on naturally-occurring advising interactions, often in institutional contexts. Qualitative analyses highlight the behavior—discourse—used to accomplish advising in these interactions, how this behavior is associated with roles, relationships, and culture, and the "meanings" or interpretive frames employed by ordinary actors. Researchers who work in this domain typically come from linguistics, socio-linguistics, sociology or English, and applied professions such as education, social work, and medicine, but some work by communication scholars aligns more closely with this paradigm than with the message paradigm (e.g., Goldsmith, 2004; Pudlinski, 2012). In this tradition, researchers often reference the definition of advice put forward by DeCapua & Dunham (1993): "opinions or counsel given by people who perceive themselves as knowledgeable" (p. 519). However, discourse analytic researchers are especially attuned to the variability of forms that "opinions and counsel" can take, including interrogative, declarative, and imperative structures (Locher & Limberg, 2012), and still more indirect or "off-record" forms, such as when advisors describe their own prior experiences and actions (Goldsmith, 2004). Much discourse analytic research has an applied dimension, with extensions to improving academic, counseling, and medical interactions (Locher & Limberg, 2012).

Most work in the discourse paradigm is conversation analytic. Conversation analysis (CA) is arguably both a method and a set of theoretical commitments (Clayman & Gill, 2012; Heritage, 2009). Starting from the assumption that social structures are created and maintained through ordinary conversations, analysts record naturally-occurring interactions and create exceptionally detailed transcriptions. Conversation analysts largely eschew "talk-extrinsic" data, and instead attempt to ground their conclusions in behavior that is "visible, hearable, displayed, and responded to, by actors in real-time interaction" (Ford, 2012). Nonetheless, many conversation analyses of advice are informed by the same theories of identity, face, and politeness that have stimulated work in the message paradigm (e.g., Brown & Levinson, 1987), and increasingly, by Heritage and colleagues' analysis of epistemic status (Heritage, 2009; 2012). Heritage's conceptual framework guides conversation analysts to consider how advisors and recipients make claims (usually implicit) to epistemic status, or "access and rights to specific domains of knowledge and information" (Heritage, 2012, p. 7)—and resist each other's claims. Some conversation analyses of advice also reference social constructionist theory (see Gubrium &

Table 8.1 Comparison of Paradigms

	Message Paradigm	Psychological Paradigm	Discourse Paradigm	Network Paradigm
Focus	Advice as message within supportive interactions, usually in personal relationships	Advice as input to individual decision making	Behavior in naturally-occurring advising interactions, often with advisors in professional or para-professional roles	Networks of advising relationships, typically between members of teams or organizations
Advice Definition	Messages that make recommendations about what to do, think, or feel, in response to a problematic situation	A recommendation about an intellective choice (i.e., one that has a correct answer)	Opinions or counsel, which can take diverse linguistic forms	Left to participants to define/defined operationally
Core Research Questions	How do advice message characteristics influence recipient evaluation and response to advice?	When do advisees utilize (or not utilize) advice? On what basis do recipients select an advisor?	What are advisor and advisee behaviors during interactions? How do they negotiate challenges, and sustain conversational goals and norms associated with roles and institutions?	Who develops an advising relationship with whom and why (i.e., network development)? How do network structures (e.g., density) affect outcomes for members of the network?
Typical Disciplinary Homes of Scholars	Communication	Psychology, business or management	Linguistics, socio-linguistics, sociology, English, communication, education, social work, and medicine	Sociology, business or management, labor and industrial relations, industrial or organizational psychology, or engineering
Data Collection and Analysis	Experiments with message manipulations, questionnaires about past advice interactions	Lab experiments with advice provided for a decision made by participants	Conversation analysis, interviews, participant-observation	Social network analysis with, sociometric sampling
Sampling of Issues Raised by Paradigm not Addressed by Message Paradigm		Cognitive and emotional processes, multiple advisors	Behavior in interaction, advising norms, roles and relationships	Multiple advisors, competing advice

Holstein, 2008) relevant to the domain of interaction (e.g., theories of learning for analyses of peer tutoring; Park, 2014).

Other discourse paradigm scholars share conversation analysts' focus on real-world enactment of advice but adopt diverse interpretive approaches to examining the meaning(s) assigned to advice in different types of interactions, relationships, and cultures. The breadth of topical focus inhibits brief summary (for a sampling, see Limberg & Locher, 2012), and methods include participant-observation, interview, and even survey (Chentsova-Dutton & Vaughn, 2011), along with diverse ways of analyzing transcripts and other texts. Scholars both invoke and contribute to social constructionist theories (Gubrium & Holstein, 2008) relevant to their context of study. For example, Goldsmith, a communication scholar whose contributions to the message paradigm were previously noted, has articulated an interpretive or rhetorical theory of supportive interaction (Goldsmith, 2004), emphasizing that both interpretation and enactment of support (including advice) are contextualized by the particularities of the relationships and cultures in which they occur (see also Goldsmith, Lindholm, & Bute, 2006).

An essential contribution of the entire discourse paradigm is highly detailed description of behavior in advising interactions. Early CA work described the adjacency pair and preference structure of advice (for reviews see Heritage, 2009; Park, 2014). An adjacency pair is a conversational sequence in which behavior by one person makes certain behaviors by another person immediately relevant. Giving advice is the first part of an adjacency pair that makes relevant the acceptance of, or resistance to, that advice, such that any response not interpretable as accepting or resisting will interrupt the flow of interaction and require explanation. For example, if a colleague says "You should really read that chapter by Scholar A," this first pair part makes relevant replies like "You're right!" or "Umm. . . . In Volume X? I already did." Acceptance is described as a "preferred" response and resistance as a "dispreferred" response, because resistance is more often marked by hesitations and qualifications (e.g., "Umm. . . . In Volume X?"), whereas acceptance is typically offered in an immediate, unhesitating form ("You're right!"). From these descriptions, CA studies have gone on to display diverse ways of offering advice (Heritage & Lindstrom, 2012; Riccioni, Bongelli, & Zuckzkowski, 2014; Waring, 2007b), such as "advice-implicative interrogatives" that inquire about the relevance of a possible future action rather than directly recommending it (Butler, Potter, Danby, Emmison, & Hepburn, 2010).

A second contribution of the discourse paradigm, closely related to the descriptive contribution, is demonstrating how certain behaviors are designed to manage issues that recur across advising interactions. For example, some work describes diverse strategies recipients can use to resist advice (Waring, 2005; 2007a) and advisors' attempts to forestall resistance (e.g., packaging the advice as a tag question that invites agreement; Hepburn & Potter, 2011). Recent work focuses on advisors' means of negotiating resistance when it occurs—e.g., expressing concern about the problem, asking questions, defending the advised action, giving alternative advice or information, and repeating or reformulating the advice (Hepburn & Potter, 2011; Heritage & Lindstrom, 2012; Pudlinski, 2012; Waring, 2007b). Goldsmith and colleagues (Goldsmith, 2004; Goldsmith et al., 2006) discuss how spouses' efforts to advise and direct may be framed as less intrusive actions, such as inquiring about one's day or initiating shared activity.

A third contribution of the discourse paradigm work is showing how advising behavior is shaped by and (re)produces roles, relationships, institutions, and cultures. For example, Heritage and colleagues' conversation analyses (e.g., Heritage & Lindstrom, 2012) connect health visitors' varied and persistent strategies for advising to their institutional mandate to ensure infant well-being. Other CA work explores how advising strategies employed by peer tutors and helpline counselors reflect institutional philosophies and training that underscore help-seekers' autonomy and self-direction (Butler et al., 2010; Park, 2012). Relying on ethnographic methods, Goldsmith and colleagues have described relational norms for giving and interpreting supportive behavior, emphasizing their dialectical character: for (some) white, middle-class, Americans advice is a way of expressing care and support, but also an intrusive boundary violation (Goldsmith & Fitch, 1997; see also Goldsmith et al., 2006). Other work explores the advice norms associated with national and ethnic cultures, such as the value Russians place on unsolicited advice motivated by mutual responsibility (Chentsova-Dutton, 2012; Chentsova-Dutton & Vaughn, 2011).

The Psychological Paradigm

In theoretical and methodological counterpoint to the discourse paradigm, the psychological paradigm focuses on cognitive and emotional processes that affect the use of advice, especially when making decisions. Researchers within this paradigm typically affiliate with psychology, business or management, or finance, and the methods are almost exclusively quantitative. Advice is usually conceptualized as "input" from an advisor to someone who needs to make a decision and operationalized as a recommendation in favor of a specific action (Bonaccio & Dalal, 2006; Dalal & Bonaccio, 2010). Psychological research is especially focused on developing theory, but practical application also informs some of this work (e.g., improving the outcomes of financial advising; Kadous, Leiby, & Peecher, 2013). Two distinctive sub-paradigms are discussed in turn: one focused on recipients' use of advice in their decisions (advice utilization research; Yaniv, 2004) and the other addressing the selection of an advisor (advisor selection research; Cross & Sproull, 2004).

Theorizing about advice utilization has drawn from the persuasion and attitude change literature (Sherif & Hovland, 1961), small group research (Kerr & Tindale, 2004), and cost-benefit analysis (Schrah, Dalal, & Sniezek, 2006). A central theoretical debate concerns the underutilization of advice, which has been explained as resulting from anchoring (attachment to one's own opinion), egocentric bias (belief in the superiority of one's own perspective) and differential information (for a review, see Yaniv, 2004). Research evidence favors the differential information account, which claims that recipients favor their own opinions because they understand their own knowledge and reasoning better than their advisors. More recently, researchers in this paradigm have tested theory addressing how emotion valence and agency (self-focused versus other-focused) affect advice utilization (de Hooge, Verlegh, & Tzioti, 2013; Gino & Schweitzer, 2008).

Studies that examine advice utilization typically employ the judge-advisor system (JAS), an experimental protocol that places participants in the role of judge or decision maker (henceforth called the recipient for consistency). Recipients are presented with a decision task, given a recommendation by an "advisor," and record a final decision; frequently they make an initial decision before receiving advice, so the initial and final decision can be compared (Yaniv & Kleinberger, 2000). The operationalization of the advisor varies; most frequently, researcher-created advice is credited to a fictitious advisor and communicated to the recipient in written form (Gino & Schweitzer, 2008), but confederate and participant advisors may be employed instead (Van Swol, 2011). Decision tasks are usually intellective (there is a correct answer), such as a multiple choice exam on the dates of historic events, and advice is given in the form of recommended answers (e.g., "choose answer 'A'," Gino, 2008). Some recent work has expanded to include judgmental choices (i.e., matters of preference without a correct answer), such as which movie to watch (Van Swol, 2011).

As previously noted, advice underutilization is a central research focus for this paradigm (Harvey & Fischer, 1997). Recipients often do not give advice enough weight to benefit from receiving it, especially when recipients have greater knowledge or experience (Yaniv, 2004), and when tasks are easier (Gino & Moore, 2007). Utilization rises when recipients invest in their advice (i.e., pay for it; Gino, 2008), and when they are induced to take the perspective of another person (Yaniv & Choshen-Hillel, 2012). Researchers in the psychological paradigm have also focused on the influence of advisor characteristics as perceived by recipients. Multiple studies show that advisors' expertise and trustworthiness are positive influences on utilization (Bonaccio & Dalal, 2006; Van Swol, 2011); indeed these may predict advice utilization more strongly and reliably than other advisor characteristics (e.g., advisor confidence, availability of other advisors; Bonaccio & Dalal, 2010).

A third research question driving advice utilization research is how recipient emotions and feelings affect the use of advice. This research indicates that emotions such as gratitude, anger, and anxiety impact advice utilization and decision accuracy even when those emotions are unrelated to the decision (Gino, Brooks, & Schweitzer, 2012; Gino & Schweitzer, 2008). Power is often negatively related to advice utilization because powerful recipients are more confident, and higher confidence leads to lower advice utilization (See, Morrison, Rothman, & Soll, 2011). Recently, de Hooge et al. (2013) synthesized advice and emotion research into a theoretical framework, proposing that positive self-focused and negative other-focused emotions decrease advice utilization, whereas negative self-focused and positive other-focused emotions increase it.

Within the psychological paradigm, the principal focus on advice utilization is complemented by a sub-paradigm focused on advisor selection. This work draws from theories of network generation (Nebus, 2006), network ties (Granovetter, 1983), and social capital (Burt, 2000), along with organization theories (Heyden, Van Doorn, Reimer, Van Den Bosch, & Volberda, 2013). Advisor selection research often utilizes egocentric sampling methods, in which participants describe their network members' qualities and behaviors, but network members' data are not obtained (Cross & Sproull, 2004; Vargas & Schafer, 2013). (As discussed later, scholars in the network paradigm also study advisor selection but with sociocentric rather than egocentric sampling.) Other studies utilize experimental methods (Bonaccio & Dalal, 2010), including some that are akin to the JAS (Gino, Shang, & Croson, 2009; Van Swol, 2011).

Findings from advisor selection research identify characteristics of advisors, tasks, and contexts that influence advisor selection. Consistent with network generation theory (Nebus, 2006), people who have few sources of advice about an issue tend to use advisors they can access easily, such as friends and family members rather than professionals (Reid et al., 2010), and those viewed as having the disposition to help (White, 2005). More generally, recipients tend to select advisors they perceive to have relevant expertise (Zagenczyk & Murrell, 2009). Similarity to the recipient (McDonald & Westphal, 2003; Van Swol, 2011) and higher status relative to the recipient (Cross & Sproull, 2004) can influence advisor selection, as does the type of problem (Heyden et al., 2013) and the cost of seeking advice (Nebus, 2006).

The Network Paradigm

A third paradigm of research on advice is characterized by its focus on networks of advising relationships, typically between members of teams or organizations, and the corresponding use of social network analysis, especially sociometric sampling methods, to examine these relationships. Researchers in this domain typically affiliate with sociology, management, or industrial-organizational psychology. Consistent with the broader paradigm of social network research (Carpenter, Li, & Jiang, 2012), an advice network is defined as a "pattern of relationships . . . in which one member asks advice from one or more members" (Wang, Tjosvold, Chen, & Luo, 2014, p. 836). Advice per se is typically left undefined, except operationally. Studies typically ask participants to identify all the individuals within some organization or context from whom they seek advice, advice in a particular domain, or advice in combination with other assistance (e.g., "help and advice," Lomi et al., 2013). Thus, the ties in advice networks are probably best understood as constructed from advice and a range of allied discourse, such as information, opinion, and assistance.

Research on advice networks addresses two related issues: the development and structure of advice networks (who has an advice relationship with whom, and why); and the influence of network structures on individuals and groups within the network. Both types of research are grounded in social capital theory (Burt, 2000), so advice networks are regarded as "main social conduits through which resource[s], knowledge, and information flow" (Lomi et al., 2013, p. 440). Scholars working in this domain have drawn from a variety of other theories, including theories of social exchange (Cropanzano & Mitchell, 2005), social status and stratification (Ravlin & Thomas, 2005), and social identity and self-categorization (Hogg & Terry, 2000), as well as theories of cooperation, leadership, and personality (Battistoni & Colladon, 2014; Wang et al., 2014; Z. Zhang & Peterson, 2011). Currently, an important theoretical question is whether advice networks are better understood as resulting from individuals' desire to improve their social status (relative social position), or from a desire to access social capital (resources available through others). In a study testing hypotheses derived from the *social status perspective* and the *social capital perspective*, Agneessens and Wittek (2012) found some support for both mechanisms, but asserted a stronger case for social capital, because social status did not generally inhibit advice seeking, except by individuals who are among the most-sought (highest-status) advisors in the network.

The network paradigm utilizes methods of social network research, especially sociocentric sampling. This method focuses on modeling the entire network of advising relationships among individuals connected within some boundary, such as a group or organization. Sociocentric methods require specialized analytic techniques to address common issues of structural autocorrelation (non-independence of observations over time and space), endogenity (predictors correlated with error terms), and sample selection bias (from non-random samples; Carpenter et al., 2012).

Research on advice network generation typically examines predictors of advice centrality, where centrality refers to the frequency with which members of a network are sought by others for advice. Research on structural factors affecting centrality indicates that advice seeking is more likely between those who share an in-group, such as a work group or professional role, than between those who do not (Creswick & Westbrook, 2010; Keith, Demirkan, & Goul, 2010). Advising relationships are also more likely when network members are "structurally equivalent," meaning that they have other advice relations in common (Copeland, Reynolds, & Burton, 2008). A variety of individual factors also affect who becomes a central advisor. Having task-relevant expertise predicts greater advisor centrality (Keith et al., 2010), as does being prototypical of one's work group (Copeland et al., 2008), and possessing certain personality traits (e.g., high in conscientiousness, Battistoni & Colladon, 2014) or behavioral characteristics (e.g., altruistic citizenship behavior and job involvement; M. Zhang, Zheng, & Wei, 2009).

Aside from centrality, other aspects of network development are beginning to receive more attention. There is evidence for a negative relationship between being sought as an advisor (centrality) and seeking advisors for oneself (Lazega, Sapulete, & Mounier, 2011), though Agneessens and Wittek (2012) suggest that this effect is limited to the most central advisors in a network. Advice-seeking behavior is also affected by individual factors, such as organizational identification. In top management teams, managers who identify more with the organization at large seek advice across corporate divisions, whereas those who identify more with their own division seek advice within that division (Lomi et al., 2013). Some research has examined the development of larger network structures. For example, Battistoni and Colladon (2014) found that people who are more conscientious and agreeable and less neurotic are more likely to inhabit larger and more connected clusters of advising relationships.

The second principal question addressed by research on advice networks is network effects, or how network structures affect outcomes for members of the network. A key construct in this research is network density, referring to the number of advice ties within a network. In general, density is positively associated with group or team effectiveness (Wang et al., 2014; Wong, 2008), which is operationalized in a variety of ways (e.g., innovation, Moolenaar, Daly, & Sleegers, 2011). Several studies have identified mechanisms, such as knowledge sharing (Wong, 2008) and shared decision-making (Moolenaar et al., 2011) by which greater network density creates positive outcomes. Network effects researchers also examine centrality, but as a characteristic of networks rather than individuals. Greater centrality in networks, indicating that advice is sought from a smaller number of individuals in that network, dampens the positive effects of density (Wang et al., 2014). Thus, for networks to benefit from the density of advice relations in the network, those relations may need to be decentralized (many people connected to many others) rather than centralized (many people connected to a few others). This conclusion is further supported by evidence that advice network outcomes improve as the number of ties to out-of-network members increases (Wong, 2008).

Comparing the Paradigms

As made evident throughout this section (and in Table 8.1), the message, discourse, psychological, and network paradigms provide different types of insight about the characteristics, functions, and outcomes of advice. At present, the message paradigm is distinctive for its focus on qualities of advice messages and the effort to predict supportive (and to a lesser extent, persuasive) outcomes for individual recipients, especially between peers, but has had much less to say about advising interactions and relationships, cognitive and emotional processes affecting advice evaluation, or organizational networks formed from the exchange of advice. The discourse paradigm provides unique insight into the structure and interpretation of advice in interactions. However, this interpretive work has focused on a limited range of advising contexts, and provides a weak basis for generalization about advising processes outside those contexts. The psychological paradigm illuminates cognitive and emotional processes that predict the use of advice in decision making, but focuses almost exclusively on persuasive outcomes and offers relatively little insight into interactions or relationships. The network paradigm highlights the utility of advice, especially in organizational contexts, but focuses on connections and global outcomes created through the exchange of advice with little attention to the interactions that create these links. The comparison between paradigms could be elaborated in ways that further highlight the value of the message paradigm. Indeed, the message paradigm accomplishes something that many scholars of interpersonal communication, social support, and social influence have prized: identifying and explaining strategies or tactics for communication behavior that show evidence of general utility (see MacGeorge et al., 2011).

However, our purpose here is not congratulatory, but motivational. We assert that the nature and influence of advice is both more complex than currently envisioned by communication scholars operating within the message paradigm (or other paradigms), and broader-reaching, such that advice is worthy of attention from scholars whose research interests range from interpersonal interactions and relationships to organizations, cultures, and computer-mediated communication. Correspondingly, we contend that the communication of advice is fruitfully examined from a greater diversity of theoretical perspectives and methods.

Toward a "Communication Paradigm"

In the following sections, we elaborate a broader vision for communication research with advice as a central focus, working toward a more useful and inclusive "communication paradigm." In part, we pull together the strengths of the discourse, psychological, and network paradigms to address the limitations of the message paradigm; these cross-paradigm comparisons indicate relevant directions while providing theoretical and methodological foundations. However, our effort to open new or little-used trails also emphasizes domains that are not well addressed by any existing paradigm, and application to important practical issues. By necessity, our recommendations are selective, but we chose them to illustrate the relevance of advice in communication contexts from the interpersonal and relational to the organizational, cultural, and computer-mediated. In the process, we encourage more research on advice that employs not only post-positivistic but interpretive and critical approaches, and we engage with theories in those domains.

Interactions and Advisors

For interpersonal communication and social support scholars, there are immediate and valuable extensions of theory and method that arise from incorporating aspects of the discourse and psychological paradigms to improve understanding of advice in interaction. By demonstrating the intricate interplay of advising interactions, the discourse paradigm highlights the message paradigm's overreliance on evaluations of researcher-constructed or recollected advice (Feng & Burleson, 2008; Feng & MacGeorge, 2010), and hints at potentially generalizable relationships between the structure of advice interactions and their outcomes for recipients. Feng's integrated model of advice (IMA; Feng, 2009, 2014a) represents an important bridge between the message and discourse paradigms, underscoring the role of emotional support and problem analysis in preparing a distressed person to consider and utilize advice (see also Burleson & Goldsmith, 1997). Recently, MacGeorge and colleagues have presented analyses of naturalistic interactions recorded in a laboratory context. This method makes advising behavior available for detailed analysis (in transcripts and video), while also permitting immediate assessment of recipients' (and advisors') advice outcomes. Initial papers from this data examine how advisor and recipient behaviors interact to influence outcomes, underscoring the role of advisor emotional support and recipient planning in determining whether advice is supportive and persuasive (MacGeorge et al., 2015; MacGeorge, Guntzviller, Branch, & Yakova, in press-a), and describing trajectories of interaction that characterize and may contribute to less satisfying advice interactions (MacGeorge, Guntzviller, Branch, & Yakova, in press-b)

The psychological paradigm highlights the value to be gained if communication scholars integrate a more explicit focus on cognition and emotion into studying advice interactions and advisors. For example, researchers in the message paradigm have spent considerable effort to describing face threat, facework, and their effects (for a review, see Goldsmith, 2004), but have not directly examined affective responses when situated identities are threatened by advice (e.g., embarrassment, anger). Moreover, people who are more anxious, guilty, or ashamed are more likely to seek and utilize advice (de Hooge et al., 2013), making it logical to assess the role of advice in reducing these negative emotions (versus indirect measures such as "coping facilitation," e.g, MacGeorge et al., 2013). Research in the psychological paradigm also highlights the discrepancy between advisors' and recipients' perceptions of advice (Danziger, Montal, & Barkan, 2012), encouraging communication scholars to pay more attention to *advisors'* perspectives, motivations, and sources of knowledge as influences on behavior and outcomes (Benjamin & Budescu, 2015; Harnish, Bridges, & Krajci, 2012). To date, a handful of communication scholars have documented variation in advisors' goals and plans for advising (Guntzviller & MacGeorge, 2013; Shi, 2013). Indeed, theories of message production (Dillard & Wilson, 2014) suggest that advisors will be more supportive and persuasive to the extent that they can address multiple goals simultaneously (e.g., problem-solving and identity management; see Wilson et al., 1998) and shift goals readily, responding to the behavior of the recipient (Feng, 2009; Samp, 2013).

A focus on the details of interaction and an effort to contribute to theories of message production or dyadic interaction need not preclude engagement with real-world advice about significant problems. Indeed, we strongly encourage "interpersonal communication" scholars (broadly defined) to continue undertaking advice research with an applied focus. One recent example of such work is research examining the details of doctors' argumentation strategies in support of their treatment advice. This work (Feng, Bell, Jerant, & Kravitz, 2011; Labrie & Schulz, 2014a, 2014b) combines a focus on naturally-occurring argument in consultations with patients (informed by the discourse paradigm; Koenig, 2011) with the goal of connecting argumentative strategies to patient outcomes (message paradigm). It is easy to imagine this work as a model for examining doctors' advice to patients about societally-relevant health concerns (e.g., antibiotic stewardship, Smith, M'ikanatha, & Read, 2014). Outside of the medical context, people often seek support from friends and family to deal with experiences of social injustice and crime, including workplace bullying (Lutgen-Sandvik & Tracy, 2012) and racial discrimination (Hanasono, Chen, & Wilson, 2014), but little work has focused directly on advice about these issues. Examining advice in interactions around significant social issues creates potential for a symbiotic relationship between traditionally post-positivistic research on advice, and a critical-activist agenda to change advice-giving practices that can harm individuals and sustain unjust conditions. For example, research on workplace bullying indicates that victims are sometimes advised to take actions that are likely to perpetuate and even worsen the situation (e.g., "just stand up to the bully," Lutgen-Sandvik & Tracy, 2012). Research focused directly on the motivations for and consequences of such advice might help to reduce its occurrence.

Advising (in) Relationships

With a few exceptions (see Feng & Magen, 2015), research in the message and psychological paradigms has typically reduced the relationship between the advisor and recipient to the recipient's perception of certain advisor qualities (e.g., liking, similarity; MacGeorge et al., 2013). This reduction of the association between advice and relationships is patently inadequate. Research in the discourse paradigm highlights relational and institutional norms for advising (Goldsmith, 2004), but leaves several valuable directions largely unexplored. One of these is simply to focus more attention on the use, evaluation, and outcomes of advice in relationships where advice is especially prevalent and consequential. Carlson (2014, in press) illustrates a multi-method approach to studying advice in the relationship between parents and emerging adult children, using interview data to explicate how emerging adults interpret advice in the context of parental knowledge and authority, and their own desire for autonomy (Carlson, 2014), and quantitative data to show how qualities of the message and relationship affect implementation (Carlson, in press). Personal relationships aside, advice is recognized as a central component of developmental relationships, such as mentoring and coaching (Allen & Eby, 2007; Passmore, Peterson, & Freire, 2013), and is integral to other professional relationships (educational, legal, financial, medical), but advice has not typically been the central focus of research attention for scholars or practitioners of these relationships.

A focus on advice meanings and consequences in relationships can be complemented by a more detailed focus on advice as a contributor to relationship development and maintenance over time. In the existing research paradigms, this type of question is addressed at a birds-eye level by the network paradigm, but links in the socio-grams largely hide the communicative work involved in generating and sustaining those connections. A scaled-up version of advice response theory (MacGeorge et al., 2013) suggests that advice will be sought most frequently over time from advisors whose advice is high quality (e.g., consistently evaluated as more efficacious and face-protective). Such evaluations should contribute in turn to positive advisor perceptions (e.g., expertise, trustworthiness, Bonaccio & Dalal, 2010), which in conjunction with access and other constraints (Nebus, 2006), could predict returning to the same advisor (and a probable positive bias toward the advice they offer). Over time, such processes could connect single advising interactions with the development of stable advising relationships. This reasoning is consistent with network evolution models (Lazega et al., 2011), in which network members with high status (due to experience) become even more central (sought for advice) over time.

Arguably, the rationale for studying advice in specific types of relationships becomes still stronger when relationships studied intersect with prevalent health and social issues. A recent model for this type of engaged scholarship on advice in relationships is provided by Wilson and colleagues (Wilson, Gettings, Hall, & Pastor, 2015), whose interpretive work identifies advising dilemmas faced by partners of military service members when they want the service members to seek mental health assistance. Correspondingly, though examples arc scarce, we see value in the application of a critical perspective on advising in relationships, asking "Who benefits?" To illustrate, in the marriages and long-term partnerships described by both Wilson et al. (2015) and Goldsmith et al. (2006), men are more typically the ones with the problems (mental health, heart condition), and women more typically face the dilemmas or challenges of advising. Scholarship based in feminist theory (see reviews by Ashcraft, 2014; Griffin, 2009) might target the gendered nature of expectations (and material conditions) that require women to wrestle with dilemmas or challenges of advising in their relationships, while men are allowed to stubbornly resist behavioral change despite the impact on their partners and families (see Loscocco & Walzer, 2013).

Organizing Advice/Advice in Organizations

Both the discourse and network paradigms do a better job of recognizing the contribution of advice in professional roles, workplaces, and other organizations than the message paradigm. However, in the gap between micro-level conversation analyses and macro-level network models of who advises whom, two large questions remain relatively unaddressed: how does advice participate in constituting organizations ("organizing"); and how can positive outcomes of advice exchange be enhanced? The first of these questions aligns with theorizing about the relationship between organizational "discourse" and "Discourse" (Fairhurst & Putnam, 2004). For example, the Montréal School theorizes organizations as "networks of practices and conversations" that are translated into collective experience, texts, and ultimately organizational representations that act as agents—which in turn affect practices and conversations (Brummans, Cooren, Robichaud, & Taylor, 2014; McPhee, Poole, & Iverson, 2014). Clearly, there are social constructionist connections between this perspective and the discourse paradigm of advice research. Yet, the Montréal School contends that advice, along with other communicative acts in organizations, does not simply facilitate decision-making or constitute an advising relationship. It is part of organizing—creating the organization through communication. Lacking examples of organizational advice studied from this perspective, we speculate that the organizing capacity of advice might be most detectable in certain communication "flows" or constitutive processes (McPhee et al., 2014), such as membership negotiation (socializing and assimilating new members; Kramer & Miller, 2014). For researchers, advice to new members about behavior within the organization might be especially transparent in training and mentoring interactions, and therefore more traceable than other types of discourse as it becomes translated into collective experience. In addition, organizational members tasked with socializing roles (e.g., trainers, co-workers) may be especially likely to "ventriloquize" advice from the organization (Cooren, 2012), providing a window on the translation from organizational representation back to practices and conversations. Advice between members of organizations should also contribute to "organizing" across multiple aspects of organizational life, as when members advise one another on work-life issues (Kirby & Buzzanell, 2014) or on responding to organizational change (Lewis, 2014).

Organizational communication scholars with a more post-positivist orientation may find value in studying how advice can be conveyed for more positive outcomes in organizations and through networks. Network paradigm studies already demonstrate that advising interactions can facilitate knowledge-sharing, decision-making, and group effectiveness (e.g., innovation, Moolenaar et al., 2011), but the dynamics of the advice exchange that support these outcomes remain largely unstudied in organizational contexts. Organizational scholars might draw on interpersonal-level analyses of advice (e.g., MacGeorge et al., 2013) as a foundation for examining the successes and failures of advice in organizational contexts. However, researchers should also think beyond the dyad to consider factors that affect whether advice that is relevant to multiple recipients actually spreads through a network. Based on diffusion of innovation theory, Dearing (2009) has argued that health interventions are more successfully disseminated to the extent that such interventions are supported by opinion leaders, who are defined as people routinely sought for advice (i.e., central in an advice network). Thus, mapping the pre-existing relational structure in an organization or population is essential for identifying opinion leaders, and recruiting them to support health interventions. Yet, Dearing also argues that opinion leaders will not be effective if asked to "advocate, persuade, promote, or educate in ways they normally would not" (2009, p. 12). This work provides fertile theoretical ground for scholars interested in connecting advice, other elements of social influence, outcomes for individuals and groups, and real-world issues (see also Kim & Dearing, 2015).

Advice and Culture

As previously reviewed, research in the message and discourse paradigms has attended to cultural influences on advice. Research in the message and psychological paradigms has focused on identifying salient characteristics of culture(s) and examined these cultural variables as predictors of cultural variation in advice giving and evaluation (Feng, 2014b; Feng & Feng, 2013; Mercier, Yama, Kawasaki, Adachi, & Van der Henst, 2014), typically contrasting European Americans or Western Europeans with people from Eastern cultures (especially, China). This work draws heavily on Hofstede's (1991) framework of cultural value orientations, especially individualism–collectivism. Consequently, explanations for cultural variation (especially at the national level) in advice seeking, provision, and evaluation have been largely restricted to these broad dimensions of cultural variation.

Scholars contributing to the message paradigm increasingly recognize that dimensions such as individualism and collectivism explain relatively small percentages of culture-related variance in advice communication (Feng, 2014b; Feng & Feng, 2013). Thus, for post-positivist scholars, alternative theoretical frameworks may be better guides for further inquiry. For example, drawing on the theory of reasoned action (Fishbein & Ajzen, 1975), research by H. Feng (2013) indicates that task-specific beliefs can explain cultural similarities and differences in support provision, including advice. Another alternative is suggested by past research on culturally-based tendencies in stress appraisal. Philosophical and religious traditions such as Buddhism and Taoism in Eastern cultures teach the virtue of enduring and accepting adverse fate (Chen, 2006); indeed individuals from many Asian cultures tend to endorse an external locus of control for stressors (Chun, Moos, & Cronkite, 2006). From this perspective, the coping strategy of actively attacking the problem may seem superfluous (Wong, Wong, & Scott, 2006), affecting how advice is given and evaluated.

From interpretive and critical perspectives, the effort to make generalizable comparisons across cultures misses essential insights about culture and communication (Halualani & Nakayama, 2010) . Research in the discourse paradigm provides some "thick" accounts of advice in particular cultural communities (e.g., Wilson et al., 2015), but this type of work remains scant, especially with regard to national or ethnic cultures (see Chentsova-Dutton & Vaughn, 2011; Fitch, 1998). One guide for future interpretive and critical study of advice and culture is the culture-centered approach (Dutta, 2008). This perspective, developed in response to the dominant paradigm in health communication, challenges Western approaches that suggest universal conceptualizations of health. Dutta and colleagues emphasize the meaningfulness of contextualized human experience, and advocate the importance of understanding participants' voices and agency (Dutta & Jamil, 2013). The culture-centered approach places special priority on hearing the voices of marginalized or "subaltern" peoples, recommending that researchers look beyond "mainstream" (e.g., Western, middle-class, young, well-educated) experiences in advice seeking, provision, and evaluation. For example, Dutta and Jamil's (2013) work with Bangladeshi immigrants suggests that doctors' advice will be understood quite differently in the context of immigration—precarious employment, no health insurance, and heavy familial obligation. The culture-centered approach also promotes a focus on advice as it participates in shaping both individual and societal responses to significant disputes and injustices. Thus, it might be used to shed light on advice about confrontations with law enforcement in urban, under-privileged, African-American communities, or Latino/Hispanic responses to legal or informal advice on immigration issues. As diverse people seek to live together harmoniously and remedy social injustice, investigating cultural influences on advising is of both theoretical and practical importance.

Advice Online

Finally, we observe that the online exchange of advice is both substantial and largely unaddressed by the existing research paradigms. The Internet has created multiple new pathways to access (and provide) information and support for virtually any problem, in a huge array of formats (e.g., traditional websites, support groups, blogs, online forums, social networking sites). In addition, most major online retailers now solicit and utilize electronic word of mouth (eWOM) that consumers then consult (often within the retail website) as a form of advice for purchasing decisions (King, Racherla, & Bush, 2014). Given space constraints, we offer brief suggestions for research on advice in the context of social networking sites (e.g., Facebook) and online forums (e.g., YahooAnswers). These sites promote a conjunction of interpersonal, group, and mass communication, termed *masspersonal* communication (O'Sullivan, 2005). In these contexts, not only can single advice-seekers interact with multiple advisors, but advisors can interact with and influence each other, as can recipients. Such online environments allow exchanges between advisors and advisees to influence a mass audience of "lurkers" who view, but do not interact.

Various forms of social support are sought and provided in masspersonal contexts, but advice and other forms of informational support often predominate (Blank et al., 2010; Sillence, 2013). Thus, these environments provide a "natural laboratory" for examining how advice seeking, giving, evaluating, and responding change as advising interactions take on characteristics of group and mass communication. For example, the phenomenon of masspersonal advice puts a spotlight on the question of multiple advisors—and interaction between multiple advisors—as influences on advice recipients. Research in the psychological tradition has examined the impact of multiple advice sources on advice judgment and utilization (Harries, Yaniv, & Harvey, 2004; Yaniv

& Milyavsky, 2007), suggesting that recipients are most likely to follow the advice closest to their original perspectives. However, in these studies, advice sources are only implied in the different pieces of advice that participants are given (Yaniv & Milyavsky, 2007), leaving the impact of interaction (and cross-advisor argument) unexamined.

More broadly, masspersonal contexts for advice interactions recommend attention to the transmission of advice from an original source, target, and context, to alternative targets and contexts (see Cappella, Kim, & Albarracín, 2014). Online environments make it easy for advisors to pass along recommendations from organizations, groups, or individuals, to use recommendations and information from those sources in support of more personalized advice, or to share information from such sources as a less direct effort to influence a recipient's actions. The prevalence, motivation, and impact of these tactics deserve attention. Given recent attention to the negative impact of misinformation in the mass media (Southwell & Thorson, 2015), one specific focus might be misinformation as the basis for giving problematic advice (e.g., anti-vaccination advice), and interpersonal advising in the face of media misinformation (see Bode & Vraga, 2015).

Research to examine how advice is sought, evaluated, utilized, and transmitted in masspersonal environments will likely require the integration of theories across traditional intra-disciplinary boundaries (dyads, groups, and mass audiences). Correspondingly, such research will generate practical knowledge for improving people's competence in advice communication and facilitate development of effective online support interventions (Barak, Boniel-Nissim, & Suler, 2008; Raghavendra, Newman, Grace, & Wood, 2013)

Advice for Communication Scholars

As this chapter indicates, advice is a significant form of interpersonal interaction, with implications for most domains of human life. We began by describing the message paradigm for research on advice, and continued by describing three alternatives: the discourse, psychological, and network paradigms. From cross-paradigm comparison, both the strengths and weaknesses of the message paradigm become more apparent. Subsequently, we sketched five areas for future research, drawing from the alternative paradigms, but also extending to domains insufficiently addressed by any prior research on advice. We sought to represent theoretically and practically relevant questions in communication contexts ranging from the dyadic to the masspersonal, and to encourage inquiry from post-positivistic, interpretive, and critical perspectives. Indeed, our review highlights how research on advice can contribute to theories of message production and dyadic interaction, relationship development and maintenance, organizing and communication in organizations, cultural influence, and computer-mediated communication—and how research on advice might be harnessed to address issues of health and social justice. Research in the four existing paradigms underscores the consequentiality of advice, but there is a wide range of questions left to be answered, with the potential to enhance communication theory and contribute to its application in the varied domains where advice is given and received. We invite scholars across our discipline to focus attention on the way that advice moves and connects us.

Notes

1   This translation from the Greek text was provided by Dr. Michele Kennerly, historian of rhetoric in the Department of Communication Arts and Sciences at Pennsylvania State University. Dr. Kennerly also provided the following context: In this play by Sophocles, Creon, the King of Thebes, intends to put Antigone to death for violating his decree forbidding the burial of enemy combatants. (She had attempted twice to bury her brother.) Being engaged to Antigone and attuned to the objections of Thebes' citizens to Creon's severity in this matter, Haemon petitions his father to grant clemency to Antigone. Creon does not heed his advice, with tragic results.

2   We recognize that people may obtain "advice" from media sources, books, or educational materials, but focus herein on recommendations by one person to another.

3   Our selected labels for these paradigms may cue for some readers broader theoretical or methodological approaches than are currently represented in research focused on advice (e.g., the discourse paradigm in organizational communication is more diverse both theoretically and methodologically; see Fairhurst, 2007). Our intention is not to diminish these larger traditions, but to use terms that adequately describe the type of work we are reviewing—and that are used by scholars who do research on advice (e.g., see Limberg & Locher, 2012).

References

Agneessens, F., & Wittek, R. (2012). Where do intra-organizational advice relations come from? The role of informal status and social capital in social exchange. *Social Networks, 34*, 333–345. doi: 10.1016/j.socnet.2011.04.002

Allen, T. D., & Eby, L. T. (Eds.). (2007). *The Blackwell handbook of mentoring: A multiple perspectives approach*. Malden, MA: Blackwell.

Ashcraft, K. L. (2014). Feminist theory. In L. L. Putnam & D. K. Mumby (Eds.), *The Sage handbook of organizational communication: Advances in theory, research, and methods* (3rd edn, pp. 127–150). Thousand Oaks, CA: Sage.

Barak, A., Boniel-Nissim, M., & Suler, J. (2008). Fostering empowerment in online support groups. *Computers in Human Behavior, 24*(5), 1867–1883.

Battistoni, E., & Colladon, A. F. (2014). Personality correlates of key roles in informal advice networks. *Learning and Individual Differences, 34*, 63–69.

Benjamin, D., & Budescu, D. V. (2015). Advice from experience: Communicating incomplete information incompletely. *Journal of Behavioral Decision Making, 28*(1), 36–49.

Blank, T. O., Schmidt, S. D., Vangsness, S. A., Monteiro, A. K., & Santagata, P. V. (2010). Differences among breast and prostate cancer online support groups. *Computers in Human Behavior, 26*(6), 1400–1404. doi: 10.1016/j.chb.2010.04.016

Bode, L., & Vraga, E. K. (2015). In related news, that was wrong: The correction of misinformation through related stories functionality in social media. *Journal of Communication, 65*, 619–638.

Bodie, G. D., & Burleson, B. R. (2008). Explaining variations in the effects of supportive messages: A dual-process framework. In C. Beck (Ed.), *Communication yearbook 32* (pp. 354–398). New York: Routledge.

Bonaccio, S., & Dalal, R. S. (2006). Advice taking and decision-making: An integrative review of the literature. *Organizational Behavior and Human Decision Processes, 101*, 127–151. doi: 10.1016/j.obhdp.2006.07.001

Bonaccio, S., & Dalal, R. S. (2010). Evaluating advisors: A policy-capturing study under conditions of complete and missing information. *Journal of Behavioral Decision-Making, 23*, 227–249. doi: 10.1016/j.obhdp.2009.11.007

Brown, P., & Levinson, S. C. (1987). *Politeness: Some universals in language usage.* Cambridge, U.K.: Cambridge University Press.

Brummans, B. H. J. M., Cooren, F., Robichaud, D., & Taylor, J. R. (2014). Approaches to the communicative constitution of organizations. In L. L. Putnam & D. K. Mumby (Eds.), *The Sage handbook of organizational communication: Advances in theory, research, and methods* (pp. 173–194). Thousand Oaks, CA: Sage.

Burleson, B. R., & Goldsmith, D. J. (1997). How the comforting process works: Alleviating emotional distress through conversationally induced reappraisals. In P. A. Andersen & L. K. Guerrero (Eds.), *Handbook of communication and emotion: Research, theory, applications, and contexts* (pp. 245–280). San Diego, CA: Academic Press.

Burleson, B. R., & MacGeorge, E. L. (2002). Supportive communication. In M. L. Knapp & J. A. Daly (Eds.), *Handbook of interpersonal communication* (3rd edn, pp. 374–424). Thousand Oaks, CA: Sage.

Burt, R. S. (2000). The network structure of social capital. *Research in Organizational Behavior, 22*, 345–423.

Butler, C. W., Potter, J., Danby, S., Emmison, M., & Hepburn, A. (2010). Advice-implicative interrogatives. *Social Psychology Quarterly, 73*(3), 265–287. doi: 10.1177/0190272510379838

Caplan, S. E., & Samter, W. (1999). The role of facework in younger and older adults' evaluations of social support messages. *Communication Quarterly, 47*, 245–264.

Cappella, J. N., Kim, H. S., & Albarracín, D. (2014). Selection and transmission processes for information in the emerging media environment: Psychological motives and message characteristics. *Media Psychology*, advance online publication.

Carlson, C. L. (2014). Seeking self-sufficiency: Why emerging adult college students receive and implement parental advice. *Emerging Adulthood, 2*(4), 257–269. doi: 10.1177/2167696814551785

Carlson, C. L. (in press). Predicting emerging adult college students' implementation of parental advice: Source, situation, relationship, and message characteristics. *Western Journal of Communication.*

Carpenter, M. A., Li, M., & Jiang, H. (2012). Social network research in organizational contexts A systematic review of methodological issues and choices. *Journal of Management, 38*(4), 1328–1361. doi: 10.1177/0149206312440119

Chen, Y.-H. (2006). Coping with suffering: The Buddhist perspective. In P. T. P. Wong & L. C. J. Wong (Eds.), *Handbook of multicultural perspectives on stress and coping* (pp. 73–89). New York: Springer.

Chentsova-Dutton, Y. E. (2012). Butting in vs. being a friend: Cultural differences and similarities in the evaluation of imposed social support. *The Journal of Social Psychology, 152*(4), 493–509. doi: 10.1080/00224545.2011.642025

Chentsova-Dutton, Y. E., & Vaughn, A. (2011). Let me tell you what to do: Cultural differences in advice-giving. *Journal of Cross-Cultural Psychology, 43*, 687–703. doi: 10.1177/0022022111402343

Chun, C.-A., Moos, R. H., & Cronkite, R. C. (2006). Culture: A fundamental context for the stress and coping paradigm. In P. T. P. Wong & L. C. J. Wong (Eds.), *Handbook of multicultural perspectives on stress and coping* (pp. 29–53). New York: Springer.

Clayman, S. E., & Gill, V. T. (2012). Conversation analysis. In J. P. Gee & M. Handford (Eds.), *The Routledge handbook of discourse analysis* (pp. 120–134). Oxon, UK: Routledge.

Cooren, F. (2012). Communication theory at the center: Ventriloquism and the communicative constitution of reality. *Journal of Communication, 62*(1), 1–20. doi: 10.1111/j.1460-2466.2011.01622.x

Copeland, M. P., Reynolds, K. J., & Burton, J. B. (2008). Social identity, status characteristics and social networks: Predictors of advice seeking in a manufacturing facility. *Asian Journal of Social Psychology, 11*, 75–87.

Creswick, N., & Westbrook, J. I. (2010). Social network analysis of medication advice-seeking interactions among staff in an Australian hospital. *International Journal of Medical Informatics, 79*(6), e116-e125. doi: 10.1016/j.ijmedinf.2008.08.005

Cropanzano, R., & Mitchell, M. S. (2005). Social exchange theory: An interdisciplinary review. *Journal of Management, 31*(6), 874–900.

Cross, R., & Sproull, L. (2004). More than an answer: Information relationships for actionable knowledge. *Organization Science, 15*(4), 446–462.

Dalal, R. S., & Bonaccio, S. (2010). What types of advice do decision-makers prefer? *Organizational Behavior and Human Decision Processes, 112*(1), 11–23. doi: 10.1016/j.obhdp.2009.11.007

Danziger, S., Montal, R., & Barkan, R. (2012). Idealistic advice and pragmatic choice: A psychological distance account. *Journal of Personality and Social Psychology, 102*(6), 1105–1117. doi: 10.1037/a0027013

Dearing, J. W. (2009). Applying diffusion of innovation theory to intervention development. *Research on Social Work Practice, 19*, 503–518.

DeCapua, A., & Dunham, J. F. (1993). Strategies in the discourse of advice. *Journal of Pragmatics, 20*(6), 519–531.

de Hooge, I. E., Verlegh, P. W. J., & Tzioti, S. C. (2013). Emotions in advice taking: The roles of agency and valence. *Journal of Behavioral Decision Making*. doi: 10.1002/bdm.1801

Dillard, J., & Wilson, S. R. (2014). Interpersonal influence. In C. R. Berger (Ed.), *Interpersonal communication*. Berlin, Germany: Walter de Gruyter.

Dutta, M. J. (2008). *Communicating health: A culture-centered approach*: Polity.

Dutta, M. J., & Jamil, R. (2013). Health at the margins of migration: Culture-centered co-constructions among Bangladeshi immigrants. *Health Communication, 28*(2), 170–182. doi: 10.1080/10410236.2012.666956

Fairhurst, G. T. (2007). *Discursive leadership: In conversation with leadership psychology*. Thousand Oaks, CA: Sage.

Fairhurst, G. T., & Putnam, L. (2004). Organizations as discursive constructions. *Communication Theory, 14*(1), 5–26. doi: 10.1111/j.1468-2885.2004.tb00301.x

Feng, B. (2009). Testing an integrated model of advice-giving in supportive interactions. *Human Communication Research, 35*, 115–129. doi: 10.1111/j.1468-2958.2008.01340.x

Feng, B. (2014a). When should advice be given? Assessing the role of sequential placement of advice in supportive interactions in two cultures. *Communication Research, 41*(7), 913–934. doi: 10.1177/0093650212456203

Feng, B. (2014b). When should advice be given?: Assessing the role of sequential placement of advice in supportive interactions in two cultures. *Communication Research, 41*, 913–934. doi: 10.1177/0093650212456203

Feng, B., & Burleson, B. R. (2008). The effects of argument explicitness on responses to advice in supportive interactions. *Communication Research, 35*, 849–874. doi: 10.1177/0093650208324274

Feng, B., & Feng, H. (2013). Examining cultural similarities and differences in responses to advice: A comparison of American and Chinese college students. *Communication Research, 40*, 623–644. doi: doi: 10.1177/0093650211433826

Feng, B., & MacGeorge, E. L. (2006). Predicting receptiveness to advice: Characteristics of the problem, the advice-giver, and the recipient. *Southern Communication Journal, 71*(1), 67–85. doi: 10.1080/10417940500503548

Feng, B., & MacGeorge, E. L. (2010). The influences of message and source factors on advice outcomes. *Communication Research, 37*, 576–598. doi: 10.1177/0093650210368258

Feng, B., & Magen, E. (2015). Relationship closeness predicts unsolicited advice giving in supportive interactions. *Journal of Social and Personal Relationships*, advance online publication. doi: 10.1177/0265407515592262

Feng, B., Bell, R. A., Jerant, A. F., & Kravitz, R. L. (2011). What do doctors say when prescribing medications?: An examination of medical recommendations from a communication perspective. *Health Communication, 26*(3), 286–296. doi: 10.1080/10410236.2010.550020

Feng, H. (2013). Understanding cultural variations in giving advice among Americans and Chinese. *Communication Research*. doi: 10.1177/0093650213486668

Fishbein, M., & Ajzen, I. (1975). *Belief, attitude, intention, and behavior: An introduction to theory and research*. Reading, MA: Addison-Wesley.

Fitch, K. L. (1998). *Speaking relationally: Culture, communication, and interpersonal connection*. New York: Guilford Press.

Ford, C. E. (2012). Clarity in applied and interdisciplinary conversation analysis. *Discourse Studies, 14*(4), 507–513. doi: 10.1177/1461445612450375

Gino, F. (2008). Do we listen to advice just because we paid for it? The impact of advice cost on its use. *Organizational Behavior and Human Decision Processes, 107*, 234–245. doi: 10.1016/j.obhdp.2008.03.001

Gino, F., & Moore, D. A. (2007). Effects of task difficulty on use of advice. *Journal of Behavioral Decision Making, 20*(1), 21–35. doi: 10.1002/bdm.539

Gino, F., & Schweitzer, M. E. (2008). Blinded by anger or feeling the love: How emotions influence advice taking. *Journal of Applied Psychology, 93*, 1165–1173. doi: 10.1037/0021-9010.93.5.1165

Gino, F., Brooks, A. W., & Schweitzer, M. E. (2012). Anxiety, advice, and the ability to discern: Feeling anxious motivates individuals to seek and use advice. *Journal of Personality and Social Psychology, 102*, 497–512. doi: 10.1037/a0026413

Gino, F., Shang, J., & Croson, R. (2009). The impact of information from similar or different advisors on judgment. *Organizational Behavior and Human Decision Processes, 108*(2), 287–302.

Goldsmith, D. J. (1992). Managing conflicting goals in supportive interaction: An integrative theoretical framework. *Communication Research, 19*, 264–286.

Goldsmith, D. J. (1994). The role of facework in supportive communication. In B. R. Burleson, T. L. Albrecht, & I. G. Sarason (Eds.), *Communication of social support: Messages, interactions, relationships, and community* (pp. 29–49). Thousand Oaks, CA: Sage.

Goldsmith, D. J. (1999). Content-based resources for giving face-sensitive advice in troubles talk episodes. *Research on Language and Social Interaction, 32*, 303–336.

Goldsmith, D. J. (2000). Soliciting advice: The role of sequential placement in mitigating face threat. *Communication Monographs, 67*, 1–19. doi: 10.1080/036377 50009376492

Goldsmith, D. J. (2004). *Communicating social support.* New York: Cambridge University Press.

Goldsmith, D. J., & Fitch, K. (1997). The normative context of advice as social support. *Human Communication Research, 23*, 454–476. doi: 10.1111/j.1468-2958.1997. tb00406.x

Goldsmith, D. J., & MacGeorge, E. L. (2000). The impact of politeness and relationship on perceived quality of advice about a problem. *Human Communication Research, 26*, 234–263. doi: 10.1111/j.1468-2958.2000.tb00757.x

Goldsmith, D. J., Lindholm, K. A., & Bute, J. J. (2006). Dilemmas of talking about lifestyle changes among couples coping with a cardiac event. *Social Science & Medicine, 63*(8), 2079–2090.

Granovetter, M. (1983). The strength of weak ties: A network theory revisited. *Sociological theory, 1*(1), 201–233.

Griffin, C. L. (2009). Feminist communication theories. In S. W. Littlejohn & K. A. Foss (Eds.), *Encyclopedia of communication theory* (Vol. 1, pp. 390–394). Thousand Oaks, CA: Sage.

Gubrium, J. F., & Holstein, H. A. (2008). The constructionist mosaic. In J. A. Holstein & J. F. Gubrium (Eds.), *Handbook of constructionist research* (pp. 3–10). New York: Guilford.

Guntzviller, L. M., & MacGeorge, E. L. (2013). Modeling interactional influence in advice exchanges: Advice giver goals and recipient evaluations. *Communication Monographs, 80*, 83–100. doi: 10.1080/03637751.2012.739707

Halualani, R. T., & Nakayama, T. K. (2010). Critical intercultural communication studies: At a crossroads. In T. K. Nakayama & R. T. Halualani (Eds.), *The handbook of critical intercultural communication* (pp. 1–16). Malden, MA: Blackwell.

Hanasono, L. K., Chen, L., & Wilson, S. R. (2014). Identifying communities in need: Examining the impact of acculturation on perceived discrimination, social support, and coping amongst racial minority members in the United States. *Journal of International and Intercultural Communication, 7*(3), 216–237.

Harnish, R. J., Bridges, K. R., & Krajci, M. D. (2012). Evaluating advice: Self-presentational biases between high and low self-monitors. *Psychology and Marketing, 29*(4), 270–278. doi: 10.1002/mar.20520

Harries, C., Yaniv, I., & Harvey, N. (2004). Combining advice: The weight of a dissenting opinion in the consensus. *Journal of Behavioral Decision Making, 17*, 333–348.

Harvey, N., & Fischer, I. (1997). Taking advice: Accepting help, improving judgment, and sharing responsibility. *Organizational Behavior and Human Decision Processes, 70*, 117–133.

Hepburn, A., & Potter, J. (2011). Designing the recipient: Managing advice resistance in institutional settings. *Social Psychology Quarterly, 74*(2), 216–241.

Heritage, J. (2009). Conversation analysis as social theory. In B. S. Turner (Ed.), *The new Blackwell companion to social theory* (pp. 300–320). West Sussex, UK: Wiley-Blackwell.

Heritage, J. (2012). Epistemics in action: Action formation and territories of knowledge. *Research on Language & Social Interaction, 45*(1), 1–29.

Heritage, J., & Lindstrom, A. (2012). Advice giving—terminable and interminable: The case of British health visitors. In H. Limberg & M. A. Locher (Eds.), *Advice in Discourse* (pp. 169–193). Amsterdam: John Benjamins.

Heyden, M. L., Van Doorn, S., Reimer, M., Van Den Bosch, F. A., & Volberda, H. W. (2013). Perceived environmental dynamism, relative competitive performance, and top management team heterogeneity: examining correlates of upper echelons' advice-seeking. *Organization Studies, 34*(9), 1327–1356.

Hofstede, G. (1991). *Cultures and organizations: Software of the mind*. London: McGraw-Hill.

Hogg, M. A., & Terry, D. I. (2000). Social identity and self-categorization processes in organizational contexts. *Academy of Management Review, 25*(1), 121–140.

Kadous, K., Leiby, J., & Peecher, M. E. (2013). How do auditors weight informal contrary advice? The joint influence of advisor social bond and advice justifiability. *The Accounting Review, 88*, 2061–2087. doi: 10.2308/accr-50529

Keith, M., Demirkan, H., & Goul, M. (2010). The influence of collaborative technology knowledge on advice network structures. *Decision Support Systems, 50*(1), 140–151.

Kerr, N. L., & Tindale, R. S. (2004). Group performance and decision making. *Annual Review of Psychology, 55*, 623–655.

Kim, D. K., & Dearing, J. W. (2015). The use of informal opinion leader-based strategy for the diffusion of public health services among international workers in South Korea. *Health Communication, 12*, 115–148.

King, R. A., Racherla, P., & Bush, V. D. (2014). What we know and don't know about online word-of-mouth: A review and synthesis of the literature. *Journal of Interactive Marketing, 28*(3), 167–183.

Kirby, E. L., & Buzzanell, P. M. (2014). Communicating work-life issues. In L. L. Putnam & D. K. Mumby (Eds.), *The Sage handbook of organizational communication: Advances in theory, research, and methods* (pp. 351–374). Thousand Oaks, CA: Sage.

Koenig, C. J. (2011). Patient resistance as agency in treatment decisions. *Social Science & Medicine, 72*(7), 1105–1114.

Kramer, M. W., & Miller, V. D. (2014). Socialization and assimilation. In L. L. Putnam & D. K. Mumby (Eds.), *The Sage handbook of organizational communication* (pp. 525–547). Thousand Oaks, CA: Sage.

Labrie, N., & Schulz, P. J. (2014a). The effects of general practitioners' use of argumentation to support their treatment advice: Results of an experimental study using video-vignettes. *Health Communication*, advance online publication. doi: 10.1080/10410236.2014.909276

Labrie, N., & Schulz, P. J. (2014b). Quantifying doctors' argumentation in general practice consultation through content analysis: Measurement development and preliminary results. *Argumentation*, advance online publication. doi: DOI 10.1007/s10503-014-9331-5

Lazega, E., Sapulete, S., & Mounier, L. (2011). Structural stability regardless of membership turnover? The added value of blockmodelling in the analysis of network evolution. *Quality & Quantity, 45*, 129–144.

Lewis, L. K. (2014). Organizational change and innovation. In L. L. Putnam & D. K. Mumby (Eds.), *The Sage handbook of organizational communication: Advances in theory, research, and methods* (3rd edn, pp. 503–524). Thousand Oaks, CA: Sage.

Limberg, H., & Locher, M. A. (Eds.). (2012). *Advice in discourse.* Amsterdam: John Benjamins.

Locher, M. A., & Limberg, H. (2012). Introduction to advice in discourse. In H. Limberg & M. Locher (Eds.), *Advice in Discourse* (pp. 1–28). Amsterdam: John Benjamins.

Lomi, A., Lusher, D., Pattison, P. E., & Robins, G. (2013). The focused organization of advice relations: A study in boundary crossing. *Organization Science, 25*, 438–457.

Loscocco, K., & Walzer, S. (2013). Gender and the culture of heterosexual marriage in the United States. *Journal of Family Theory & Review, 5*(1), 1–14.

Lutgen-Sandvik, P., & Tracy, S. J. (2012). Answering five key questions about workplace bullying how communication scholarship provides thought leadership for transforming abuse at work. *Management Communication Quarterly, 26*(1), 3–47.

MacGeorge, E. L., & Hall, E. D. (2014). Relationship advice. In C. Agnew (Ed.), *Social influences on close relationships: Beyond the dyad* (pp. 188–208). Cambridge, UK: Cambridge University Press.

MacGeorge, E. L., Feng, B., & Burleson, B. R. (2011). Supportive communication. In M. L. Knapp & J. A. Daly (Eds.), *The Sage handbook of interpersonal communication* (4th edn, pp. 317–354). Thousand Oaks, CA: Sage.

MacGeorge, E. L., Feng, B., & Thompson, E. R. (2008). "Good" and "bad" advice: How to advise more effectively. In M. T. Motley (Ed.), *Studies in Applied Interpersonal Communication* (pp. 145–164). Thousand Oaks, CA: Sage.

MacGeorge, E. L., Lichtman, R. M., & Pressey, L. C. (2002). The evaluation of advice in supportive interactions: Facework and contextual factors. *Human Communication Research, 28*, 451–463. doi: 10.1111/j.1468-2958.2002.tb00815.x

MacGeorge, E. L., Feng, B., Butler, G. L., & Budarz, S. K. (2004). Understanding advice in supportive interactions: Beyond the facework and message evaluation paradigm. *Human Communication Research, 30*, 42–70. doi: 10.1111/j.1468-2958.2004.tb00724.x

MacGeorge, E. L., Guntzviller, L. M., Branch, S., & Yakova, L. (in press-a). Advice in interaction: Quantity and placement of problem-solving behaviors. *Communication Research.*

MacGeorge, E. L., Guntzviller, L. M., Branch, S., & Yakova, L. (in press-b). Mediocre counsel: An interpretive analysis of trajectories associated with less satisfying advice interactions. *Journal of Language and Social Psychology.*

MacGeorge, E. L., Guntzviller, L. M., Hanasono, L. K., & Feng, B. (2013). Testing advice response theory in interactions with friends. *Communication Research*, advance online publication. doi: 10.1177/0093650213510938

MacGeorge, E. L., Guntzviller, L. M., Bailey, L., Brisini, K., Salmon, S., Severen, K., . . . Cummings, R. (2015). *The influence of emotional support quality on advice evaluation and outcomes.* Paper presented at the annual convention of the International Communication Association, San Juan, Puerto Rico.

Marsden, M., Zick, C., & Mayer, R. (2011). The value of seeking financial advice. *Journal of Family and Economic Issues, 32*(4), 625–643. doi: 10.1007/s10834-011-9258-z

McDonald, M. L., & Westphal, J. D. (2003). Getting by with the advice of their friends: CEOs' advice networks and firms' strategic responses to poor performance. *Administrative Science Quarterly, 48*(1), 1–32.

McPhee, R. D., Poole, M. S., & Iverson, J. (2014). Structuration theory. In L. L. Putnam & D. K. Mumby (Eds.), *The Sage handbook of organizational communication* (pp. 75–99). Thousand Oaks, CA: Sage.

Mercier, H., Yama, H., Kawasaki, Y., Adachi, K., & Van der Henst, J.-B. (2014). Is the use of averaging in advice taking modulated by culture? *Journal of Cognition and Culture*, advance online publication.

Miller-Ott, A. E., & Durham, W. T. (2011). The role of social support in young women's communication about the genital HPV vaccine. *Women's Studies in Communication, 34*, 183–201.

Moolenaar, N. M., Daly, A. J., & Sleegers, P. J. (2011). Ties with potential: Social network structure and innovative climate in Dutch schools. *Teachers College Record, 113*(9), 1983–2017.

Nebus, J. (2006). Building collegial information networks: A theory of advice network generation. *The Academy of Management Review, 31*(3), 615–637. doi: 10.2307/20159232

O'Sullivan, P. B. (2005). *Masspersonal communication: Rethinking the mass interpersonal divide*. Paper presented at the 55th annual convention of the International Communication Association, New York, NY.

Park, I. (2012). Seeking advice: Epistemic asymmetry and learner autonomy in writing conferences. *Journal of Pragmatics, 44*(14), 2004–2021.

Park, I. (2014). Stepwise advice negotiation in writing center peer tutoring. *Language and Education, advance online publication*. doi: 10.1080/09500782.2013.873805

Passmore, J., Peterson, D. B., & Freire, T. (Eds.). (2013). *The Wiley-Blackwell handbook of the psychology of coaching and mentoring*. Malden, MA: Wiley-Blackwell.

Pudlinski, C. (2012). The pursuit of advice on US peer telephone helplines: Sequential and functional aspects. In H. Limberg & M. A. Locher (Eds.), *Advice in Discourse* (pp. 233–252). Amsterdam: John Benjamins.

Raghavendra, P., Newman, L., Grace, E., & Wood, D. (2013). "I could never do that before": effectiveness of a tailored Internet support intervention to increase the social participation of youth with disabilities. *Child: Care, Health and Development, 39*(4), 552–561.

Ravlin, E. C., & Thomas, D. C. (2005). Status and stratification processes in organizational life. *Journal of Management, 31*(6), 966–987.

Reid, J., Schmied, V., & Beale, B. (2010). "I only give advice if I am asked": Examining the grandmother's potential to influence infant feeding decisions and parenting practices of new mothers. *Women and Birth, 23*(2), 74–80. doi: 10.1016/j.wombi.2009.12.001

Riccioni, I., Bongelli, R., & Zuckzkowski, A. (2014). Mitigation and epistemic positions in troubles talk: The giving advice activity in close interpersonal relationships. Some examples from Italian. *Language and Communication, 39*, 51–72. doi: 10.1016/j.langcom.2014.08.001

Samp, J. A. (2013). Goal variability and message content during relational discussions. *Communication Studies, 64*(1), 86–105.

Schrah, G. E., Dalal, R. S., & Sniezek, J. A. (2006). No decision-maker is an island: Integrating expert advice with information acquisition. *Journal of Behavioral Decision Making, 19*, 43–60.

See, K. E., Morrison, E. W., Rothman, N. B., & Soll, J. B. (2011). The detrimental effects of power on confidence, advice taking, and accuracy. *Organizational Behavior and Human Decision Processes, 116*, 272–285. doi: 10.1016/j.obhdp.2011.07.006

Sherif, M., & Hovland, C. I. (1961). *Social judgment: Assimilation and contrast effects in communication and attitude change.* New Haven, CT: Yale University Press.

Shi, X. (2013). Cognitive responses in advice planning: An examination of thought content and its impact on message features under high versus low effortful thinking modes. *Journal of Language and Social Psychology, 32,* 311–334. doi: 10.1177/0261927X12470112

Sillence, E. (2013). Giving and receiving peer advice in an online breast cancer support group. *Cyberpsychology, Behavior, and Social Networking, 16*(6), 480–485.

Smith, R. A., M'ikanatha, N. M., & Read, A. F. (2014). Antibiotic resistance: A primer and call to action. *Health Communication, 30,* 309–314.

Southwell, B. G., & Thorson, E. A. (2015). The prevalence, consequence, and remedy of misinformation in mass media systems. *Journal of Communication, 65,* 589–595.

Van Swol, L. M. (2011). Forecasting another's enjoyment versus giving the right answer: Trust, shared values, task effects, and confidence in improving the acceptance of advice. *International Journal of Forecasting, 27,* 103–120. doi: 10.1016/j.ijforecast.2010.03.002

Vargas, N., & Schafer, M. H. (2013). Diversity in action: Interpersonal networks and the distribution of advice. *Social science research, 42*(1), 46–58.

Wang, Z., Tjosvold, D., Chen, Y.-f. N., & Luo, Z. (2014). Cooperative goals and team performance: Examining the effects of advice network. *Asia Pacific Journal of Management, 31*(3), 835–852.

Waring, H. Z. (2005). Peer tutoring in a graduate writing centre: Identity, expertise, and advice resisting. *Applied Linguistics*(26), 141–168. doi: 10.1093/applin/amh041

Waring, H. Z. (2007a). Complex advice acceptance as a resource for managing asymmetries. *Text & Talk, 27*(1), 107–137. doi: 10.1515/TEXT.2007.005

Waring, H. Z. (2007b). The multi-functionality of accounts in advice giving. *Journal of Sociolinguistics, 11,* 367–391.

White, T. B. (2005). Consumer trust and advice acceptance: The moderating roles of benevolence, expertise, and negative emotions. *Journal of Consumer Psychology, 15,* 141–148.

Wilson, S. R., & Kunkel, A. W. (2000). Identity implications of influence goals: Similarities in perceived face threats and facework across sex and close relationships. *Journal of Language and Social Psychology, 19,* 195–221. doi: 10.1177/0261927X00019002002

Wilson, S. R., Aleman, C. G., & Leatham, G. B. (1998). Identity implications of influence goals: A revised analysis of face-threatening acts and application to seeking compliance with same-sex friends. *Human Communication Research, 25,* 64–96.

Wilson, S. R., Gettings, P. E., Hall, E. D., & Pastor, R. G. (2015). Dilemmas families face in talking with returning US military service members about seeking professional help for mental health issues. *Health Communication, 30*(8), 772–783.

Wong, P. T. P., Wong, L. C. J., & Scott, C. (2006). Beyond stress and coping: The positive psychology of transformation. In P. T. P. Wong & L. C. J. Wong (Eds.), *Handbook of multicultural perspectives on stress and coping* (pp. 1–26). New York: Springer.

Wong, S.-S. (2008). Task knowledge overlap and knowledge variety: the role of advice network structures and impact on group effectiveness. *Journal of Organizational Behavior, 29*(5), 591–614.

Wong, S.-S., & Boh, W. F. (2014). The contingent effects of social network sparseness and centrality on managerial innovativeness. *Journal of Management Studies, 51*(7), 1180–1203. doi: 10.1111/joms.12086

Yaniv, I. (2004). Receiving other people's advice: Influence and benefit. *Organizational Behavior and Human Decision Processes, 93*, 1–13. doi: 10.1016/j.obhdp.2003.08.002

Yaniv, I., & Choshen-Hillel, S. (2012). When guessing what another person would say is better than giving your own opinion: Using perspective-taking to improve advice-taking. *Journal of Experimental Social Psychology, 48*(5), 1022–1028.

Yaniv, I., & Kleinberger, E. (2000). Advice taking in decision making: Egocentric discounting and reputation formation. *Organizational Behavior and Human Decision Processes, 84*, 260–281. doi: 10.1006/obhd.2000.2909

Yaniv, I., & Milyavsky, M. (2007). Using advice from multiple sources to revise and improve judgments. *Organizational Behavior and Human Decision Processes, 103*, 104–120. doi: http://dx.doi.org/10.1016/j.obhdp.2006.05.006

Zagenczyk, T., & Murrell, A. (2009). It is better to receive than to give: Advice network effects on job and work-unit attachment. *Journal of Business & Psychology, 24*(2), 139–152. doi: 10.1007/s10869-009-9095-3

Zhang, M., Zheng, W., & Wei, J. (2009). Sources of social capital: Effects of altruistic citizenship behavior and job involvement on advice network centrality. *Human Resource Development Quarterly, 20*(2), 195–217.

Zhang, Z., & Peterson, S. J. (2011). Advice networks in teams: The role of transformational leadership and members' core self-evaluations. *Journal of Applied Psychology, 96*(5), 1004–1017.

Part III

Place, Boundaries, and Exchange in Organizational Communication

CHAPTER CONTENTS

9 Organizational Space and Place beyond Container or Construction

Exploring Workspace in the Communicative Constitution of Organizations

Elizabeth D. Wilhoit

Brian Lamb School of Communication, Purdue University

Space (measurable, objective) and place (meaningful space) are foundational elements of all organizations and organizing. However, extant literature on organizational space has focused on material space as a container for organizations or socially constructed places within organizations. Such an understanding contrasts research from critical geography that has demonstrated the centrality of space to all social life. Using geography and a constitutive approach to organizing, I propose that space and place be understood as both constitutive of, and constituted by, organizational communication. I conclude by proposing several areas for organizational communication research on space and general communication research.

Introduction

Over the past decade, whimsical, yet reportedly effective, workplaces like Google have entered the popular imagination (Levy, 2011; Meyerson & Ross, 2003), teleworking is on the rise (Fonner & Roloff, 2010), and technology enables work to be done outside the office (Golden & Geisler, 2007). In light of these changes, the nature and meaning of workspace are increasingly important issues for organizational scholars. Although other communication subfields like rhetoric (e.g., Barney, 2014; Dunn, 2011; Endres & Senda-Cook, 2011), environmental communication (e.g., Cantrill, 2012; Milstein, Anguiano, Sandoval, Chen, & Dickinson, 2011; Porter, 2013), and media studies (Adams & Jansson, 2012) have studied space and place, organizational communication has not dealt with it extensively. This lack of scholarship is problematic because, as the above examples show, space is central to organizations and organizing.

Where work takes place matters, not just as context or background for work, but as a constitutive element. Although sites are one of the three kinds of materiality identified by Ashcraft, Kuhn, and Cooren (2009) and are a fundamental aspect of organizational life (Dale & Burrell, 2007), there has been little organizational communication research focused on organizational space. There is existing literature on organizational space from fields including facilities management, organization studies, and management. However, within this scholarship, there tends to be a division between studies that see space as a social construction and those that understand space as material.

In this review, I demonstrate the problem of seeing organizational space as either primarily material or social. Both aspects need to be considered in studying organizational space: material space provides organizations with some stability and durability, while socially constructed places contribute to the fluid and performative nature of organizations. I propose that the communication constitutes organizations (CCO) approach, with its view of agency as a product of multiple agents of varying ontologies (including non-humans; Cooren 2004; 2006), offers an appropriate framework for understanding both the material and social aspects of organizational space. By integrating space and place's social and material facets through communication theory, communication becomes a means for better theorizing space as well as using space to better understand specific organizational communication phenomena. Although the focus of this review is on physical space in organizations and organizational communication, this constitutive approach to space can be applied to online spaces and other areas of communication, particularly as they intersect with organizing. To this end, the review concludes by suggesting directions for research in online spaces and for other areas of communication.

Constitutive Approaches to Organizational Communication and Non-Human Agency

Following the review of extant spatial literature, I suggest that a constitutive approach to organizational space can address the problems present in existing research. That proposal is made assuming a constitutive approach to organizations and that non-humans can have agency. The premise of CCO scholarship is that organizational communication is not something that happens in organizations, but that communication is what makes organizations (Taylor & Van Every, 2000). Organizations, therefore, only exist because of communication (McPhee & Zaug, 2000; Taylor & Van Every, 2000). As a result, organizations are the product of ongoing communicative performances and are not stable, but change as communication does (Putnam, Nicotera, & McPhee, 2008; Taylor, Cooren, Giroux, & Robichaud, 1996). Organizations then have their being in interaction and one must study that interaction or communication to understand an organization (Taylor & Van Every, 2000).

This means that the organization as an actor is constituted by those actors who manifest the organization; the micro becomes the macro (Kuhn, 2012). However, it is not only human actors who communicate an organization into being. Non-humans including bodies, sites, and objects also enter into the plenum of agencies present in organizing (Ashcraft et al., 2009; Cooren, 2006). For example:

> Aren't the United States of America as much embodied in their constitu-
> tion, flag or official buildings as they are in their President when he [sic]

presents the State of the Union address, speaks to his [sic] collaborators or responds to journalist?

(Cooren, Fox, Robichaud, & Talih, 2005, p. 266)

Non-humans thus play an equally important role in constituting organizations through communication. Additionally, action is never attributable to only a human or non-human, rather all action is the result of hybrid agency (Cooren, 2010; Latour, 2005).

In light of this, some CCO scholarship has considered space (Cooren et al., 2005; Vásquez, 2013; Vásquez & Cooren, 2013). The present review and research agenda builds on and extends existing CCO spatial work. At first glance, these studies are similar to the present work, arguing that spacing is a hybrid achievement of actors of varying ontological statuses (Cooren et al., 2005) and that space is an ongoing sociomaterial construction that constitutes organizations (Vásquez & Cooren, 2013). However, these studies present a somewhat more constrained view of organizational space and materiality than I do here. As most Montréal School CCO research does, these studies use conversation analysis to study how specific interactions constitute organizations while focusing on immaterial non-humans and examining materiality as manifest in conversation or as intentionally used or manipulated by humans (Wilhoit & Kisselburgh, 2015). These CCO studies have explored how space is materialized in conversation and how communication can transport organizations through space and time. These studies are valuable for demonstrating how space is constructed through interaction, but give little attention to material realities other than how an organization is made present in and across space through communication (Vásquez, 2013; Vásquez & Cooren, 2013). Here, I aim to understand space as constitutive beyond conversation and to consider materiality more broadly (see Wilhoit & Kisselburgh, 2015).

Space

An obvious question to ask at this point is, "What is space?" It is evident that space and place are central to human experience (Massey, 1994) and this fundamental role is represented in the many ways that people refer to space in language; it is part of humanity's common sense, embodied, and social experiences of the world (Cresswell, 2015; Merleau-Ponty, 1962). However, space's essential nature has not made it easier to define and many conflicting definitions of space have been proposed. In this section, I describe two definitions of space: one in relation to time and the other in relation to place. Following that, I briefly introduce some of the major thinkers and ideas of critical geography[1] and how they have reconceptualized space and/or place. Much of the organizational research presented in this review has been influenced by the field of critical geography and this scholarship thus provides a foundation for understanding space in organizations.

Space and Time

Historically, space and time have been understood as opposites (Massey, 2005). Space was seen as unchanging while time was continuous and moving (Foucault, 1980). Later scholars have read this division as one that privileged time over space (Tuan, 1977) and the masculine (time) over the feminine (space; Massey, 1994). Critical geography seeks to overturn this idea of static space and recognize it instead as the product of intersecting flows (Castells, 1999; Massey, 2005) and dynamic, changing, and always-under-construction (Thrift, 2006). Space is then "'the series of simultaneity,' or what coexists together at one instance" (Latour, 1998, p. 99). Rather than being something static and immutable (in opposition to time), space becomes the site of action and dynamism.

Space and Place

The other way to define space is in relationship to place. Although many organizational scholars refer to space, it will become clear that many of them actually mean place. In general, space refers to objective space. It is what can be measured and relates to notions of scale (Agnew, 2011). Place, in contrast, is lived space or a meaningful location (Cresswell, 2015) or practiced space (de Certeau, 1984).[2] Place then marks humans as unique from other species. Although humans are territorial about place in the same way that many animals are, humans have an emotional attachment to their places, giving them meaning (Tuan, 1976). For example, when moving into a new house, one likely understands it as space: the number and size of rooms, the distance of the house from the grocery store and work. However, once one begins to personalize the space with their belongings and it begins to be the site of personal history, space is transformed into place as it is lived and made meaningful. This understanding also demonstrates that what might be space to one can be place for another. For example, one experiences their new house as space, but the old owner would understand it as place, even with their personal belongings removed because of the memories and history they associate with it.

Place is then socially constructed and a communicative process. Massey (1994) proposed a four-fold progressive concept of place that is reminiscent of communication theory, demonstrating the importance of studying place in communication. First, place emerges as the result of interaction and is therefore a process, rather than something static. Second, places do not have boundaries; they are not simple enclosures. Third, places are full of internal conflict and do not have single identities. Fourth, the specificity of place is an ongoing reproduction, rather than a once-produced historical truth. From this understanding, place is a shifting construction (Massey, 1994). These four statements could be applied to many phenomena constituted by communication and therefore demonstrate the role that communication plays in creating places.

Critical Geography

These understandings of space and time and space and place have emerged from critical geography, a movement that began within the field of geography in the later 20th century to understand space not only as measurable object of study but also the site of power and social production (e.g., Harvey, 2001; Massey, 1994; Soja, 1989; Thrift, 2008). Much of this work has been influenced by Marxism and its major theme is the plasticity, contingency, and production of space (Cresswell, 2015). Space is understood as a performance that is contingent and changing (Thrift 2006; 2008). Space is therefore socially produced, but this construction is a political struggle connected to the dominant means of production (Lefebvre, 1991).

Those in power try to change and fix the meanings of space and claim its identity in a certain way (Massey, 1994). However, given the multiplicity of flows always present in a given space, it is impossible to fix a space's meaning (Lefebvre, 1991). For example, de Certeau (1984) has shown how the pedestrian can create alternate spatial meanings through practice by breaking rules like walking the wrong way or cutting a corner. To illustrate these theories and how they are used, I will summarize Lefebvre's theory of the social production of space. Lefebvre's scholarship has not only been foundational to critical geography, but has also influenced what Beyes and Steyaert (2011) termed "organization theory's minor spatial turn" (p. 48).

Lefebvre's (1991) theory of social space emerged as a reaction to his understanding that space had become the domain of mathematicians and was seen as an empty container. Lefebvre proposed that space is socially produced. From this perspective, space is not homogenous or always experienced the same way. Lefebvre (1991) proposed a spatial triad to express his spatial theory. First, perceived space is physical and produced by spatial practice. It is the space of experience and where local activity takes place. It includes particular locations and spatial characteristics experienced through the body. In an organization, one's lived, embodied experience of one's office would be perceived space. Second, conceived space is mental. It is produced by representations of space and is the domain of planners. An office floor plan is an organizational example. Third, lived space is social and produced by representational space. It is thus associated with symbolic meanings and imagination and incorporates perceived and conceived space without being reducible to either (Zhang, 2006). For example, the symbolic power of the large, corner office is an organizational representational space (Dale, 2005). Through this triad, and the relationships of the elements, Lefebvre's understanding of space is productive, multiple, and shifting. As this review will show, these interpenetrations and layers of space in time have appealed to many fields across the social sciences (see Warf & Arias, 2009), including some scholars of organizations (see Dale & Burrell, 2007) and communication (see Ashcraft et al., 2009).

The Spatial Turn

Following critical geography, many social scientific and humanistic disciplines began to adopt these new understandings of space (Cresswell, 2015). This move has been called "the spatial turn," a shift in thinking that recognizes the socially constructed, conflicting, and changing nature of space and the essential role it plays in many areas of human life (Warf & Arias, 2009). The spatial turn recognizes that "geography matters not for the simplistic and overly used reason that everything happens in space, but because *where* things happen is critical to knowing *how* and *why* they happen" (Warf & Arias, 2009, p. 1). The importance of understanding *where* to know *how* and *why* is key in organizational communication as well. However, as this review demonstrates, organizational communication and allied fields often do not consider space and place or do so in a limited way. I suggest that organizational communication is well positioned to lead future scholarship on the spatial turn by using communication to integrate space's social and material facets.

Space in Organizations

I now turn to space in organizations. What differentiates this review from others on organizational space (Davis, Leach, & Clegg, 2011; Elsbach & Pratt, 2007; Taylor & Spicer, 2007) is an emphasis on how space can be understood in ways that are more and less material. My concern in this review is to focus specifically on the spectrum of material to symbolic, or discursive emphases on space across disciplines concerned with organization, to demonstrate how communication research may be able to provide a unique constitutive understanding of space that accounts for space's symbolic *and* material aspects. As I show, although space is understood in both material and symbolic ways, these approaches are rarely integrated (see also Ashcraft et al., 2009 for this argument). I suggest that communication research may be able to study space in a more comprehensive, integrative manner: considering how the materiality of space and its social, symbolic, and discursive elements are integrated in hybrid agency to construct organizations as well as how space and place are constructed in organizing processes.

In organizing this literature around more symbolic and more material approaches to space, materiality and discourse are distinguished by the fact that what makes something material is that it has some enduring qualities not found in human activity (Gieryn, 2002; Leonardi, 2012). For example, the materiality of an automatic door closer is more enduring and reliable than a person whose job it is to close the door (Latour, 1992). In this review, there are very few instances of immaterial non-humans, so an emphasis on materiality (rather than the umbrella category of non-humans) is appropriate. When I refer to symbolic understandings of space, I mean that which is not inevitable: the socially constructed meanings that people have attached to spaces (Hacking, 2000).

Many forms of materiality (e.g., an organization's headquarters) are not inevitable and in many ways social and material factors cannot be distinguished (Latour, 2005). Still, the material is different from the symbolic in that it has a unique obduracy because there are aspects of it that cannot be changed through language (Latour, 1992). The walls in an office may have socially-produced meanings about power, surveillance, and separation, but changing one's interpretation of a wall does not allow one to suddenly be able to walk through it. Although the social and the material always operate in tandem, they function differently. This review proceeds by first discussing literature from management, organization studies, organizational communication, and other related fields that approach space materially. Second, I review literature that views organizational space as socially constructed. Third, I address the small body of literature that considers both aspects of space.

Space as a Backdrop, Container, or Variable

The first way that space has often been studied in organizational literature is as a static material object that can be manipulated by humans. Historically, the physical layout of organizations, or "space as distance" (Taylor & Spicer, 2007), has been a significant topic in studies of organizations. This research takes advantage of the durability of material space that allows one to make material changes to space and expect it to behave consistently (Latour, 1992). Although this research rarely uses the language of affordances, it has an implicit focus on spatial affordances or how certain behaviors are facilitated or constrained as people interact with material features of the environment (Leonardi, 2011). Systematic research in this area began with the Hawthorne studies and its findings about the role of physical environment on both informal interactions and productivity (Roethlisberger & Dickson, 1939; Zhong & House, 2012). Since then, numerous studies have been conducted to understand how the physical work environment affects work practices (Elsbach & Pratt, 2007). Considering space as the context of communication has also been one way that space has been incorporated into organizational communication (Eaves & Leathers, 1991; Haslett, 2013; Sillince, 2007).

In general, this research has been conducted with an objective, social scientific approach, viewing space as a backdrop for action, a container for organizing, or a variable that can be changed and manipulated to optimize work performance. In this section, I review literature that understands organizational space primarily as material and demonstrates how "buildings stabilize social life. They give structure to social institutions, durability to social networks, and persistence to behavior patterns. What humans build solidifies society against time and its incessant forces for change" (Gieryn, 2002, p. 35). This is an extensive body of literature and reviewing it in its entirety is outside the scope of this review. Instead, I highlight major themes as well as research topics that deal specifically with issues of interaction and communication.

Configuring Office Space

The most basic level at which the physical space in organizations has been studied is by viewing space as an independent variable. There are several reasons to study the physical environment of organizations this way. First, the major aspects of the physical environment of an organization (e.g., physical structure, physical stimuli, and symbolic artifacts) all influence organizational behavior (Davis, 1984; Värlander, 2011). As a result, design decisions need to be made carefully because they are usually expensive and relatively permanent (Chan, Beckman, & Lawrence, 2007; Elsbach & Pratt, 2007). Therefore, designers and managers must understand how space functions objectively to optimize workspaces (van Meel, Martens, & Jan van Ree, 2010). Second, the aesthetics of a building can be used as part of organizational strategy and a building communicates an organization's identity and image (Vischer, 2005; Wasserman, 2011). Third, the environment of an organization is important for recruitment and retention of workers, particularly younger employees (Earle, 2003) and increasing organizational commitment (Morrow, McElroy, & Scheibe, 2012). Therefore, choosing the physical configuration of an office can be one of the most important (and difficult) tasks for management (Chan et al., 2007; Elsbach & Pratt, 2007).

In their review of the literature on physical work environment, Elsbach and Pratt (2007) found that there are no elements of physical organizational space that are always correlated with positive outcomes. The four aspects of physical workplace environment that they found most frequently discussed in the literature were: (a) barriers and enclosures; (b) adjustable work arrangements, equipment, and furnishings; (c) personalization of workspace and display of symbols; and (d) nature-like ambient surroundings. They found that there were both positive and negatives associated with each of these four aspects of workspace and that there are often tensions and trade-offs in choosing which aspects to incorporate into a given office. Their review demonstrated that there is no single optimal workplace configuration and that what is best for a given organization may be contextual.

Increasing Informal Interaction, Creativity, and Innovation

One arena where there has been an ongoing concern with improving workspaces regards how to increase informal interaction (for an early example see Steele, 1973). Although research has presented conflicting results, there is interest in the potential relationship between physical organization, informal interaction, and collaboration and creativity (Fayard & Weeks, 2007; Oksanen & Ståhle, 2013). In an early and classic study on informal interaction, Allen and Fustfeld (1975) found that there is a logarithmic relationship between distance and communication indicating that even small distances between workers can limit communication. This finding suggests that propinquity is essential for communication, collaboration, and innovation. Subsequent research has confirmed the relationship between propinquity and collaboration and communication (Fayard & Weeks, 2007; Leiva-Lobos, De Michelis, & Covarrubias, 1997). Additionally, spatial proximity, among other factors, affects how employees perceive the level of collaboration supported by the physical environment (Hua, Loftness, Heerwagen, & Powell, 2010).

Another concern has been which spaces best facilitate creativity (Moultrie et al., 2007). Scholarly conclusions about creative space have been mixed. Although many studies have found that physical environment can improve or diminish creativity (Dul & Ceylan, 2011; 2014; Jankowska & Atlay, 2008; McCoy & Evans, 2010; Oksanen & Ståhle, 2013; Vithayathawornwong, Danko, & Tolbert, 2003), these studies do not present a consensus on what makes a more creative space. As a result, some have argued that organizations need a variety of spaces to facilitate creativity (e.g., spaces to facilitate both group and individual creativity; Haner, 2005; Hemlin, Allwood, & Martin, 2008; Sailer, 2011). Additionally, it is unclear whether space designed for creativity is effective because the physical environment led to innovation or that people are instructed to use it in specific ways (Magadley & Birdi, 2009). There is therefore not a consensus on whether space does make a difference in creativity and, if so, what is the optimal space (Davis et al., 2011).

Open Offices

Another related area that has received extensive study, often in relationship to issues of collaboration, communication, and creativity, has been whether open office plans are better for work than traditional office plans where each worker has an assigned, closed off space (Davis et al., 2011). Open offices are increasing in popularity and have entered the popular imagination through examples like Google's offices (Levy, 2011). Open offices present advantages including cost-saving (Vischer, 2005), flexibility (Duffy, 1997; Myerson & Ross, 2003), increased communication and interaction (Brookes & Kaplan, 1972; Sundstrom & Sundstrom, 1986), more informal communication (Brennan, Chugh, & Kline, 2002), increased organizational commitment (Morrow et al., 2012), and communication of organizational identity and values (Davis, 1984; McElroy & Morrow, 2010). Disadvantages of open offices include employee hesitancy to adopt such a design (Cairns, 2002; Våland, 2011), distractions, interruption, and over-stimulation (McElroy & Morrow, 2010; Oldham & Brass, 1979), loss of employee identity (Elsbach, 2003), lack of privacy (Oldham & Brass, 1979; Pepper, 2008; Sundstrom & Sundstrom, 1986), and increased surveillance and exertion of power (Cairns, 2002; Thanem, Värlander, & Cummings, 2011). In light of these mixed results, some studies have suggested that the decision to move to an open office needs to be based on a specific organization's goals (McElroy & Morrow, 2010; Pepper, 2008; Thanem et al., 2011). Given the conflicting research about open-office plans, more research needs to be conducted that organizations can use for evidence-based design (Lindahl, 2004; Sailer, Budgen, Lonsdale, Turner, & Penn, 2010).

This cross-section of literature reflects an understanding of organizational space in which space is an objective variable that can be manipulated to change organizational outcomes. These studies recognize that material space presents a level of stability that often acts and is responded to in predictable ways. Although there are many other specific topics that this body of literature has studied, this review represents some of the recent major concerns. As a result of approaching space this way, space comes to be understood as a container for organizing or a background upon which organizational activity takes place. This assumption can be seen in making the design of space a managerial task with the assumption that management can change the organization as they shape its space (Chan et al., 2007). This research thus attends to the material aspects of organizations, but does not consider how workers might attach alternative meanings to or interact discursively with space.

Place as a Social Construct

In contrast to the studies on physical space in organizations that see space as an objective variable, other studies have considered the symbolic aspects of space. In recent years there has been an interest in organizational space from subjective and critical perspectives as illustrated by two edited volumes (de Vaujany & Mitev, 2013; van Marrewijk & Yanow, 2010) and two additional books (Dale & Burrell, 2007; Hernes, 2004). This area of research is often, but not always, influenced by critical geography (Dale & Burrell, 2007; Taylor & Spicer, 2007) and reflects a move away from seeing the material as something fixed or essential to understand how humans might hold matter together rather than the other way around (Anderson & Wylie, 2009). Although scholars doing this research tend to use the term space for their object of study, I suggest that in many cases they are studying place: the social, lived, and constructed aspects of space (Tuan, 1977). I have therefore used place in the title of this section, although I follow the authors I review in their terminology.

Many of these studies have been concerned with raising awareness of the importance of studying space in organizations and theorizing organizational space—research aiming to "bring space back in" (Kornberger & Clegg, 2004, p.1095). In this vein, Dale and Burrell (2007) suggested that organizational space can be thought about in two ways: organizations as consisting of spaces and organizations as space for human action and interaction. This makes space a proxy for organization and one avenue for approaching organizational research. Space can therefore be both a central analytic theme as well as a means for understanding other organizational topics (Taylor & Spicer, 2007). In the following section, I review organizational research that theorizes the social aspects of space. In particular, I note the organizational communication studies that have taken this approach.

Multiplicity of Organizational Space

A major theme of scholarship that treats space as a social construction is the multiplicity of organizational space. For example, managers and employees construct spaces differently as they impose certain discourses and meanings on space and interact with a space in both personal and impersonal ways (Kingma, 2008). This finding demonstrates that the meaning of a space is not absolute or stable (Dale & Burrell, 2007). Following the critical geography literature, organizational space is not static, but a process and performance that is multiple and constructed through mundane activity. As a result, space must be studied in terms of what it does (Kornberger & Clegg, 2004) and the process of producing space (Beyes & Steyaert, 2011), rather than what it contains.

In general, organizational scholars have illustrated the multiplicity of space through two theories. First, many studies have used Lefebvre's three-part theory of the social production of space to show that space is not static, but that objective, conceived, and lived space can exist simultaneously and present conflicting meanings (Dale, 2005; Dobers & Strannegard, 2004; Kingma, 2008; Wapshott & Mallett, 2011; Wasserman, 2011; Watkins, 2005; Zhang, Spicer, & Hancock, 2008). For example, Wapshott and Mallett (2011) studied working from home from a Lefebvrian perspective that collapses the demarcation between work and home. The authors used this integrated perspective to understand how homeworkers' multiple meanings of work and place can coexist rather than needing to compete.

Second, other scholars have used Foucault's (1984) concept of heterotopia (anti-utopias that are socially-sanctioned places of conflict and multiplicity) to show the multiplicity of organizational space (Beyes & Michels, 2011; Cairns, McInnes, & Roberts, 2003; Dobers & Strannegard, 2004; Hjorth, 2005; Kingma, 2008). Organizational scholars have extended Foucault to demonstrate that casinos (Kingma, 2008), business schools (Beyes & Michels, 2011), and creative workplaces (Hjorth, 2005) are heterotopias in which difference becomes productive. Organizations are thus composed of multiple spaces. As a result, depending on which organizational space an employee is in, they may have different identities, subjectivities, or draw on different discourses (Halford & Leonard, 2005). It is important to note that, in addition to these postmodern approaches, earlier research not taking a postmodern approach came to similar conclusions about the multiplicity of space. For example, Schein (2010), demonstrated how artifacts in organizations (including space) can have different meanings for different people, especially for those who are inside or outside of the organization's culture. All of these approaches show that organizational space has multiple layers of meaning and discourse, redefining space not as something fixed, given, or monolithic, but as a dynamic, conflicted, and constructed aspect of an organization (Knox, O'Doherty, Vurdubakis, & Westrup, 2008; Kornberger & Clegg, 2004).

In organizational communication, one specific area where the multiplicity and conflicting nature of space has been studied is in work/life research. For contemporary workers, work and home as social spaces are seldom clearly distinguished by the physical spaces of an office and a house. Instead, work and home are discursive and negotiated constructions that often prevent conflicts as they overlap and bump up against each other in challenging ways (Golden, 2013; Golden & Geisler, 2007; Halford, 2005; Kirby, Golden, Medved, Jorgenson, & Buzzanell, 2003; Turner & Norwood, 2013). As more people work from home, these social constructions about what is work space and what is personal space within the physical space of the home become more nuanced and complicated (Butler & Modaff, 2008; Walker, Wang, & Redmond, 2008; Wapshott & Mallett, 2011).

Similarly, several studies have examined how teleworkers construct their workspace as legitimate in the face of discourses that suggest otherwise. Hylmö (2006) studied how employees in a telecommuting-friendly organization legitimized their choice of workspace (office or home) as well as showing that employees normalized telework by discursively positioning the office as relative space (Hylmö & Buzzanell, 2002). Additionally, Chinese teleworkers legitimize the home as an appropriate workspace to their friends and family and negotiate the potential danger of missing out on social relationships by not being co-located (Long, Kuang, & Buzzanell, 2013). These contemporary examples demonstrate how different stakeholders create varying meanings of space that may vary across time and context.

Power and Resistance

One way that critical geography has transformed the study of space is by introducing a political element to space and demonstrating how the use and creation of space can be an exercise of power (Harvey, 2001; Massey, 2005; Soja, 1989). For example, de Certeau (1984) has been influential in comparing spatial activity to communication and describing how transgressive spatial behaviors can be resistant. This theme has been carried into studies of organizational space with a particular concern for not only how power is imposed, but also how workers spatially resist (Dale & Burrell, 2007; Taylor & Spicer, 2007).

First, research has shown how power is exerted through space, particularly managerially ascribed spatial meanings (Sage & Dainty, 2012). Examples of research in this area have shown that employees can embrace a Panopticon because of positive managerial discourses about it (Dale, 2005), hierarchical power is produced through everyday spatial interactions (Zhang & Spicer, 2013), workspace is often gendered as masculine, exerting patriarchal power (Tyler & Cohen, 2010), space can be the basis for surveillance (Collinson & Collinson, 1997), ideology and discourses can be embedded in and imposed through architecture and design (Guillén, 1998; Hurdley, 2010), and the color white can be used as a form of symbolic institutional power (Connellan, 2013).

If space can be a location of power, it can also be a resource for resistance. Following Foucault (1984), organizational space is heterotopian, consisting of multiple times and spaces that create knowledge, power, and resistance in a multiplicity of ways rather than the singularity of a Panopticon (Cairns et al., 2003). Since power is symbolically constructed through organizational space that same space becomes the place from which a subject is able to resist, demonstrating the co-constitutive nature of power and resistance from organizational space (Ball & Wilson, 2000; Panayiotou & Kafiris, 2010; Zhang et al., 2008). Resistance often involves creating a discursive space from which workers can speak (Prasad & Prasad, 2000) and many studies of resistance in factory settings have demonstrated how workers challenge the dominant meanings of spaces to resist either implicitly or explicitly (Burawoy, 1979; Graham, 1995; Kondo, 1990; Levidow, 1991; Ong, 1987; Rofel, 1992). However, the connection between power and resistance can also be found in surprising sites like workplace aesthetics that offer freedom to workers through incorporating the human senses into organization (Cairns, 2002).

People can also create spaces and places from which to organize in order to resist. By creating a space for action, activists can find each other and organize, both intentionally (Haug, 2013) and unintentionally (Wilhoit & Kisselburgh, 2015). Additionally, research on transnational organizing examines how individuals organize across spatial differences, create spatial imaginaries that re-draw boundaries and play with spatial scale, and create participative counter spaces that offer a voice to participants while destabilizing dominant structures (Conway, 2008; Dempsey, Parker, & Krone, 2011; Parker, 2014). These social movements organize by creating and connecting places, acknowledging the importance of local place while also transcending it through the construction of alternative spaces and networks (McFarlane, 2009).

Issues of power and resistance have also been an arena for connecting organizational communication theory and space by demonstrating how employees resist and create alternative meanings to managerial discourses and rules about space. For instance, Murphy (1998) described how flight attendants only obeyed a rule to wear high heels in airports where they might be seen and caught; in other settings, they wore flats. Resistance was tied to certain spaces. Breastfeeding mothers transformed closets, restrooms, and phone booths into places where they could pump breast milk, resisting by articulating new purposes for these spaces (Turner & Norwood, 2013). Office folklore, photocopied cartoons and signs that clerical workers hung up in their workspaces, represent another reappropriation of organizational space (Bell & Forbes, 1994). Just as spaces are discursively constructed by those in power, those subjected to those discourses can resist by attaching alternative meanings to spaces.

Identity and Identification

Another area where the socially constructed nature of space is evident is in studies of organizational identity and identification. Both individual organizational members' identities (e.g., Elsbach, 2004) and the identity of the entire organization can be constituted by space (e.g., van Marrewijk & Broos, 2012). Additionally, the space through which identity is constructed can include physical space, geographic location, and the meaningfully constructed place (Halford & Leonard, 2005; O'Neill & McGuirk, 2003). One common way that workers express and construct identity through space is by personalizing their workspaces (Brown, Lawrence, & Robinson, 2005; Elsbach, 2003; 2004; O'Toole & Were, 2008; Pierce, Kostova, & Dirks, 2001). Through these symbolic representations, workers share about themselves, build relationships with others, focus on their goals, and establish their desired boundary or integration between work and non-work (Byron & Laurence, 2015).

In organizational communication, the role of space and place in the development of identity and identification is one area where space has been widely considered. Several studies have examined how geographic place affects one's identity. Larson and Pearson (2012) studied high-tech entrepreneurs in Montana who used aspects of place (e.g., lifestyle, home, challenge) as discursive resources to manage their work identities, demonstrating that place is not only a context for action, but can have agency. Similarly, Gill and Larson (2013) and Kuhn (2006) studied how local place-based discourses (e.g., religious discourses from Mormonism in Utah or discourses about taking advantage of the outdoor recreation available in the American west) intersect with larger organizational or career discourses. Moving away from geography towards workspace, Rooney et al. (2010) found that those employees with the highest identification with organizational place were lowest in the organization and had the most difficult time adapting to changes to organizational space.

Overall, these more symbolic approaches to understanding organizational space demonstrate how organizational members attach meanings to organizational spaces that may or may not be related to the materiality of the space. These studies also show that there will always be multiple, often contradictory spaces within an organization, reflecting messy social realities. These studies are then useful for revealing this reality of organizational life. However, in privileging the social, most of these studies do not consider the physical, material aspects of organizational space, a reality that cannot be ignored or communicated away.

Organizational Space and Place Integrated

The research reviewed up to this point has generally focused on either the material aspects of space or the symbolic aspects of place. Of course, most of these studies do mention both material and social aspects of space, but there are few studies that take seriously both the structuring stability of materiality and the shifting multiplicity of the social. Before suggesting why this is a serious gap and how it might be remedied, I detail the few studies that do understand space as a material reality that affords and constrains certain actions as well as recognizing the symbolic dimensions that humans project onto spaces. These studies illustrate the potential for an integrated study of the material and discursive aspects of both organizational space and place.

Several of these studies deal with the relationship between what was intended in designing an organizational space versus how users interpreted and attached meaning to that space. Peltonen (2011) and Pepper (2008) both demonstrated how new buildings designed to communicate certain managerial intentions can be misinterpreted by employees. For example, Pepper (2008) showed how a building designed to symbolize and foster openness was used in ways that decreased communication and openness. These studies demonstrated that the material structure of buildings does shape users' perceptions and uses, but users also attach different meanings or behaviors to this materiality than was intended. Similarly, Elsbach (2003) studied how employees in a non-territorial office (where no one had a fixed workspace) resisted identity threats by manipulating both material and symbolic artifacts to re-assert identity while breaking rules about the new work configuration. Ewalt and Ohl (2013) have also approached place-based identity in both material and discursive ways by looking at how soldiers' identities are tied both to material (e.g., war zone versus home) and social spaces (e.g., occupational space, identity).

Returning to informal interaction, Fayard and Weeks (2007) studied the copy rooms at three organizations and how the privacy and propinquity of copy rooms affect their use, as well as how social designation of who was supposed to use the space played a role in interaction. Additionally, Gieryn (2000; 2002) has shown how the sociomaterial nature of organizational spaces means that buildings can be reconfigured in both material (e.g., rebuilding, changing the layout) and discursive (e.g., re-naming, changing goals) ways (Gieryn, 2002). Yanow (1995; 1998) has theorized buildings by suggesting they be understood as stories in which landscaping, interior design, and other material elements are interpreted to reveal the power, policies, and history of the building. Finally, Palmås (2013) has shown how rice paddies are made to speak, demonstrating how material space can be made to embody and speak for certain discourses. These examples demonstrate what the study of organizational space that incorporates both material and symbolic aspects might look like. I now conclude by suggesting future lines of inquiry and research questions in this vein.

A Constitutive Approach to Organizational Space and Place

In the preceding review of literature on organizational space, I established two problems that are present in the organizational space literature: extant research almost always treats space as either an entirely material phenomenon or as something that is primarily socially constructed. This dichotomy is problematic because the stability and durability of material spaces and the fluidity of social places are both important to organizational life and the nature and ontology of the organization itself. Communication theory that does not consider how both humans and non-humans act and interact will always be incomplete (Kuhn, 2011). Therefore, both materiality and discourse are essential to understanding organizations and organizational space. I propose that this division can be overcome by developing a communicative understanding of organizational space.

This communicative understanding can be built on critical geography. Massey (2005) has presented a general constitutive view of space that can be applied to and extended within an organizational communication context. Although Massey has focused specifically on gender (1994) and globalization (2005), her approach can be expanded into a fuller understanding of communicatively constituted space that is commensurate with a CCO perspective. Using Massey's (2005) three central propositions as an organizing framework, I briefly describe the features and advantages of a CCO approach to space. The goal of this section is not to present a complete CCO theory of organizational space, but to demonstrate its necessity and to open up avenues for fruitful research directions in this area.

First, Massey (2005) has shown that space is the product of interaction. Similarly, a CCO understanding of space recognizes space as the product of communication. This means that space is no longer one of many features of organizations, but an integral part of it. The nature of a space—crowded, empty, bleak, colorful, flexible, fixed—will shape not only interaction between employees and productivity, but also the nature and being of the organization. Similarly, the nature of the organization—innovative, traditional, small, large, hierarchical, flat—will affect the type of space. Although I have used the term "organizational space" throughout this review, the research reviewed here has not dealt with organizational space in the truest sense of the term. These studies have been concerned with *space in organizations*, but not with how space reflects or contributes to the organization itself or organizing. The ability to study space and organizing is a major advantage of a constitutive approach to space. Additionally, moving somewhat beyond Massey, a CCO approach recognizes the scaling up of agency—the idea that micro interactions scale up to create the organization as an actor with agency (Kuhn, 2012). This provides the possibility for space and place themselves to become agents and subjects, rather than only being products of communication as suggested by Vásquez and Cooren (2013).

Second, Massey (2005) has shown that space is the coexistence of multiplicity and plurality:

> The specifically spatial . . . is produced by that—sometimes happenstance, sometimes not—arrangement-in-relation-to-each-other that is the result of there being a multiplicity of trajectories. In spatial configurations, otherwise unconnected narratives may be brought into contact, or previously connected ones may be wrenched apart.
>
> (p. 111)

Similarly, communication theory acknowledges multiplicity and the varying stories and realities present in any interaction (or organization; see Ashcraft et al., 2009). Additionally, CCO acknowledges the role of non-human agency and heterogeneous actors in constituting organizations (Cooren, 2004). From a CCO approach, it is this "arrangement-in-relation-to-each-other" that allows actors of varying ontological statuses to interact with each other, communicating the organization into being. A CCO approach to space would then recognize how the coming together of multiple discourses, actors, narratives, and objects is constitutive of organizational space. One result of this is an equal regard for materiality and discourse in the constitution of space.

Third, Massey has demonstrated that space is always under construction, again aligning with a CCO approach that recognizes how reality is the result of communicative performances (Cooren, 2010). Just as organizations are not stable, neither is organizational space. However, a CCO approach can challenge this premise somewhat by exploring how the material aspects of space provide some stability or structure at least in the short term. This is something that many spatial scholars have hesitated to do. For example, Massey (2005) has shown how even geological features like continents or mountains are not fixed. Following critical geography, a CCO perspective on space would be characterized by the production of space through communicative interaction, a co-existing and productive multiplicity of both agents and activities, and a tension between the quasi-stability provided by material space and the performed, changing nature of discursive place.

A Research Agenda for Organizational Communication Space and Place

Following this proposed constitutive approach to organizational space, I suggest research questions that can be asked about organizational space. These questions reflect the fact that communication scholars can study space for space's sake, but also use it as a framework to understand other areas of organizational communication research (Dale & Burrell, 2007; Taylor & Spicer, 2007). Either approach provides a new approach for asking questions about organizations and organizing, allowing communication scholars to develop a constitutive understanding of organizational space while better understanding other organizational phenomena by incorporating space. They also offer an opportunity for communication scholars to lead spatial research by overcoming the material/social divide present in much existing literature.

Proposed Research Questions

Organizational Boundaries and Presence

First, research can further explore organizational space and place by asking where an organization is. Such research would entail looking at the spaces of an organization, not only in terms of its offices, but also how employees travelling for business, delivery trucks, or organizational brochures manifest the organization and are also organizational spaces and places, both materially and discursively. Asking these questions extends extant CCO research on the "presentification" of an organization, or how an organization is made present by its constitutive agents (Cooren, 2010; Vásquez & Cooren, 2013). Such tracing of where an organization is and what its spaces and places are will help better define organizational space and place through carefully delineating what is and is not space and/or place. Research in this area would also contribute to broader organizational theory on what makes an organization and organizational boundaries, including whether organizations and spaces even have boundaries.

One specific direction in this area would be to ask what metaphors are appropriate for organizations and organizing in the twenty-first century. Although contemporary scholars tend to look back on earlier organizational communication research and see the misguided use of a container metaphor for organizations (Putnam & Mumby, 2014; Smith, 1993), it seems that the container metaphor is still implicit in much organizational scholarship (and not only scholarship on organizational space). By considering the nature of organizational presence and boundaries, communication scholars may be able to develop helpful new metaphors for organizations and organizing.

Place as Internally and Externally Constitutive

Second, one unique aspect of space and place is that they exist as both internally and externally constitutive elements. All organizations are located in a larger space (e.g., online space, the geographic locale where the organization's headquarters are located, or the homes of teleworkers). This space of location is then externally constitutive of organizations as local discourses, regulations, natural and human resources, and other elements play a constitutive role in the organization. At the same time, each organization has its unique place: its website, its headquarters, the desks in teleworkers' homes, and other places where the organization is made present. Internally, these aspects are also constitutive of organizations. This makes space and place unique constitutive elements in that they function both from the inside and outside of an organization. Future research should ask how this makes space a different kind of constituent element and what the difference is between internal and external spatial constitution. It also provides an opportunity to contribute to larger spatial theory by asking whether all spaces are the same or if different kinds of spaces act in unique ways.

Studying space from this perspective also allows scholars to attend to the increasingly rapid pace of the economy and need for organizations to be flexible and innovative to remain relevant and meet changing demands (Brown, 2008; Leonardi, 2011). As organizations are changing their workspaces to be more innovative, creative, and playful (Meyerson & Ross, 2003), and more people telework (Fonner & Roloff, 2010) or cowork (Spinuzzi, 2012), scholars need to consider how organizations are constituted by the spaces inside and outside of organizations. Additionally, physical workspaces can become one way to study the constitution of flexible, innovative organizations through both material changes and managerial discourses.

Online Spaces

Third, this review has largely assumed that spaces are physical, geographic locations, privileging physical space over the virtual. However, organizations increasingly also exist in online spaces. There is some research that theorizes online space (e.g., Cohen, 2007; Mitra, 2001; Sassen 2002), but this thinking needs to be extended into organizational contexts to understand how these spaces function and are constitutive of/constituted by organizations. Studying online space also presents opportunities to ask fundamental questions about what makes an organization, challenging traditional organizational theory that has assumed an organization has a physical location. Studying online spaces for organizations also offers the opportunity to study spaces of organizing, rather than only formal organizations. Because this is an area still being theorized, it is one where communication research and a constitutive approach could have an important impact.

Conclusion

Although the focus of this review has been specifically on organizational communication, such an approach also offers fruitful directions for other areas of communication research. All communication can be understood as constitutive (Craig, 1999) and many other communication subfields intersect with organizing. Other areas of communication could therefore benefit from a constitutive approach to space, particularly as their interests intersect with organizing. For example, health communication often deals with healthcare organizations and could consider the role that space plays in constituting the patient/provider relationship. Research has examined how the built environment of healthcare settings affects patient experiences (Douglas & Douglas, 2005). However, this scholarship could go further with a constitutive view of space to understand how meanings about space (e.g., the hospital as a space of healing, fear, or distrust) as well as the material aspects (e.g., institutional furniture or doctors' diplomas on the wall) together constitute the experience of medical treatment and patient-provider interaction. Such an approach could also challenge ideas about where medical institutions exist, exploring other spaces like hospital websites, pharmacies, and the home as places where medical interaction and activity takes place, connecting health communication, organizational communication, and space.

Similarly, family communication can be considered from an organizational perspective as families organize through communication. Research in this area could consider how family spaces like the home or car constitute the family. Again, family members will have constructed discursive meanings about these spaces while also dealing with their material realities. How these aspects intersect in space to both reflect and act on family structures and communication could be studied. Additionally, media scholars could further study the constitutive nature of online and/or mediated spaces, particularly how organizing takes place in online spaces. As mentioned above, some work has begun to theorize online spaces, but these theories can be extended, particularly to explore how user experience of a space affects the resultant organization. This is not an exhaustive list of topics or communication subfields that could use such an approach, but provides some examples of ways a communicatively constitutive understanding of space could be applied outside organizational communication.

In this review, I have demonstrated that existing literature on organizational space tends to either treat space as entirely material or as totally socially constructed. Both tendencies are problematic because space exists as a stable, durable, material thing *and* a fluid, constructed, social construction. The material and social both contribute to the nature of organizations and organizing and therefore both need to be incorporated in theorizing on organizational space. I have suggested that this problem can be resolved by developing a CCO understanding of space founded on critical geography. This approach provides a language and framework for studying space itself as well as a new lens for investigating other organizational issues. Although space has not been widely considered within communication research up to this point, I hope that communication scholars might find its study to be a fruitful avenue, both for the study of space itself and for better understanding communication, organizations, and organizing.

Notes

1   Although disciplinary distinctions are not always clear, I follow Aitken and Valentine (2006) and see human geography as an overarching field characterized by its distinction from physical geography. Within human geography, there are many approaches and methods. Here, I deal primarily with humanistic geography that privileges human activity and experience (e.g., de Certeau, 1984; Tuan, 1976) and critical geography that uses Marxist theory to critique the uneven development of space (e.g., Harvey, 2001; Lefebvre, 1991, Massey, 1994; 2005; Soja, 1989; Thrift, 2008). Critical geographers tend to take a poststructuralist approach to space and as a result are sometimes referred to as postmodern or poststructuralist geographers. Although one could be a non-critical postmodern geographer, in practice these subfields of human geography tend to be the same.
2   In English translation, de Certeau's terminology for space and place are reversed. Here I have kept his meaning while using the more common usage of the terms.

References

Adams, P. C., & Jansson, A. (2012). Communication geography: A bridge between disciplines. *Communication Theory, 22*, 299–318. doi: 10.1111/j.1468-2885.2012.01406.x

Agnew, J. (2011). Space and place. In J. Agnew & D. Livingstone (Eds.), *Handbook of geographical knowledge* (pp. 316–330). London, UK: Sage.

Aitken, S. and Valentine, G. (Eds.). (2006). *Approaches to human geography*. London, UK: Sage.

Allen, T. J., & Fustfeld, A. R. (1975). Research laboratory architecture and the structuring of communications. *R&D Management, 5*, 153–163. doi: 10.1111/j.1467-9310.1975.tb01230.x

Anderson, B., & Wylie, J. (2009). On geography and materiality. *Environment and Planning A, 41*, 318–335. doi: 10.1068/a3940

Ashcraft, K. L., Kuhn, T. R., & Cooren, F. (2009). Constitutional amendments: "Materializing" organizational communication. *The Academy of Management Annals, 3*, 1–64. doi: 10.1080/19416520903047186

Ball, K., & Wilson, D. C. (2000). Power, control and computer-based performance monitoring: Repertoires, resistance and subjectivities. *Organization Studies, 21*, 539–565. doi: 10.1177/0170840600213003

Barney, T. (2014). Diagnosing the third world: The "map doctor" and the spatialized discourses of disease and development in the Cold War. *Quarterly Journal of Speech, 100*, 1–30. doi: 10.1080/00335630.2014.887215

Bell, E., & Forbes, L. C. (1994). Office folklore in the academic paperwork empire: The interstitial space of gendered (con)texts. *Text and Performance Quarterly, 14*, 181–196. doi: 10.1080/10462939409366082

Beyes, T., & Michels, C. (2011). The production of educational space: Heterotopia and the business university. *Management Learning, 42*, 521–536. doi: 10.1177/1350507611400001

Beyes, T., & Steyaert, C. (2011). Spacing organization: Non-representational theory and performing organizational space. *Organization, 19*, 45–61. doi: 10.1177/1350508411401946

Brennan, A., Chugh, J. S., & Kline, T. (2002). Traditional versus open office design: A longitudinal study. *Environment and Behavior, 34*, 279–299. doi: 0.1177/0013916502034003001

Brookes, M. J., & Kaplan, A. (1972). The office environment: Space planning and affective behavior. *Human Factors and Ergonomics in Manufacturing, 14*, 373–391.

Brown, G., Lawrence, T. B., & Robinson, S. L. (2005). Territoriality in organizations. *Academy of Management Review, 30*, 577–594. doi: 10.5465/AMR.2005.17293710

Brown, T. (2008). Design thinking. *Harvard Business Review, 86*(6), 84–92, 141.

Burawoy, M. (1979). *Manufacturing consent: Changes in the labor process under monopoly capitalism.* Chicago, IL: University Of Chicago Press.

Butler, J. A., & Modaff, D. P. (2008). When work is home: Agency, structure, and contradictions. *Management Communication Quarterly, 22*, 232–257. doi: 10.1177/0893318908323151

Byron, K., & Laurence, G. A. (2015). Diplomas, photos, & tchotchkes as symbolic self-representations: Understanding employees' individual use of symbols. *Academy of Management Journal, 58*, 298–323. doi: 10.5465/amj.2012.0932

Cairns, G. (2002). Aesthetics, morality and power: Design as espoused freedom and implicit control. *Human Relations, 55*, 799–820. doi: 10.1177/0018726702055007541

Cairns, G., McInnes, P., & Roberts, P. (2003). Organizational space/time: From imperfect panoptical to heterotopian understanding. *Ephemera, 3*, 126–139.

Cantrill, J. G. (2012). Amplifiers on the commons: Using indicators to foster place-based sustainability initiatives. *Environmental Communication, 6*, 5–22. doi: 10.1080/17524032.2011.640703

Castells, M. (1999). Grassrooting the space of flows. *Urban Geography, 20*, 294–302. doi: 10.2747/0272-3638.20.4.294

Chan, J. K., Beckman, S. L., & Lawrence, P. G. (2007). Workplace design: A new managerial imperative. *California Management Review, 49*, 6–23. doi: 10.2307/41166380

Cohen, J. E. (2007). Cyberspace as/and space. *Columbia Law Review, 107*, 210–256.

Collinson, D., & Collinson, M. (1997). Delayering managers: time–space surveillance and its gendered effects. *Organization, 4*, 375–407. doi: 10.1177/135050849743005

Connellan, K. (2013). The psychic life of white: Power and space. *Organization Studies*, *34*, 1529–1549. doi: 10.1177/0170840613495331

Conway, J. (2008). Geographies of transnational feminisms: The politics of place and scale in the World March of Women. *Social Politics*, *15*, 207–231. doi: 10.1093/sp/jxn010

Cooren, F. (2004). Textual agency: How texts do things in organizational settings. *Organization*, *11*, 373–393. doi: 10.1177/1350508404041998

Cooren, F. (2006). The organizational world as a plenum of agencies. In F. Cooren, J. R. Taylor, & E. J. Van Every (Eds.), *Communication as organizing: Empirical and theoretical explorations in the dynamic of text and conversation* (pp. 81–100). Mahwah, NJ: Lawrence Erlbaum Associates.

Cooren, F. (2010). *Action and agency in dialogue: Passion, incarnation and ventriloquism.* Amsterdam, Netherlands: John Benjamins Publishing Company.

Cooren, F., Fox, S., Robichaud, D., & Talih, N. (2005). Arguments for a plurified view of the social world: Spacing and timing as hybrid achievements. *Time & Society*, *14*, 265–282. doi: 10.1177/0961463X05055138

Craig, R. T. (1999). Communication theory as a field. *Communication Theory, 9*, 119–161. doi: 10.1111/j.1468-2885.1999.tb00166.x

Cresswell, J. (2015). *Place: A short introduction.* Malden, MA: John Wiley & Sons.

Dale, K. (2005). Building a social materiality: Spatial and embodied politics in organizational control. *Organization*, *12*, 649–678. doi: 10.1177/1350508405055940

Dale, K., & Burrell, G. (2007). *Spaces of organization and the organization of space: Power, identity and materiality at work.* Basingstoke, UK: Palgrave Macmillan.

Davis, M. C., Leach, D. J., & Clegg, C. W. (2011). The physical environment of the office: Contemporary and emerging issues. In G. P. Hodgkinson & J. K. Ford (Eds.), *International Review of Industrial and Organizational Psychology* (Vol. 26). Chichester, UK: John Wiley & Sons. doi: 10.1002/9781119992592.ch6

Davis, T. R. V. (1984). The influence of the physical environment in offices. *The Academy of Management Review*, *9*, 271–283. doi: 10.2307/258440

de Certeau, M. (1984). *The practice of everyday life.* (S. Rendall, trans.). Berkeley, CA: University of California Press.

de Vaujany, F. X., & Mitev, N. (Eds.). (2013). *Materiality and space: Organizations, artefacts and practices.* London, UK: Palgrave Macmillan.

Dempsey, S. E., Parker, P. S., & Krone, K. J. (2011). Navigating socio-spatial difference, constructing counter-space: Insights from transnational feminist praxis. *Journal of International and Intercultural Communication*, *4*, 201–220. doi: 10.1080/17513057.2011.569973

Dobers, P., & Strannegard, L. (2004). The cocoon—A traveling space. *Organization*, *11*, 825–848. doi: 10.1177/1350508404047253

Douglas, C. H., & Douglas, M. R. (2005). Patient-centered improvements in health-care built environments: Perspectives and design indicators. *Health Expectations, 8*, 264–276. doi: 10.1111/j.1369-7625.2005.00336.x

Duffy, F. (1997). *The new office.* London, UK: Conran Octopus.

Dul, J., & Ceylan, C. (2011). Work environments for employee creativity. *Ergonomics*, *54*, 12–20. doi: 10.1080/00140139.2010.542833

Dul, J., & Ceylan, C. (2014). The impact of a creativity-supporting work environment on a firm's product innovation performance. *Journal of Product Innovation Management*, *31*, 1254–1267. doi: 10.1111/jpim.12149

Dunn, T. R. (2011). Remembering "a great fag": Visualizing public memory and the construction of queer space. *Quarterly Journal of Speech*, 97, 435–460. doi: 10.1080/00335630.2011.585168

Earle, H. A. (2003). Building a workplace of choice: Using the work environment to attract and retain top talent. *Journal of Facilities Management*, 2, 244–257. doi: 10.1108/14725960410808230

Eaves, M. H., & Leathers, D. G. (1991). Context as communication: McDonald's vs. Burger King. *Journal of Applied Communication Research*, 19, 263–289. doi: 10.1080/00909889109365309

Elsbach, K. D. (2003). Relating physical environment to self-categorizations: Identity threat and affirmation in a non-territorial office space. *Administrative Science Quarterly*, 48, 622–654. doi: 10.2307/3556639

Elsbach, K. D. (2004). Interpreting workplace identities: The role of office décor. *Journal of Organizational Behavior*, 25, 99–128. doi: 10.1002/job.233

Elsbach, K. D., & Pratt, M. G. (2007). The physical environment in organizations. *The Academy of Management Annals*, 1, 181–224. doi: 10.1080/078559809

Endres, D., & Senda-Cook, S. (2011). Location matters: The rhetoric of place in protest. *Quarterly Journal of Speech*, 97, 257–282. doi: 10.1080/00335630.2011.585167

Ewalt, J., & Ohl, J. (2013). "We are still in the desert": Diaspora and the (de)territorialization of identity in discursive representations of the US soldier. Culture & Organization, 19, 209–226. doi: 10.1080/14759551.2013.802167

Fayard, A. L., & Weeks, J. (2007). Photocopiers and water-coolers: The affordances of informal interaction. Organization Studies, 28, 605–634. doi: 10.1177/0170840606068310

Fonner, K. L., & Roloff, M. E. (2010). Why teleworkers are more satisfied with their jobs than are office-based workers: When less contact is beneficial. *Journal of Applied Communication Research*, 38, 336–361. doi: 10.1080/00909882.2010.513998

Foucault, M. (1980). *Power/knowledge: Selected interviews and other writings, 1972–1977.* (C. Gordon, Ed.). New York, NY: Vintage.

Foucault, M. (1984). Of other spaces, heterotopias. *Architecture, Mouvement, Continuité*, 5, 46–49.

Gieryn, T. F. (2000). A space for place in sociology. *Annual Review of Sociology*, 26, 463–496. doi: 10.1146/annurev.soc.26.1.463

Gieryn, T. F. (2002). What buildings do. *Theory and Society*, 31, 35–74. doi: 10.1023/A:1014404201290

Gill, R., & Larson, G. S. (2013). Making the ideal (local) entrepreneur: Place and the regional development of high-tech entrepreneurial identity. *Human Relations*, 67, 519–542. doi: 10.1177/0018726713496829

Golden, A. G. (2013). The structuration of information and communication technologies and work–life interrelationships: Shared organizational and family rules and resources and implications for work in a high-technology organization. *Communication Monographs*, 80, 101–123. doi: 10.1080/03637751.2012.739702

Golden, A. G., & Geisler, C. (2007). Work-life boundary management and the personal digital assistant. *Human Relations*, 60, 519–551. doi: 10.1177/0018726707076698

Graham, L. (1995). *On the line at Subaru-Isuzu: The Japanese model and the American worker*. Ithaca, NY: Cornell University Press.

Guillén, M. (1998). Scientific management's lost aesthetic: Architecture, organization, and the Taylorized beauty of the mechanical. *Administrative Science Quarterly*, 42, 682–715.

Hacking, I. (2000). *The social construction of what?* Cambridge, MA: Harvard University Press.

Halford, S. (2005). Hybrid workspace: Re-spatialisations of work, organisation and management. *New Technology, Work and Employment, 20,* 19–33. doi: 10.1111/j.1468-005X.2005.00141.x

Halford, S., & Leonard, P. (2005). Place, space and time: Contextualizing workplace subjectivities. *Organization Studies, 27,* 657–676. doi: 10.1177/0170840605059453

Haner, U. E. (2005). Spaces for creativity and innovation in two established organizations. *Creativity and Innovation Management, 14,* 288–298. doi: 10.1111/j.1476-8691.2005.00347.x

Harvey, D. (2001). *Spaces of capital: Towards a critical geography.* New York, NY: Routledge.

Haslett, B. B. (2013). Structurational interaction. *Management Communication Quarterly, 27,* 615–622. doi: 10.1177/0893318913504037

Haug, C. (2013). Organizing spaces: Meeting arenas as a social movement infrastructure between organization, network, and institution. *Organization Studies, 34,* 705–732. doi: 10.1177/0170840613479232

Hemlin, S., Allwood, C. M., & Martin, B. R. (2008). Creative knowledge environments. *Creativity Research Journal, 20,* 196–210. doi: 10.1080/10400410802060018

Hernes, T. (2004). *The spatial construction of organization.* Philadelphia, PA: John Benjamins Publishing Company.

Hjorth, D. (2005). Organizational entrepreneurship: With de Certeau on creating heterotopias (or spaces for play). *Journal of Management Inquiry, 14,* 386–398. doi: 10.1177/1056492605280225

Hua, Y., Loftness, V., Heerwagen, J. H., & Powell, K. M. (2010). Relationship between workplace spatial settings and occupant-perceived support for collaboration. *Environment and Behavior, 43,* 807–826. doi: 10.1177/0013916510364465

Hurdley, R. (2010). The power of corridors: Connecting doors, mobilising materials, plotting openness. *The Sociological Review, 58,* 45–64. doi: 10.1111/j.1467-954X.2009.01876.x

Hylmö, A. (2006). Telecommuting and the contestability of choice: Employee strategies to legitimize personal decisions to work in a preferred location. *Management Communication Quarterly, 19,* 541–569. doi: 10.1177/0893318905284762

Hylmö, A., & Buzzanell, P. M. (2002). Telecommuting as viewed through cultural lenses: an empirical investigation of the discourses of utopia, identity, and mystery. *Communication Monographs, 69,* 329–356. doi: 10.1080/03637750216547

Jankowska, M., & Atlay, M. (2008). Use of creative space in enhancing students' engagement. *Innovations in Education and Teaching International, 45,* 271–279. doi: 10.1080/14703290802176162

Kingma, S. F. (2008). Dutch casino space or the spatial organization of entertainment. *Culture and Organization, 14,* 31–48. doi: 10.1080/14759550701863324

Kirby, E. L., Golden, A. G., Medved, C. E., Jorgenson, J., & Buzzanell, P. M. (2003). An organizational communication challenge to the discourse of work and family research: From problematics to empowerment. In P. J. Kalbfleisch (Ed.), *Communication Yearbook 27* (pp. 1–43). New York, NY: Routledge. doi: 10.1207/s15567419cy2701_1

Knox, H., O'Doherty, D., Vurdubakis, T., & Westrup, C. (2008). Enacting airports: Space, movement and modes of ordering. *Organization, 15,* 869–888. doi: 10.1177/1350508408095818

Kondo, D. K. (1990). *Crafting selves: Power, gender, and discourses of identity in a Japanese workplace*. Chicago, IL: University of Chicago Press.

Kornberger, M., & Clegg, S. R. (2004). Bringing space back in: Organizing the generative building. *Organization Studies, 25*, 1095–1114. doi: 10.1177/0170840604046312

Kuhn, T. R. (2006). A "demented work ethic" and a "lifestyle firm": Discourse, identity, and workplace time commitments. *Organization Studies, 27*, 1339–1358. doi: 10.1177/0170840606067249

Kuhn, T. R. (2011). Introduction: Engaging materiality, communication and social problems. In T. R. Kuhn (Ed.), *Matters of communication: Political, cultural, and technological challenges to communication theorizing* (pp. 1–10). Cresskill, NJ: Hampton Press.

Kuhn, T. R. (2012). Negotiating the micro-macro divide: Thought leadership from organizational communication for theorizing organization. *Management Communication Quarterly, 26*, 543–584. doi: 10.1177/0893318912462004

Larson, G. S., & Pearson, A. R. (2012). Placing identity: Place as a discursive resource for occupational identity work among high-tech entrepreneurs. *Management Communication Quarterly, 26*, 241–266. doi: 10.1177/0893318911435319

Latour, B. (1992). Where are the missing masses? The sociology of a few mundane artifacts. In W. Beijker & J. Law (Eds.), *Shaping Technology* (pp. 225–258). Cambridge, MA: MIT Press.

Latour, B. (1998). Ein Ding ist ein Thing: A philosophical platform for a left European party. *Concepts and Transformation, 3*, 97–111. doi: 10.1075/cat.3.1-2.06lat

Latour, B. (2005). *Reassembling the social: An introduction to actor-network theory*. Oxford, UK: Oxford University Press.

Lefebvre, H. (1991). *The production of space*. Oxford, UK: Blackwell Publishing.

Leiva-Lobos, E. P., De Michelis, G., & Covarrubias, E. (1997). Augmenting and multiplying spaces for creative design. Proceedings from *ACM 1997*.

Leonardi, P. M. (2011). When flexible routines meet flexible technologies: Affordance, constraint, and the imbrication of human and material agencies. *MIS Quarterly, 35*, 147–167.

Leonardi, P. M. (2012). Materiality, sociomateriality, and socio-technical systems: What do these terms mean? How are they different? Do we need them? In P. M. Leonardi, B. A. Nardi, & J. Kallinikos (Eds.), *Materiality and organizing: Social interaction in a technological world* (pp. 25–48). Oxford, UK: Oxford University Press.

Levidow, L. (1991). Women who make the chips. *Science as Culture, 2*, 103–124. doi: 10.1080/09505439109526294

Levy, S. (2011). *In the plex: How Google thinks, works, and shapes our lives*. New York, NY: Simon & Schuster.

Lindahl, G. A. (2004). The innovative workplace: An analytical model focusing on the relationship between spatial and organisational issues. *Facilities, 22*, 253–258. doi: 10.1108/02632770410555977

Long, Z., Kuang, K., & Buzzanell, P. M. (2013). Legitimizing and elevating telework: Chinese constructions of a nonstandard work arrangement. *Journal of Business and Technical Communication, 27*, 243–262. doi: 10.1177/1050651913479912

Magadley, W., & Birdi, K. (2009). Innovation labs: An examination into the use of physical spaces to enhance organizational creativity. *Creativity and Innovation Management, 18*, 153–163. doi: 10.1111/j.1467-8691.2009.00540.x

Massey, D. (1994). *Space, place, and gender*. Minneapolis, MN: University of Minnesota Press.

Massey, D. (2005). *For space*. London, UK: Sage.

McCoy, J. M., & Evans, G. W. (2010). The potential role of the physical environment in fostering creativity. *Creativity Research Journal, 14*, 409–426. doi: 10.1207/S15326934CRJ1434_11

McElroy, J. C., & Morrow, P. C. (2010). Employee reactions to office redesign: A naturally occurring quasi-field experiment in a multi-generational setting. *Human Relations, 63*, 609–636. doi: 10.1177/0018726709342932

McFarlane, C. (2009). Translocal assemblages: Space, power and social movements. *Geoforum, 40*, 561–567. doi: 10.1016/j.geoforum.2009.05.003

McPhee, R. D., & Zaug, P. (2000). The communicative constitution of organizations: A framework for explanation. *Electronic Journal of Communication, 10*(1–2).

Merleau-Ponty, M. (1962). *Phenomenology of perception*. New York, NY: Routledge.

Meyerson, J., & Ross, P. (2003). *The 21st century office*. London, UK: Laurence King.

Milstein, T., Anguiano, C., Sandoval, J., Chen, Y. W., & Dickinson, E. (2011). Communicating a "new" environmental vernacular: A sense of relations-in-place. *Communication Monographs, 78*, 486–510. doi: 10.1080/03637751.2011.618139

Mitra, A. (2001). From cyber space to cybernetic space: Rethinking the relationship between real and virtual Spaces. *Journal of Computer Mediated Communication, 7*, 1–14. doi: 10.1111/j.1083-6101.2001.tb00134.x

Morrow, P. C., McElroy, J. C., & Scheibe, K. P. (2012). Influencing organizational commitment through office redesign. *Journal of Vocational Behavior, 81*, 99–111. doi: 10.1016/j.jvb.2012.05.004

Moultrie, J., Nilsson, M., Dissel, M., Haner, U. E., Janssen, S., & Van der Lugt, R. (2007). Innovation spaces: Towards a framework for understanding the role of the physical environment in innovation. *Creativity and Innovation Management, 16*, 53–65. doi: 10.1111/j.1467-8691.2007.00419.x

Murphy, A. G. (1998). Hidden transcripts of flight attendant resistance. *Management Communication Quarterly, 11*, 499–535. doi:10.1177/0893318998114001

O'Neill, P., & McGuirk, P. (2003). Reconfiguring the CBD: Work and discourses of design in Sydney's office space. *Urban Studies, 40*, 1751–1767. doi: 10.1080/0042098032000106582

O'Toole, P., & Were, P. (2008). Observing places: Using space and material culture in qualitative research. *Qualitative Research, 8*, 616–634. doi: 10.1177/1468794108093899

Oksanen, K., & Ståhle, P. (2013). Physical environment as a source for innovation: investigating the attributes of innovative space. *Journal of Knowledge Management, 17*, 815–827. doi: 10.1108/JKM-04-2013-0136

Oldham, G. R., & Brass, D. J. (1979). Employee reactions to an open-plan office: A naturally occurring quasi-experiment. *Administrative Science Quarterly, 24*, 267–284. doi: 10.2307/2392497

Ong, A. (1987). *Spirits of resistance and capitalist discipline: Factory women in Malaysia*. Albany, NY: State University of New York Press.

Palmås, K. (2013). The production of chemical worlds: Territory and field science in global agribusiness. *Culture and Organization, 19*, 227–241. doi: 10.1080/14759551.2013.802169

Panayiotou, A., & Kafiris, K. (2010). Viewing the language of space: Organizational spaces, power, and resistance in popular films. *Journal of Management Inquiry, 20*, 264–284. doi: 10.1177/1056492610389816

Parker, P. S. (2014). Difference and organizing. In L.L. Putnam & D.K. Mumby (Eds.), *The Sage handbook of organizational communication* (pp. 619–642). Thousand Oaks, CA: Sage.

Peltonen, T. (2011). Multiple architectures and the production of organizational space in a Finnish university. *Journal of Organizational Change Management, 24,* 806–821. doi: 10.1108/09534811111175760

Pepper, G. L. (2008). The physical organization as equivocal message. *Journal of Applied Communication Research, 36,* 318–338. doi: 10.1080/0090988080 2104882

Pierce, J. L., Kostova, T., & Dirks, K. T. (2001). Toward a theory of psychological ownership in organizations. *Academy of Management Review, 26,* 298–310. doi: 10.5465/AMR.2001.4378028

Porter, N. (2013). "Single-minded, compelling, and unique": Visual communications, landscape, and the calculated aesthetic of place branding. *Environmental Communication, 7,* 231–254. doi: 10.1080/17524032.2013.779291

Prasad, P., & Prasad, A. (2000). Stretching the iron cage: The constitution and implications of routine workplace resistance. *Organization Science, 11,* 387–403. doi: 10.1287/orsc.11.4.387.14597

Putnam, L. L., & Mumby, D. K. (2014). Introduction: Advancing theory and research in organizational communication. In L. L. Putnam & D. K. Mumby (Eds.), *The Sage handbook of organizational communication* (pp. 1–18). Thousand Oaks, CA: Sage.

Putnam, L. L., Nicotera, A. M., & McPhee, R. D. (2008). Introduction: Communication constitutes organization. In L. L. Putnam & A. M. Nicotera (Eds.), *Building theories of organization: The constitutive role of communication* (pp. 1–20). New York, NY: Routledge.

Roethlisberger, F., & Dickson, W. (1939). *Management and the worker: An account of research program conducted by the Western Electric Company, Hawthorne Works, Chicago.* Cambridge, MA: Harvard University Press.

Rofel, L. (1992). Rethinking modernity: Space and factory discipline in China. *Cultural Anthropology, 7,* 93–114. doi: 10.1525/can.1992.7.1.02a00070

Rooney, D., Paulsen, N., Callan, V. J., Brabant, M., Gallois, C., & Jones, E. (2010). A new role for place identity in managing organizational change. *Management Communication Quarterly, 24,* 44–73. doi: 10.1177/0893318909351434

Sage, D. J., & Dainty, A. (2012). Understanding power within project work: The neglected role of material and embodied registers. *Engineering Project Organization Journal, 2,* 202–215. doi: 10.1080/21573727.2011.648619

Sailer, K. (2011). Creativity as social and spatial process. *Facilities, 29,* 6–18. doi: 10.1108/02632771111101296

Sailer, K., Budgen, A., Lonsdale, N., Turner, A., & Penn, A. (2010). Pre and post occupancy evaluations in workplace environments: Theoretical reflections and practical implications. *The Journal of Space Syntax, 1,* 199–213.

Sassen, S. (2002). Towards a sociology of information technology. *Current Sociology, 50,* 365–388. doi: 10.1177/0011392102050003005

Schein, E. H. (2010). *Organizational culture and leadership* (4th edn). San Francisco, CA: John Wiley & Sons.

Sillince, J. A. A. (2007). Organizational context and the discursive construction of organizing. *Management Communication Quarterly, 20,* 363–394. doi: 10.1177/0893318906298477

Smith, R. C. (1993). Images of organizational communication: Root-metaphors of the organization-communication relation. Paper presented at the annual convention of the International Communication Association, Washington DC.

Soja, E. (1989). *Postmodern geographies: The reassertion of space in critical social theory*. London, UK: Verso.

Spinuzzi, C. (2012). Working alone together: Coworking as emergent collaborative activity. *Journal of Business and Technical Communication, 26,* 399–441. doi: 10.1177/1050651912444070

Steele, F. I. (1973). *Physical settings and organization development*. Reading, MA: Addison-Wesley.

Sundstrom, E., & Sundstrom, M. G. (1986). *Work places: The psychology of the physical environment in offices and factories*. New York, NY: Cambridge University Press.

Taylor, J. R., Cooren, F., Giroux, N., & Robichaud, D. (1996). The communicational basis of organization: Between the conversation and the text. *Communication Theory, 6,* 1–39. doi: 10.1111/j.1468-2885.1996.tb00118.x

Taylor, J. R., & Van Every, E. J. (2000). *The emergent organization: Communication as its site and surface*. Mahwah, NJ: Lawrence Erlbaum.

Taylor, S., & Spicer, A. (2007). Time for space: A narrative review of research on organizational spaces. *International Journal of Management Reviews, 9,* 325–346. doi: 10.1111/j.1468-2370.2007.00214.x

Thanem, T., Värlander, S., & Cummings, S. (2011). Open space = open minds? The ambiguities of pro-creative office design. *International Journal of Work Organisation and Emotion, 4,* 78–98. doi: 10.1504/IJWOE.2011.041532

Thrift, N. (2006). Space. *Theory, Culture & Society, 23,* 139–146. doi: 10.1177/0263276406063780

Thrift, N. (2008). *Non-representational theory: Space, politics, affect*. New York, NY: Routledge.

Tuan, Y. F. (1976). Humanistic geography. *Annals of the Association of American Geographers, 66,* 266–276. doi: 10.1111/j.1467-8306.1976.tb01089.x

Tuan, Y. F. (1977). *Space and place: The perspective of experience*. Minneapolis, MN: University of Minnesota Press.

Turner, P. K., & Norwood, K. (2013). Unbounded motherhood: Embodying a good working mother identity. *Management Communication Quarterly, 27,* 396–424. doi: 10.1177/0893318913491461

Tyler, M., & Cohen, L. (2010). Spaces that matter: Gender performativity and organizational space. *Organization Studies, 31,* 175–198. doi: 10.1177/0170840609357381

Våland, M. S. (2011). Between organisation and architecture: End-user participation in design. *International Journal of Work Organisation and Emotion, 4,* 42–60. doi: 10.1504/IJWOE.2011.041530

van Marrewijk, A., & Broos, M. (2012). Retail stores as brands: Performances, theatre and space. *Consumption Markets & Culture, 14,* 374–391. doi: 10.1080/10253866.2012.659438

van Marrewijk, A., & Yanow, D. (Eds.). (2010). *Organizational spaces: Rematerializing the workaday world*. Cheltenham, UK: Edward Elgar Publishing.

van Meel, J., Martens, Y., & Jan van Ree, H. (2010). *Planning office spaces: A practical guide for managers and designers*. London, UK: Laurence King.

Värlander, S. (2011). Individual flexibility in the workplace: A spatial perspective. *The Journal of Applied Behavioral Science, 48,* 33–61. doi: 10.1177/0021886311407666

Vásquez, C. (2013). Spacing organization: Or how to be here and there at the same time. In D. Robichaud & F. Cooren (Eds.), *Organization and organizing: Materiality, agency, and discourse* (pp. 127–149). Newbury Park, CA: Routledge.

Vásquez, C., & Cooren, F. (2013). Spacing practices: The communicative configuration of organizing through space-times. *Communication Theory, 23*, 25–47. doi: 10.1111/comt.12003

Vischer, J. C. (2005). *Space meets status: Designing workplace performance*. Oxford, UK: Routledge.

Vithayathawornwong, S., Danko, S., & Tolbert, P. (2003). The role of the physical environment in supporting organizational creativity. *Journal of Interior Design, 29*, 1–16. doi: 10.1111/j.1939-1668.2003.tb00381.x

Walker, E., Wang, C., & Redmond, J. (2008). Women and work-life balance: Is home-based business ownership the solution? *Equal Opportunities International, 27*, 258–275. doi: 10.1108/02610150810860084

Wapshott, R., & Mallett, O. (2011). The spatial implications of homeworking: A Lefebvrian approach to the rewards and challenges of home-based work. *Organization, 19*, 63–79. doi: 10.1177/1350508411405376

Warf, B., & Arias, S. (2009). Introduction: The reinsertion of space into the social sciences and humanities. In B. Warf & S. Arias (Eds.), *The Spatial Turn* (pp. 1–10). Oxford, UK: Routledge.

Wasserman, V. (2011). To be (alike) or not to be (at all): Aesthetic isomorphism in organisational spaces. *International Journal of Work Organisation and Emotion, 4*, 22. doi: 10.1504/IJWOE.2011.041529

Watkins, C. (2005). Representations of space, spatial practices and spaces of representation: An application of Lefebvre's spatial triad. *Culture and Organization, 11*, 209–220. doi: 10.1080/14759550500203318

Wilhoit, E. D., & Kisselburgh, L. G. (2015). Collective action without organization: The material constitution of bike commuters as collective. *Organization Studies, 36*, 573–592. doi: 10.1177/0170840614556916

Yanow, D. (1995). Built space as story: The policy stories that buildings tell. *Policy Studies Journal, 23*, 407–423. doi: 10.1111/j.1541-0072.1995.tb00520.x

Yanow, D. (1998). Space stories: Studying museum buildings as organizational spaces while reflecting on interpretive methods and their narration. *Journal of Management Inquiry, 7*, 215–239. doi: 10.1177/105649269873004

Zhang, Z. (2006). What is lived space? *Ephemera, 6*, 219–223.

Zhang, Z., & Spicer, A. (2013). "Leader, you first": The everyday production of hierarchical space in a Chinese bureaucracy. *Human Relations, 67*, 739–762. doi: 10.1177/0018726713503021

Zhang, Z., Spicer, A., & Hancock, P. (2008). Hyper-organizational space in the work of J.G. Ballard. *Organization, 15*, 889–910. doi: 10.1177/1350508408095819

Zhong, C. B., & House, J. (2012). Hawthorne revisited: Organizational implications of the physical work environment. *Research in Organizational Behavior, 32*, 3–22. doi: 10.1016/j.riob.2012.10.004

CHAPTER CONTENTS

10 Exploring the Effects of Workplace Health Promotions

A Critical Examination of a Familiar Organizational Practice

Jessica L. Ford and Emily N. Scheinfeld

University of Texas, Austin

As workplaces become sites where health issues are addressed, organizations have an ever-increasing presence in the personal lives of workers. The purpose of this chapter is to illustrate how workplace health promotions (WHPs) violate four types of boundaries: (a) cultural, (b) privacy, (c) confidentiality, and (d) ethical, all of which are managed through communication. We apply Petronio's (2002) communication privacy management theory to frame health-related boundary negotiations between employee and employer. This chapter concludes with a call for more research on WHPs from interpretive, critical, feminist, and postcolonial approaches.

The leading cause of occupational disease, which is largely responsible for organizational turnover, absenteeism, and job performance, is occupational stress (Dollard, Winefield, Winefield, & Jonge, 2000; Leigh & Schnall, 2000; Michie & Williams, 2003). Whether this rise in occupational stress is the result of technological advancements propelling individuals to work faster, the demand for increased productivity in light of a recovering world economy, or simply the result of corporate downsizing—the cost of occupational stress on organizations incentivizes workplace health promotions (Berry, Mirabito, & Baun, 2010; Farrell & Geist-Martin, 2005; Geist-Martin, Horsley, & Farrell, 2003a). In the United States alone, the annual economic impact of time off work due to poor health, or work-related health, was last estimated, in 2014, at $300 billion (American Institute on Stress, 2015). Additionally, American organizations report an annual loss of $6 billion due to poor productivity stemming from their workers' personal problems (Turvey & Olsen, 2006). In an effort to combat the economic hit from poor health, organizations increasingly provide wellness initiatives to their employees (Baicker, Cutler, & Song, 2010). The most recent statistics show that 45% of all full-time workers in the private sector have access to employee assistance programs (U.S. Bureau of Labor Statistics, 2011) and 76% of full-time workers in the public sector have these programs at their work (U.S. Bureau of Labor Statistics, 2009).

Although U.S. policies, which place the responsibility on organizations to provide their employees with health care, feed the economic incentives for workplace health promotions (WHPs), the medicalization of the workplace is not exclusively a U.S. practice (Csiernik & Csiernik, 2012). The impact of absenteeism due to health issues affects the bottom-line of any organization, regardless of location (Cartwright & Cooper, 2014). For instance, work-related stress is the second leading cause of illness in Europe (European Agency for Safety and Health at Work, 2015). Unsurprisingly, organizations around the world buy into the potential for workplace health interventions to establish a healthy and productive workforce (see related research on organizations based in the United Kingdom, Japan, Canada, Sweden, Finland, and Australia; Arthur, 2000; Csiernik & Csiernik, 2012; Gånedahl, Viklund, Carlén, Kylberg, & Ekberg, 2015; Ichikawa et al., 2006; Kirk & Brown, 2003; Kuoppala & Kekoni, 2013).

Despite reports that WHPs can yield a positive return on businesses (Baicker et al., 2010), the problem with these initiatives is that they confound the role of an employer with the role of a physician as well as impinge upon employees' personal boundaries (Farrell & Geist-Martin, 2005; May, 1998). When poor productivity or absenteeism is seen as the result of an individual's health choices, managers play the role of physicians encouraging or incentivizing certain healthy behaviors (May, 1998). For example, employee assistance programs (EAPs) which focus on identifying, referring, and providing treatment for troubled workers—typically those with substance abuse or mental health issues—rely on supervisors to detect troubled employees and refer them to these services (Dickman, 2009; May, 2015). Farrell and Geist-Martin (2005) acknowledge the potential issues with the medicalization of the work stating, "As boundaries between their professional and personal lives are crossed, employees may feel ill at ease or even embarrassed, not wanting supervisors or coworkers to become aware of their personal health issues" (p. 543).

Recognizing the centrality of communication in constructing the social environment of a workplace (Geist-Martin & Scarduzio, 2011), research assessing the effects of WHPs should focus on the ways communication structures health information boundary negotiations. Previous scholarship, however, largely focuses on the effectiveness of WHPs and the ways management can encourage compliance and participation (Freimuth, Edgar, & Fitzpatrick, 1993; Rogers, 1996; Schaeffer, Snelling, Stevenson, & Karch, 1994). Research on the organizational impact of WHPs suggests there is potential for these programs to increase worker productivity (Brown, 1996; Jensen, 2011), self-esteem (Arneson & Ekberg, 2005), and morale (Stewart, Ricci, Chee, & Morganstein, 2003), while decreasing turnover intent (Grawitch, Trares, & Kohler, 2007) and absenteeism (Brown, 1996; Hamar, Coberley, Pope, & Rula, 2015). Yet this research neglects to examine the role communication plays in marginalizing, stigmatizing, and even silencing employees with health concerns. Although communication scholars address several problems with the medicalization of work, which we detail in this chapter (see Farrell & Geist-Martin, 2005;

Geist-Martin et al., 2003a; Geist-Martin & Scarduzio, 2011, 2014; Kirby & Krone, 2002; Parrot & Lemieux, 2003; Zoller, 2003, 2004, 2005; Zook, 1994), there are rich opportunities to build on extant literature.

This chapter examines the ways WHPs foster an ever-increasing organizational reach into the personal lives of workers, transforming the worksite into a place where employers monitor the physical condition of workers bodies in addition to evaluating their work-related tasks. Our goal is to illustrate how these wellness initiatives cross four types of boundaries: (a) cultural, (b) privacy, (c) confidentiality, and (d) ethical, all of which are managed through communication. This chapter uses communication privacy management (CPM) theory to address the ways individuals employ communication as a means of structuring information boundaries (Petronio, 2002, 2010). According to CPM, people create privacy rules to guide decisions regarding the amount of information they are willing to give others (i.e., boundary permeability). Additionally, CPM helps frame the problems with information co-ownership in the workplace, which occurs when employees share health-related information with their employer. Unlike doctor's visits, disclosing health information at work is not protected under the same doctor-patient code of confidentiality. This chapter concludes with an appeal to apply alternative meta-theoretical lenses in WHP research. In particular, we encourage more research from interpretive, critical, feminist, and postcolonial approaches to provide a more complete understanding of the problems with the medicalization of work. To begin, it is useful to make explicit the definitions of widely used terms in this chapter as well as the motivations for these initiatives.

Key Concepts and Economic Underpinnings of Workplace Health Promotions

The prevailing assumption within organizations promoting health at work is that "wellness cannot be delegated, but can be encouraged and facilitated," (Berry & Mirabito, 2011, p. 335). Oftentimes, the terms *health* and *wellness* can be used interchangeably. However, the definition of health seems to vary across fields (e.g., medical versus health communication). Communication scholars commonly refer to health as the "absence of disease" (Sharf & Vanderford, 2003, p. 13). Albeit simple, this definition neglects other components of health, such as psychological and spiritual health (Geist-Martin & Scarduzio, 2014). For the purpose of this chapter, and according to the World Health Organization, *health* is defined as "a state of complete physical, social, and mental well-being, and not merely the absence of disease or infirmity" (Nutbeam, 1998, p. 351). In other words, some health is outwardly noticeable whereas evaluating employees' mental well-being is harder to detect. *Health communication*, then, is "the symbolic process by which people individually and collectively, understand, shape, and accommodate to health and illness" (Geist-Martin, Ray, & Sharf, 2003b, p. 3). Health communication scholarship is particularly useful in unpacking how everyday discourse contains health beliefs rooted in sociocultural, contextual, and political sources (Sharf & Vanderford, 2003).

Despite the characteristics of health, which by definition are not always observable, organizations mistakenly equate poor health with physical qualities such as unacceptable dietary habits, inactivity, and smoking (Scarduzio & Geist Martin, 2015; Zoller, 2012). Not only does a superficial view of health ignore an individual's social, psychological, and spiritual well-being (Geist-Martin et al., 2003a), but it also makes health the product of individual actions rather than systemic issues. As a result of this belief, the solution to poor health is more money for program participation. For example, in 2011 the U.S Department of Health and Human Services allocated $10 million to help companies create more programs designed to foster health (Churchill, Gillespie, & Herbold, 2014). This government initiative, called *Health People 2020*, outlines the necessary elements for any comprehensive workplace health program: (a) health education; (b) a supportive environment both socially and physically; (c) ties to similar programs (i.e., employee assistance programs); (d) workplace screening and education; and (e) integration of the program into the organization's structure (Harris, Hannon, Beresford, Linnan, & McLellan, 2014). Regardless of the comprehensiveness of a workplace wellness program, or the reservoir of goodwill these initiatives may help generate (May & Roper, 2014), it is appropriate to consider whether organizations should function as health promoters at all.

The fundamental goal of an organization is to sustain business (Jensen, 2002). This is not an immoral objective, but it is does raise ethical issues concerning the role of organizations in promoting the health of their employees (Broadfoot et al., 2008; Kirby, 2007). Understandably, organizations develop WHPs in an effort to reduce sick days, turnover, and other financial hits from unhealthy employees (Geist-Martin & Scarduzio, 2011; Machen, Cuddihy, Reaburn, & Higgins, 2010). In the United Kingdom, for example, the annual cost of workers' mental illness was last estimated at £77.4 billion ($154 billion USD; Sainsbury Centre for Mental Health, 2007). Undeniably, healthy employees are less taxing on organizations in terms of cost, sick leave, and turnover (Churchill et al., 2014; Danna & Griffin, 1999; Fielding, 1984; Tully, 1995). Many U.S. organizations broadcast high financial rewards due to WHPs, such as a six-to-one return on their investment in employee health simply by altering employees' health behaviors (Baicker et al., 2010; Berry et al., 2010). In fact, Johnson & Johnson has estimated saving $250 million since 2000 due to its workplace wellness initiatives (Berry et al., 2010). On average, U.S. organizations who implement WHPs see a $3.27 decrease in medical care costs for every dollar spent promoting health in the workplace (Baicker et al., 2010).

Although organizations depend on a stable workface, organizational life itself appears to be the culprit of infirmity (Leigh & Schnall, 2000). Occupational stress is the leading cause of occupational disease, which contributes to a number of health issues such as anxiety, depression, autoimmune deficiencies, cardiovascular disease, and exhaustion (Michie & Williams, 3003; Sapolsky,

2003). Occupational stress occurs when individuals perceive their work demands as exceeding their capacity to meet them (Farrell & Geist-Martin, 2005). Occupational stress can be the result of perceived lack of time, resources, knowledge, and skills (French, Caplan, & Van Harrison, 1982; Noblet & LaMontagne, 2006). Studies on chronic job stress link it to organizational outcomes such as turnover, poor job performance, and absenteeism (Dollard et al., 2000; Michie & Williams, 2003). Unsurprisingly, the primary aim of many WHPs is to combat these organizational plagues by attempting to manage occupational stress (Berry & Mirabito, 2011; Noblet & LaMontagne, 2006). In effect, an organizational double-bind is created; workplaces both cause stress and disseminate messages that instruct employees to improve their health. A closer analysis of WHPs reveals the inherent problem with organizations incentivizing health outcomes. In particular, the medicalization of work violates four types of boundaries: cultural, privacy, confidentiality, and ethical. Petronio's (2002) CPM theory argues that individuals are the owners of their personal information and that forced or reluctant disclosure creates relational turbulence due to boundary violations. As such, CPM offers a suitable lens for studying how employees manage violated information boundaries. Before unpacking the four types of boundary violations due to WHPs, we highlight how research in this area provides an opportunity to apply and extend CPM.

Extending Communication Privacy Management to Workplace Health Promotions

Communication privacy management theory explains the process by which individuals manage privacy boundaries to either retain ownership of information or become co-owners of shared information (Petronio, 2002). To date, scholarship framed by CPM explores the experiences of those who disclose or conceal health or family information (e.g., Caughlin, Petronio, & Middleton, 2013; Greene, Derlega, Yep, & Petronio, 2003). Applying CPM to an organizational setting provides opportunities to extend this theory conceptually. Given that the medicalization of work—as evidenced by WHPs—shifts privacy boundaries, CPM helps scholars and practitioners to understand how employees manage health information at work. To highlight the applicability of CPM in assessing workplace wellness initiatives, this chapter reviews the three key concepts from this theory: (a) privacy boundaries, (b) privacy rules, and (c) boundary turbulence (Petronio, 2002). These three concepts help frame the communicative process that undergirds employees' perceptions of WHP initiatives. The following provides an explanation of Petronio's (2002) privacy boundaries, privacy rules, and boundary turbulence as they relate to WHPs.

Privacy Boundaries

One of the main axioms of CPM is that individuals construct and manage privacy boundaries concerning private information (Petronio, 2002). These boundaries mark the extent of control and ownership a person possess over private information (Caughlin et al., 2013). After all, CPM states that "people own information they consider belonging to them and are co-owners, or stakeholders in, private information that is shared by others" (Caughlin et al., 2013, p. 322). The idea of information ownership is particularly salient considering the sensitive nature of health (Kelly & Macready, 2009).

WHPs challenge traditional notions of health information management where individuals are the sole owner of information (May, 1998). Instead, organizations incentivizing health assessments often place employees' health and workplace goals at odds with one another and abuse privacy boundaries. For example, consider the 2014 class action lawsuit against CVS, a U.S. based pharmacy chain, brought by one of its own employees. According to Roberta Watterson, the plaintiff, CVS requires its employees to take an on-site "Wellness Exam" or receive a $600 fine. However, the exam asks a variety of personal questions, including sexual activity, alcohol consumption, and smoking history—information Watterson was not comfortable providing to her employer (Murno, 2014). This example illustrates how WHPs can coerce employees to provide *linkages*, or access to private information, to their employers (Petronio, 2002). According to CPM, any information that is shared with another becomes co-owned, even if the receiver does not claim to be an information owner (Petronio 2002, 2010). Thus, once health information, such as Waterson's sexual activity, is shared with an employer it becomes co-owned between the employee and employer. After this point of disclosure, the employee loses autonomous control over how their information is used. In an attempt to retain control of private information in the workplace, employees may develop rules for disclosure.

Privacy Rules

Managing privacy boundaries is a process requiring the formation of rules between the information owner and co-owner (Petronio, 2002). According to CPM, information owners establish two types of privacy rules: protection rules and accessibility rules. These two rule categories stem from various influences such as gender, culture, context, personal motivations, and the risk-benefit ratio (Bute & Vik, 2010; Durham, 2008; Petronio & Durham, 2008; Petronio & Martin, 1986; Thorson, 2009). For example, Bute and Vik's (2010) study on women's openness about infertility demonstrates how privacy rules are not fixed behavioral guidelines, but rather continually renegotiated in every interpersonal interaction. Extending this finding to an organizational setting, privacy rules protecting health information may also require constant renegotiation as circumstances change. For instance, the ability of certain U.S. organizations to deny employees birth control forces female workers to either remain silent and buy birth control out-of-pocket or confront their employer to request coverage of this prescription. One worker describes the humiliating experience of discussing family planning options with her HR director after her workplace stopped covering birth control.

The HR director told me that birth control is something the university should never be expected to cover, and that I should be more responsible for my reproduction and "proud" of my child. . . . Ever since that conversation, the HR director gives me dirty looks whenever I pass him in the hallway. . . . I love my job and can't afford to lose it, which is why I bite my tongue when I see the HR director, and why I'm not using my real name in this blog. But I should not have to choose between keeping my job and losing my dignity.

(American Civil Liberties Union, 2014, para. 5)

Also, considering the role culture plays in prescribing appropriate openness about health issues (Geist-Martin et al., 2003b), more attention is needed to understand the ways organizations employing a diverse workforce violate individual's privacy boundaries. Simmons' (2012) research on foreign English teachers in Japan, for example, shows how the cultural value of cooperation creates a work environment where keeping health information private is selfish and a threat to group harmony. Consequently, western foreign workers in Japan experience information boundary violations due to the profuse sharing of medical information between doctors and employers (Simmons, 2012). One teacher explained that in order to use a sick day, he had to present a doctor's note to his supervisor, which outlined the reason for his doctor's visit, his diagnosis, and prescription. This common practice forces sick employees to either share health information with their employer or continue coming to work despite being sick in order to keep personal information private (Simmons, 2012). Recognizing the role culture plays in managing privacy rules, CPM offers a useful lens for looking at cultural constructions of privacy. This situation also exemplifies how expectations for privacy are not always consistent between the original information owner and subsequent co-owners, which disrupts privacy boundaries and results in boundary turbulence.

Boundary Turbulence

Navigating privacy boundaries can be difficult in the workplace, and privacy rules often remain unclear and are ineffective in functioning properly (Petronio, Jones, & Morr, 2004). Without proper boundary coordination, the "negotiation of ownership, rule formation, and rule usage" is likely to ensue (Petronio, 2000, p. 43; Petronio, 2007; Petronio & Durham, 2008). Boundary turbulence is the disruption of the way people perceive boundaries surrounding private information, and results when already established privacy rules are violated (Petronio, 2002). Petronio (2002) predicts that, in the event of boundary turbulence, individuals attempt to take action and make adjustments to return to a level of homeostasis and control over their private information. Boundary turbulence is therefore exhibited when employees try to gain control of their health information (Hawk, Hale, Raaijmakers, & Meeus, 2008), despite organizational attempts to obtain this information. For example, Simmons (2012) found that foreign English teachers in Japan actively concealed their health needs by either remaining silent at work, neglecting physician care when sick, or by asking a non-work friend for medical assistance. In one case, a teacher with ADHD smuggled her prescription of Adderall to work in vitamin bottles to hide her condition from others (Simmons, 2012).

The practice of WHPs may contribute to employees' perceived boundary turbulence. As May (2015) states, these workplace wellness initiatives "focus more and more often upon what have traditionally been 'private' areas of workers' health and well-being" (p. 7). Despite the value WHPs bring to the bottom-line of an organization by increasing productivity (Jensen, 2011), decreasing absenteeism (Hamar et al., 2015), and lowering health insurance costs for U.S. companies (Baicker et al., 2010; Berry et al., 2010), communication scholars must consider alternative matrixes for assessing WHPs. Instead of measuring the health and financial outcomes of these programs, it is important to consider how these initiatives impact workplace communication and create boundary turbulence as employees are pressured to reveal their health issues (Kirby & Buzzanell, 2014). For instance, organizations encouraging employees to participate in athletic competitions may create anxiety in individuals who do not want to disclose a physical ailment, such as asthma or a heart condition, as this type of disclosure may increase health insurance policy rates or stigmatize individuals. Employees, therefore, may experience boundary turbulence when asked why they do not want to participate in health promotions at work.

Workplace Health Promotions and Boundary Violations

This chapter argues for increased attention to the ways WHPs confound the role of an employer with the role of a physician, in effect violating traditional privacy boundaries. Recognizing the value of Petronio's (2002) CPM in framing future studies on the ways employees communicatively construct privacy boundaries, we now address how these wellness initiatives violate four worker boundaries. Specifically, we call attention to the ways organizations pressure employees through WHPs to change their preferred (a) cultural, (b) privacy, (c) confidentiality, and (d) ethical boundaries. First, we begin with a look at how organizational attempts to improve health may violate cultural boundaries.

Cultural Boundary Issues

The meanings and value individuals imbue on health and privacy differs from culture to culture. Yet, "cultures are now less bounded and homogeneous and more porous and self-conscious than ever before, and cultural differences— of religion, gender, language, ethnicity, sexual orientation, and so on—are no longer contained within old geopolitical boundaries" (Barbash & Taylor, 1997, p. 5). Perhaps there is no better picture of cultural integration than organizations, which are the "containers" of cultural diversity. In this chapter we define *culture* as any group of people with a shared set of beliefs and meaning attached to their behaviors (Geertz, 1973; Gudykunst, Ting-Toomey, & Chua, 1988; Kreps & Kunimoto, 1994). Assumptions guiding health care decisions are often different for members of cultural groups (Geist-Martin et al., 2003b), yet previous research on WHPs indicates that organizations not only neglect to see individual health differences, but that health differences are used as a means of discrimination (see May, 1993, 1998, 2015). Here, we highlight how sexual orientation and gender serve as cultural boundaries that organizations violate in their attempts to promote a healthy workforce. Even if organizations commit to a whole person approach to wellness, where physical, social, psychological, and spiritual wellness are encouraged (Scarduzio & Geist-Marin, 2015), it is difficult to expunge culturally biased views of health in the workplace. Thus, we ask whether it is the role of an organization to be an educator and promoter of health in the first place.

Sexual Orientation in the Workplace

Although there is growing awareness of workplace bullying and discrimination towards individuals of the LGBTQ community (Lewis, 2009), this does not mean that all organizations recognize when these instances of abuse occur. Even if organizations espouse an inclusive atmosphere to LGBTQ individuals, these organizations may send conflicting messages when their health benefits deny access to these same individuals (Hornsby, 2006). For example, an organization may hire LGBTQ individuals, but refuse to provide health insurance for same-sex spouses. Although same-sex marriage must be recognized in the United States after the SCOTUS ruling, organizations that self-insure their employees are still under no legal obligation to cover a same-sex spouse (Silverman, 2015).

Despite some organizations claiming to provide an inclusive atmosphere for their employees, other employers may intentionally create an environment where certain sexual orientations and identities are unwelcome (Hornsby, 2006). Previous research by Schultz (1994) brings to light Coors' practice of encouraging employees to fill out a Health Hazard Appraisal, which asks about employees' sexual history and orientation. Similarly, May's (1993) research on EAPs reveals that, under the auspices of "wellness," employees have been terminated on the basis of sexual orientation. Recent research continues to highlight how LGBTQ workers feel silenced because of the ways coworkers discuss family life (Dixon & Dougherty, 2014; Lucas & Buzzanell, 2006). According to Dixon and Dougherty (2014), traditional family expectations at work produce an environment where individuals who identify as LGBTQ feel both invisible and hyper-visible. As a means of controlling the feeling of hyper-visibility, LGBTQ workers may hide or lie about their identity (Dixon & Dougherty, 2014). However, organization's orientation to health, which is made visible through WHPs, does not acknowledge health differences based on sexual orientation. Consequently, WHPs may further marginalize, stigmatize, and silence employees who identify as LGBTQ.

Communication scholars are well suited to address the experience of employees on the receiving end of conflicting messages about the acceptance of their sexual identity at work. Previous work demonstrates how vulnerable identities become muted or silenced within the workplace (Dixon & Dougherty, 2014; Meares, Oetzel, Torres, Derkacs, & Ginossar, 2004), whereas other research indicates that EAPs ousted members of the LGBTQ community (May, 1993; Schultz, 1994). Recognizing that debates over identifying individuals' sexual orientation at work is fundamentally an issue over work and personal boundaries (Dixon & Dougherty, 2014; Lewis, 2009), more research needs to address how members of marginalized sexual identities communicatively construct these boundaries at work.

Gender in the Workplace

Organizations do not operate detached from broader political, social, and economic factors. Thus, the present gender disparities in health are likely occurring at the organizational level as well. Not only is female health different from male health on a reproductive level, but also certain medical issues present themselves differently based on sex (Eckman, 1998). According to Watkins and Whaley (2000), women are less likely to report good health, and account for two-thirds of all medical visits. Researchers regularly attribute these differences in health to structural issues that interrupt the equal dispersion of poverty, abuse, stress, and childrearing responsibilities (Zoller, 2005).

Yet, within the workplace, health initiatives do not recognize males and females as having different health needs (Zoller, 2005). In particular, feminist scholars must make the point of addressing how health promotions continue to disadvantage women in the workplace while providing added benefits to men. Buzzanell's (1994) research on the consequences of traditional gender workplace interactions provides a framework for addressing the issues of gendered identity found in Zoller's (2004) study. In this study, Zoller (2004) exposed how a workplace gym unabashedly catered to males. Female workers described feeling unwelcome in the workplace gym because it was a "masculine space" primarily used for playing basketball and lifting weights (Zoller, 2004, p. 291). As a result of these indirect messages discouraging females from using the workplace gym, the female workers avoided this space (Zoller, 2004).

Kirby and Krone (2002) also address the impact of indirect gendered messages in their study of work-family policies. Women reported feeling resentment for taking their maternity leave, even when their organization offers a maternity leave policy. Employees in this organization felt more pressure from their peers, rather than their supervisors, to not use work-family leave policies. One employee stated, "No one talked to me directly and said, 'Gee, I resent the fact that you were on maternity leave,' but I know that people felt that way" (Kirby & Krone, 2002, p. 50). Similarly, research on women who breastfeed at work illuminates how women's bodies become contested sites of organizational control (Turner & Norwood, 2013, 2014). Considering that maternity leave is considerably shorter in the United States than other countries, many women return to work while still breastfeeding. As a result, women who decide to pump breast milk at work report having to do so in the presence of their coworkers when their organization does not offer a designated private room for breastfeeding (Turner & Norwood, 2013). Given that this act brings the materiality of motherhood into the workplace, women report having to navigate between the ideals of a "good worker" who does not let personal obligations interfere with her job, and that of a "good mother" who puts nothing else before her child's needs (Turner & Norwood, 2013). These finding highlight how communication structures the way employees interpret their access to health benefits as well as the value placed on their physical bodies at work. For women in the workplace, messages regarding what constitute appropriate health behaviors clearly restrict subsequent health decisions. The influence of organizational life on women's health behaviors exposes larger privacy boundary issues being negotiated within our places of work—an issue ripe for more attention from communication scholars.

Privacy Boundary Issues

Strategic health programs, which incentivize certain health behaviors, raise considerable privacy issues. Although under the guise of promoting health, WHPs ultimately serve the economic interests of the organization: maintaining productivity, decreasing absenteeism and in some social states, decreasing overhead on healthcare (Goetzel et al., 2002; Pelletier, 2005). It is no surprise then, to witness employers mandating or pressuring their employees to provide private information related to their health. Considering the definition of *privacy* as the ability to control the availability and circumstances surrounding the sharing of personal information (Westin, 2003), a natural counterpoint to privacy is surveillance. Drawing on Lyon's (2001) description of surveillance as "any collecting or processing of personal data, whether identifiable or not, for the purposes of influencing or managing those whose data have been gathered" (p. 2), we argue that technology facilitates obtrusive surveillance of employees' private lives.

In the name of health and employee care, organizations offering health promotions increasingly use technology to monitor what their employees do at work and at home (Guttman, 2000). Wearable technology, in particular, allows organizations to track an employee's steps, heart rate, caloric consumption, body mass index, metabolic rate, weight, and even brain activity (Lupton, 2014a). In fact, the wearable technology manufacturer, Fitbit®, has created partnerships with organizations looking to make biometric health surveillance part of their wellness program (Olson & Tilley, 2014). Clearly, technology companies are well aware of the potential profit of selling biometric monitoring devices to organizations. In 2013 alone, 14,000 BP employees and 6,000 spouses of BP workers were given Fitbits to monitor their health (Olson & Tilley, 2014). By 2018, another 13 million wearable devices are projected to be integrated into existing WHP initiatives (Zielinski, 2014).

In the wake of revelations regarding the use of personal data for corporate means (i.e., Snowden's WikiLeaks), it is appropriate to question what corporations are doing with the data from these wearable devices (Lupton, 2014b). Recent reports indicate there is an unsettling absence of information from health app developers concerning their handling of personal data (Till, 2014). Barcena's (2014) review of over 1,000 health apps found that 60% contained privacy concerns, including users not being protected against the availability of their health information, how it is being used, or even if their private health information is being distributed (e.g., strategic marketing). Thus, in addition to the information that U.S. worksites already collect from employees wearing biometric monitoring devices, employees' information may also be subject to the app developers' flawed privacy boundaries. The use of employees' biometric data as figures for algorithmic calculations on whether or not an individual is a "health risk" to an organization is a breeding ground for potential health-based discrimination (Lupton, 2014b). Take Lori, for example, an employee at a U.S. based health insurance company who was penalized $4,200 for refusing to complete her organization's on-site health screening because of a desire to keep her health information private (Begley, 2015).

Despite the health benefits that may come with personal tracking devices at work (see Faghri et al., 2008), there is something inherently unsettling about organizations collecting information on the physical activity of employees, and in some cases, their spouses (Olson & Tilley, 2014). Now, in addition to assessing workers' completion of job-related tasks, organizations become places where their entire body is audited, appraised, and encouraged to do more. Not only does this on-the-job physical monitoring of employees breach conventional privacy boundaries, these devices are also worn off the job, effectively extending the surveillance of employees beyond traditional organizational boundaries (Broadfoot et al., 2008; Kirby & Buzzanell, 2014). Although employees consent to being monitored (Lupton, 2014a), these biometric screening tactics coerce employee involvement through financial incentives, which is not the same as unadulterated participation (Moore, 2000). Essentially, employee assistance programs "provide an endorsed means of surveillance and social control" (Vickers, 2006, p. 276). Thus, scholars must not confuse WHP participation with success as most organizations do. Instead communication researchers must examine the ways employer power creates privacy boundary turbulence for employees who are tagged and monitored by these wearable technologies. Similar to Panopticon prison designs, which allow a single guard to watch all inmate activity from a centralized location (Bentham, 1798), wearables may also be a "mechanism of power" executed through continuous organizational observation under the guise of health promotion (Foucault, 1977, p. 205).

Confidentiality Boundaries

The medicalization of work also ushers in new forms of workplace discrimination as personal health history, treatment, and even genetic predispositions become known to employers. Whereas the trust between patient and physician rests on strict codes of confidentiality, programs offered through work—such as on-site counseling—gather information on employees that ultimately serve the employers' economic interests. May (1998) explains how "corporations control access to employee medical records [obtained through employee assistance programs], and the information is often used to deny worker's compensation claims or to defeat worker lawsuits regarding unfair hiring or firing practices" (p. 23). Organizational scholars must address two central questions related to the confidentiality of personal information obtained through WHPs: (a) who has access to this information? and (b) how is this information being used by organizations to make decisions about an employees' value or risk to their organization?

To answer these questions, we draw upon two cases to illustrate how the economic interests driving employers to provide health services create the conditions for confidentiality boundary infringement. The first case examines the use of drug testing at work and the second explores the issues surrounding genetic testing to identify health risks. It is important to note that information obtained through services, like employee assistance programs, is not protected under the doctor-patient code of confidentiality. Instead, this information belongs to the company providing this service. "Although some [U.S.] state laws do give limited protection to alcohol and drug treatment records, the release forms most workers sign in order to receive health insurance automatically give employers access to their medical records" (May, 1998, p. 23). As a result, organizations are able to use this information in ways that protect the financial interests of the company.

One of the most common organizational violations of confidential information is drug testing (Rosenberg, 2005). Employee assistance programs often provide indiscriminate drug testing, but these tests do not directly measure job-impairment. Instead, a positive drug test only shows that a drug was ingested but cannot differentiate between habitual and occasional use (American Civil Liberties Union, 2015). Moreover, urine analyses also disclose other aspects of an employee's heath. According to the National Workrights Institute (2010), these tests also show if an employee is pregnant, being treated for depression, diabetes, a heart condition, or even epilepsy. In 1988, for example, the Washington D.C. police department admitted to secretly using these drug screenings to determine if female officers were pregnant (Rosenberg, 2005). The concern over how organizations use private medical information is still present today, especially considering the ease of access to health information through electronic medical records (Pyper, Amery, Watson, & Crook, 2004).

As medical technologies advance, so do the fears surrounding the use of this information. Survey data suggests that people fear possible discrimination from their employer based on genetic testing (Feldman, 2012). For instance, if workplaces pressure employees to take part in genetic testing in order to lower health insurance premiums, and subsequently find that an employee has a gene associated with cancer, there is a great temptation to use this information against the individual (Cohen, 2012). Possible repercussions for employees include job termination, denying raises, or other earned benefits (Feldman, 2012). Recognizing the lure for organizations to discriminate against their employees with at-risk genetic markers led to the Genetic Information Nondiscrimination Act (GINA), which was passed in the United States in 2008. Although this act prohibits employers from using genetic information to make employment decisions, such as physical examinations prior to employment, information obtained through workplace wellness programs is not forbidden because it is deemed as "voluntary." However, individuals are unable to make voluntary decisions at work, where organizational power structures constrain employees' ability to make unbiased choices. According to the U.S. Equal Employment Opportunity Commission, which files genetic discrimination cases, "genetic information (such as family medical history) may be obtained as part of health or genetic services, including wellness programs, offered by the employer on a voluntary basis" (2015, para. 9).

Unsurprisingly, the substantial loophole in GINA opens the door for genetic discrimination in the workplace. In the 2014 fiscal year alone, there were 333 genetic-discrimination complaints filed to the Equal Employment Opportunity Commission, the agency responsible for enforcing federal employment laws in America (U.S. Equal Employment Opportunity Commission, 2015). A 2012 *Time* article highlights the case of one worker who filed a lawsuit claiming that her employer had fired her because of a genetic test that revealed her high risk of cancer (Cohen, 2012). Cases like these indicate that organizations are violating confidentiality boundaries and, in effect, ushering in a new age of information and privacy negotiation between worker and employer. "Even though this sort of medical information should remain private, employers and insurance companies will have strong financial incentives to get access to it— and use it to avoid people who are most likely to get sick" (Cohen, 2012, para. 4). Outside of the United States, discussions regarding genetic discrimination are also on the rise considering some nations, like Canada, do not have any legislation protecting this information from employer's misuse (Walker, 2014).

When organizations incentivize health assessments, like urine analysis or genetic testing, how do employees communicate to maintain their confidentiality boundaries? Communication scholars must address how employees and organizations communicatively construct their confidentiality boundaries. Afifi (2003) argues that boundary tensions generate uncertainty about the amount of information an individual should reveal versus conceal. According to CPM, there are consequences for either revealing or concealing personal information (Petronio, 2002, 2010). Extending the findings from interpersonal communication scholars on secrets, it is likely that concealing personal health information from co-workers and supervisors creates stress and tension at work (Frijns & Finkenauer, 2009; Kelly, 2002). For example, if an employee does not want to disclose a terminal medical illness to others, this worker may withdraw from social situations and feel disconnected from his or her colleagues. Yet, disclosing a terminal diagnosis at work may change the way the affected employee is treated, and possibly the extent to which he or she is considered for advancement opportunities.

Future research needs to explore how employees communicatively manage violated boundaries. Are there similar discursive patterns in the narratives of employees who have suffered work consequences due to their health status? What communicative strategies do employees use to reveal and conceal health information at work? Also, considering that much of the research on CPM focuses on the person who is either revealing or concealing information, it is useful to examine the experiences of confidants in organizations. How do these individuals respond to health disclosures and negotiate subsequent information ownership? Even in cases where employees voluntarily reveal health information at work, it is important to evaluate how disclosure impacts their well-being at work.

Ethical Boundary Violations

The medicalization of work creates a slew of ethical issues, which communication researchers have only begun to uncover (see May, 1993, 1998, 2015). These ethical dilemmas stem from problematic organizational power and control. Previously, "a fair day's work for a fair day's pay" was the assumption undergirding employees' contracts (May, 1998, p.19). Now, employees must also satisfy the conditions of good health set by the organization or face penalties (Jones, 2012; Kirby, 2007). As organizational observation extends beyond work, so does the level of influence organizations have over their workers. This section describes the ethical considerations scholars must address when examining WHPs, namely how these initiatives: (a) place employers in a physician's role; (b) create a conflict of interest based on monetary motives; and (c) fail to consider the complexities of health.

First, WHPs confuse the role of an employer with the role of a physician. This problem is most evident in organizations with employee assistance programs, which rely on supervisors to refer their employees to counseling or substance abuse programs (Kirk & Brown, 2003). As a result, poor worker productivity is an indicator of personal health issues that necessitate an intervention (May, 1998). Not only does this approach fail to recognize systemic influences on health—such as an employee's work environment—but it also places an unfair burden on supervisors to intervene in personal health choices. Acknowledging that occupational stress is the leading cause of occupational disease (Dollard et al., 2000; Leigh & Schnall, 2000; Michie & Williams, 2003), WHPs wrongly blame individual choices as the sole culprit of health problems (May, 1998).

Second, WHPs represent a conflict of interests, which deceives employees into believing that their organization has pure motivations for promoting health. Receiving health messages at work is problematic because the main function of an organization is not to promote health, but to protect the bottom line (Jensen, 2002). Workers may disclose health information to their employer under the assumption that the organization has a vested interest in their personal health, only to find out that this information is used against them. For example, consider employees who agree to wear a device that monitors their physical activity. Employees may be surprised to find their physical activity plays a role in determining their future health insurance costs (Olson & Tilley, 2014). Moreover, employees cannot make truly "voluntary" decisions within an organization whose power structures influence their livelihood. Thus, allowing organizations to retrieve genetic information through voluntary health promotions is inherently unethical. Although WHPs may help certain employees meet their personal health goals (Baicker et al., 2010), these programs ultimately serve the organizations' interest in reducing the cost of sick employees.

Third, WHPs create an ethical dilemma by incentivizing certain health outcomes without taking into consideration the complexity of health. Modifying an individual's diet and exercise does not guarantee certain health outcomes, because it neglects other aspects to health including psychological, spiritual, and social wellness (Scarduzio & Geist-Martin, 2015). Mujtaba and Cavico (2013) capture the problem with having a one-size-fits-all approach to health:

> Perhaps an employee cannot lose weight because of a medical condition, such as a thyroid problem; and if so the employer risks legal sanctions for disclosing and/or penalizing an employee for his or her weight, as well as moral opprobrium for treating the employee's weight problem in a demeaning fashion.
>
> (p. 46)

Employers are not medical experts, thus the advice of WHPs may incentivize behaviors that may put the health of certain individuals at risk. Whereas previous research recognizes how workplace wellness programs fail to address health holistically (Geist-Martin & Scarduzio, 2011; Scarduzio & Geist-Martin, 2015), this chapter asks whether any type of WHP, regardless of its comprehensiveness, is appropriate. A further exploration of WHPs requires scholars to consider how these health messages violate ethical boundaries by marginalizing, stigmatizing, and even silencing certain workers.

Future Considerations: Employing Other Meta-Theoretical Lenses

The purpose of this chapter is to examine how the medicalization of work infringes on four types of boundaries: cultural, privacy, confidentiality, and ethical. Given that the management of boundaries takes place through communication (Petronio, 2002), we urge communication scholars to further investigate how individuals manage their health information at work. Specifically, we call for a diverse range of meta-theoretical lenses to better capture the consequences of WHPs within organizations around the world. The majority of research exploring issues related to health and organizations has post-positivists roots (Bandura, 2004; Leshner, Bolls, & Thomas, 2009; Moran & Sussman,

2014; Prestin & Nabi, 2012), which fosters scholarship that looks at the effectiveness of WHPs on organizational productivity (Putnam & Cheney, 1985) and healthy behavior adoption (Finnegan & Viswanath, 1990). Other perspectives, specifically interpretive, critical, feminist, and postcolonial approaches, offer questions that are not well represented in WHP scholarship (see Kirby, 2007; Zoller & Kline, 2008 for notable exceptions).

An interpretive lens offers a more nuanced understanding of the way in which employees attach meaning to WHPs through their everyday interactions with coworkers, managers, and family members (Zoller & Kline, 2008). Through an interpretive paradigm, scholars examine how interactions at work help to develop health beliefs that impact participation in workplace wellness initiatives. To date, studies address how culture and socioeconomic status shape health beliefs and impact the success of public health campaigns (Kreuter, Lukwago, Bucholtz, Clark, & Sanders-Thompson, 2003; Najib Balbale, Schwingel, Chodzko-Zajko, & Huhman, 2014; Rimer & Kreuter, 2006). Yet, research exploring how culture and health beliefs influence the way employees make sense of workplace wellness initiatives is scant (see Dutta-Bergman, 2005; Zoller, 2004 for exceptions). Thus, one avenue for future research from an interpretive orientation could investigate the ways external influences—such as culture, religion, and socioeconomic status—alter how individuals attribute meaning to WHPs. Do these wellness initiatives change an individual's daily experience of work? And in what ways do employees discursively create and maintain privacy boundaries regarding their health?

A critical examination of the medicalization of work helps to capture the ways organizational power may be (un)intentionally pressuring employees to change their preferred boundaries between work and health. Although interpretive and critical work stems from the belief that reality is based on meanings assigned through social construction (Lindlof & Taylor, 2010), critical perspectives are less concerned with offering thick descriptions than interpretive work (see Geertz, 1973), and more concerned with challenging power structures and other taken-for-granted assumptions (Lupton, 2014a; 2014b; Zoller & Kline, 2008). Organizational communication has a history of encouraging research that questions workplace power dynamics (Mumby & Ashcraft, 2006). May and Roper (2014) succinctly describe the plight of critical organizational communication research stating, "Critical researchers seek out both overt and covert differences and dissensus in order to show how organizational practices have become naturalized and normalized to the benefit of some over others" (p. 776). Accordingly, critical research should explore how WHPs create new forms of controlling workers, which results in certain employees feeling marginalized, stigmatized, and even silenced by these initiatives. For instance, Zoller's (2004) research highlights how workplace wellness initiatives, like a workplace gym, do not make all employees feel equally welcome, resulting in the silencing of certain employees.

Building on the present chapter, future critical work on WHPs should examine how cultural, privacy, confidentiality, and ethical boundaries become contested sites harboring worker marginalization. Furthermore, critical approaches to WHP must confront how the power inequalities between employee and employer unfairly pressure employees to participate in health programs. What power systems contribute to the silencing of certain employees? How do employees resist pressure from their employer to disclose personal health information? Attending to these questions offers a unique perspective to the present research on WHPs which largely addresses the effectiveness of these programs without considering how these programs affect workplace communication and the social environment created at work (Baicker et al., 2010; Berry & Mirabito, 2011; Jensen, 2011; Stewart et al., 2003). Although there are exceptions to this general pattern of WHP research (see Geist-Martin & Scarduzio, 2011; May, 1998, 2015; Scarduzio & Geist-Martin, 2015; Zoller, 2003, 2004, 2005; Zoller & Kline, 2008), more research from a critical perspective needs to bring attention to the ways these health initiatives usher in a new type of work—where individuals' bodies and work tasks are evaluated.

A feminist lens affords the opportunity to assess how organizations infuse WHPs with meaning surrounding what male and female health should look like. Previous scholarship advocates for organizational communication to address how "gender organizes every aspect of our social and work lives including how we formally and informally communicate in organizational settings" (Buzzanell, 1994, p. 327; see also Allen, 1996; Ashcraft, 2000, 2005, 2014). Buzzanell and Liu (2005) show how women who go on maternity leave face hostility and criticism from coworkers and managers who insinuate that they are no longer the "ideal worker" (p. 12). As a result, women discursively construct their identity as the ideal worker by reining in their joy for motherhood and submitting to their boss' paternalistic health beliefs—implying that he/she knows what is best for working mothers (Buzzanell & Liu, 2005). Tracy and Rivera (2010) articulate how work-life problems (e.g., maternity leave) are considered "women's issues"; however, men who take paternity leave also experience resentment from others and discrimination in the workplace (Hall, 2013; Petroski & Edley, 2006). Extending this research, feminist communication researchers should investigate how organizations (un)knowingly produce and reproduce certain gender ideologies that shape workplace wellness programs. Possible research questions guided by a feminist framework include: how do organizations produce and reproduce meaning around what constitutes as acceptable female and male health? In what ways do organizational structures privilege male health? And how do organizations use communication to foster a bias toward male health problems? Recognizing that feminist theorizing cannot be characterized by a single principle (Buzzanell, 1994), these questions provide a starting point for future feminist scholarship on workplace health programs, but are not representative of the entire spectrum of feminist theory.

Lastly, a postcolonial approach to WHP research helps reframe organizational practices that are widely taken for granted (Broadfoot & Munshi, 2007). Considering that in the United States alone, 45% of private sector workers and 76% of public sector workers have access to some type of workplace health program (U.S. Bureau of Labor Statistics, 2009, 2011), it is appropriate to view this common organizational practice as largely taken for granted. A postcolonial lens is particularly suitable for organizational communication research because it "offers a uniquely radical and ethically informed critique of Western modernity and modernity's overdetermined accouterments like capitalism, Eurocentrism, science, and the like" (Banerjee & Prasad, 2008, p. 33). Admittedly, employee assistance programs, while originating in the United States, now find their form in organizations around the world (Csiernik & Csiernik, 2012; Gånedahl et al., 2015; Kuoppala & Kekoni, 2013). Not only is a Western view of health problematic within organizations in the West, but also this narrow understanding of health clearly influences the rise of WHP practices around the world.

Postcolonial organizational scholarship helps deconstruct the visible forms of social and economic power (Broadfoot & Munshi, 2007), and thus, appropriately frames research on WHP programs. Considering the economic motivations for WHPs and the influence of Western health beliefs on these initiatives, postcolonial approaches enable an alternative perspective that asks: how can we begin to address health differently in the workplace? Why are WHPs the way they are and how can they be undone or redone? How can organizations creatively restructure health messages apart from a Western influence of what it means to be healthy? To date, much of the research using a postcolonial approach stems from critical management studies (Banerjee & Prasad, 2008; Jack, Westwood, Srinivas, & Sardar, 2011), with an apparent oversight from organization communication (Broadfoot & Munshi, 2007). Thus, we encourage scholars to enter the challenging arena of postcolonial thinking to address WHPs from this unique perspective.

Certainly, no single approach to research will ever capture the complexity of communication. Cheney (2000) advocated for multiple perspectives in communication research in order to fully capture a given phenomenon, which is especially true for the study of health behaviors that reflect myriad systemic influences. In an attempt to encourage scholars to use multiple perspectives when assessing workplace wellness programs, this chapter demonstrates the usefulness of interpretive, critical, feminist, and postcolonial approaches. However, future WHP research is not limited to these four lenses. Regardless of the meta-theoretical lens selected to examine WHPs, communication scholars ought to draw upon perspectives that raise questions regarding the role of organizations to improve the health of their employees. As a starting point, more research needs to confront the ways employees' cultural, privacy, confidentially, and ethical boundaries are violated as a result of the medicalization of work.

Closing

There were two main goals for this chapter: (a) illustrate how WHP initiatives violate employees' cultural, privacy, confidentiality, and ethical boundaries; and (b) encourage future research on WHPs to use meta-theoretical lenses that bring attention to the ways these programs marginalize, stigmatize, and silence certain employees. Communicating about health at work is complex. For instance, unlike health communication in interpersonal settings, the relationship between employee and employer is ridden with power structures, economic motives, and ethical dilemmas. The implications of WHPs create the need for organizational members to communicatively maintain, and at times, renegotiate the boundaries that guard personal health information. Although we use Petronio's (2002) CPM as the theoretical framework for understanding boundary negotiations, we also advocate for scholarship that extends and generates new theories to address how the medicalization of work changes organizational communication.

As there is much to be explored within this area of research, this chapter encourages communication scholars from all backgrounds and meta-theoretical approaches to continue studying how WHPs impact employees' health beliefs both at work and at home. Communication scholars are well suited to address how social processes and organizational messages influence employee participation in workplace wellness initiatives (Harrison, 2015). Specifically, we highlight the rich opportunities for interpretive, critical, feminist, and postcolonial approaches to make meaningful contributions to the literature on workplace wellness programs. Irrespective of the meta-theoretical lens scholars select for future work on WHPs, there is a need to balance out the voluminous research on the benefits that these programs offer organizations' bottom-line with research that examines the ways these programs induce new forms of organizational control. As WHPs continue to infringe on cultural, privacy, confidentially, and ethical boundaries, communication scholars must address how health messages in the workplace change traditional notions of work.

References

Afifi, T. (2003). 'Feeling caught' in stepfamilies: Managing boundary turbulence through appropriate communication privacy rules. *Journal of Social and Personal Relationships, 20,* 729–755. doi: 10.1177/0265407503206002.

Allen, B. J. (1996). Feminist standpoint theory: A black woman's (re)view of organizational socialization. *Communication Studies, 47,* 257–271. doi: 10.1080/105 10979609368482

American Civil Liberties Union. (2014). *My employer shamed me for using birth control.* https://www.aclu.org/blog/my-employer-shamed-me-using-birth-control

American Civil Liberties Union. (2015). *Privacy in America: Workplace drug testing.* Retrieved from https://www.aclu.org/privacy-america-workplace-drug-testing

American Institute on Stress. (2015). *Stress impact statistics.* Retrieved from www.stress.org/daily-life/

Arneson, H., & Ekberg, K. (2005). Evaluation of empowerment processes in a workplace health promotion intervention based on learning in Sweden. *Health Promotion International, 20,* 351–359. doi: 10.1093/heapro/dai023

Arthur, A. R. (2000). Employee assistance programmes: The emperor's new clothes of stress management? *British Journal of Guidance & Counselling, 28,* 549–559. doi: 10.1080/03069880020004749

Ashcraft, K. L. (2000). Empowering "professional" relationships: Organizational communication meets feminist practice. *Management Communication Quarterly, 13*, 347–392. doi: 10.1177/0893318900133001

Ashcraft, K. L. (2005). Feminist organizational communication studies: Engaging gender in public and private. In S. May & D. K. Mumby (Eds.), *Engaging organizational communication theory & research: Multiple perspectives* (pp. 141–170). Thousand Oaks, CA: Sage.

Ashcraft, K. L. (2014). Feminist theory. In L. L. Putnam & D. K. Mumby (Eds.), *The Sage handbook of organizational communication: Advances in theory, research, and methods* (3rd ed., pp. 767–789). Thousand Oaks, CA: Sage.

Baicker, K., Cutler, D., & Song, Z. (2010). Workplace wellness programs can generate savings. *Health Affairs, 2*, 304–311. doi: 10.1377/hlthaff.2009.0626

Bandura, A. (2004). Health promotion by social cognitive means. *Health Education & Behavior, 31*, 143–164. doi: 10.1177/1090198104263660

Banerjee, S., & Prasad, A. (2008). Introduction to the special issue on "critical reflections on management and organizations: A postcolonial perspective." *Critical Perspectives on International Business, 4*, 90–98. doi: 10.1108/17422040810869963

Barbash, I., & Taylor, L. (1997). *Cross-cultural filmmaking: A handbook for making documentary and ethnographic films and videos.* Berkeley, CA: University of California Press.

Barcena, M. B. (2014). *How safe is your quantified self?* Retrieved from www.symantec.com/content/en/us/enterprise/media/security_response/whitepapers/how-safe-is-your-quantified-self.pdf

Begley, S. (2015). *Coming soon to a workplace near you: 'Wellness or else'.* Retrieved from www.reuters.com/article/2015/01/13/us-usa-healthcare-wellness-insight-id USKBN0KM17C20150113

Bentham, J. (1798). *Proposal for a new and less expensive mode of employing and reforming convicts.* Retrieved from http://oll.libertyfund.org/titles/2234

Berry, L. L., & Mirabito, A. M. (2011). Partnering for prevention with workplace health promotion programs. *Mayo Clinic Proceedings, 86*, 335–337. doi: 10.4065/mcp.2010.0803

Berry, L. L., Mirabito, A. M., & Baun, W. B. (2010). What's the hard return on employee wellness programs? *Harvard Business Review, 88*, 104–112. Retrieved from https://hbr.org/2010/12/whats-the-hard-return-on-employee-wellness-programs

Broadfoot, K. J., & Munshi, D. (2007). Diverse voices and alternative rationalities: Imagining forms of postcolonial organizational communication. *Management Communication Quarterly, 21*, 249–267. doi: 10.1177/0893318907306037

Broadfoot, K. J., Carlone, D., Medved, C. E., Aakhus, M., Gabor, E., & Taylor, K. (2008). Meaning/ful work and organizational communication: Questioning boundaries, positionalities, and engagements. *Management Communication Quarterly, 22*, 152–161. doi: 10.1177/0893318908318267

Brown, M. (1996, July). Survival of the fittest. *Management Today*, 74–76. Retrieved from http://schd.ws/hosted_files/dallassapinsightsuperuserco2014/9b/SAP_Kerry_Brown_Survival%20of%20the%20Fittest.pdf

Bute, J. J., & Vik, T. A. (2010). Privacy management as unfinished business: Shifting boundaries in the context of infertility. *Communication Studies, 61*, 1–20. doi: 10.1080/10510970903405997

Buzzanell, P. M. (1994). Gaining a voice feminist organizational communication theorizing. *Management Communication Quarterly, 7*, 339–383. doi: 10.1177/0893318994007004001

Buzzanell, P. M., & Liu, M. (2005). Struggling with maternity leave policies and practices: A poststructuralist feminist analysis of gendered organizing. *Journal of Applied Communication Research, 33*, 1–25. doi: 10.1080/00909880420003 18495

Cartwright, S., & Cooper, C. L. (2014). Towards organizational health: Stress, positive organizational behavior, and employee well-being. In G. F. Bauer & O. Hämmig (Eds.), *Bridging occupational, organizational and public health* (pp. 29–42). Dordrecht, Netherlands: Springer Netherlands.

Caughlin, J. P., Petronio, S., & Middleton, A. V. (2013). When families manage private information. In A. Vangelisti (Ed.), *The Routledge handbook of family communication* (pp. 321–337). New York, NY: Routledge.

Cheney, G. (2000). Interpreting interpretive research: Toward perspectivism without relativism. In S. R. Corman & M. S. Poole (Eds.), *Perspectives on organizational communication: Finding common ground* (pp. 17–45). New York, NY: Guilford.

Churchill, S. A., Gillespie, H., & Herbold, N. H. (2014). The desirability of wellness program and incentive offerings for employees. *Benefits Quarterly, 30*, 48–57. Retrieved from http://web.b.ebscohost.com.ezproxy.lib.utexas.edu/ehost/pdfviewer/ pdfviewer?sid=fc9fbca9-b5d7-4cf5-b457-f9f281640b27%40sessionmgr113&vid= 1&hid=128

Cohen, A. (2012, February). Case Study: Can you be fired for your genes? *Time*. Retrieved from http://ideas.time.com/2012/02/20/can-you-be-fired-for-your-genes/

Csiernik, R., & Csiernik, A. (2012). Canadian employee assistance programming: An overview. *Journal of Workplace Behavioral Health, 27*, 100–116. doi: 10.1080/ 15555240.2012.666465

Danna, K., & Griffin, R. W. (1999). Health and well-being in the workplace: A review and synthesis of the literature. *Journal of Management, 25*, 357–384. doi: 10.1177/014920639902500305

Dickman, F. (2009). Ingredients of an effective employee program. In M. A. Richard (Ed.), *Employee assistance programs: Wellness/enhancement programming* (4th edn, pp. 48–54). Springfield, IL: Charles C. Thomas Publisher Ltd.

Dixon, J., & Dougherty, D. S. (2014). A language convergence/meaning divergence analysis exploring how LGBTQ and single employees manage traditional family expectations in the workplace. *Journal of Applied Communication Research, 42*, 1–19. doi: 10.1080/00909882.2013.847275

Dollard, M. F., Winefield, H. R., Winefield, A. H., & Jonge, J. (2000). Psychosocial job strain and productivity in human service workers: A test of the demand—control—support model. *Journal of Occupational and Organizational Psychology, 73*, 501–510. doi: 10.1348/096317900167182.

Durham, W. T. (2008). The rules-based process of revealing/concealing the family planning decisions of voluntarily child-free couples: A communication privacy management perspective. *Communication Studies, 59*, 132–147. doi: 10.1080/10510970802062451

Dutta-Bergman, M. J. (2005). Theory and practice in health communication campaigns: A critical interrogation. *Health Communication, 18*, 103–122. doi: 10.1207/ s15327027hc1802_1

Eckman, A. K. (1998). Beyond the "Yentyl" Syndrome": Making women visible in post-1990 women's health discourse. In P. A. Treichler, L. Cartwright, & C. Penley (Eds.), *The visible woman: Imaging technologies, gender, and science* (pp. 130–168). New York, NY: New York University Press.

European Agency for Safety and Health at Work. (2015). *Managing stress and psychological risks at work*. Retrieved from https://www.healthy-workplaces.eu/en/ tools-and-resources/publications

Faghri, P. D., Omokaro, C., Parker, C., Nichols, E., Gustavesen, S., & Blozie, E. (2008). E-technology and pedometer walking program to increase physical activity at work. *The Journal of Primary Prevention, 29,* 73–91. doi: 10.1007/s10935-007-0121-9

Farrell, A., & Geist-Martin, P. (2005). Communicating social health perceptions of wellness at work. *Management Communication Quarterly, 18,* 543–592. doi: 10.1177/0893318904273691

Feldman, E. A. (2012). The Genetic Information Nondiscrimination Act (GINA): Public policy and medical practice in the age of personalized medicine. *Journal of General Internal Medicine, 27,* 743–746. doi: 10.1007/s11606-012-1988-6

Fielding, J. E. (1984). *Corporate health management.* Boston, Massachusetts: Addison-Wesley Publishing Company.

Finnegan, J. R. J., & Viswanath, K. (1990). Health and communication: Medical and public health influences on the research agenda. In E. B. Ray & L. Donohew (Eds.), *Communication and health: Systems and applications* (pp. 9–24). Hillsdale, NJ: Erlbaum.

Foucault, M. (1977). *Discipline and punish: The birth of the prison.* New York, NY: Vintage.

Freimuth, V. S., Edgar, T., & Fitzpatrick, M. A. (1993). The role of communication in health promotion. *Communication Research, 20,* 509–516. doi: 10.1177/009365 093020004001

French, J. R., Caplan, R. D., & Van Harrison, R. (1982). The mechanisms of job stress and strain. *Administrative Science Quarterly, 29,* 124–127. doi: 10.2307/2393087

Frijns, T., & Finkenauer, C. (2009). Longitudinal associations between keeping a secret and psychosocial adjustment in adolescence. *International Journal of Behavioral Development, 33,* 145–154. doi: 10.1177/0165025408098020

Gånedahl, H., Viklund, P. Z., Carlén, K., Kylberg, E., & Ekberg, J. (2015). Work-site wellness programmes in Sweden: A cross-sectional study of physical activity, self-efficacy, and health. *Public Health, 129,* 525–530. doi: 10.1016/j.puhe.2015.01.023

Geertz, C. (1973). *The interpretation of culture.* New York, NY: Basic Books.

Geist-Martin, P., & Scarduzioj. (2011). Working well: Re-considering health communication at work. In T. Thompson, R. Parrott, & J. F. Nussbaum (Eds.), *Handbook of health communication* (2nd edn, pp. 117–131). Mahwah, NJ: Erlbaum.

Geist-Martin, P., & Scarduzioj. (2014). Working well. In T. Thompson (Ed.), *Encyclopedia of Health Communication* (pp. 1478–1479). Los Angeles, CA: Sage.

Geist-Martin, P., Horsley, K., & Farrell, A. (2003a). Working well: Communicating individual and collective wellness initiatives. In T. L. Thompson, A. M. Dorsey, K. I. Miller, & R. Parrott (Eds.), *Handbook of health communication* (pp. 423–443). Mahwah, NJ: Erlbaum.

Geist-Martin, P., Ray, E. B., & Sharf, B. F. (2003b). *Communicating health.* Belmont, CA: Wadsworth/Thomson Learning.

Goetzel, R. Z., Ozminkowski, R. J., Bruno, J. A., Rutter, K. R., Isaac, F., & Wang, S. (2002). The long-term impact of Johnson & Johnson's health & wellness program on employee health risks. *Journal of Occupational and Environmental Medicine, 44,* 417–424. doi: 10.1097/00043764-200205000-00010

Grawitch, M. J., Trares, S., & Kohler, J. M. (2007). Healthy workplace practices and employee outcomes. *International Journal of Stress Management, 14,* 275. doi: 10.1037/1072-5245.14.3.275

Greene, K., Derlega, V. J., Yep, G. A., & Petronio, S. (Eds.) (2003). *Privacy and disclosure of HIV in interpersonal relationships: A sourcebook for researchers and practitioners.* Mahwah, NJ: Erlbuam.

Gudykunst, W. B., Ting-Toomey, S., & Chua, E. (1988). *Culture and interpersonal communication.* Newbury Park, CA: Sage.

Guttman, N. (2000). *Public health communication interventions: Values and ethical dilemmas.* Thousand Oaks, CA: Sage.

Hall, J. (2013). Why men don't take paternity leave. *Fortune.* Retrieved from www.fortune.com.

Hamar, B., Coberley, C., Pope, J. E., & Rula, E. Y. (2015). Well-being improvement in a midsize employer: Changes in well-being, productivity, health risk, and perceived employer support after implementation of a well-being improvement strategy. *Journal of Occupational and Environmental Medicine, 57,* 367–373. doi: 10.1097/JOM.0000000000000433

Harris, J. R., Hannon, P. A., Beresford, S. A., Linnan, L. A., & McLellan, D. L. (2014). Health promotion in smaller workplaces in the United States. *Annual Review of Public Health, 35,* 327–342. doi: 10.1146/annurev-publhealth-032013-182416

Harrison, T. R. (2015). The social diffusion of health messages in organizations. In T. R. Harrison & E. Williams (Eds.), *Organizations, health, and communication* (in press). New York, NY: Routledge.

Hawk, S. T., Hale, W. W., Raaijmakers, Q. A. W., & Meeus, W. (2008). Adolescents' perceptions of privacy invasion in reaction to parental solicitation and control. *Journal of Early Adolescence, 28,* 583–608. doi: 10.1177/0272431608317611.

Hornsby, E. E. (2006). Using policy to drive organizational change. *New Directions for Adult and Continuing Education, 2006,* 73–83. doi: 10.1002/ace.238

Ichikawa, K., Matsui, T., Nishikawa, A., Tsunoda, T., Teruya, K., Takeda, N., & Okamoto, H. (2006). Applicability of the international program evaluation tool of employee assistance programs (EAP) onto Japan. *International Congress Series, 1294,* 163–166. doi: 10.1016/j.ics.2006.01.077

Jack, G., Westwood, R., Srinivas, N., & Sardar, Z. (2011). Deepening, broadening and re-asserting a postcolonial interrogative space in organization studies. *Organization, 18,* 275–302. doi: 10.1177/1350508411398996

Jensen, J. D. (2011). Can worksite nutritional interventions improve productivity and firm profitability? A literature review. *Perspectives in Public Health, 131,* 184–192. doi: 10.1177/1757913911408263

Jensen, M. C. (2002). Value maximization, stakeholder theory, and the corporate objective function. *Business Ethics Quarterly, 12,* 235–256. doi: 10.2307/3857812

Jones, L. E. (2012). Framing of fat: Narratives of health and disability in fat discrimination litigation. *N.Y.U. Journal of International Law and Politics, 87,* 1996–2039. Retrieved from www.nyulawreview.org/sites/default/files/pdf/NYULawReview-87-6-Jones_0.pdf

Kelly, A., & Macready, D. (2009). Why disclosing to a confidant can be so good (or bad) for us. In T. Afifi & W. Afifi (Eds.), *Uncertainty, information management, and disclosure decisions: Theories and applications* (pp. 384–402). New York, NY: Routledge.

Kelly, A. E. (2002). *The psychology of secrets.* New York, NY: Kluwer Academic/Plenum.

Kirby, E. L. (2007, November). *Doing (private/unpaid) work on the body to be a good (public/paid) worker: How organizational wellness programs are recasting the meaning of where "work" begins.* Paper presented at the annual Organizational Communication Division of the National Communication Association preconference seminar, Chicago.

Kirby, E. L., & Buzzanell, P. M. (2014). Communicating work-life issues. In L. L. Putnam & D. K. Mumby (Eds.), *The Sage handbook of organizational communication: Advances in theory, research, and methods* (3rd edn, pp. 351–373). Thousand Oaks, CA: Sage.

Kirby, E. L., & Krone, K. J. (2002). "The policy exists but you can't really use it": Communication and the structuration of work-life policies. *Journal of Applied Communication Research, 30*, 50–77. doi: 10.1080/00909880216577

Kirk, A. K., & Brown, D. F. (2003). Employee assistance programs: A review of the management of stress and wellbeing through workplace counselling and consulting. *Australian Psychologist, 38*, 138–143. doi: 10.1080/00050060310001707137

Kreps, G. L., & Kunimoto, E. N. (1994). *Effective communication in multicultural health care settings.* Thousand Oaks, CA: Sage.

Kreuter, M. W., Lukwago, S. N., Bucholtz, D. C., Clark, E. M., & Sanders-Thompson, V. (2003). Achieving cultural appropriateness in health promotion programs: Targeted and tailored approaches. *Health Education & Behavior, 30*, 133–146. doi: 10.1177/1090198102251021

Kuoppala, J., & Kekoni, J. (2013). At the sources of one's well-being: Early rehabilitation for employees with symptoms of distress. *Journal of Occupational and Environmental Medicine, 55*, 817–823. doi: 10.1097/JOM.0b013e31828dc930

Leigh, J. P., & Schnall, P. (2000). Costs of occupational circulatory disease. *Occupational Medicine, 15*, 257–267. Retrieved from www.workhealth.org/OMSTAR/OMSTAR%20chapter%2011.pdf

Leshner, G., Bolls, P., & Thomas, E. (2009). Scare 'em or disgust 'em: The effects of graphic health promotion messages. *Health Communication, 24*, 447–458. doi: 10.1080/10410230903023493

Lewis, A. P. (2009). Destructive organizational communication and LGBT workers' experiences. In P. Lutgen-Sandvik & B. D. Sypher (Eds.), *Destructive organizational communication: Processes, consequences, and constructive ways of organizing* (pp. 184–202). New York, NY: Routledge.

Lindlof, T. R., & Taylor, B. C. (2010). *Qualitative communication research methods.* Thousand Oaks, CA: Sage.

Lucas, K., & Buzzanell, P. M. (2006). Employees "without families": Discourses of family as an external constraint to work-life balance. In L. H. Turner & R. West (Eds.), *The family communication sourcebook* (pp. 335–352). Thousand Oaks, CA: Sage.

Lupton, D. (2014a). Health promotion in the digital era: A critical commentary. *Health Promotion International, 30*, 174–183. doi: 10.1093/heapro/dau091

Lupton, D. (2014b). Apps as artefacts: Towards a critical perspective on mobile health and medical apps. *Societies, 4*, 606–622. doi: 10.3390/soc4040606

Lyon, D. (2001). *Surveillance society: Monitoring in everyday life.* Buckingham, U.K.: Open University Press.

Machen, R., Cuddihy, T. F., Reaburn, P., & Higgins, H. (2010). Development of a workplace wellness promotion pilot framework: A case study of the Blue Care Staff Wellness Program. *Asia-Pacific Journal of Health, Sport and Physical Education, 1*, 13–20. doi: 10.1080/18377122.2010.9730327

May, S. (1993). *Employee assistance programs and the troubled worker: A discursive study of knowledge, power, and subjectivity.* Unpublished Ph.D. dissertation. Salt Lake City, UT: University of Utah.

May, S. (1998). Health care and the medicalization of work: Policy implications. *Marriner S. Eccles biennial policy yearbook* (pp. 5–36). Salt Lake City, UT: University of Utah.

May, S. (2015). Corporate social responsibility and employee health. In T. R. Harrison & E. Williams (Eds.), *Organizations, health, and communication* (in press). New York, NY: Routledge.

May, S. K., & Roper, J. (2014). Corporate social responsibility and ethics. In L. L. Putnam & D. K. Mumby (Eds.), *The sage handbook of organizational communication: Advances in theory, research, and methods* (3rd edn, pp. 767–789). Thousand Oaks, CA: Sage.

Meares, M. M., Oetzel, J. G., Torres, A., Derkacs, D., & Ginossar, T. (2004). Employee mistreatment and muted voices in the culturally diverse workplace. *Journal of Applied Communication Research, 32*, 4–27. doi: 10.1080/0090988042000178121

Michie, S., & Williams, S. (2003). Reducing work related psychological ill health and sickness absence: A systematic literature review. *Occupational and Environmental Medicine, 60*, 3–9. doi: 10.1136/oem.60.1.3

Moore, A. D. (2000). Employee monitoring and computer technology: Evaluative surveillance v. privacy. *Business Ethics Quarterly, 10,* 697–709. doi: 10.2307/3857899

Moran, M. B., & Sussman, S. (2014). Translating the link between social identity and health behavior into effective health communication strategies: An experimental application using antismoking advertisements. *Health Communication, 29*, 1–10. doi: 10.1080/10410236.2013.832830

Mujtaba, B. G., & Cavico, F. J. (2013). A review of employee health and wellness programs in the United States. *Public Policy and Administration Research, 3*, 1–15. Retrieved from http://iiste.org/Journals/index.php/PPAR/article/viewFile/5331/5438

Mumby, D. K., & Ashcraft, K. L. (2006). Organizational communication studies and gendered organization: A response to Martin and Collinson. *Gender, Work & Organization, 13*, 68–90. doi: 10.1111/j.1468-0432.2006.00296.x

Murno, D. (2014). Are workplace wellness programs legal? *Forbes.* Retrieved from www.forbes.com/sites/danmunro/2014/07/16/are-workplace-wellness-programs-legal/

Najib Balbale, S., Schwingel, A., Chodzko-Zajko, W., & Huhman, M. (2014). Visual and participatory research methods for the development of health messages for underserved populations. *Health Communication, 29*, 728–740. doi: 10.1080/10410236.2013.800442

National Workrights Institute. (2010). *Drug testing in the workplace.* Retrieved from http://workrights.us/?products=drug-testing-in-the-workplace

Noblet, A., & LaMontagne, A. D. (2006). The role of workplace health promotion in addressing job stress. *Health Promotion International, 21*, 346–353. doi: 10.1093/heapro/dal029

Nutbeam, D. (1998). Health promotion glossary. *Health Promotion International, 13*, 349–373. doi: 10.1093/heapro/13.4.349

Olson, P., & Tilley, A. (2014). The quantified other: Nest and Fitbit chase a lucrative side business. *Forbes.* Retrieved from www.forbes.com/sites/parmyolson/2014/04/17/the-quantified-other-nest-and-fitbit-chase-a-lucrative-sidebusiness/

Parrott, R., & Lemieux, R. (2003). When the worlds of work and wellness collide: The role of familial support on skin cancer control. *Journal of Family Communication, 3*, 95–106. doi: 10.1207/S15327698JFC0302_02

Pelletier, K. R. (2005). A review and analysis of the clinical and cost-effectiveness studies of comprehensive health promotion and disease management programs at the worksite: Update VI 2000–2004. *Journal of Occupational & Environmental Medicine, 47*, 1051–1058. doi: 10.1097/01.jom.0000174303.85442.bf.00043764-200510000-00012.

Petronio, S. (2000). The boundaries of privacy: Praxis of everyday life. In S. Petronio (Ed.), *Balancing the secrets of private disclosures* (pp. 37–50). Mahwah, NJ: LEA Publishers.

Petronio, S. (2002). *The boundaries of privacy: Dialectics of disclosure.* New York, NY: State University of New York Press.

Petronio, S. (2007). Translational endeavors and the practices of communication privacy management. *Journal of Applied Communication Research, 35,* 218–222. doi: 10.1080/00909880701422443.

Petronio, S. (2010). Communication privacy management theory: What do we know about family privacy regulation? *Journal of Family Theory & Review, 2,* 175–196. doi: 10.1111/j.1756-2589.2010.00052.x

Petronio, S., & Durham, W. T. (2008). Communication privacy management theory. In L. Baxter & D. O. Braithwaite (Eds.), *Engaging theories in interpersonal communication: Multiple perspectives* (pp. 309–322). Thousand Oaks, CA: Sage.

Petronio, S., & Martin, J. N. (1986). Ramifications of revealing private information: A gender gap. *Journal of Clinical Psychology, 42,* 499–506. doi: 10.1002/1097-4679(198605)42:3<499::AID-JCLP2270420317>3.0.CO;2-I

Petronio, S., Jones, S., & Morr, M. C. (2004). Family privacy dilemmas: Managing communication boundaries within family groups. In L. R. Frey (Ed.). *Group communication in context: Studies of bona fide groups* (pp. 23–55), Mahway, NJ: Erlbaum.

Petroski, D. J., & Edley, P. P. (2006). Stay-at-home fathers: Masculinity, family, work, and gender stereotypes. *Electronic Journal of Communication, 16.* Retrieved from www.cios.org/EJCPUBLIC/016/3/01634.HTML

Prestin, A., & Nabi, R. L. (2012). Examining determinants of efficacy judgments as factors in health promotion message design. *Communication Quarterly, 60,* 520–544. doi: 10.1080/01463373.2012.704572

Putnam, L. L., & Cheney, G. (1985). Organizational communication: Historical development and future directions. In T. W. Benson (Ed.), *Speech communication in the 20th century* (pp. 130–156). Carbondale, IL: Southern Illinois University Press.

Pyper, C., Amery, J., Watson, M., & Crook, C. (2004). Patients' experiences when accessing their on-line electronic patient records in primary care. *British Journal of General Practice, 54,* 38–43. Retrieved from http://bjgp.org/content/bjgp/54/498/38.full.pdf

Rimer, B. K., & Kreuter, M. W. (2006). Advancing tailored health communication: A persuasion and message effects perspective. *Journal of Communication, 56,* S184–S201. doi: 10.1111/j.1460-2466.2006.00289.x

Rogers, E. M. (1996). Up-to-date report. *Journal of Health Communication, 1,* 15–24. doi: 10.1080/108107396128202

Rosenberg, S. R. (2005). The technological assault on ethics in the modern workplace. In J. W. Budd, & J. G. Scoville (Eds.), *The ethics of human resources and industrial relations* (pp. 141–172). Champaign, IL: Cornell University Press.

Sainsbury Centre for Mental Health. (2007). *Mental health at work: Developing the business case* (Policy Paper 8). London, U.K.: Author.

Sapolsky, R. (2003). Taming stress. *Scientific American, 289,* 86–95. doi: 10.1038/scientificamerican0903-86

Scarduzio, J, & Geist-Martin, P. (2015). Workplace wellness campaigns: The four dimensions of a whole person approach. In T. R. Harrison & E. Williams (Eds.), *Organizations, health, and communication* (ahead of press). New York, NY: Routledge.

Schaeffer, M. A., Snelling, A. M., Stevenson, M. O., & Karch, R. C. (1994). Worksite health promotion evaluation. In J. P. Opatz (Ed.), *Economic impact of worksite health promotion* (pp. 67–98). Champaign, IL: Human Kinetics Publishers.

Schultz, E. E. (1994, May 18). Open secrets: Medical data gathered by firms can prove less than confidential. *The Wall Street Journal,* A1–A3. Retrieved from http://legacy.library.ucsf.edu/tid/aas52f00/pdf;jsessionid=F2D459CE492A20A5B8D3EF1EB7D9D40C.tobacco03

Sharf, B. F., & Vanderford, M. L. (2003). Illness narratives and the social construction of health. In T. L. Thompson, A. M. Dorsey, K. I. Miller, & R. Parrott (Eds.), *Handbook of health communication* (pp. 9–34). Mahwah, NJ: Erlbaum.

Silverman, R. E. (2015, June). What employers need to know about Supreme Court gay marriage ruling. *The Wall Street Journal.* Retrieved from http://blogs.wsj.com/atwork/2015/06/26/what-the-supreme-court-gay-marriage-ruling-means-for-employers/

Simmons, N. (2012). Tales of gaijin: Health privacy perspectives of foreign English teachers in Japan. *Kaleidoscope: A Graduate Journal of Qualitative Communication Research, 11*, 17–38. Retrieved from http://opensiuc.lib.siu.edu/kaleidoscope/vol11/iss1/3

Stewart, W. F., Ricci, J. A., Chee, E., & Morganstein, D. (2003). Lost productive work time costs from health conditions in the United States: Results from the American Productivity Audit. *Journal of Occupational and Environmental Medicine, 45*, 1234–1246. doi: 10.1097/01.jom.0000099999.27348.78

Thorson, A. R. (2009). Adult children's experiences with their parent's infidelity: Communicative protection and access rules in the absence of divorce. *Communication Studies, 60*, 32–48. doi: 10.1080/10510970802623591

Till, C. (2014). Exercise as labour: Quantified self and the transformation of exercise into labour. *Societies, 4*, 446–462. doi: 10.3390/soc4030446

Tracy, S. J., & Rivera, K. D. (2010). Endorsing equity and applauding stay-at-home moms: How male voices on work-life reveal aversive sexism and flickers of transformation. *Management Communication Quarterly, 24*, 3–42. doi: 10.1177/0893318909352248

Tully, S. (1995). America's healthiest companies. *Fortune, 131*, 98–100. Retrieved from www.ncbi.nlm.nih.gov/pubmed/10143880.

Turner, P. K., & Norwood, K. (2013). Unbounded motherhood: Embodying a good working mother identity. *Management Communications Quarterly, 27*, 396–424. doi: 10.1177/0893318913491461

Turner, P. K., & Norwood, K. (2014). "I had the luxury . . ." Organizing breastfeeding support as privatized privilege. *Human Relations, 67*, 849–874. doi: 10.1177/0018726713507730

Turvey, M. D., & Olson, D. H. (2006). *Marriage and family wellness: Corporate America's business?* Minneapolis, MN: Live Innovations.

U.S. Bureau of Labor Statistics. (2009). *Access to wellness and employee assistance programs in the U.S.* Washington, DC: U.S. Department of Labor. Retrieved from www.bls.gov/opub/mlr/cwc/access-to-wellness-and-employee-assistance-programs-in-the-united-states.pdf

U.S. Bureau of Labor Statistics. (2011). *Health, wellness, and employee assistance: A holistic approach to employee benefits.* Washington, DC: U.S. Department of Labor. Retrieved from www.bls.gov/opub/mlr/cwc/health-wellness-and-employee-assistance-a-holistic-approach-to-employee-benefits.pdf

U.S. Equal Employment Opportunity Commission. (2015). *Genetic information discrimination.* Washington, DC: EEOC. Retrieved from www.eeoc.gov/laws/types/genetic.cfm

Vickers, M. H. (2006). Towards employee wellness: Rethinking bullying paradoxes and masks. *Employee Responsibilities and Rights Journal, 18*, 267–281. doi: 10.1007/s10672-006-9023-x

Walker, J. (2014). *Genetic discrimination and Canadian law* (Research Report No. 2014-90-E). Retrieved from www.parl.gc.ca/Content/LOP/ResearchPublications/2014-90-e.pdf

Watkins, P. L., & Whaley, D. (2000). Gender role stressors and women's health. In R. M. Eisler & M. Hersen (Eds.), *Handbook of gender, culture, and health* (pp. 43–62). Mahwah, NJ: Erlbaum.

Westin, A. F. (2003). Social and political dimensions of privacy. *Journal of Social Issues, 59*, 431–453. doi: 10.1111/1540-4560.00072

Zielinski, D. (2014). Incorporating fitness trackers into the workplace wellness. *Society of Human Resource Management, 59.* Retrieved from www.shrm.org/publications/hrmagazine/editorialcontent/2014/1014/pages/1014-wearable-fitness-trackers.aspx

Zoller, H. M. (2003). Health on the line: Identity and disciplinary control in employee occupational health and safety discourse. *Journal of Applied Communication Research, 31*, 118–139. doi: 10.1080/00909880320000064588

Zoller, H. M. (2004). Manufacturing health: Employee perspectives on problematic outcomes in a workplace health promotion initiative. *Western Journal of Communication, 68*, 278–301. doi: 10.1080/10570310409374802

Zoller, H. M. (2005). Women caught in the multi-causal web: A gendered analysis of Healthy People 2010. *Communication Studies, 56*, 175–192. doi: 10.1080/00089570500078809

Zoller, H. M. (2012). Communicating health: Political risk narratives in an environmental health campaign. *Journal of Applied Communication Research, 40*, 20–43. doi: 10.1080/00909882.2011.634816

Zoller, H. M., & Kline, K. N. (2008). Theoretical contributions of interpretive and critical research in health communication. In C. S. Beck (ed.), *Communication Yearbook 32* (pp. 89–135). Thousand Oaks, CA: Sage.

Zook, E. G. (1994). Embodied health and constitutive communication: Toward and authentic conceptualization of health communication. In S. A. Deetz (ed.), *Communication Yearbook 17* (pp. 344–377). Thousand Oaks, CA: Sage.

CHAPTER CONTENTS

11 Newcomer Socialization Research

The Importance and Application of Multilevel Theory and Communication

Brian Manata and Vernon D. Miller

Portland State University

Briana N. DeAngelis

University of Minnesota

Jihyun Esther Paik

University of Wisconsin, Madison

Although multiple conceptualizations and measures of newcomer socialization have been offered, most approaches to measuring socialization efforts (a) confound distinctions between multilevel influences and (b) overlook critical communicative aspects (i.e., who-says-what-to-whom-and-how). Advocating for a shift in theory and measurement, this paper reviews three popular approaches in the socialization corpus (i.e., contextual, content, and memorable messages) and then critiques their inattention to the multilevel and communicative nature of socialization processes. This paper concludes with recommendations for future research on the dynamics of newcomer socialization, especially as they occur across multiple levels of analysis.

Socialization scholars have produced a bevy of narrative reviews that scrutinize the state of newcomer socialization research (e.g., Ashforth, Sluss, & Harrison, 2007; Bauer & Erdogan, 2011; Chao, 2012; Kramer & Miller, 1999; 2014). These reviews typically promote the importance of prominent socialization theories, often leaving readers with the impression that socialization efforts are vital predictors of newcomer adjustment, learning, and productivity. This impression, however, is somewhat at odds with the results of recent meta-analyses, which suggest that relationships between socialization tactics and newcomer adjustment variables are relatively small to moderate in size (e.g., Bauer, Bodner, Erdogan, Truxillo, & Tucker, 2007; Saks, Uggerslev, & Fassina, 2007).

Although we maintain that these meta-analytic findings hold considerable value, we also contend that consideration of *communicative influences* that originate at *multiple levels* of analysis (e.g., individual-level, unit-level, organizational-level) are essential for advancing theory and knowledge related to newcomer socialization. Specifically, accounting for multilevel effects and communicative phenomena simultaneously will enable socialization scholars to make more accurate assessments of the relationships that occur among various socialization tactics and newcomer adjustment outcomes (Anderson & Thomas, 1996; Klein & Heuser, 2008; Rink, Kane, Ellemers, & Van der Vegt, 2013). Hence, the purpose of this chapter is to explicate multilevel effects and communicative phenomena as they occur during newcomer socialization, which advances our ultimate goal of guiding future newcomer socialization scholarship.

Throughout this chapter, we argue that popular measurement approaches used by socialization scholars confound or disregard theoretical distinctions made between individual-, unit-, and organizational-levels of socialization efforts, which undermines the ability to examine cross-level effects (Klein & Kozlowski, 2000) and compromises the construct validity of existing measures (Edwards, 2003; Messick, 1995). Furthermore, despite scholars' insistence that communication is a central process by which newcomer socialization occurs, explicit assessments of *how* and *what* information is exchanged between newcomers and incumbents are often avoided (Kramer & Miller, 2014). Such exclusions make it difficult to unearth communication variables that are at play during newcomer socialization, which limits our ability to delineate the unique effects that multilevel socialization efforts have on newcomers. In light of these omissions, this chapter promotes opportunities for communication scholarship that, we hope, will begin to illuminate the intricate, multilevel nature of newcomer socialization.

We begin the chapter with an overview of three popular approaches to studying newcomer socialization. Next, we illustrate the multilevel nature of socialization and the value of assessing communication, and then critique the current state of research in each of the three popular areas. Our illustrations follow primarily from a quantitative perspective, which we argue affords a clear articulation of how communication variables might manifest across numerous types of multilevel models (Miller et al., 2011). Although this approach may seem somewhat restrictive to those who prefer qualitative approaches, our general aims are to draw attention to lingering communication issues within newcomer socialization and to provide a detailed discussion of multilevel theory; aims that we believe cut-across methodological perspectives. We conclude the chapter by offering principles that are intended to guide future socialization scholarship on the issues of multilevel theory and communication.

Popular Approaches to Studying Socialization

The first efforts to assess the process of organizational socialization appeared in the mid-1970s (e.g., Bibby & Brinkeroff, 1974; Feldman, 1976). Van Maanen and Schein's (1979) seminal explication of organizational socialization, which emphasized "the process by which an individual acquires the social knowledge and skills necessary to assume an organizational role" (p. 211), appeared shortly thereafter. In the time since Van Maanen and Schein's theoretical explication, three broad approaches have guided a majority of socialization research. For our purposes, we refer to these approaches as (a) contextual, (b) content, and (c) memorable-messages (see Table 11.1). To set the stage for materials that will emphasize multilevel and communicative aspects of socialization, brief reviews of each approach and of the primary measures associated with each approach are provided below (for extensive reviews of each approach, see Ashforth et al., 2007; Bauer & Erdogan, 2011; Chao, 2012; Kramer & Miller, 2014).

Contextual Approach

Researchers who adopt the most extensively published approach to studying socialization focus on the socially engineered *contexts* in which newcomers learn their roles. This approach stems from Van Maanen and Schein's (1979) early explication of socialization strategies, in which Van Maanen and Schein described aspects of the unique contexts in which newcomers learn preferred organizational behaviors. Specifically, Van Maanen and Schein argued that a range of socialization contexts are described by mixtures of six primary tactics, or dimensions, that pertain to the structure and organization of socialization processes (i.e., collective-individual, formal-informal, sequential-random, fixed-variable, serial-disjunctive, and investiture-divestiture). Building on Van Maanen and Schein's work, Jones (1986) proposed that these tactics can be thought of as distinguishing between two basic ways of processing people into organizations: institutionalized vs. individualized. Specifically, collective, formal, sequential, fixed, serial, and investiture tactics offer institutionalized or structured experiences; whereas individual, informal, random, variable, disjunctive, and divestiture tactics offer individualized or unstructured experiences. Jones ultimately conceded that it is more accurate to think of socialization contexts as being described by their unique classifications along all six tactical dimensions (rather than as different mixtures or sub-sets of tactics).

Researchers interested in the contextual features of organizational socialization typically measure socialization contexts via Jones' (1986) organizational socialization tactic instrument, which includes scales for each of Van Maanen and Schein's (1979) six dimensions of socialization. In line with Van Maanen and Schein's theorizing, research on the validity of Jones' instrument is consistent with a six-factor solution (Ashforth, Saks, & Lee, 1998; for a critique of Jones' scale, however, see Ashforth & Saks, 1996). Thus, scholars generally recommend that researchers treat each of the six contextual tactics as distinct constructs to allow for a rich picture of the process by which socialization occurs (Bauer et al., 2007; Saks et al., 2007). Moreover, the predictive validity of the contextual socialization tactics is supported by recent meta-analyses (Bauer et al., 2007; Saks et al., 2007). Saks and colleagues (2007), for instance,

Table 11.1 Summary of Three Primary Approaches to Measuring Organizational Socialization

Characteristics and Critiques	Approach to Measurement		
	Contextual	Content	Memorable Messages
Primary Focus	How organizations process people (i.e., socialization tactics)	Focal content areas of socialization	Messages that have a lasting impact on newcomers
Example Measure(s)	Jones (1986)	Chao et al. (1994)	Barge & Schlueter (2004); Stohl (1986)
Dimensions	Six tactics: 1. formal-informal 2. individual-collective 3. sequential-random 4. fixed-variable 5. serial-disjunctive 6. investiture-divestiture	Six content areas: 1. history 2. language 3. politics 4. people 5. organizational goals and values 6. performance proficiency	Evidence for validity of taxonomy not available; Emergent/unique to situation
Contributions	Acknowledges influence from organization, work-group, and individuals Recognizes the influence of context	Assesses information acquired by newcomers Emphasizes social & task-related content	Assesses the content & source of messages that newcomers receive Focuses on rich information; descriptive data
General Concerns	Mixes items that refer to one's job with items that refer to one's career Dynamic nature of context(s) rarely considered	Does not address the perceived value or importance of information Does not distinguish between knowledge acquired through intentional socialization efforts versus proactive behaviors or pre-entry	Issues of verbatim recall compromise validity Memorable messages may not stem from intentional socialization efforts

Multilevel Concerns	Co-mingling of referents within dimensions	Some dimensions mix items that target different levels of influence	Information about message sources lacks specificity necessary to assess multilevel validity
	Non-independence is not assessed, despite referencing multilevel properties	There may be between-unit variance in the importance attributed to content areas	Existing studies do not assess similarity of messages or of message sources between individuals within the same work-unit
Multilevel Suggestions	Modify items to target a single level (of interest)	Modify item content to specific level of interest	Examine similarity of memorable messages & sources for employees within work-units, departments, etc.
	Model non-independence when multilevel properties are assumed	Assess whether the impact of specific types of content differ between units of analysis	
Communication Concerns	Does not capture message sources or message content	Does not capture message sources or delineate within message types (e.g., which organizational values?)	Relies on single message recall
	Does not account for newcomers' perceived value of the tactics	Does not assess newcomers' perceived value of the knowledge	Does not account for whether messages were solicited or unsolicited
Communication Suggestions	Use multiple sources to assess others' perceptions of shared socialization tactics (e.g., incumbents, supervisors)	Measure who imparts content knowledge	Develop primers and validation for conversation recall
	Examine the interplay of communication content and context	Validate perceptions by asking message sources about information that they emphasized	Link memorable messages with specific socialization events
		Include measures to assess perceived value of received socialization messages	Validate with other socialization measurement approaches

concluded that the "social or interpersonal aspects of socialization [from serial and investiture tactics]" (p. 440) are essential to successful newcomer adjustment. Similarly, Bauer et al. (2007) concluded that contextual socialization tactics are key predictors of role clarity, self-efficacy, and social acceptance.

Content Approach

Whereas researchers who adopt a contextual approach to studying socialization focus on the settings in which newcomers learn their roles, researchers who adopt a *content* approach attempt to uncover specific domains of information to which newcomers are exposed during organizational socialization (Klein & Heuser, 2008). In the main, researchers who adopt a content approach assume that there are values, standards, and behaviors that newcomers must learn in order to attain organizational success (Brim, 1966; Hyde, 1966; Zurcher, 1983). For instance, Chao, O'Leary-Kelly, Wolf, Klein, and Gardner (1994) proposed six general content areas in which employees can accumulate organizational knowledge: (a) history—knowledge of the organization's traditions, customs, and background; (b) language—mastery of specialized slang and jargon; (c) politics—knowledge of the influential members and how things "really work"; (d) people—acceptance into the workgroup; (e) goals and values—understanding and support for organizational goals and values; and (f) performance proficiency—mastery of required tasks and skills. Using this system of classification, Chao and colleagues (1994) found evidence that greater knowledge in all six content domains was associated positively with newcomers' subsequent career effectiveness.

Unlike the relative uniformity in measurement observed in studies that have examined the contexts of socialization, marked variation in measurement is observable across studies that have examined socialization content. Since Chao et al. (1994) published their instrument for measuring content areas of organizational knowledge, a number of researchers have modified the original instrument. Hart (2012; Hart & Miller, 2005), for instance, revised the items in Chao et al.'s (1994) instrument to measure the extent to which newcomers received messages from organizational incumbents about each of the six content areas.

Other researchers have proposed more radical deviations from Chao et al.'s original instrument. For instance, Haueter, Macan, and Winter (2003) raised concerns about the construct validity of Chao et al.'s measurement; they proposed a new instrument (i.e., the newcomer socialization questionnaire) to assess newcomers' perceived levels of organizational-, group-, and task-knowledge. Myers and colleagues (Gailliard, Myers, & Seibold, 2010; Myers & Oetzel, 2003) also developed a unique instrument to measure socialization content, which focuses on measuring both knowledge acquired (e.g., "I feel like I know my supervisor pretty well") and newcomer acclimation (e.g., "I have figured out efficient ways to do my work"). Regardless of the specific instruments utilized, scholars adopting a content approach examine how social and task-related content affects newcomer-related outcomes (e.g., job performance).

Memorable Messages Approach

Scholars guided by the third approach to studying newcomer socialization focus on *memorable messages,* or messages that recipients perceive as particularly influential and that are remembered for a long time (Stohl, 1986). These scholars conceptualize the transmission of, and the recollection of, memorable messages as a process by which newcomers acquire organizational knowledge. Researchers who adopt a memorable messages approach to studying socialization aim to understand the nature, context, and impact of salient messages that newcomers use to (a) understand organizational norms and expectations and (b) align their behaviors with the organization's values (Barge & Schlueter, 2004; Stohl, 1986). For instance, Barge and Schlueter (2004) asked participants "to describe in detail a single memorable message that made an impact on their work life when they first entered the organization" (p. 240), and then to explain how they used the memorable message.

Unlike researchers who adopt contextual or content approaches to study socialization, researchers who adopt a memorable messages approach do not use pre-defined scales to measure socialization experiences. Rather, memorable message scholars rely on open-ended responses to questions that ask organizational members to recall messages that they received during their organizational socialization experiences. Then, the messages are coded and analyzed (Stohl, 1986) or used to identify predominant themes that emerge in socialization discourse (Barge & Schlueter, 2004). For instance, Stohl (1986) interviewed organizational members and asked them to recall messages that were received during their organizational tenure and that were particularly influential in their work life. After recording these memorable messages, Stohl coded their content into categories based on a coding scheme that was developed in previous memorable message research. In using this methodological approach, Stohl found descriptive evidence that a majority of memorable messages transferred requisite knowledge for newcomer survival (i.e., norms, values, expectations, and rules) which newcomers used to make sense of their environment and to align their actions with the norms valued by the organization.

A more recent example of research guided by the memorable messages approach is Barge and Schlueter's (2004) examination of memorable messages recalled by organizational newcomers. Unlike Stohl (1986), Barge and Schlueter (2004) developed their own categorization scheme using an inductive approach to identifying qualitative themes in newcomers' memorable messages. Despite their different approach, Barge and Schlueter found evidence consistent with the conclusions drawn by Stohl (1986). Specifically, Barge and Schlueter found that a majority of messages conveyed requisite information about organizational performance and important office polemics. Taken together, it is clear that adopting a memorable messages approach to studying newcomer socialization renders rich information regarding the messages that newcomers receive during socialization.

New Directions

Research guided by the contextual, content, and memorable messages approaches offers unique insights regarding newcomers' organizational entry experiences. Namely, socialization research guided by a contextual approach has contributed to our understanding of the structure and organization of the social settings in which newcomers are socialized. Research informed by a content approach to studying socialization has shed light on the domains of information that newcomers receive during socialization. And research guided by a memorable messages approach has contributed to our understanding of socialization discourse that newcomers perceive as particularly impactful during their organizational entry.

Despite their contributions to our understanding of newcomer socialization, the contextual, content, and memorable messages approaches are not without shortcomings. As will be seen upon closer inspection, research guided by each approach is marked by limitations that have impeded progress in our theorizing about, and our understanding of, (a) the multilevel nature of newcomer socialization and (b) the influence of communication during socialization. Consider, for instance, how departmental policies and espoused values have substantial downward influence on common socialization practices in some units but not in others. Also, consider how almost every workgroup differs in how they socialize their newcomers (see Moreland & Levine, 1982; 2001). With current research designs and measures, researchers are hard-pressed to analyze such differences in a systematic way. We argue that failure to account for multilevel effects inherently limits our understanding of how newcomer socialization operates (Kozlowski & Bell, 2012).

We also seek to address the ever-present role of communication in newcomer socialization activities (Ashforth et al., 2007; Bauer & Erdogan, 2014; Kramer & Miller, 2014). Consistent with earlier calls (e.g., Jablin, 2001; Kramer & Miller, 2014), we note that current newcomer socialization researchers have largely excluded communication from their research domain. We note that such methodological and theoretical practices have obfuscated our understanding of how key communication processes operate during socialization. Presumably, documenting communication as a process will help explicate the subtleties of dyadic and group interaction and, thus, should begin to shed light on numerous socialization practices (e.g., the impact of receiving information from different sources on newcomer learning; Ostroff & Kozlowski, 1992, 1993).

We begin our push for new directions by noting the general omission of multilevel theory, and then we shift our attention to communication as an important process variable. Given the momentum these issues have gained in other literatures (e.g., management) and domains of communicative inquiry (e.g., social influence), these two subjects are both prominent and relevant to socialization scholarship.

Multilevel Considerations

Fundamental to multilevel theory is the assumption that organizations are systems comprised of numerous *interdependent units* (Scott, 1987). Given this, it is minimally assumed that (a) multiple levels exist within organizations, (b) some levels may be more influential than others, and (c) forces of influence from numerous levels may be operating concurrently (Kozlowski, 2012). Thus, contemporary multilevel theory posits that researchers must contemplate the dynamic nature of influence as it occurs both within and between individuals, groups, organizations, and even external environments (Kozlowski & Klein, 2000). When applied to socialization phenomena, it is presumed that newcomers' socialization experiences depend largely on factors that originate at multiple levels of analysis (e.g., departmental- and organizational-level; Kozlowski & Bell, 2012).

A Primer on Multilevel Theory

Theorizing about cross-level effects that occur during newcomer socialization involves consideration of two primary types of effects: *contextual* (top-down) and *emergent* (bottom-up). A contextual effect occurs "when factors at a higher level influence or constrain phenomena at the lower level" (Kozlowski, 2012, p. 266). Thus, consideration of contextual effects may entail identification of organizational- or group-level factors that influence individuals' actions in a *downward* fashion. For instance, in his seminal article on the effects of "concertive control," Barker (1993) explicates how team-level norms constrain newcomer behaviors. Specifically, Barker described a process in which newcomers experience coordinated pressure from team-members to assimilate to established, team-level normative behaviors (e.g., the team agrees that all members must come to work on time). Thus, Barker documented a process in which a higher-level contextual factor (e.g., team-level norms) influenced units at a lower level of analysis (i.e., individual behaviors) in a top-down fashion.

Conversely, an emergent effect originates "in the cognition, affect, behaviors, or other characteristics of individuals, is amplified by their interactions, and manifests as a higher-level, collective phenomenon" (Kozlowski & Klein, 2000, p. 55). Scholars distinguish between forms of emergent effects based on the extent to which the construct of interest is isomorphic across levels (Kozlowski, 2012; Kozlowski & Klein, 2000); scholars label these forms *composition* and *compilation* emergence.

If a construct retains structural equivalence across levels of analysis (i.e., similar measurement and representation), *composition emergence* is said to occur. Thus, composition emergence occurs when a group-level property emerges as a result of group members' shared properties. For example, as individuals' perceptions of trust in the team become shared by all members, trust in the team emerges as a collective, group-level belief (De Jong & Dirks, 2012). Alternatively, *compilation emergence* occurs when a construct does not retain structural equivalence across levels. Hence, a group-level property emerges as a result of a unique combination of group members' characteristics (i.e., the group-level property exists because of variance within the group). For example, if a diverse group of experts formed a team, then the team's expertise would emerge as a compilation of unshared knowledge stores (e.g., transactive memory; Kozlowski & Ilgen, 2006; Kozlowski & Klein, 2000). Stated differently, the expertise of any one group member would fail to equal the team's total expertise.

Illustrating the Multilevel Nature of Socialization

To clarify the importance of multilevel theory within the context of newcomer socialization, an illustration may be of some assistance. Corporation XYZ is a fictitious organization that consists of multiple departments, each of which contains numerous project teams. Upon being hired at XYZ, all newcomers are assigned to project teams within departments. Because considerable variation exists between departments and project teams, however, newcomers' socialization experiences vary substantially. We present the socialization experiences of four newcomers: Devon, Lisa, Tony, and Rebecca.

Suppose that Devon and Lisa, two organizational newcomers, are placed within the Advertising department upon being hired at XYZ. Despite being placed within the same department, Devon and Lisa are assigned to different teams (Devon to team *A* and Lisa to team *B*) and, as it would happen, their socialization experiences are relatively different. Whereas Devon experiences mutually supportive interactions and finds that his team is characterized by relatively high intra-team trust, Lisa experiences little support and finds that her team is characterized by relatively low intra-team trust. Furthermore, because teams *A* and *B* have conflicting opinions regarding how departmental matters should be handled, Devon and Lisa learn that interactions between teams are relatively unsupportive and department-level unity is largely absent.

The remaining newcomers, Tony and Rebecca, are also assigned to different teams within the Product Development department (Tony to team *Blue* and Rebecca to team *Green*) at XYZ. Unlike Devon and Lisa's experiences in the Advertising department, Tony and Rebecca learn that the Product Development department is very cohesive and fosters supportive interactions both within and between teams (i.e., supportive communication and trust do not differ between Product Development teams). The unity of the Product Development department is achieved, in part, through a standardized department-level orientation (contextual, or top-down, influence), in which newcomers are introduced to the department's values. As a result of these department-level properties, Tony and Rebecca's initial socialization experiences do not differ, despite their assignment to different teams.

Theorizing multilevel effects is essential for capturing systematic differences in newcomer socialization, such as those described in the experiences of Devon, Lisa, Tony, and Rebecca. Distinguishing between Devon's and Lisa's socialization experiences within the Advertising department, for instance, requires consideration of team-level effects (e.g., mutual supportive communication and intra-team trust). Alternatively, capturing the differences between Devon and Lisa's experiences (in the Advertising department) and Tony and Rebecca's experiences (in the Product Development department) might require consideration of department-level effects. Further, as Devon and his colleagues become established organizational members, their experiences are likely to change over time. In the same way that Devon and the others are nested within teams (or departments), one could theorize that different *time-points* are nested within Devon and the other newcomers (i.e., individuals are treated at the higher-level of analysis, whereas time is treated as a lower-level variable; Raudenbush & Bryk, 2002; Singer, 1998; Singer & Willett, 2003).

As this example highlights, multilevel theory affords the inclusion of multiple effects, many of which likely occur within and between organizations as well as across time. To wit, although the effects referenced here make note of between-team and between-departmental differences, examination of other variables may lead researchers to find that they are instead interested in between-organizational differences. Conversely, at a more micro-level, researchers may come to find that they are instead interested in assessing how individuals change over time (Singer & Willett, 2003). Thus, identifying potential multilevel effects is critical for advancing theory and knowledge related to newcomer socialization.

Level-specification during the research conceptualization stage also forms the basis for valid measurement. Suppose that we have an opportunity to collect data from Devon, Lisa, Tony, Rebecca, and other newcomers at XYZ for the purpose of examining the relationship between supportiveness and employee satisfaction. Are we interested in measuring team-level support or department-level support? Likewise, are we interested in measuring individual-level, team-level, or departmental-level satisfaction? As we will argue, specifying the level(s) of these variables allows us to create valid measures that reflect our conceptual and theoretical variables of interest. If, for instance, we overlook the possibility that support can occur at multiple levels, we likely end up creating overly generic survey items that attempt to measure supportiveness (e.g., "How supportive is your work environment?"). Devon, for one, would have difficulty responding to such items because his immediate workgroup (i.e., his assigned teammates) is very supportive, but employees who are outside of his immediate team are not very supportive. Inversely, level-specification prior to constructing measures would have allowed for the creation of more specific items that reflect our theoretical level of interest (e.g., "How supportive is your team's work environment?").

In essence, traditional socialization research designs and socialization measurement approaches attempt to generalize from individuals' entry experiences and researchers rarely consider whether departmental affiliations or organizational norms for socializing newcomers exist (Kramer & Miller, 2014). Thus, the ability to capture composition and compilation emergence is severely constrained. In contrast, multilevel analyses reflect the nature of organizations and enable scholars to specify multiple factors that originate at multiple levels and that influence the processes and constructs of interest to newcomer socialization scholars. Socialization researchers interested in multilevel phenomena, for example, are tasked with considering how individuals influence groups (Gallagher & Sias, 2009), groups influence individuals (Rink et al., 2013), organizations influence groups (Scott & Myers, 2010), and even how levels external to the organization foretell member socialization experiences (e.g., Jablin, 2001; Teboul, 1994). Although daunting, integration of multilevel theory into the design and development of measures used by newcomer socialization scholars is necessary for fidelity in measurement.

In the following sections, we offer a critique of extant measures used in socialization research in which we highlight concerns that arise when considering their use within the context of multilevel socialization. Our critique is organized by the three main approaches expounded in our earlier review of the literature (i.e., contextual, content, and memorable messages approaches). Note, however, that the criticisms concerning both contextual and content approaches are presented together, whereas the criticisms concerning the memorable messages approach are presented in isolation. This division was made due to the quantitative nature of both the contextual and content approaches (e.g., questionnaires), which differs from the primarily qualitative nature of the memorable messages approach (e.g., discourse analysis). We also note that a majority of our criticisms make use of the common distinction made between individual- and team-levels of analysis. This was done with the intention of forwarding a parsimonious argument, but our logic generalizes to all theoretical levels of analysis (e.g., time, individuals, departments, organizations).

Multilevel Critique of Contextual and Content Approaches

Research guided by contextual and content approaches to understanding organizational socialization reflects consideration of multiple levels of influence; however, current measures used in research guided by these approaches confound influences that occur at multiple levels. For instance, although Jones' (1986) items reflect consideration of multiple levels of influence, items within the six scales refer to influences that occur at multiple levels of analysis, including the organizational level (e.g., "The organization puts all newcomers through the same set of learning experiences," p. 277) and at the level of coworker interactions (e.g., "Almost all of my colleagues have been supportive of me personally," p. 278). Given that researchers have demonstrated that individuals respond differently to items that use individual- versus group-referents (e.g., Klein, Conn, Smith, & Sorra, 2001), mixing items that refer to different levels of analysis poses a threat to validity. For instance, Klein and colleagues (2001) observed greater between-group variability when group-level (vs. individual-level) referents were used. If item referents are able to change how individuals respond to survey items, one is left wondering whether changing referents changes the meaning of the underlying construct under question. In the case that changing referents does change the meaning of the construct, mixing referents within a given scale undermines the goal of creating an instrument that measures a single construct of interest (Schwarz, 1999). As such, confounds observed in extant measures may preclude our ability to assess contextual influences in a valid manner.

Measures used in research guided by the content approach also reflect consideration of multiple levels of influence. However, their manifestation is different than the manifestations observed in Jones' (1986) contextual measure. For instance, in their attempt to assess work relationships, Chao et al.'s (1994) measure of "People" content includes items that refer to the workgroup- and organizational-levels (e.g., "Within my work group, I would be easily identified as 'one of the gang,'" and "I am pretty popular in the organization," p. 734). As noted above, a failure to specify the source or level of influence when creating items leads to co-mingling of referents, which poses a threat to construct validity (Klein, Dansereau, & Hall, 1994; Miller et al., 2011; Schwarz, 1999).

A second problem embedded in contextual and content approaches is the assumption of unit-level phenomena (e.g., teams, departments, organizations) in the absence of evidence supporting the existence of unit-level properties. The assumption of unit-level properties introduces the potential for analyzing data at the incorrect level of analysis (Kozlowski & Klein, 2000). When researchers are interested in shared unit-level properties, rather than assuming homogeneity across units or an entire organization, it is vital to verify (a) that a unit-level property exists and (b) that it retains the same meaning across workgroups or organizations (Roberts, Hulin, & Rousseau, 1978). To do this, researchers often establish non-independence or within-group agreement (i.e., homogeneity) using either intra-class correlations or R_{wg} values, respectively (Bliese, 2000; for a discussion of R_{wg} values, see James, Demaree, & Wolf, 1993; Kozlowski & Hattrup, 1992; Schmidt & Hunter, 1989). Such statistics are usually deemed essential for assessing whether multilevel constructs are in operation and for determining whether aggregation and multilevel analyses are warranted (Kozlowski & Klein, 2000; Miller et al., 2011). To the best of our knowledge, organizational scholars using the Jones (1986) and Chao et al. (1994) scales have not examined within-group agreement or non-independence, which increases the odds of analyzing data at an incorrect level of analysis (Bliese, 2000; Miller et al., 2011). Furthermore, these practices leave open the possibility that researchers have confounded key multilevel variables and effects (Klein et al., 1994; Klein & Kozlowski, 2000).

Multilevel Critique of the Memorable Messages Approach

Scholars guided by the memorable messages approach leave open the possibility of multiple levels of influence; however, this approach precludes the ability to establish multilevel validity. Stohl (1986), for instance, argued that memorable messages are generally "received from someone directly in one's work area" (p. 245), which implies that memorable messages may manifest as a group-level property. The generality of Stohl's (1986) reporting, however, hinders the assessment of whether "one's work area" refers to one's department, one's team, or some other organizational unit. Similarly, although Barge and Schlueter (2004) distinguished between message-sources (e.g., cohort, manager, co-worker), their data are not presented in a manner that would allow for examination of unit-level properties. For example, if one were to claim that a memorable message originated from their unit manager, should this be coded as a unit- or organizational-level influence? Although the manager is technically on the unit's roster, extant evidence suggests that message espousal from supervisors may be perceived as embodying organizational values (e.g., Eisenberger et al., 2010).

Communication Considerations

In addition to clouding the multilevel nature of organizational socialization, research guided by the three primary approaches to studying socialization often overlooks the role of communication within socialization activities (Ashforth et al., 2007; Bauer & Erdogan, 2014; Jablin, 2001; Kramer & Miller, 2014). Communication scholars from an information processing perspective generally acknowledge that *what* and *how* information is conveyed can influence reception, perceptions, and interpretations of the information (e.g., Jablin, 2001; Poole, 2010). Despite this acknowledgement, scholars often fall short of capturing message content and meaning, message sources, and the nature of communicative interactions, all of which are essential to understanding the communicative processes that occur during newcomer socialization (Jablin, 2001; Klein & Heuser, 2008; Poole, 2010).

   Although the importance of examining communication variables is evident in the work of some scholars—such as that of Hart and Miller (2005), who found that performance proficiency messages mediated the relationships between socialization tactics and role ambiguity—researchers often stop short of examining message content and other features of communicative interactions. As is argued below, because of these oversights, research guided by both contextual and content approaches often contributes relatively little to our understanding of how communication operates during socialization. Furthermore, despite the prominence of communication variables in research guided by a memorable messages approach (Barge & Schlueter, 2004; Stohl 1986), a review of the literature suggests that a number of key communication variables have yet to be examined by memorable messages scholars.

Communication Critique of Contextual and Content Approaches

As discussed earlier, researchers adopting the contextual and content approaches to examining socialization often use existing measures to study organizational socialization. Thus, research guided by these approaches is replete with short-comings imposed by the popularity of measures that are employed, despite their limitations. For example, Jones' (1986) measure of socialization tactics is used extensively by researchers who are interested in understanding the situations in which newcomers learn preferred behaviors and orientations within organizations. Although Jones' measure includes items that are related to communication within organizations (e.g., "Almost all of my colleagues have been supportive of me personally," and "I have little or no access to people who have previously performed my role in this organization" p. 278), the content and form of these tactics (i.e., *what* and *how* support and information is conveyed) is not captured (Jablin, 2001). Thus, insofar as the majority of scholars who adopt the contextual approach use Jones' socialization scales, most of the research guided by this approach provides scant information regarding potentially influential communicative elements (e.g., the source and content of messages). Given the importance of message content and the potential influence of message sources, additional research that examines these, and other, communication variables would contribute to our understanding of newcomer socialization.

Much like the omission of important communication variables in research guided by the contextual approach, researchers who adopt the content approach to studying socialization (e.g., Hart & Miller, 2005; Haueter et al., 2003) are also limited by the shortcomings that characterize popular content measures, including frequent exclusion of important communication variables. For example, although Chao et al.'s (1994) measure of socialization content can be useful for capturing information that describes incumbents' perceived knowledge in various domains, the measure does not capture important communication elements, such as the source and timing of the information that incumbents receive. Therefore, research guided by the content approach falls short of providing insight regarding factors that influence the efficiency with which newcomers develop knowledge schemas or the efficacy of different techniques that are intended to enhance newcomers' knowledge. Future efforts that examine how newcomers build their knowledge store, such as assessing where newcomers get information and how the information is conveyed, will contribute to our understanding of how newcomers successfully acquire relevant organizational information.

In addition, researchers interested in socialization content rarely assess newcomers' perceived value of, and acceptance of, content that falls within Chao et al.'s (1994) six knowledge areas (Klein & Heuser, 2008). With few exceptions (e.g., Hart, 2012; Myers & McPhee, 2006), researchers guided by the content approach overlook potential relationships that may be found among the receipt of messages and newcomers' subsequent values, attitudes, and behaviors (Brim, 1966). Thus, the extent to which newcomers agree or comply with messages that convey socialization content remains unclear. In addition, we also know relatively little about whether newcomers perceive such messages as helpful (Barge & Schlueter, 2004; Kammeyer-Mueller &

Wanberg, 2003) and whether or how such messages influence newcomer behaviors and attitudes across different contextual environments. Chen (2005), for instance, found that newcomers placed on high performing teams outperformed those placed on low performing teams. Although this finding is useful, our ability to explain why newcomers' performance differed between high and low performing teams requires examination of potential mechanisms, such as the specific socialization content and the nature of messages espoused by high and low performing teams.

Communication Critique of the Memorable Messages Approach

Unlike organizational scholars who adopt contextual and content approaches, researchers guided by the memorable messages approach (Barge & Schlueter, 2004; Stohl, 1986) focus explicitly on the source, content, and value of messages received by organizational incumbents. For instance, researchers who adopt this approach to studying socialization ask organizational members to recall specific messages that are provided by coworkers (or other prominent organizational members), which are perceived as having had a substantial impact on members' work life. The open-ended nature of memorable message responses allows researchers to capture specific message content, which can provide rich insights into the information needs of newcomers and their role readiness (Jablin, 2001) as well as insights into how memorable messages structure the experiences of newcomers (McPhee & Zaug, 2000).

This method of studying communication during socialization, however, is not without its shortcomings. Specifically, researchers who solicit memorable messages rely on organizational members' retrospective self-reports to gather information about influential messages, sometimes requiring respondents to recall messages that were received 20 years previously (Barge & Schlueter, 2004; Stohl, 1986). Recalled messages may be highly dependent on personal (or recent) circumstances, which could influence messages that are deemed particularly salient or influential at the time of data collection (Sias, 1996). In addition, because memorable messages are recalled from memory, the content validity of reported messages becomes suspect (Stafford & Daly, 1984). Future investigations might begin to address this issue by employing longitudinal study designs that include solicitation of memorable messages at multiple time-points, or by implementing diverse methods that enable comparisons between original messages and recalled messages. For example, obtaining communication records for employees working in virtual/remote locations would allow researchers to compare original message content to the memorable messages reported by employees. In doing so, one might better assess the extent to which memorable messages are recalled accurately, while also examining the extent to which messages are memorable across certain circumstances and contexts.

Scholars might also employ additional methodological approaches to look at memorable messages to help reduce reliance on pure recall. Utilizing a diary method in which newcomers keep a journal of impactful messages

(Waddington, 2005), or conversational reconstruction of memorable message exchanges (Sias, 1996), might help elucidate the specific contexts in which memorable messages are most likely to be received (e.g., Barge & Schlueter, 2004). Such methodologies might also illuminate the unique characteristics that make messages both meaningful and memorable to message recipients (Barge & Schlueter, 2004; Jablin, 2001; Saks et al., 2007).

Applying Multilevel Theory and Examining Communication in Future Research on Organizational Socialization

Current approaches to measuring socialization (e.g., Chao et al., 1994; Jones, 1986; Stohl, 1986) will require rigorous adaptation if the goal is to capture important communicative and multilevel phenomena. Although communicative interactions within one's specific work unit are said to influence newcomers' attitudes and behaviors (Jablin, 2001; Kozlowski & Bell, 2012; Kramer, 2010), inadequate methodological developments have prevented researchers from substantiating the direction and degree of both multilevel and communicative influences that occur during socialization. Recent efforts to create guidelines and primers for developing and testing multilevel theory are now readily available (Kashy & Kenny, 2000; Klein & Kozlowski, 2000; Miller et al. 2011; Scott & Myers, 2010; Slater, Synder, & Hayes, 2006), thus rendering this an opportune time to begin engaging in rigorous multilevel thinking.

Multilevel Theory Applications

Whether constructing new or adopting older psychometric batteries, it is essential that measures reflect researchers' conceptualizations of the construct(s) of interest. When studying multilevel systems, theorizing about the level(s) at which the phenomenon of interest manifests itself is of paramount importance when defining the constructs and specifying their level of analysis (Klein et al., 1994; Pan & McLeod, 1991; Slater et al., 2006). Future theorizing should also include considerations regarding constructs that are likely to emerge during the process of socialization, including properties that emerge through compositional and compilational processes. These basic considerations will allow researchers to assess whether the phenomenon of interest is best represented by single-level, cross-level, or homologous models.

In its current state, the socialization corpus contains an overabundance of single-level models in comparison to its multilevel nature (Kramer & Miller, 2014). *Single-level models* are used to represent relationships among constructs that are specified at the same level of analysis (e.g., predictors and outcomes are both situated at one specific level of analysis; Klein & Kozlowski, 2000). For example, a single-level model could be used to represent the relationship between newcomers' individualized socialization entry context, information seeking behaviors, subsequent role clarity, etc. (Bauer et al., 2007; Miller & Jablin, 1991). Alternatively, researchers could use a single-level model to represent the relationship between team-level efficacy and team-level effectiveness (Stajkovic, Lee, & Nyberg, 2009), or between organization-level onboarding practices, organizational-level mentoring systems, and organizational-level productivity (Bauer, Erdogan, & Simon, 2014).

Cross-level models are used to represent relationships among constructs that exist at different levels of analysis (Klein & Kozlowski, 2000). For instance, Chen, Kanfer, DeShon, Mathieu, and Kozlowski (2009) examined a cross-level model of the relationships between team performance, individuals' self-efficacy, and individuals' goal-striving efforts. Researchers can also examine more complex cross-level models, such as models that include cross-level moderation (e.g., organizational performance that cross-moderates the relationship between departmental efficacy and departmental performance; see Figure 11.1 for a general visualization of this model). Within the socialization corpus, recent work conducted by Myers and McPhee (2006) provides evidence of group-level variables (i.e., crew performance) combining non-additively with individual-level predictors (e.g., acculturation, involvement) to affect individual-level outcomes (e.g., commitment).

A third type of model, *homologous models*, is used to represent functional equivalence in addition to similar magnitudes and directions of relationships between constructs at multiple levels of analysis (Klein & Kozlowski, 2000). The classic Staw, Sandelands, and Dutton (1981) argument for threat-rigidity effects operating at individual-, group-, and organizational-levels is one of the more well-known uses of a homologous model. More recently, DeShon, Kozlowski, Schmidt, Milner, and Wiechmann (2004) found evidence that team-regulatory feedback processes aided team-level performance, which was similar to how individual self-regulatory feedback processes increased individual performance. Self-regulatory feedback processes thus operated similarly across two different levels of analysis, which provided evidence of homology. In terms of socialization phenomena, documenting the parallel effects of supportiveness on communication climate as they occur across team-, department-, and organizational-levels of analysis would also provide evidence for homology.

As noted earlier, readers can find a more detailed discussion of these multilevel models in Klein and Kozlowski (2000) and Klein et al. (1994). In its most basic form, however, multilevel theorizing requires researchers to begin with specification of the locus at which the primary constructs of interest reside. After establishing the level at which the constructs exist, specifying how the primary constructs of interest relate to other constructs both within and between organizational levels of interest is crucial to multilevel theorizing. For example, researchers may theorize that organizational-level variables have direct effects on team-level variables, and thus specify their relationships at those theoretical levels of analysis. Conversely, other research may hypothesize that commonly used individual-level variables (e.g., giving or receiving social support, proactive information seeking behaviors) impact newcomer learning and sense-making over time. Such multilevel considerations will build

MULTILEVEL THEORY AND COMMUNICATION

Single-level Model(s)

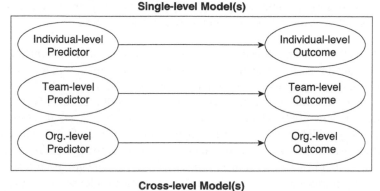

Cross-level Model(s)

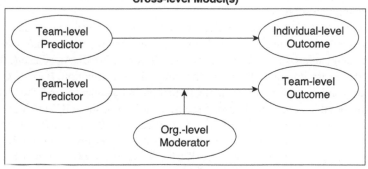

Homologous Model(s)

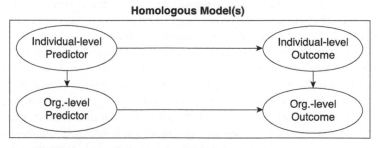

Figure 11.1 General Forms of Multilevel Models

foundational links between constructs as they exist within single-level, cross-level, or homologous models, ultimately forming the basis for understanding socialization as a multilevel process. In light of these multilevel considerations, we offer the first principle (P1) for guiding future socialization scholarship:

Principle 1. Before attempting any empirical investigations, theorize about how the phenomena of interest occur both within and between levels of analysis.

Principle 1a. At minimum, single-level, cross-level, and homologous models should be specified, whereby individual, team, and organizational levels of analysis are considered. Incorporation of other theoretical levels of analysis (e.g., time, sub-groups, departments) and more complex models will also inform the newcomer socialization corpus.

In addition to explicating constructs at the specific level(s) of theoretical interest (e.g., organizational-level socialization practices), testing for non-independence or within-group agreement is essential to justifying the use of multilevel statistics and establishing group-level construct validity (Bliese, 2000; Hofmann, Griffin, & Gavin, 2000; Klein & Kozlowski, 2000). Researchers need to rely on empirical evidence, not unfounded assumptions, to argue for the existence and effects of higher level contextual factors. Thus, prior to aggregating scores, researchers should test to see if there is a basis for generating group-level scores (substantial within-group agreement) and conducting multilevel analyses (non-independence in scores).

Intra-class correlations, for instance, have been used to evaluate the degree to which individuals within a designated unit (e.g., department) are *non-independent* or interchangeable (Bliese, 2000; Kozlowski & Klein, 2000). As Bliese (2000) notes, the most common form of the intra-class correlation (i.e., ICC[1]) has been used by others to estimate both non-independence and the extent to which member scores are homogeneous. That is, a positive ICC(1) indicates that member responses are clustered and in agreement (Bartko, 1976), which is why some scholars use it to justify the aggregation of lower-level scores to higher levels of analysis (for procedure, see Kashy & Kenny, 2000; see also Bliese, 2000). Others interpret the ICC(1) as the proportion of variance that is due to the theoretical level of interest (e.g., group, department, organization). For example, a positive ICC(1) of .20 derived from a random coefficient model indicates that 20% of the variance in the outcome measure is attributable to between-unit differences (Bliese, 2000; Kashy & Kenny, 2000; Raudenbush & Bryk, 2002; Singer & Willett, 2003). Establishing non-independence in the outcome measure is necessary to justify the use of a multilevel model; to wit, there is little reason to believe that higher-level contextual factors will explain much variance in the outcome measure if it fails to vary between units. An informative discussion of numerous types of intra-class correlations and their myriad intricacies can be found in Algina (1978), Bartko (1976), McGraw and Wong (1996), and Schrout and Fleiss (1979).

Multilevel research thus requires the implementation of two important steps: (1) to provide statistical evidence that documents the existence of group-level properties (e.g., shared group-member perceptions); and (2) to show that member scores depend on some higher-level contextual factor (e.g., group affiliation). In the absence of sufficient evidence documenting within-group agreement or non-independence, whether one is investigating unit-level properties becomes questionable. In addition, when examining phenomena that occur both within and between units, estimating non-independence in one's dataset is crucial because many statistical procedures (e.g., regression) are appropriate only when independence of observations is assumed. Specifically, if there is evidence of substantial non-independence in the data (i.e., if responses cluster by groups), alternative statistical procedures are necessary as traditional statistical models (e.g., OLS regression) provide disparate answers. Techniques have been developed that allow researchers to test for multilevel effects, such as hierarchical linear modeling (Park, 2011; Raudenbush & Bryk, 2002; Singer, 1998). Statistical procedures for assessing organizational networks are also able to establish the existence of groups and analyze non-independent data (Borgatti, Mehra, Brass, & Labianca, 2009; Butts, 2009; Newman, 2010). Upon mapping the network of interest by establishing theoretically relevant nodes and ties, researchers can use various cluster analyses (e.g., Q-statistic; Newman, 2006) or the external-internal index (Hanneman & Riddle, 2005) to establish the existence of pertinent organizational units (e.g., teams, departments). Similar to ICCs, these network statistics are used to establish the existence of group-level phenomena, as such evidence is typically necessary to conclude that we are in fact looking at group-level properties. With this in mind, we offer a second principle (P2):

Principle 2. Align theory (P1) and methods by providing evidence for the existence of contextual factors, and then conduct empirical explorations at the correct level of analysis.

Principle 2a. Assess non-independence and within-group agreement when higher-level contextual factors are assumed. These analyses will help determine the extent to which variables vary both within and between levels of analysis, and whether planned statistical analyses are applicable.

Communication Applications

Explication of the *process* by which meaning is conveyed and derived among organizational incumbents constitutes one of the most valuable contributions of communication scholarship (Poole, 2010). At a minimum, investigating the process of socialization requires that communication scholars investigate message content, sources, and the nature (e.g., timing, content) by which role-sending and role-taking occurs (Jablin, 2001; Klein & Heuser, 2008; Kramer, 2010). Without making such fine theoretical distinctions, the probability of successfully understanding important socialization elements decreases substantially.

To illustrate the importance of this point, we present an example of a non-communication study. Research by Chen and colleagues (2005; Chen & Klimoski, 2003) suggests that newcomer performance levels increase when presented with high team expectations. That is, team-level expectations, as constituted by team performance levels, are said to influence individual-level newcomer behavior. However, the communicative nature (e.g., content, manner) of incumbent expectations and their timing were not in the purview of these studies. This exclusion makes it difficult to discern exactly how team expectations influenced member behaviors. From a communication perspective, empirical

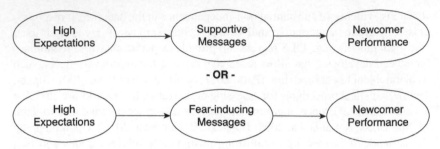

Figure 11.2 An Instance in which the Mediating Nature of Communicative Phenomena May Change a Causal Model.

evidence indicates that high expectations can be communicated in ways that instill confidence by conveying notions of belief (e.g., Pygmalion; Harris & Rosenthal, 1985), or, alternatively, in ways that instill fear (e.g., concertive control; Barker, 1993). Thus, depending on *what* and *how* expectations are conveyed, the causal model postulating the expectation-performance link may change (see Figure 11.2). It is possible that Chen and colleagues' assumptions will be substantiated over time, but it is important to test the communication constructs underlying such assumptions.

Theoretical awareness should guide scholars to consider the specific manifestations of communicative instances that are most likely associated with their phenomenon of interest. Such contemplations are likely to drive key communicative hypotheses, and thus illuminate important relationships (cf. Bunge, 2004; cf. Ilgen, Hollenbeck, Johnson, & Jundt, 2005) that drive key socialization outcomes (e.g., learning, well-being, performance). Moreover, in conjunction with multilevel analyses, researchers can investigate differences in communication acts and experiences as they occur between and across levels of analysis. Researchers, for instance, can explore differences in how teams socialize newcomers by examining the consistency in content as it is conveyed between teams. To wit, rather than simply inferring acts of communication (e.g., Chen, 2005), researchers can theorize about them as they occur during socialization:

> **Principle 3**. Consider communicative processes as they occur during new-comer socialization. At minimum, this requires consideration of message content (*what*), message sources (*who*), and interaction contexts (*when* and *how* interactions occur). These communicative variables will likely manifest as mediators, but can also take on the role of independent or dependent variables.
>
> **Principle 3a**. Communicative processes that take place during socialization can occur at and across numerous levels, such that they can occur at a single level of analysis (e.g., individual → individual), or between differ-ent levels of analysis (e.g., organizational → departmental).

With this principle, we contend that socialization scholarship can be advanced via the thoughtful explication of message conveyance and meaning creation as it occurs across multiple levels of analysis. Contributions that stem from these theoretical advancements, however, will only come to light as scholars enrich current methodological approaches or develop new ones. To be sure, the systematic measurement of key communicative phenomena that occur during socialization is of paramount importance (e.g., Jablin, 2001; Klein & Heuser, 2008; Kramer & Miller, 2014). We agree and also contend that such efforts geared toward the systematic measurement of communication will offer a more thorough examination of how numerous unit-initiated messages influence myriad unit- or organizational-level variables (e.g., work climates; McPhee & Zaug, 2000; Poole, 2010). As such, a fourth principle is offered that emphasizes the importance of moving beyond mere theorizing to implementing measures that capture myriad communicative phenomena in a valid manner:

Principle 4. Advancements in newcomer socialization research will stem from using valid measurement that captures key communicative phenomena.

Principle 4a. These advancements will come from both adopting and reframing common socialization measures and methods, as well as developing new ones.

We believe that the integration of these four principles will advance knowledge about fundamental micro-level communicative processes that are common to organizational entry experiences as they occur across similar levels of analysis (e.g., organization to organization; Contractor, Wasserman, & Faust, 2006), or between levels of analysis (e.g., team to individual; Myers & McPhee, 2006). Moreover, despite our general focus on the important role of mediation, adoption of these principles will allow for situations in which communication variables are treated more broadly as either independent or dependent variables. For instance, instead of evaluating how supportive messages mediate the relationship between high team expectations and newcomer performance (Figure 11.2), one might theorize about how supportive messages either predict, or are predicted by, other important socialization variables. Accumulating knowledge about these fundamental communicative processes will, in turn, be integral to modeling myriad socialization outcomes as emergent phenomena (cf. Kozlowski & Klein, 2000). In their constitutive approach to studying organizations, for example, McPhee and Zaug (2000) explicated numerous communicative message flows (e.g., activity coordination, institutional positioning) that allow for the eventual emergence of the organization (see also Putnam & Nicotera, 2009). Similarly, Barker's (1993) explication of norm emergence is based on the premise that acceptable group-level behavior is established via nuanced discussion between members as they complete tasks and make sense of their environment. Indeed, understanding how various contextual factors emerge (e.g., team goals; DeShon et al., 2004) during newcomer socialization will require, at minimum, the modeling and application of our central communicative mantra (P3): *who*, *what*, *when*, and *how*. Such modeling will presumably allow scholars to move beyond basic information sharing to conceptualizing communication as a back-and-forth process that emerges over time in a complex manner. In consequence, we offer a fifth and final principle:

> **Principle 5.** Modeling emergence will be aided by the careful consideration and integration of all four principles. As this integration occurs, incorporation of other non-communication variables (e.g., group cohesion, departmental trust) will also inform the newcomer socialization corpus.

Concluding Remarks

With few exceptions (e.g., Myers & McPhee, 2006), research considering both socialization and communication has been entirely at the individual-level of analysis and, as this review points out, fraught with validity issues. As a result, Klein and Heuser's (2008) observations of socialization scholarship continue to reflect the state of socialization research,

> There have been a few studies examining socialization at multiple levels . . . but precisely how the content of what needs to be learned differs across those different levels has received little attention and, as a result, the academic basis for recommending what content needs to be mastered for each level is limited.
>
> (p. 310)

In an effort to mitigate these criticisms, we contend that adopting multilevel research practices that account for communicative variables can provide greater explanatory power and yield additional insights into communicative processes that occur at all levels of the organization (Jablin, 2001; Kramer & Miller, 2014; Scott & Myers, 2010). Indeed, we believe that implementing the principles set-forth in this chapter will help advance socialization scholarship beyond its current state, in which communicative behaviors are often *inferred* or implied (e.g., Chen, 2005), to a state in which researchers *theorize* about communication and *measure* communicative acts as they occur across multiple levels of analysis.

Additional Remarks

Five additional points merit mentioning for those interested in measuring multilevel properties and communication during newcomer socialization. First, when working with constructs at multiple levels of analysis, it is important to (a) ensure that variables vary between units of analysis (Klein & Kozlowski, 2000) and (b) consider sample size (Maas & Hox, 2005). To be sure, ensuring substantial between-unit variance in one's independent measure(s) is critical for testing multilevel models (Klein & Kozlowski, 2000). Specifically, if an independent, higher-level contextual factor lacks substantial between-unit variation (e.g., departments within an organization are indistinguishable), then aggregation is unwarranted. Similarly, if variance in a criterion variable is not due to unit-level differences, then variation in the criterion variable is likely explained by other non-contextual factors. Scholars must thus seek to capture substantial between-unit variation in both independent and dependent variables if they hope to give their models a fair, testable shake (Kozlowski & Klein, 2000).

Moreover, when working with higher-level constructs (e.g., teams, departments, organizations), organizational scholars often have no choice but to work with smaller sample sizes (Maas & Hox, 2005). In contrast to samples of 300 to 400 participants, which are more easily amassed in studies of individual-level properties, obtaining large samples for assessing macro-level effects is often not feasible. Thus, studies examining macro-level effects are inherently plagued by low statistical power (Maas & Hox, 2005). Working with larger (and many) organizations (which presumably contain substantial variance between a large number of sub-units) is one way that researchers can try to minimize these limitations when studying multilevel effects.

Second, investigating the *dynamic process* of socialization will require the theoretical and statistical treatments of time and its relevant counterparts (Chen, 2005; Klein & Heuser, 2008; Kozlowski & Bell, 2012; Kozlowski, Chao, Grand, Braun, & Kuljanin, 2013; Kozlowski & Ilgen, 2006; Kramer & Miller, 2014; Miller & Dibble, 2009; Monge, 1990). Indeed, as newcomers acquire knowledge and develop integral role-related competencies, socialization agents may alter the content and timing of socialization experiences (Ashforth & Saks, 1996; Chao, 1997; Klein & Heuser, 2008; Reichers, 1987; Wanous, Reichers, & Malik, 1984), especially if these experiences involve apprenticeship periods (Perrot et al., 2014), job enlargements, or promotions (Kramer & Hoelscher, 2014). Longitudinal studies that assess incremental changes in patterns of communication over time may help researchers better delineate unique phases as organizational members develop and negotiate their roles (Kramer, 2009; 2010), as well as *when* socialization messages have their greatest impact on newcomers (Klein & Heuser, 2008; Miller & Dibble, 2009).

Third, investigations of socialization as a dynamic process will also begin to allow for the study of emergent communicative phenomena, especially as they manifest at multiple levels of analysis (P5). As a caveat, however, it is important to note that modeling emergence is a difficult methodological problem that is still in development. Attempting to model emergence with HLM (a popular tool used for assessing multilevel hypotheses), for instance, is inappropriate because the hierarchical nature of the model assumes that influence between levels occurs in top-down fashion (Hofmann et al., 2000). A potential solution to this problem includes the integration of Agent Based Modeling (ABM), where researchers attempt to simulate the emergence of various macro-level phenomena by stipulating the micro-level processes deemed responsible for emergence (Railsback & Grimm, 2011). Such modeling may be useful for testing the validity of myriad constitutive hypotheses in which emergent outcomes (e.g., organization; McPhee & Zaug, 2000) are predicted by numerous micro-level processes. ABM, however, is unlikely the perfect solution, as such modeling is primarily used for theoretical purposes and becomes excessively complicated when attempting to reproduce actual data. Understanding how interpersonal behaviors manifest and become meaningful at higher levels of analysis will likely come from implementing different methodological techniques (either quantitative or qualitative), many of which are either under-developed or do not yet exist.

Fourth, of the socialization measures that do exist, however, it is clear that scholars would benefit from redeveloping and validating long-forgotten scales (P4). Pascale (1985), for instance, posited that successful "strong culture" organizations shape the workforce by accentuating seven important aspects of the socialization process (e.g., humility inducing experiences, reinforcing folklore). Although little work has been done using Pascale's theoretical framework (e.g., Caldwell, Chatman, & O'Reilly, 1990; Chatman, 1991), attempting to unearth the integral dimensions of organizational culture as it occurs across organizational levels strikes us as a laudable pursuit. Moreover, targeted uses of other promising scales that have already begun to address some of the issues presented in this manuscript also appear to be worthwhile research endeavors. Some efforts of note include Myers and colleagues' (Gailliard et al., 2010; Myers & Oetzel, 2003) organizational assimilation instrument, Riddle, Anderson, and Martin's (2000) small group communication scale, and Wright and Barker's (2000) concertive control scale.

Fifth, the measurement of multilevel phenomena and communication as it occurs during socialization can also benefit from a range of methodological approaches. Investigating the long-term impact of socialization contexts or message content via mixed methods, for instance, will certainly help provide a richer picture of the socialization process (Myers, 2011). Methodological approaches might include observing or interviewing newcomers during organizational entry to discover messages and stories received as well as information learned about the job, unit, and organization. These factors can then be examined in relation to the emergence of norms, informal structures, and patterns of communication (e.g., Barker, 1993; Dailey & Browning, 2014; Scott & Myers, 2010).

Using qualitative approaches to implement the principles presented herein, however, will require the special consideration of certain challenges, such as how to establish within-group agreement or non-independence (e.g., Principle 2). Although we do not address how our quantitatively-geared principles can be integrated with more qualitative approaches—a true limitation of this chapter—we do not feel as though the task is insurmountable. As Taylor and Trujillo (2001) point out, there is a variety of means by which claims of validity can be supported, depending on the epistemological position that one adopts. We encourage qualitative researchers to conduct emic and inductive analyses (Taylor & Trujillo, 2001) across extensive samples, with triangulation of multiple data sources and levels and checks to provide evidence of commonality in newcomers' communicative experiences. Similarly, negative case analysis (Taylor & Trujillo, 2001) may be a valuable tool for showing that a given communication construct (e.g., supportiveness) is not present at the group or organizational level. Providing qualitative evidence that a unit-level construct fails to be reproduced as theorized is of considerable value; it offers researchers opportunities to distinguish between sources of influence, such as separating individual versus unit influences and identifying whether or not there are differences between units (Kramer & Miller, 2014).

We conclude by reminding the reader that a review of socialization literature highlights the need for more multilevel theorizing and measures that capture both communicative and multilevel influences. To be sure, despite naming only a few communication constructs, many of which may serve as either independent, mediating, or dependent variables, the field of communication is replete with constructs that may help illuminate the process of newcomer socialization. Quantitative and qualitative investigations, for instance, have yet to examine communicative elements such as supervisor or coworker communication competence in message sending or receptivity, the ability to enact an authoritative text that supersedes others' articulations, and how individual incumbents communicatively reinforce group norms. Explorations of Scott and Myer's (2010) notion of organizational norm reproduction and discursive consciousness also hold great value. The importance of exploring these basic aspects becomes even more apparent when embracing a multilevel perspective. Researchers and practitioners alike have interest in discovering why some units appear to develop newcomers more readily than others, how memorable messages at the individual level may contribute to the unit or organizational culture, and why some norm reinforcement efforts lead to concertive control whereas others lead to supportive work environments. Indeed, as others have begun to echo (e.g., Klein & Heuser, 2008; Kramer & Miller, 2014), acknowledgement of socialization as a multilevel process through which communication plays an important role is certain to broaden our knowledge, measurement, and practice of newcomer socialization.

Acknowledgments

We would like to thank Karen Myers and the two anonymous reviewers for their comments and suggestions on earlier versions of this manuscript.

References

Algina, J. (1978). Comment on Bartko's "On various intraclass correlation reliability coefficients." *Psychological Bulletin, 85*, 135–138. doi: 10.1037/0033-2909.85.1.135
Anderson, N., & Thomas, H. D. C. (1996). Work group socialization. In M. A. West (ed.), *Handbook of work group psychology* (pp. 423–450). Chichester, England: Wiley.

Ashforth, B. E., & Saks, A. M. (1996). Socialization tactics: Longitudinal effects on newcomer adjustment. *Academy of Management Journal, 39,* 149–178. doi: 10.2307/256634

Ashforth, B. E., Saks, A. M., & Lee, R. T. (1998). Socialization and newcomer adjustment: The role of organizational context. *Human Relations, 51,* 897–926. doi: 10.1023/A:1016999527596

Ashforth, B. E., Sluss, D. M., & Harrison, S. H. (2007). Socialization in organizational contexts. In G. P. Hodgkinson, & J. K. Ford (Eds.), *International review of industrial and organizational psychology* (Vol. 22, pp. 1–70). Chichester, UK: Wiley.

Barge, K. J., & Schlueter, D. W. (2004). Memorable messages and newcomer socialization. *Western Journal of Communication, 68,* 233–256. doi: 10.1080/105703 10409374800

Barker, J. R. (1993). Tightening the iron cage: Concertive control in self-managing teams. *Administrative Science Quarterly, 38,* 408–437. doi: 10.2307/2393374

Bartko, J. J. (1976). On various intraclass correlation reliability coefficients. *Psychological Bulletin, 83*(5), 762–765. doi: 10.1037/0033-2909.83.5.762

Bauer, T. N., & Erdogan, B. (2011). Organizational socialization: The effective onboarding of new employees. In S. Zedeck (Ed.), *APA handbook of industrial and organizational psychology* (Vol. 2, pp. 51–64). Washington, DC: American Psychological Association.

Bauer, T. N., & Erdogan, B. (2014). Delineating and reviewing the role of newcomer capital in organizational socialization. *Annual Review of Organizational Psychology and Organizational Behavior, 1,* 439–457. doi: 10.1146/annurev-orgpsych-031413-091251

Bauer, T. N., Erdogan, B., & Simon, L. (2014). Effective new employee socialization: A review of the critical role of communication. In V. D. Miller, & M. E. Gordon (Eds.), *Meeting the challenges of human resource management: A communication perspective* (pp. 52–63). New York, NY: Routledge.

Bauer, T. N., Bodner, T., Erdogan, B., Truxillo, D. M., & Tucker, J. S. (2007). Newcomer adjustment during organizational socialization: A meta-analytic review of antecedents, outcomes, and methods. *Journal of Applied Psychology, 92,* 707–721. doi: 10.1037/0021-9010.92.3.707

Bibby, R. W., & Brinkerhoff, M. B. (1974). When proselytizing fails: An organizational analysis. *Sociological Analysis, 35,* 189–200. doi: 10.2307/3710649

Bliese, P. (2000). Within-group agreement, non-independence, and reliability: Implications for data aggregation and analysis. In K. J. Klein, & S. W. J. Kozlowski (Eds.), *Multilevel theory, research and methods in organizations* (pp. 349–381). San Francisco, CA: Jossey-Bass.

Borgatti, S. P., Mehra, A., Brass, D. J., & Labianca, G. (2009). Network analysis in the social sciences. *Science, 323,* 892–895. doi: 10.1126/science.1165821

Brim, O. G., Jr. (1966). Socialization through the life cycle. In O. G. Brim Jr., & S. Wheeler (Eds.), *Socialization after childhood: Two essays* (pp. 1–49). New York, NY: Wiley.

Bunge, M. (2004). How does it work? The search for explanatory mechanisms. *Philosophy of the Social Sciences, 34,* 182–210. doi: 10.1177/0048393103262550

Butts, C. T. (2009). Revisiting the foundations of network analysis. *Science, 325,* 414–416. doi: 10.1126/science.1171022

Caldwell, D. F., Chatman, J. A., & O'Reilly, C. A. (1990). Building organizational commitment: A multifirm study. *Journal of Occupational Psychology, 63,* 245–261. doi: 10.1111/j.2044-8325.1990.tb00525.x

Chao, G. T. (1997). Unstructured training and development. In K. Ford & Associates (Eds.), *Improving training effectiveness in work organizations* (pp. 129–151). Mahwah, NJ: Lawrence Erlbaum Associates.

Chao, G. T. (2012). Organizational socialization: Background, basics, and blueprint for adjustment at work. In S. W. J. Kozlowski (Ed.), *The Oxford handbook of organizational psychology* (pp. 579–614). New York, NY: Oxford University Press.

Chao, G. T., O'Leary-Kelly, A. M., Wolf, S., Klein, H. J., & Gardner, P. D. (1994). Organizational socialization: Its content and consequences. *Journal of Applied Psychology, 79*, 730–743. doi: 10.1037/0021-9010.79.5.730

Chatman, J. A. (1991). Matching people and organizations: Selection and socialization in public accounting firms. *Administrative Science Quarterly, 36*, 459–484. doi: 10.5465/AMBPP.1989.4980837

Chen, G. (2005). Newcomer adaptation in teams: Multilevel antecedents and outcomes. *Academy of Management Journal, 48*, 101–116. doi: 10.5465/AMJ.2005. 15993147

Chen, G., & Klimoski, R. J. (2003). The impact of expectations on newcomer performance in teams as mediated by work characteristics, social exchanges, and empowerment. *Academy of Management Journal, 46*, 591–607. doi: 10.2307/30040651

Chen, G., Kanfer, R., DeShon, R. P., Mathieu, J. E., & Kozlowski, S. W. J. (2009). The motivating potential of teams: Testing and extension of Chen and Kanfer's (2006) cross-level model of motivation in teams. *Organizational Behavior and Human Decision Processes, 110*, 45–55. doi: 10.1016/j.obhdp.2009.06.006

Contractor, N. S., Wasserman, S., & Faust, K. (2006). Testing multitheoretical, multilevel hypotheses about organizational networks: An analytic framework and empirical example. *Academy of Management Review, 31*, 681–703. doi: 10.5465/ amr.2006. 21318925

Dailey, S. L., & Browning, L. (2014). Retelling stories in organizations: Understanding the functions of narrative repetition. *Academy of Management Review, 39*, 22–43. doi: 10.5465/amr.2011.0329

De Jong, B. A., & Dirks, K. T. (2012). Beyond shared perceptions of trust and monitoring in teams: Implications of asymmetry and dissensus. *Journal of Applied Psychology, 97*, 391–406. doi: 10.1037/a0026483

DeShon, R. P., Kozlowski, S. W. J., Schmidt, A. M., Milner, K. R., & Wiechmann, D. (2004). A multiple-goal, multilevel model of feedback effects on the regulation of individual and team performance. *Journal of Applied Psychology, 89*, 1035–1056. doi: 10.1037/0021-9010.89.6.1035

Edwards, J. R. (2003). Construct validation in organizational behavior research. In J. Greenberg (Ed.), *Organizational behavior: The state of the science* (2nd edn, pp. 327–371). Mahwah, NJ: Erlbaum.

Eisenberger, R., Karagonlar, G., Stinglhamber, F., Neves, P., Becker, T. E., Gonzalez-Morales, M. G., & Steiger-Mueller, M. (2010). Leader-member exchange and affective organizational commitment: The contribution of supervisor's organizational embodiment. *Journal of Applied Psychology, 95*, 1085–1103. doi: 10.1037/ a0020858

Feldman, D. C. (1976). A contingency theory of socialization. *Administrative Science Quarterly, 21*, 433–452.

Gailliard, B. M., Myers, K. K., & Seibold, D. R. (2010). Organizational assimilation: A multidimensional reconceptualization and measure. *Management Communication Quarterly, 24*, 552–578. doi: 10.1177/0893318910374933

Gallagher, E. B., & Sias, P. M. (2009). The new employee as a source of uncertainty: Veteran employee information seeking about new hires. *Western Journal of Communication, 73*, 23–46. doi: 10.1080/10570310802636326

Hanneman, R. A., & Riddle, M. (2005). *Introduction to social network methods.* Riverside, CA: University of California, Riverside.

Harris, M. J., & Rosenthal, R. (1985). Mediation of interpersonal expectancy effects: 31 meta-analyses. *Psychological Bulletin, 97*, 363–386. doi: 10.1037/0033-2909.97. 3.363

Hart, Z. (2012). Message content and sources during organizational socialization. *Journal of Business Communication, 49*, 191–209. doi: 10.1177/0021943612446731

Hart, Z., & Miller, V. D. (2005). Context and message content during organizational socialization. *Human Communication Research, 31*, 295–309. doi: 10.1093/hcr/31.2.295

Haueter, J. A., Macan, T. H., & Winter, J. (2003). Measurement of newcomer socialization: Construct validation of a multidimensional scale. *Journal of Vocational Behavior, 63*, 20–39. doi: 10.1016/S0001-8791(02)00017-9

Hofmann, D. A., Griffin, M. A., & Gavin, M. B. (2000). The application of hierarchical linear modeling to organizational research. In K. J. Klein, & S. W. J. Kozlowski (Eds.), *Multilevel theory, research and methods in organizations* (pp. 467–511). San Francisco, CA: Jossey-Bass.

Hyde, D. (1966). *Dedication and leadership: Learning from the communists.* Notre Dame, IN: University of Notre Dame Press.

Ilgen, D. R., Hollenbeck, J. R., Johnson, M., & Jundt, D. (2005). Teams in organizations: From input-process-output models to IMOI models. *Annual Review of Psychology, 56*, 517–543. doi: 10.1146/annurev.psych.56.091103.070250

Jablin, F. M. (2001). Organizational entry, assimilation, and disengagement/ exit. In F. M. Jablin, & L. L. Putnam (Eds.), *The new handbook of organizational communication: Advances in theory, research, and methods* (pp. 732–818). Thousand Oaks, CA: Sage.

James, L. R., Demaree, R. G., & Wolf, G. (1993). r_{wg}: An assessment of within group agreement. *Journal of Applied Psychology, 78*, 306–309. doi: 10.1037/0021-9010.78.2.306

Jones, G. R. (1986). Socialization tactics, self-efficacy, and newcomers' adjustments to organizations. *Academy of Management Journal, 29*, 262–279. doi: 10.2307/256188

Kammeyer-Mueller, J. D., & Wanberg, C. R. (2003). Unwrapping the organizational entry process: Disentangling multiple antecedents and their pathways to adjustment. *Journal of Applied Psychology, 88*, 779–794. doi: 10.1037/0021-9010.88.5.779

Kashy, D. A., & Kenny, D. A. (2000). The analysis of data from dyads and groups. In H. T. Reis, & C. M. Judd (Eds.), *Handbook of research methods in social and personality psychology* (pp. 451–477). Cambridge, UK: Cambridge University Press.

Klein, H. J., & Heuser, A. E. (2008). The learning of socialization content: A framework for researching orientating practices. *Research in Personnel and Human Resource Management, 27*, 279–336. doi: 10.1016/S0742-7301(08)27007-6

Klein, K. J., & Kozlowski, S. W. J. (2000). *Multilevel theory, research, and methods in organizations: Foundations, extensions, and new directions.* San Francisco, CA: Jossey-Bass.

Klein, K. J., Dansereau, F., & Hall, R. J. (1994). Levels issues in theory development, data collection, and analysis. *Academy of Management Review, 19*, 195–229. doi: 10.5465/AMR.1994.9410210745

Klein, K. J., Conn, A. B., Smith, D. B., & Sorra, J. S. (2001). Is everyone in agreement?: An exploration of within-group agreement in employee perceptions of the work environment. *Journal of Applied Psychology, 86,* 3–16. doi: 10.1037/0021-9010.86.1.3

Kozlowski, S. W. J. (2012). Groups and teams in organizations: Studying the multilevel dynamics of emergence. In A. B. Hollingshead, & M. S. Poole (Eds.), *Research methods for studying groups and teams: A guide to approaches, tools, and technologies* (pp. 260–283). New York, NY: Routledge.

Kozlowski, S. W. J., & Bell, B. S. (2012). Work groups and teams in organizations: Review update. In N. Schmitt, & S. Highhouse (Eds.), *Handbook of psychology: Industrial and organizational psychology* (2nd edn, Vol. 12, pp. 412–469). London, UK: Wiley.

Kozlowski, S. W. J., & Hattrup, K. (1992). A disagreement about within-group agreement: Disentangling issues of consistency versus consensus. *Journal of Applied Psychology, 77,* p. 161–167. doi: 10.1037/0021-9010.77.2.161

Kozlowski, S. W. J., & Ilgen, D. R. (2006). Enhancing the effectiveness of work groups and teams. *Psychological Science in the Public Interest, 7,* 77–124. doi: 10.1111/j.1529-1006.2006.00030.x

Kozlowski, S. W. J., & Klein, K. J. (2000). A multilevel approach to theory and research in organizations: Contextual, temporal, and emergent processes. In K. J. Klein, & S. W. J. Kozlowski (Eds.), *Multilevel theory, research and methods in organizations: Foundations, extensions, and new directions* (pp. 3–90). San Francisco, CA: Jossey-Bass.

Kozlowski, S. W. J., Chao, G. T., Grand, J. A., Braun, M. T., & Kuljanin, G. (2013). Advancing multilevel research design: Capturing the dynamics of emergence. *Organizational Research Methods, 16,* 581–615. doi: 10.1177/1094428113493119

Kramer, M. W. (2009). Role negotiations in a temporary organization: Making sense during role development in an educational theater production. *Management Communication Quarterly, 23,* 188–217. doi: 10.1177/0893318909341410

Kramer, M. W. (2010). *Organizational socialization joining and leaving organizations.* Cambridge, UK: Polity.

Kramer, M. W., & Hoelscher, C. S. (2014). Promotions and transfers. In V. D. Miller, & M. E. Gordon (Eds.), *Meeting the challenges of human resource management: A communication perspective* (pp. 64–75). New York, NY: Routledge.

Kramer, M. W., & Miller, V. D. (1999). A response to criticisms of organizational socialization research: In support of contemporary conceptualizations of assimilation. *Communication Monographs, 66,* 358–367. doi: 10.1080/03637759909376485

Kramer, M. W., & Miller, V. D. (2014). Socialization and assimilation: Theories, processes, and outcomes. In L. L. Putnam, & D. Mumby (Eds.), *The Sage handbook of organizational communication* (3rd edn). Thousand Oaks, CA: Sage.

Maas, C. J. M., & Hox, J. J. (2005). Sufficient sample sizes for multilevel modeling. *Methodology, 1,* 86–96. Doi: 10.1027/1614-2241.1.3.86

McGraw, K. O., & Wong, S. P. (1996). Forming inferences about some intraclass correlation coefficients. *Psychological Methods, 1,* 30–46. doi: 10.1037/1082-989x.1.4.390

McPhee, R. D., & Zaug, P. (2000). The communicative constitution of organizations: A framework for explanation. *Electronic Journal of Communication, 10* (1-2), 1–17.

Messick, S. (1995). Standards of validity and the validity of standards in performance assessment. *Educational Measurement: Issues and Practice, 14*(4), 5–8. doi: 10.1111/j.1745-3992.1995.tb00881.x

Miller, V. D., & Dibble, J. (2009, May). *Organizational socialization and communication processes.* Paper presented at the 59th Annual Meeting of the International Communication Association, Chicago, IL.

Miller, V. D., & Jablin, F. M. (1991). Information seeking during organizational entry: Influence, tactics, and a model of the process. *Academy of Management Review, 16,* 92–120. doi: 10.5465/AMR.1991.4278997

Miller, V. D., Poole, M. S., Seibold, D. R., Meyers, K., Park, H. S., Monge, P. R., Fulk, J., Frank, L., Margolin, D., Schultz, C., Cuihua, S., Weber, M., Lee, S., & Shumate, S. (2011). Advancing research in organizational communication through quantitative methodology. *Management Communication Quarterly, 25,* 1–43. doi: 10.1177/0893318910390193

Monge, P. R. (1990). Theoretical and analytical issues in studying organizational processes. *Organization Science, 1,* 406–430. doi: 10.1287/orsc.1.4.406

Moreland, R. L., & Levine, J. M. (1982). Group socialization: Temporal changes in individual-group relations. In L. Berkowitz (Ed.), *Advances in experimental social psychology* (pp. 137–192). New York, NY: Academic Press.

Moreland, R. L., & Levine, J. M. (2001). Socialization in organizations and work groups. In M. E. Turner (Ed.), *Groups at work: Theory and research* (pp. 69–112). Mahwah, NJ: Lawrence Erlbaum Associates.

Myers, K. K. (2011). Mixed methods. In V. D. Miller, M. S. Poole, D. R. Seibold, & Associates, Advancing research in organizational communication through quantitative methodology. *Management Communication Quarterly, 25,* 12–16. doi: 10.1177/0893318910390193

Myers, K. K., & McPhee, R. D. (2006). Influences on member assimilation in workgroups in high reliability organizations: A multilevel analysis. *Human Communication Research, 32,* 440–468. doi: 10.1111/j.1468-2958.2006.00283.x

Myers, K. K., & Oetzel, J. G. (2003). Exploring the dimensions of organizational assimilation: Creating and validating a measure. *Communication Quarterly, 51,* 438–457. doi: 10.1080/01463370309370166

Newman, M. E. J. (2006). Modularity and community structure in networks. *Proceedings of the National Academy of Sciences, 103,* 8577–8582. doi: 10.1073/pnas.0601602103

Newman, M. E. J. (2010). *Networks: An introduction.* New York, NY: Oxford.

Ostroff, C., & Kozlowski, S. W. J. (1992). Organizational socialization as a learning process: The role of information acquisition. *Personnel Psychology, 45,* 849–874. doi: 10.1111/j.1744-6570.1992.tb00971.x

Ostroff, C., & Kozlowski, S. W. J. (1993). The role of mentoring in the information gathering processes of newcomers during early organizational socialization. *Journal of Vocational Behavior, 42,* 170–183. doi: 10.1006/jvbe.1993.1012

Pan, Z., & McLeod, J. M. (1991). Multilevel analysis in mass communication research. *Communication Research, 18,* 140–173. doi: 10.1177/009365091018002002

Park, H. S. (2011). Multilevel analysis. In V. D. Miller, M. S. Poole, D. R. Seibold, & Associates, Advancing research in organizational communication through quantitative methodology. *Management Communication Quarterly, 25,* 17–23. doi: 10.1177/0893318910390193

Pascale, R. (1985). The paradox of corporate culture: Reconciling ourselves to socialization. *California Management Review, 27,* 26–40. doi: 10.2307/41165127

Perrot, A., Bauer, T. N., Abonneau, D., Campoy, E., Erdogan, B., & Liden, R. C. (2014). Organizational socialization tactics and newcomer adjustment: The moderating role of perceived organizational support. *Group & Organization Management, 39*, 247–273. doi: 10.1177/1059601114535469

Poole, M. S. (2010). Communication. In S. Zedeck (Ed.), *APA handbook of industrial and organizational psychology* (pp. 249–270). Washington, DC: APA Books.

Putnam, L. L., & Nicotera, A. M. (2009). *Building theories of organization: The constitutive role of communication.* New York, NY: Routledge.

Railsback, S. F., & Grimm, V. (2011). *Agent-based and individual-based modeling: A practical introduction.* Princeton, NJ: Princeton University Press.

Raudenbush, S. W., & Bryk, A. S. (2002). *Hierarchical linear models: Applications and data analysis methods* (Vol. 1). Thousand Oaks, CA: Sage.

Reichers, A. E. (1987). An interactionist perspective on newcomer socialization rates. *Academy of Management Review, 12*, 278–287. doi: 10.5465/AMR.1987.4307838

Riddle, B. L., Anderson, C. M., & Martin, M. M. (2000). Small group socialization scale: Development and validity. *Small Group Research, 31*, 554–572. doi: 10.1177/104649640003100503

Rink, F., Kane, A. A., Ellemers, N., & Van der Vegt, G. (2013). Team receptivity to newcomers: Five decades of evidence and future research themes. *Academy of Management Annals, 7*, 247–293. doi: 10.1080/19416520.2013.766405

Roberts, K. H., Hulin, C. L., & Rousseau, D. M. (1978). *Developing an interdisciplinary science of organizations.* San Francisco, CA: Jossey-Bass.

Saks, A. M., Uggerslev, K. L., & Fassina, N. E. (2007). Socialization tactics and newcomer adjustment: A meta-analytic review and test of a model. *Journal of Vocational Behavior, 70*, 413–446. doi: 10.1016/j.jvb.2006.12.004

Schmidt, F. L., & Hunter, J. E. (1989). Interrater reliability coefficients cannot be computed when only one stimulus is rated. *Journal of Applied Psychology, 74*, 368–370. doi: 10.1037/0021-9010.74.2.368

Schwarz, N. (1999). Self-reports: How the questions shape the answers. *American Psychologist, 54*, 93–105. doi: 10.1037/0003-066X.54.2.93

Scott, C., & Myers, K. (2010). Toward an integrative theoretical perspective on organizational membership negotiations: Socialization, assimilation, and the duality of structure. *Communication Theory, 20*, 79–105. doi: 10.1111/j.1468-2885.2009.01355.x

Scott, W. R. (1987). *Organizations: Rational, natural, and open systems* (2nd edn). Englewood Cliffs, NJ: Prentice-Hall.

Shrout, P. E., & Fleiss, J. L. (1979). Intraclass correlations: Uses in assessing rater reliability. *Psychological Bulletin, 86*, 420–428. doi: 10.1037/0033-2909.86.2.420

Sias, P. M. (1996). Constructing perceptions of differential treatment: An analysis of coworker discourse. *Communication Monographs, 63*, 171–187. doi: 10.1080/03637759609376385

Singer, J. D. (1998). Using SAS PROC MIXED to fit multilevel models, hierarchical models, and individual growth models. *Journal of Educational and Behavioral Statistics, 23*, 323–355. doi: 10.3102/10769986023004323

Singer, J. D., & Willett, J. B. (2003). *Applied longitudinal data analysis: Modeling change and event occurrence.* New York, NY: Oxford University Press.

Slater, M. D., Synder, L., & Hayes, A. F. (2006). Thinking and modeling at multiple levels: The potential contribution of multilevel modeling to communication theory and research. *Human Communication Research, 32*, 375–384. doi: 10.1111/j.1468-2958.2006.00280.x

Stafford, L., & Daly, J. A. (1984). Conversational memory: The effects of recall mode and memory expectancies on remembrances of natural conversations. *Human Communication Research, 10,* 379–402. doi: 10.1111/j.1468-2958.1984.tb00024.x

Stajkovic, A. D., Lee, D., & Nyberg, A. J. (2009). Collective efficacy, group potency, and group performance: Meta-analyses of their relationships, and test of a mediating model. *Journal of Applied Psychology, 94,* 814–828. doi: 10.1037/a0015659

Staw, B. M., Sandelands, L. E., & Dutton, J. E. (1981). Threat rigidity effects in organizational behavior: A multilevel analysis. *Administrative Science Quarterly, 26,* 501–524. doi: 10.2307/2392337

Stohl, C. (1986). The role of memorable messages in the process of organizational socialization. *Communication Quarterly, 34,* 213–249. doi: 10.1080/01463378609369638

Taylor, B. C., & Trujillo, N. (2001). Qualitative research methods. In F. M. Jablin, & L. L. Putnam (Eds.), *The new handbook of organizational communication: Advances in theory, research, and methods* (pp. 161–194). Thousand Oaks, CA: Sage.

Teboul, J. B. (1994). Facing and coping with uncertainty during organizational encounter. *Management Communication Quarterly, 8,* 190–224. doi: 10.1177/0893318994008002003

Van Maanen, J., & Schein, E. H. (1979). Toward a theory of organizational socialization. *Research in Organizational Behavior, 1,* 209–264.

Waddington, K. (2005). Using diaries to explore the characteristics of work-related gossip: Methodological considerations from exploratory multimethod research. *Journal of Occupational and Organizational Psychology, 78,* 221–236. doi: 10.1348/096317905X40817

Wanous, J. P., Reichers, A. E., & Malik, S. D. (1984). Organizational socialization and group development: Toward an interactionist perspective. *Academy of Management Review, 9,* 670–683. doi: 10.5465/AMR.1984.4277394

Wright, B. M., & Barker, J. B. (2000). Assessing concertive control in the term environment. *Journal of Occupational and Organizational Psychology, 73,* 345–361. doi: 10.1348/096317900167065

Zurcher, A. L. (1983). *Social roles: Conformity, conflict and creativity.* Beverly Hills, CA: Sage.

12 A Comprehensive Review and Communication Research Agenda of the Contextualized Workgroup

The Evolution and Future of Leader-Member Exchange, Coworker Exchange, and Team-Member Exchange

Leah M. Omilion-Hodges

Western Michigan University

Jennifer K. Ptacek

Purdue University

Deirdre H. Zerilli

University of Missouri

Although leader-member exchange (LMX), coworker exchange (CWX), and team-member exchange (TMX) serve distinct yet related purposes in workgroups, these relationships remain segregated in scholarship, thus providing an incomplete view of the most prevalent communicative relationships in the workplace. The purpose of this comprehensive review and research agenda is to present the current state of workplace exchange relationships and offer compelling reasoning for why these relationships should be examined in concert. Areas for future scholarship are suggested, including the refinement of epistemological perspectives, replication of studies to explore current contradictions, and need for more multilevel examinations of workgroup relationships.

Some (e.g., Hackman & Johnson, 2009) have suggested that leadership is composed of two ingredients: the people and the tasks. However, in review of extant literature the people examined are virtually always individual members at the expense of an exploration of the collective effects of leader-member relationships on other salient workgroup associations. This obscures the communicative processes that occur within workgroups including setting and completing individual and group goals, establishing and managing boundaries, and navigating social interactions (Mathieu, Maynard, Rapp, & Gilson, 2008). Fairhurst (2007) notes that leadership is a process ascribed by followers and may be performed by many members within an organization, arguing that communication itself constitutes these relationships and is the very basis upon which perceptions are made. Considering this, anchoring focus primarily on formal leaders promotes a rudimentary understanding of leading while the interdependence of leader, peer, and team relationships is neglected (Fairhurst & Uhl-Bien, 2012).

Literature is replete with studies exploring the antecedents and consequences of differentiated leader-member relationships (Ma & Qu, 2010), but by and large this line of inquiry overlooks the contextualized work of communicating, relating, and leading within groups and organizations. Communication scholars (Bakar & Sheer, 2013; Fairhurst & Connaughton, 2014) continue to acknowledge the lack of depth in leadership research, reiterating the need to holistically explore leadership within the milieu of the workgroup to recognize the messiness (Denis, Langley, & Rouleau, 2010), the meaningful dialogues (Cook & Leathard, 2004), and the overall physical and social environment (Liden & Antonakis, 2009) produced from a collection of varied leader-member relationships. To that end, we argue that current approaches to examining leadership are insular, where instead, as a field communication scholars must explore leadership within the contextualized workgroup inclusive of leader-member (LMX; Dansereau, Graen, & Haga, 1975), coworker (CWX; Sherony & Green, 2002), and team (TMX; Seers, 1989) relationships.

Arguably the three most important relationships for organizational members include the relationship they share with their leader, peer couplings, and the sum of all workgroup associations. Leader-member exchange theory (LMX; Dansereau et al., 1975), a dyadic and relational approach to exploring leadership through varied leader-follower associations, is currently celebrating its fortieth year of utility. LMX presumes that a leader develops unique relationships with each follower where these differentiated leader-member relationships create bifurcations within the workgroup (Dansereau et al., 1975). Coworker exchange theory (CWX; Sherony & Green, 2002) describes the relationship of two peers who report to the same direct manager with research indicating that individual LMXs directly impact employee development of peer relationships. While LMX and CWX detail dyadic exchange relationships, team-member exchange (TMX; Seers, 1989) accounts for the sum of workgroup relationships, inclusive of the leader(s) and members. Though often studied in isolation, the aggregation of these relationships forges an employee's communicative and relational work experience.

Thus we argue that, as a field, scholars must move from considering workplace relationships as points of a triangle to the stakes of a teepee (see Figure 12.1). When examined individually, leader, coworker, and team relationships, if illustrated, may be represented as the points on the larger triangle of workplace relationships. Although connected as parts of the same structure, the triangle approach does little to suggest how these relationships interact and are dependent on one another. Rather, a more accurate illustration of these relationships may be as the foundations of a teepee, each relationship representing a different

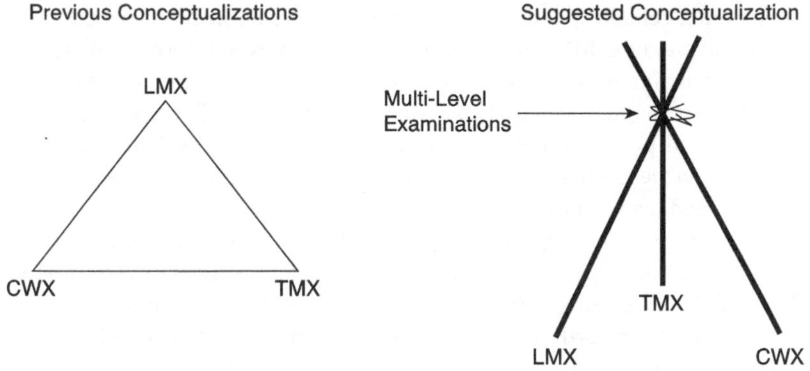

Previous Conceptualizations

Suggested Conceptualization

Figure 12.1 Previous and Suggested Conceptualizations of Exchange Research

stake and offering a three-dimensional view of workplace complexity. The more relationships and perspectives considered, the more support the overall structure has—however, at its very core, the argument must consider multiple perspectives in order to stand alone and to give an increasingly accurate depiction of how these relationships are interdependent. Research that considers multilevel effects of myriad relationships in tandem, or contextualized research, is what binds the teepee together. Put simply, contextualized research accounts for the dynamic and complex entanglement of leader, coworker, and team associations, holistically considering how these pivotal relationships may impact organizational life for any individual employee, but also how an employee's associations may subsequently impact others' leader, coworker, and team relationships. As communication is at the heart of workplace relationships (Fairhurst, 2007), one of the best approaches to contextualized research comes from the communication discipline.

Communication scholars are especially well-placed to examine the complexities inherent in individual and intersecting workplace relationships. In fact, the communication field has yielded some of the most intricate understandings of workplace relationships, ranging from integrative negotiation between managers and employees (Meiners & Boster, 2012) to the effects of cooperative communication on group cohesion (Bakar & Sheer, 2013). Bakar, Dilbeck, and McCroskey (2010), for example, explored how supervisory communication practices influenced leader-member relationships and workgroup commitment. Similarly, Sheer (2014) recently argued that LMX should be recast as a behavior-based construct, where work and social communication are the two most pivotal components of leader-member relationships. Through an experimental design, Omilion-Hodges and Baker (2013) found that after watching only three minutes of simulated leader-member and coworker communication, participants were able to accurately deduce the quality of their leader-member and peer relationships. Moreover, Sias and colleagues (Sias, 1996; Sias, 2005; Sias, Gallagher, Kopaneva, & Pedersen, 2012) have explored communication-related phenomena within peer relationships, specifically discourse surrounding differential treatment, the employee information experience, and the maintenance of workplace friendships. In sum, communication scholars have remained an important staple in this vein of research and are particularly well positioned to remain at the forefront as the field begins to uncover the nuances imbued within the contextualized workgroup, inclusive of leader, peer, and team relationships.

The current scholarship argues for a more holistic examination of workgroup relationships, where the effects of one relationship (i.e., LMX, CWX, or TMX) are considered when interpreting other relational associations. LMX pioneers criticized the then-standard average leadership style approach (ALS; Evans, 1970) as obtuse and suggested that researchers must examine differences between leader-member dyads. Thus we argue that the field is at the intersection where communication scholars have the opportunity to transcend into the next natural extension of leadership communication research—the contextualized workgroup. Workgroups can be thought of as a web where, despite a researcher's best intentions, it is impossible to disentangle the influence of one relationship from the remainder (Liden & Antonakis, 2009). Considering this, we argue for a systems theory approach, where we seek to explain functions of part of the workgroup in relation to the whole. Similarly, to focus on a singular workgroup relationship at the exclusion of others obscures the co-constructed character of communication (Johansson, Miller, & Hamrin, 2014). Finally, each of these pivotal workgroup relationships is undergirded by social exchange theory (Blau, 1964), which inherently accounts for the context in which relationships are embedded (Kamdar & Van Dyne, 2007).

Taken together, workgroup relationships are in a constant state of flux (Omilion-Hodges & Baker, 2013) where the quality of one's associations influences employees' other associations. This may lead to increased access to resources—such as praise, promotion, and latitude—or it may lead to relative isolation. As a means to propel leadership communication research forward, we begin by laying the theoretical foundation with a discussion of social exchange and systems theory and then trace the evolution of LMX, CWX, and TMX. Then we turn our attention to discussing the prevalent approaches to conducting research from this area and offer concrete suggestions for communication scholars regarding future research and practice.

Theoretical Framework

Systems Theory

Systems theory, which relies on the metaphor of the human body for understanding organizational processes, helps to illustrate the interdependence of system components such as leader, peer, and team relationships (Weick, Sutcliffe, & Obstfeld, 2005). In the context of the workgroup, systems theory can help to explain how workgroups may become more resilient and adaptable due to the existing mutually dependent relationships among a leader, individual members, and the sum of the group. The metatheory perspective acknowledges a natural hierarchical order and the presence of smaller subsystems and larger suprasystems. For example, workgroups are a mosaic of leader, coworker, and team relationships that are embedded within and interact with other departments and the organization as a whole. Thus, this impresses the importance of examining the system and subsystems holistically because a reductionist approach masks the culmination of the relationships anchored within. Moreover, as communication scholars (e.g., Fairhurst, 2007) have long argued, leadership is not confined to or done by one particular individual, but rather emerges from the relational interactions of actors (Lichtenstein et al., 2006).

However, at the same time systems theory does not diminish the role of an individual member, due to their unique role of influencing the system in a variety of positive and negative ways. Moreover, systems theory specifically accounts for leadership in and of complex adaptive systems (Uhl-Bien & Marion, 2009, p. 631). In using the imagery of the teepee, systems theory describes how each stake plays an important role in supporting the overall structure. Although the structure is based on the interconnection of multiple roles and relationships, the individual posts each represent an essential component to the overall functioning, stability, and survival of the construct.

Fostering an open system is among the most efficacious means recommended for helping a system to function effectively (Golden & Geisler, 2007). Open systems are those that interact with their environment, engaging in the two-way exchange of information and resources to remain prosperous. Unlike closed systems, open systems use the exchange of information to remain adaptive, using new knowledge to amend goals, plans, and processes as is necessary (Golden, 2009). It is because of the exchange and flow of additional information among system and subsystem members that open systems are competitively advantaged and less susceptible to atrophy.

Applied to the workgroup context, this suggests that, in place of isolating various relationships, both researchers and organizations are more likely to benefit from examining and encouraging the development of strong leader-member, peer, and team relationships (see Table 12.1). In this sense, the consistent flow of information among members is likely to help the group move beyond the hidden profile paradigm (Wittenbaum, Hollingshead, & Botero, 2004) and result in more realistic and attainable goals, enhanced decision-making, and more thoughtful collaborations (Herdman, Yang, & Arthur, 2014). Put simply, leader, peer, and team relationships constitute a malleable organization structure, where individual and the collective set of relationships impact the overall functioning of the system. In this sense, systems theory provides a foundation for understanding leader, peer, and team relationships interdependently, yet it is evident that our explanatory power of these associations increases when coupled with an understanding of the ways in which individual actors engage in exchange.

Social Exchange Theory

Social exchange theory (SET; Blau, 1964) posits that social actors engage in interdependent exchanges where the costs and benefits of such exchanges are considered (Emerson, 1976), produce obligation (Gouldner, 1960), and may ultimately lead to the development of high-quality relationships. Just as some relationships will mature into mutually beneficial, trusting associations, others will not transcend an exchange relationship where actors keep track of what is contributed relative to what is received, careful not to upset a state of equity (Homans, 1958). Though the theory possesses a variety of subtleties, SET continues to be hailed as one of the most popular explanatory mechanisms for exploring and interpreting workplace behavior (Cropanzano & Mitchell, 2005).

In addition to being an influential means for examining behavior within organizations, social exchange theory undergirds leader-member exchange, coworker exchange, and team-member exchange (Liao, Liu, & Loi, 2010; Wayne, Shore, & Liden, 1997). In fact, SET has been used to explain how LMX and TMX influence social loafing within groups (Murphy, Wayne, Liden, & Erdogan, 2003), how LMX and TMX impact task and citizenship performance (Kamdar & Van Dyne, 2007), how leader-member relationships impact coworker exchange relationships (Sherony & Green, 2002), the ways in which LMX, perceived organizational support, and TMX influence social exchange of the entire workplace (Cole, Schaninger, & Harris, 2002), and how LMX may impact employee reactions including in regard to the development of peer relationships (Hooper & Martin, 2008) and workplace friendships (Tse, Dasborough, & Ashkanasy, 2008), among other outcomes.

In regard to the contextualized workgroup, interpersonal relationships develop over time through a series of exchanges (Wayne et al., 1997). However, employees are astute in their ability to keep track of exchanges and in their assessments of the perceived value of exchanges. For example, in regard to leader-member relationships, Graen and Scandura (1987), explain that "each party must offer something that the other party sees as valuable and each party must see the exchange as equitable or relatively fair" (p. 82). Unlike traditional exchange theories, SET (Homans, 1958) acknowledges that actors may exchange intangible communication-based goods such as information or friendship; which may be perceived to hold greater value than other exchanges (Foa & Foa, 1974). As a case in point, Dotan (2009) acknowledged employees may exchange with others and ultimately develop relationships in order to secure a trusting workplace association, to fill the role of other friends while at work, or simply for a sanity check. Thus, within the context of the workgroup, scholars can begin to see how members exchange in varied ways with their leader, individual peers, and the sum of the group as a means to satisfy individual and interpersonal needs (Shutz, 1966). In doing so, it is useful to reference the intent of the theorists of each named exchange relationship (see Table 12.1). The literature on each relationship will be explored in the following sections, beginning with LMX.

Table 12.1 Exchange Relationship Definitions

Relationship	Definition
Leader-Member Exchange (LMX)	"Leader-member exchange (LMX) theory emphasizes that leaders develop a differential quality of dyadic relationships with followers such that within work groups, they form low-quality transactional relationships with some and high-quality socioemotional relationships with others" (Dansereau, Graen, & Haga, 1975, p. 974).
LMX differentiation	Also commonly referred to as Relative LMX; "the degree of variability in the quality of LMX relationships formed within work groups" (Liden, Erdogan, Wayne, & Sparrowe, 2006, p. 723).
Relative LMX (RLMX)	"An employee's LMX quality relative to the average LMX quality of others in a workgroup" (Tse, Ashkanasy, & Dasborough, 2012, p. 2).
Coworker Exchange (CWX)	"Exchanges among coworkers who report to the same supervisor" (Sherony & Green, 2002, p. 542).
Team-Member Exchange (TMX)	"The exchange relationship [of the individual member's perception of his or her exchange relationship with the peer group as a whole] is defined in the context of an ongoing work group as the member interacts with interdependent members of the role set" (Seers, 1989, p. 119).

Leader-Member Exchange Relationships

Leader-member exchange (LMX; Dansereau et al., 1975) is a communication-based theory of leadership (Baker & Omilion-Hodges, 2013), which details the exchange relationship shared between an employee and his or her direct manager. LMX revolutionized the organizational communication field and related others (i.e., management, organizational behavior, industrial and organizational psychology, etc.) in suggesting a modernized approach to studying leader-follower relations. At its core, LMX suggests that leaders develop differential exchange relationships with each member that can range from a low-quality transactional association to one that is typified by mutual trust, respect, and openness (Graen, Novak, & Sommerkamp, 1982). Since its inception, LMX has undergone numerous refinements (see Graen & Uhl-Bien, 1995 for an early theoretical review) and has yielded myriad antecedents and outcomes of the leader-member communicative relationship.

Evolution of LMX Research

In their seminal article, Dansereau and colleagues (1975) levied two critiques on extant leadership literature: firstly, researchers made the erroneous assumption that all members were "sufficiently homogenous" and secondly, that a leader "behaves in essentially the same prescribed manner toward each of his [sic] members," (p. 47). Thus, early LMX research (Dansereau et al., 1975; Graen & Cashman, 1975) transcended the narrow parameters tacitly followed by fellow scholars. In its place, the ground-breaking researchers (Dansereau et al., 1975) anchored exploration around both members within the dyad to allow for the cases in which each leader-member coupling is "radically different" and for cases when "each are essentially the same" (p. 47). This initial questioning of the traditional conventions of leader-member exchange relationships induced a deluge of LMX research over the course of the next four decades.

While scholarship examining individual level effects (i.e., satisfaction, commitment, behavioral tendencies, etc.) composes the bulk of extant LMX research (Hu & Liden, 2013), we focus on the most recent innovation in this vein of leadership literature: an examination of leader-member exchange relationships through group and organizational lenses, where scholars account for the context of workgroups in not only considering, but also in observing, measuring, and describing how individual LMXs impact peer LMXs, ultimately influencing the workgroup as a whole. While the call to examine the effects of LMX at the group level is not new (e.g., Graen & Cashman, 1975), LMX differentiation research (also commonly referred to as Relative LMX) has become the new standard. While LMX differentiation research continues to gain momentum (Harris, Li, & Kirkman, 2014; Omilion-Hodges & Baker, 2013), scholars continue to encourage others to remember that "LMX is embedded within the wider social context of teams," (Hu & Liden, 2013, p. 127). Thus while awareness of the importance of conducting contextualized leadership research continues to grow, a number of early empirical studies have laid a foundation for the now ripe area of study.

LMX differentiation and communication serve as natural partners, considering the term refers to "the distinctiveness of the interpersonal relationships that exist among managers and the subordinates they directly manage" (Henderson, Wayne, Shore, Bommer, & Tetrick, 2008, p. 1210). Consequently, much of the early exploration of the effects of LMX differentiation was from a communication perspective. For example, in a series of studies, Fairhurst and colleagues (Fairhurst & Chandler, 1989; Fairhurst, Rogers, & Sarr, 1987) revealed numerous communication differences between leaders and their members based on LMX including distinct discourse patterns and varied uses of interpretive and conversational resources. Similarly, Sias and Jablin (1995) illustrated that leader-member relationships impacted others in the workgroup, where coworkers employed communication to confer with others to determine the fairness of differentiated leader behavior. These early studies regarding the effects of varied LMXs may not have explicitly used the term, but nonetheless examined how individual LMX relationships impacted other leader-member associations in regard to specific communication phenomena.

LMX Differentiation

LMX differentiation research has sought to not only re-examine individual level outcomes previously studied from an individual LMX perspective, but has been systematic in extending the field's knowledge by accounting for contextual factors allowing for a richer, nuanced understanding of leadership in the modern organization. Henderson, Liden, Glibkowski, and Chaudhry (2009) argue for a meso-model of LMX differentiation in their review of antecedents and outcomes, acknowledging that variability in LMX patterns within groups affects four distinct levels simultaneously: individual-leader, individual-member, workgroup, and organization. Other related studies have found that high LMX variability within groups is related to relative deprivation among low LMX employees (Bolino & Turnley, 2009), decreases in employee well-being and job satisfaction (Hooper & Martin, 2008), declines in peer sharing of resources (Omilion-Hodges & Baker, 2013), increased team conflict (Boies & Howell, 2006), and diminished group effectiveness (Wu, Tsui, & Kinicki, 2010). While there are notable negative implications of varied LMX relationships, several encouraging outcomes have also been revealed: positive relationships between LMX differentiation and psychological contract fulfillment (Henderson et al., 2008), increased team performance (Naidoo, Scherbaum, Goldstein, & Graen, 2011) and commitment (Le Blanc & González-Romá, 2012); improved performance in low LMX members (Liden, Erdogan, Wayne, & Sparrowe, 2006), increases in organizational citizenship behaviors (Vidyarthi, Liden, Anand, Erdogan, & Ghosh, 2010) and employee voice (Zhao, 2014), correlations with task performance and innovative behavior (Li, Feng, Liu, & Cheng, 2014), surges in social identification (Tse, Ashkanasy, & Dasborough, 2012), and increases in self-efficacy, in-role performance, OCB, and job satisfaction (Hu & Liden, 2013). While LMX examines the dyadic relationship shared between a leader and member, coworker exchange theory (CWX) like LMX is undergirded by social exchange theory, and details the dyadic relationship of two employees who report to the same direct manager. The following section explores the progression of CWX.

Coworker Exchange Relationships

Research on coworkers has examined many facets of the peer relationship. In its simplest form, coworker exchange (CWX) refers to "exchanges among coworkers who report to the same supervisor" (Sherony & Green, 2002, p. 542). Although LMX is undoubtedly an important relational influence, in recent years CWX has also been shown to affect outcomes independently of leader influences, with coworker support being uniquely and positively related to job involvement, job satisfaction, and organizational commitment (Chiaburu & Harrison, 2008). In some scholarship, coworkers were believed to have the strongest effect of all the workplace relationships (Takeuchi, Yun, & Wong, 2011). Coworkers with excellent communication relationships can act as social referents to one another, shaping how the employee views his or her workplace (Takeuchi et al., 2011). Scholars' examination of mentors suggests that both leaders and coworkers are better at achieving goal outcomes than formal mentors (Kram & Isabella, 1985; Raabe & Beehr, 2003). That is, mentor and leader relationships naturally forged by employees may be equally or more influential than formal mentoring relationships set up through organizational means. This suggests that although the organizational setting may have a significant influence on the nature of the coworker relationship, the communication that occurs between employees can allow for a more intricate relationship than is generally acknowledged.

Evolution of CWX Research

Although coworker exchange remains a fairly new topic in scholarly discourse, peer relationships have been studied for several years. One of the earliest influences on peer relationship scholarship is Kram and Isabella's (1985) typology of relationships. This research delineated three particular peer relationships that are distinguished by both developmental and psychosocial function: (a) information peer, (b) collegial peer, and (c) special peer. Although Kram and Isabella's typology differs in many ways from the coworker exchange research of today, this study remains widely referenced and has served as a defining categorization in peer communication research. In more recent scholarship, this typology has served to determine that higher-quality relationships (i.e., collegial and special peer) are related to affinity seeking (Gordon & Hartman, 2009), open communication strategies (Myers, Knox, Pawlowski, & Ropog, 1999), and functional communication skills (Myers et al., 1999). Another influential concept in coworker relationship literature is the "blended friendship," a term used to describe the strong friendships that can form between work associates (Bridge & Baxter, 1992). Blended friends encounter a number of dialectical tensions where these strains are negatively associated with the closeness of the relationship (Bridge & Baxter, 1992). In order to understand how these close friendships develop at work, Sias and Cahill (1998) identified three major transitions—coworker to friend, friend to close friend, and close friend to almost best friend—similar to Kram and Isabella's classification of peer relationships.

A more direct comparison to LMX, coworker exchange (CWX) originated in Sherony and Green's (2002) research on the propensity of two coworkers' LMX to predict the relationship between the coworkers themselves. Specifically, results indicate that two coworkers who share a similar quality of relationship with their leader will have a high-quality relationship with each other (regardless if the LMX association is high- or low-quality), while coworkers with dissimilar leader relationships will have a poor-quality relationship with one another (Sherony & Green, 2002). Research on the underlying mechanisms of coworker exchange has yielded important insights on the development and maintenance of peer relationships. In particular, relationship conflict between coworkers is detrimental to coworker trust (Lau & Cobb, 2010), while coworker relational maintenance tactics are positively related to communication satisfaction, job satisfaction, and organizational commitment (Madlock & Booth-Butterfield, 2012). In addition, research on the benefits of high-quality coworker exchange has revealed that being perceived as trustworthy by one's coworkers is positively related to employee performance (Dirks & Skarlicki, 2009). Furthermore, coworker satisfaction is correlated with life satisfaction (Simon, Judge, & Halvorsen-Ganepola, 2010). While CWX looks specifically at the relationship between a coworker dyad, team member exchange theory focuses on the exchanges among members of a team. We now trace the evolution of team-member exchange.

Team-Member Exchange Relationships

Team-member exchange (TMX) explicates the social exchange relationships between a member and the sum of his/her team, and "refers to the extent to which information, help, and recognition between a member and other members of the workgroup is reciprocal" (Bakar & Sheer, 2013, p. 445). The definition of *team* includes individuals within an organization who work together to perform tasks interdependently and share common goals (Banks et al., 2014). TMX differs from LMX and CWX because rather than focusing on a dyadic relationship, it concentrates on how the worker identifies as a member of a group as a whole (Seers, 1989). Since team effectiveness relies on the quality of exchange between team members, interpersonal relationships are an integral element (Tse et al., 2008). Each exchange relationship is unique from those of other members, as the individual member decides how he or she will interact with their workgroup peers (Bakar & Sheer, 2013).

Evolution of TMX Research

In light of increased acknowledgement of the importance of work teams within organizations, scholars have expanded research on social exchange to include team member relationships (Banks et al., 2014). Influenced by LMX, TMX was developed to address perceptions of exchange quality between an individual and the members within his or her team (Seers, 1989). Seers found that TMX quality helps to predict job attitudes by leader-member exchange quality, and that it varies according to factors such as group autonomy (for a more thorough examination of TMX, see Seers, 1989). Drawing from this foundational research, Seers, Petty, and Cashman (1995) found that as TMX quality increased so did cohesiveness and satisfaction in members of self-managing workgroups. Recently, Banks et al. incorporated TMX in conjunction with LMX in a meta-analysis to show how TMX affects some organizational outcomes more than LMX, arguing for consideration of both exchange relationships in tandem. Moreover, scholars have measured a number of antecedents and outcomes of team-member exchange including team performance (De Jong, Cursea, &

Leenders, 2014), cohesion (Bakar & Sheer, 2013), and effectiveness (Mathieu et al., 2008).

Workgroup Relationships in Context

While the breadth of extant research has explored these communicative workgroup relationships individually, it is important to acknowledge that these relationships do not develop nor exist in a vacuum and therefore must be considered in concert (Fairhurst & Uhl-Bien, 2012). Below we present research that explores two or more of these exchange relationships in tandem. For ease of understanding, we have separated these findings by individual exchange relationship.

We follow by parceling out trends and gaps in this area of research where we conclude with an agenda on where communication scholars can continue to extend the field's collective knowledge. It is important to note that only articles that explicitly use LMX, CWX, and TMX are presented here; that is, research that uses other means to conceptualize or operationalize the leader-member, peer, or team associations fall outside of the scope of this particular review because other conceptualizations may not be built on the same foundation of social exchange theory (Blau, 1964) or may not be psychometrically sound for direct comparison as LMX, CWX, and TMX are. Nonetheless, we do not wish to discredit such research, but merely could not include it in the present comprehensive review.

Leader-Member Relationships in Context

Considering the storied past and continuous evolution of LMX, it is not surprising that scholars have begun to explore the ways in which leader-member dyads influence other workgroup relationships, namely coworker and team associations. This particular section reviews articles where LMX is the primary relational focus, whereas subsequent sections will revolve around scholarship where CWX and TMX, respectively, are presented as the predominant exchange relationship.

LMX and CWX serve as natural comparison partners because varied leader-member dyadic relationships naturally create in- (i.e., partnership, cadre) and out-groups (managership, hired hands; Liden & Maslyn, 1998). Thus the presence of qualitatively different leader-member relationships sparks curiosity regarding the ways in which varied LMXs influence peers' propensities to develop relationships with each other. McClane (1991) initiated this area of inquiry when exploring how LMX differentiation influenced members' treatment of their least preferred coworkers. Sias and Jablin (1995) quickly followed by examining how differentiated leader-member relationships influenced employee perceptions of fairness and coworker communication. Scholarship continues to echo these early findings, reiterating that LMX differentiation impacts coworker relationships and often does so in negative ways.

For illustration, Erdogan and Bauer (2010) found that variance in LMXs led to poorer coworker relationships, more negative work attitudes, and higher levels of withdrawal behaviors which aligns with other research (Tse, Lam, Lawrence, & Huang, 2013) that found LMX differentiation increased contempt for workgroup peers. In a series of studies, Omilion-Hodges and Baker (2013) sought to further contextualize the role of LMX differentiation within the workgroup. The researchers found that individual LMX had a strong positive relationship with CWX, where increases in CWX sparked increased organizational citizenship behaviors. LMX has also been widely applied to the team sports arena, where Cranmer and Myers (2014) recently explored how varied coach-athlete dyads influenced athlete-teammate communication. While some have examined the intersection of LMX and CWX, others have looked exclusively at the ways in which differentiated LMX relationships impact the team as a whole. Though it has been suggested that researchers have "merely scratched the surface" of understanding the junction of LMX and CWX (Baker & Omilion-Hodges, 2013, p. 321), team level examinations of varied LMX relationships are much more ample.

Scholars continue to discover that differentiated LMX relationships yield mixed results for teams just as they do for peer associations. For instance, variance within group LMX and TMX negatively impacted employee creativity and self-efficacy (Liao, Liu, & Loi, 2010) and is harmful to group agreement on climate (Ford & Seers, 2006). Kamdar and Van Dyne (2007) found that perceptions of social exchange relationships (i.e., LMX and TMX) moderate the personality-work relationship, particularly for those with low-quality exchange relationships. In other words, developing high-quality leader-member and team relationships can counteract the negative work performance of an employee low in consciousness or agreeableness.

Coworker Exchange Relationships in Context

Since CWX founders (Sherony & Green, 2002) conceived CWX within Heider's (1958) balance theory, CWX has rarely been studied as a single exchange relationship, but rather is most often studied in conjunction with leader-member exchange. In early CWX research, LMX was thought to exert a strong influence on coworker exchange, as similarity between coworkers' LMX was correlated with either high-quality (similar LMX) or low-quality (dissimilar LMX) coworker exchange (Sherony & Green, 2002). Research extending these findings further correlated LMX variability with coworker contempt and sympathy (Tse, Lawrence, & Lam, 2010). Other literature shows that subordinates may look to their leaders for behavioral cues, as a leader's trust of a subordinate can act as a precursor of coworkers' trust (Lau & Liden, 2008). LMX has shaped coworker relationships, but also coworker conversation, as researchers believe that differential LMX sparks dialogue between coworkers that create and reinforce perceptions of this differential treatment (Sias, 1996).

While the majority of contextual research has considered either LMX or CWX to be most impactful, more recent literature has given credence to the potentially equal influence of both LMX and CWX. When LMX and CWX were compared as equally impactful constructs, high-quality exchange in both domains was related to organizational citizenship behaviors (Ma & Qu, 2011) and work-family integration (Major, Fletcher, Davis, & Germano, 2008). When LMX, CWX, and organizational support were examined, results suggested that all three relationships acted as virtually equal predictors of change-oriented citizenship (Chiaburu, Lorinkova, & Van Dyne, 2013). Similarly, workers and leaders have also been shown to possess a virtually identical influence on employee turnover, as both relied on persuasive strategies that were not rooted in legitimate power (Cox, 1999). This line of literature shows promising indications that all workplace relationships are equally impactful, and argues against the belief that there are finite influences on any given workplace outcome.

Recent scholarship has extended examination of the coworker relationship to include unconventional relationships that spread beyond the basic premises of LMX and CWX. In one such study of LMX and coworkers, some leaders coped with coworker conflict by exhibiting abusive supervisory behaviors toward their subordinates, namely those with whom they had low leader-member exchange relationships (Harris, Li, & Kirkman, 2014). This finding introduces a new intricacy to the importance of coworker exchange. If previous understandings of CWX hold true, the implications of a leader's coworker exchange may eventually influence the entire workplace through the decreased quality of LMX with select members, thus further polarizing the previously defined in-group and out-group behavior.

Team-Member Exchange Relationships in Context

Research indicates several interesting relationships between TMX and LMX, where contextual factors such as team-based and traditional management approaches must be considered (Seers, 1989). For illustration, LMX quality is less likely to have an effect on teams that are more autonomous than those that are more traditionally led. Therefore, it is important to consider both of these exchange relationships in the context of the workgroup.

Seers (1989) noted that while role-making research has been focused primarily on the leader, peer relationships have not been considered. Seers suggested that TMX affects job satisfaction similarly to that of LMX, and TMX quality fluctuates between groups in terms of autonomy given to the group by management. Dose (1999) integrated TMX and LMX to look at work values and found that while perceived similarity on work ethics were positively associated with LMX, TMX was positively associated with actual similarity. TMX and LMX have also been viewed as parallel constructs that can be used to understand the relationship between newcomers with their team members and supervisors (Lam, 2003). Lam uncovered that high-quality TMX can improve organizational commitment and high LMX has a positive effect on turnover intentions.

These findings suggest that exchange relationships with both the leader and team members play significant yet separate roles in employee outcomes, and therefore must be considered in conjunction. Tse, Dasborough, and Ashkanasy (2008) found that workplace friendships are positively related to TMX and mediate the relationship between TMX and LMX. Furthermore, these scholars found that affective climate moderates the connection between LMX and workplace friendships at the team level, suggesting that LMX relationships play a role in workplace friendships between employees (Tse et al., 2008).

Recently, Bakar and Sheer (2013) combined LMX and TMX with cooperative communication to look at interpersonal exchange relationships among leaders, teams, and coworkers, and acknowledged that both theories must be considered to explain the relationships between supervisors and coworkers. Findings illustrate that LMX is related to TMX at the individual level, and perceived cohesion between LMX and TMX is negotiated through perceived cooperative communication at the team level (Bakar & Sheer, 2013). Another recent study (Banks et al., 2014) revealed the significance of incorporating TMX in LMX research, because while LMX affects many workplace outcomes, TMX can be even more critical in some areas, as Banks et al. found that while LMX has incremental validity for job performance and turnover intentions, TMX exceeds LMX in influencing employee commitment and job satisfaction.

While the above studies have recognized the importance of considering both TMX and LMX together, there are no published studies that simultaneously examine TMX and CWX to date, although both these constructs relate to important workplace outcomes. As TMX considers an employee's relationship with their team as a whole (Seers, 1989) and CWX refers to a dyadic relationship (Sherony & Green, 2002), there may be important outcomes that arise from the direct comparison of these constructs in a single workgroup. This remains a fruitful area of future research.

Trends in LMX, CWX, and TMX Research

There are several trends in LMX, CWX, and TMX research worth noting. In review of these important social exchange relationships, similarities in studies arose around reliance on cross-sectional survey data virtually always conducted from the post-positivist paradigm, and more recently, an exploration of exchange relationships in unique cultural contexts, and novel measures and applications to further nuance the workgroup experience (Vidyarthi, Erdogan, Anand, Liden, & Chaudhry, 2014). Moreover, data is predominantly collected from the member perspective (Hiller, DeChurch, Murase, & Doty, 2011). Likewise, there are also striking similarities in antecedent and outcome variables used in examining LMX, CWX, and TMX individually and in unison (see Figures 12.2–12.4).

A post-positivist reliance on self-report surveys is a marked change from early LMX research conducted by communication scholars (Fairhurst & Chandler, 1989; Fairhurst et al., 1987; Sias & Jablin, 1995) that employed a variety of interpretive and discursive approaches including participant observations, interviews, and review of leader-member communicative interactions. At the time of writing, in examination of LMX differentiation or relative LMX, CWX, and TMX articles, over 70% were explored at least in part through a self-report survey. While surveys offer participants a chance to respond confidentially (and often anonymously), and are relatively quick and cost effective to administer, they are plagued by common method bias, psychometric limitations or unreliability, and have been critiqued for obscuring the messiness of organizational life (Hu, Ou, Chiou, & Lin, 2012). While there are few recent longitudinal studies (Naidoo et al., 2011; Tordera & González-Romá, 2013) and experiments (Omilion-Hodges & Baker, 2013), the field is dominated by one particular approach to exploring communicative workplace relationships. This is in sharp contrast to calls (Alexopoulos & Buckley, 2013) for future scholarship that employs varied methods and paradigmatic approaches to exploring workgroup relationships. For example, Fairhurst and Connaughton (2014) note a lack of cross-paradigmatic work within leadership research and suggest communication scholars are distinctively primed to integrate multiple methodologies. Similarly, communication scholar Fritz (2014) explicitly argues for the need to apply qualitative organizational research to the study of workplace relationships.

Another recent trend in exchange relationship research is an examination of unique cultural contexts. As traditional and widely-generalizable outcome measures such as satisfaction, commitment, and turnover intentions (Raabe & Beehr, 2003; Agarwal & Bhargava, 2014; Harris, Li, & Kirkman, 2014) became known in the research, scholars have turned their attention to more novel applications of exploring these communicative relationships. One such trend includes exploration of LMX differentiation, CWX, and TMX in various ethnic settings including with Indian managers (Agarwal & Bhargava, 2014) and in Indian organizations (Vidyarthi et al., 2010), with employees in Hong Kong (Chan & Mak, 2012; Takeuchi, Yun, & Wong, 2011; Lam, 2003) and Mexico (Tierney, Bauer, & Potter, 2002), with diverse occupations in Australia (Tse et al., 2012; Hooper & Martin, 2008), with Dutch municipal water employees (van Breukelen, Konst, & van der Vlist, 2002), with Taiwanese teams (Chin-Yun, Long-Sheng, Ing-Chuang, & Kuo-Chin, 2010), and with employees in Malaysia (Bakar & Sheer, 2013; Bakar et al., 2010). Moreover, Chen, Yu, and Son (2014) recently examined LMX differentiation in indigenous cultures.

An additional thread that is tightly woven into this area of inquiry is the consistent use of member-centric data (Hiller et al., 2011). Indeed, after reviewing 25 years of LMX literature, Hiller and colleagues found that nearly 85% of studies measure LMX from the member's perspective, whereas only 13% of studies employed the leader's perspective to examine outcome measures (Hiller et al., 2011). Others (Wilson, Sin, & Conlon, 2010) too have questioned why the leader is so often absent in examinations of leader-member exchange. Though this may appear to be a concern exclusive to LMX research, as more research is conducted on the contextualized workgroup, where leader-member relationships are explored in concert with coworker and team associations, scholars should endeavor to capture both leader and member perspectives.

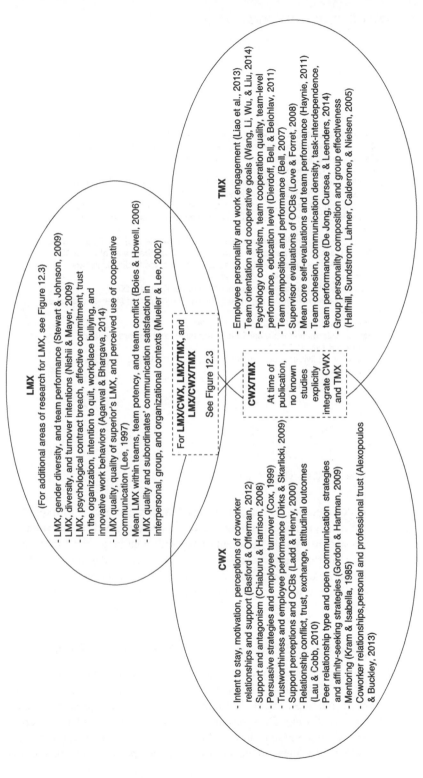

LMX

(For additional areas of research for LMX, see Figure 12.3)

- LMX, gender diversity, and team performance (Stewart & Johnson, 2009)
- LMX, diversity, and turnover intentions (Nishii & Mayer, 2009)
- LMX, psychological contract breach, affective commitment, trust in the organization, intention to quit, workplace bullying, and innovative work behaviors (Agarval & Bhargava, 2014)
- LMX quality, quality of superior's LMX, and perceived use of cooperative communication (Lee, 1997)
- Mean LMX within teams, team potency, and team conflict (Boies & Howell, 2006)
- LMX quality and subordinates' communication satisfaction in interpersonal, group, and organizational contexts (Mueller & Lee, 2002)

TMX

- Employee personality and work engagement (Liao et al., 2013)
- Team orientation and cooperative goals (Wang, Li, Wu, & Liu, 2014)
- Psychology collectivism, team cooperation quality, team-level performance, education level (Dierdoff, Bell, & Belohlav, 2011)
- Team composition and performance (Bell, 2007)
- Supervisor evaluations of OCBs (Love & Forret, 2008)
- Mean core self-evaluations and team performance (Haynie, 2011)
- Team cohesion, communication density, task-interdependence, team performance (De Jong, Cursea, & Leenders, 2014)
- Group personality composition and group effectiveness (Halfhill, Sundstrom, Lahner, Calderone, & Nielsen, 2005)

For **LMX/CWX, LMX/TMX,** and **LMX/CWX/TMX**

See Figure 12.3

CWX/TMX

At time of publication, no known studies explicitly integrate CWX and TMX

CWX

- Intent to stay, motivation, perceptions of coworker relationships and support (Basford & Offerman, 2012)
- Support and antagonism (Chiaburu & Harrison, 2008)
- Persuasive strategies and employee turnover (Cox, 1999)
- Trustworthiness and employee performance (Dirks & Skarlicki, 2009)
- Support perceptions and OCBs (Ladd & Henry, 2000)
- Relationship conflict, trust, exchange, attitudinal outcomes (Lau & Cobb, 2010)
- Peer relationship type and open communication strategies and affinity-seeking strategies (Gordon & Hartman, 2009)
- Mentoring (Kram & Isabella, 1985)
- Coworker relationships, personal and professional trust (Alexopoulos & Buckley, 2013)

Figure 12.2 Areas of Research and Overlap for LMX, CWX, and TMX

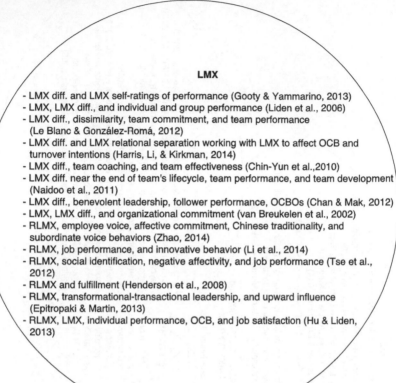

LMX

- LMX diff. and LMX self-ratings of performance (Gooty & Yammarino, 2013)
- LMX, LMX diff., and individual and group performance (Liden et al., 2006)
- LMX diff., dissimilarity, team commitment, and team performance
  (Le Blanc & González-Romá, 2012)
- LMX diff. and LMX relational separation working with LMX to affect OCB and
  turnover intentions (Harris, Li, & Kirkman, 2014)
- LMX diff., team coaching, and team effectiveness (Chin-Yun et al.,2010)
- LMX diff. near the end of team's lifecycle, team performance, and team development
  (Naidoo et al., 2011)
- LMX diff., benevolent leadership, follower performance, OCBOs (Chan & Mak, 2012)
- LMX, LMX diff., and organizational commitment (van Breukelen et al., 2002)
- RLMX, employee voice, affective commitment, Chinese traditionality, and
  subordinate voice behaviors (Zhao, 2014)
- RLMX, job performance, and innovative behavior (Li et al., 2014)
- RLMX, social identification, negative affectivity, and job performance (Tse et al.,
  2012)
- RLMX and fulfillment (Henderson et al., 2008)
- RLMX, transformational-transactional leadership, and upward influence
  (Epitropaki & Martin, 2013)
- RLMX, LMX, individual performance, OCB, and job satisfaction (Hu & Liden,
  2013)

Figure 12.3 Areas of Research for LMX (continued)

Examining leader-member exchange from the leader's perspective is likely to yield a new and more contextualized perspective. For example, through primary data collection and meta-analytic techniques, Sin, Nahrgang, and Morgeson (2009) found moderate agreement ($p = .37$) between leader and member judgments of the relationship. Thus, the work that has been conducted can be interpreted with confidence; but again, endeavoring to include the leader's perspective will only help to further nuance this area of inquiry.

Future Application and Extension of LMX, CWX, and TMX

While this work was originally designed to address future applications and extensions for each exchange relationship separately, examination of extant research revealed numerous parallels among the associations. Although future areas of LMX, CWX, and TMX research are essentially boundless, several concrete avenues for communication scholars are suggested, including: (a) discussion and/or refinement of epistemological perspectives and methods;

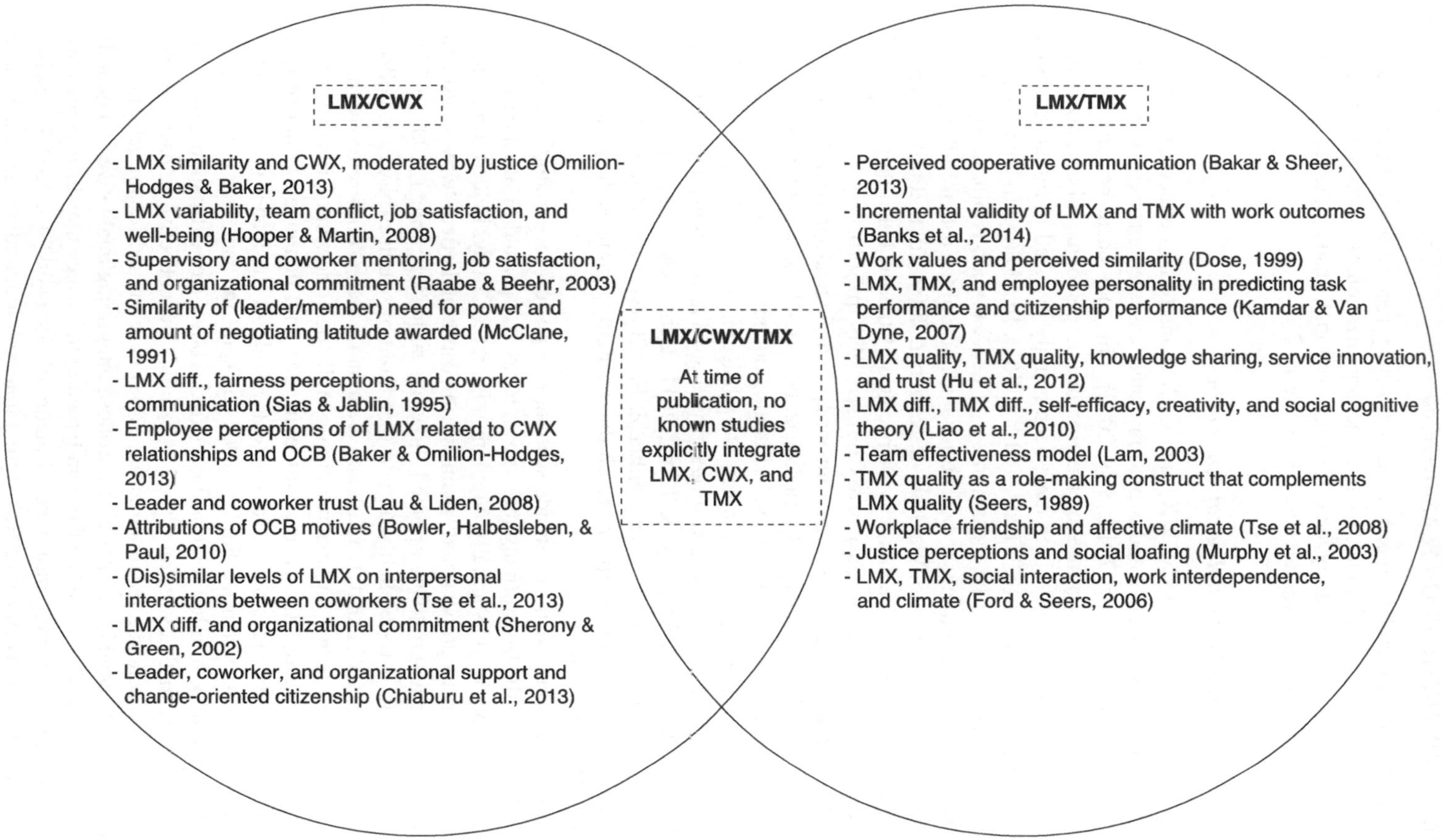

LMX/CWX

- LMX similarity and CWX, moderated by justice (Omilion-Hodges & Baker, 2013)
- LMX variability, team conflict, job satisfaction, and well-being (Hooper & Martin, 2008)
- Supervisory and coworker mentoring, job satisfaction, and organizational commitment (Raabe & Beehr, 2003)
- Similarity of (leader/member) need for power and amount of negotiating latitude awarded (McClane, 1991)
- LMX diff., fairness perceptions, and coworker communication (Sias & Jablin, 1995)
- Employee perceptions of LMX related to CWX relationships and OCB (Baker & Omilion-Hodges, 2013)
- Leader and coworker trust (Lau & Liden, 2008)
- Attributions of OCB motives (Bowler, Halbesleben, & Paul, 2010)
- (Dis)similar levels of LMX on interpersonal interactions between coworkers (Tse et al., 2013)
- LMX diff. and organizational commitment (Sherony & Green, 2002)
- Leader, coworker, and organizational support and change-oriented citizenship (Chiaburu et al., 2013)

LMX/TMX

- Perceived cooperative communication (Bakar & Sheer, 2013)
- Incremental validity of LMX and TMX with work outcomes (Banks et al., 2014)
- Work values and perceived similarity (Dose, 1999)
- LMX, TMX, and employee personality in predicting task performance and citizenship performance (Kamdar & Van Dyne, 2007)
- LMX quality, TMX quality, knowledge sharing, service innovation, and trust (Hu et al., 2012)
- LMX diff., TMX diff., self-efficacy, creativity, and social cognitive theory (Liao et al., 2010)
- Team effectiveness model (Lam, 2003)
- TMX quality as a role-making construct that complements LMX quality (Seers, 1989)
- Workplace friendship and affective climate (Tse et al., 2008)
- Justice perceptions and social loafing (Murphy et al., 2003)
- LMX, TMX, social interaction, work interdependence, and climate (Ford & Seers, 2006)

LMX/CWX/TMX

At time of publication, no known studies explicitly integrate LMX, CWX, and TMX

Figure 12.4 Areas of Research and Overlap for LMX/CWX, LMX/TMX, and LMX/CWX/TMX

(b) replication of studies to explore contradictory results; and (c) examination within multilevel (individual, group, and organizational) workgroup studies. We also present future study ideas for organizational, group, interpersonal, and health communication researchers (see Table 12.2).

Perspectives and Methodological Approaches

Research regarding LMX, CWX, and TMX tends to be conducted from the post-positivist perspective and is predominately assessed through quantitative, self-report surveys (Fritz, 2014; Sias, 2009). This may occur because "workplace relationships rest at the intersection of interpersonal and organizational communication, both of which have been heavily invested in research from a post-positivist perspective," (Fritz, 2014, p. 461). In addition to being heavily quantitatively focused, the measurement of LMX (which is often adapted for CWX and TMX) continues to be critiqued because of the use of multiple measurement devices (Avolio, Walumbwa, & Weber, 2009; Yukl, 2006), which do not seem to evolve systematically or because of theory, but rather on an "ad hoc" basis (Schriesheim, Castro, & Cogliser, 1999, p. 100).

In place of privileging research from one epistemological approach, Sias (2009) encourages scholars to not only appreciate, but actively seek out post-positivist, social constructionist, critical, and structuration perspectives. Interestingly, if workplace relationships are examined as a whole, that is, inclusive and exclusive of LMX, CWX, and TMX, a vast quantity of qualitative scholarship (Ashcraft, Kuhn, & Cooren, 2009; Fay & Kline, 2011; Lutgen-Sandvik, Riforgiate, & Fletcher, 2011; Sias, Heath, Perry, Silva, & Fix, 2004) exists. However, there is a notable dearth in qualitative research that explicitly examines the joint impact of LMX, CWX, and TMX.

As was discussed in the trends section, though few recent studies employ qualitative methods—utilizing interviews, focus groups, and/or observations—they are likely to substantially augment this area of study. Indeed, traditional research has been preoccupied "in answering cause-and-effect 'why' questions than the more descriptively oriented 'how' questions" (Fairhurst, 2007, p. 15). Some scholars have explicitly argued that future research explore the collective effects of CWX and TMX, where Lau and Liden (2008) reiterate that it is necessary to garner an "examination of full social networks, rather than to rely on self-reports" (p. 1136). This coincides with continued criticism that LMX largely excludes the social context outside of the leader-member dyad (Hogg, Abrams, Otten, & Hinkle, 2004), despite the fact that LMX occurs within a system of other relationships (Yukl, 2009). Notwithstanding the lack of qualitative methods recently used to examine the collective impact of these relationships, scholars (Mathieu et al., 2008) have argued for the adoption of this approach. Mathieu et al. (2008) propose integrating qualitative and quantitative methods to create a "new research paradigm," which may be a useful way to "capture the inherent multifaceted nature of teamwork" (p. 463). Likewise, Alexopoulos and Buckley (2013) argued that both longitudinal and qualitative methods would be helpful in understanding the relationship between trust and knowledge transfer among coworkers. It is important to continue to bolster our understanding of leader and workgroup relationships through discourse studies, such as those done by Fairhurst and colleagues (Fairhurst & Chandler, 1989; Fairhurst et al., 1987), and employ qualitative methods such as journaling, focus groups, and observations to identify the "how" of these relationships.

Replication of Contradictory Results

This review of literature also suggests the value of replication of LMX, CWX, and TMX studies, as many tout results that are at odds with other published works. For example, LMX differentiation has been linked to diminished group effectiveness (Wu et al., 2010) and increased team performance (Le Blanc & González-Romá, 2012). Similarly, while some have found that varied LMX relationships attenuate employee commitment (van Breukelen et al., 2002), others have found that LMX differentiation leads to marked increases (Naidoo et al., 2011). While LMX quality has been found to have a significant influence on job satisfaction and commitment to workgroups (Bakar & McCann, 2014), some suggest that TMX has a much greater impact on these variables, beyond that of LMX (Banks et al., 2014). Additionally, some have found that mentoring is critical early on in a career (Kram & Isabella, 1985), but others found that mentoring had little effect on mentee outcomes compared to relationships with a leader and coworkers (Raabe & Bechr, 2003). Thus, replication of such studies can help to further clarify the outcomes of these relationships.

Multilevel Studies

The final recommendation for LMX, CWX, and TMX scholarship includes conducting research that labors to even further contextualize our understanding of the workgroup because examination of these relationships in isolation or only in tandem (rather than collectively) obscures the interdependent nature of the collective communicative processes and relationships resulting in a partial understanding of individual and group-level outcomes (e.g., Le Blanc & González-Romá, 2012). To that end, we encourage communication scholars to commence new research by considering these pivotal workplace relationships as stakes of a teepee, departing from traditional approaches that virtually always positioned these associations as points of a triangle (see Figure 12.1). We also suggest that scholars not only consider the effects of various patterns of LMX behaviors within groups, but further explore how coworker and team relationships are impacted. For example, several researchers have argued for future research considering more organizational outcomes (Bakar & Sheer, 2013), such as team-oriented results (Banks et al., 2014), team trust in various contexts (Haynie, 2011), and work engagement (Liao, Yang, Wang, Drown, & Shi, 2013). Basford and Offermann (2012) found that positive coworker relationships increase one's intention to stay, and thus suggest it is important to explore the specific mechanisms that influence coworker relationships and employee motivation. Relatedly, Cox (1999) calls for an examination of communication strategies peers may use to prompt coworkers to leave positions. Gooty and Yammarino (2013) argue that it is time to look at how both leaders and followers can contribute to the relationship, and scholars should consider the communication processes therein. As stated succinctly by Omilion-Hodges & Baker (2013),

> while the leader–member relationship is often utilized as the starting point for examining and explaining organizational phenomena, it may be more fruitful to address the effect that these dyadic relationships have on other relationships within the work unit and beyond.
>
> (p. 948)

Leader-member relationship scholars believe that this will lead to important revelations on the team level (Omilion-Hodges & Baker, 2013), particularly in culturally diverse groups (Tse et al., 2013).

Peer scholars are also interested in the effect differential LMX will have on coworker relationships (Bowler, Halbesleben, & Paul, 2010) and across varying cultures (Tse, Lawrence, & Lam, 2010). Team researchers, too, are calling for multilevel examinations (Liao et al., 2010), particularly focusing on the reciprocal influences of team and leader relationships. From a communication perspective, Sias (1996) noted the importance of contextualized understanding of workplace relationships by stating, "Dyadic relationships are embedded within a larger social context and . . . this embeddedness created the possibility that dyadic relationships influence and are influenced by that larger context" (p. 171). Although each communicative relationship has remained relatively isolated, a unifying theme across these lines of research is the call for a more contextualized viewpoint of the associations that occur within the workgroup.

Discussion

It has been suggested that peers make the place (Chiaburu & Harrison, 2008) and others, too, have argued the far-reaching ramifications of leader (e.g., Casimir, Ng, Wang, & Ooi, 2014) and team relationships (e.g., Banks et al., 2014). However, we take the stance that it is the collection of leader, peer, and team associations that color employees' work experiences. Again, we argue we should move from thinking of workplace relationships as merely points of a triangle to more like stakes of a teepee. As scholars seek to understand the entangled nature of multilevel relationships, the web of workplace complexity will continue to bind the stakes of the teepee that support the structure. While an associate's relationship with his or her leader will impact individual access to information, decision-making latitude, work satisfaction, organizational commitment, and promotion and earning potential (Han, 2010; Law, Wang, & Hui, 2009), individual LMX relationships in large part determine employee

Table 12.2 Suggestions for Future Study and Extension

Communication Specialization	*Areas for future study and extension*
Health Communication	Future research should consider the impacts of conflict, social support, and burnout and turnover among health care employees in consideration of individual traits and organizational structures (Wright & Nicotera, in press).
	While research in areas such as social support and conflict have suggested the influence that various workplace relationships have on a number of outcomes (Simon, Judge, & Halvorsen-Ganepola, 2010), further study is needed on the effects of peer, leader, and subordinate relationships on employee health and ability to cope with work stress.
	Support from leaders and coworkers is an under-researched area which may help us to understand the connection to employee burnout and turnover, as posed in the question "Why do positive coworker relationships increase employee motivation and intent to stay?" (Basford & Offermann, 2012, p. 815).
	The integration of systems theory may help to explain communication issues and processes within a number of health care organization contexts (Real & Poole, in press).
Interpersonal Communication	Tse, Dasborough, and Ashkanasy (2008) suggest "future research should adopt experimental and longitudinal designs that strengthen conclusions about the casual direction between LMX, workplace friendship, and TMX" (p. 207).
	Future research should consider the influence of social networks on the leader and member relationship (Bowler, Halbesleben, & Paul, 2010).
	Tse, Ashkanasy, and Dasborough (2012) stress the importance of studying interpersonal communication within work exchanges by suggesting that "interpersonal exchange relationships between leaders, subordinates, and coworkers are interconnected and embedded within a larger social network in organizations. This suggests that these exchange relationships are interdependent and can influence each other" (p. 2).
	A broad range of emotions should be examined when examining how workers respond to coworkers' (dis)similar LMX. Tse, Lam, and Lawrence (2013) add that "Balance theory suggests that while triadic imbalance cause negative interpersonal sentiments, triadic balance induces positives interpersonal emotions" (p. 985).
Organizational Communication	Mathieu, Maynard, Rapp, and Gilson (2008) argue for the integration of qualitative and quantitative methods to create a "new research paradigm," which may be a useful way to "capture the inherent multifaceted nature of teamwork" (p. 463).
	Future studies should expand research to a wider range of outcomes than have currently been explored and further investigate how communication influences workplace relationships and outcomes such as turnover (Bakar & Sheer, 2013). Bakar and Sheer also suggest training in cooperative communication as a way to improve organizational outcomes.

Communication Specialization	Areas for future study and extension
	Further replication of LMX, CWX, and TMX research is needed to clarify inconsistent results between studies (Henderson, Wayne, Shore, Bommer, & Tetrick, 2008).
Group Communication	Subgroups should be examined in terms of how they work together and influence workgroup and the organization (Omilion-Hodges & Baker, 2013).
	Banks et al. (2014) argue for "a re-focused research agenda that includes better reporting practices, the inclusion of theoretically meaningful moderators, and a broader range of outcomes (e.g., team-oriented outcomes)" and that "more research is needed in order to identify, under differing conditions, the relative and unique contributions of TMX and LMX quality within work groups" (p. 290).
	Consideration of Foa and Foa's (1974) resource theory may help in examining how "differential exchanges of resources influence outcomes at the individual, group, and higher theoretical levels" (Henderson, Liden, Glibkowski, & Chaudhry, 2009, p. 532).
	Future study must consider a more contextualized view of the workplace as context plays an integral part in group-level outcomes (Le Blanc & González-Romá, 2012).

peer relationships (Sherony & Green, 2002). Employees are most likely to develop high-quality exchange relationships with workgroup peers who share leader-member relationships similar to their own (Sherony & Green). Thus, individuals who already have access to increased information, flexibility, trust, and respect, etc. because of the high-quality relationship they share with their leader are also more likely to develop substantive associations with other in-group members. It is for this reason that some researchers (Omilion-Hodges & Baker, 2013) have warned that just as certain LMXs are better advantaged than others, the benefits associated with superior leader-member associations pervade other relationships, increasing the division between workgroup members. Moreover, just as an employee's LMX influences CWX relationships, both of these associations have the potential to positively and negatively impact team relationships (Hooper & Martin, 2008). For example, variability within group LMXs can not only diminish employee job satisfaction, but may also have deleterious effects on one's wellbeing (Hooper & Martin, 2008; van Breukelen et al., 2002). Considering the pervasive influence of contextualized workgroup relationships, it is an area ripe for communication inquiry both in regard to theoretical advances and pragmatic implications.

Theoretical Implications

If current leadership literature is anchored in the dyadic leader-member relationship, but we know that LMX variation impacts coworker and team relationships, the fissure is teeming with phenomena for organizational, group, and interpersonal communication researchers to explore. However, regardless of the particular approach, it is time to depart from the longstanding insular approach to studying workgroup relationships where dyadic exchanges are studied in seclusion. Instead, we must now explore how these relationships are constructed, maintained, and negotiated communicatively. Doing so privileges a contextualized view that we have only gleaned cursory glances of thus far and allows us to further extant theory.

As was discussed, two primary theories undergird this line of reasoning: social exchange (Blau, 1964) and systems theory (Boulding, 1956). Social exchange theory posits that some relationships will transcend simple economic or exchange-based relationships to develop into associations based on trust and respect (Cropanzano & Mitchell, 2005). Social exchange partners, such as close leader-member, peer, and team couplings, exchange openly and without expecting immediate or future repayment because these relationships are typified by trust and support. However, not all relationships mature into two-way, reciprocal relationships, thus introducing interesting dynamics in the interplay of varied leader-member, peer, and team associations (Bagger & Li, 2014). In this vein, systems theory helps to further augment our understanding of the contextualized workgroup.

It has long been asserted that organizations are complex and adaptive systems, in part due to the high interdependence of leadership and contextual factors (Schneider & Somers, 2006). In other words, leadership and context reciprocally define one another. We propose this same tenet is true for not only leadership, but multiple workplace relationships. General systems theory (Boulding, 1956) holds explanatory power that can be applied to a number of disciplines, because it accounts for a number of sophisticated phenomena such as diverse and interdependent populations, the inter-relationships among individuals within their environments, and strives for homeostasis. In this regard, systems theory privileges a means to explore how these interconnected workgroup exchange relationships influence one another, adapt and change within the parameters of the workgroup, and ultimately how the collection of leader-member, peer, and team relationships settle to find equilibrium. In sum, the utility of social exchange theory coupled with systems theory provides a substantive foundation for communication scholars to continue leadership research within the contextualized workgroup.

Pragmatic Implications

Just as this research has yielded theoretical implications, there are also pragmatic effects. By illustration, the often employed traditional approach to understanding leadership has focused on the individual "top-down" control of leaders, where other members and social contexts have been pushed to the side (Fairhurst & Uhl-Bien, 2012). Fairhurst and Uhl-Bien (2012) remind us that, "A relational view recognizes leadership not as a trait or behavior of an individual leader, but as a phenomenon generated in the interactions among people acting in context" (p. 1043). In doing so, we are likely to engender new suggestions for the development of workgroup relationships.

For example, in considering how these three relationships are interdependent, managers may encourage employees to work to develop at least one high-quality relationship within their workgroup. This one strong association is likely to be noted by other workgroup members, where others begin to amend their perceptions of the participant based on their own relationships. Moreover, managers should be coached on the importance of workgroup relationships in order to better facilitate collaboration among members. It is valuable for leaders to be mindful that the influence of member communication is far-reaching, as much so as their own. However, for some of the more drastic outcomes of workplace relationships (e.g., turnover), decisions are often made based on a myriad of communicative pressures that are not exclusive to the leader (Cox, 1999). Communication scholars are well situated to examine the nuances of these decisions, as all workplaces are communicatively maintained. Thus, to sum up, the workplace environment as a whole will likely prove a more fruitful area for practical recommendations. If studied on the micro-level, an antagonistic relationship does not readily provide an understanding of what other members could do to change the overall environment. Organizational communication scholars, in particular, often have a stake in providing useful recommendations to practitioners and scholars alike.

References

Agarwal, U. A., & Bhargava, S. (2014). The role of social exchange on work outcomes: A study of Indian managers. *The International Journal of Human Resource Management, 25*, 1484–1504. doi: 10.1080/09585192.2013.870316

Alexopoulos, A. N., & Buckley, F. (2013). What trust matters when: The temporal value of professional and personal trust for effective knowledge transfer. *Group & Organization Management, 38*, 361–391. doi: 10.1177/1059601113488939

Ashcraft, K. L., Kuhn, T. R., & Cooren, F. (2009). Constitutional amendments: "Materializing" organizational communication. *The Academy of Management Annals, 3*, 1–64. doi: 10.1080/19416520903047186

Avolio, B. J., Walumbwa, F. O., & Weber, T. J. (2009). Leadership: Current theories, research, and future directions. *Annual Review of Psychology, 60*, 421–449. doi: 10.1146/annurev.psych.60.110707.163621

Bagger, J., & Li, A. (2014). How does supervisory family support influence employees' attitudes and behaviors? A social exchange perspective. *Journal of Management, 40*, 1123–1150. doi: 10.1177/0149206311413922 10.1177/0149206311413922

Bakar, H. A., & McCann, R. M. (2014). Matters of demographic similarity and dissimilarity in supervisor–subordinate relationships and workplace attitudes. *International Journal of Intercultural Relations, 41*, 1–16. doi: 10.1016/j.ijintrel.2014.04.004

Bakar, H. A., & Sheer, V. C. (2013). The mediating role of perceived cooperative communication in the relationship between interpersonal exchange relationships and perceived group cohesion. *Management Communication Quarterly*, *27*, 443–465. doi: 10.1177/0893318913492564

Bakar, H. A., Dilbeck, K. E., & McCroskey, J. C. (2010). Mediating role of supervisory communication practices on relations between leader–member exchange and perceived employee commitment to workgroup. *Communication Monographs*, *77*, 637–656. doi: 10.1080/03637751.2010.499104

Baker, C. R., & Omilion-Hodges, L. M. (2013). The effect of leader-member exchange differentiation within work units on coworker exchange and organizational citizenship behaviors. *Communication Research Reports*, *30*, 313–322. doi: 10.1080/088 24096.2013.837387

Banks, G. C., Batchelor, J. H., Seers, A., O'Boyle Jr., E. H., Pollack, J. M., & Gower, K. (2014). What does team-member exchange bring to the party? A meta-analytic review of team and leader social exchange. *Journal of Organizational Behavior*, *35*, 273–295. doi: 10.1002/job.1885

Basford, T. E., & Offermann, L. R. (2012). Beyond leadership: The impact of coworker relationships on employee motivation and intent to stay. *Journal of Management & Organization*, *18*, 807–817. doi: 10.1017/S1833367200000456

Bell, S. T. (2007). Deep-level composition variables as predictors of team performance: A meta-analysis. *Journal of Applied Psychology*, *92*, 595–615. doi: 10.1037/0021-9010.92.3.595

Blau, P. M. (1964). *Exchange and power in social life*. New York, NY: Wiley.

Boies, K., & Howell, J. M. (2006). Leader–member exchange in teams: An examination of the interaction between relationship differentiation and mean LMX in explaining team-level outcomes. *The Leadership Quarterly*, *17*, 246–257. doi: 10.1016/j.leaqua.2006.02.004

Bolino, M. C., & Turnley, W. H. (2009). Relative deprivation among employees in lower-quality leader-member exchange relationships. *The Leadership Quarterly*, *20*, 276–286. doi: 10.1016/j.leaqua.2009.03.001

Boulding, K. E. (1956). General systems theory: The skeleton of science. *Management Science*, *2*, 197–208. doi: 10.1287/mnsc.2.3.197

Bowler, W. M., Halbesleben, J. R., & Paul, J. R. (2010). If you're close with the leader, you must be a brownnose: The role of leader-member relationships in follower, leader, and coworker attributions of organizational citizenship behavior motives. *Human Resource Management*, *20*, 309–316. doi: 10.1016/j.hrmr.2010.04.001

Bridge, K., & Baxter, L. (1992). Blended relationships: Friends as work associates. *Western Journal of Communication*, *56*, 200–225. doi: 10.1080/10570319209374414

Casimir, G., Ng, Y. N. K., Wang, Y. K., & Ooi, G. (2014). The relationships amongst leader-member exchange, perceived organizational support, affective commitment, and in-role performance: A social exchange perspective. *Leadership & Organizational Development Journal*, *35*, 366–385. doi: 10.1108/LODJ-04-2012-0054

Chan, S. C., & Mak, W. M. (2012). Benevolent leadership and follower performance: The mediating role of leader–member exchange (LMX). *Asia Pacific Journal of Management*, *29*, 285–301. doi: 10.1007/s10490-011-9275-3

Chen, Y., Yu, E., & Son, J. (2014). Beyond leader–member exchange (LMX) differentiation: An indigenous approach to leader–member relationship differentiation. *The Leadership Quarterly*, *25*, 611–627. doi: 10.1016/j.leaqua.2013.12.004

Chiaburu, D. S., & Harrison, D. A. (2008). Do peers make the place? Conceptual synthesis and meta-analysis of coworker effects on perceptions, attitudes, OCBs, and performance. *Journal of Applied Psychology*, *93*, 1082–1103. doi: 10.1037/0021-9010.93.5.1082

Chiaburu, D. S., Lorinkova, N. M., & Van Dyne, L. (2013). Employees' social context and change-oriented citizenship: A meta-analysis of leader, coworker, and organizational influences. *Group & Organization Management*, *38*, 291–333. doi: 10.1177/1059601113476736

Chin-Yun, L., Long-Sheng, L., Ing-Chuang, H., & Kuo-Chin, L. (2010, November). Exploring the moderating effects of LMX quality and differentiation on the relationship between team coaching and team effectiveness. In *Management Science and Engineering (ICMSE), 2010 International Conference on* (pp. 886–892). IEEE. doi: 10.1109/ICMSE.2010.5719903

Cole, M. S., Schaninger, W. S., & Harris, S. G. (2002). The workplace social exchange network: A multilevel, conceptual examination. *Group Organizational Management*, *27*, 142– 167. doi: 10.1177/1059601102027001008

Cook, M. J., & Leathard, H. L. (2004). Learning for clinical leadership. *Journal of Nursing Management*, *12*, 436–444. doi: 10.1111/j.1365-2834.2004.00420.x

Cox, S. (1999). Group communication and employee turnover: How coworkers encourage peers to voluntarily exit. *The Southern Communication Journal*, *64*, 181–192. doi: 10.1080/10417949909373133

Cranmer, G. A., & Myers, S. A. (2014). Sports teams as organizations: A leader–member exchange perspective of player communication with coaches and teammates. *Communication & Sport*, *3*, 100–118. doi: 10.1177/2167479513520487

Cropanzano, R., & Mitchell, M. S. (2005). Social exchange theory: An interdisciplinary review. *Journal of Management*, *31*, 874–900. doi: 10.1177/0149206305279602

Dansereau, F., Graen, G., & Haga, W. J. (1975). A vertical dyad linkage approach to leadership within formal organizations: A longitudinal investigation of the role making process. *Organizational Behavior and Human Performance*, *13*, 46–78. doi: 10.1016/0030- 5073(75)90005-7

De Jong, J. P., Cursea, P. L, & Leenders, R. T. A. J. (2014). When do bad apples not spoil the barrel? Negative relationships in teams, team performance, and buffering mechanisms. *Journal of Applied Psychology*, *99*, 514–522. doi: 10.1037/a0036284

Denis, J., Langley, A., & Rouleau, L. (2010). The practice of leadership in the messy world of organizations. *Leadership*, *6*, 67–88. doi: 10.1177/1742715009354233

Dierdoff, E. C., Bell, S. T., & Belohlav, J. A. (2011). The power of "we": Effects of psychological collectivism on team performance over time. *Journal of Applied Psychology*, *96*(2), 247–262. doi: 10.1037/a0020929

Dirks, K. T., & Skarlicki, D. P. (2009). The relationship between being perceived as trustworthy by coworkers and individual performance. *Journal of Management*, *35*, 136–157. doi: 10.1177/0149206308321545

Dose, J. J. (1999). The relationship between work value similarity and team-member and leader–member exchange relationships. *Group Dynamics: Theory, Research, and Practices*, *3*, 20–32. doi: 10.1037/1089-2699.3.1.20

Dotan, H. (2009). Workplace friendships: Origins and consequences for managerial effectiveness. *Academy of Management Proceedings*, *86*, 1–6. doi: 10.5465/AMBPP.2009.44244633

Emerson, R. M. (1976). Social exchange theory. *Annual Review of Sociology*, *2*, 335–362. Retrieved from www.jstor.org/stable/2946096

Epitropaki, O., & Martin, R. (2013). Transformational–transactional leadership and upward influence: The role of relative leader–member exchanges (RLMX) and perceived organizational support (POS). *The Leadership Quarterly, 24*(2), 299–315. doi: 10.1016/j.leaqua.2012.11.007

Erdogan, B., & Bauer, T. N. (2010). Differentiated leader–member exchanges: The buffering role of justice climate. *Journal of Applied Psychology, 95,* 1104–1120. doi: 10.1037/a0020578

Evans, M. G. (1970). The effects of supervisory behavior on the path–goal relationship. *Organizational Behavior and Human Performance, 5*(3), 277–298. doi: 10.1016/0030-5073(70)90021-8.

Fairhurst, G. T. (2007). *Discursive leadership: In conversation with leadership psychology.* Thousand Oaks, CA: Sage.

Fairhurst, G. T., & Chandler, T. A. (1989). Social structure in leader-member interaction. *Communication Monographs, 56,* 215–239. doi: 10.1080/03637758909390261

Fairhurst, G. T., & Connaughton, S. L. (2014). Leadership: A communicative perspective. *Leadership, 10,* 7–35. doi: 10.1177/1742715013509396

Fairhurst, G. T., & Uhl-Bien, M. (2012). Organizational discourse analysis (ODA): Examining leadership as a relational process. *The Leadership Quarterly, 23,* 1043–1062. doi: 10.1016/j.leaqua.2012.10.005

Fairhurst, G. T., Rogers, L. E., & Sarr, R. A. (1987). Manager-subordinate control patterns and judgements about the relationship. In M. McLaughlin (Ed.) *Communication Yearbook 10* (395–415). Beverly Hills: Sage, 1987.

Fay, M. J., & Kline, S. L. (2011). Coworker relationships and informal communication in high-intensity telecommuting. *Journal of Applied Communication Research, 39,* 144–163. doi: 10.1080/00909882.2011.556136

Foa, U. G., & Foa, E. B. (1974). *Societal structures of the mind.* Springfield, IL: Charles C Thomas.

Ford, L. R., & Seers, A. (2006). Relational leadership and team climates: Pitting differentiation versus agreement. *The Leadership Quarterly, 17,* 258–270. doi: 10.1016/j.leaqua.2006.02.005

Fritz, J. H. (2014). Researching workplace relationships: What can we learn from qualitative organizational studies? *Journal of Social and Personal Relationships, 31,* 460–466. doi: 10.1177/0265407514522888

Golden, A. G. (2009). Employee families and organizations as mutually enacted environments: A sensemaking approach to work-life interrelationships. *Management Communication Quarterly, 22,* 385–415. doi: 10.1177/0893318908327160

Golden, A. G., & Geisler, C. (2007). Work–life boundary management and the personal digital assistant. *Human Relations, 60,* 519–551. doi: 10.1177/0018726707076698

Gooty, J., & Yammarino, F. J. (2013). The leader–member exchange relationship: A multisource, cross-level investigation. *Journal of Management,* 1–21. doi: 10.1177/0149206313503009

Gordon, J., & Hartman, R. L. (2009). Affinity-seeking strategies and open communication in peer workplace relationships. *Atlantic Journal of Communication, 17,* 115–125. doi: 10.1080/15456870902873184

Gouldner, A. W. (1960). The norm of reciprocity: A preliminary statement. *American Sociological Review, 25,* 161–177. Retrieved from www.jstor.org/stable/2092623

Graen, G. B., & Cashman, J. (1975). A role-making model of leadership in formal organizations: A developmental approach. In J. G. Hunt & L. L. Larson (Eds.), *Leadership Frontiers* (pp. 143–166). Kent, OH: Kent State University Press.

Graen, G. B., & Scandura, T. A. (1987). Toward a psychology of dyadic organizing. In B. M. Staw, & L. L. Cummings (Eds.), *Research in organizational behavior* (pp. 175–208). Greenwich, CT: JAI Press.

Graen, G. B., & Uhl-Bien, M. (1995). Development of leader–member exchange (LMX) theory of leadership over 25 years: Applying a multi-level multi-domain perspective. *Leadership Quarterly, 6*, 219–247. doi: 10.1016/1048-9843(95)90036-5

Graen, G. B., Novak, M., & Sommerkamp, P. (1982). The effects of leader-member exchange and job design on productivity and satisfaction: Testing a dual attachment model. *Organizational Behavior and Human Performance, 30*, 109–131. doi: 10.1016/0030- 5073(82)90236-7

Hackman, M. Z., & Johnson, C. E. (2009). *Leadership: A communication perspective* (5th edn). Long Grove, IL: Woodward.

Halfhill, T., Sundstrom, E., Lahner, J., Calderone, W., & Nielsen, T. M. (2005). Group personality composition and group effectiveness: An integrative review of empirical research. *Small Group Research, 36*, 83–105. doi: 10.1177/1046496404268538

Han, G. (2010). Trust and career satisfaction: The role of LMX. *Career Development International, 15*, 437–458. doi: 10.1108/13620431011075321

Harris, T. B., Li, N., & Kirkman, B. L. (2014). Leader–member exchange (LMX) in context: How LMX differentiation and LMX relational separation attenuate LMX's influence on OCB and turnover intention. *The Leadership Quarterly, 25*, 314–328. doi: 10.1016/j.leaqua.2013.09.001

Haynie, J. J. (2011). Core self evaluations and team performance: The role of team-member exchange. *Small Group Research, 43*, 315–329. doi: 10.1177/1046496411 428357

Heider, F. (1958). *The psychology of interpersonal relations*. New York, NY: Wiley.

Henderson, D. J., Liden, R. C., Glibkowski, B. C., & Chaudhry, A. (2009). LMX differentiation: A multilevel review and examination of its antecedents and outcomes. *The Leadership Quarterly, 20*, 517–534. doi: 10.1016/j.leaqua.2009.04.003

Henderson, D. J., Wayne, S. J., Shore, L. M., Bommer, W. H., & Tetrick, L. E. (2008). Leader-member exchange, differentiation, and psychological contract fulfillment: A multilevel examination. *Journal of Applied Psychology, 93*, 1208–1219. doi: 10.1037/a0012678

Herdman, A. O., Yang, J., & Arthur, J. B. (2014). How does leader-member exchange disparity affect teamwork behavior and effectiveness in work groups? The moderating role of leader-leader exchange. *Journal of Management, 20*, 1–26. doi: 10.1177/0149206314556315

Hiller, N. J., DeChurch, L. A., Murase, T., & Doty, D. (2011). Searching for outcomes of leadership: A 25-year review. *Journal of Management, 37*, 1137–1177. doi: 10.1177/0149206310393520

Hogg, M. A., Abrams, D., Otten, S., & Hinkle, S. (2004). The social identity perspective intergroup relations, self-conception, and small groups. *Small Group Research, 35*, 246–276. doi: 10.1177/1046496404263424

Homans, G. C. (1958). Social behavior as exchange. *American Journal of Sociology, 63*, 597–606. Retrieved from www.jstor.org/stable/2772990

Hooper, D. T., & Martin, R. (2008). Beyond personal leader-member exchange (LMX) quality: The effects of perceived LMX variability on employee reactions. *The Leadership Quarterly, 19*, 20–30. doi: 10.1016/j.leaqua.2007.12.002

Hu, J., & Liden, R. C. (2013). Relative leader–member exchange within team contexts: How and when social comparison impacts individual effectiveness. *Personnel Psychology, 66*, 127–172. doi: 10.1111/peps.12008

Hu, M. M., Ou, T., Chiou, H., & Lin, L. (2012). Effects of social exchange and trust on knowledge sharing and service innovation. *Social Behavior and Personality, 40,* 783–800. doi: 10.2224/sbp.2012.40.5.783

Johansson, C., Miller, V. D., & Hamrin, S. (2014). Conceptualizing communicative leadership: A framework for analyzing and developing leaders' communication competence. *Corporate Communications: An International Journal, 19,* 147–165. doi: 10.1108/CCIJ- 02-2013-0007

Kamdar, D., & Van Dyne, L. (2007). The joint effects of personality and workplace social exchange relationships in predicting task performance and citizenship performance. *Journal of Applied Psychology, 92,* 1286–1298. doi: 10.1037/0021-9010.92.5.1286

Kram, K., & Isabella, L. A. (1985). Mentoring alternatives: The role of peer relationships in career development. *Academy of Management Journal, 28,* 110–132. doi: 10.2307/256064

Ladd, D., & Henry, R. A. (2000). Helping coworkers and helping the organization: The role of support perceptions, exchange ideology, and conscientiousness. *Journal of Applied Social Psychology, 30,* 2028–2049. doi: 10.1111/j.1559-1816.2000.tb02422.x

Lam, T. (2003). Leader-member exchange and team-member exchange: The roles of moderators in new employees' socialization. *Journal of Hospitality and Tourism Research, 27,* 48–68. doi: 10.1177/1096348002238880

Lau, D. C., & Liden, R. C. (2008). Antecedents of coworker trust: Leaders' blessings. *Journal of Applied Psychology, 93,* 1130–1138. doi: 10.1037/0021-9010.93.5.1130

Lau, R. S., & Cobb, A. T. (2010). Understanding the connections between relationship conflict and performance: The intervening roles of trust and exchange. *Journal of Organizational Behavior, 31,* 898–917. doi: 10.1002/job.674

Law, K. S., Wang, H., & Hui, C. (2009). Currencies and exchange of global LMX: How they affect employee task performance and extra-role performance. *Asia Pacific Journal of Management, 27,* 625–646. doi: 10.1007/s10490-009-9141-8

Le Blanc, P. M., & González-Romá, V. (2012). A team level investigation of the relationship between leader–member exchange (LMX) differentiation, and commitment and performance. *The Leadership Quarterly, 23,* 534–544. doi: 10.1016/j.leaqua.2011.12.006

Lee, J. (1997). Leader-member exchange, the "Pelz effect," and cooperative communication between group members. *Management Communication Quarterly, 11*(2), 266–287. doi: 10.1177/0893318997112004

Li, H., Feng, Z., Liu, C., & Cheng, D. (2014). The impact of relative leader-member exchange on employees' work behaviors as mediated by psychological contract fulfillment. *Social Behavior and Personality: An International Journal, 42,* 79–88. doi: 10.2224/sbp.2014.42.1.79

Liao, F., Yang, L., Wang, M., Drown, D., & Shi, J. (2013). Team-member exchange and work engagement: Does personality make a difference? *Journal of Business Psychology, 28,* 63–77. doi: 10.1007/s10869-012-9266-5

Liao, H., Liu, D., & Loi, R. (2010). Looking at both sides of the social exchange coin: A social cognitive perspective on the joint effects of relationship quality and differentiation on creativity. *Academy of Management Journal, 53,* 1090–1109. doi: 10.5465/AMJ.2010.54533207

Lichtenstein, B. B., Uhl-Bien, M., Marion, R., Seers, A., Orton, J. D., & Schreiber, C. (2006). Complexity leadership theory: An interactive perspective on leading in complex adaptive systems. *Complexity and Organization, 8,* 2–12. Retrieved from http://digitalcommons.unl.edu/managementfacpub/8

Liden, R. C., & Antonakis, J. (2009). Considering context in psychological leadership research. *Human Relations, 62*, 1587–1605. doi: 10.1177/0018726709346374

Liden, R. C., & Maslyn, J. M. (1998). Multidimensionality of leader–member exchange: An empirical assessment through scale development. *Journal of Management, 24*, 43–73. doi: 10.1016/S0149-2063(99)80053-1

Liden, R. C., Erdogan, B., Wayne, S. J., & Sparrowe, R. T. (2006). Leader-member exchange, differentiation, and task interdependence: Implications for individual and group performance. *Journal of Organizational Behavior, 27*, 723–746. doi: 10.1002/job.409

Love, M. S., & Forret, M. (2008). Exchange relationships at work: An examination of the relationship between team-member exchange and supervisor reports of organizational citizenship behavior. *Journal of Leadership & Organizational Studies, 14*, 342–352. doi: 10.1177/1548051808315558

Lutgen-Sandvik, P., Riforgiate, S., & Fletcher, C. (2011). Work as a source of positive emotional experiences and the discourses informing positive assessment. *Western Journal of Communication, 75*, 2–27. doi: 10.1080/10570314.2010.536963

Ma, E., & Qu, H. (2011). Social exchange as motivators of hotel employees' organizational citizenship behavior: The proposition and application of a new three-dimensional framework. *International Journal of Hospitality Management, 30*, 680–688. doi: 10.1016/j.ijhm.2010.12.003

Ma, L., & Qu, Q. (2010). Differentiation in leader–member exchange: A hierarchical linear modeling approach. *The Leadership Quarterly, 21*, 733–744. doi: 10.1016/j.leaqua.2010.07.004

Madlock, P. E., & Booth-Butterfield, M. (2012). The influence of relational maintenance strategies among coworkers. *Journal of Business Communication, 49*, 21–47. doi: 10.1177/0021943611425237

Major, D. A., Fletcher, T. D., Davis, D. D., & Germano, L. M. (2008). The influence of workfamily culture and workplace relationships on work interference with family: A multilevel model. *Journal of Organizational Behavior, 29*, 881–897. doi: 10.1002/job.502

Mathieu, J. E., Maynard, M. T., Rapp, T., & Gilson, L. (2008). Team effectiveness 1997–2007: A review of recent advancements and a glimpse into the future. *Journal of Management, 34*, 410–476. doi: 10.1177/0149206308316061

McClane, W. E. (1991). Implications of member role differentiation analysis of a key concept in the LMX model of leadership. *Group & Organization Management, 16*, 102–113. doi: 10.1177/105960119101600107

Meiners, E. B., & Boster, F. J. (2012). Integrative process in manager-employee negotiations: Relational and structural factors. *Journal of Applied Communication Research, 40*, 208–228. doi: 10.1080/00909882.2011.636374

Mueller, B. H., & Lee, J. (2002). Leader-member exchange and organizational communication satisfaction in multiple contexts. *Journal of Business Communication, 39*(2), 220–244. doi: 10.1177/0021943602039002204

Murphy, S. M., Wayne, S. J., Liden, R. C., & Erdogan, B. (2003). Understanding social loafing: The role of justice perceptions and exchange relationships. *Human Relations, 56*, 61–84. doi: 10.1177/0018726703056001450

Myers, S. A., Knox, R. L., Pawlowski, D. R., & Ropog, B. L. (1999). Perceived communication openness and functional communication skills among organizational peers. *Communication Reports, 12*, 71–83. doi: 10.1080/08934219909367712

Naidoo, L. J., Scherbaum, C. A., Goldstein, H. W., & Graen, G. B. (2011). A longitudinal examination of the effects of LMX, ability, and differentiation on team performance. *Journal of Business and Psychology*, *26*, 347–357. doi: 10.1007/s10869-010-9193-2

Nishii, L. H., & Mayer, D. M. (2009). Do inclusive leaders help to reduce turnover in diverse groups? The moderating role of leader-member exchange in the diversity to turnover relationship. *Journal of Applied Psychology*, *94*(6), 1412–1426. doi: 10.1037/a0017190

Omilion-Hodges, L. M., & Baker, C. R. (2013). Contextualizing LMX within the workgroup: The effects of LMX and justice on relationship quality and resource sharing among peers. *The Leadership Quarterly, 24*, 935–951. doi: 10.1016/j.leaqua.2013.10.004

Raabe, B., & Beehr, T. A. (2003). Formal mentoring versus supervisor and coworker relationships: Differences in perceptions and impact. *Journal of Organizational Behavior*, *24*, 271–293. doi: 10.1002/job.193

Real, K., & Poole, M. S. (in press). A systems framework for health care team communication. In T. R. Harrison & E. A. Williams (Eds.), *Organizations, communication, and health* (pp. 1–17). New York, NY: Routledge.

Schneider, M., & Somers, M. (2006). Organizations as complex adaptive systems: Implications of complexity theory for leadership research. *The Leadership Quarterly*, *17*, 351–365. doi: 10.1016/j.leaqua.2006.04.006

Schriesheim, C. A., Castro, S. L., & Cogliser, C. C. (1999). Leader-member exchange (LMX) research: A comprehensive review of theory, measurement, and data-analytic practices. *Leadership Quarterly*, *10*, 63–113. doi: 10.1016/S1048-9843(99)80009-5

Seers, A. (1989). Team-member exchange quality: A new construct for role-making research. *Organizational Behavior and Human Decision Processes*, *43*, 118–135. doi: 10.1016/0749-5978(89)90060-5

Seers, A., Petty, M. M., & Cashman, J. F. (1995). Team-member exchange under team and traditional management: A naturally occurring quasi-experiment. *Group & Organization Management*, *20*, 18–38. doi: 10.1177/1059601195201003

Sheer, V. C. (2014). "Exchange lost" in leader–member exchange theory and research: A critique and a reconceptualization. *Leadership*, *11*, 1–17. doi: 10.1177/1742715014530935

Sherony, K. M., & Green, S. G. (2002). Coworker exchange: Relationships between coworkers, leader-member exchange, and work attitudes. *Journal of Applied Psychology*, *87*, 542–548. doi: 10.1037//0021-9010.87.3.542

Shutz, W. (1966). *The interpersonal underworld*. Palo Alto, CA: Science and Behavior Books.

Sias, P. M. (1996). Constructing perceptions of differential treatment: An analysis of coworker discourse. *Communications Monographs*, *63*, 171–187. doi: 10.1080/03637759609376385

Sias, P. M. (2005). Workplace relationship quality and employee information experiences. *Communication Studies*, *56*, 375–395. doi: 10.1080/10510970500319450

Sias, P. M. (2009). *Organizing relationships: Traditional and emerging perspectives on workplace relationships*. Thousand Oaks, CA: Sage Publications.

Sias, P. M., & Cahill, D. J. (1998). From coworkers to friends: The development of peer friendships in the workplace. *Western Journal of Communication*, *62*, 273–299. doi: 10.1080/10570319809374611

Sias, P. M., & Jablin, F. M. (1995). Differential superior-subordinate relations, perceptions of fairness, and coworker communication. *Human Communication Research, 22*, 5–38. doi: 10.1111/j.1468-2958.1995.tb00360.x

Sias, P. M., Gallagher, E. B., Kopaneva, I., & Pedersen, H. (2012). Maintaining workplace friendships: Perceived politeness and predictors of maintenance tactic choice. *Communication Research, 39*, 239–268. doi: 10.1177/0093650210396869

Sias, P. M., Heath, R. G., Perry, T., Silva, D., & Fix, B. (2004). Narratives of workplace friendship deterioration. *Journal of Social and Personal Relationships, 21*, 321–340. doi: 10.1177/0265407504042835

Simon, L. S., Judge, T. A., & Halvorsen-Ganepola, M. D. K. (2010). In good company? A multi-study, multi-level investigation of the effects of coworker relationships on employee well-being. *Journal of Vocational Behavior, 76*, 534–546. doi: 10.1016/j.jvb.2010.01.006

Sin, H. P., Nahrgang, J. D., & Morgeson, F. P. (2009). Understanding why they don't see eye to eye: An examination of leader-member exchange (LMX) agreement. *Journal of Applied Psychology, 94*, 1048–1057. doi: 10.1037/a0014827

Stewart, M. M., & Johnson, O. E. (2009). Leader-member exchange as a moderator of the relationship between work group diversity and team performance. *Group & Organization Management, 34*(5), 507–535. doi: 10.1177/1059601108331220

Takeuchi, R., Yun, S., & Wong, K. F. E. (2011). Social influence of a coworker: A test of the effect of employee and coworker exchange ideologies on employees' exchange qualities. *Organizational Behavior and Human Decision Processes, 115*, 226–237. doi: 10.1016/j.obhdp.2011.02.004

Tierney, P., Bauer, T. N., & Potter, R. E. (2002). Extra-role behavior among Mexican employees: The impact of LMX, group acceptance, and job attitudes. *International Journal of Selection and Assessment, 10*, 292–303. doi: 10.1111/1468-2389.00219

Tordera, N., & González-Romá, V. (2013). Leader-member exchange (LMX) and innovation climate: The role of LMX differentiation. *The Spanish Journal of Psychology, 16*, 1–8. doi: 10.1017/sjp.2013.83

Tse, H. H., Ashkanasy, N. M., & Dasborough, M. T. (2012). Relative leader–member exchange, negative affectivity and social identification: A moderated-mediation examination. *The Leadership Quarterly, 23*, 354–366. doi: 10.1016/j.leaqua.2011.08.009

Tse, H. H., Dasborough, M. T., & Ashkanasy, N. M. (2008). A multi-level analysis of team climate and interpersonal exchange relationships at work. *The Leadership Quarterly, 19*, 195–211. doi: 10.1016/j.leaqua.2008.01.005

Tse, H. H., Lawrence, S. A., & Lam, C. K. (2010). Interpersonal work relationships and emotional reactions in teams: A co-worker dyadic analysis. In *24th Annual Australian and New Zealand Academy of Management Conference*. ANZAM. Retrieved from www.anzam.org/wp-content/uploads/pdf-manager/861_ANZAM2010-147.PDF

Tse, H. H., Lam, C. K., Lawrence, S. A., & Huang, X. (2013). When my supervisor dislikes you more than me: The effect of dissimilarity in leader–member exchange on coworkers' interpersonal emotion and perceived help. *Journal of Applied Psychology, 98*, 974– 988. doi: 10.1037/a0033862

Uhl-Bien, M., & Marion, R. (2009). Complexity leadership in bureaucratic forms of organizing: A meso model. *The Leadership Quarterly, 20*, 631–650. doi: 10.1016/j.leaqua.2009.04.007

van Breukelen, W., Konst, D., & van der Vlist, R. (2002). Effects of LMX and differential treatment on work unit commitment. *Psychological Reports, 91*, 220–230. doi: 10.2466/pr0.2002.91.1.220

Vidyarthi, P. R., Erdogan, B., Anand, S., Liden, R. C., & Chaudhry, A. (2014). One member, two leaders: Extending leader–member exchange theory to a dual leadership context. *Journal of Applied Psychology, 99*, 468–483. doi: 10.1037/a0035466

Vidyarthi, P. R., Liden, R. C., Anand, S., Erdogan, B., & Ghosh, S. (2010). Where do I stand? Examining the effects of leader–member exchange social comparison on employee work behaviors. *Journal of Applied Psychology, 95*, 849–861. doi: 10.1037/a0020033

Wang, Z., Li, C., Wu, J., & Liu, L. (2014). The mediating effect of cooperative goals on the relationship between team orientation and team member exchange. *Social Behavior and Personality, 42*(4), 685–694. doi: 10.2224/sbp.2014.42.4.685

Wayne, S. J., Shore, L. M., & Liden, R. C. (1997). Perceived organizational support and leader-member exchange: A social exchange perspective. *Academy of Management Journal, 40*, 82–111. doi: 10.2307/257021

Weick, K. E., Sutcliffe, K. M., & Obstfeld, D. (2005). Organizing and the process of sensemaking. *Organization Science, 16*, 409–421. doi: 10.1287/orsc.1050.0133

Wilson, K. S., Sin, H. P., & Conlon, D. E. (2010). What about the leader in leader-member exchange? The impact of resource exchanges and substitutability on the leader. *Academy of Management Review, 35*, 358–372. doi: 10.5465/AMR.2010.51141654

Wittenbaum, G. M., Hollingshead, A. B., & Botero, I. C. (2004). From cooperative to motivated information sharing in groups: Moving beyond the hidden profile paradigm. *Communication Monographs, 71*, 286–310. doi: 10.1080/0363452042000299894

Wright, K. B., & Nicotera, A. M. (in press). Conflict, social support and burnout/turnover among health care workers: A review of developments in organizational conflict theory and practice. In T. R. Harrison & E. A. Williams (Eds.), *Organizations, communication, and health* (pp. 1–19). New York, NY: Routledge.

Wu, J. B., Tsui, A. S., & Kinicki, A. J. (2010). Consequences of differentiated leadership in groups. *Academy of Management Journal, 53*, 90–106. doi: 10.5465/AMJ.2010.48037079

Yukl, G. (2006). *Leadership in organizations.* Upper Saddle River, NJ: Pearson/Prentice Hall.

Yukl, G. (2009). Leading organizational learning: Reflections on theory and research. *The Leadership Quarterly, 20*, 49–53. doi: 10.1016/j.leaqua.2008.11.006

Zhao, H. (2014). Relative leader-member exchange and employee voice: Mediating role of affective commitment and moderating role of Chinese traditionality. *Chinese Management Studies, 8*, 3–3. doi: 10.1108/CMS-01-2013-0016

CHAPTER CONTENTS

13 Mixing Methods in Organizational Communication Research

Current State and Prospects for Advancing Knowledge

Elizabeth J. Carlson

Central Michigan University

Katherine R. Cooper

Northwestern University

Andrew Pilny

University of Kentucky

In this review, we examine current practices in mixing methods in communication research. We examined 209 mixed-method organizational communication articles published between 1994 and 2014. Our analysis revealed four trends: (1) the dominance of single-paradigm, interpretive studies; (2) the preponderance of triangulation, complementarity, and development as purposes for mixing methods; (3) varied combinations of methods; and (4) a lack of mixed methods citations. In response to findings, we clarify the value proposition of mixing methods, suggest criteria for when communication researchers should or should not consider mixing methods, and recommend strategies for greater transparency in the reporting of mixed-method research.

When designing large empirical projects, communication researchers often include multiple forms of data collection—sometimes even using multiple methodologies, such as qualitative and quantitative. Deciding how to analyze, interpret, and report about multiple forms of data, however, can be difficult. The researcher can treat each type of data separately, analyzing them separately and publishing them in separate articles. This kind of research design produces multiple-method, or *multi-method*, research. Alternatively, the researcher can design the project such that the analysis of one form of data informs the collection, analysis, or interpretation of another form of data within the same study; this is called *mixing methods* (Greene, 2007). Mixing methods may help researchers bolster their confidence in their findings, understand complex phenomena in a more nuanced way, or generate insights about the implications of findings that reflect a simultaneous awareness of ontological, epistemological, disciplinary, and pragmatic concerns. At the same time, however, conducting mixed-method research brings a host of challenges: how to execute the methods themselves; how to draw conclusions that neither understate nor overstate the case; how to describe data collection and analysis with an appropriate level of transparency; and how to defend one's methodological choices to a broad audience of reviewers and readers.

In this paper, we examine how mixed-method approaches have been applied in communication research, and we consider how advances in mixed-methodological thinking could enhance these practices. Our primary purpose is to help communication scholars make more informed choices about whether to mix, how to mix, and how to report on what has been mixed. Secondarily, we explore how mixed-method research has advanced communication scholarship, and we envision how it could continue to do so. As a disclaimer to this stance of advocacy, we acknowledge that mixing methods is by no means a panacea for the complexities of social scientific research, nor is a mixed-method approach advisable for every project. We believe, however, that mixed-method approaches have the potential to generate uniquely innovative, credible, and practical insights. In addition, we have observed that many scholars routinely collect multiple forms of data for a single project, and we wish to empower those scholars to consider additional ways to maximize the knowledge gained from such projects.

In order to investigate the current status of mixed-method research in communication, we made a strategic decision to focus on published empirical research in one sub-discipline: organizational communication. We chose organizational communication for three reasons. First, mixed methodologists have observed that mixed-method approaches appear to be more prevalent and more widely accepted in applied research settings (Alise & Teddlie, 2010), and much of organizational communication research consists of field studies that take into account, if not originate from, the needs and interests of practitioners. Second, two recent publications indicate an emerging conversation about the use of mixed methods in organizational communication research. In 2011, *Management Communication Quarterly* published a methodological review that promoted the use of quantitative research methods in organizational communication (Miller et al., 2011), which addressed the possibility of mixing methods. In addition, the most recent edition of the *SAGE Handbook of Organizational Communication*, published in 2013, included a chapter by Karen Myers entitled "Mixed Methods: When More Really Is More." These pieces indicate a readiness among organizational communication scholars to reflect on their practices and perhaps even to pursue methodological innovation. The third and final reason that we chose to focus on published research in organizational communication is the feasibility of the review project. While organizations serve as the context for these studies, we anticipate that the insights represented here will be helpful to any communication scholar interested in mixing methods.

The premise of our study was that of gap analysis: if we compare our current state to a desirable future state, we can generate ideas about how to get from one to the other. In that spirit, our review was guided by two questions: (1) What are the most common applications of mixed methods in published organizational communication studies; and (2) What advances in mixed methodological thinking from outside the field of communication might enhance these practices? To address the first question, we established sampling criteria and collected articles from a set of nine prominent journals in communication and organizational communication, spanning the years 1994–2014. In the end, our sample included 209 articles. We then analyzed the articles using a review guide, and we generated a set of four holistic trends. We addressed the second question by considering how each trend compared to recent advances in mixed methodology.

This paper is organized as follows: first, we contextualize our review in a brief history of mixed methodology and an assessment of the prevalence of published mixed-method research in organizational communication. Second, we describe the framework of mixed-methods concepts that informed our review. Third, we present four trends from our review of the data, illustrated using descriptive statistics and snapshots of exemplar articles. Finally, we discuss the implications of our review for future mixed-methods work in organizational communication. We hope that our recommendations spark field-wide conversations about ways to continue to enhance the contributions of communication scholars, whether through conducting innovative mixed-method research or through engaging in cross-paradigmatic conversations.

Foundations and Context for the Review

In mixed-method research designs, the researcher makes strategic use of the results from one method to inform decisions related to design or interpretation of another method. Mixed-method research designs can involve sequential or simultaneous data collection, and mixing may occur during design, data collection, data transformation, or interpretation (Greene, 2007). This flexible definition includes everything from studies that integrate two or more social scientific research paradigms (e.g., the critical perspective and interpretivism) to studies that use data from one-on-one interviews to help interpret statistics that describe survey results. In contrast, multi-method research uses multiple methods but keeps data, analysis, and interpretation separate, while mixed-method research strategically integrates (i.e., mixes) materials.

The term "mixed methods" is often associated with the mixing of quantitative and qualitative data (as emphasized in Myers, 2013 and Miller et al., 2011), but this need not be the case. A mixed methods study may also mix "within" a methodology (Greene, 2007), as in a multi-trait, multi-method validity test (Campbell & Fiske, 1959) or an ethnography that incorporates observation and interview. Mixing may occur at any of the following levels: (a) data, as in mixing numbers and text; (b) methods, as in mixing data collection methods (e.g., questionnaire) and data analysis techniques (e.g., thematic analysis); (c) design; (d) epistemology; (e) ontology; (f) purpose/s of the research, for example, to explain, to understand, and to transform; and (g) practical roles of research, for example, to posit an argument to the scholarly community or to advocate for policy change (from Biesta, 2010).

The value proposition of mixing methods relates to the generation of insights that could not be achieved with a single method. In the vein of pragmatism, mixed-method research has long been defined by its prioritization of the research question or problem in the selection of methods and research design (Teddlie & Tashakkori, 2009); as such, mixing methods can help the researcher understand a practical issue in a practical way.[1] In recent years, mixed methodologists have commented that the value of mixing methods is not only pragmatic but extends to the development of findings and implications that simultaneously address ontological, epistemological, disciplinary, and pragmatic concerns, as in Greene's (2007) "mixed methods way of thinking," (p. 20). On a more tactical level, mixing methods can strengthen arguments for the stability of findings that emerge from triangulated methods, the validity of instruments (e.g., questionnaires, interview guides, coding schemes) designed from context-specific data, or the insights gained by exploring non-overlapping findings that emerge from different methods.

Published research using mixed methods is generally more prevalent in applied fields of social inquiry—such as program evaluation, health sciences, nursing, and education—but it can also be found in "pure disciplines" like psychology and sociology (Teddlie & Tashakkori, 2009, p. 78). Alise and Teddlie (2010) assessed the prevalence of mixed-method studies, as compared to non-mixed quantitative and qualitative studies, in a sample of social and behavioral science journals. They found that the prevalence rate of mixed-method studies was 16% in applied disciplines and 6% in pure disciplines. Taking into account prior prevalence studies, they estimated that the overall prevalence rate of mixed methods studies in social and behavioral science journals was roughly 10–15%. Similarly, Molina-Azurin (2011) found that approximately 11% of strategic management publications used mixed methods. The present study suggests similar rates for organizational communication; see Table 13.1 for details.

From these foundations, we devised the present review of published articles on organizational communication topics that used mixed-method approaches. The constructs that comprised the classification scheme are described in the upcoming section, "Framework for the Review," and the review process from design to analysis can be found in Table 13.2.

Framework for the Review

Through the process outlined in Table 13.2, we generated a sample of 209 published articles for the review. In order to classify them, we developed a review guide (see Table 13.2 for development process). This section describes the conceptual categories used in our review. Tables 13.3 and 13.4 summarize key concepts. For an at-a-glance overview of the classification scheme, see the sample entry in the Appendix (Table A1).

Table 13.1 Prevalence of the Publication of Mixed-Method Studies in Organizational Communication, 1994–2014

Journal	Prevalence Rate: All Articles	Prevalence Rate: Organizational Articles
	(%)	(%)
Communication Monographs	6.3	14.3
Communication Reports	1.9	6.6
Communication Research	0.3	4.2
Human Communication Research	2.7	11.0
Journal of Applied Communication Research	11.2	18.6
Journal of Business and Technical Communication	3.6	20.6
Journal of Business Communication	6.7	20.6
Journal of Communication	0.5	1.4
Management Communication Quarterly	7.7	13.2
All of the above	4.3	12.3

Note: "Prevalence Rate: All Articles" describes the percentage of articles, out of all published articles in the journal, that both: (a) mix methods, and (b) emphasize organizational communication topics or theories. To calculate the denominator of this rate, non-empirical articles, such as theory essays, rhetorical studies, introductions to special issues, and editors' introductions were included, while erratum, author acknowledgements, calls for papers, and indices were excluded. "Prevalence Rate: Organizational Articles" describes the percentage of articles, out of the total number of studies identified as at least nominally related to communication and organizations, compiled in the first stage of this review (see Table 13.2 for review process).

Classifying Methods, Methodologies, and Paradigms

A mixed-method approach may mix methods within a methodology, across methodologies, within a paradigm, or across paradigms. To make classifications about what is being mixed, one must first distinguish between a *method* and a *methodology*. Corbin and Strauss (2008) defined *methods* as "techniques and procedures for gathering and analyzing data" and *methodologies* as "way[s] of thinking about and studying social phenomena" (p. 1). For example, participant observation and in-depth interviewing are methods; ethnography is a methodology. A researcher conducting an ethnographic study may or may not use these particular methods, and the researcher might conduct a wide range of procedures in the execution of either method. Ethnography, as a methodology, provides a way of thinking about how the methods should be implemented— for example, that the observer should record descriptive details in her field notes—but not a requisite set of procedures or rules.

When mixing across methodologies, one is also likely to mix across paradigms. Methodologies and paradigms are often linked by epistemological warrants and ontological assumptions (Corman & Poole, 2000; Greene, 2007; Poole, McPhee, & Canary, 2003). Baxter and Babbie's (2004) communication research textbook defines a paradigm as a "model or framework that shapes both what we see and how we understand it" (p. 426). The term "mixed methods" is

Table 13.2 Review Process from Design to Analysis: Six Phases

Phase	Procedures	Outcomes
Phase 1: Selected journals from which articles will be reviewed.	Inclusion criteria for journals: • Indexed in all three of the following communication abstract aggregation databases: Communication & Mass Media Complete (EBSCO), Communication Abstracts (EBSCO), and ComAbstracts (CIOS) • Title does not indicate a geographic or regional affiliation • Title indicates no sub-discipline of communication other than management or business communication • Journal publishes primarily empirical studies	A set of nine journals: *Communication Monographs* *Communication Reports* *Communication Research* *Human Communication Research* *Journal of Applied Communication Research* *Journal of Business and Technical Communication* *Journal of Business Communication* *Journal of Communication* *Management Communication Quarterly*
Phase 2: Identified the population of articles from Phase 1 journals related to organizations or organizing.	Used full text search function in EBSCO database to identify articles from each journal meeting the following criteria: • Published between January 1994 and December 2014 • Contains the word "organization" or any variant	Produced a list of 257 (*Communication Reports*) to 949 (*Journal of Communication*) unique articles to be considered from each journal – approximately 5,000 across all nine journals
Phase 3: Determined which articles from Phase 2 constituted published mixed-method research in organizational communication.	1. Manually reviewed abstracts of all articles identified in Phase 2 to select articles that: • Used multiple methods of data collection and/or transformation • Illustrated organizational communication scholarship[1] 2. Skimmed the methods and results sections of each article to determine whether the methods were actually mixed (Note: Articles that used multiple methods but collected, analyzed, and interpreted the data separately were excluded.)	Final sample consisted of 209 articles. Number of articles in sample from each journal: *Communication Monographs* (31) *Communication Reports* (4) *Communication Research* (2) *Human Communication Research* (14) *Journal of Applied Communication Research* (57) *Journal of Business and Technical Communication* (14) *Journal of Business Communication* (36) *Journal of Communication* (5) *Management Communication Quarterly* (47)
Phase 4: Developed the review guide.	Developed review guide based on three sources: • A mixed method study review guide by Gannon and Sun (unpublished seminar project, undated) • Greene, Caracelli, and Graham's (1989) review of educational policy research • The mixed methods typologies and definitions found in Greene's (2007) mixed methods textbook[2]	Produced the review guide (see sample entry in Appendix Table A1)

| Phase 5: Applied the review guide's classification schemes (i.e., coded). | 1. Classified each of the 209 articles according to fields in review guide

2. Assessed inter-rater reliability in the three categories that required the most inference:
• Number of paradigms represented
• Whether the paradigms (if multiple) were of equal or unequal weight
• Purpose for mixing[3] | • First wave of coding: Cohen's Kappa for inter-rater agreement ranged from 0.700 to 0.810 for the three categories ($p < 0.001$)[4]
• Second wave: Cohen's Kappa for inter-rater agreement ranged from 0.778 to 0.860 ($p < 0.001$) |
| Phase 6: Conducted thematic analysis of trends. | Analyzed the review guide classification results inductively, seeking themes (see Ezzy, 2002), specifically:
(1) Individually reviewed quantitative and qualitative summaries of the data (classification frequencies, coders' notes, and article texts);
(2) Created and presented individual summaries of 'trends' (i.e., themes);
(3) Discussed summaries with research team members and reached consensus on four trends.[5] | Produced the four trends described in the "Results" section of the study |

Note:
1 To evaluate whether an article constituted organizational communication research, we considered whether the study addressed one or more of the theories or topics found in an undergraduate-level organizational communication textbook, such as Miller (2015).

2 In addition to Greene, authors such as Creswell, Plano Clark, Gutmann, and Hanson (2003) and Teddlie and Tashakkori (2006) have proposed various typologies, but we selected Greene's text because it was the most comprehensive (i.e., it included typologies for each of the categories in our review guide) and concise (i.e., the typologies were easiest to understand, apply, and explain to readers).

3 Authors rarely explained these features of their work explicitly. Consequently, we often had to make inferences about authors' goals or intentions. In order to classify their work, we relied on the text of the articles themselves. When in doubt, we consulted with one another, using exact quotations from the article, to discuss ambiguous cases and to clarify classification standards.

4 We coded the data in two waves. In the first wave, we coded 95 articles. We assigned multiple coders to a randomly selected 30% of that sample, discussed and resolved disagreements, and developed additional classification guidelines to address the types of disagreements that occurred. Next, we assigned multiple coders to a randomly selected 20% of the sample, and we used this coding to gauge inter-rater reliability. In the second wave of the coding process, we coded an additional 114 articles. We assigned multiple coders to 20% of that sample. Of the whole sample ($n = 209$), and including those articles coded by more than author to assess reliability, the first author coded 148 articles, the second author coded 73 articles, and the third author coded 61 articles.

5 More specifically, the discussion involved connecting similar observations into a concise list of conceptually distinct trends. For example, we all noted the prevalence of interpretive approaches in our sample, but we decided that this fell under a broader trend related to the prevalence of single paradigm studies. This inductive process allowed us to acknowledge "the interplay of data and conceptualization" (Bulmer, 1979, p. 672) and, consequently, to ensure that our conclusions were grounded in the data.

Table 13.3 Definitions of Key Concepts in Mixed Methodology

Key Term	Definition
Methods	Techniques and procedures for gathering and analyzing data (Corbin & Strauss, 2008, p. 1)
Methodology	A way of thinking about and studying social phenomena (Corbin & Strauss, 2008, p. 1)
Paradigm	A model or framework that shapes both what we see and how we understand it (Baxter & Babbie, 2004, p. 426)

often associated with the mixing of data collected via quantitative and qualitative methodologies (e.g., questionnaire data, interview data), which implicates the mixing of post-positivist and interpretive paradigms. This is the kind of mixing emphasized in Miller et al., (2011), but it is also possible to mix methods within a single paradigm, as suggested in the prior example of an ethnographic study employing participant observation and in-depth interviewing.

Purposes for Mixing

Researchers may mix methods for different reasons. The five mixed methods purposes developed by Greene, Caracelli, and Graham (1989) for program evaluation have become standard terminology across disciplines. Each of the purposes—triangulation, complementarity, development, initiation and expansion—is defined in Table 13.4.

Table 13.4 Reasons for Mixing Methods from Greene (2007)

Mixed Methods Purpose	Description
Triangulation	"Seeks convergence, corroboration, or correspondence of results from multiple methods . . . In a mixed methods study with a triangulation intent, different methods are used to measure the *same phenomenon*" (p. 100).
Complementarity	Refers to the purpose of obtaining "broader, deeper, and more comprehensive social understandings by using methods that tap into different facets or dimensions of the *same complex phenomenon*. [. . .] results from the different methods serve to elaborate, enhance, deepen, and broaden the overall interpretations and inferences from the study" (p. 101).
Development	"The results of one method are used to inform the development of the other method, where development is broadly construed to include sampling and implementation, as well as actual instrument construction" (p. 102).
Initiation	"The most generative" of these purposes, as "different methods are implemented to assess various facets of the *same complex phenomenon*, much like complementarity, but the intended result is indeed divergence or dissonance" (pp. 102–103).
Expansion	Refers to a study in which "different methods are used to assess *different phenomena*" (p. 103).

Results of the Review

Our results reflect two forms of analysis: a quantitative analysis of the coding of articles according to the review guide, and a qualitative thematic analysis of overall trends in the application of mixed methods. With respect to the former, inter-rater reliability ranged from 0.700 to 0.860 for all coded categories. Additional information related to both forms of analysis can be found in Table 13.2.

Four Trends in Mixing Methods in Organizational Communication Research

Based on our review, we identified four trends related to how scholars have employed mixed-method approaches in published organizational communication research: (a) the predominance of single-paradigm studies and, in particular, the interpretive paradigm; (b) triangulation, complementarity, and development as the three most popular purposes for mixing; (c) the diversity of data collection methods and how they were used in combination; and (d) the overall lack of mixed methodology citations. Each trend is elaborated in detail below.

Single-Paradigm Studies and the Interpretive Paradigm Predominate

For each article, we labeled the paradigm or paradigms present using three categories: critical, interpretive, and post-positivist. Authors rarely stated their guiding paradigm(s) (i.e., in fewer than 15% of cases), but we could readily make inferences based upon the paradigmatic assumptions demonstrated in the authors' work. We found that 64% of the articles (133 out of 209) could be classified as "single paradigm"—that is, employing the assumptions of only one paradigm. Of the single-paradigm articles, 110 employed the interpretive paradigm (53% of the entire sample), and 22 employed the post-positivist paradigm (11%). In summary, roughly two-thirds of the articles mixed methods within a single paradigm rather than across paradigms, and roughly half the articles mixed methods within the interpretive paradigm. The roughly one-third of articles in the sample that did mix across paradigms demonstrated a variety of different orientations toward balancing and integrating the paradigmatic assumptions of the multiple paradigms upon which they drew (see Table A2 in the Appendix).

Whether used alone or in combination with other paradigms, the interpretive paradigm predominated. Overall, 90% of the articles in the sample incorporated the interpretive paradigm. By contrast, 36% of the articles involved the post-positivist paradigm, and just 13% engaged the critical paradigm. In short, the interpretive paradigm was strongly represented in mixed-method studies, while the post-positivist and critical paradigms appeared somewhat under-represented by comparison. Although some scholars associate the term *mixed methods* with a mix of quantitative and qualitative data, we found that the vast majority of mixing was happening within the interpretive paradigm.

Triangulation, Complementarity, and Development as Popular
Purposes for Mixing

In Table 13.4, we summarized Greene's (2007) five purposes for mixing methods: triangulation, complementarity, development, initiation, and expansion. When classifying purposes, we found that the only purpose that authors explicitly identified was triangulation (16 out of 209). Other authors used verbs that strongly suggested a particular purpose, such as "to complement" (generally, complementarity) or "to support" (generally, triangulation). In many cases, however, the authors provided no justification for mixing.

Among those studies whose authors did not explicitly identify a purpose for mixing, our classifications indicated that triangulation was the most common purpose for mixing in the sample overall (48%). Close behind were complementarity at 31% and development at 15%. Expansion was relatively uncommon, at 5%, and we classified only four articles (2%) as initiation. In our classification process, one of the most difficult distinctions to make was that between complementarity and triangulation, particularly in studies in the interpretive paradigm. The defining characteristic of triangulation is that the researcher uses multiple methods to assess or measure the same concept; the researcher then evaluates the degree to which these assessments of the focal concept converge (Greene, 2007). Complementarity, by contrast, seeks to understand different facets or aspects of a single complex phenomenon— something broader than a concept. Among the articles in our sample, authors' descriptions provided varying degrees of clarity about the extent to which their investigation targeted a single focal concept or multiple aspects of a complex phenomenon. For example, McGuire's (2010) study of spiritual labor included interviews about participants' experiences of and responses to "the spiritual expectations of their work," as well as an analysis of documents and artifacts "to understand how spirituality might be commodified" (p. 82). We concluded that spiritual labor functioned as a focal concept in this article, so we classified the purpose for mixing as triangulation. One might reasonably argue, however, that the quoted text reflects different aspects of spiritual labor as a complex phenomenon.

We saw a similar lack of clarity in much of the purist interpretive work in our sample; in such cases, authors seemed to implicitly invoke a paradigmatic justification for mixing qualitative data through holistic analytical techniques, such as thematic analysis or case study methodology. Because so many of the articles in our sample (about one-third) self-identified as case studies, we sought clarification about whether the methodology itself specifies a purpose for mixing. According to Yin (2003), "The case study inquiry [. . .] relies on multiple sources of evidence, with data needing to converge in a triangulation fashion" (p. 13). Such a description seems inclusive of complementarity, as well as triangulation. Since the concept of triangulation originated in the post-positivist paradigm (e.g., Jick, 1979), the difficulty may originate in the challenge of translating the concept across paradigms. Along similar lines, mixed methodologists have argued that the label "triangulation" has been rendered imprecise by popular usage (Greene, Caracelli, & Graham, 1989) and that there are multiple ways of mixing that seek convergence in findings. In our sample, descriptions of how researchers sought triangulating or complementary evidence were often opaque or altogether absent.

Diverse Combinations of Methods and Ways of Mixing

Our analysis illuminated the variety of data collection methods and how they have been combined and mixed. The term "mixed methods" encompasses many combinations of research methodologies. In order to illustrate the diversity of methods mixed, we found it helpful to condense the list of methods used into nine emic categories, namely: eight categories of data collection methods (participant observation, non-participant observation, individual interviews, focus groups, archival records and documents, other text, questionnaire with closed and/or open-ended items, and experimental design), as well as one category for data transformation, namely coding and content analysis.

The most frequently occurring data collection method, overall, was interviewing. In our sample, 81% of the studies included individual interviews among their data. In our sample as a whole, interviewing had been combined with each of the eight other categories of methods. Non-participant observation (39%), archival records or documents (39%), and questionnaires (33%) were the other most frequently used methods.

We observed a variety of ways of mixing data from these and other methods. The methods most likely to be combined were non-participant observation and interviews. Because the sample studies were so diverse, studies that mixed just these two methods constituted only 12% of the sample. The combination of non-participant observation, interviews, and archival records or documents also represented 12% of the studies in the sample. Overall, studies that mixed non-participant observation and interviews with one or more additional methods constituted approximately one-third of the sample (34%). By providing just two examples from the former category—the observation and interview mix— we hope to give a glimpse of the diversity of ways of mixing that we observed in our sample. Treem (2012) and Eisenberg, Murphy, and Andrews (1998) exemplify two different sequential approaches. Eisenberg et al. studied the process of hiring a university provost by observing search committee meetings, observing candidate interviews, and then conducting follow-up interviews with search committee members and other stakeholders "for their description and impressions of the process" (p. 7). Treem (2012) applied a reverse approach:

> The goal of the first stage was to investigate the criteria used by workers to determine who is an expert among team members. To achieve this goal, I examined the interview data through a process of "selective coding." [. . .] Next, a threshold was implemented to focus on themes widely agreed upon among subjects across the sites. [. . .] [W]e still do not know what specific

behaviors an actor needed to engage in to for an observer to make the relevant attributions about expertise. To uncover these behaviors, I turned to the observational data.

(pp. 29–30)

While these examples were both sequential, many other studies collected or analyzed observational and interview data concurrently (e.g., Turner & Krizek, 2006) or iteratively (e.g., member checking, as in Scarduzio, 2011). Interpretive scholars tended to mix ethnographic observation with interviews (e.g., Edley, 2000; Parker, 2001; Robinson, 2011; Scarduzio, 2011; Shuler & Sypher, 2000; Turner & Krizek, 2006). While it appeared, in most cases, that the data were collected concurrently and mixed during collection, analysis, and presentation, authors did not regard this as mixing but as subsumed under qualitative analysis techniques like thematic analysis, open coding, and constant comparative techniques.

The next most common combination of methods was interviews and questionnaires (only the two, 9%; with additional methods, 20%). In such cases, interview data were often treated as a supplement to questionnaire data, as exemplified by Russo (1998). Development was also a common purpose guiding the interview-questionnaire combination; authors used data of one kind to develop an instrument or identify a sample to collect a different kind of data. Xu (2011) interviewed faculty members at Chinese universities to develop questionnaire items based on their descriptions of a good leader. Similarly, Myers and Oetzel (2003) used interviews to determine dimensions of organizational assimilation, followed by the use of questionnaire data to develop and validate a measure. Waldeck, Seibold, and Flanagin (2004) used interviews as a preliminary step to developing a scenario-based questionnaire to ensure that scenarios "represented prototypical, natural, and recognizable organizational assimilation experiences" (p. 172). Warisse Turner, Grube, Tinsley, Lee, and O'Pell (2006) developed research questions in response to the quantitative results of a questionnaire.

In total, we logged 53 different permutations of our nine categories of data collection and transformation methods, with a maximum of five methods in a single study. As these relatively small distributions suggest, the permutations of methods mixed were diverse.

Lack of Mixed-Method Citations

To investigate which articles in our sample cited mixed-method literature, we defined "mixed-method literature" as published articles or books that explicitly addressed methodological concerns related to mixing methods within or across paradigms. The majority of studies reviewed, 84%, did not cite any mixed-method literature. Most authors used citations to provide further justification and explanation of their analytical techniques. The majority of our sample fell within the interpretive paradigm; consequently, we saw many authors cite seminal qualitative analysis sources such as Glaser and Strauss (1967) or Strauss and Corbin (1990), but these same authors tended not to cite any sources to support their rationale for collecting data using multiple methods. As we discussed in the prior section on purposes for mixing, it seems reasonable to assume that qualitative methodologies are compatible with the idea that analyses of multiple data sources would seek convergence, but perhaps the more interesting question is how a more targeted approach might improve the researcher's argument for conclusions related to both similarities and differences related to the phenomena of study. As a disciplinary norm, it appeared that organizational communication scholars are socialized to cite methodological sources for individual methodologies but not for mixed-method approaches.

Among the articles that cited mixed-method literature, only a few citations were used by multiple studies in the sample. The most-frequently cited sources were Miles and Huberman (1994) and Rossman and Wilson (1985). Additionally, two authors appeared frequently, although no particular work was cited more than once: Alan Bryman (1988; 2006; also, with co-authors, Deacon, Bryman, & Fenton, 1998) and John W. Creswell (1994; 1998; 2003). Consistent with their reputations, Bryman was cited regarding the mixing of quantitative and qualitative methods, while Creswell was cited regarding mixing methods in qualitative inquiry.

Reflections and Recommendations Based on the Corpus of Work Reviewed

The purpose of this paper was to examine and characterize the status of mixed methods research in organizational communication. Here, we present our reflections and recommendations in two veins. First, we give suggestions regarding whether and how to mix more effectively; we believe that these suggestions, if implemented, would advance our field methodologically. Second, we discuss how greater visibility for mixed-methods research and thinking would advance our field's contributions to knowledge and society.

Suggestions for Whether and How to Mix Methods

In this section, we present implications for each trend subsumed within a set of considerations for those who would consider mixing, each with a default approach to be avoided and a corresponding recommendation.

Intentionality

First and foremost, we want to encourage researchers to choose the method or methods that best suit the research context, question, and theoretical perspective, as well as the researcher's mental model. Myers (2013) asked readers to challenge the assumption that, in research design, "more is more"; instead, she advocated for intentional mixed-method designs in which "more really is more" (p. 297). We wish to echo and extend that argument in light of the findings from our review.

Default approach: Mixing as habit. With respect to the question of when *not* to mix methods, one answer is not to mix methods in an unexamined or habitual way. As our first trend illustrated, the single-paradigm interpretive studies that dominated the sample typically had a number of different types of data, but the authors did not necessarily indicate which data had been mixed, at what point, or to what extent the mixing of data informed the findings. While these may be common practices, mixed methodology suggests opportunities for thoughtful reflection on the purpose for mixing—as well as its implications for data collection and analysis—even within a single paradigm. Similarly, popular cross-paradigmatic sequential designs, like using interview data to develop a questionnaire, are only strengthened by context-specific explanations of what was expected and what was actually gained from the mixed-method design.

Recommendation: Make the rationale for mixing more explicit and methodologically specific. The fourth trend from our review described how authors often did not cite relevant, existing mixed-method literature. We recommend that researchers who mix methods express their rationales for mixing using mixed-methods terminology. They may also find it useful to refer the reader to methodological sources that support their research design (e.g., Creswell, 2003; Creswell, Plano Clark, Gutmann, & Hanson, 2003; Teddlie & Tashakkori, 2006) or the legitimacy of their paradigmatic stance (Greene, 2007). For an example of an explanation and justification of a mixed-method approach that uses mixed methodological citations, see the excerpt from Lammers, Atouba, and Carlson (2013) in the appendix.

We believe that citing relevant mixed-method literature in communication research will benefit both individual researchers and the field as a whole. For the researcher, using mixed-methods terminology will enhance the transparency of the methods section and showcase the intentionality of the author's methodological decisions. On a field level, citing relevant methodological literature will help develop normative best practices for communication scholars. Even simply including the term "mixed methods" in an article's abstract or keywords will help other scholars find examples of mixed methods within the field. Not only will these practices improve the impact of individual studies; in time, they may help establish mixed methods as a distinct methodology in social inquiry.

Convergence

One implication of our findings is that researchers who mix methods appear to be more comfortable pursuing and reporting convergent findings than divergent findings. We attribute this, at least in part, to an overreliance on triangulation as the predominant rationale for mixing methods. When considering whether and how to mix methods, we encourage researchers to think about how important it is to them that the results of their methods fully converge and how they might respond to divergent results.

Default approach: Privilege full convergence. Our second trend related to the prevalence of triangulation as a purpose for mixing methods. Recall that, in triangulation, each of the multiple methods employed should be applied to the same construct or phenomenon (Greene, 2007). Although the results may fully converge, partially converge, or diverge (Jick, 1979), scholars predominantly seek and report convergent results. In other words, triangulation is largely used for confirmation rather than disconfirmation or more nuanced comparison. As such, the overreliance on using mixed methods for confirming preconceived theories or ideas runs the risk of confirmation bias (e.g., Evans, 1989). We suspect that scholars may feel pressure not to report partially or fully divergent results, but discovering and reporting such results would be very helpful for breaking new ground conceptually, theoretically, or in a relatively unexplored research context.

Recommendation: Consider seeking, as well as reporting, divergent results. Regarding the question of whether or when to mix methods, we suggest that mixing methods can be effective for exploring an emerging communicative or social problem, or a new research context. If focusing on a single construct, as in triangulation, the researcher should be sure to give consideration to divergent findings, as they may suggest fruitful directions for continued study. For example, after describing the extensive data she collected as a participant, Tracy (2005) noted that she conducted interviews "to elaborate issues and inconsistencies noted in participant observation" (p. 266) in her study of correctional officers. Tracy (2005) went on to mention one such instance in the study, in which she recounted an observation and later questioned the officer about the incident in an interview. Noting dissonances, rather than dismissing them, gave the researcher the opportunity to dig deeper during data collection and better convey the nuanced relationship between perceptions and actions.

Alternatively, other purposes for mixing—and corresponding research designs—are also possible. While triangulation focuses on a single construct, mixed methods can also be applied to different but related phenomena; for example, for the purpose of expansion, initiation, or development. For example, Lammers, Atouba, and Carlson's (2013) study of organizational and group identification among IT workers collected individual interviews after analyzing questionnaire results for the purpose of expansion—specifically, to provide researchers with examples of context-specific communication behaviors and messages that illustrated "oneness" and other perceptual concepts from the questionnaire. As purposes for mixing, expansion, initiation, and development can emphasize exploration rather than confirmation.

Innovation

Creativity involves making meaningful connections between unrelated ideas. Similarly, social scientists can innovate by using accepted methods in unforeseen ways. When considering whether to mix methods, some researchers may find appeal in challenging themselves by incorporating a method, methodology, or paradigm that they do not typically engage. As specialists, scholars may see this as risky, but the combination of perspectives or traditions may yield unexpectedly insightful results.

Default approach: When in doubt, add semi-structured interviews. Our third trend illustrated that there are many accepted methods, many ways to conduct them, and many ways to combine them. Even so, the most common method to be mixed with other methods was the semi-structured interview. We see more exciting opportunities for pursuing methodological innovation through the use of mixed-method designs.

Recommendation: Mixing to incorporate an unconventional method. Acknowledging the popularity of interviewing as a method, we also wish to encourage researchers to consider the variety of ways that interviewing could be conducted and combined with other methods. Interviews can vary widely in approach (e.g., structured, semi-structured), analysis (e.g., constructivist grounded theory, discourse analysis, content analysis), and potential for mixing (see Sandelowski, Voils, & Knafl, 2009; Teddlie & Tashakkori, 2009). For example, Chewning, Lai, and Doerfel (2013) developed an extensive coding system to transform data from a longitudinal interview design into network data that illustrated the evolution of an inter-organizational communication network.

Beyond interviews, we see mixed-method approaches as conducive to using unconventional methods or to using familiar methods in unconventional ways. For instance, there is a growing trend towards collecting Big Data and applying computational social science methods in communication research (e.g., Lazer et al., 2009; Welles, Vashevko, Bennett, & Contractor, 2014). Mixing such computational methods—like machine learning—with methods that are more familiar—like regression—might be a fruitful way to introduce unconventional methods to a broader audience. Across a range of methods, scholars wishing to push methodological boundaries may find that mixing methods allows them more freedom to experiment.

Advancing the Field's Contributions to Knowledge and Society

Moving from a tactical view to a strategic view, we see three levels at which the use and knowledge of mixed methods can advance communication research: (1) on the macro level, a move toward more common disciplinary ground; (2) on the meso level, a move toward more nuanced understandings of communication phenomena; and (3) on the micro level, a move toward more individual scholars enjoying the documented career benefits of being a 'multilingual' researcher.

Communication—and, more specifically, organizational communication—is an eclectic field, consisting of diverse intellectual traditions and methods. Because methods are deeply tied to specific paradigmatic assumptions (see also Abbott, 2004, p. 54), we believe that the training, use, and acceptance of mixed methods can help the field find what Corman and Poole (2000) referred to as common ground: a deeper disciplinary unification and collective interest. Some of the benefits of finding common ground, according to the essays in Corman and Poole's (2000) collection, include moving beyond simplistic and antagonistic binary thinking, recognizing the limitations of our own preferred perspectives, avoiding unproductive and chronic conflict, shifting efforts from abstract disagreements to more practical social problems, and creating an overall culture of hospitality rather than hostility. Similarly, Miller et al. (2011) urged that scholars who were entrenched in either quantitative or qualitative preferences "must change their current practice of largely ignoring each other's work. Only through understanding each other's contributions and limitations can quantitative and interpretive-critical scholars identify potential complementarities" (p. 41). A move toward greater common ground would not only improve the dialogue within the discipline of communication, but also its contributions to interdisciplinary conversations. Many communication scholars have found cross-disciplinary collaborators and audiences by contributing to projects that compare some form of communication data with data of another type, such as behavioral, consumer, biophysical, cognitive, perceptual, or performance data. In this way, mixed-methods approaches could be a gateway to becoming, as Kuhn (2005) proposed, "meaningfully interdisciplinary" (p. 625).

Moving from a macro level to a meso level, we reiterate a second advantage of using mixed methods: namely, the potential for more nuanced understanding of a topic of inquiry. The studies included in our review resulted from researchers' interest in understanding a phenomenon in ways that transcended the limitations of a single method or paradigm. As Myers (2013), citing Molina-Azorin (2011), suggested, mixed-method studies may even garner greater readership and citation counts than single-method studies.

Finally, there are individual advantages for understanding best practices of mixed methods research, especially for a new generation of doctoral students. We tend to agree with Putnam (2008) that doctoral students in organizational communication often lack a deeper understanding of the philosophical assumptions and basic limitations underlying different research methods (quoted in Hample, 2008). Thus, a more holistic training in mixed methods research—in concert with the basic histories, assumptions, and limitations of distinct methodologies—could prevent early career scholars from developing methodological tunnel vision. Krone (2000) has noted some of the individual advantages of training in mixed method research, especially for doctoral students, including improved ability to collaborate in interdisciplinary projects, teach introductory research method courses, and hold intelligent conversations with prospective colleagues during job interviews. These examples point to a sort of intellectual empathy that can be gained from mixed-methods training, which is something that is likely to yield tangible benefits for the early career scholar.

Conclusion

Our review sought to analyze how methods have been mixed in published organizational communication research over the past twenty years. In addition, we considered how mixed-method approaches could advance communication research in the future. From the review, we identified four trends: (a) the dominance of single-paradigm, interpretive studies; (b) the preponderance of triangulation, complementarity, and development as purposes for mixing methods; (c) varied combinations of methods; and (d) a lack of mixed-methods citations. We concluded by discussing the implications of these trends for communication researchers seeking guidance on whether or how to mix, as well as the ways in which greater visibility for mixed-method approaches can advance the field of communication.

We believe that the promotion of mixed methodology in organizational communication scholarship will not only help individual scholars to work in a more 'multilingual' fashion, but will help us as researchers, collectively, to broaden and deepen our discoveries. Insightful research employing mixed methods will be poised to captivate and enlighten scholars of all persuasions and disciplines.

Appendix A

Table A1 Mixed Method Review Guide: Organizational Communication Empirical Examples (Adapted from Gannon & Sun, unpublished)

Citation	Ashcraft, K. L., & Kedrowicz, A. (2002). Self-direction or social support? Nonprofit empowerment and the tacit employment contract of organizational communication studies. *Communication Monographs, 69*(1), 88–110. doi: 10.1080/03637750216538
Paradigm: Post-positivist, Systems, Interpretive (Constructive), Critical, Participation (Greene, 2007, p. 52, and Baxter & Babbie, 2004, p. 47)	Interpretive
Methods used/mixed	Non-participant observation, interviews; label methodology as "organizational ethnography"
How do they describe reasons, purposes, justification for mixing? Quote directly from authors.	"Done well, organizational ethnography informs larger theoretical and practical concerns, lending variation, incongruity, process, nuance, and texture to more conventional accounts. . . . The study involved approximately 230 hours of participant observation across multiple forums, such as volunteer training and support meetings, staff meetings and retreats, social functions, and informal interaction at the shelter. [. . .] Additionally, the data include in-depth interviews [. . .]. Interview questions probed perceptions of the philosophy, structure, and practice of empowerment at Haven." (pp. 95–96)
Purpose of mixing (Greene, 2007, p. 98–104, 123, 125)	Complementarity
Notes on analysis (how did they mix?)	"Our analytic methods reflect the sort of inductive, iterative process that generally suits ethnographic data" (p. 96).
Cited any MM literature? (Include any references)	No

Table A2 Frequency of Multiple-Paradigm Studies and Balance of Paradigms Mixed

Paradigms Balanced?	Paradigms Represented	Frequency[a] (n=75)	Example
Balanced	Interpretive and Post-positivist	24	Leonardi (2009) analyzed ethnographic data (field notes and recorded conversations) using selective coding, constant comparison, and a hierarchical linear regression model of coded communication behaviors. The results section gives roughly equal weight to results of qualitative and quantitative analysis.
Unbalanced	Post-positivist, Primary; Interpretive, Secondary	18	Miller and Koesten (2008) collected data using questionnaires and interviews, but they stated that the interviews would serve as an "illustration of the quantitative results rather than as a central focus of the research" (p. 19).
Balanced	Interpretive and Critical	18	Scarduzio (2011) analyzed data from observations and interviews to answer three research questions related to emotional labor, emotional deviance (i.e., resistance), power, and status. Observations related to power and status appeared throughout the presentation of inductively-generated themes.
Unbalanced	Interpretive, Primary; Critical, Secondary	6	Harter, Scott, Novak, Leeman, and Morris (2006) analyzed data from participant observation, interviews, and organizational documents to explore a non-profit organization's efforts to integrate people with disabilities into the community through collaborative artistic projects. Although the study related to the topic of empowerment, concepts like power, oppression, and hegemony were implied rather than explicitly considered.
Unbalanced	Interpretive, Primary; Post-positivist, Secondary	5	Thomas et al. (2006) asked participants to keep a five-day log of e-mails received and to nominate one "illustrative" e-mail for closer inspection. The authors performed a close textual analysis of such illustrative e-mail chain and conducted a focus group in which participants reacted to the same text. Additionally, however, the authors also measured and reported on the number of e-mails logged and the length of e-mails.

Paradigms Balanced?	Paradigms Represented	Frequency[a] (n=75)	Example
Unbalanced	Interpretive, Primary; Critical, Secondary; Post-positivist, Tertiary	3	Hamel (2009) used a survey, interviews, and a focus group to explore how female executives made sense of barriers to career advancement for women. Perhaps because most of the research questions were "how" questions, the results section drew heavily on the qualitative data and gave numeric response distributions for only one questionnaire item.
Unbalanced	Post-positivist, Primary; Critical, Secondary; Interpretive, Tertiary	1	Shefner-Rogers, Rao, Rogers, and Wayangankar (1998) evaluated an entrepreneurship program intended to empower women dairy farmers in India. In addition to their primary method, a questionnaire, the authors reported that they conducted in-depth interviews with dairy farmers and observed program activities, which "enriched the quantitative data that [they] collected about empowerment" (p. 330). In the paper, however, no qualitative data is directly reported, only quantitative results.

Note: (a) Among studies in sample with multiple paradigms (75 out of 209)

Appendix B

Sample Explanation of Mixed-Methods Approach with Methodological References:

> In order to investigate differences among identities we used a mixed-methods approach. Many scholars advocate for mixing methods in order to capitalize on the "complementary strengths" of the elements that they are mixing—or to compensate for those elements' individual limitations (Greene, Caracelli, & Graham, 1989). Mixing methods can also prompt discovery by illuminating researchers' paradigmatic assumptions.
>
> A mixed-methods approach was particularly valuable to this study due to the exploratory nature of the project of differentiating among targets of identification. In mixed methodologists' terminology, our purpose for mixing methods was expansion (Greene, Caracelli, & Graham, 1989; Teddlie & Tashakkori, 2009). The qualitative analysis of interviews was used to expand on the initial understanding gained from the quantitative analysis of the survey data. In sum, we opted to use a mixed-method approach to more completely analyze the data in search of illustrations, explanations, and further understanding of the findings from the survey

analysis in the participants' own words. The qualitative data also provided more insight into particular communication behaviors and messages that participants associated with their "oneness" with a target of identification. Research designs of this kind have been classified as the explanatory sequential mixed data analysis strategy (Creswell & Plano Clark, 2007; Teddlie & Tashakkori, 2009). An explanatory sequential mixed data analysis design refers to a mixed methods research design in which the quantitative phase of the study occurs before the qualitative phase of the study, with the qualitative phase emerging from or related to the quantitative phase (Teddlie & Tashakkori, 2009). When the purpose of mixing methods is expansion, a sequential mixed design is an appropriate strategy (Teddlie & Tashakkori, 2009).

(Lammers, Atouba, & Carlson, 2013, pp. 514–515)

Acknowledgments

The authors wish to thank the editor and editorial staff of *Communication Yearbook 40*, as well as the anonymous reviewers, for their very helpful feedback.

Note

1   For example, studies of organizational communication networks increasingly collect self-reported networks (e.g., survey responses that indicate individuals' reports of communication ties), observed networks (e.g., the investigator's observations of actual communication), and chain-of-command networks (e.g., organizational charts or other records that indicate with whom individuals are supposed to communicate) in order to characterize an organization's communication structure.

References

(NB Single asterisk indicates references included in the review. Double asterisk indicates references included in the review and directly cited in the text or appendices.)

Abbott, A. (2004). *Methods of discovery: Heuristics for the social sciences*. New York: W.W. Norton & Company, Inc.
Alise, M. A., & Teddlie, C. (2010). A continuation of the paradigm wars? Prevalence rates of methodological approaches across the social/behavioral sciences. *Journal of Mixed Methods Research, 4*, 103–126. doi: 10.1177/1558689809360805
*Allen, M. W., Walker, K. L., & Brady, R. (2012). Sustainability discourse within a supply chain relationship: Mapping convergence and divergence. *Journal of Business Communication, 49*, 210–236. doi: 10.1177/0021943612446732
*Anderson, D. L. (2004). The textualizing functions of writing for organizational change. *Journal of Business and Technical Communication, 18*, 141–164. doi: 10.1177/1050651903260800

*Apker, J. (2001). Role development in the managed care era: A case of hospital-based nursing. *Journal of Applied Communication Research, 29*, 117–136. doi: 10.1080/00909880128106

*Ashcraft, K. L. (2000). Empowering "professional" relationships: Organizational communication meets feminist practice. *Management Communication Quarterly, 13*, 347–392. doi: 10.1177/0893318900133001

*Ashcraft, K. L. (2006). Feminist-bureaucratic control and other adversarial allies: Extending organized dissonance to the practice of "new" forms. *Communication Monographs, 73*, 55–86. doi: 10.1080/03637750600557081

**Ashcraft, K. L., & Kedrowicz, A. (2002). Self-direction or social support? Nonprofit empowerment and the tacit employment contract of organizational communication studies. *Communication Monographs, 69*, 88–110. doi: 10.1080/0363775021 6538

*Ashcraft, K. L., & Pacanowsky, M. E. (1996). "A woman's worst enemy": Reflections on a narrative of organizational life and female identity. *Journal of Applied Communication Research, 24*, 217–239. doi: 10.1080/00909889609365452

*Ballard, D. I., & Seibold, D. R. (2004a). Communication-related organizational structures and work group temporal experiences: The effects of coordination method, technology type, and feedback cycle on members' construals and enactments of time. *Communication Monographs, 71*, 1–27. doi: 10.1080/0363452041000 1691474

*Ballard, D. I., & Seibold, D. R. (2004b). Organizational members' communication and temporal experience. *Communication Research, 31*, 135–172. doi: 10.1177/ 0093650203261504

*Barbour, J. B., & Gill, R. (2014). Designing communication for the day-to-day safety oversight of nuclear power plants. *Journal of Applied Communication Research, 42*, 168–189. doi: 10.1080/00909882.2013.859291

*Barge, J. K. (2004). Reflexivity and managerial practice. *Communication Monographs, 71*, 70–96. doi: 10.1080/03634520410001691465

*Barge, J. K., Lee, M., Maddux, K., Nabring, R., & Townsend, B. (2008). Managing dualities in planned change initiatives. *Journal of Applied Communication Research, 36*, 364–390. doi: 10.1080/00909880802129996

*Barker, J. R., & Cheney, G. (1994). The concept and the practices of discipline in contemporary organizational life. *Communications Monographs, 61*, 19–43. doi: 10.1080/03637759409376321

*Barley, W. C., Leonardi, P. M., & Bailey, D. E. (2012). Engineering objects for collaboration: Strategies of ambiguity and clarity at knowledge boundaries. *Human Communication Research, 38*, 280–308. doi: 10.1111/j.1468-2958.2012.01430.x

*Bastien, D. T. (1994). A feedback loop model of postmerger performance: Customers and competitors. *Management Communication Quarterly, 8*, 46–69. doi: 10.1177/0893318994008001003

Baxter, L. A., & Babbie, E. R. (2004). *The basics of communication research*. Belmont, CA: Wadsworth/Thomson Learning.

*Bennett, W. L., Foot, K., & Xenos, M. (2011). Narratives and network organization: A comparison of fair trade systems in two nations. *Journal of Communication, 61*, 219–245. doi: 10.1111/j.1460-2466.2011.01538.x

*Berkelaar, B. L., Buzzanell, P. M., Kisselburgh, L. G., Tan, W., & Shen, Y. (2012). "First, it's dirty. Second, it's dangerous. Third, it's insulting": Urban Chinese children talk about dirty work. *Communication Monographs, 79*, 93–114. doi: 10.1080/03637751.2011.646490

Biesta, G. J. J. (2010). Pragmatism and the philosophical foundations of mixed methods research. In A. Tashakkori & C. Teddlie (Eds.), *Sage Handbook of mixed methods in social and behavioral research*. Thousand Oaks, CA: Sage.

*Bird, S. (2007). Sensemaking and identity. *Journal of Business Communication, 44*, 311–339. doi: 10.1177/0021943607306135

*Bolkan, S., & Daly, J. A. (2009). Organizational responses to consumer complaints: An examination of effective remediation tactics. *Journal of Applied Communication Research, 37*, 21–39. doi: 10.1080/00909880802592656

*Bolkan, S., Goodboy, A. K., & Daly, J. A. (2010). Consumer satisfaction and repatronage intentions following a business failure: The importance of perceived control with an organizational complaint. *Communication Reports, 23*, 14–25. doi: 10.1080/08934211003598767

*Borden, S. L. (1997). Choice processes in a newspaper ethics case. *Communication Monographs, 64*, 65–81. doi: 10.1080/03637759709376405

*Bremner, S. (2014). Genres and processes in the PR industry: Behind the scenes with an intern writer. *Journal of Business Communication, 51*, 259–278. doi: 10.1177/2329488414525398

*Browning, L. D., & Beyer, J. M. (1998). The structuring of shared voluntary standards in the U.S. semiconductor industry: Communicating to reach agreement. *Communication Monographs, 65*, 220–243. doi: 10.1080/03637759809376449

Bryman, A. (1988). *Quantity and quality in social research*. London: Unwin Hyman.

Bryman, A. (2006). Integrating quantitative and qualitative research: How is it done? *Qualitative Research, 6*, 97–113. doi: 10.1177/1468794106058877

Bulmer, M. (1979). Concepts in the analysis of qualitative data. *Sociological Review, 27*, 651–677. doi: 10.1111/1467-954X.ep5462736

*Buzzanell, P. M., & Burrell, N. A. (1997). Family and workplace conflict: Examining metaphorical conflict schemas and expressions across context and sex. *Human Communication Research, 24*, 109–146. doi: 10.1111/j.1468-2958.1997.tb00589.x

*Buzzanell, P. M., & Liu, M. (2005). Struggling with maternity leave policies and practices: A poststructuralist feminist analysis of gendered organizing. *Journal of Applied Communication Research, 33*, 1–25. doi: 10.1080/0090988042000318495

Campbell, D. T., & Fiske, D. W. (1959). Convergent and discriminant validation by the multitrait-multimethod matrix. *Psychological Bulletin, 56*(2), 81–105. doi: 10.1037/h0046016

*Canary, H. (2010). Constructing policy knowledge: Contradictions, communication, and knowledge frames. *Communication Monographs, 77*, 181–206. doi: 10.1080/03637751003758185

**Chewning, L. V., Lai, C., & Doerfel, M. L. (2013). Organizational resilience and using information and communication technologies to rebuild communication structures. *Management Communication Quarterly, 27*, 237–263. doi: 10.1177/0893318912465815

*Chiles, A. M., & Zorn, T. E. (1995). Empowerment in organizations: Employees' perceptions of the influences on empowerment. *Journal of Applied Communication Research, 23*, 1–25. doi: 10.1080/00909889509365411

*Conaway, R. N., & Wardrope, W. J. (2010). Do their words really matter? Thematic analysis of U.S. and Latin American CEO letters. *Journal of Business Communication, 47*, 141–168. doi: 10.1177/0021943610364523

*Cooper, K. R., & Shumate, M. (2012). Interorganizational collaboration explored through the bona fide network perspective. *Management Communication Quarterly, 26*, 623–654. doi: 10.1177/0893318912462014

Corbin, J., & Strauss, A. (2008). *Basics of qualitative research* (3rd edn). Los Angeles: Sage.

Corman, S. R., & Poole, M. S. (2000). *Perspectives on organizational communication: Finding common ground.* New York: Guilford Press.

*Cornelissen, J. P., & Thorpe, R. (2001). The organisation of external communication disciplines in UK companies: A conceptual and empirical analysis of dimensions and determinants. *Journal of Business Communication, 38,* 413–438. doi: 10.1177/002194360103800402

Creswell, J. W. (1994). *Research design: Qualitative, quantitative, and mixed methods approaches* (1st edn). Thousand Oak, CA: Sage.

Creswell, J. W. (1998). *Qualitative inquiry and research design: Choosing among five traditions.* Thousand Oaks, CA: Sage.

Creswell, J. W. (2003). *Research design: Qualitative, quantitative, and mixed methods approaches* (2nd edn). Thousand Oak, CA: Sage.

Creswell, J. W. (2008). *Educational research: Planning, conducting and evaluating quantitative and qualitative research* (3rd edn). Upper Saddle River, NJ: Pearson/Merrill Prentice Hall.

Creswell, J. W., & Plano Clark, V. L. (2007). *Designing and conducting mixed methods research.* Thousand Oaks, CA: Sage.

Creswell, J. W., Plano Clark, V. L., Gutmann, M. L., & Hanson, W. E. (2003). Advanced mixed methods research designs. In A. Tashakkori & C. Teddlie (Eds.), *Handbook of mixed methods research in social and behavorial research.* Thousand Oaks, CA: Sage.

Deacon, D., Bryman, A., and Fenton, N. (1998). Collision or collusion? A discussion of the unplanned triangulation of quantitative and qualitative research methods. *International Journal of Social Research Methodology, 1,* 47–63. doi: 10.1080/13645579.1998.10846862

*Dempsey, S. E. (2007). Negotiating accountability within international contexts: The role of bounded voice. *Communication Monographs, 74,* 311–322. doi: 10.1080/03637750701543485

*D'Enbeau, S., & Buzzanell, P. M. (2011). Selling (out) feminism: Sustainability of ideology–viability tensions in a competitive marketplace. *Communication Monographs, 78,* 27–52. doi: 10.1080/03637751.2010.542472

*DiSanza, J. R. (1995). Bank teller organizational assimilation in a system of contradictory practices. *Management Communication Quarterly, 9,* 191–218. doi: 10.1177/0893318995009002003

*Ditlevsen, M. (2012). Telling the story of Danisco's annual reports (1935 through 2007–2008) from a communicative perspective. *Journal of Business and Technical Communication, 26,* 92–115. doi: 10.1177/1050651911421132

*Dougherty, D., & Smythe, M. J. (2004). Sensemaking, organizational culture, and sexual harassment. *Journal of Applied Communication Research, 32,* 293–317. doi: 10.1080/0090988042000275998

*Downing, J. R. (2004). "It's easier to ask someone I know". *Journal of Business Communication, 41,* 166–191. doi: 10.1177/0021943603262140

*Downing, J. R. (2007). No greater sacrifice: American airlines employee crisis response to the September 11 attack. *Journal of Applied Communication Research, 35,* 350–375. doi: 10.1080/00909880701611078

**Edley, P. P. (2000). Discursive essentializing in a woman-owned business: Gendered stereotypes and strategic subordination. *Management Communication Quarterly, 14,* 271–306. doi: 10.1177/0893318900142003

**Eisenberg, E. M., Murphy, A., & Andrews, L. (1998). Openness and decision making in the search for a university provost. *Communication Monographs, 65*, 1–23. doi: 10.1080/03637759809376432

*Ellingson, L. L. (2003). Interdisciplinary health care teamwork in the clinic backstage. *Journal of Applied Communication Research, 31*, 93. doi: 10.1080/00909880320000 64579

*Erbert, L. A. (2014). Antagonistic and nonantagonistic dialectical contradictions in organizational conflict. *Journal of Business Communication, 51*, 138–158. doi: 10.1177/2329488414525194

*Erhardt, N., & Gibbs, J. L. (2014). The dialectical nature of impression management in knowledge work: Unpacking tensions in media use between managers and subordinates. *Management Communication Quarterly, 28*, 155–186. doi: 10.1177/ 0893318913520508

Evans, J. (1989). *Bias in human reasoning: Causes and consequences*. Hillsdale, NJ: Lawrence Erlbaum.

Ezzy, D. (2002). Coding data and interpreting texts: Methods of analysis. In D. Ezzy, *Qualitative Analysis: Practice and Innovation* (pp. 80–110). London: Routledge.

*Fairhurst, G. T., Cooren, F., & Cahill, D. J. (2002). Discursiveness, contradiction, and unintended consequences in successive downsizings. *Management Communication Quarterly, 15*, 501–540. doi: 10.1177/0893318902154001

*Flanagin, A. J., Monge, P., & Fulk, J. (2001). The value of formative investment in organizational federations. *Human Communication Research, 27*, 69–93. doi: 10.1111/j.1468-2958.2001.tb00776.x

*Forbes, D. A. (2009). Commodification and co-modification explicating black female sexuality in organizations. *Management Communication Quarterly, 22*, 577–613. doi: 10.1177/0893318908331322

*Ford, W. S. Z. (1995). Evaluation of the indirect influence of courteous service on customer discretionary behavior. *Human Communication Research, 22*, 65–89. doi: 10.1111/j.1468-2958.1995.tb00362.x

*Franz, C. R., Gregory Jin, K., & Jin, K. G. (1995). The structure of group conflict in a collaborative work group during information systems development. *Journal of Applied Communication Research, 23*, 108–127. doi: 10.1080/009098895093 65418

*Gibson, M. K., & Papa, M. J. (2000). The mud, the blood, and the beer guys: Organizational osmosis in blue-collar work groups. *Journal of Applied Communication Research, 28*, 68–88. doi: 10.1080/00909880009365554

*Gilsdorf, J. W. (1998). Organizational rules on communicating: How employees are— and are not—learning the ropes. *Journal of Business Communication, 35*, 173–201. doi: 10.1177/002194369803500201

Glaser, B., & Strauss, A. (1967). *The discovery of grounded theory*. Chicago: Aldine.

*Gossett, L. (2002). Kept at arm's length: Questioning the organizational desirability of member identification. *Communication Monographs, 69*, 385–404. doi: 10.1080/ 03637750216548

*Gossett, L. M. (2006). Falling between the cracks: Control and communication challenges of a temporary workforce. *Management Communication Quarterly, 19*, 376–415. doi: 10.1177/0893318905280327

Greene, J. C. (2007). *Mixed methods in social inquiry*. San Francisco, CA: Joessy-Bass.

Greene, J. C. (2008). Is mixed methods social inquiry a distinctive methodology? *Journal of Mixed Methods Research, 2*, 7–22. doi: 10.1177/1558689807309969

Greene, J. C., Caracelli, V. J., & Graham, W. F. (1989). Toward a conceptual framework for mixed-method evaluation designs. *Educational Evaluation and Policy Analysis, 11*, 255–274. doi: 10.3102/01623737011003255

*Haas, C., & Witte, S. P. (2001). Writing as an embodied practice: The case of engineering standards. *Journal of Business and Technical Communication, 15*, 413–457. doi: 10.1177/105065190101500402

*Haas, J. W., & Arnold, C. L. (1995). An examination of the role of listening in judgments of communication competence in co-workers. *Journal of Business Communication, 32*, 123–139. doi: 10.1177/002194369503200202

*Hacker, K. L., Goss B., Townley, C, & Horton, V. J. (1998). Employee attitudes regarding electronic mail policies. *Management Communication Quarterly, 11*, 422–452. doi: 10.1177/0893318998113004

*Hale, J. E., Dulek, R. E., & Hale, D. P. (2005). Crisis response communication challenges. *Journal of Business Communication, 42*, 112–134. doi: 10.1177_0021943605274751

**Hamel, S. A. (2009). Exit, voice, and sensemaking following psychological contract violations. *Journal of Business Communication, 46*, 234–261. doi: 10.1177/0021943608328079

Hample, D. (2008) Issue forum: Breadth and depth of knowledge in communication, *Communication Monographs, 75*, 111–135. doi: 10.1080/03637750802088323

*Hansen, C. J. (1995). Writing the project team: Authority and intertextuality in a corporate setting. *Journal of Business Communication, 32*, 103–122. doi: 10.1177/002194369503200201

*Harrison, T. R., & Morrill, C. (2004). Ombuds processes and disputant reconciliation. *Journal of Applied Communication Research, 32*, 318–342. doi: 10.1080/0090988042000276005

**Harter, L. A., Scott, J. A., Novak, D. R., Leeman, M., & Morris, J. F. (2006). Freedom through flight: Performing a counter-narrative of disability. *Journal of Applied Communication Research, 34*, 3–29. doi: 10.1080/00909880500420192

*Harter, L. M. (2004). Masculinity(s), the agrarian frontier myth, and cooperative ways of organizing: Contradictions and tensions in the experience and enactment of democracy. *Journal of Applied Communication Research, 32*, 89–118. doi: 10.1080/0090988042000210016

*Harter, L. M., & Krone, K. J. (2001). The boundary-spanning role of a cooperative support organization: Managing the paradox of stability and change in non-traditional organizations. *Journal of Applied Communication Research, 29*, 248–277. doi: 10.1080/00909880128111

*Heath, R. G. (2007). Rethinking community collaboration through a dialogic lens: Creativity, democracy, and diversity in community organizing. *Management Communication Quarterly, 21*, 145–171. doi: 10.1177/0893318907306032

*Heath, R. G., & Sias, P. M. (1999). Communicating spirit in a collaborative alliance. *Journal of Applied Communication Research, 27*, 356. doi: 10.1080/00909889909365545

*Heiss, S. N., & Carmack, H. J. (2012). Knock, knock; who's there? Making sense of organizational entrance through humor. *Management Communication Quarterly, 26*, 106–132. doi: 10.1177/0893318911414914

*Hong, J., & Engeström, Y. (2004). Changing principles of communication between Chinese managers and workers Confucian authority chains and guanxi as social networking. *Management Communication Quarterly, 17*, 552–585. doi: 10.1177/0893318903262266

*Hovde, M. R. (2000). Tactics for Building Images of Audience in Organizational Contexts: An Ethnographic Study of Technical Communicators. *Journal of Business and Technical Communication, 14*, 395–444. doi: 10.1177/105065190001400401

*Howard, L. A., & Geist, P. (1995). Ideological positioning in organizational change: The dialectic of control in a merging organization. *Communication Monographs, 62*, 110–131. doi: 10.1080/03637759509376352

*Hylmö, A. (2006). Telecommuting and the contestability of choice. *Management Communication Quarterly, 19*, 541–569. doi: 10.1177/0893318905284762

*Hylmö, A., & Buzzanell, P. (2002). Telecommuting as viewed through cultural lenses: An empirical investigation of the discourses of utopia, identity, and mystery. *Communication Monographs, 69*, 329–356. doi: 10.1080/03637750216547

*Iverson, J. O., & McPhee, R. D. (2008). Communicating knowing through communities of practice: Exploring internal communicative processes and differences among CoPs. *Journal of Applied Communication Research, 36*, 176–199. doi: 10.1080/0090 9880801923738

Jablin, F. M., & Putnam, L. L. (2001). *The new handbook of organizational communication: Advances in theory, research, and methods*. Thousand Oaks, CA: Sage.

*Jackson, M. H., & Poole, M. S. (2003). Idea-generation in naturally occurring contexts. *Human Communication Research, 29*, 560–591. doi: 10.1111/j.1468-2958.2003. tb00856.x

Jick, T. D. (1979). Mixing qualitative and quantitative methods: Triangulation in action. *Administrative Science Quarterly, 24*(4), 602–611. doi: 10.2307/2392366

*Jones, S. L. (2005). From writers to information coordinators: Technology and the changing face of collaboration. *Journal of Business and Technical Communication, 19*, 449–467. doi: 10.1177/1050651905278318

*Jones, T. S., & Bodtker, A. (1998). A dialectical analysis of a social justice process: International collaboration in South Africa. *Journal of Applied Communication Research, 26*, 357–373. doi: 10.1080/00909889809365514

*Jovanovic, S., & Wood, R. V. (2006). Communication ethics and ethical culture: A study of the ethics initiative in Denver city government. *Journal of Applied Communication Research, 34*, 386–405. doi: 10.1080/0090988060090 8633

*Kahn, R. L. (2000). The effect of technological innovation on organizational structure: Two case studies of the effects of the introduction of a new technology on informal organizational structures. *Journal of Business and Technical Communication, 14*, 328–347. doi: 10.1177/105065190001400305

*Kankaanranta, A., & Planken, B. (2010). BELF competence as business knowledge of internationally operating business professionals. *Journal of Business Communication, 47*, 380–407. doi: 10.1177/0021943610377301

*Katz, S. M. (1998). A newcomer gains power: An analysis of the role of rhetorical expertise. *Journal of Business Communication, 35*, 419–442. doi: 10.1177/00219436 9803500401

*King III, G., & Hermodson, A. (2000). Peer reporting of coworker wrongdoing: A qualitative analysis of observer attitudes in the decision to report versus not report unethical behavior. *Journal of Applied Communication Research, 28*, 309. doi: 10.1080/00909880009365579

*Kirby, E., & Krone, K. (2002). "The policy exists but you can't really use it": communication and the structuration of work-family policies. *Journal of Applied Communication Research, 30*, 50–77. doi: 10.1080/00909880216577

*Kolb, J. A. (1995). Leader behaviors affecting team performance: Similarities and differences between leader/member assessments. *Journal of Business Communication, 32*, 233–248. doi: 10.1177/002194369503200302

*Kolb, J. A. (1996). A comparison of leadership behaviors and competencies in high-and average-performance teams. *Communication Reports, 9*, 173–183. doi: 10.1080/08934219609367649

*Kramer, M. W. (1995). A longitudinal study of superior-subordinate communication during job transfers. *Human Communication Research, 22*, 39–64. doi: 10.1111/j.1468-2958.1995.tb00361.x

*Kramer, M. W. (2005). Communication in a fund-raising marathon group. *Journal of Communication, 55*, 257–276. doi: 10.1111/j.1460-2466.2005.tb02671.x

*Kramer, M. W. (2006). Shared leadership in a community theater group: Filling the leadership role. *Journal of Applied Communication Research, 34*, 141–162. doi: 10.1080/00909880600574039

*Kramer, M. W. (2009). Role negotiations in a temporary organization: Making sense during role development in an educational theater production. *Management Communication Quarterly, 23*, 188–217. doi: 10.1177/0893318909341410

*Kramer, M. W. (2011). Toward a communication model for the socialization of voluntary members. *Communication Monographs, 78*, 233–255. doi: 10.1080/03637751.2011.564640

*Kramer, M. W., & Noland, T. L. (1999). Communication during job promotions: A case of ongoing assimilation. *Journal of Applied Communication Research, 27*, 335. doi: 10.1080/00909889909365544

*Kramer, M. W., Dougherty, D. S., & Pierce, T. A. (2004). Managing uncertainty during a corporate acquisition. *Human Communication Research, 30*, 71–101. doi: 10.1111/j.1468-2958.2004.tb00725.x

Krone, K. J. (2000). Becoming deeply multi-perspectival: Commentary on finding common ground in organizational communication research. In S. Corman & M. S. Poole (Eds.), *Perspectives on organizational communication: Finding common ground* (pp. 144–151). New York: Guilford Press.

Kuhn, T. (2005). The institutionalization of Alta in organizational communication studies. *Management Communication Quarterly, 18*, 618–627. doi: 10.1177/0893318904273851

*Kuhn, T., & Corman, S. R. (2003). The emergence of homogeneity and heterogeneity in knowledge structures during a planned organizational change. *Communication Monographs, 70*, 198–229. doi: 10.1080/0363775032000167406

*Kuhn, T., & Nelson, N. (2002). Reengineering identity: A case study of multiplicity and duality in organizational identification. *Management Communication Quarterly, 16*, 5–38. doi: 10.1177/0893318902161001

*Kuhn, T., & Poole, M. S. (2000). Do conflict management styles affect group decision making? Evidence from a longitudinal field study. *Human Communication Research, 26*, 558–590. doi: 10.1111/j.1468-2958.2000.tb00769.x

*Kupritz, V. W., & Cowell, E. (2011). Productive management communication. *Journal of Business Communication, 48*, 54–82. doi: 10.1177/0021943610385656

*Kupritz, V. W., & Hillsman, T. (2011). The impact of the physical environment on supervisory communication skills transfer. *Journal of Business Communication, 48*, 148–185. doi: 10.1177/0021943610397269

*Lammers, J. C., & Garcia, M. A. (2009). Exploring the concept of "profession" for organizational communication research: Institutional influences in a veterinary

organization. *Management Communication Quarterly, 22*, 357–384. doi: 10.1177/0893318908327007

**Lammers, J. C., Atouba, Y. L., & Carlson, E. J. (2013). Which identities matter? A mixed-method study of group, organizational, and professional identities and their relationship to burnout. *Management Communication Quarterly, 27*, 503–536. doi: 10.1177/0893318913498824

*Larson, G. S., & Pepper, G. L. (2003). Strategies for managing multiple organizational identifications. *Management Communication Quarterly, 16*, 528–557. doi: 10.1177/0893318903251626

*Larson, G. S., & Tompkins, P. K. (2005). Ambivalence and resistance: A study of management in a concertive control system. *Communication Monographs, 72*, 1–21. doi: 10.1080/0363775052000342508

*Lauring, J. (2011). Intercultural organizational communication: The social organizing of interaction in international encounters. *Journal of Business Communication, 48*, 231–255. doi: 10.1177/0021943611406500

Lazer, D., Pentland, A. Adamic, L., Aral, S., Barabasi, A., Brewer, D., Christakis, N., Contractor, N., Fowler, J., Gutmann, N., Jebara, T., King, G., Macy, M., Roy, D., & Van Alstyne, M. (2009, 6 February). Computational social science. *Science, 323*, 721–723.

*Lee, J., & Jablin, F. M. (1995). Maintenance communication in superior-subordinate work relationships. *Human Communication Research, 22*, 220–257. doi: 10.1111/j.1468-2958.1995.tb00367.x

*LeGreco, M. (2012). Working with policy: Restructuring healthy eating practices and the circuit of policy communication. *Journal of Applied Communication Research, 40*, 44–64. doi: 10.1080/00909882.2011.636372

**Leonardi, P. M. (2009). Why do people reject new technologies and stymie organizational changes of which they are in favor? Exploring misalignments between social interactions and materiality. *Human Communication Research, 35*, 407–441. doi: 10.1111/j.1468-2958.2009.01357.x

*Leonardi, P. M., & Rodriguez-Lluesma, C. (2013). Occupational stereotypes, perceived status differences, and intercultural communication in global organizations. *Communication Monographs, 80*, 478–502. doi: 10.1080/03637751.2013.828155

*Levine, K. J., Muenchen, R. A., & Brooks, A. M. (2010). Measuring transformational and charismatic leadership: Why isn't charisma measured?. *Communication Monographs, 77*, 576–591. doi: 10.1080/03637751.2010.499368

*Lewis, L. K. (2000). Communicating change: Four cases of quality programs. *Journal of Business Communication, 37*, 128–155. doi: 10.1177/002194360003700201

*Lin, C., & Clair, R. P. (2007). Measuring Mao Zedong thought and interpreting organizational communication in China. *Management Communication Quarterly, 20*, 395–429. doi: 10.1177/0893318907299177

*Lindsley, S. L. (1999). A layered model of problematic intercultural communication in US-owned maquiladoras in Mexico. *Communications Monographs, 66*, 145–167. doi: 10.1080/03637759909376469

*Livesey, S. M., Hartman, C. L., Stafford, E. R., & Shearer, M. (2009). Performing sustainable development through eco-collaboration. *Journal of Business Communication, 46*, 423–454. doi: 10.1177/0021943609338664

*Lynch, O. H. (2009). Kitchen antics: The importance of humor and maintaining professionalism at work. *Journal of Applied Communication Research, 37*, 444–464. doi: 10.1080/00909880903233143

*Lyon, A. (2004). Participants' use of cultural knowledge as cultural capital in a dot-com start-up organization. *Management Communication Quarterly, 18*, 175–203. doi: 10.1177/0893318904267721

*Mangrum, F. G., Fairley, M. S., & Wieder, D. L. (2001). Informal problem solving in the technology-mediated work place. *Journal of Business Communication, 38*, 315–336. doi: 10.1177/002194360103800307

**Marshall, A., & Stohl, C. (1993). Participating as participation: A network approach. *Communication Monographs, 60*, 137–157. doi: 10.1080/03637759309376305

*Martin, D. M. (2004). Humor in middle management: women negotiating the paradoxes of organizational life. *Journal of Applied Communication Research, 32*, 147–170. doi: 10.1080/0090988042000210034

*Mattson, M., & Buzzanell, P. M. (1999). Traditional and feminist organizational communication ethical analyses of messages and issues. *Journal of Applied Communication Research, 27*, 49–72. doi: 10.1080/00909889909365523

*McCarthy, J. E., T. Grabill, J., Hart-Davidson, W., & McLeod, M. (2011). Content management in the workplace: Community, context, and a new way to organize writing. *Journal of Business and Technical Communication, 25*, 367–395. doi: 10.1177/1050651911410943

*McEachern, R. W. (1998). Meeting minutes as symbolic action. *Journal of Business and Technical Communication, 12*, 198–216. doi: 10.1177/1050651998012002002

**McGuire, T. (2010). From emotions to spirituality: Spiritual labor as the commodification, codification, and regulation of organizational members' spirituality. *Management Communication Quarterly, 24*(1), 74–103. doi: 10.1177/0893318909351432

*Mckinney, J. H., Barker, J. R., Davis, K. J., & Smith, D. (2005). How swift starting action teams get off the ground. *Management Communication Quarterly, 19*, 198–237. doi: 10.1177/0893318905278539

*McNamee, L. G. (2011). Faith-based organizational communication and its implications for member identity. *Journal of Applied Communication Research, 39*, 422–440. doi: 10.1080/00909882.2011.608697

*McNamee, L. G., & Peterson, B. L. (2014). Reconciling "third space/place": Toward a complementary dialectical understanding of volunteer management. *Management Communication Quarterly, 28*, 214–243. doi: 10.1177/0893318914525472.

McPhee, R. D., & Zaug, P. (2009). The communicative constitution of organizations: A framework for explanation. In L. Putman & A. Nicotera (Eds.), *Building theories of organization: The constitutive role of communication* (pp. 21–48). New York: Routledge.

*Medved, C. E., Morrison, K., Dearing, J. W., Larson, R. S., Cline, G., & Brummans, B. H. (2001). Tensions in community health improvement initiatives: Communication and collaboration in a managed care environment. *Journal of Applied Communication Research, 29*, 137–152. doi: 10.1080/00909880128107

Mertens, D. M. (2003). Mixed methods and the politics of human research: The transformative-emancipatory perspective. In A. Tashakkori & C. Teddlie (Eds.), *Handbook of mixed methods in social and behavioral research* (pp. 135–164). Thousand Oaks, CA: Sage.

Miles, M. and Huberman, M. (1994). *Qualitative Data Analysis: An Expanded Sourcebook.* London: Sage.

*Miller, B. M., & Horsley, J. S. (2009). Digging deeper: Crisis management in the coal industry. *Journal of Applied Communication Research, 37*, 298–316. doi: 10.1080/00909880903025903

Miller, K. (2012). *Organizational communication: Approaches and processes.* Boston, MA: Wadsworth.

**Miller, K., & Koesten, J. (2008). Financial feeling: An investigation of emotion and communication in the workplace. *Journal of Applied Communication Research, 36,* 8–32. doi: 10.1080/00909880701799782

*Miller, K., Joseph, L., & Apker, J. (2000). Strategic ambiguity in the role development process. *Journal of Applied Communication Research, 28,* 193–214. doi: 10.1080/00909880009365571

*Miller, K., Birkholt, M., Scott, C., & Stage, C. (1995). Empathy and burnout in human service work: An extension of a communication model. *Communication Research, 22,* 123–147. doi: 10.1177/009365095022002001

Miller, V. D., Poole, M. S., Seibold, D. R., Myers, K. K., Hee Sun Park, Monge, P., . . . Shumate, M. (2011). Advancing research in organizational communication through quantitative methodology. *Management Communication Quarterly, 25,* 4–58. doi: 10.1177/0893318910390193

*Mills, C. (2002). The hidden dimension of blue-collar sensemaking about workplace communication. *Journal of Business Communication, 39,* 288–313. doi: 10.1177/002194360203900301

Molina-Azurin, J. F. (2011). The use and added value of mixed methods in management research. *Journal of Mixed Methods Research, 5,* 7–24. doi: 10.1177/1558689810384490

Morgan D. (2007). Paradigms lost and pragmatism regained: Methodological implications of combining qualitative and quantitative methods. *Journal of Mixed Methods Research, 1,* 48–76. doi: 10.1177/2345678906292462

*Morgan, J., & Krone, K. (2001). Bending the rules of "professional" display: Emotional improvisation in caregiver performances. *Journal of Applied Communication Research, 29,* 317–340. doi: 10.1080/00909880128114

*Murphy, A. (2001). The flight attendant dilemma: an analysis of communication and sensemaking during in-flight emergencies. *Journal of Applied Communication Research, 29,* 30–53. doi: 10.1080/00909880128100

*Myers, K. K. (2005). A burning desire. *Management Communication Quarterly, 18,* 344–384. doi: 10.1177/0893318904270742

Myers, K. K. (2013). Mixed methods: When more really is more. In L. L. Putnam & D. K. Mumby (Eds.), *The SAGE handbook of organizational communication: Advances in theory, research, and methods,* 3rd edn, (pp. 297–320). Thousand Oaks, CA: Sage.

*Myers, K. K., & McPhee, R. D. (2006). Influences on member assimilation in workgroups in high-reliability organizations: A multilevel analysis. *Human Communication Research, 32,* 440–468. doi: 10.1111/j.1468-2958.2006.00283.x

**Myers, K. K., & Oetzel, J. G. (2003). Exploring the dimensions of organizational assimilation: Creating and validating a measure. *Communication Quarterly, 51,* 438–457. doi: 10.1080/01463370309370166

Newman, I., Ridenour, C. S., Newman, C., & DeMarco, G. M. P. (2003). A typology of research purposes and its relationship to mixed methods. In A. Tashakkori & C. Teddlie (Eds.), *Handbook of mixed methods research in social and behavioral research* (pp. 189–208). Thousand Oaks, CA: Sage.

*Norander, S., & Harter, L. M. (2012). Reflexivity in practice: Challenges and potentials of transnational organizing. *Management Communication Quarterly, 26,* 74–105. doi: 10.1177/0893318911415607

*Norton, T. (2009). Situating organizations in politics: A diachronic view of control–resistance dialectics. *Management Communication Quarterly, 22*, 525–554. doi: 10.1177/0893318908331099

*Norton, T., Sias, P., & Brown, S. (2011). Experiencing and managing uncertainty about climate change. *Journal of Applied Communication Research, 39*, 290–309. doi: 10.1080/00909882.2011.585397

*Novak, J. M., & Sellnow, T. L. (2009). Reducing organizational risk through participatory communication. *Journal of Applied Communication Research, 37*, 349–373. doi: 10.1080/00909880903233168

*Pal, M., & Buzzanell, P. M. (2008). The Indian call center experience. *Journal of Business Communication, 45*, 31–60. doi: 10.1177/0021943607309348

*Papa, M. J., Mohammad, A. A., & Singhal, A. (1997). Organizing for social change within concertive control systems: Member identification, empowerment, and the masking of discipline. *Communication Monographs, 64*, 219–249. doi: 10.1080/03637759709376418

**Parker, P. S. (2001). African American women executives' leadership communication within dominant-culture organizations: (Re)Conceptualizing notions of collaboration and instrumentality. *Management Communication Quarterly, 15*, 42–82. doi: 10.1177/0893318901151002

*Pazos, P., Chung, J. M., & Micari, M. (2013). Instant messaging as a task-support tool in information technology organizations. *Journal of Business Communication, 50*, 68–86. doi: 10.1177/0021943612465181

*Pepper, G. L. (2008). The physical organization as equivocal message. *Journal of Applied Communication Research, 36*, 318–338. doi: 10.1080/00909880802104882

*Pepper, G. L., & Larson, G. S. (2006). Cultural identity tensions in a post-acquisition organization. *Journal of Applied Communication Research, 34*, 49–71. doi: 10.1080/00909880500420267

*Pierce, T., & Dougherty, D. S. (2002). The construction, enactment, and maintenance of power-as-domination through an acquisition: The case of TWA and Ozark Airlines. *Management Communication Quarterly, 16*, 129–164. doi: 10.1177/089331802237232

Poole, M. S. (1981). Decision development in small groups I: A comparison of two models. *Communication Monographs, 48*, 1–24. doi: 10.1080/03637758109376044

Poole, M. S. (1983a). Decision development in small groups II: A study of multiple sequences in decision making. *Communication Monographs, 50*, 206–232. *doi:* 10.1080/03637758309390165

Poole, M. S. (1983b). Decision development in small groups III: A multiple sequence model of group decision development. *Communication Monographs, 50*, 321–341. doi: 10.1080/03637758309390173

**Poole, M. S., & Holmes, M. E. (1995). Decision development in computer-assisted group decision making. *Human Communication Research, 22*(1), 90–127. doi: 10.1111/j.1468-2958.1995.tb00363.x

Poole, M. S., & Roth, J. (1989a). Decision development in small groups IV: A typology of group decision paths. *Human Communication Research, 15*, 323–356. doi: 10.1111/j.1468-2958.1989.tb00188.x

Poole, M. S., & Roth, J. (1989b). Decision development in small groups V: Test of contingency model. *Human Communication Research, 15*, 549–589. doi: 10.1111/j.1468-2958.1989.tb00199.x

Poole, M. S., McPhee, R. D., & Canary, D. J. (2003). Theory-method complexes. In M. L. Knapp & G. R. Miller (Eds.), *Handbook of interpersonal communication*. Newbury Park, CA: Sage.

*Porter, A. J. (2013). Emergent organizing and responsive technologies in crisis: Creating connections or enabling divides? *Management Communication Quarterly, 27*, 6–33. doi: 10.1177/0893318912459042

Putnam, L., & Mumby, D. K. (2014). *The Sage handbook of organizational communication: Advances in theory, research, and methods* (3rd edn). Los Angeles: Sage.

Putnam, L. L. (2008). Developing breadth in organizational communication doctoral training. In D. Hample (Ed.), Issue forum: Breadth and depth of knowledge in communication (p. 111–135). *Communication Monographs, 75*.

*Redden, S. M. (2013). How lines organize compulsory interaction, emotion management, and "emotional taxes": The implications of passenger emotion and expression in airport security lines. *Management Communication Quarterly, 27*, 121–149. doi: 10.1177/0893318912458213.

*Reid, S. A., & Ng, S. H. (2006). The dynamics of intragroup differentiation in an intergroup social context. *Human Communication Research, 32*, 504–525. doi: 10.1111/j.1468-2958.2006.00285.x

*Renz, M. A. (2006). Paving consensus: Enacting, challenging, and revising the consensus process in a cohousing community. *Journal of Applied Communication Research, 34*, 163–190. doi: 10.1080/00909880600574088

*Riedlinger, M. E., Gallois, C., McKay, S., & Pittam, J. (2004). Impact of social group processes and functional diversity on communication in networked organizations. *Journal of Applied Communication Research, 32*, 55–79. doi: 10.1080/0090988042000178130

**Robinson, S. (2011). Convergence crises: News work and news space in the digitally transforming newsroom. *Journal of Communication, 61*, 1122–1141. doi: 10.1111/j.1460-2466.2011.01603.x

*Rogers, P. S., & Song Mei, L. W. (2003). Reconceptualizing politeness to accommodate dynamic tensions in subordinate-to-superior reporting. *Journal of Business and Technical Communication, 17*, 379. doi: 10.1177/1050651903255401

*Rogers, P. S., Mian Lian, H., Thomas, J., Wong, I. H., & Ooi Lan Cheng, C. (2004). Preparing new entrants for subordinate reporting. *Journal of Business Communication, 41*, 370–401. doi: 10.1177/0021943604268442

*Rosenfeld, L. B., Richman, J. M., & May, S. K. (2004). Information adequacy, job satisfaction and organizational culture in a dispersed network organization. *Journal of Applied Communication Research, 32*, 28–54. doi: 10.1080/0090988042000178112

Rossman, G. B., & Wilson, B. L. (1985). Numbers and words. *Evaluation Review, 9*(5), 627–643. doi: 10.1177/0193841x8500900505

**Russo, T. C. (1998). Organizational and professional identification. *Management Communication Quarterly, 12*, 72–111. doi: 10.1177/0893318998121003

**Ruud, G. (2000). The symphony: Organizational discourse and the symbolic tensions between artistic and business ideologies. *Journal of Applied Communication Research, 28*, 117–143. doi: 10.1080/00909880009365559

*Salvador, M., & Markham, A. (1995). The rhetoric of self-directive management and the operation of organizational power. *Communication Reports, 8*(1), 45–53. doi: 10.1080/08934219509367606

Sandelowski, M., Voils, C. I., & Knafl, G. (2009). On quantitizing. *Journal of Mixed Methods Research, 3*, 208–222. doi: 10.1177/1558689809334210

**Scarduzio, J. A. (2011). Maintaining order through deviance? The emotional deviance, power, and professional work of municipal court judges. *Management Communication Quarterly, 25*, 283–310. doi: 10.1177/0893318910386446

*Schryer, C. F. (2000). Walking a fine line: Writing negative letters in an insurance company. *Journal of Business and Technical Communication, 14*, 445. doi: 10.1177/105065190001400402

*Schwarz, G. M., Watson, B. M., & Callan, V. J. (2011). Talking up failure: How discourse can signal failure to change. *Management Communication Quarterly, 25*, 311–352. doi: 10.1177/0893318910389433

*Scott, C., & Myers, K. K. (2005). The socialization of emotion: Learning emotion management at the fire station. *Journal of Applied Communication Research, 33*, 67–92. doi: 10.1080/0090988042000318521

*Scott, C. R., & Rains, S. A. (2005). Anonymous communication in organizations: Assessing use and appropriateness. *Management Communication Quarterly, 19*, 157–197. doi: 10.1177/0893318905279191

*Scott, C. R., & Trethewey, A. (2008). Organizational discourse and the appraisal of occupational hazards: Interpretive repertoires, heedful interrelating, and identity at work. *Journal of Applied Communication Research, 36*, 298–317. doi: 10.1080/00909880802172137

*Scott, C. R., Connaughton, S. L., Diaz-Saenz, H. R., Macguire, K., Ramirez, R., Richardson, B., Shaw, S. P., & Morgan, D. (1999). The impacts of communication and multiple identifications on intent to leave: A multimethodological exploration. *Management Communication Quarterly, 12*, 400–435. doi: 10.1177/0893318999123002

*Seeger, M., & Ulmer, R. (2002). A post-crisis discourse of renewal: The cases of Malden Mills and Cole Hardwoods. *Journal of Applied Communication Research, 30*, 126–142. doi: 10.1080/00909880216578

*Seiter, J. S. (1995). Surviving turbulent organizational environments: A case study examination of a lumber company's internal and external influence attempts. *Journal of Business Communication, 32*, 363–382. doi: 10.1177/002194369503200404

*Sellnow, T. L., Seeger, M. W., & Ulmer, R. R. (2002). Chaos theory, informational needs, and natural disasters. *Journal of Applied Communication Research, 30*, 269–292. doi: 10.1080/00909880216599

**Shefner-Rogers, C. L., Rao, N., Rogers, E. M., & Wayangankar, A. (1998). The empowerment of women dairy farmers in India. *Journal of Applied Communication Research, 26*, 319–337. doi: 10.1080/00909889809365510

*Shelby, A. N., & Reinsch Jr, N. L. (1995). Positive emphasis and you-attitude: An empirical study. *Journal of Business Communication, 32*, 303–327. doi: 10.1177/002194369503200401

*Shockley-Zalabak, P. (2002). Protean places: Teams across time and space. *Journal of Applied Communication Research, 30*, 231–250. doi: 10.1080/00909880216587

*Shuler, S., & Sypher, B. D. (2000.) Seeking emotional labor: When managing the heart enhances the work experience. *Management Communication Quarterly, 14*, 50–89. doi: 10.1177/0893318900141003

*Sias, P. M., & Wyers, T. D. (2001). Employee uncertainty and information-seeking in newly formed expansion organizations. *Management Communication Quarterly, 14*, 549–573. doi: 10.1177/0893318901144001

*Silva, D., & Sias, P. M. (2010). Connection, restructuring, and buffering: How groups link individuals and organizations. *Journal of Applied Communication Research, 38*, 145–166. doi: 10.1080/00909881003639510

*Smith, F. L., & Keyton, J. (2001). Organizational storytelling metaphors for relational power and identity struggles. *Management Communication Quarterly, 15*, 149–182. doi: 10.1177/0893318901152001

Smith, M. L. (1997). Mixing and matching: Methods and models. *New Directions for Evaluation, 1997,* (74), 73–85. doi: 10.1002/ev.1073

*Stahley, M. B., & Boyd, J. (2006). Winning is(n't) everything: The paradox of excellence and the challenge of organizational epideictic. *Journal of Applied Communication Research, 34,* 311–330. doi: 10.1080/00909880600908575

*Stephens, K. K., Cho, J. K., & Ballard, D. I. (2012). Simultaneity, sequentiality, and speed: Organizational messages about multiple-task completion. *Human Communication Research, 38,* 23–47. doi: 10.1111/j.1468-2958.2011.01420.x

Strauss, A., & Corbin, J. (1990). *Basics of qualitative research: Grounded theory procedures and techniques.* Newbury Park, CA: Sage.

Suchan, J. (1995). The influence of organizational metaphors on writers' communication roles and stylistic choices. *Journal of Business Communication, 32,* 7–29. doi: 10.1177/002194369503200101

*Suchan, J. (1998). The effect of high-impact writing on decision making within a public sector bureaucracy. *Journal of Business Communication, 35,* 299–327. doi: 10.1177/002194369803500301

*Swarts, J. (2004). Technological mediation of document review: The use of textual replay in two organizations. *Journal of Business and Technical Communication, 18,* 328–360. doi: 10.1177/1050651904264037

Tashakkori, A., & Teddlie, C. (1998). *Mixed methodology: Combining qualitative and quantitative approaches.* Thousand Oaks, CA: Sage.

Teddlie, C., & Tashakkori, A. (2003). *Handbook of mixed methods research in social and behavorial research.* Thousand Oaks, CA: Sage.

Teddlie, C., & Tashakkori, A. (2006). A general typology of research designs featuring mixed methods. *Research in the Schools, 13*(1), 12–28.

Teddlie, C., & Tashakkori, A. (2009). *Foundations of mixed methods research: Integrating quantitative and qualitative approaches in the social and behavioral sciences.* Thousand Oaks, CA: Sage.

**Thomas, G., King, C. L., Baroni, B., Cook, L., Keitelman, M., Miller, S., & Wardle, A. (2006). Reconceptualizing e-mail overload. *Journal of Business and Technical Communication, 20,* 252–287. doi: 10.1177/1050651906287253

*Thompson, I. K., & Rothschild, J. M. (1995). Stories of three editors: A qualitative study of editing in the workplace. *Journal of Business and Technical Communication, 9,* 139–169. doi: 10.1177/1050651995009002001

*Tracy, K., & Ashcraft, C. (2001). Crafting policies about controversial values: How wording disputes manage a group dilemma. *Journal of Applied Communication Research, 29,* 297–316. doi: 10.1080/00909880128115

*Tracy, S. J. (2004). Dialectic, contradiction, or double bind?: Analyzing and theorizing employee reactions to organizational tension. *Journal of Applied Communication Research, 32,* 119–146. doi: 10.1080/0090988042000210025

**Tracy, S. J. (2005). Locking up emotion: Moving beyond dissonance for understanding emotion labor discomfort. *Communication Monographs, 72,* 261–283. doi: 10.1080/03637750500206474

*Tracy, S. J., & Tracy, K. (1998). Emotion labor at 911: A case study and theoretical critique. *Journal of Applied Communication Research, 26,* 390–411. doi: 10.1080/00909889809365516

*Tracy, S. J., Myers, K. K., & Scott, C. W. (2006). Cracking jokes and crafting selves: Sensemaking and identity management among human service workers. *Communication Monographs, 73*, 283–308. doi: 10.1080/03637750600889500

**Treem, J. W. (2012). Communicating expertise: Knowledge performances in professional-service firms. *Communication Monographs, 79*, 23–47. doi: 10.1080/03637751.2011.646487

*Treem, J. W. (2013). Technology use as a status cue: The influences of mundane and novel technologies on knowledge assessments in organizations. *Journal of Communication, 63*, 1032-1053. doi: 10.1111/jcom.12061

*Trethewey, A. (1997). Resistance, identity, and empowerment: A postmodern feminist analysis of clients in a human service organization. *Communications Monographs, 64*, 281–301. doi: 10.1080/03637759709376425

**Turner, P. K., & Krizek, R. L. (2006). A meaning-centered approach to customer satisfaction. *Management Communication Quarterly, 20*, 115–147. doi: 10.1177/0893318906288276

*Van Praet, E. (2009). Staging a team performance. *Journal of Business Communication, 46*, 80–99. doi: 10.1177/0021943608325754

*Veil, S. R., Sellnow, T. L., & Petrun, E. L. (2012). Hoaxes and the paradoxical challenges of restoring legitimacy: Dominos' response to its YouTube crisis. *Management Communication Quarterly, 26*, 322–345. doi: 10.1177/0893318911426685

*Volkema, R. J., & Niederman, F. (1996). Planning and managing organizational meetings: An empirical analysis of written and oral communications. *Journal of Business Communication, 33*(3), 275–296. doi: 10.1177/002194369603300304

**Waldeck, J. H., Seibold, D. R., & Flanagin, A. J. (2004). Organizational assimilation and communication technology use. *Communication Monographs, 71*, 161–183. doi: 10.1080/03637750423331302497

*Warisse Turner, J., & Reinsch Jr., N. L. (2007). The business communicator as presence allocator. *Journal of Business Communication, 44*, 36–58. doi: 10.1177/0021943606295779

**Warisse Turner, J., Grube, J. A., Tinsley, C. H., Lee, C., & O'Pell, C. (2006). Exploring the dominant media: How does media use reflect organizational norms and affect performance? *Journal of Business Communication, 43*(3), 220–250. doi: 10.1177/0021943606288772

*Way, D., & Tracy, S. J. (2012). Conceptualizing compassion as recognizing, relating and (re) acting: a qualitative study of compassionate communication at hospice. *Communication Monographs, 79*, 292–315. doi: 10.1080/03637751.2012.697630

Welles, B. F., Vashevko, A., Bennett, C., & Contractor, N. (2014). Dynamic models of communication in an online friendship network. *Communication Methods and Measures, 8*, 223–243. doi: 10.1080/19312458.2014.967843

*Whittle, A., Mueller, F., & Mangan, A. (2008). In search of subtlety: Discursive devices and rhetorical competence. *Management Communication Quarterly, 22*, 99–122. doi: 10.1177/0893318908318515

*Wieland, S. M. (2010). Ideal selves as resource for the situated practice of identity. *Management Communication Quarterly, 24*, 503–528. doi: 10.1177/0893318910374938

*Wieland, S. M. (2011). Struggling to manage work as a part of everyday life: Complicating control, rethinking resistance, and contextualizing work/life studies. *Communication Monographs, 78*, 162–184. doi: 10.1080/03637751.2011.564642

*Wilson, S. R., Wilkum, K., Chernichky, S. M., MacDermid Wadsworth, S. M., & Broniarczyk, K. M. (2011). Passport toward success: Description and evaluation of a program designed to help children and families reconnect after a military deployment. *Journal of Applied Communication Research, 39*, 223–249. doi: 10.1080/00909882.2011.585399

*Witherspoon, P. D., & Wohlert, K. L. (1996). An approach to developing communication strategies for enhancing organizational diversity. *Journal of Business Communication, 33*, 375–399. doi: 10.1177/002194369603300402

**Xu, K. (2011). An empirical study of Confucianism. *Management Communication Quarterly, 25*, 644–662. doi: 10.1177/0893318911405621

*Yates, J., & Orlikowski, W. (2002). Genre systems: Structuring interaction through communicative norms. *Journal of Business Communication, 39*, 13–35. doi: 10.1177/002194360203900102

Yin, R. K. (2003). *Case study research: Design and methods* (3rd edn, Vol. 5). Thousand Oaks, CA: Sage.

*Zak, M. W. (1994). 'It's like a prison in there': Organizational fragmentation in a demographically diversified workplace. *Journal of Business and Technical Communication, 8*, 281–299. doi: 10.1177/1050651994008003002

*Zimmermann, S., Sypher, B. D., & Haas, J. W. (1996). A communication metamyth in the workplace: The assumption that more is better. *Journal of Business Communication, 33*, 185–204. doi: 10.1177/002194369603300206

*Zoller, H. M. (2003). Health on the line: Identity and disciplinary control in employee occupational health and safety discourse. *Journal of Applied Communication Research, 31*, 118–139. doi: 10.1080/0090988032000064588

*Zorn, T. E., Roper, J., Broadfoot, K., & Weaver, C. K. (2006). Focus groups as sites of influential interaction: Building communicative self-efficacy and effecting attitudinal change in discussing controversial topics. *Journal of Applied Communication Research, 34*, 115–140. doi: 10.1080/00909880600573965

Part IV

Emerging Issues in Communication Research

CHAPTER CONTENTS

14 Communicating Energy in a Climate (of) Crisis

Danielle E. Endres

University of Utah

Brian Cozen

University of Nevada, Las Vegas

Joshua Trey Barnett

University of Utah

Megan O'Byrne

University of Pennsylvania

Tarla Rai Peterson

University of Texas, El Paso

We review energy communication, an emerging subfield of communication studies that examines the role of energy in society, and argue that it is dominated by a crisis frame. Whereas this frame can be productive, it can also be limiting. In response, we propose three areas for future energy communication research—internal rhetoric of science, comparative studies, and energy in everyday life—as starting points for rethinking and expanding energy communication. This expanded focus will continue to contribute to communication theory, add to interdisciplinary energy studies, and supply practical resources for the creation and deployment of just and sustainable energy futures.

Energy is foundational to the functioning of all human societies. Industrial and post-industrial societies rely heavily on the production of energy from fossil fuels and nuclear fission to power the infrastructure and technologies to which they have grown accustomed. Non-industrial and emerging societies, though perhaps not fully embedded in a large-scale system of energy production and consumption, similarly rely on energy to sustain everyday life. Heightened societal awareness of and controversies about the connections between energy security, economic growth, and energy systems demonstrate these interconnections between energy and society (Tyfield & Urry, 2014). In this chapter, we focus on communication about energy as a significant and emerging subfield in communication studies that not only reflects opportunities for further theorizing the role of communication in diverse contexts but also positions communication research as a resource for addressing ongoing deliberation about the role of energy in society. Our review of communication scholarship on energy reveals a history of research that primarily responds to crises, from particular energy crisis events (e.g., Fukushima nuclear disaster 2011) to the more encompassing climate crisis. After reviewing this history, we call for new lines of research that expand beyond the crisis frame into a focus on energy as a central aspect of human society, even in times of perceived normalcy.

But first, a few preliminary definitions are in order. We define *energy* as power that may be used to operate the infrastructures of the human-built environment. Humans derive that power from resources such as fossil fuels, solar, wind, hydroelectric, nuclear, biofuels, and geothermal sources that are extracted and harnessed, prepared, and distributed in a cycle of energy production. We use the term *energy resources* to discuss sources of energy, *energy production* to describe the cradle-to-grave process whereby energy is supplied to human-built infrastructures, and *energy consumption* to refer to the processes wherein people use energy resources to power infrastructure, technology, and other activities. We define *energy communication research* as the study of symbolic practices surrounding material experiences with energy resources, production, and consumption, including related practices of research, development, deployment, and policy.

A guiding assumption of energy communication research, we argue, is that communication influences not only how people understand energy resources, production, and consumption but also the societal implications that emerge from those understandings. As we will demonstrate in this chapter, much of the *ad hoc* research on energy communication relates to the rapid rate of climate change that has resulted from industrial society's use of fossil fuels. Climate change, although confirmed through a long-standing scientific consensus (IPCC, 2015), currently "presents perhaps the most profound and complex challenge to have confronted human social, political, and economic systems" (Dryzek, Norgaard, & Schlosberg, 2011, p. 17). It can be seen as an existential crisis because of its ability to threaten the future of humanity if it is not curtailed (Klein, 2014; see also Bostrom, 2013 on existential risks). However, developing and implementing policies to mitigate climate change remains a significant political issue that has thus far eluded solution (Dryzek et al., 2011). The challenges posed by climate change, along with the threat that climate change mitigation policies may derail ways of life built largely on fossil fuel-based energy systems, constitutes the perfect storm for academic researchers across the disciplines, including communication.

Although much attention has been paid to the emerging study of climate change communication (e.g., Koteyko, Nerlich & Hellsten, 2015; Moser &

Dilling, 2007), less attention has been paid to communication scholarship centered on energy. Since climate change mitigation requires fundamental transformations in how energy is understood, communication is one of the main challenges in creating and implementing different energy futures. Even though scholarship in energy communication extends beyond responses to climate change, it remains the most pressing exigency for research in energy communication. Climate change has also sparked research supporting normative arguments for the need to shift energy futures. Thus, like the field of environmental communication, energy communication is emerging as a crisis discipline (Cox, 2007). In addition to building and expanding communication theory, much energy communication research is concerned with ameliorating the climate crisis and developing more sustainable and just energy systems.

In addition to climate change, energy communication research has also responded to particular crisis events in energy production by analyzing the mediated, political, organizational, and public reactions to these disasters. Events that spurred energy communication research include: Three Mile Island, Exxon Valdez, Fukushima, and the BP oil spill (e.g., Cotton, Veil, & Iannarino, 2015; Farrell & Goodnight, 1981; Harlow et al., 2011; Rubin, 1987). For example, the 2011 Fukushima Daiichi nuclear disaster not only raised questions among publics and policy makers about the continued viability of nuclear power, but also provoked academic research that responded to the crisis (e.g., Kinefuchi, 2015; Kinsella, 2012a; 2012b). Indeed, Kinsella (2012b) organized a forum in *Environmental Communication* that highlights the crisis frame: "Communicative Action in Response to a Nuclear Crisis." As these examples reveal, recent energy communication research is responsive not just to the climate crisis, but also to seemingly isolated crisis events in which energy production is embedded.

Climate change represents a different type of crisis from these more bounded crisis events. The climate crisis is temporally and geographically expansive, impacting various publics and geographies continuously yet differently across an indefinite period of time. Even before climate change became a household word, scientists recognized and warned of the greenhouse effect, increasing fossil fuel emissions, and global warming. While the climate crisis may have only reached broad societal consciousness recently, climate charge has been a reality since as early as the 1800s when the first evidence of the Industrial Revolution's impacts on increasing CO_2 emerged (IPCC, 2015). Given the scale of the climate crisis, smaller crisis events in energy production are always embedded within the larger climate context. As such, the climate crisis has served as an overarching frame for energy communication research, which often evaluates whether energy entrenches or ameliorates the climate crisis.

Although the crisis frame animating energy communication research can be productive and valuable, it can also be limiting (Killingsworth, 2007; Senecah, 2007). Focusing on climate change and other crisis events may divert attention from questions regarding the role of energy in everyday life. Expanding and reframing energy communication research to address the everydayness of energy serves as a starting point for research that examines how communication structures' understandings of energy policy enable and constrain past, current, and future energy deployment and function as a perceptual filter for larger social processes, such as how energy discourses are embedded within national mythologies (Jasanoff & Kim, 2009; Kitch, 2007). Energy communication research will have more impact and longer staying power if it addresses the values, dispositions, and issues that are routinely de-emphasized within crisis-oriented research. Enlarging energy communication research to include context-oriented research that expands beyond crises to everyday energy communication will contribute to communication theory, add a needed perspective to interdisciplinary energy studies, and supply practical resources for the creation and deployment of just and sustainable energy futures.

In the following pages, we begin by calling for the recognition of energy communication as a distinct subfield of communication studies. Next, we highlight three themes in the history of energy communication research that display the crisis frame. We then suggest three areas for further research that each offer ways of considering energy communication more broadly. We conclude by developing a context-responsive frame for energy communication research that encourages continued attention to the climate crisis as well as expansion into new areas of inquiry.

Communication Research on Energy

Although communication research about energy has existed since as early as the 1980s (e.g., Farrell & Goodnight, 1981; Medhurst, 1987), this research has accumulated in a largely *ad hoc* manner across an array of subareas in communication studies such as rhetoric, organizational communication, crisis communication, media studies, and public relations. Rather than drawing from a single area, this research combines the theoretical and practical resources of communication studies with topics related to energy resources, production, and consumption. Though research in disciplines such as sociology (e.g., McLachlan, 2010) and linguistics (e.g., Scollon, 2009) overlaps with communicative questions regarding energy, and while communication research has important implications for interdisciplinary research on energy, this review is primarily focused on bringing together the diverse research related to energy in the field of communication studies.

In undertaking our review of communication scholarship on energy, we found two things. First, energy is a common topic in communication research. Even in the absence of a defined subarea of energy communication, research on energy occurs regularly in communication studies' journals and books. Energy communication is a content-oriented subfield, similar to other subfields such as environmental communication, peace and conflict studies, and health communication that are held together across diverse theoretical and methodological traditions. In energy communication, as with these similar subfields, it is neither the medium of communication (e.g., interpersonal, social media, and television media) nor the type of communication (e.g., rhetorical, organizational, and persuasive) but the interest in energy content that determines the subfield. As such, energy communication cannot be contained within an extant subarea of communication. Although environmental communication is perhaps the closest subarea, energy communication exceeds the field of environmental communication and offers a wealth of material for communication research given energy's fundamental role in the function of human society.

Second, we found that the majority of energy communication research falls within what we call a crisis frame. While communication research on energy is not synonymous with the subfield of crisis communication, some of the research does overlap since perceived crises often motivate energy communication research. This research does not only study the communicative dynamics of crises, but societal crises over energy and climate change undergird the communicative dimensions of energy resources, production, and consumption. The crisis frame materializes in two ways. The first set of research examines the communicative dynamics of specific energy-related crises through a variety of lenses. The type of crisis ranges depending on the energy resource, but oil and nuclear energy are particularly prominent since both have precipitated major crisis events. Oil-related crises include large-scale oil spills, such as the Exxon Valdez disaster (Dyer, Miller, & Boone, 1991; Hearit, 1995; Peterson & Peterson, 1996; Sellnow, 1993; Williams & Olaniran, 1994; Williams & Treadaway, 1992), the BP Deepwater Horizon disaster (Breeze, 2012; Chewning, 2015; Choi, 2012; Harlow et al., 2011; Muralidharan, Dillistone, & Shin, 2011; Russell & Babrow, 2011; Schultz, Kleinnijenhuis, Oegema, Utz, & van Atteveldt, 2012; Spangler & Pompper, 2011), and lesser known spills (Jeong, 2009; Liska, Petrun, Sellnow, & Seeger, 2012; Maresh & Williams, 2007, 2009). In terms of nuclear energy, the disasters at Chernobyl (Eribo & Gaddy, 1992; Gorney, 1992; Luke, 1987; Young & Launer, 1991), Three Mile Island (Dionisopoulos & Crable, 1988; Farrell & Goodnight, 1981; Rubin, 1987), and Fukushima (Cotton et al., 2015; Kinsella, 2012a; Tateno & Yokoyama, 2013; Visschers & Siegrist, 2013; Yeo et al., 2014) provoked much research within (and beyond) the field of communication. This second set of research comes from an underlying normative perspective that assumes a need to change our energy choices (often away from fossil fuels) to ameliorate the existential crisis of climate change (Klein, 2014). Under the pressures of climate change, the entire field of energy production and policy is in a transformative upheaval. Although we present these two manifestations of the crisis frame as discrete, there is overlap between them.

The Crisis Frame in Energy Research

The crisis frame is a dominant theme in communication research on energy. In this section, we offer a review of previous energy communication research that highlights the many theories and methodologies (crossing many established subareas of communication) that are brought to bear in analyses of the communicative dynamics of energy. In particular, we examine three noteworthy themes that emerged from our review: 1) the role of media in covering energy crises; 2) analyses of corporate communication surrounding crises; and 3) discourses of decision-making about energy in the context of crises. These themes do not correspond with a particular subarea of communication (e.g., media, organizational). Taken together, they highlight how the crisis frame, in its two overlapping manifestations, plays out in energy communication research.

Media Coverage of Energy Crisis

Crises in energy resources, production, and consumption have been a common topic or case study for research in media studies (e.g., Doyle, 2011; Eklöf & Mager, 2013; Evensen, Clarke & Stedman, 2014; Feldpausch-Parker, Ragland, et al., 2013; Feldpausch-Parker, O'Byrne, et al., 2013; Feldpausch-Parker & Peterson, 2014; Kitch, 2007; Kittle Autry & Kelly, 2012; Langheim et al., 2014; Monani, 2008; Skjølsvold, 2012; Smith & Lindenfeld, 2014; Stephens, Rand, & Melnick, 2009) and journalism (e.g., Abe, 2013; Bacon & Nash, 2012; Burt, 2011; Erfle & McMillan, 1989; Harcup, 2011; Kim, Besley, Oh, & Kim, 2014; Vraga, Tully, Akin, & Rojas, 2012; Watson, 2012; Wood, Shabajee, Schien, Hodgson, & Preist, 2014). These studies address the role of various media—newspapers, social media, websites, and films—in communication about particular crises and the broader crisis of climate change.

Following major crises in energy production or consumption, researchers routinely study the relationship between media and specific crises. For example, after the Chernobyl nuclear disaster, studies examined how the crisis was communicated by news media and how that coverage influenced public understanding and public opinion about nuclear power (Eribo & Gaddy, 1992; Gorney, 1992; Luke, 1987; Young & Launer, 1991). Gorney (1992), for instance, argues that media coverage of the Chernobyl crisis was less sensationalistic than she expected, even with the use of loaded words such as "radiation" and "meltdown." Notably, while there are a number of articles addressing Chernobyl in the late 1980s and early 1990s—soon after the crisis event in 1986—articles on this topic trail off in favor of different crisis events. Currently, there is an uptick in research examining the relationship between the Fukushima crisis and media (Binder, 2012; Friedman, 2011; Lazic & Kaigo, 2013; Utz, Schultz, & Glocka, 2013; Wei, Lo, Lu, & Hou, 2015). For example, Utz, Schultz, and Glocka (2013) examine the role of social media in crisis communication about Fukushima and argue that the media type has a stronger effect than crisis type on public perception.

In addition to studies that address specific crisis events, energy communication research approaches the relationship between energy and the larger climate crisis as it is presented to the public through media. Framing analysis is a dominant approach for making sense of news media coverage of energy processes. We use the term "framing" to describe how humans communicate about reality through a series of lenses or perspectives. As Horsbøl (2013) states, "Frames are constitutive of the construction and interpretation of issues" (p. 23). Drawing on a diversity of approaches to framing literature (Druckman & Bolsen, 2011;

Entman, 1993; Gamson & Modigliani, 1989; Nisbet, Maibach, & Leiserowitz, 2011), these studies show how news media construct narratives related to energy futures in the context of the climate crisis. Some of these studies examine newspaper coverage of various energy sources, from US coverage on biofuels (Kim et al., 2014), to smart grids (Langheim et al., 2014), to wind (Stephens et al., 2009), to carbon-based energy sources (Feldpausch-Parker & Peterson, 2014; Koteyko, Thelwall, & Nerlich, 2010) and alternative energy in general (Haigh, 2010). For example, Stephens et al. (2009) argue that despite wind power's critical importance to climate change mitigation, news media coverage of wind's contribution to climate mitigation has been limited. In another example, Oltra, Delicado, Prades, Pereira, and Schmidt (2014) reveal that Internet-based media coverage of nuclear fusion presents it as a viable solution to world energy problems in the context of climate change. These studies assume a crisis lens by examining competing frames in the context of the crisis over energy futures in relation to climate change.

Other energy communication research examines media frames to understand how media influence public opinion of energy. These studies of public opinion are contextualized by both specific crisis events and the larger need to examine which energy resources are perceived to be best for addressing the climate crisis. For example, Gamson and Modigliani (1989) analyze the interpretive frames of nuclear power—pronuclear progress, energy independence, the antinuclear soft path, and the devil's bargain—from 1945 to 1989, reflecting on how these frames respond to particular crisis events in nuclear power such as Three Mile Island and larger societal discourses about energy futures. Butler, Parkhill, and Pidgeon (2011) update these interpretive frames in a post-Fukushima era. These mediated interpretive frames are associated with policy implications as they relate to public acceptance of energy technologies within a context of both crisis events and climate change. Bickerstaff, Lorenzoni, Pidgeon, Poortinga, and Simmons (2008), for example, categorize the public's opinion of linking nuclear energy to climate change as "reluctant acceptance," which in turn has implications for energy policy.

Beyond characterizing the role of media frames in public opinion and policy outcomes related to energy, other studies take a critical normative approach premised on using communication research to explicitly contribute to ameliorating the climate crisis (see Cox, 2007 for a discussion of how crisis-oriented research is normative). Smith and Lindenfeld (2014), for example, integrate climate change media analyses into the growing corpus of transdisciplinary research focused on finding solutions to climate change and the crisis it presents. Their analytical efforts, characterizing frames and ideological narratives within various media, are meant as contributions to effectively aiding such solutions.

Corporate Communication about Crisis

A second theme of energy communication research analyzes the discourse of energy corporations in response to or in anticipation of future crises surrounding energy resources, production, and consumption in the context of the ongoing climate crisis. These studies draw heavily from the theoretical resources of organizational communication, crisis communication, and public relations (e.g., Barbour & Gill, 2014; Chewning, 2015; Choi, 2012; Collis, Bianco, Margaryan, & Waring, 2005; Cotton et al., 2015; Dyer, Miller, & Boone, 1991; Hynes & Prasad, 1997; Idemudia, 2009; Kinsella, 1999; 2014; Livesey, 2002; Miller, 2010; O'Connor & Gronewold, 2013; Prasad & Mir, 2002; Sellnow, 1993; Spangler & Pompper, 2011; Vandenberghe, 2011), but also expand across other subareas of the field. Studies range from promoting best practices for corporate communication in response to crises to critical studies that interrogate corporate discourses for complicity within larger structures that sustain the climate crisis.

Regarding the former, numerous studies examine specific energy crises to draw out best (and worst) practices for corporate communication. Breeze (2012), for example, assesses the justification strategies used by corporate actors to legitimate British Petroleum (BP) after the 2010 Deepwater Horizon oil catastrophe in the Gulf of Mexico. Case studies of this sort show, for instance, how strategies should differ at varied stages of crises and how strategies useful in one instance may be less successful in others (Williams & Olaniran, 1994; Williams & Treadaway, 1992).

In addition to research that examines and categorizes the strategies employed by particular institutions in response to an energy crisis event, other research in this area emphasizes the importance of an anticipatory model for crisis communication so that energy companies' communications in times of crises are interpreted more favorably (Olaniran & Williams, 2008). For example, Cotton et al. (2015) demonstrate how TEPCO, the Japanese power company held responsible for the Fukushima Daiichi disaster, failed in their post-crisis attempts at "renewal"—discourse designed to rebuild its reputation through a focus on rebuilding in the future—due in part to unsuccessful pre-crisis framing strategies. Along these lines, research on corporate energy communication often examines best practices for creating a positive image that can then be relied on in times of crisis. Miller's research, for instance, focuses on how public audiences perceive marketplace advocacy—designed to encourage public acceptance for a product, service, or industry sector—in the coal industry (Miller, 2010; Miller & Lellis, 2015).

Some scholars also take a critical normative stance in their analyses of corporate energy marketing campaigns, particularly fossil fuels. Unlike research that focuses on best practices for crisis communication in specific crisis events, this research takes climate change as an underlying crisis that calls for research examining corporate efforts to perpetuate the status quo or for research that advocates for alternate energy futures that would lessen the impact of climate change. For example, Bsumek, Schneider, Schwarze, and Peeples (2014) offer the term "corporate ventriloquism" to explain how coal corporations appropriate non-corporate discourses through the persona of "dummy" grassroots organizations to align corporate positions with cultural values and promote coal as a "clean" energy option. They call for further interrogations of how energy corporations present coal and other fossil fuels as common sense, despite what the authors perceive to be a clear need to move away from fossil fuels. In another study that critiques the rhetoric of energy corporations, Peeples, Bsumek, Schwarze, and Schneider (2014) argue that corporate discourse from the coal industry combines apocalyptic rhetoric with ridicule (or the burlesque frame as they call it) to denigrate environmentalist opposition. Smerecnik and Renegar (2010), Plec and Pettenger (2012), and Cozen (2010) similarly criticize fossil fuel advertising campaigns, elaborating on the ideological undercurrents in these campaigns that maintain the status quo of fossil fuel production and worsen climate change. These critical analyses often attempt "to help critics observe the ideological work accomplished by" energy corporation communication strategies (Bsumek et al., 2014, p. 27). These studies not only critically analyze these strategies but also advance normative desires to generate energy futures that move away from the climate crisis. For instance, while Plec and Pettenger (2012) focus on compliance-gaining strategies and appeals to expertise in ExxonMobil campaigns, they also explicitly argue for a move toward a reduction of energy consumption in light of the climate crisis.

Decision-Making in the Context of Crisis

Still other studies focus on decision-making related to energy production in times of crisis. The overarching urgency of the climate crisis informs contemporary decision-making about energy technologies due to the perceived necessity of the rapid deployment of low-carbon energy technologies to address climate change (Fleishman, De Bruin, & Morgan, 2010; Stephens, Wilson, & Peterson, 2015). Such studies explore how various stakeholders come into play when a decision must be made about energy technologies.

Publics make up an important stakeholder group in energy policy decision-making. Public attitudes and beliefs can have a profound impact on ensuing deliberation, but those attitudes and beliefs are often formed in relation to crisis events and acceptance (or rejection) of the climate crisis. Regarding the former, particular crisis events can influence, trigger, or reinforce public opposition to a particular technology. The Fukushima crisis, for example, caused several stakeholder groups to re-evaluate their position on nuclear power, often creating an assessment that weighed the risks of nuclear disasters against the perceived benefits of nuclear power as a low-carbon alternative to fossil fuels (Besley & Oh, 2014; Butler et al., 2011; Juraku, 2013; Kinsella, 2012b; Kittle Autry & Kelly, 2012; Visschers & Seigrist, 2013).

Absent a major crisis event, public perceptions of energy resources are still tied to broader discourses about climate change, low-carbon energy technologies, and the need to transform energy policy to prevent future crises. When looking at newer energy technologies that may not have experienced a major crisis event, public understanding of science (PUS) and public perception research focus on making sense of how publics comprehend new energy technologies and their potential roles in intensifying or mitigating climate change. While each type of energy resource involves some questions of public acceptance, research in this area primarily focuses on public opinions regarding new(er) technologies, such as carbon capture and storage (e.g., Bradbury et al., 2009), geothermal (e.g., Gross, 2013), wind (e.g., Aitken, 2010b; Swofford & Slattery, 2010), and biofuels (e.g., Cacciatore, Binder, Scheufele, & Shaw, 2012; Cacciatore, Scheufele, & Shaw, 2012; Fung, Choi, Scheufele, & Shaw, 2014; Raza, Kumar, & Singh, 2011; Van de Velde, Verbeke, Popp, & Van Huylenbroeck, 2011; Vraga et al., 2012). Much of the research on wind energy, for example, evaluates how negative public perceptions of wind energy influence the political viability of this low-carbon climate mitigating energy resource (e.g., Aitken, 2010a; Devine-Wright, 2009; Fischlein et al., 2010; Fischlein, Feldpausch-Parker, Peterson, Stephens, & Wilson 2014; Fischlein, Wilson, Peterson, & Stephens, 2013; Maillé & Saint-Charles, 2014; Stephens et al., 2009; Swofford & Slattery, 2010; Wolsink, 2006). Yet, this research is not only focused on new(er) low-carbon energy resources. Even in light of the role of fossil fuels in worsening the climate crisis, there has been a rise in unconventional forms of fossil fuel extraction such as hydraulic fracturing ("fracking"; Newell & Raimi, 2014). Research has focused on understanding public opinion and understanding about this controversial energy production technology (e.g., Boudet et al., 2014; Clarke et al., 2015).

Because energy production requires land use, it often provokes political crises related to the different ways in which space is inhabited and animated. Siting locations for power plants, wind farms, and waste facilities is a significant issue that raises conflicts among stakeholders across a variety of energy resources. The ubiquitous Not-In-My-Backyard (NIMBY) framework oversimplifies the many factors at play in siting decisions as well as broader public support for energy technologies (Aitken, 2010a; Devine-Wright, 2005; 2009; Endres, 2012; Sjöberg & Drottz-Sjöberg, 2001; Wolsink, 2000; 2012). Debates over siting practices are particularly intense for wind and nuclear technologies. In the case of wind energy, research has examined how local populations react to locating wind farms in their areas (Aitken, 2010a; Devine-Wright, 2005; Maillé & Saint-Charles, 2014; Wolsink, 2000). For example, Maille and Saint-Charles (2014) examine how a wind farm developer's communication strategies affected the diffusion of information in the community and ultimately led to opposition to the project. The claim that opposition is rooted in the NIMBY phenomenon fails to adequately describe how opposition developed in this community.

Stakeholder tension is also apparent in communication research on nuclear siting practices. While the nuclear renaissance discourse calls for more nuclear power to respond to the exigencies of climate change, the renaissance has not yet materialized in many tangible proposals for new sites (Kinsella, Kelly, & Kittle Autry, 2013). Yet, in countries like South Korea that are actively pursuing nuclear power, the issue of siting remains significant. Song, Kim, and Han

(2013), for instance, highlight that perceived efficacy positively influenced while perceived risk negatively influenced social acceptance of nuclear plants in South Korea. Moreover, Juraku (2013) provides a historical account of Japan's decision to build multiple plants on single sites to avoid greater public dissent. Yet, this study also illustrates the relationship between siting decisions and future crises by pointing out that while the Japanese strategy of multiple power plants on one site minimized dissent in the short term, the Fukushima disaster reveals the future risks and intensified crisis events involved in such a decision. Thus, siting becomes an integral part of the crisis frame, particularly when poor siting decisions precipitate and exacerbate crises.

What is even more contested in terms of nuclear siting is the location of high-level nuclear waste sites. Much research directly responds to the international crisis of nuclear waste (Clarke, 2010; Endres, 2009a; 2009b; 2009c; 2012; 2013; Fan, 2006a; 2006b; Freudenburg, 2004; Peeples, Krannich, & Weiss, 2008; Ratliff, 1997). For example, Clarke (2010) and Endres (2009c; 2012; 2013) have analyzed the (often silenced) rhetorical arguments of Native American stakeholders in nuclear waste siting decisions in the US. As with wind, these cases reveal that siting decisions are more complicated than a NIMBY framework would suggest, with some groups opposing and some groups openly calling for nuclear waste facilities on or near Native American lands. Yet, in all cases, discussions about nuclear waste siting and its relevance to national interests further the crisis framing of energy communication.

Energy decision-making also features discussions of risk (e.g., Boyd et al., 2013; Kinsella, 2012a; Kuchinskaya, 2010; Remillard, 2011; Russell & Babrow, 2011; Song et al., 2013; Tateno & Yokoyama, 2013; Yeo et al., 2014). As Kinsella (2012a) notes, risk communication "fundamentally constitute[s] the world on which decision-makers, organizations, and communities act" (p. 251). Discussion of risk (of major crisis events) is particularly prominent in the case of nuclear energy. Mirel (1994) argues that, for nuclear energy where the risks are potentially catastrophic, risk communication teaches us that the purpose of communication is not persuasion but presenting information to let people come to their own position. The Fukushima crisis provoked an uptick in research on risk perception among publics and stakeholders. For example, Tateno and Yokoyama (2013) focus on Japanese publics' perceptions of risk post-Fukushima that exposed a lack of trust in experts and officials. In the US context, Yeo et al. (2014) examine how risk perceptions after Fukushima varied across different ideological sub-populations. Although risk communication is prevalent in nuclear energy, it also relates to other energy resources, such as analysis of public risk perception in a large carbon capture and sequestration demonstration project (Boyd et al., 2013).

Broadly, energy communication research calls forth expertise from a variety of different communication theories and methodologies. In this review, we have shown that research in energy communication cannot be contained within an existing communication subfield, such as environmental or crisis communication. Rather, what binds communication research on energy is its responsiveness to perceived energy-related crises, both specific crisis events and the climate crisis. Further, we organized extant energy communication research in terms of the most dominant themes in the crisis frame. While these three themes cannot cover all energy communication research, they do reveal the varied ways in which the majority of this research responds implicitly or explicitly to crises. Next, we discuss how the crisis-frame can be limiting for the field of energy communication.

Moving Beyond Crisis: Energy in Everyday Life

Operating under the crisis frame, energy communication research has missed out on fully exploring the role of energy in everyday life. In much of the industrialized world, energy is assumed to be available, reliable, and affordable. Thus, people often overlook energy in its mundanity and are drawn to it only in times of crisis. In order to ameliorate this gap we identify three areas of future research, each of which points to some of the more commonplace aspects of energy. Not all of these studies completely extricate themselves from the crisis frame (indeed, climate change is an ever-present existential crisis from which it is hard to escape), but they do show some ways of moving away from a reactive stance to a proactive one that is focused on the role of energy in everyday life.

Internal Rhetoric of Energy Science

Focusing on the internal expert-to-expert communication practices among energy technology professionals—for example, conference talks, face-to-face conversations, and laboratory cultures—could shed light on the backstage processes of producing energy technology. In the everyday circuits of communicative exchange between energy scientists and engineers, we might make sense of the ways in which public discourses about energy (which have been the primary focus of the research we reviewed) relate to the discourses of the technoscientists who research and develop commercial applications of energy technologies. These expert-to-expert rhetorics are especially critical as they significantly shape the future of particular aspects of energy resources, production, and consumption. Rhetorical scholars, however, have concentrated more on the ways in which public audiences understand the science behind particular energy technologies. Lyne and Miller (2009) argue, "Rhetoricians usually feel most comfortable in the spaces of civic and cultural life and may be reluctant to take on the internal discourse of a natural science or other discipline outside their own" (p. 170). By moving past this reluctance to grapple with the internal rhetorics of energy scientists and engineers, we argue, communication scholars could add substantially to our collective understanding of how energy systems are developed, deliberated, and deployed through communication.

Although few energy communication researchers have explored the internal rhetoric of energy scientists (e.g., Endres, Cozen, O'Byrne, & Feldpausch-Parker, 2013), rhetorical scholars have long recognized the value of studying the internal rhetorics of science. These expert-to-expert modes of persuasive communication significantly shape the symbolic and material conditions of life beyond the laboratory and the field (Wander, 1976). By exploring some aspects of internal rhetoric, scholars have shed light on the ways in which scientific knowledge is produced. These communicative exchanges range from the rhetorical figures of science (Fahnestock, 1999) to argumentative patterns (Prelli, 1989) to the constitutive aspects of science rhetoric (Ceccarelli, 2001) to the formation of collaborative objects (Barley, Leonardi, & Bailey, 2012), and from citizen science projects (Hartman, 1997) and rhetorical interactions between scientists and policy makers (Besel, 2011) to the role of analogies in the laboratory (Graves, 1998).

In addition to providing nuanced understandings of how scientific knowledge about energy is produced, research on the internal rhetorics of energy scientists and engineers can avoid some of the traps of crisis-driven research. By shifting their attention away from publicly circulating texts and onto the less formal, rhetorical exchanges between scientists and engineers, scholars can grapple with how, for example, prudential (pragmatic, ethical, and value-based) reasoning influences the production of scientific knowledge in energy technology systems. Although appeals to particular values may not appear explicitly in scientific texts, they are certainly present in the internal rhetorical exchanges between scientists that take place in hotel lobbies and office corridors, at conference receptions and departmental dinner parties (Heath, 1998; Krauss, 2011; Lorenz-Meyer, 2012; Marcus, 1995). Everyday, mundane scientific practices like lab meetings, casual conversations, and informal research presentations are richly rhetorical scenes of knowledge production where these prudential forms of reasoning can be glimpsed and appreciated. In the case of energy science and engineering, which has a close relationship to ongoing societal and policy deliberation about energy, such examinations might yield significant insight into whether and how topics in internal rhetoric make their way to public discourse.

Research about the internal rhetoric of scientists has already yielded important insights. For example, in *Science in Action,* Latour (1987) traced many of the social, political, and economic forces that impinge upon the everyday actions of scientists and engineers. In our current research, we are examining various forms of reasoning employed by scientists and engineers working on nuclear, wind, and carbon sequestration technologies. Exploring not only the technical but also the prudential forms of reasoning engaged by scientists in these fields of study, we are undertaking ethnographic research at professional conferences, in-depth interviews with scientists and engineers, and archival and textual analyses of internal rhetorics. Focusing on these aspects of knowledge production enables researchers to uncover and critique the ways in which energy scientists deploy certain forms of reasoning in some contexts and not others. In doing so, they construct a more complete picture of the scientific process and, in turn, enable a broader view of how science impacts society.

By shifting attention to the everyday practices of scientists and engineers in energy technology fields, especially the informal rhetorical exchanges that shape the day-to-day rhythms of knowledge production, we argue that energy communication scholars can fill some of the gaps in the crisis frame and open up new paths of understanding. When energy science is viewed from this perspective, it is no longer possible or practical to overemphasize the role of publicly circulating texts at the expense of the ordinary rhetorical exchanges that always and importantly shape the conditions of possibility for broader public understandings of the role of energy in society. Although we have focused primarily on the rhetoric of science in this section, we suggest that it would also be productive to examine expert-to-expert communication practices among energy scientists and engineers from other communication approaches, such as organizational communication, science communication, as well as other methodological approaches, such as quantitative social scientific research.

Comparative Studies

Most of the studies we reviewed focus on a particular energy resource (e.g., wind, nuclear, coal, etc.). Comparative studies across energy resources would allow energy communication researchers to discern broader themes across the energy landscape. Comparative studies can show how energy—regardless of the specific type—influences society and everyday life. Although the climate change crisis has provoked some comparative studies that transcend particular crises (Pralle & Boscarino, 2011), many of these studies still situate energy communication as a reaction to crises rather than an everyday part of life.

Everyday energy production and deployment occurs in an energy resource ecosystem. Stephens, Peterson, and Wilson (2014) developed a framework for analyzing the multiple sociocultural factors in play when people interact with the electric grid. They argue that, because actors engage in multiple ways and are interested in different aspects of electricity system change, one of the most valuable contributions that communication scholarship offers is its examination of the symbolic interactions through which individual (and corporate) members of social systems attempt to understand and influence each other. For example, electric utilities are in the business of producing and selling electricity, so changes in markets become central concerns. Government actors are responsible for ensuring that the system serves the public interest, which includes the complicated process of identifying that interest within particular locations and times. Some actors may see themselves as consumers who simply want reliable and high quality power that is easily affordable. Still others, the early adopters of new technologies, enthusiastically embrace "smart" technologies that enable them to play a more active part in maximizing the role played by renewable energy resources such as wind and solar. Expanding energy communication scholarship beyond the crisis frame opens additional opportunities for contributing to theory and practice, both within the communication discipline and across the social and policy sciences.

From an infrastructure perspective, Todd and Wood (2006) illustrate how the grid combines various resources into one overarching channel: the continuous flow of electricity. Everyday interactions with energy are not necessarily experienced in terms of crisis. Nor are they experienced in terms of a particular (or single) form of energy. Rather, in developed countries energy is experienced in terms of a grid system that activates when one flips a switch. The act of turning on a light may not signal a particular energy resource for the actor. Further studies of the grid and people's everyday experiences with energy could reveal how people can simultaneously carry strong feelings about particular energy resources but also not know which energy resources come together when they turn on the lights. Comparative research can also show how arguments about energy in society map across geographic, cultural, economic, and political contexts. Reiteration of themes across resource types, as well as across stakeholder groups, could suggest common modes of understanding energy. It may also suggest the chronic persistence of energy production and consumption in peoples' day-to-day lives: whether through siting and living near a production plant or waste repository, or the uses of energy resources in one's everyday consumption habits.

Finally, comparative studies of energy can show how support for one energy resource can entail support for, or opposition toward, another energy resource. For example, nuclear energy proponents may support or contest the development of other renewables, depending on how that other energy resource impacts nuclear power production. Comparative aspects can also open up considerations of how particular energy resources are viable solutions in some but not all cases. Nuclear power production, for example, is an international market with regionally specific determinants of its deployment (Jewell, 2011). These examples suggest that thinking about energy resources from a comparative perspective has implications for the composition of energy policy. Comparative studies of energy, coming from a diverse mix of theoretical and methodological approaches in communication, encourages movement away from the crisis frame by (re)centering the fundamental role of energy as a heuristic that guides the conduct of everyday life as opposed to thinking about particular energy resources.

Energy in Everyday Life

Theorizing energy in everyday life not only moves beyond the crisis frame, but also focuses attention on the broader relationships between current energy production practices and societal structures that assume a steady or increasing demand for energy. The crisis frame for energy communication selects, reflects, and deflects (Burke, 1966) the way people think about energy in their everyday lives. Speaking about energy primarily in terms of risks and crises then calls for actions that respond to risks and crises (Kinsella, 2012a; Russell & Babrow, 2011), conditioning people to think about energy only when disaster strikes. A shift away from the crisis frame can encourage people to reflect on the way that energy production is a ubiquitous but mainly hidden process in the everyday production and maintenance of society, the human-built environment, and infrastructural networks. While the chronic climate crisis could also be characterized as a ubiquitous and everyday reality, it is more likely to be seen in light of the crisis events it produces as well as particular climatic crisis events, such as the "snowpocalypse" and Hurricane Katrina (Hilfinger Messias, Barrington, & Lacy, 2012). That is, even though the chronic crisis of climate change needs to be addressed, much of the research that comes out of energy communication responds by examining the smaller crisis events that are indicative of the larger climate crisis. We contend that more research on the everyday nature of energy production in individual lives and collective society is also needed to address the everyday realities of climate change and global warming.

We encourage energy communication scholars to follow a similar trajectory as the one taken in the special issue "Energy & Society" in the journal *Theory, Culture & Society* (Tyfield & Urry, 2014). This special issue raises important questions about power and the structuring influence of energy in society. Many of its essays focus on shifts in everyday practice as starting points for shifting energy futures toward more just and sustainable energy production practices. For instance, Shove and Walker (2014) consider energy through its everyday social practices and Sheller (2014) considers the history of energy's mutual constitution with industrial development. Such emphases point to how energy is enmeshed in larger social processes and examine how social change can occur given the pervasive interrelationship between energy and contemporary society. For example, Tyfield (2014) argues that moves toward alternative energy in light of the chronic climate crisis actually contribute to a resurgence in coal production because coal is positioned as a stable energy resource that is needed when renewables falter. This position assumes that current or increased levels of energy production are a constant need to fuel contemporary society. It also fails to challenge the underlying premise that society needs forms of energy production that continue the status quo both for individuals wanting to maintain their current lifestyles and for societies with energy-intensive infrastructures already in place. As Shove and Walker (2014) argue, larger societal changes that minimize demand for energy may enable us to envision and implement more just and sustainable energy practices and futures that can also address climate change.

Likewise, energy communication research would benefit from more attention to and reflection on mundane individual and societal energy consumption needs and desires. To interrogate how energy exists in everyday practice is also to ask questions that are less focused on particular energy crisis events and particular types of energy and more focused on the mundane social practices that make up energy demand in times of relative normalcy in energy production. In their special issue on climate change communication, Carvalho and Peterson (2009) highlight essays that emphasize "the importance of research that looks beyond traditionally defined texts, into how they are embedded in social life and are subject to varying processes of interpretation" (p. 132).

Because communication both reproduces ways of knowing and opens up new possibilities, communication scholars are uniquely positioned to theorize the development of new energy futures in proactive ways. It could be argued that this focus on everyday energy does not move beyond a climate crisis orientation in energy communication. Yet, the current link between the chronic climate crisis and particular crisis events that we have articulated in this essay suggests that there is room for alternative lines of research that focus on addressing climate change through shifting attention from episodic crisis events to the everyday nature of climate change and its relationship with everyday energy practices. For example, Schneider and Miller (2011) offer alternative hedonism—an "approach to ethical practice that is concerned with the 'good life' that is not based on an unexamined consumer identity or overwork" (p. 468)—as a positive and pleasurable alternative to crisis-oriented approaches that rely on fear of the apocalypse. If we are to address the existential crisis posed by climate change, then we need to address everyday habits and ways of living that fall under the larger societal systems, such as capitalism (Klein, 2014), and offer new options such as alternative hedonism.

Conclusion

In this chapter we argued that energy communication is a significant emerging area of study for communication scholars. Yet our review revealed that much extant scholarship in energy communication is reactive to particular crisis events or more broadly to the climate crisis. Although the crisis frame is useful for producing applied research that responds to tangible problems, it is also limiting in terms of thinking through the everyday nature of energy production and consumption. We proposed three directions for future research that are more attentive to mundane communicative practices that often go unnoticed. By studying the internal rhetoric of scientists and engineers, by engaging in comparative studies, and by exploring the roles of energy in society, energy communication scholars can more proactively account for how energy impacts ordinary life and offer different pathways towards just and sustainable energy futures.

Although we have highlighted some of the constraints of a crisis-oriented approach to energy communication, we do not advocate that this line of research be eradicated. Rather, we suggest an expansion beyond the crisis frame that can retain its value while also bringing in new communicative resources to engage with everyday aspects of energy. This expanded framework for energy communication research would emphasize the importance of *context* over crisis and reaction. As communication scholars have known for decades, context matters. Energy communication scholars should never ignore the social, political, and cultural contexts of energy production and consumption decisions. Yet, both particular crisis events and the chronic climate crisis are only two possible contexts for energy communication research. Moving from a crisis-responsive to context-oriented position allows for continued research on crises while also encouraging examination of broader societal structures that impact energy production. Further, within the context of climate change, energy communication should strive towards creative composition. Latour (2010) asserts that the insights of social science research risk irrelevance if they stop at critique and fail to explicitly account for power imbalances. In line with what Sismondo (2008) calls the engaged program of science and technology studies research, there is an urgent need to use the insights of energy communication scholarship to inform policy choices related to phenomena that demand immediate attention, such as energy policy in relation to climate change. In an attempt to respond to the need for immediate, yet thoughtful, policy action, Latour (2010) proposes the metaphor of *composition*, which "acknowledges that things have to be put together (Latin-*componere*) while retaining their heterogeneity" (pp. 473–474). This metaphor enables a way of thinking about energy communication research that is not just responsive, but also proactive in terms of composing untapped opportunities for developing energy policy.

More emphasis on context and composition in future energy communication research can enhance communication theory, contribute to interdisciplinary studies of energy, and provoke practical and applied research about and for just energy futures. Energy communication research already contributes to communication theory across a variety of subareas of the field. In the sources cited throughout this chapter, we have seen contributions to organizational communication, risk communication, rhetoric, media studies, and more. Under the crisis frame, we have seen numerous theoretical resources from communication brought to bear on particular crises. By thinking more broadly about the contexts of energy communication and more specifically about the everyday practices of energy, we might open up new theoretical streams in energy communication research.

Further, energy communication research is poised to contribute to interdisciplinary studies of energy that often miss out on the importance of communication. For instance, research that draws from rhetoric (Bedsworth, Lowenthal, & Kastenberg, 2004) and framing (Pralle & Boscarino, 2011) can point to the importance of communication in energy policy and decision-making, highlighting the essential role of communication in such deliberations. Controversies over future energy policies, choices, and technologies all have communicative elements. Communication is primed to extend emergent themes into further research trajectories regarding energy resource development.

Finally, a context-oriented emphasis allows for the development of applied research that seeks to make a difference in both crisis-oriented energy communication and energy in everyday life. Of course, current research in energy communication already has significant applications in ongoing energy crisis events. Expanding on the crisis frame that currently guides much research in energy communication enhances the possibilities for application and composition with meaningful consequences for society. Given the importance of energy resources, production, and consumption to policy, there continues to be a need to engage in what Endres, Sprain, and Peterson (2008) describe as praxis-based research. A proactive context orientation might enable energy communication researchers to develop heuristics that strengthen the communication discipline and are socially pragmatic even in times of non-crisis, times we hope will become more common in our energy futures.

Acknowledgments

This publication is a part of a larger project that was funded by the National Science Foundation (SES-1329563).

References

Abe, Y. (2013). Critical communication history: Risk assessment of nuclear power by Japanese newspapers following the Chernobyl nuclear disaster. *International Journal of Communication, 7*, 1968–1989.

Aitken, M. (2010a). Why we still don't understand the social aspects of wind power: A critique of key assumptions within the literature. *Energy Policy, 38*(4), 1834–1841. doi: 10.1016/j.enpol.2009.11.060

Aitken, M. (2010b). Wind power and community benefits: Challenges and opportunities. *Energy Policy, 38*(10), 6066–6075. doi: 10.1016/j.enpol.2010.05.062

Bacon, W., & Nash, C. (2012). Playing the media game: The relative (in)visibility of coal industry interests in media reporting of coal as a climate change issue in Australia. *Journalism Studies, 13*(2), 243–258. doi: 10.1080/1461670X.2011.646401

Barbour, J. B., & Gill, R. (2014). Designing communication for the day-to-day safety oversight of nuclear power plants. *Journal of Applied Communication Research, 42*(2), 1–22. doi: 10.1080/00909882.2013.859291

Barley, W. C., Leonardi, P. M., & Bailey, D. E. (2012). Engineering objects for collaboration: Strategies of ambiguity and clarity at knowledge boundaries. *Human Communication Research, 38*, 280–308. doi: 10.1111/j.1468-2958.2012.01430.x

Bedsworth, L. W., Lowenthal, M. D., & Kastenberg, W. E. (2004). Uncertainty and regulation: The rhetoric of risk in the California low-level radioactive waste debate. *Science, Technology, & Human Values, 29*(3), 406–427. doi: 10.1177/0162243904264904

Besel, R. D. (2011). Opening the "black box" of climate change science: Actor-network theory and rhetorical practice in scientific controversies. *Southern Communication Journal, 76*(2), 120–136. doi: 10.1080/10417941003642403

Besley, J. C., & Oh, S. H. (2014). The impact of accident attention, ideology, and environmentalism on American attitudes toward nuclear energy. *Risk Analysis, 34*, 949–964. doi: 10.1111/j.1539-6924.2011.01664.x

Bickerstaff, K., Lorenzoni, I., Pidgeon, N. F., Poortinga, W., & Simmons, P. (2008). Reframing nuclear power in the UK energy debate: Nuclear power, climate change mitigation and radioactive waste. *Public Understanding of Science, 17*(2), 145–169. doi: 10.1177/0963662506066719

Binder, A. R. (2012). Figuring out #Fukushima: An initial look at functions and content of US Twitter commentary about nuclear risk. *Environmental Communication, 6*(2), 268–277. doi: 10.1080/17524032.2012.672442.

Bostrom, N. (2013). Existential risk prevention as global priority. *Global Policy, 4*(1), 15–31. doi: 10.1111/1758-5899.12002.

Boudet, H., Clarke, C., Bugden, D., Maibach, E., Roser-Renouf, C., & Leiserowitz, A. (2014). "Fracking" controversy and communication: Using national survey data to understand public perceptions of hydraulic fracturing. *Energy Policy, 65,* 57–67. doi: http://dx.doi.org/10.1016/j.enpol.2013.10.017

Boyd, A. D., Liu, Y., Stephens, J. C., Wilson, E. J., Pollak, M., Peterson, T. R., . . . Meadowcroft, J. (2013). Controversy in technology innovation: Contrasting media and expert risk perceptions of the alleged leakage at the Weyburn carbon dioxide storage demonstration project. *International Journal of Greenhouse Gas Control, 14,* 259–269. doi: 10.1016/j.ijggc.2013.01.011

Bradbury, J., Ray, I., Peterson, T., Wade, S., Wong-Parodi, G., & Feldpausch, A. (2009). The role of social factors in shaping public perceptions of CCS: Results of multi-state focus group interviews in the US. *Energy Procedia, 1*(1), 4665–4672. doi: 10.1016/j.egypro.2009.02.289

Breeze, R. (2012). Legitimation in corporate discourse: Oil corporations after Deepwater Horizon. *Discourse & Society, 23*(1), 3–18. doi: 10.1177/0957926511431511

Bsumek, P. K., Schneider, J., Schwarze, S., & Peeples, J. (2014). Corporate ventriloquism: Corporate advocacy, the coal industry, and the appropriation of voice. In J. Peeples & S. Depoe (Eds.), *Voice and environment communication* (pp. 21–43). London: Palgrave MacMillan.

Burke, K. (1966). *Language as symbolic action: Essays on life, literature, and method.* Berkeley: University of California Press.

Burt, E. V. (2011). Shocking atrocities in Colorado: Newspapers' responses to the Ludlow Massacre. *American Journalism, 28*(3), 61–83. doi: 10.1080/08821127.2011. 10677788

Butler, C., Parkhill, K. A., & Pidgeon, N. F. (2011). Nuclear power after Japan: The social dimensions. *Environment: Science and Policy for Sustainable Development 53*(6), 3–14. doi: 10.1080/00139157.2011.623051.

Cacciatore, M. A., Scheufele, D. A., & Shaw, B. R. (2012). Labeling renewable energies: How the language surrounding biofuels can influence its public acceptance. *Energy Policy, 51,* 673–682. doi: 10.1016/j.enpol.2012.09.005

Cacciatore, M. A., Binder, A. R., Scheufele, D. A., & Shaw, B. R. (2012). Public attitudes toward biofuels: Effects of knowledge, political partisanship, and media use. *Politics and the Life Sciences, 31*(1-2), 36–51. doi: 10.2990/31_1-2_36

Carvalho, A., & Peterson, T. R. (2009). Discursive constructions of climate change: Practices of encoding and decoding. *Environmental Communication, 3*(2), 131–133. doi: 10.1080/17524030902935434

Ceccarelli, L. (2001). *Shaping science with rhetoric: The Cases of Dobzhansky, Schrödinger, and Wilson.* Chicago: University of Chicago Press.

Chewning, L. V. (2015). Multiple voices and multiple media: Co-constructing BP's crisis response. *Public Relations Review, 41(1).* doi: 10.1016/j.pubrev.2014.10.012

Choi, J. (2012). A content analysis of BP's press releases dealing with crisis. *Public Relations Review, 38*(3), 422–429. doi: 10.1016/j.pubrev.2012.03.003

Clarke, C., Hart, P. S., Evensen, D. T., Boudet, H., Jacquet, J. B., Schuldt, J. P., & Stedman, R. C. (2015). Public opinion on energy development: The interplay of issue framing, top-of-mind associations, and political ideology. *Energy Policy, 81,* 131–140. doi: http://dx.doi.org/10.1016/j.enpol.2015.02.019

Clarke, T. (2010). Goshute Native American tribe and nuclear waste: Complexities and contradictions of a bounded-constitutive relationship. *Environmental Communication: A Journal of Nature and Culture, 4*(4), 387–405. doi: 10.1080/17524032.2010.520724

Collis, B., Bianco, M., Margaryan, A., & Waring, B. (2005). Putting blended learning to work: A case study from a multinational oil company. *Education, Communication & Information, 5*(3), 233–250. doi: 10.1080/14636310500350471

Cotton, A. J., Veil, S. R., & Iannarino, N. T. (2015). Contaminated communication: TEPCO and organizational renewal at the Fukushima Daiichi nuclear power plant. *Communication Studies, 66*(1), 27–44. doi: 10.1080/10510974.2013.811427

Cox, R. (2007). Nature's "crisis disciplines": Does environmental communication have an ethical duty? *Environmental Communication: A Journal of Nature and Culture, 1*(1), 5–20. doi: 10.1080/17524030701333948

Cozen, B. (2010). This pear is a rhetorical tool: Food imagery in energy company advertising. *Environmental Communication: A Journal of Nature and Culture, 4*(3), 355–370. doi: 10.1080/17524032.2010.499212

Devine-Wright, P. (2005). Beyond NIMBYism: Towards an integrated framework for understanding public perceptions of wind energy. *Wind Energy, 8*, 125–139. doi: 10.1002/we.124

Devine-Wright, P. (2009). Rethinking NIMBYism: The role of place attachment and place identity in explaining place-protective action. *Journal of Community & Applied Social Psychology, 19*(6), 426–441. doi: 10.1002/casp.1004

Dionisopoulos, G. N., & Crable, R. E. (1988). Definitional hegemony as a public relations strategy: The rhetoric of the nuclear power industry after Three Mile Island. *Central States Speech Journal, 39*(2), 134–145. doi: 10.1080/10510978809363244

Doyle, J. (2011). Acclimatizing nuclear? Climate change, nuclear power and the reframing of risk in the UK news media. *International Communication Gazette, 73*(1-2), 107–125. doi: 10.1177/1748048510386744

Druckman, J., & Bolsen, T. (2011). Framing, motivated reasoning, and opinions about emerging technologies. *Journal of Communication, 61*, 659–688. doi: 10.1111/j.1460-2466.2011.01562.x

Dryzek, J. S., Norgaard, R. B., & Schlosberg, D. (2011). Climate change and society: Approaches and responses. In J. S. Dryzek, R. B. Norgaard, & D. Schlosberg (Eds.), *The Oxford handbook of climate change and society* (pp. 3–17). Oxford, UK: Oxford University Press.

Dyer, S. C., Miller, M. M., & Boone, J. (1991). Wire service coverage of the Exxon Valdez crisis. *Public Relations Review, 17*(1), 27–36. doi: 10.1016/0363-8111(91)90004-5

Eklöf, J., & Mager, A. (2013). Technoscientific promotion and biofuel policy: How the press and search engines stage the biofuel controversy. *Media, Culture & Society, 35*(4), 454–471. doi: 10.1177/0163443713483794

Endres, D. (2009a). From wasteland to waste site: The role of discourse in nuclear power's environmental injustices. *Local Environment: The International Journal of Justice and Sustainability, 14*(10), 917–937. doi: 10.1080/13549830903244409

Endres, D. (2009b). Science and public participation: An analysis of public scientific argument in the Yucca Mountain controversy. *Environmental Communication: A Journal of Nature and Culture, 3*(1), 49–75. doi: 10.1080/17524030802704369

Endres, D. (2009c). The rhetoric of nuclear colonialism: Rhetorical exclusion of American Indian arguments in the Yucca Mountain nuclear waste siting decision. *Communication and Critical/Cultural Studies, 6*(1), 39–60. doi: 10.1080/14791420802632103

Endres, D. (2012). Sacred land or national sacrifice zone: The role of values in the Yucca Mountain participation process. *Environmental Communication: A Journal of Nature and Culture, 6*(3), 328–345. doi: 10.1080/17524032.2012.688060

Endres, D. (2013). Animist intersubjectivity as argumentation: Western Shoshone and Southern Paiute arguments against a nuclear waste site at Yucca Mountain. *Argumentation, 27*(2), 183–200. doi: 10.1007/s10503-012-9271-x

Endres, D., Sprain, L., & Peterson, T. R. (2008). The imperative of praxis-based environmental communication research: Suggestions from the Step It Up 2007 national research project. *Environmental Communication: A Journal of Nature and Culture, 2*(2), 237–245. doi: 10.1080/17524030802141794

Endres, D., Cozen, B., O'Byrne, M., & Feldpausch-Parker, A. M. (2013). Putting the U in carbon capture and storage: Performances of rupture within the CCS scientific community. Presented at the Conference on Communication and the Environment, Upsalla, Sweden.

Entman, R. M. (1993). Framing: Toward a clarification of a fractured paradigm. *Journal of Communication, 43*(4), 51–58. doi: 10.1111/j.1460-2466.1993.tb01304.x

Erfle, S., & McMillan, H. (1989). Determinants of network news coverage of the oil industry during the late 1970s. *Journalism Quarterly, 66*(1), 121–128. doi: 10.1177/107769908906600116

Eribo, F., & Gaddy, G. D. (1992). Pravda's coverage of the Chernobyl nuclear accident at the threshold of Glasnost. *Howard Journal of Communications, 3*(3-4), 242–252. doi: 10.1080/10646179209359753

Evensen, D. T., Clarke, C., & Stedman, R. C. (2014). A New York or Pennsylvania state of mind: Social representations in newspaper coverage of shale gas development in the Marcellus Shale. *Journal of Environmental Studies and Sciences, 4*, 65–77. doi: 10.1007/s13412-013-0153-9

Fahnestock, J. (1999). *Rhetorical figures in science*. New York: Oxford University Press.

Fan, M. F. (2006a). Environmental justice and nuclear waste conflicts in Taiwan. *Environmental Politics, 15*(3), 417–434. doi: 10.1080/09644010600627683

Fan, M. F. (2006b). Nuclear waste facilities on Tribal Land: The Yami's struggles for environmental justice. *Local Environment: The International Journal of Justice and Sustainability, 11*(4), 433–444. doi: 10.1080/13549830600785589

Farrell, T. B., & Goodnight, G. T. (1981). Accidental rhetoric: The root metaphors of Three Mile Island. *Communication Monographs, 48*(4), 271–300. doi: 10.1080/03637758109376063

Feldpausch-Parker, A. M., & Peterson, T. R. (2014). Communicating the science behind carbon sequestration: A case study of US Department of Energy and regional partnership websites. *Environmental Communication, 0*(0), 1–20. doi: 10.1080/17524032.2014.955039

Feldpausch-Parker, A. M., O'Byrne, M., Endres, D., & Peterson, T. R. (2013). The Adventures of Carbon Bond: Using a melodramatic game to explain CCS as a mitigation strategy for climate change. *Greenhouse Gases: Science and Technology, 3*(1), 21–29. doi: 10.1002/ghg.1298

Feldpausch-Parker, A. M., Ragland, C. J., Melnick, L. L., Chaudhry, R., Hall, D. M., Peterson, T. R., . . . Wilson, E. J. (2013). Spreading the news on carbon capture and storage: A state-level comparison of US media. *Environmental Communication: A Journal of Nature and Culture, 7*(3), 336–354. doi: 10.1080/17524032.2013.807859

Fischlein, M., Wilson, E. J., Peterson, T. R., & Stephens, J. C. (2013). States of transmission: Moving towards large-scale wind power. *Energy Policy, 56*, 101–113. doi: 10.1016/j.enpol.2012.11.028

Fischlein, M., Feldpausch-Parker, A. M., Peterson, T. R., Stephens, J. C., & Wilson, E. J. (2014). Which way does the wind blow? Analysing the state context for renewable energy deployment in the United States. *Environmental Policy and Governance*, *24*(3), 169–187. doi: 10.1002/eet.1636

Fischlein, M., Larson, J., Hall, D. M., Chaudhry, R., Rai Peterson, T., Stephens, J. C., & Wilson, E. J. (2010). Policy stakeholders and deployment of wind power in the subnational context: A comparison of four U.S. states. *Energy Policy*, *38*(8), 4429–4439. doi: 10.1016/j.enpol.2010.03.073

Fleishman, L. A., De Bruin, W. B., & Morgan, M. G. (2010). Informed public preferences for electricity portfolios with CCS and other low-carbon technologies. *Risk Analysis*, *30*, 1399–1410. doi: 10.1016/j.enpol.2010.03.073

Freudenburg, W. R. (2004). Can we learn from failure? Examining US experiences with nuclear repository siting. *Journal of Risk Research*, *7*(2), 153–169. doi: 10.1080/1366987042000171285

Friedman, S. M. (2011). Three Mile Island, Chernobyl, and Fukushima: An analysis of traditional and new media coverage of nuclear accidents and radiation. *Bulletin of the Atomic Scientists*, *67*(5), 55–65.

Fung, T. K. F., Choi, D. H., Scheufele, D. A., & Shaw, B. R. (2014). Public opinion about biofuels: The interplay between party identification and risk/benefit perception. *Energy Policy*, *73*, 344–355. doi: 10.1016/j.enpol.2014.05.016

Gamson, W. A., & Modigliani, A. (1989). Media discourse and public opinion on nuclear power: A constructionist approach. *American Journal of Sociology*, *95*(1), 1–37. doi: 10.2307/2780405

Gorney, C. (1992). Numbers versus pictures: Did network television sensationalize Chernobyl coverage? *Journalism & Mass Communication Quarterly*, *69*(2), 455–465. doi: 10.1177/107769909206900219

Graves, H. (1998). Marbles, dimples, rubber sheets, and quantum wells: The role of analogy in the rhetoric of science. *Rhetoric Society Quarterly*, *28*(1), 25–48. doi: 10.1080/02773949809391111

Gross, M. (2013). Old science fiction, new inspiration: Communicating unknowns in the utilization of geothermal energy. *Science Communication*, *35*(6), 810–818. doi: 10.1177/1075547012469184

Haigh, M. M. (2010). Newspapers use three frames to cover alternative energy. *Newspaper Research Journal*, *31*(2), 47–62.

Harcup, T. (2011). Reporting the voices of the voiceless during the miners' strike: An early form of "citizen journalism." *Journal of Media Practice*, *12*(1), 27–39. doi: 10.1386/jmpr.12.1.27_1

Harlow, W. F., Brantley, B. C., & Harlow, R. M. (2011). BP initial image repair strategies after the Deepwater Horizon spill. *Public Relations Review*, *37*(1), 80–83. doi: 10.1016/j.pubrev.2010.11.005

Hartman, J. (1997). The popularization of science through citizen volunteers. *Public Understanding of Science*, *6*(1), 69–86. doi: 10.1088/0963-6625/6/1/005

Hearit, K. M. (1995). "Mistakes were made": Organizations, apologia, and crises of social legitimacy. *Communication Studies*, *46*(1-2), 1–17. doi: 10.1080/10510979509368435

Heath, D. (1998). Locating genetic knowledge: Picturing Marfan Syndrome and its traveling constituencies. *Science, Technology & Human Values*, *23*(1), 71–97. doi: 10.1177/016224399802300104

Hilfinger Messias, D. K., Barrington, C., & Lacy, E. (2012). Latino social network dynamics and the Hurricane Katrina disaster. *Disasters*, *36*(1), 101–121. doi: 10.1111/j.1467-7717.2011.01243.x

Horsbøl, A. (2013). Energy transition in and by the local media: The public emergence of an "energy town." *Nordicom Review*, *34*(2), 19–34. doi: 10.2478/nor-2013-0051

Hynes, T., & Prasad, P. (1997). Patterns of "mock bureaucracy" in mining disasters: An analysis of the Westray coal mine explosion. *Journal of Management Studies*, *34*(4), 601–623. doi: 10.1111/1467-6486.00065

Idemudia, U. (2009). Oil extraction and poverty reduction in the Niger delta: A critical examination of partnership initiatives. *Journal of Business Ethics*, *90*(S1), 91–116. doi: 10.1007/s10551-008-9916-8

Intergovernmental Panel on Climate Change (IPCC). (2015) *Climate Change 2014 Synthesis Report*. Geneva, Switzerland: IPCC.

Jasanoff, S., & Kim, S.-H. (2009). Containing the atom: Sociotechnical imaginaries and nuclear power in the United States and South Korea. *Minerva*, *47*(2), 119–146. doi: 10.1007/s11024-009-9124-4

Jeong, S.-H. (2009). Public's responses to an oil spill accident: A test of the attribution theory and situational crisis communication theory. *Public Relations Review*, *35*(3), 307–309. doi: 10.1016/j.pubrev.2009.03.010

Jewell, J. (2011). Ready for nuclear energy?: An assessment of capacities and motivations for launching new national nuclear power programs. *Energy Policy*, *39*(3), 1041–1055. doi: 10.1016/j.enpol.2010.10.041

Juraku, K. (2013). Social structure and nuclear power siting problems revealed. In R. Hindmarsh (Ed.), *Nuclear disaster at Fukushima Daiichi: Social, political and environmental issues* (pp. 41–56). New York: Routledge.

Killingsworth, M. J. (2007). A phenomenological perspective on ethical duty in environmental communication. *Environmental Communication: A Journal of Nature and Culture*, *1*(1), 58–63. doi: 10.1080/17524030701334243

Kim, S.-H., Besley, J. C., Oh, S.-H., & Kim, S. Y. (2014). Talking about bio-fuel in the news: Newspaper framing of ethanol stories in the United States. *Journalism Studies*, *15*(2), 218–234. doi: 10.1080/1461670X.2013.809193

Kinefuchi, E. (2015). Nuclear power for good: Articulations in Japan's nuclear power hegemony. *Communication, Culture & Critique*, n/a–n/a. doi: 10.1111/cccr.12092

Kinsella, W. J. (1999). Discourse, power, and knowledge in the management of "Big Science": The production of consensus in a nuclear fusion research laboratory. *Management Communication Quarterly*, *13*(2), 171–208. doi: 10.1177/0893318999132001

Kinsella, W. J. (2012a). Environments, risks, and the limits of representation: Examples from nuclear energy and some implications of Fukushima. *Environmental Communication: A Journal of Nature and Culture*, *6*(2), 251–259. doi: 10.1080/17524032.2012.672928

Kinsella, W. J. (2012b). Forum communicative action in response to a nuclear crisis: Representations of Fukushima across communication contexts. *Environmental Communication: A Journal of Nature and Culture*, *6*(2), 250. doi: 10.1080/17524032.2012.675346

Kinsella, W. J. (2014). Rearticulating nuclear power: Energy activism and contested common sense. *Environmental Communication: A Journal of Nature and Culture*, *0*(0), 1–21. doi: 10.1080/17524032.2014.978348

Kinsella, W. J., Kelly, A. R., & Kittle Autry, M. (2013). Risk, regulation, and rhetorical boundaries: Claims and challenges surrounding a purported nuclear renaissance. *Communication Monographs*, *80*(3), 278–301.doi: 10.1080/03637751.2013.788253

Kitch, C. (2007). Mourning "men joined in peril and purpose": Working-class heroism in news repair of the Sago miners' story. *Critical Studies in Media Communication*, *24*(2), 115–131. doi: 10.1080/07393180701262727

Kittle Autry, M., & Kelly, A. R. (2012). Merging Duke Energy and Progress Energy: Online public discourse, post-Fukushima reactions, and the absence of environmental communication. *Environmental Communication: A Journal of Nature and Culture*, *6*(2), 278–284. doi: 10.1080/17524032.2012.672444

Klein, N. (2014). *This changes everything: Capitalism vs. the climate*. New York: Simon & Schuster.

Koteyko, N., Nerlich, B., & Hellsten, I. (2015). Climate change communication and the internet: Challenges and opportunities for research. *Environmental Communication*, *9*(2), 149–152. doi: 10.1080/17524032.2015.1029297.

Koteyko, N., Thelwall, M., & Nerlich, B. (2010). From carbon markets to carbon morality: Creative compounds as framing devices in online discourses on climate change mitigation. *Science Communication*, *32*(1), 25–54. doi: 10.1177/1075547009340421

Krauss, W. (2011). Migratory birds, migratory scientists, and shifting fields: The political ecology of a northern coastline. In S. Coleman & P. von Hellerman (Eds.), *Multi-sited ethnography: Problems and possibilities in the translocation of research methods* (pp. 146–160). New York: Routledge.

Kuchinskaya, O. (2010). Articulating the signs of danger: Lay experiences of post-Chernobyl radiation risks and effects. *Public Understanding of Science*, *20*(3), 405–421. doi: 10.1177/0963662509348862

Langheim, R., Skubel, M., Chen, X., Maxwell, W., Peterson, T. R., Wilson, E., & Stephens, J. C. (2014). Smart grid coverage in US newspapers: Characterizing public conversations. *The Electricity Journal*, *27*(5), 77–87. doi: 10.1016/j.tej.2014.05.008

Latour, B. (1987). *Science in action: How to follow scientists and engineers through society*. Cambridge, MA: Harvard University Press.

Latour, B. (2010). An attempt at a "Compositionist Manifesto." *New Literary History*, *41*(3), 471–490. doi: 10.1353/nlh.2010.0022

Lazic, D., & Kaigo, M. (2013). US press coverage of the Fukushima nuclear power plant accident: Frames, sources and news domestication. *Media Asia*, *40*(3), 260–273.

Liska, C., Petrun, E. L., Sellnow, T. L., & Seeger, M. W. (2012). Chaos theory, self-organization, and industrial accidents: Crisis communication in the Kingston coal ash spill. *Southern Communication Journal*, *77*(3), 180–197. doi: 10.1080/1041794X.2011.634479

Livesey, S. M. (2002). Global warming wars: Rhetorical and discourse analytic approaches to Exxonmobil's corporate public discourse. *Journal of Business Communication*, *39*(1), 117–146. doi: 10.1177/002194360203900106

Lorenz-Meyer, D. (2012). Locating excellence and enacting locality. *Science, Technology & Human Values*, *37*(2), 241–263. doi: 10.1177/0162243911409249

Luke, T. W. (1987). Chernobyl: The packaging of transnational ecological disaster. *Critical Studies in Mass Communication*, *4*(4), 351–375. doi: 10.1080/15295038709360145

Lyne, J., & Miller, C. R. (2009). Rhetoric across the disciplines: Rhetoric, disciplinarity, and fields of knowledge. In A. A. Lunsford (Ed.), *The SAGE handbook of rhetorical studies* (pp. 167–174). Thousand Oaks, CA: SAGE Publications.

Maillé, M. È., & Saint-Charles, J. (2014). Fuelling an environmental conflict through information diffusion strategies. *Environmental Communication*, *8*(3), 305–325. doi: 10.1080/17524032.2013.851099

Marcus, G. E. (1995). Ethnography in/of the world system: The emergence of multi-sited ethnography. *Annual Review of Anthropology*, *24*, 95–117. doi: 10.1146/annurev.an.24.100195.000523

Maresh, M. M., & Williams, D. E. (2007). Responding to oil industry crises: The case of Phillips Petroleum in Pasadena, Texas. *American Communication Journal, 9*(2), 1–12.

Maresh, M. M., & Williams, D. E. (2009). Oil industry crisis communication. In W. T. Coombs & S. Holladay (Eds.), *The handbook of crisis communication* (pp. 285–300). Chichester: Wiley-Blackwell.

McLachlan, C. (2010). Technologies in place: Symbolic interpretations of renewable energy. *The Sociological Review, 57,* 181–199. doi: 10.1111/j.1467-954X.2010. 01892.x

Medhurst, M. J. (1987). Eisenhower's "Atoms for Peace" speech: A case study in the strategic use of language. *Communication Monographs, 54*(2), 204–220. doi: 10.1080/03637758709390226

Miller, B. M. (2010). Community stakeholders and marketplace advocacy: A model of advocacy, agenda building, and industry approval. *Journal of Public Relations Research, 22*(1), 85–112. doi: 10.1080/10627260903170993

Miller, B. M., & Lellis, J. C. (2015). Response to marketplace advocacy messages by sponsor and topic within the energy industry: Should corporations or industry trade groups do the talking? *Journal of Applied Communication Research, 43*(1), 66–90. doi: 10.1080/00909882.2014.982684

Mirel, B. (1994). Debating nuclear energy: Theories of risk and purposes of communication. *Technical Communication Quarterly, 3*(1), 41–65. doi: 10.1080/10572259 409364557

Monani, S. (2008). Energizing environmental activism? Environmental justice in *Extreme Oil: The Wilderness* and *Oil on Ice. Environmental Communication: A Journal of Nature and Culture, 2*(1), 119–127. doi: 10.1080/17524030801936772

Moser, S. C., & Dilling, L. (2007). *Creating a climate for change: Communicating climate change and facilitating social change.* Cambridge, UK: Cambridge University Press.

Muralidharan, S., Dillistone, K., & Shin, J.-H. (2011). The Gulf Coast oil spill: Extending the theory of image restoration discourse to the realm of social media and beyond petroleum. *Public Relations Review, 37*(3), 226–232. doi: 10.1016/j. pubrev.2011.04.006

Newell, R. G., & Raimi, D. (2014). Implications of shale gas development for climate change. *Environmental Science & Technology, 48,* 8360-8368. doi: 10.1021/es4046154

Nisbet, M. C., Maibach, E., & Leiserowitz, A. (2011). Framing peak petroleum as a public health problem: Audience research and participatory engagement in the United States. *American Journal of Public Health, 101,* 1620–1626. doi: 10.2105/ AJPH.2011.300230

O'Connor, A., & Gronewold, K. L. (2013). Black gold, green earth: An analysis of the petroleum industry's CSR environmental sustainability discourse. *Management Communication Quarterly, 27*(2), 210–236. doi: 10.1177/0893318912465189

Olaniran, B. A., & Williams, D. E. (2008). Applying anticipatory and relational perspectives to the Nigerian delta region oil crisis. *Public Relations Review, 34*(1), 57–59. doi: 10.1016/j.pubrev.2007.11.005

Oltra, C., Delicado, A., Prades, A., Pereira, S., & Schmidt, L. (2014). The Holy Grail of energy? A content and thematic analysis of the presentation of nuclear fusion on the Internet. *Journal of Science Communication, 13*(4), 1–18.

Peeples, J., Bsumek, P., Schwarze, S., & Schneider, J. (2014). Industrial apocalyptic: Neoliberalism, coal, and the burlesque frame. *Rhetoric & Public Affairs, 17*(2), 227–253. doi: 10.1353/rap.2014.0023

Peeples, J. A., Krannich, R. S., & Weiss, J. (2008). Arguments for what no one wants: The narratives of waste storage proponents. *Environmental Communication: A Journal of Nature and Culture*, 2(1), 40–58. doi: 10.1080/17524030701642751

Peterson, T. R., & Peterson, M. J. (1996). Valuation analysis in environmental policy making: How economic models limit possibilities for environmental advocacy. In C. J. Oravec & J. C. Cantrill (Eds.), *The symbolic earth: Discourse and our creation of the environment* (pp. 198–218). Lexington, KY: University of Kentucky Press.

Plec, E., & Pettenger, M. (2012). Greenwashing consumption: The didactic framing of Exxonmobil's energy solutions. *Environmental Communication*, 6(4), 459–476. doi: 10.1080/17524032.2012.720270

Pralle, S., & Boscarino, J. (2011). Framing trade-offs: The politics of nuclear power and wind energy in the age of global climate change. *Review of Policy Research 28*(4), 323–346. doi: 10.1111/j.1541-1338.2011.00500.x.

Prasad, A., & Mir, R. (2002). Digging deep for meaning: A critical hermeneutic analysis of CEO letters to shareholders in the oil industry. *Journal of Business Communication*, 39(1), 92–116. doi: 10.1177/002194360203900105

Prelli, L. J. (1989). *A rhetoric of science: Inventing scientific discourse*. Columbia, SC: University of South Carolina Press.

Ratliff, J. N. (1997). The politics of nuclear waste: An analysis of a public hearing on the proposed Yucca Mountain nuclear waste repository. *Communication Studies*, 48(4), 359–380. doi: 10.1080/10510979709368512

Raza, G., Kumar, P. V. S., & Singh, S. (2011). Public understanding of environment and bioenergy resources. *Journal of Science Communication*, 10(3), 1–7.

Remillard, C. (2011). Picturing environmental risk: The Canadian oil sands and the National Geographic. *International Communication Gazette*, 73(1-2), 127–143. doi: 10.1177/1748048510386745

Rubin, D. M. (1987). How the news media reported on Three Mile Island and Chernobyl. *Journal of Communication*, 37(3), 42–57. doi: 10.1111/j.1460-2466.1987.tb00993.x

Russell, L. D., & Babrow, A. S. (2011). Risk in the making: Narrative, problematic integration, and the social construction of risk. *Communication Theory, 21*(3), 239–260. doi: 10.1111/j.1468-2885.2011.01386.x

Schneider, J., & Miller, G. (2011). The impact of "no impact man": Alternative hedonism as environmental appeal. *Environmental Communication*, 5(4), 467–484. doi: 10.1080/17524032.2011.611524

Schultz, F., Kleinnijenhuis, J., Oegema, D., Utz, S., & van Atteveldt, W. (2012). Strategic framing in the BP crisis: A semantic network analysis of associative frames. *Public Relations Review*, 38(1), 97–107. doi: 10.1016/j.pubrev.2011.08.003

Scollon, S. W. (2009). Peak oil and climate change in a rural Alaskan community: A sketch of a nexus analysis. *Journal of Applied Linguistics*, 6(3), 357–377. doi: 10.1558/japl.v6i3.357

Sellnow, T. L. (1993). Scientific argument in organizational crisis communication: The case of Exxon. *Argumentation and Advocacy*, 30(1), 28–42.

Senecah, S. L. (2007). Impetus, mission, and future of the environmental communication commission/division: Are we still on track? Were we ever? *Environmental Communication: A Journal of Nature and Culture, 1*(1), 21–33. doi: 10.1080/17524030 701334045

Sheller, M. (2014). Global energy cultures of speed and lightness: Materials, mobilities and transnational power. *Theory, Culture & Society, 31*(5), 127–154. doi: 10.1177/0263276414537909

Shove, E., & Walker, G. (2014). What is energy for? Social practice and energy demand. *Theory, Culture & Society, 31*(5), 41–58. doi: 10.1177/0263276414536746

Sismondo, S. (2008). Science and technology studies and an engaged program. In E. J. Hackett, O. Amsterdamska, M. Lynch, & J. Wajcman (Eds.), *The handbook of science and technology studies* (pp. 13–31). Cambridge, MA: MIT Press.

Sjöberg, L., & Drottz-Sjöberg, B.-M. (2001). Fairness, risk and risk tolerance in the siting of a nuclear waste repository. *Journal of Risk Research, 4*(1), 75–101. doi: 10.1080/136698701456040

Skjølsvold, T. M. (2012). Curb your enthusiasm: On media communication of bioenergy and the role of the news media in technology diffusion. *Environmental Communication: A Journal of Nature and Culture, 6*(4), 512–531. doi: 10.1080/17524032.2012.705309

Smerecnik, K. R., & Renegar, V. R. (2010). Capitalistic agency: The rhetoric of BP's Helios Power campaign. *Environmental Communication: A Journal of Nature and Culture, 4*(2), 152–171. doi: 10.1080/17524031003760879

Smith, H. M., & Lindenfeld, L. (2014). Integrating media studies of climate change into transdisciplinary research: Which direction should we be heading? *Environmental Communication: A Journal of Nature and Culture, 8*(2), 179–196. doi: 10.1080/17524032.2014.906479

Song, Y., Kim, D., & Han, D. (2013). Risk communication in South Korea: Social acceptance of nuclear power plants (NPPs). *Public Relations Review, 39*(1), 55–56. doi: 10.1016/j.pubrev.2012.10.002

Spangler, I. S., & Pompper, D. (2011). Corporate social responsibility and the oil industry: Theory and perspective fuel a longitudinal view. *Public Relations Review, 37*(3), 217–225. doi: 10.1016/j.pubrev.2011.03.013

Stephens, J., Wilson, E. J., & Peterson, T. R. (2015). *Smart grid (r)evolution: Electric power struggles.* New York: Cambridge University Press.

Stephens, J. C., Peterson, T. R., & Wilson, E. J. (2014). Socio-political evaluation of energy deployment (SPEED): A framework applied to smart grid. *UCLA L. Rev., 61*, 1930–2068.

Stephens, J. C., Rand, G. M., & Melnick, L. L. (2009). Wind energy in US media: A comparative state-level analysis of a critical climate change mitigation technology. *Environmental Communication: A Journal of Nature and Culture, 3*(2), 168–190. doi: 10.1080/17524030902916640

Swofford, J., & Slattery, M. (2010). Public attitudes of wind energy in Texas: Local communities in close proximity to wind farms and their effect on decision-making. *Energy Policy, 38*(5), 2508–2519. doi: 10.1016/j.enpol.2009.12.046

Tateno, S., & Yokoyama, H. M. (2013). Public anxiety, trust, and the role of mediators in communicating risk of exposure to low dose radiation after the Fukushima Daiichi Nuclear Plant explosion. *Journal of Science Communication, 12*(2), 1–22.

Todd, A. M., & Wood, A. (2006). "Flex your power:" Energy crises and the shifting rhetoric of the grid. *Atlantic Journal of Communication, 14*(4), 211–228. doi: 10.1207/s15456889ajc1404_2

Tyfield, D. (2014). "King coal is dead! Long live the king!": The paradoxes of coal's resurgence in the emergence of global low-carbon societies. *Theory, Culture & Society, 31*(5), 59–81. doi: 10.1177/0263276414537910

Tyfield, D., & Urry, J. (Eds.). (2014). Energy & society [Special issue]. *Theory, Culture & Society, 31*(5).

Utz, S., Schultz, F., & Glocka, S. (2013). Crisis communication online: How medium, crisis type and emotions affected public reactions in the Fukushima Daiichi Nuclear Disaster. *Public Relations Review*, *39*(1), 40–46. doi: 10.1016/j.pubrev.2012.09.010.

Vandenberghe, J. (2011). Repsol meets YPF: Displaying competence in cross-border M&A press releases. *Journal of Business Communication*, *48*(4), 373–392. doi: 10.1177/0021943611414686

Van de Velde, L., Verbeke, W., Popp, M., & Van Huylenbroeck, G. (2011). Trust and perception related to information about biofuels in Belgium. *Public Understanding of Science*, *20*(5), 595–608. doi: 10.1177/0963662509358641

Visschers, V. H., & Siegrist, M. (2013). How a nuclear power plant accident influences acceptance of nuclear power: Results of a longitudinal study before and after the Fukushima disaster. *Risk Analysis, 33,* 333–347. doi: 10.1111/j.1539-6924.2012.01861.x

Vraga, E. K., Tully, M., Akin, H., & Rojas, H. (2012). Modifying perceptions of hostility and credibility of news coverage of an environmental controversy through media literacy. *Journalism*, *13*(7), 942–959. doi: 10.1177/1464884912455906

Wander, P. C. (1976). The rhetoric of science. *Western Speech Communication*, *40*(4), 226–235. doi: 10.1080/10570317609373907

Watson, B. R. (2012). Ideologies drive journalists' attitudes toward oil industry. *Newspaper Research Journal*, *33*(2), 6-22.

Wei, R., Lo, V. H., Lu, H. Y., & Hou, H.-Y. (2015). Examining multiple behavioral effects of third-person perception: Evidence from the news about Fukushima nuclear crisis in Taiwan. *Chinese Journal of Communication*, *8*(1), 95–111. doi: 10.1080/17544750.2014.972422.

Williams, D. E., & Olaniran, B. A. (1994). Exxon's decision-making flaws: The hypervigilant response to the Valdez grounding. *Public Relations Review*, *20*(1), 5–18. doi: 10.1016/0363-8111(94)90110-4

Williams, D. E., & Treadaway, G. (1992). Exxon and the Valdez accident: A failure in crisis communication. *Communication Studies*, *43*(1), 56–64. doi: 10.1080/10510979209368359

Wolsink, M. (2000). Wind power and the NIMBY-myth: Institutional capacity and the limited significance of public support. *Renewable Energy*, *21*, 49–64. doi: 10.1016S0960-1481(99)00130-5

Wolsink, M. (2006). Invalid Theory Impedes Our Understanding: A Critique on the Persistence of the Language of NIMBY. *Transactions of the Institute of British Geographers*, *31*(1), 85–91. doi: 10.1111/j.1475-5661.2006.00191.x

Wolsink, M. (2012). Undesired reinforcement of harmful "self-evident truths" concerning the implementation of wind power. *Energy Policy*, *48*, 83–87. doi: 10.1016/j.enpol.2012.06.010

Wood, S., Shabajee, P., Schien, D., Hodgson, C., & Preist, C. (2014). Energy use and greenhouse gas emissions in digital news media: Ethical implications for journalists and media organisations. *Digital Journalism*, *2*(3), 284–295. doi: 10.1080/21670811.2014.892759

Yeo, S. K., Cacciatore, M. A., Brossard, D., Scheufele, D. A., Runge, K., Su, L. Y., . . . Corley, E. A. (2014). Partisan amplification of risk: American perceptions of nuclear energy risk in the wake of the Fukushima Daiichi disaster. *Energy Policy*, *67*, 727–736. doi: 10.1016/j.enpol.2013.11.061

Young, M. J., & Launer, M. K. (1991). Redefining Glasnost in the Soviet media: The recontextualization of Chernobyl. *Journal of Communication*, *41*(2), 102–124. doi: 10.1111/j.1460-2466.1991.tb02312.x

CHAPTER CONTENTS

15 Communication Infrastructure and Civic Engagement in the ICT Era

A Synthetic Approach

Seok Kang

University of Texas, San Antonio

Communication infrastructure as a collective storytelling system contributing to civic engagement needs to reflect the prominence of information and communication technologies (ICTs). This chapter, therefore, proposes that civic engagement is implemented through the synthesis of ICT and daily communication practices at different levels. Drawing on communication infrastructure theory and communicative ecology, this chapter suggests that ICT, traditional media and face-to-face communication are key factors of civic engagement. These storytelling agents operate at different levels from micro- to meso- and macro-levels. Communication infrastructure that reflects ICT becomes an ecological foundation that comprehensively explicates the process of civic engagement.

Communication scholars have defined communication infrastructure as a collective storytelling system, through storytelling networks and communication action contexts (Ball-Rokeach, Kim, & Matei, 2001; Kim & Ball-Rokeach, 2006). Research has suggested that shared discourse and lived experiences in storytelling networks, grounded in conducive social contexts, contribute to constructive civic engagement (Anderson, 1996; Offe, 1980; Wilkin, 2013). Communication infrastructure theory involves public deliberation not only as a tool of using networks and action contexts and making collective decisions but also as a process of reaching a mutual understanding through various channels. Recently, communication infrastructure theory in the information and communication technology (ICT) era has been under scrutiny, because multiple communicative agents in increased communication channels have come into play in the storytelling process. Communicative agents—from family and friends to local organizations and national and global interactions for storytelling—can construct a communication infrastructure that provides a sphere for civic engagement opportunities.

ICT is broadly defined as the integrated formats of telecommunication, computers, and data systems that support, store, and transmit communication resources (Alena & Libor, 2012). As such, ICT deals with new telecommunication technologies in terms of devices or systems such as the Internet, wireless networks, or the mobile phone (Andronie & Andronie, 2014). This definition provides a guideline for media outlets by distinguishing ICT from traditional media, including television, radio, newspaper, and magazines.

Based on the increased importance of ICT, the goals of this chapter are twofold. First, this chapter discusses the role of ICT in the paths to civic engagement by claiming that communication infrastructure theory alone, without discussing ICTs as communicative agents, has limitations in explicating substantial factors influencing active citizenship. Second, this chapter elaborates on the significance of an expanded communication infrastructure in ICT formats at the different levels—including micro-, meso-, and macro-levels—through which civic engagement is fulfilled. The dynamic processes of communication need to be addressed to understand the role of communicative formats and levels in civic engagement. In this view, current communication infrastructure theory (CIT), which predicts the relationship between storytelling agents and civic engagement, needs to reflect the ecological aspects of ICT. Furthermore, the associations among the communicative agents at multiple levels, from the communication ecological perspective, can be contingent upon action contexts.

A considerable amount of communication research has articulated the implementation of social participation in terms of social engagement, civic involvement, and civic engagement (e.g., Ganesh & Zoller, 2012; Kang, 2013; Paek, Yoon, & Shah, 2005; Shah, McLeod, & Yoon, 2001; Shklovski, & Valtysson, 2012). The factors driving the public's civic engagement have been of keen interest among scholars. Scholars' development and delineation of theories have been added to improve the explanatory power of theoretical models that account for the factors contributing to civic engagement. Communication infrastructure theory can be articulated with the deliberation of widespread ICT formats. To do justice to the new, complex convergence in expanded communication outlets, CIT needs to be complemented by a more holistic, ecological perspective on storytelling agents at the micro-, meso-, and macro-levels.

This chapter first discusses the meaning of human and media storytelling networks in CIT. Second, ICT is explicated in terms of communicative ecology. Third, this chapter attempts a synthesis of CIT and communicative ecology. Fourth, communication action agents are delineated as contextual factors. Fifth, civic engagement is detailed as a consequence of human storytelling agents and ICT combination. Finally, a synthetic model as an expansion of communicative agents in the ICT era in terms of formats and levels is proposed.

Storytelling Networks as Civic Engagement Agents

A communication infrastructure involves facilitating factors for active citizenship. Some societies possess rich communication infrastructures, but other societies possess weak infrastructures (Kim & Ball-Rokeach, 2006). Communication infrastructures are based on the media system dependency theory (MSD; Ball-Rokeach, 1998), which postulates that the mass media and individuals interact with each other to facilitate the growth of individuals and society. MSD focuses mainly on power dependency relations between individuals and the mass media system, which confines its range to media communicative agents. Meanwhile, communication infrastructure is inclusive of human communicative agents—such as everyday conversations or local meetings—in addition to the mass media (Kim & Ball-Rokeach, 2006). Therefore, communication infrastructure theory follows the concept of dependency and expands to a broader level.

Communication infrastructure is theoretically delineated in communication infrastructure theory (CIT). CIT states that the members of a society build connections to a feasible storytelling network in order to anticipate a successful engagement. Storytelling networks in a communication action context are initiators of collective action. As members of a society communicate with each other, they develop a sense of togetherness within the society.

CIT considers three key storytelling agents as elements for engagement and action. Interpersonal communication agents such as family, friends, and next-door neighbors (i.e., the Internet such as neighborhood social network sites) are the first agents, at the micro-level (Lake & Huckfeldt, 1998). The second storytelling agent refers to local organizations and local media outlets (e.g., geo-ethnic media, community social network sites) at the meso-level (Kim & Ball-Rokeach, 2006). The third storytelling agent includes mainstream media (e.g., national TV news, Internet news) for national or global issues and communication with individuals at the macro-level (Kim & Ball-Rokeach, 2006). These agents, as integrated communication storytelling networks (ICSN), contribute to engendering and engaging action at the micro-, meso-, and macro-levels (Wilkin & Ball-Rokeach, 2011).

Community growth processes are shaped and attained by building a firm communication infrastructure in which citizens effectively leverage communicative formats at different levels for optimal outcomes. The efforts of harnessing the elements of communication infrastructure are a precursor to the development of social, political, cultural, and global capital (Ball-Rokeach et al., 2001).

The eventual goal of the use of communication infrastructure is the realization of democracy and civil society (Habermas, 1989). The neighborhood, community, or country continually experiences changes for improvement through the influx of external forces, physical or administrative relocating, expansion, or contraction. In each different circumstance, citizens make use of different communication strategies to achieve intended outcomes through face-to-face or mediated communication.

Habermas (1984; 1989) articulates the power of storytelling networks and communication action in building civil society. Habermas (1989) emphasized the importance of the "lifeworld" rather than the "social system" for the future of civil society. To Habermas (1989), the "lifeworld" is where citizens gather and discuss the issues they face. This storytelling process is based on mutual understanding. If storytelling remains stagnant and the communication action context does not support the storytelling process, then society experiences problems and eventually faces difficulties in functioning in a healthy way. When storytelling and a sustained communication action context cease to exist, citizens invariably lose their public sphere. In a society such as this, citizens lose the opportunity to resolve their social problems, and social development becomes unattainable.

Habermas (1984) distinguishes four types of social actions as a result of "life-world" dialogs: teleological, normative, dramaturgical, and communicative. The teleological action model proposes that human actors are competitors for the success or failure of the objective world. This model is directed by effectiveness and purposiveness. The normative action model refers to a situation where citizens orient their actions to common values. Widespread social norms and rules, such as pure procedural justice, govern public deliberations (Elster, 1998). The dramaturgical action model focuses on the presentation of self through interaction. In this dialogic setting, human actors check their own intentions, thoughts, and desires. "Lifeworld" talks or democratic discussions at a town hall meeting are two examples of the dramaturgical action model. The communicative action model refers to the interaction of two or more actors in society in reaching a consensus for action. Cooperation and interaction in a community for a better outcome are examples of the communicative action model.

In summary, citizens use diverse storytelling agents to build communication infrastructures. Today's daily life is heavily dependent on ICT, so if the existing technological environment does not support society, then citizens' civic engagement can lag compared to other societies.

Communicative Ecology for Civic Engagement

In discussing communication infrastructure, a communicative format can be used in the social process of communication for civic engagement. By definition, a communicative format refers to the selection, organization, and presentation of experience and information through direct (e.g., face-to-face communication) or indirect channels (e.g., mediated communication; Snow, 1983). The implementation or change of communicative formats contributes to civic engagement both implicitly and explicitly.

Human interactions use the formats at different levels, from micro- to meso- and macro-levels. Therefore, a communicative level refers to the realms of communication in terms of size. Individuals can discuss public affairs with next-door neighbors (micro-level), members of community organizations (meso-level), and global activists (macro-level). The discussions can take place through different communicative formats—such as face-to-face meetings, traditional media (e.g., television, radio, newspaper, magazines), or ICTs (e.g., Internet, wireless networks, mobile phone). In this process, communication action context agents, including demographic backgrounds or living environments, are contingent factors.

Communicative formats with an emphasis on ICT have been detailed in the communicative ecology perspective. Communicative ecology is the communication process in context (Altheide, 1994). The parameters of communication come into play in understanding the way social activities are organized and social orders are implied.

Communicative ecology is defined as human interaction and ICT use for communicative matters. Communicative ecology also implies interdependence, mutuality, and coexistence in human society. From a communication infrastructure perspective, communicative ecology refers to the network of communication resources built by individuals in a communication environment in pursuit of knowledge or goals (Broad et al., 2013). Citizens' interdependence and mutual communication in the community for a cause—either through push or pull communication—have the potential to evoke communicative action. Communicative ecology continues to mutate, enhance, or withdraw. In turn, communicative ecology is a fluid structure, discourse, story, frame, and network. In this sense, communicative ecology enriches the discussion of communication infrastructure for civic engagement in terms of social interaction and ICT (Figure 15.1).

In biology, ecology refers to organic systems functioning dynamically to maintain equilibrium. Communication infrastructure as ecology in human society can contribute to social equilibrium through interactions. The dynamics of human networks are adjusted naturally and culturally for human adaptation. As such, communication infrastructure theory may indicate human behaviors functioning in a biological way (Cappella, 1991). Communicative ecology takes a holistic approach to identifying micro-, meso-, and macro-dimensions of communicative channels that facilitate civic engagement. Media ecology (Postman, 1971) underpins the importance of an approach to understanding the role of media in our conception of time and space. Communicative ecology emphasizes equally both human and ICT factors in the civic engagement process, whereas media ecology is oriented to technological determinism—this puts more weight on media and ICT factors than on human communication.

While communication infrastructure theory focuses on individual activities of goal seeking in discourse at multiple levels, communicative ecology maintains that communication processes expand the levels from temporal to spatiotemporal, and the formats from face-to-face to ICT (Coleman & Firmstone, 2014; Foth & Hearn, 2007). In other words, communication used to be primarily based in the past (time) and offline (space). Communicative ecology, however, offers individuals with ICT experience an expansion of communication in both time (e.g., online and offline connection either synchronously or asynchronously) and space (e.g., online and offline spaces). Therefore, the successful implementation of communicative ecology should be interpreted contextually from the ecological perspective. The media dimension of communication infrastructure

Figure 15.1 Communicative Ecology for Civic Engagement

theory can be expanded to ICT use for both local and global information attainment. Furthermore, these dimensions need additional outlets for citizens to use in the communication process. The Internet, wireless networks, and the mobile phone as ICTs in micro-, meso-, and macro-sectors are integrated into pre-existing communication patterns (Poell, 2014; Tacchi, 2006).

Communicative ecology is derived from the embeddedness of communication in context. Members of society become involved in symbolic interactions in everyday conversation (Blumer, 1969). Through symbolic interactions, people interpret and define the actions of others. People object to or agree with each other's reactions. Citizens conduct inner or outer conversations in interactions. Interactions also occur at micro-, meso-, and macro-levels. With the prevalence of ICT, communication outlets are more diversified than ever.

The Ecological Infrastructure of Communication

Communicative ecology, from a communication infrastructure perspective, refers to the network of communication resource relations constructed by human interaction and ICT in pursuit of a goal in a communication environment (Broad et al., 2013). Communicative ecology consists of micro-, meso-, and macro-ecology, and symbolizes multi-modal communication connections shaped by social and cultural conditions. Human actors employ the connections through interaction and ICT as a means to construct knowledge and to achieve civic goals.

The empowerment of communication is attained through diverse communication formats and levels (Ball-Rokeach, Rokeach, & Grube, 1984; Ball-Rokeach, 1998). At the micro-level, interwoven communicative behaviors in everyday life provide reasons for action. Civic action occurs when communicative formats and levels interact. Micro-level human interaction and ICT use can be the beginnings of a social ecology for civic engagement.

Having expanded from the micro-level to the meso-level, other factors come into play. Community citizens are exposed to storytelling opportunities provided by social sectors (e.g., local government). As an example, a local government's new program for recent immigrants can be announced on the city's website, on social network site (SNS) applications, and on local information websites. This push method encourages the potential participation of immigrants at the meso-level. On the other hand, pull communication occurs when citizens seek particular information about opportunities for community togetherness and further participation. In this way, communication infrastructures, in connection with communicative ecology, are formulated in both push and pull communication modes.

Communicative ecology also enables citizens to expand the array of symbols of control and surveillance to the macro-level. Human interaction and ICT at the macro-level have played a dominant role in the surveillance and monitoring of society thus far. The prevalence of ICT has expanded their roles to a wider population. Citizens have become the agents of surveillance of social affairs that could have been manipulated by the practitioners who did not produce them.

All distal communication involves messages via channels. In fact, numerous human activities are mediated by the logic of ICT. ICT enables citizens to create, organize, transmit, store, and retrieve information and interaction at the micro-, meso-, and macro-levels. From the static Internet to the mobile phone, ICT creates spaces for discussion and accounts for the informational territoriality of space (Lemos, 2011). Spaces created through ICT encompass physical places through location-based services (LBSs) or virtual spaces through the mobile phone or SNS. The exchange of mobile phone calls and LBS posts about civic affairs through applications can create new mobilizations such as voting or petition signing and new forms of synchronicity or meeting people. In LBS, locating and mapping services position and change the way citizens interact with other individuals and gather information at the broader level (Ito & Daisuke, 2005; Katz & Aakhus, 2002; Kavanaugh et al., 2014).

In this way, communication infrastructure, from an ecological perspective, encourages the formation of a participatory culture (Valcanis, 2011). The interconnection of ICT with communicative storytelling agents is necessary in order to embrace the comprehensive behaviors at micro-, meso-, and macro-levels that lead to civic engagement. This chapter argues that communicative ecology theory relatively tones down the importance of face-to-face communication practices for active citizenship. On the other hand, communication infrastructure describes only a limited role for ICT in the civic engagement process. The synthesis of these two theoretical perspectives with communication action context elements deserves theoretical attention in order to empower communication infrastructure for civic engagement in the ICT era.

Communicative Action in the ICT Era

Habermas (1984) described communicative action as discursive forms or interactive speech acts. Communicative action originally referred to "the interaction of at least two subjects to establish interpersonal relations" (Habermas, 1984, p. 85). Another view is that communicative action is contextual (Kim & Ball-Rokeach, 2006)—the context allows interactions to be expanded to a broader level. Ranging from the degree of involvement with civic discussion to the degree of residential stability, the circumstantial statuses of citizens affects communicative action.

By utilizing communicative formats at multiple levels, citizens participate in discussions and meetings to develop small changes or large transformations. Variances in socioeconomic background—such as gender, age, income, social castes, ethnicity, immigration duration, and religion—are action factors of civic engagement. All citizens endure different communicative conflicts. Their approach to problem-solving varies depending on their background.

As well as socioeconomic backgrounds, several other communication context agents have received scholarly attention. Ethnic identity is one of them. Immigrants with solid ethnic identities are more likely to have high levels of civic engagement in their respective ethnic communities than in mainstream society (Seo & Moon, 2013). Expressiveness in family communication is a catalyst for the development of ethnic identity, which then moves on to membership of a formal group (Pearson, Semlak, Western, & Herakova, 2010).

Personality is another communication action context in civic engagement, particularly in ICT settings. For example, SNS use has been found to positively influence civic engagement (Kim, Hsu, & de Zúñiga, 2013). In their study, SNS use by introverted people contributed to discussion network heterogeneity and civic engagement. Another study found that extroverted citizens are more likely than introverted citizens to participate in civic activities (Omoto, Snyder, & Hackett, 2010). The contrasting results of the two studies imply that participatory media—such as SNS—as an ecological storytelling agent can be used as a catalyst of civic engagement for both introverted and extroverted citizens.

In summary, civic engagement results from the interrelationships among human interaction, ICT, and communication action agents at micro-, meso-, and macro-levels. This chapter stresses the role of ICT by expanding communication infrastructure theory. ICTs can be described as communicative formats, which are embedded in every sector of human interaction in today's communication environment.

Civic Engagement in the ICT Era

Civic engagement is an element of active citizenship (Hoffman & Thomson, 2009). Citizenship is described as political and civic engagement (Erentaitė, Žukauskienė, Beyers, & Pilkauskaitė-Valickienė, 2012). Political engagement consists of actions aimed at targeting government policy or the election of public officials (Zukin, Keeter, Andolina, Jenkins, & Delli Carpini, 2006). Civic engagement is usually carried out in cooperation with others, as collective action, to change or improve the social conditions, in the public interest (Adler & Goggin, 2005; Nissen, 2010). In recent studies, both political and civic engagement are called civic engagement, with the view that citizens take action in the public interest both politically and socially.

Civic engagement consists of attached feelings, intentions, and behaviors. The discussion of local issues with families and neighbors at the micro-level increases bonding capital (Ellison, Steinfield, & Lampe, 2007; Park, Kee, & Valenzuela, 2009; Steinfield, Ellison, & Lampe, 2008). Bonding capital refers to trusting and cooperative relations between members of a network who see themselves as being similar and share the same social norms (Szreter & Woolcock, 2004). In communication infrastructure, Kim and Ball-Rokeach (2006) label the feeling of attachment as neighborhood belonging. In this view, neighborhood belonging shares its definition with bonding capital.

Civic engagement in the ICT era means that online or mobile communication should be taken into account, to a significant degree, in active citizenship. The role of ICT in civic engagement at different levels is echoed by research evidence. At the micro-level, for example, expressiveness in family and news use in online media fosters youths' civic engagement (Lee, Shah, & McLeod, 2013). At the meso-level, e-participation has been proposed as a way of eliciting citizens' engagement in local government policies—citizens' participation in government policymaking can be achieved through partnership, consultation, or control of citizen access (de Reuver, Stein, & Hampe, 2013). An example of e-participation is local mobile elections—for example, the election of a Home Owners Association president, held in the city of Daejeon in South Korea. This mobile election was deemed successful in terms of the level of citizens' interest in the election and the high voter turnout (Cho, 2013). At the macro-level, the Internet enables citizens to facilitate political expression due to the low cost of transactions, ease of access, and large social network reach (Lagos, Coopman, & Tomhave, 2014). This social-technical interaction at the national level demonstrates the potential for social movements on a large scale. Therefore, civic engagement in the ICT era is not only explained by face-to-face communication practices and the mass media but also by ICT experiences at different levels.

Storytelling Agents for Civic Engagement in the ICT Era: An Expansion

Communication infrastructure in the ICT era covers a comprehensive communicative environment that encompasses personal interaction, social information flow, and online and offline interconnections. Ellul (1990) pointed out that the expansion of communication infrastructure through media convergence sets up networks to which individuals can adapt. Competition and tension among communication components in individuals' daily lives leads to adaptations in society. Some communication components are more appropriate than others, depending on the nature of the communication and the background of the communicators.

The ownership of ICT enables users to foster a Habermasian "public sphere" of participatory culture in a neighborhood, local city, or global cyber sphere. At the micro-level, being attentive to everyday dialog is the easiest way to see the degree to which citizens are personally or socially engaged in resolving personal or social agendas using ICT (Campbell & Kwak, 2010).

At the meso-level, local government programs and publicity can be examined by conducting a survey of citizens on the subject of civic engagement. Program information can be included in the survey to find out to what extent citizens participate in programs. Mobilizing citizens for a cause to improve the current status of the community is implemented through ICT. Communication infrastructure of online and offline behaviors is created and modified through the use of ICT, thereby giving rise to a new communication format.

At the macro-level, the symbolic environment of society is contextualized, implying that communication occurs in a "social matrix" of action-meaning systems (Altheide, 1994). The expansion of communication formats breaks down bureaucratic society, which is characterized by monitoring and surveillance.

In the ICT era, monitoring and surveillance are conducted in social sectors. For instance, companies with "big data" consumer information use advanced computer algorithms to detect fraudulent behaviors. In the era of "big data," communicators are responsible for efficiently building a storytelling network in society. The expansion of communicative formats embraces the current practice of human interaction via both face-to-face communication and ICT for social action. Identifying the protocols of ecological infrastructure is the key component of this chapter. Given the discussions of communication infrastructure theory and communicative ecology, communicative formats at the micro-, meso-, macro-levels contribute to civic engagement. The newly proposed model in this chapter states that communicative formats at different levels in a communication action context are likely associated with civic engagement. Communication infrastructure theory (CIT) falls short of emphasizing the role of ICT in the civic engagement process. Meanwhile, the communicative ecology perspective states that the roles of both human interaction and ICT in the human communication environment exist in developing civic engagement. However, the communicative ecology perspective pays less attention to various human storytelling agents. The pitfalls of each theoretical typology are complemented to intensify the explanatory power of communication infrastructure for civic engagement in the ICT era. In the current chapter, the model adopts the strengths of both perspectives and reflects the importance of ICT use in today's communication. This model is presented visually in Figure 15.2.

A large body of research confirms that ICTs are facilitators, rather than deterrents, of civic engagement. The Internet is an outlet with low-cost transactions and ease-of-use social networking, which enhances civic participation opportunities (Lagos et al., 2014; Xenos & Moy, 2007). As a prevailing communication channel on the Internet, SNS use is positively related to political consumerism, a form of civic engagement (de Zúñiga, Copeland, & Bimber, 2014). In addition to traditional media use, SNS use also explains social capital development and political participation (de Zúñiga, 2012). Mobile phone use for texting, calling, and exploring the Internet plays an enhanced role in civic involvement and political behavior (Campbell & Kwak, 2010; 2011). Although these studies do not categorize the influencing factors into formats and levels, the evidence suggests that ICT is a storyteller for civic engagement.

Drawn from the review of factors influencing civic engagement, this chapter categorizes storytellers derived from communication infrastructure and communicative ecology perspectives into three formats: ICT, traditional media, and face-to-face communication. Communicative action context variables are considered as contingent factors. All of the storytelling agents act at the micro-, meso-, and macro-levels.

ICTs are the technologies or the devices that run through the telecommunication infrastructure, including the Internet, wireless network, or mobile phone. Traditional media are the existing mass media formats, such as TV, radio, newspaper, and magazines. Face-to-face communication indicates human interaction.

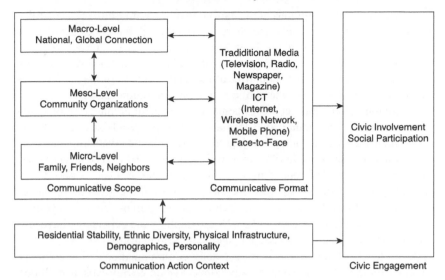

Figure 15.2 A Process Model of Communicative Formats and Levels for Civic Engagement

When people use ICT to discuss personal stories or public affairs with friends, families, and close neighbors, they are practicing ICT storytelling at the micro-level. Email, texting, and instant messaging are used for the encouragement of civic engagement through e-newsletters or direct messages (Hampton, 2010; 2011). Traditional media can be used for neighborhood discussions when they cover local issues such as gate security or road construction. Face-to-face communication occurs when families or neighbors meet at gatherings.

Citizens also use phone calling, texting, chatting applications, web applications, and mobile SNS to share and exchange local issues with members of local organizations, local governments, and professionals at the meso-level. The discussion of county issues through mobile chat and SNS applications is meso-level storytelling. Local media targeting municipal or regional areas and populations can be used for civic engagement opportunities. Research suggests that geo-ethnic media are contributors to civic engagement by meeting local residents' information and communication needs (Moy, McCluskey, McCoy, & Spratt, 2004; Rothenbuhler, Mullen, DeLaurell, & Ryu, 1996). Face-to-face meetings with community members at city or community conferences or hearings are examples of meso-level communicative formats. Club gatherings create networks among community members where they become engaged in civic activities (Meshram & O'Cass, 2013).

Macro-level storytelling occurs when citizens use ICT to read or view national or international issues. For example, the mobile Internet provides both textual and visual information in the form of articles and videos on global affairs. Teleconferencing and web applications allow citizens to communicate with others in different regions of the nation. In other words, citizens can utilize ICT to communicate virtually and share domestic or global issues that they or other communities face (Shklovski & de Souza e Silva, 2013). Exposure to the mass media for national or global issues can lead to civic action. Meeting with people from other regions or countries at national or international conferences enables communicators to take public action on a common cause.

Communication action context agents are the social architecture of living space that makes communicative formats at multiple levels strong or weak. Residential stability, including residential tenure or home ownership, has been a factor in active citizenship (Wilkin & Ball-Rokeach, 2011). The level of civic engagement has varied depending on ethnicity (Okten & Osili, 2004). Other physical infrastructures—such as libraries, transportation, schools, resources for family, and healthcare—are also factors operating in the civic engagement process (Kim & Ball-Rokeach, 2006). Demographics and personality have also been related to variations in civic engagement (Kim et al., 2013).

At all levels of communicative formats in communication action contexts, *connectedness* is the interweaving key concept (Kim & Ball-Rokeach, 2006). Face-to-face storytelling networks at micro-, meso-, and macro-levels can be initiated by exposure to ICT and traditional media. In this regard, storytelling networks are integrated rather than segmented in the ICT era.

At the same time, however, scholars acknowledge some challenges in the integration of human communication factors with ICT in the civic engagement process. There can be a technological divide among citizens in ICT use (Hargittai, 2008). Being active online and using ICT does not always translate into active offline participation—this is called slacktivism (Penney, 2015). Therefore, in order for the integration of human communication with ICT connection to occur in civic engagement, motivations and efficacy of the "will to self-performance" and the "will to conformity" in the community are necessary (Macek, 2013). When such challenges are overcome, the synthetic practice of human communication and ICTs can be a vehicle for implementing social action.

Conclusion: Synthetic Networks for Civic Engagement

This chapter aimed to address how civic engagement is shaped by the communication infrastructure, supplemented by communicative ecology, in the ICT era. To aid our theoretical discussion, we first started by considering human storytelling agents and mass media in CIT. Second, communicative ecology was delineated to emphasize the role of ICT. Third, an attempt to synthesize CIT and communicative ecology was made in terms of formats and levels. Fourth, communication action agents as contextual factors were incorporated into the discussion. Fifth, detail on the meaning of civic engagement in the ICT era was offered at different levels. Finally, a theoretical model as an expansion of communicative formats at different levels was proposed in order to synthesize CIT and communicative ecology factors in active citizenship in conjunction with communication action agents.

This chapter suggested that, for active citizenship, the formats and levels of communication are implicated in the everyday lives of different social groups. Communication for civic engagement embraces communication formats through which active interactions occur in communication action contexts. Interaction among ICTs, traditional media, and face-to-face communication engenders significant social processes that transform the way people become engaged in civic life. The provision of a structure, logic, and competence in communication plays a role in social action. Diverse communication formats are integrated into human activities for different purposes. In the ICT era, when societies face desperate needs, citizens and the government work side by side in the effective development of a communicative ecology.

Personal and social communication infrastructures are shaped by the degree to which citizens depend on communicative formats at different levels. "Doing it" and "sharing it" are bound together by ICT, traditional media, and face-to-face communication. ICT plays a more invasive and pervasive role in civic action. The massive integration of a plethora of media outlets has created a circuitry of surveillance in social life. Extensive feedback or looping of signals informs activities and patterns established in citizen culture and organizational culture at micro-, meso-, and macro-levels.

The expansion of communicative formats is illustrated by ICTs, most of which are based on the networked circuitry that permits and depends on extensive feedback and looping of signals, discourse, and narratives as part of the process of making communicative activity and production. Hence, communication infrastructure can be expanded to the formats that intertwine ICTs in everyday affairs.

Communication infrastructure has been emerging in society for the past several decades. It is evident that today's communication infrastructure cannot be discussed without considering ICTs (Kim & Shin, 2016). E-government offers decision support systems which involve citizens in policymaking, and geographical information systems which engage citizens in public planning (Freeman, 2013; Kang & Gearhart, 2010). ICT has become an integral part of everyday life for ordinary people (de Reuver et al., 2013). Citizens have become more informed due, in part, to the increased stability, connectivity, and functionality of ICT devices. Formats are derived from meanings and the use of human actors in their communication infrastructure. Human actors rely on online and offline communication at the personal and social levels to set and accomplish certain collective goals. The accomplishment of these goals is an indication of civic engagement. The communicative formats illustrate how new activities and logics have been modified to fit the discourse of exchange, productivity, and effectiveness in public affairs.

Communicative formats at different levels inform the engagement process, in which challenges to the situation occur in the forms of control, support, or resistance. In the ecological communication infrastructure, competent social actors forge definitions of communicative situations. Ecological communication infrastructure creates symbolic boundaries so that freedom and constraints are routinized. Social actions are reflective because human actors learn what to do by watching and learning in various communication contexts.

Communication infrastructure in the ICT era is formed by coordination and a reciprocal consensus. Additionally, deviance and resistance reflect a communicative ecology. Communication infrastructure theory comprises formats of online and offline communicative logics that grow in a broad cultural context. Civic engagement at the micro-level includes homeowners' association memberships and volunteering to clean up the neighborhood. Meso-level civic engagement encompasses city reform or community elections. Civic engagement at the macro-level includes participation in national issues—such as healthcare act reform, abortion, and charity giving in response to international disasters.

Communication infrastructure in the ICT era, therefore, is meta-communication within which human actors through different formats and systems change social affairs in certain directions. The expanded communicative formats define symbolic spaces of communicative activities. Communication infrastructure today is increasingly constructed through a synthesis of ICT, traditional media, and face-to-face communication agents.

This chapter—which recognizes the conceptual intersections and integrations between communication infrastructure and communicative ecology— identified the ecological infrastructure of communication as a synthetic structure of communication agents for civic engagement. ICT can be a format that is spontaneous, informal, and non-purposive as well as deliberative, speculative, formal, and impactful in the process of civic engagement (Campbell & Kwak, 2010). Supplementing the view of storytelling networks in communication action contexts, this chapter proposes expanding the formats of communication infrastructure beyond the storytelling agent systems to the ICT sphere. This chapter postulates that the essential impact of communicative ecology in the ICT era at multiple levels will be found in the quality of communication. Future researchers on civic engagement need to explore the conditions that reflect the ecological elements of ICT that people use in their everyday lives.

References

Adler, R. P., & Goggin, J. (2005). What do we mean by "civic engagement"? *Journal of Transformative Education, 3*(3), 236–253. doi: 10.1177/1541344605276792

Alena, B., & Libor, G. (2012). Green ICT adoption survey focused on ICT lifecycle from the consumer's perspective. *Journal of Competitiveness, 4*(4), 109–122. doi: 10.7441/joc.2012.04.08

Altheide, D. L. (1994). An ecology of communication: Toward a mapping of the effective environment. *The Sociological Quarterly, 35*(4), 665–683. doi: 10.1111/j.1533-8525.1994.tb00422.x

Anderson, C. J. (1996). Political social integration. *American Politics Quarterly, 24*(1), 105–124. doi: 10.1177/1532673X9602400106

Andronie, M., & Andronie, M. (2014). Information and communication technologies (ICT) used for education and training. *Contemporary Readings in Law & Social Justice, 6*(1), 378–386.

Ball-Rokeach, S. J. (1998). A theory of media power and a theory of media use: Different stories, questions, and ways of thinking. *Mass Communication & Society, 1*(1/2), 5–40. doi: 10.1080/15205436.1998.9676398

Ball-Rokeach, S. J., Kim, Y. C., & Matei, S. (2001). Storytelling neighborhood: Paths to belonging in diverse urban environments. *Communication Research, 28*(4), 392–428. doi: 10.1177/009365001028004003

Ball-Rokeach, S. J., Rokeach, M., & Grube, J. W. (1984). *The great American values test: Influencing behaviors and belief through television.* New York: Free Press.

Blumer, H. (1969). *Symbolic interactionism: Perspective and method.* Englewood Cliffs, NJ: Prentice Hall.

Broad, G. M., Ball-Rokeach, S. J., Ognyanova, K., Stokes, B., Picasso, T., & Villanueva, G. (2013). Understanding communication ecologies to bridge communication research and community action. *Journal of Applied Communication Research, 41*(4), 325–345. doi: 10.1080/00909882.2013.844848

Campbell, S. W., & Kwak, N. (2010). Mobile communication and civil society: Linking patterns and places of use to engagement with others in public. *Human Communication Research, 37*(2), 207–222. doi: 10.1111/j.1468-2958.2010.01399.x

Campbell, S. W., & Kwak, N. (2011). Mobile communication and strong network ties: Shrinking or expanding spheres of public discourse? *New Media & Society, 14*(2), 262–280. doi: 10.1177/1461444811411676

Cappella, J. N. (1991). The biological origin of automated patterns of human interaction. *Communication Theory, 1,* 4–35.

Cho, H. P. (2013, October 23). The first mobile election of HOA president held in Deajeon. *Maeil Economy.* Retrieved from http://news.mk.co.kr/newsRead.php?year=2013&no=1054552

Coleman, S., & Firmstone, J. (2014). Contested meanings of public engagement: Exploring discourse and practice within a British city council. *Media, Culture & Society, 36*(6), 826–844. doi: 10.1177/0163443714536074.

de Reuver, M., Stein, S., & Hampe, F. (2013). From eParticipation to mobile participation: Designing a service platform and business model for mobile participation. *Information Polity, 18*(1), 57–73. doi: 10.3233/IP-2012-0276

de Zúñiga, H. G. (2012). Social media use for news and individuals' social capital, civic engagement, and political participation. *Journal of Computer-Mediated Communication.* 17(3), 319–336. doi: 10.1111/j.1083-6101.2012.01574.x

de Zúñiga, H. G., Copeland, L., & Bimber, B. (2014). Political consumerism: Civic engagement and the social media connection. *New Media & Society, 16*(3), 488–506. doi: 10.1177/1461444813487960

Ellison, N., Steinfield, C., & Lampe, C. (2007). The benefits of Facebook "friends:" Social capital and college students' use of online social network sites. *Journal of Computer-Mediated Communication, 12*(4), 1143–1168. doi: 10.1111/j.1083-6101.2007.00367.x

Ellul, J. (1990). *The technological bluff* (G. W. Bromiley, Trans.). Grand Rapids, MI: Eerdmans.

Elster, J. (1998). *Deliberative democracy.* Cambridge, UK: Cambridge University Press.

Erentaitė, R., Žukauskienė, R., Beyers, W., & Pilkauskaitė-Valickienė, R. (2012). Is news media related to civic engagement? The effects of interest in and discussions about the news media on current and future civic engagement of adolescents. *Journal of Adolescence.* 35(3), 587–597. doi: 10.1016/j.adolescence.2011.12.008

Foth, M., & Hearn, G. (2007). Networked individualism of urban residents: Discovering the communicative ecology in inner-city apartment buildings. *Information, Communication & Society, 10*(5), 749–772. doi: 10.1080/13691180701658095

Freeman, J. (2013). E-government in the context of monitory democracy: Public participation and democratic reform. *Media Asia, 40*(4), 352–362.

Ganesh, S., & Zoller, H. M. (2012). Dialogue, activism, and democratic social change. *Communication Theory, 22*(1), 66–91. doi: 10.1111/j.1468-2885.2011.01396.x

Habermas, J. (1984). *The theory of communication action: Vol 1., Reason and the rationalization. of society* (T. McCarthy, Trans.). Boston: Beacon Press.

Habermas, J. (1989). *The structural transformation of the public sphere: An inquiry into a category of bourgeois society.* Cambridge, MA: MIT Press.

Hampton, K. N. (2010). Internet use and the concentration of disadvantage: Glocalization and the urban underclass. *American Behavioral Scientist, 53*(8), 1111–1132. doi: 10.1177/0002764209356244

Hampton, K. N. (2011). Comparing bonding and bridging ties for democratic engagement. *Information, Communication & Society, 14*(4), 510–528. doi: 10.1080/1369118X.2011.562219

Hargittai, E. (2008). The digital reproduction of inequality. In D. Grusky (Ed.), *Social stratification* (pp. 936–944). Boulder, CO: Westview Press.

Hoffman, L. H., & Thomson, T. L. (2009). The effect of television viewing on adolescents' civic participation: political efficacy as a mediating mechanism. *Journal of Broadcasting & Electronic Media, 53*(1), 3–21. doi: 10.1080/08838150802643415

Ito, M., & Daisuke O. (2005). Technosocial situations: Emergent structurings of mobile email use. In M. Ito, D, Okabe, & M. Matsuda (Eds.), *Personal, portable, pedestrian: Mobile phones in Japanese life* (pp. 257–273). Cambridge: MIT Press.

Kang, S. (2013). The elderly population and community engagement in the Republic of Korea: The role of community storytelling network. *Asian Journal of Communication, 23*(3), 302–321. doi: 10.1080/01292986.2012.725176

Kang, S., & Gearhart, S. (2010). E-government and civic engagement: How is citizens' use of city web sites related with civic involvement and political behaviors? *Journal of Broadcasting & Electronic Media, 54*(3), 443–462. doi: 10.1080/08838151.2010.498847

Katz, J., & Aakhus, M. (Eds.). (2002). *Perpetual contact: Mobile communication, private talk, public performance.* Cambridge: Cambridge University Press.

Kavanaugh, A., Krishnan, S., Pérez-Quiñones, M., Tedesco, J., Madondo, K., & Ahuja, A. (2014). Encouraging civic participation through local news aggregation. *Information Polity: The International Journal of Government & Democracy in the Information Age, 19*(1), 35–56. doi: 10.3233/IP-140332

Kim, Y. C., & Ball-Rokeach, S. J. (2006). Civic engagement from a communication infrastructure perspective. *Communication Theory, 26*(2), 173–197. doi: 10.1111/j.1468-2885.2006.00267.x

Kim, Y. C., & Shin, E. K. (2016). Localized use of information and communication technologies in Seoul's urban neighborhood. *American Behavioral Scientist, 60*(1), 81–100. doi: 10.1177/0002764215601713

Kim, Y., Hsu, S, & de Zúñiga, H. G. (2013). Influence of social media use on discussion network heterogeneity and civic engagement: The moderating role of personality traits. *Journal of Communication, 63*(3), 498–516. doi: 10.1111/jcom.12034

Lagos, T. G., Coopman, T. M., & Tomhave, J. (2014). "Parallel poleis": Towards a theoretical framework of the modern public sphere, civic engagement and the structural advantages of the internet to foster and maintain parallel socio-political institutions. *New Media & Society. 16*(3), 398–414. doi: 10.1177/1461444813487953

Lake, R. L. D., & Huckfeldt, R. (1998). Social capital, social networks, and political participation. *Political Psychology, 19*(3), 567–584. doi: 10.1111/0162-895X. 00118

Lee, N., Shah, D. V., & McLeod, J. M. (2013). Processes of political socialization: A communication mediation approach to youth civic engagement. *Communication Research, 40*(5), 669–697. doi: 10.1177/0093650212436712

Lemos, A. (2011). Pervasive computer games and processes of specialization: Informational territories and mobile technologies. *Canadian Journal of Communication, 36*(2), 277–294.

Macek, J. (2013). More than a desire for text: Online participation and the social curation of content. *Convergence: The International Journal of Research into New Media Technologies, 19*(3), 295–302. doi: 10.1177/1354856513486530

Meshram, K., & O'Cass, A. (2013). Exploring civic engagement through seniors' good citizenship behavior within clubs. *Journal of Nonprofit & Public Sector Marketing, 25*(3), 256–283. doi: 10.1080/10495142.2013.816196

Moy, P., McCluskey, M. R., McCoy, K., & Spratt, M. A. (2004). Political correlates of local news media use. *Journal of Communication, 54*(3), 532–546. doi: 10.1111/ j.1460-2466.2004.tb02643.x

Nissen, B. (2010). Political activism as part of a broader civic engagement: The case of SEIU Florida Healthcare Union. *Labor Studies Journal, 35*, 51–72. doi: 10.1177/0160449X09353038

Offe, C. (1980). Two logics of collective action: Theoretical notes on social class and organizational form. *Political Power and Social Theory, 1*, 67–115.

Okten, C., & Osili, U. (2004). Contributions in heterogeneous communities: Evidence from Indonesia. *Journal of Population Economics, 17*(4), 603–626. doi: 10.1007/ s00148-004-0189-y

Omoto, A. M., Snyder, M., & Hackett, J. D. (2010). Personality and motivational antecedents of activism and civic engagement. *Journal of Personality, 78*(6), 1703–1734. doi: 10.1111/j.1467-6494.2010.00667.x

Paek, H. J., Yoon, S. H., & Shah, D. V. (2005). Local news, social integration, and community participation: Hierarchical linear modeling of contextual and cross-level effects. *Journalism & Mass Communication Quarterly, 82*(3), 587–606. doi: 10.1177/ 107769900508200307

Park, N., Kee, K. F., & Valenzuela, S. (2009). Is there social capital in a social network site? Facebook use and college students' life satisfaction, trust, and participation. *Journal of Computer-Mediated Communication, 14*(4), 875–901. doi: 10.1111/j.1083-6101.2009.01474.x

Pearson, J. C., Semlak, J. L., Western, K. J., & Herakova, L. L. (2010). Answering a call for service: An exploration of family communication schemata and ethnic identity's effect on civic engagement behaviors. *Journal of Intercultural Communication Research, 39*(1), 49–68. doi: 10.1080/17475759.2010.520838

Penney, J. (2015). Social media and symbolic action: Exploring participation in the Facebook Red Equal Sign Profile Picture Campaign. *Journal of Computer-Mediated Communication, 20*(1), 52–66. doi: 10.1111/jcc4.12092

Poell, T. (2014). Social media and the transformation of activist communication: Exploring the social media ecology of the 2010 Toronto G20 protests. *Information, Communication & Society, 17*(6), 716–731. doi: 10.1080/1369118X.2013.812674

Postman, N. (1971). What is media ecology? Media Ecology Association. Retrieved from www.media-ecology.org/media_ecology/#What is Media Ecology?

Rothenbuhler, E. W., Mullen, L. J., DeLaurell, R., & Ryu, C. R. (1996). Communication, community attachment, and involvement. *Journalism & Mass Communication Quarterly, 73*(2), 445–466. doi: 10.1177/107769909607300214

Seo, M., & Moon, S. (2013). Ethnic identity, acculturative stress, news uses, and two domains of civic engagement: A case of Korean immigrants in the United States. *Mass Communication & Society, 16*(2), 245–267. doi: 10.1080/15205436.2012. 696768

Shah, D. V., McLeod, J. M., & Yoon, S. (2001). Communication, context, and community: An exploration of print, broadcast, and Internet influences. *Communication Research, 28*(4), 464–506. doi: 10.1177/009365001028004005

Shklovski, I., & de Souza e Silva, A. (2013). An urban encounter. *Information, Communication & Society, 16*(3), 340–361. doi: 10.1080/1369118X.2012.756049

Shklovski, I., & Valtysson, B. (2012). Secretly political: Civic engagement in online publics in Kazakhstan. *Journal of Broadcasting & Electronic Media, 56*(3), 417–433. doi: 10.1080/08838151.2012.705196

Snow, R. P. (1983). *Creating media culture*. Newbury Park, CA: Sage.

Steinfield, C., Ellison, N. B., & Lampe, C. (2008). Social capital, self-esteem, and use of online social network sites: A longitudinal analysis. *Journal of Applied Developmental Psychology, 29*(6), 434–445. doi: 10.1016/j.appdev.2008.07.002

Szreter, S., & Woolcock, M. (2004). Health by association? Social capital, social theory, and the political economy of health. *International Journal of Epidemiology, 33*(4), 650–667. doi: 10.1093/ije/dyh013

Tacchi, J. (2006). Studying communicative ecologies: An ethnographic approach to information and communication technologies. Paper presented at the 56th Annual Conference of the International Communication Association, Dresden, Germany.

Valcanis, T. (2011). An iPhone in every hand: Media ecology, communication structures, and the global village. *ETC: A Review of General Semantics, 68*(1), 33–45.

Wilkin, H. A. (2013). Exploring the potential of communication infrastructure theory for informing efforts to reduce health disparities. *Journal of Communication, 63*(1), 181–200. doi: 10.1111/jcom.12006

Wilkin, H. A., & Ball-Rokeach, S. J. (2011). Hard-to-reach? Using health access status as a way to more effectively target segments of the Latino audience. *Health Education Research, 26*(2), 239–253. doi: 10.1093/her/cyq090

Xenos, M., & Moy, P. (2007). Direct and differential effects of the Internet on political and civic engagement. *Journal of Communication, 57*(4), 704–718. doi: 10.1111/j.1460-2466.2007.00364.x

Zukin, C., Keeter, S., Andolina, M., Jenkins, K., & Delli Carpini, M. X. (2006). *A new engagement? Political participation, civic life, and the changing American citizen.* New York: Oxford University Press.

Epilogue

Elisia L. Cohen

University of Kentucky

Communication Yearbook began as an annual review sponsored by the International Communication Association. Transaction Books, in New Brunswick, New Jersey, published the first five volumes of the series. The founding volumes edited by Brent Rubin (Rutgers, State University of New Jersey) were organized first by their inclusion of disciplinary-wide reviews and commentaries. A second means of facilitating synthesis was annual "overviews" prepared by ICA division chairs or their designee to examine the trends in theory and research in their subdomains. Finally, the book included competitively selected original research studies presented at the annual conference of the International Communication Association.

Led by editor Brent Rubin, *Communication Yearbook*'s first decade included invited communication reviews and commentaries, adding theoretical perspectives to a developing discipline. In Volumes 3 and 4, Dan Nimmo (deceased), working from the University of Tennessee, began to "internationalize" *Communication Yearbook* by adding a section of review and commentary pieces dealing with the developing study of communication around the world. Nimmo continued with the tradition set in the first two volumes, where each section of the yearbook then presented topical overviews by ICA divisions, and top papers selected for the annual conference. Nimmo also included emerging developments in substantive problems of importance. For example, the fourth volume contained a research statement on androgyny and communication.

Michael Burgoon (deceased) led the fifth and sixth volumes of *Communication Yearbook: An Annual Review Published of the International Communication Association*. During his editorship he moved to change the composition of the volume entirely, competitively accepting all manuscripts under a peer review process. In 1982 he wrote "It was my thought that these opening pieces were a very important part of past volumes, and that the steps should be taken to open up this section to anyone who thought he or she had something important to say." Additionally, he reported in the volume that the division overviews were dropped in *Communication Yearbook 6* due to the unevenness between the essays submitted from divisions providing state of the art reviews. Instead, for Burgoon's sixth volume top papers submitted to *Communication Yearbook* became subject to peer review. The sixth volume was also significant as it marked a change in publisher from Transaction Books to Sage Publications.

Communication Yearbook 7 and *8* edited by Robert N. Bostrom (deceased) continued this tradition. First, review and commentary chapters were competitively selected following a call for papers "issuing critiques of substantive matters of generic interest and relevance that transcend the more specialized concerns of scholars working in the highly diversified discipline of communication science" (1983, p. 17). Second, *Communication Yearbook* was a means of publishing edited versions of selected studies from the 34th Annual Conference of the ICA held in 1984 in San Francisco. In his preface, Bostrom detailed the potential of electronic peer review leveraging "the vast information-processing capacity of a typical computing installation for our annual information exchange," describing a process of divisional referee review process. He imagined a system where referees could "log on the home computer using a remote facility and either have the files dumped (I love that particular interactive command—there is something fun about telling the computer to DUMP when you really mean transfer a file)" (p. 14). Alas, he also predicted that *Yearbook* submissions would be similarly easy for submission and peer review.

Margaret McLaughlin's (University of Southern California) editorship followed Bostrum's. Her editorship provided for the inclusion of the broadest group of consulting editors from outside the United States into the *Communication Yearbook* process to date. Her consulting editorial board included faculty from the University of Bristol, University of Leicester, Hebrew University of Jerusalem, University of Sheffield, Universidade Federal De Santa Maria (Brazil), University of Gothenburg, and Njmegen University in addition to ICA scholars in the United States. Volume 9's chapters provided topical reviews and commentaries ranging across the history and present state of topical research in countries such as Japan (e.g., "Mass Communication Research in Japan"), to advances in methodology (e.g., "Revised Lag Sequential Analysis"), to early commentaries on controversies of the time, including a 1990 examination of "Gender Differences in Adolescents' Use of and Attitudes Toward Computers." McLaughlin maintained this approach for the *Communication Yearbook 10* as well.

In the preface to Volume 9, McLaughlin noted that "What makes this volume different is that the Reviews and Commentaries section contains a significant number of contributions from scholars outside the United States, indicative of the international vitality of the discipline of communication" (1986, p. 13). Accordingly, she used an editorial board international in scope to review these manuscripts. This was a noteworthy departure from past volumes, as the divisional selections made by the ICA selection committees, divisions, and interest groups were led by faculty appointed solely at U.S. institutions.

When James Anderson (University of Utah) became *Communication Yearbook* editor for Volumes 11 through 14, he did so after ICA decided to split commissioned works from convention papers (the latter to be published in a *Proceedings* of the ICA). In the first volume under his editorship, Volume 11, Anderson enunciated three principles for the *Yearbook*. First, that the series would seek articles speaking to the field at large, written from the perspectives of the authors. Second, that rather than appear in an encyclopedic chapter function, readers should profit from reading the volume as a whole, seeing the connections between its pieces. Finally, Anderson hoped "to represent many different working perspectives" or to provide a pluralistic vision of communication inquiry from the work published (1988, p. 11). The resulting volume included monographs with connective commentaries proposed by the editor and selected by the author to address tensions in communication theories or explanations of communication processes identified by monograph authors. It differed from prior volumes as each chapter consisted of a monograph and two criticisms of it. Throughout his editorship, Anderson focused on diverse topics including: the theory of mediation; health care communication; feminist criticism of television; discourse and relationships; intercultural relationships and cultural identity; technology and communication systems; and organizational culture, interpersonal communication and interaction goals.

Under his editorship, Anderson also changed the peer review process. Rather than a public editorial board, his volumes included a specific acknowledgment of ten reviewers on the volume and generally acknowledged "several dozen colleagues who advised" him on individual pieces (1988, p. 19). This editorial methodology continued through Volume 14, and was largely followed by Stan Deetz (University of Colorado, Boulder) who edited Volumes 15 through 18.

In Volume 15, Deetz wrote

> following Jim Anderson's lead, I have asked authors to say more and to position their studies to engage in more general questions, to situate their own mode of knowledge production (sometimes with success). The literature reviews explicitly develop points of view as well as report and summarize the studies of the last several years. . . . The commentaries are not just the opening up of the later stages of the review process to the public it is hoped that they will help the reader to engage in the debate that any good work generates and will open debates that the essays themselves overlook or suppress. The goal is not to determine how good a study is with paradigmatic standards, but to ask whether being good makes a difference.
>
> (1992, p. xii)

One major change under Deetz's editorship was a topical focus for each *Yearbook*. Deetz's first volume (Volume 15) had a mass media focus with monographs and commentaries related to mass entertainment, audience mediation and politics; mass media messages and influence; interaction in the social context; and the person in interaction. Later, Volume 16 focused on comparative (American and European) perspectives on organizational communication, technologies and multiculturalism, and the social construction of identity, media messages, and media, culture, and diversity concerns: Section 1 studied communication within corporate organizations from American and European perspectives and Section 2 communication and social change.

Volume 17 concluded his editorship with attention given to interpersonal inter-action studies.

Brant R. Burleson (deceased) followed Deetz's topical approach to organiz-ing the yearbook. *Communication Yearbook 18,* published in 1994, focused on cognitive approaches to communication study, developments in health and envi-ronmental risk communication, and a potpourri section examining discourse, relationships, technology and ideology. Each section had commentaries, rather than each monograph. *Communication Yearbook* Volumes 19 and 20 took a step away from the commentary approach, and published ten integrative research reviews on diverse topics. These reviews presented findings, as well as "pen-etrating discussions" of theories, methods, problems and directions for future research in the field.

Under the editorship of Michael E. Roloff (Northwestern University), *Communication Yearbook 21* continued the tradition of publishing state-of-the-art literature reviews that were proposed from "all interest areas in communication" and selected "based entirely upon their judged quality" (1999, p. xi). The types of reviews ranged from narrative and historical accounts to research studies using meta-analytic techniques on a range of topical issues including: organizational democracy and change; intercultural negotiation; crisis management; and contemporary challenges in journalism and broadcasting. In Volume 22, Roloff (1999, p. xi) provided specialized focus on including essays addressing a pressing communication problem: how to communicate with people from different backgrounds or cultures, in addition to scholarly reviews from other domains. Similarly, Volume 23 includes specialized essays discussing the relationship between communication and emotional processes across interpersonal, family, organizational, and public contexts. The volume then followed with review and critical syntheses articles that offer research reviews of topical interest representing the breadth of the field.

When William B. Gudykunst (deceased) was appointed editor of *Communi-cation Yearbook*, he planned to continue publishing review essays similar to those in Burleson and Roloff's edited volumes. However, he added two new features to the volumes he edited. First, he specified that he would devote "one volume under my editorship to essays summarizing the state of the art of research and theory in the ICA's various divisions and interest groups" (2001, p. xi). Second, he indicated that he "wanted to include state-of-the-art review essays of research published in languages other than English and state-of the-art reviews of senior scholars' lines of research" (2001, p. xi). Volume 24 was the volume dedicated to summarizing the "state of the ICA," while Volumes 25 and 26 followed the format of Volumes 19–23.

Importantly, for Volume 24 Gudykunst posed four questions in the call for papers and in instructions to authors:

1   What are the parameters of the division/interest group, and what is the relationship of the division/interest group to other divisions/interest groups?

2   What are the major theories used in the division/interest group, and what research is there to support these theories?
3   What are the major lines of research in the division/interest group?
4   What are the major issues with which scholars in the division/interest group must cope with in the next century?

Gudykunst's introduction to the volume noted the difficulty in eliciting competitive state-of-the-art essays about each subarea or interest group area, as there was unevenness in the quality of submissions from across the field. However, he thought the goal was important and so he invited authors to write essays "to fill in the gaps left by the proposals" he received (2001, p. xii). Additionally, Linda Putnam, president-elect of the ICA at the time, wrote an overview focusing on the discipline as a whole that was co-authored by Stan Deetz (a former *CY* editor and 1996–1997 ICA President). The resulting Volume 24 provided "a state-of-the-discipline review as represented by the International Communication Association at the end of the 20th century" (2001, p. xiii). Gudykunst's final volume garnered essays of research published in languages other than English and state-of the-art reviews of senior scholars' lines of research from outside of the United States. During Gudykunst's editorship, Lawrence Erlbaum Associates (LEA) began publishing *CY* with Volume 25, transitioning to Routledge/Taylor & Francis in 2007, when Taylor & Francis purchased LEA .

Following Gudykunst's editorship, Volume 27, edited by Pamela J. Kalbfleisch (University of North Dakota), marked a change in the organization of the *Yearbook*. Kalbfleisch's call for papers requested chapters that would address "what each reviewed area has to say about an issue of collective concern—empowerment" (2003, p. xii). Similarly, Volume 38 represented "the best literature reviews submitted in response to the published call for reviews of communication research addressing the theme of community" (2004, p. xii). In addition, Kalbfleisch invited literature reviews from four sets of scholars engaged in communication research, addressing community concerns within diverse domains of the discipline. In her final volume, Kalbfleisch sought research reviews addressing the theme of "Communication and the Future." She noted that:

> this volume addresses questions such as: Has the discipline of communication kept up with change? Have we adapted to new technology and moved forward in our thinking? What do we as a discipline have to say about the future? . . . The focus of this volume is on what we can do as communication scholars to make a difference in everyday life and in the future.
>
> (2005, p. x)

Moving away from the thematic volume strategy established under Kalbfleisch's editorship, Christina S. Beck's (Ohio University) editorship marked the beginning of a decade-long quest to offer *Communication Yearbook* as a volume offering a wide range of reviews of literature on topics of importance to the discipline. Although Beck describes how many of the contributions to Volumes 30, 31, 32, and 33 "contributed to larger conversations about legitimacy . . . the dialectic of fluidity and stability (see, especially, *CY31*), the position of communication as co-constructed, co-negotiated, and consequential (see, especially, *CY32*), and communication as implicitly persuasive and power-lade (see, especially, *CY33*)" these connections were made during the proposal development and editing process rather than as thematic volumes (2009, p. xvi). Importantly, Beck's editorial process solicited proposals for development into chapters. Compared to its earlier instantiations, Beck's volumes were highly selective, with acceptance rates hovering around 15% after reviewing more than 70 proposals. After blind, peer-review Beck selected chapters from authors from inside and outside of the United States with a goal of addressing "issues that truly pervade our discipline, span communication contexts, and affect our daily lives as individuals, family members, organizational participants, media consumers, and citizens" (2009, p. xviii).

When Charles T. Salmon (Nanyang Technological University) became editor of *Communication Yearbook 34* it had been nearly a decade that the *Yearbook* had been utilized to provide commentary on the growth of the field. Salmon's editorship included a mix of invited commentaries and competitively selected review essays of topics of theoretical, practical, or empirical importance to the field.

As an exemplar of invited scholarship, Part I of Salmon's first edited volume (34) was titled, "The Seeds of Mass Communication Research." The section leveraged Elihu Katz's public remarks written on the occasion of an honorary degree from the University of Bucharest tracing the development of four strands of mass communication scholarship to provide historical insight into the history of the field. Four other scholars—Kurt Lang, Gladys Lang, Gertrude Robinson, and Mihai Coman—agreed to serve as commentators on Katz's remarks, serving as the cornerstone for Volume 35. The sections that followed included competitive essays on contemporary communication problems and commentaries on these groups of essays written by senior scholars.

At the same time, his goal was to "make *CY* the most international and interdisciplinary of all ICA publications" (2013, p. xii). Indeed, throughout his editorship his use of associate editors from outside of the United States combined with his movement as an editor from Michigan State University, to the Interdisciplinary Center in Herzliya, Israel, to Nanyang Technological University, Singapore supported international submissions to his final volume from authors calling nine different countries their home, making contributions from a diverse set of disciplinary perspectives. As he created his final volume, each contributed essay had a counter-point in commentary offering theoretical criticism, extension, analysis of the hypotheses, theoretical perspectives, or even veritable disagreements of scientific understanding related to the reviews presented.

Chuck Salmon also initiated a conversation within the International Communication Association executive board on the future of *Communication Yearbook*. Specifically, there was an apparent tension between the *Yearbook*'s goals of being an edited volume with international reach and its availability to scholars across the globe. The publisher experimented with making *Communication Yearbook* an "e-book" and made individual chapters available for electronic purchase. Additionally, more of *Communication Yearbook* became available for electronic preview, including the front matter, first page and table of contents of recent volumes. However, the limitations of an annual in book form remained, and these efforts to make the book more accessible coincided with the desirability of ICA having an electronic journal that accepted longer monographs and reviews. The review process for the editor was also cumbersome as the *Yearbook* lacked the electronic manuscript review platform support that a journal would need. When I was selected as the *Communication Yearbook* editor, I did so expecting that the *Yearbook* may face a transition in the coming years. As I wrote in *Communication Yearbook 37:*

> As I began editing my first volume in this *Communication Yearbook* series, I did so with the goal for the volume to reflect the scholarly research and objectives of its sponsoring organization, the International Communication Association (ICA). To that end, I sent a broad call for papers to all division and interest group chairs and announcements to ICA members. I recruited a set of internationally recognized scholars to serve on the editorial board, and encouraged its members to recommend authors submit manuscripts for peer review that traversed broad terrain pushing disciplinary boundaries.
>
> (p. xxi)

One of ICA's goals in continuing the *Yearbook* tradition was to publish reviews of the literature in each of the areas represented by the divisions and interest groups of the ICA. Importantly, given the growth in the number of ICA divisions and diversity in submissions, the volume of submissions and the variance in quality of non peer-reviewed "commentaries," I decided to discontinue the latter tradition of including commentaries in the volume. Instead, the manuscripts submitted for publication and published in Volumes 37–40 are state-of-the-art reviews that address questions about our capacity as communication scholars to study complex, often multileveled, communication phenomena. The volumes also offer essays which transverse divisional boundaries and discuss advances and applications in methodology to advance the quality and effectiveness of communication research.

In this culminating volume of *Communication Yearbook*, the number of submissions for consideration from an international group of scholars grew in scope and number. I expanded the scope of the editorial board and list of ad-hoc reviewers to keep up with the demand for these submissions to receive peer review within the short window for inclusion in the annual *Communication Yearbook*.

Communication Yearbook published in its book format (although it has also transitioned to full digital e-book available during my editorship) has found itself challenged to be relevant to scholars and authors in the new "digital" era. Put simply, in this era the ICA and its scholars place a premium on the ability of authors to be discoverable, internationally accessible, with its research published in a timely manner. Numerous editors examined these issues in their reports to the ICA Board, and to address this historical but growing challenge, Francois Heinderyckx (Université libre de Bruxelles) led the publications committee and the ICA Board to prepare for a transition of the series to a journal.

Given the need for an electronic manuscript submission system to support the next editor, and the demand for *Communication Yearbook* to have a global access, reach and scope, the ICA Publication Committee's discussions to transition *Communication Yearbook* to an online journal format, with an annual print compendium for libraries, will preserve its history while providing an audience for ICA as international in scope as its members. In 2015, David Ewoldsen was selected by the ICA Board to lead the development of *Communication Yearbook*'s successor publication. Although when I assumed the editorship I did not do so intending to be the last editor of the *Communication Yearbook* series, David Ewoldson's vision for the re-branded "Annals" of the International Communication Association will include the best of *Communication Yearbook*'s tradition while extending its reach and impact in service to the ICA membership.

About the Editor

Elisia L. Cohen earned her Ph.D. in Communication from the University of Southern California, and is Chair of the Department of Communication at the University of Kentucky where she holds the Gifford Blyton Endowed Professorship. She is a Member of the Markey Cancer Center and is the Director of the College of Communication and Information's Health Communication Research Collaborative. At the University of Kentucky, she was awarded the Sarah Bennett Holmes award for her leadership, research, and service. Her research has been supported by the Centers for Disease Control and Prevention, National Institutes of Health, and private industry. Her research on public understanding of disease has appeared in such journals as: *Health Communication, Health Education and Behavior, Journal of Applied Communication Research, Journal of Broadcasting and Electronic Media, Journal of Communication, Journal of Communication in Healthcare, Journal of Health Communication, Qualitative Health Research,* and *Prometheus.* She currently chairs the publications committee for the International Communication Association. She is married and has one daughter, Addison Lydia.

About the Contributors

Joshua Trey Barnett is a doctoral student in the Department of Communication at the University of Utah, where he is also a research fellow at the Global Change and Sustainability Center. His research on environmental communication has been published in the *Quarterly Journal of Speech* and elsewhere.

Ann Burnett (Ph.D., University of Utah) is a Professor of Communication and Director of the Women and Gender Studies program at North Dakota State University. Her current research in interpersonal communication focuses on how the fast pace of life impacts relationships.

Elizabeth J. Carlson (Ph.D., University of Illinois, Urbana-Champaign) is an Assistant Professor in the Communication and Dramatic Arts Department at Central Michigan University. Elizabeth studies collaboration, coordination, and conflict in inter-organizational and inter-disciplinary teams. She is particularly interested in collaboration in the context of multi-agency disaster response training exercises.

Jonathan Cohen (Ph.D., University of Southern California) is an Associate Professor in the Department of Communication, University of Haifa, Israel. His research and teaching focus on narrative persuasion, audience relationships with media characters and perceptions of media influence. His recent publications on these topics have appeared in such journals as the *Journal of Communication, Media Psychology* and *Communication Research*, among others. He is currently an associate editor of *Communication Theory*.

Katherine R. Cooper (Ph.D., University of Illinois, Urbana-Champaign) is a research associate at Northwestern University, where she serves as the associate director of the Network for Nonprofit and Social Impact. Kate studies organizational communication, with an emphasis on the nonprofit sector; her main research interest is cross-sector collaboration in response to social problems.

Brian Cozen (Ph.D., University of Utah) is a Visiting Assistant Professor of Communication Studies at the University of Nevada, Las Vegas. His research focuses on environmental rhetoric with specific emphases in energy discourse, critical/cultural studies, and communication geography. His research has been published in *Environmental Communication, Communication Theory,* and *Argumentation and Advocacy.*

Claes H. de Vreese (Ph.D., University of Amsterdam) is Professor and Chair of Political Communication at the Amsterdam School of Communication Research at the University of Amsterdam, The Netherlands. His research interests include comparative journalism research, the effects of news, public opinion and European integration, and the effects of information and campaigning on elections, referendums and direct democracy. He has published more than 100 articles in international peer-reviewed journals, including *Communication Research, Journal of Politics, Journalism Studies, Political Communication, Journal of Communication,* and *Public Opinion Quarterly.*

Briana DeAngelis (M.A., Michigan State University) is a Research Assistant and Coordinator with the Behavioral Medicine Laboratories and the Duluth Medical Research Institute at the University of Minnesota Medical School, Duluth. Her research interests span the social and behavioral sciences. Her primary research interests include communication and cognition within the context of social influence and group dynamics.

Marya L. Doerfel (Ph.D., University at Buffalo) is Associate Professor at the School of Communication and Information at Rutgers University. Her research focuses on networked forms of organizing with a particular interest in disrupted networks and community resilience. She has been funded by the National Science Foundation and has published her research in journals such as *Communication Monographs, Management Communication Quarterly, Human Communication Research, the Journal for the Association for Information Science and Technology, New Media & Society, Voluntas,* and *Public Relations Review.*

Danielle Endres (Ph.D., University of Washington) is an Associate Professor of Communication and faculty in the Environmental Humanities Masters Program at the University of Utah. She is a rhetorical theorist and critic with expertise in environmental communication, science communication, social movements, and Native American cultures. Her research focuses on the rhetoric of environmental and science controversies and social movements including nuclear waste siting decisions, climate change activism, Native American environmental activism, and low carbon energy policy. Danielle is the co-editor of *Social Movement to Address Climate Change: Local Steps for Global Action* (Cambria Press, 2009) and has published in *Quarterly Journal of Speech, Communication and Critical Cultural Studies, Rhetoric & Public Address, Western Journal of Communication, Environmental Communication, Argumentation & Advocacy, Argumentation,* and *Local Environment.* She has also received Department of Energy and National Science Foundation funding for her research.

Bo Feng (Ph.D., Purdue University) is an Associate Professor in the Department of Communication at the University of California, Davis. Her research program centers on supportive communication, investigating the processes through which people conceptualize, seek, provide, and respond to various forms of support, such as comforting and advice, and how these processes are similar and different for people of different cultures, genders, and across contexts. In addition to examining supportive communication in traditional face-to-face and close relationship contexts, Bo studies technologically-mediated supportive communication that occurs in virtual environments.

Jessica L. Ford is a doctoral candidate in Organizational Communication and Technology at The University of Texas at Austin. Next year, she will join the faculty at Ohio University's School of Communication Studies. Her research explores how individuals communicatively manage information about their health and safety within organizations. Specifically, her dissertation investigates the influences on risk and safety information seeking among employees working in high-risk jobs. Jessica's work can be found in *Communication Teacher, Communication Education, The Journal of Homeland Security and Emergency Management,* and the *International Journal of Information Systems for Crisis Response and Management.* Additionally, she is the editor of a communication textbook titled *Professional Communication Skills.*

Lisa Guntzviller (Ph.D., Purdue University) is an Assistant Professor in the Department of Communication at the University of Illinois at Urbana-Champaign. Her research focuses on interpersonal communication in health and family contexts, specifically examining the link between communication quality and individual and dyadic perceptions of complex interactions. She has focused on language-brokering interactions—in which a bilingual child culturally and linguistically mediates between a primarily Spanish-speaking parent and an English speaker—and advice-giving interactions—such as parent-to-child advice on exercise and physical activity.

Seok Kang (Ph.D., University of Georgia) is an Associate Professor in the Department of Communication at the University of Texas at San Antonio (UTSA). His research interests are communicative ecology of mobile media, impact of social media, communication infrastructure for civic engagement, information and communication technology for sustainable urban development, and immersive journalism in the mobile era. His research has appeared in over 32 international journals such as *Journal of Broadcast and Electronic Media, Mass Communication and Society, Journal of Health Communication, Asian Journal of Communication,* and *International Journal of Communication,* among others. He has authored one book, *Digital Message Design: The Path to Multimedia Production* (2013).

Sophie Lecheler (Ph.D., University of Amsterdam) is an Associate Professor of Political Communication and Journalism at the Amsterdam School of Communication Research at the University of Amsterdam, The Netherlands. Her research interests include political communication, framing theory, news media effects and digital journalism. Her work has been published in a range of international journals, such as *Communication Research, Communication Theory, Journal of Communication* and *Journalism & Mass Communication Quarterly*.

Erina MacGeorge (Ph.D., University of Illinois) is an Associate Professor in the Department of Communication at the Pennsylvania State University. Her primary research program examines the intersection of social support and social influence, in the form of interpersonal advice. She studies advice in both personal and professional contexts, with a current focus on how advice recipients evaluate the content and style of advice messages, and how those evaluations are influenced by other behaviors in supportive interactions, such as planning. In related work, Erina examines supportive and persuasive communication, especially about matters of health, including miscarriage, bipolar disorder, breast cancer, and antibiotic resistance.

Brian Manata (Ph.D., Portland State University) was an instructor at Michigan State University. His research interests include communication, organizational behavior and psychology, and quantitative methods, especially as they apply to groups and teams.

Vernon Miller (Ph.D., University of Texas, Austin) is an Associate Professor in the Department of Communication and Department of Management at Michigan State University. His research focuses on the communicative aspects of the employment interview, organizational entry, and role negotiation and appears in journals such as *Management Communication Quarterly, Human Communication Research, Journal of Applied Communication Research,* and *Academy of Management Review*. With Professor Mike Gordon of Rutgers University, he has authored, *Conversations about Job Performance: A Communication Perspective on the Appraisal Process* and *Meeting the Challenges of Human Resource Management: A Communication Perspective*.

Patricia J. Moore (MCIS, Rutgers University), is a doctoral student at the Brian D. Lamb School for Communication at Purdue University. Her emphasis is in communication technology and society. Her research focuses on online communities as sites where former members of social outgroups engage in reconfiguring their identities. She has been published in *Information, Communication and Society* and has presented her work at the National Communication Association and the Social Media and Society conferences.

Paul Clemens Murschetz (Ph.D., Vienna School of Economics and Business Administration) is Senior Scientist of Media Management and Organizational Communications at the Alpen-Adria-University of Klagenfurt, Austria. His research work focuses on strategic media management, media economics, media convergence and media innovation management. He has published in journals such as *The International Journal on Media Management*, the *European Journal of Communication*, ICA's *Communication Yearbook*, and is a frequent conference speaker on issues of media management and economics (German Communication Association, World Media Economics Conference, European Media Management Association).

Megan O'Byrne is a Ph.D. candidate in the Department of Communication at the University of Utah and Visiting Assistant Professor at Kutztown University. She is a critical/cultural rhetorician particularly interested in social movements and music. She has examined environmental, anti-war, and feminist social movements, with a particular interest in the role of music in those movements. Megan has published in *Southern Journal of Communication* and elsewhere. She has also worked on projects funded by the Department of Energy and the National Science Foundation.

Leah M. Omilion-Hodges (Ph.D., Wayne State University) is Assistant Professor in the School of Communication at Western Michigan University. Her research focuses on leadership and health communication within the larger context of organizational communication. Her work explores workgroup dynamics within applied settings to examine the influence of leader-member, peer, and team associations on relationship development, status distinctions, and sharing of resources. Her work has been featured in venues such as *Health Communication*, *the Leadership Quarterly*, and *Computers in Human Behavior*.

Jihyun Esther Paik (M.A., Michigan State University and M.S., University of Michigan-Ann Arbor) is a doctoral student in the Department of Communication Arts at University of Wisconsin-Madison. Her academic interest lies in interpersonal and group communication, more specifically, seeking and receiving advice, distorted feedback, and deception.

Tarla Rai Peterson (Ph.D., Washington State University) is a Professor of Communication at the University of Texas, El Paso and Guest Professor of Environmental Communication at the Swedish University of Agricultural Sciences. Her research focuses on resonance between communication, democracy, and environmental policy. She studies how this resonance enables and constrains policy options and public life related to energy system change, environmental planning, and wildlife conservation. Her professional goal is to conduct research that facilitates the emergence and implementation of more sustainable policy, while critiquing the normativity associated with sustainability. She has developed an active *Theory to Practice* Program that includes design and evaluation of best practices for facilitating public participation in related issues. Her most recent books are *Environmental Conflict Management, Smart Grid (R) Evolution: Electric Power Struggles*, and *The Housing Bomb: Why our Addiction to Houses is Destroying the Environment and Threatening our Society*.

Andrew Pilny (Ph.D., University of Illinois, Urbana-Champaign) is an Assistant Professor in the Department of Communication at the University of Kentucky. He is interested in organizational/small group communication and computational social science. He also specializes in social movements, team performance, and network analysis.

Carrie Anne Platt (Ph.D., University of Southern California) is an Associate Professor of Communication at North Dakota State University. She researches and teaches classes on gender, technology, and culture, with a focus on how social discourses shape our understanding and use of emerging technologies. Her research has been published in *Argumentation and Advocacy, Communication Teacher, Rhetoric Society Quarterly, Journal of Online Learning and Teaching, Quarterly Journal of Speech*, among other venues.

Jennifer K. Ptacek (M.A., Western Michigan University) is a Ph.D. student in the Brian Lamb School of Communication at Purdue University. Her research interests include applying qualitative approaches to studying interpersonal and health communication within organizations. Her research focuses on various types of workplace relationships and the influences of antagonism and support on coping with stress. Recent work has explored the use of metaphors and communication behaviors of close nurse friends and admission handoff communication between emergency and hospitalist physicians.

Amber N. W. Raile (Ph.D., Michigan State University) is an Assistant Professor of Management and Director of the Business Communications Curriculum in the Jake Jabs College of Business & Entrepreneurship at Montana State University. Her research focuses on the social organizing functions of communication and communication influence.

Stephen A. Rains (Ph.D., University of Texas, Austin) is an Associate Professor in the Department of Communication at the University of Arizona. His research examines communication and technology, health communication, and social influence. He is particularly interested in the use and implications of new communication technologies for social support processes. His work on this topic can be found in journal such as *Human Communication Research, Communication Monographs, Communication Research, Journal of Computer-Mediated Communication, Health Communication*, and *Journal of Health Communication*.

Emily Scheinfeld (M.A., University of Georgia) is finishing her Ph.D. in Interpersonal Communication from The University of Texas at Austin. Her research interests center on how emerging adults and their parents communicate about health behaviors, including sex, safe sex practices, and weight management practices. She is interested in examining how familial health communication differs from family communication and the process of disclosure during emerging adulthood in order to seek out social support. She has published in *Health Communication* and the *American Journal of Infection Control*.

Daniela M. Schlütz (Ph.D., University of Music, Drama and Media Hanover) is Assistant Professor at the Department of Journalism and Communication Research at the University of Music, Drama and Media Hanover (Germany). Her research and teaching interests are media entertainment (especially quality TV series), advertising, and empirical research methods. Her habilitation treatise is on quality TV as an entertainment phenomenon and deals with development, characteristics, use, and reception of complex television series like The Sopranos, The Wire, or Breaking Bad.

Nurit Tal-Or (Ph.D., University of Haifa, 2001) is a Senior Lecturer in the Department of Communication, University of Haifa, Israel. Her research and teaching focus on media psychology and interpersonal communication. Her publications on these topics have appeared in journals such as the *Journal of Communication*, *Human Communication Research*, *Media Psychology* and *Communication Research*.

Elizabeth Wilhoit (M.A., Purdue University) is a doctoral candidate in the Brian Lamb School of Communication at Purdue University. Her research examines materiality and non-human agency in organizing and organizational communication, seeking to understand how the stability offered by materiality intersects with the dynamism of communication and social construction. Her work has been published in journals including *Organization Studies*, *Gender, Work & Organization*, and *Field Methods*.

Kevin B. Wright (Ph.D., University of Oklahoma) is a Professor in the Department of Communication at George Mason University. His research focuses on health communication, social support, and new communication technologies. He is the author of five books, including *Health Communication in the 21st Century* and *Computer-Mediated Communication in Personal Relationships*. He has published over 75 articles and book chapters, and his research appears in numerous journals such as *Communication Monographs, Journal of Computer-Mediated Communication, Journal of Communication, Health Communication, Journal of Health Communication, Journal of Applied Communication Research, Journal of Personal and Social Relationships, Communication Quarterly, Communication Studies.*

Deirdre H. Zerilli (M.A., Western Michigan University) is a Ph.D. student in the School of Communication at the University of Missouri under the advisement of Dr. Debbie Dougherty. Her area of interest is organizational communication, with a specific interest in the creation and maintenance of organizational out-groups. Her most recent work focuses on organization around the topics of victim blaming and dis/ability. She has presented her work at various conferences including the National Communication Association and the Central States Communication Association.

About the Editorial Assistants

Rachael A. Record (Ph.D., University of Kentucky) is an Assistant Professor in the School of Communication at San Diego State University. Her research interests include methodological and theoretical explorations of message design and campaign efforts aimed at fostering health-related behavior change. Specifically, her research has focused in the area of tobacco, including topics of policy, cessation, air quality, and secondhand smoke. Her publications have appeared in the journals of *Health Communication*, *Journal of Health Communication*, *Journal of Applied Communication Research*, *Nursing Clinics of North America*, and *Public Health Nursing*.

Jenna E. Reno (Ph.D., University of Kentucky) is a Postdoctoral Research Fellow with the Adult and Child Center for Health Outcomes Research and Delivery Science (ACCORDS) at the University of Colorado, Denver. Her research is centered around mediated, technological, and social influences on health behaviors. Specifically, her research has focused on problems affecting college students and campus communities, particularly the role that social media plays in promoting problematic behaviors. Additionally, her work involves examining the most effective ways to develop, implement, and evaluate health campaigns in a changing media environment. Her publications appear in journals such as *Health Communication, Public Relations Review, Clinical Journal of Oncology Nursing,* and *Psycho-Oncology.*

Author Index

Subject Index

Please note that page numbers relating to Tables will be in italics followed by the letter 't', whereas numbers relating to Figures will contain the letter 'f'. Notes will contain the letter 'n'.